A HISTORY OF TELEVISION
IN 100 PROGRAMMES

Also by Phil Norman:

The Great British Tuck Shop (with Steve Berry)
A History of Sweets in 50 Wrappers (with Steve Berry)

A HISTORY (
IN 100 PR

*Th
A His*

A HISTORY OF TELEVISION IN 100 PROGRAMMES

Phil Norman

The Friday Project
An imprint of HarperCollins*Publishers*
1 London Bridge Street
London SE1 9GF

www.harpercollins.co.uk

First published in Great Britain by The Friday Project in 2015

1

Phil Norman asserts the moral right to be identified as the author of this work

A catalogue record for this book is available from the British Library

ISBN 978-0-00-757549-7

Typeset by Palimpsest Book Production Ltd,
Falkirk, Stirlingshire

Printed and bound in Great Britain by Clays Ltd, St Ives plc

MIX
Paper from
responsible sources
FSC
www.fsc.org   **FSC™ C007454**

Find out more about HarperCollins and the environment at
www.harpercollins.co.uk/green

CONTENTS

INTRODUCTION

There is no holding down the modern inventor. He rides the waves of the ether with the conquering skill of a master in a celestial rodeo. Give him a valve and there is no holding him. It is almost certain that within a few years we shall have all our entertainment available within our own four walls. Press but the button and a stereoscopic talking film will happen over the mantelpiece.

'Seen and Heard', *Manchester Guardian*,
1 April 1930

IT HAD AN AURA about it, a presence. By today's standards it was tiny, but it dominated the room in a way its technically superior descendants never quite manage. It catered directly for two of the senses, but in operation it affected them all. The flicker and the glare of the bulbous, grey-green screen. The hum and whine of the tube heating up. The crackle of static when it turned off, the tang of burnt dust in the air when it was repaired. For decades the television set was the most advanced piece of technology to be found in any house. How it worked was a mystery, but it was literally part of the furniture.

It was also an instant portal to a cavalcade of smart, witty house guests with inexhaustible supplies of information, anecdotes, opinions and vibrant sweaters. Miraculous and commonplace at the same time, television occupied a unique position in the national imagination. Detractors claimed it hijacked the national imagination – formerly a cultural Arcadia of chamber music and well-made plays – for its own base ends, but at its best it brought classes and

1

cultures into each other's homes without prejudice. By the late 1960s even the press admitted that TV, coming from nowhere, was beating them at their own game and several new ones of its own invention.

The birth of television in the mid-1920s garnered more fuss than a royal baby. The race to perfect a workable system was matched by the rush to predict imminent social catastrophe. Newspapers, radio, theatre and even the motor car (why drive somewhere you can see at the flick of a switch?) were pronounced doomed many times. Rumour and misconception abounded. Professor A. M. Low worried about the effect on international relations if Americans could use the new device to view their British neighbours engaged in 'frightful' activities, such as drinking cocktails.[1] Meanwhile, R. H. Hill of Oxford University demanded, 'How could one have a bath in comfort if all the neighbours could look in?'[2] Noted physicist Sir Oliver Lodge fretted that broadcasting's electro-magnetic waves might make planes fall out of the sky, though he didn't expect TV to become a working reality 'for a good many years yet, perhaps not for a century'.[3]

More usefully, Lodge worried about content, noting that the majority of messages sent by another recent scientific triumph – the transatlantic telegraph cable – were 'rubbishy'. 'It is no use enlarging our powers of communication,' he warned, 'if we have nothing worthwhile to say.'[4] The insubstantial nature of the early demonstrations didn't help – even John Logie Baird provoked a wave of cheap laughs when he based his first telerecording demo around a cabbage.

Initially the preserve of the rich, the take up of TV spread after the Second World War as prices dropped and services improved. Older media, who had originally described it as an elitist fad for well-to-do stay-at-homes, now tried to dismiss it as a pernicious influence on those less stable, less educated than themselves. A snobbish line in the fifties had it that people were raising H-shaped aerials over their houses to make up for all the 'H's dropped inside them.

It may have projected a serene, slightly aloof air on screen, but behind the cameras post-war television was paddling like mad, inventing a new medium on the hoof, often with whatever came to hand. Studios looked less like the glistening caverns of today and more like the shop floor of an engineering works under the stewardship of a hyperactive ten-year-old. A profession was being steadily built through years of committed bodging.

America initially lagged behind Britain, Germany, France, Italy, Russia and Japan in television take up, but soon made up for lost time. NBC's first electronic transmission in 1936, featuring comedian Ed Wynn, ignited an industrial boom that in little over a decade would result in four national television networks broadcasting to over four million set-equipped homes. The US network system, commercially funded and powered by the twin big tickets of sports and vaudeville, was voracious and unstoppable. By the late 1940s its diverse schedule offered programmes that were sombre (*Court of Current Issues, People's Platform*), sophisticated (*Café de Paris, Champaign and Orchids*) and silly (*Buzzy Wuzzy, Campus Hoopla*).

This last category caused unease back in Britain, where ITV's arrival in the mid-1950s threatened the state-run BBC order. The US broadcasts of Elizabeth II's coronation had included grinning appearances by NBC's mascot, chimpanzee J. Fred Muggs, and there were concerns about a similar crassness creeping in to British broadcasting. The Tories championed ITV, Labour vilified it, while Liberal councillor Paul Rose reminded both sides that 'there is always freedom of the knob.'[5]

Technological advance was an enduring obsession, if not always taking place as quickly as predicted: a committee set up in 1943 to prepare for British television's post-war return anticipated the swift invention not only of colour, but 1000-line high definition and 3D.[6] A quarter of a century later, round the clock coverage of the Apollo missions fused the Television Age with the Space Age for as long as the latter held out, and made a star of James Burke, who went on to present the most lavish science programmes ever made, travelling further on a BBC expense account than Armstrong ever managed in a *Saturn V*. On a smaller scale, potting shed innovation was everywhere, from the BBC's home computer sideline to abortive plans in the late 1960s for contestants on *The Golden Shot* to operate the game show's famous crossbow from their own front rooms, via a Golden Joystick in a James Bond-style Golden Suitcase, specially delivered in a Golden Car. The technology, the producers made clear, boasted Golden safety features as 'we don't want any nut shooting Bob Monkhouse.'[7]

Around this time came the first symptoms of two ailments that would dog the medium for evermore. The first was the transformation of the social embarrassment surrounding television among the middle classes into an ironic 'guilty pleasure'. As John Osborne confessed to Kenneth Tynan in 1968, 'When TV is dreadful, it's thoroughly enjoyable. After you've seen *The Golden Shot* a couple of times, it acquires a special horror of its own.'[8] The second, closely related to the first, was nostalgia. In the dying days of 1969, ITV screened *A Child of the Sixties*, taking the temperature of the decade with a rummage in the archive. This sort of thing was nothing new in itself, but for the first time whimsical talking heads were added, including 'the impressions they made on a receptive young mind' – an Oxford undergraduate named Gyles Brandreth. The bar for retro-punditry was set from that moment.

The study of television doesn't have to be so apologetic. Television may not be high art, but many artists have worked in it, regardless of its condemnation as unclean by the world's cultural custodians. Samuel Beckett wrote for it. Kingsley Amis presented a pop music show on it. Carol Ann Duffy laboured in it writing cockney gags for Joe Brown's snakes and ladders game show *Square One* on her way to becoming Poet Laureate.

As a vivid source of graphic reportage, television transformed our relationship with the world at large. When the Vietnam War stopped being a few fuzzy black and white images accompanied by sober paragraphs of text and became an avalanche of explicit, full-colour moving horrors, western populations seriously considered the wisdom of military adventures. Dramatists, meanwhile, found a unique new medium that was more intimate than cinema, more precise than the theatre and which could pluck the hearts of millions. Worries about the creation of a world of antisocial couch ornaments were outweighed by a sense of barriers and borders vaulted by satellite, a shift in the way we looked at the world that wouldn't happen again until the advent of the Internet.

If that arrival meant the writing was on the wall for television's place in the media vanguard, for most it was hard to read. Prestel, the British Post Office's pioneering online data service, was struggling by 1982. Punters predicted that staring at a load of text was so passé in the age of the image it would never catch on. 'Prestel and *The Two Ronnies* . . . have no more in common than the *Financial Times* and Hammond Innes,' reasoned Hamish McRae. 'It would further follow that it is pointless to give people who want to watch *The Two Ronnies* a Prestel set that tells them the time of the trains to Newcastle.'[9] Such faultless logic buoyed TV's unassailable self-image until it was far too late, at which point panic set in.

Factual programmes in particular are acutely conscious of the Internet looking over their shoulders. Current affairs channels pride themselves as vital parts of the democratic machine, but TV could never make on-screen democracy work. In May 1982, *World in Action* tried to atone for the scarcity of news coming out of the Falklands Conflict with a high-tech viewer vote. This consisted of 75 homes being equipped to give instant reaction to the big questions of warfare. The set-up worked fine, but a naively honest on-screen tally of the total votes showed less than half the audience, specially wired in at great fuss, were actually bothering. Viewer participation remains largely a token gesture – and, thanks to premium rate phone lines, often the token that pays for the programme.

Before the Internet took its place as the number one scourge of decent society, television's constant stream bred disdain. A novel takes its place in the literary canon. A film lines up in the cinematic pantheon. Television programmes just float there, then vanish. While films relate to other films at a distance, via elegant homage or the critic's comparative whim, a TV show arrives surrounded by other shows before and after, on other channels, from other seasons. It's an adaptation of this Danish show, a reboot of that long-forgotten space opera, or a strange amalgam of those two 1970s programmes presented by that newsreader who's suddenly all over the place after she showed how game she was, doing that soap opera parody on a charity special. Never mind placing a programme in context, it's an afternoon's work just to pull the thing out of the undergrowth.

Small wonder that early critics, fearful of getting their hands dirty with this suspicious new medium, contented themselves with a few tentative pokes and prods at TV as a whole – muttering darkly about 'admass' and 'diachronic flow', and treating it with the disinterested loftiness of the anthropologist. For these early critics, TV could best be understood as the by-product of some industrial process or quaintly exotic lower culture: it was an experimental new plastic from the labs of ICI, or the campfire story of a backward tribe. Aside from the odd accidentally interesting curio, artistic judgement was hardly appropriate. The *Guardian*'s TV editor Peter Fiddick noted that TV's lowly status could lead, at worst, to 'know-nothings writing for care-nothings about stuff that [is] worth nothing.'[10] That was in 1982. Things have got worse since.

So here's an attempt to revisit and revive the history of the idiot's lantern. A hundred programmes have been gathered to chart eighty-odd years of televisual evolution. It is, admittedly, a predominantly Anglophone, western collection. Though the Global Village has lately begun to live up to its name, TV around the world has overwhelmingly followed blueprints drawn up by British and American hands.

A crudely calibrated Hundred Greatest, a solemn Hall of Fame, would give only a fraction of the picture. This book aims to celebrate and mimic the serendipitous joy of that scheduling jumble which, in the days of restricted channel numbers, threw up dizzy juxtapositions daily: an earnest play might be followed by a big broad variety spectacular; a horror anthology that drove children behind furniture followed a sketch show that chewed the carpet. This riotous mix, now slowly disappearing as themed channels and on-demand services take over, may have downgraded TV's importance in the eyes of aesthetes, but gave it a community feel other media lacked. No-one ever turned up at a cinema half an hour early for a screening of *Three Colours: Red* and got thirty minutes of *Slam Dunk Ernest* for their trouble.

This isn't a book about how much 'better' television once was, but how much stranger it used to be – much braver, more foolhardy, unselfconscious and creatively energetic before commerce knocked those fascinating corners off its character. At its best and at its worst, television is brutally honest and charmingly deceitful, sentimentally partisan and coldly dispassionate, obscenely lavish and ludicrously cheap. Its screen bulges with obsessive perfectionists and clueless amateurs, sociopathic monsters and all-round good eggs. It can't be contained by a neat little narrative. It's chaos all the way down.

No countdown of the top hundred shows can do television full justice. But maybe a more varied hundred can make a better stab at exploring it: a rough guide antidote to the standard lists of well-worn greats. What follows is one such alternative trek. Overlooked gems and justly wiped follies, overcooked spectaculars and underfunded experiments are as much a part of TV history as the national treasures and stone cold classics. They can tell us just as much, and sometimes more, about the nature of television, those who crafted it and those who lapped it up. Here, then, are tales of the days when television was at the most exciting, creative stage of any medium: a cottage industry with the world at its feet.

TELE-CRIME (1938–9)
BBC

The original TV drama series.

When the BBC asks a question, it isn't just a question, it's a 'viewer participation programme'.

Grace Wyndham Goldie,
Listener, 2 March 1939

IN BBC TELEVISION'S BRIEF life before the war, drama meant the theatre: simple studio productions of acknowledged classics or extracts from a show currently running in the West End. These unofficial trailers were either recreated in the studio (with as much of the theatre's scenery as could be blagged) or occasionally and chaotically broadcast live from their home turf. Champions of theatre broadcasts claimed the presence of an audience added atmosphere and upped the actors' game – the fact that the cameras often ended up chasing them about the stage, like a football match filmed by a bunch of drunken fans, was a small price to pay.

Visuals took a back seat at first. Early TV equipment produced low-definition pictures in murky black and grimy white. Faces had to be held in tight close-up to enable recognition, and wide shots couldn't be that wide due to the Beeb's tiny Lime Grove studios. Sets and lighting just about did the job, and nothing more. Directors couldn't cut between cameras – a change of shot had to be done by mixing, which could take several seconds. With all these restrictions, wrote the critic Philip Hope-Wallace, 'the television screen is much less a stage . . . than a checking-board helping us listen to good talk.'[11]

The first step on the road to the modern drama series was taken by what critic Grace Wyndham Goldie, later to run the BBC's current affairs department, called 'an interesting experiment in presentation'.[12] Mileson Horton had made a name for himself in the mid-1930s writing 'Photocrime', an immensely popular series of whodunit photo-stories starring the intrepid Inspector Holt, published in *Weekly Illustrated*. These bare bones procedurals, simply told and visually direct, were just what TV producers were after. Horton was hired to script a series of twenty-minute Holt adventures for the small screen.

Take a typical episode of *Tele-crime*, 'The Fletcher Case'. A man's body is found sprawled on the floor of his bedroom, with a gun in his right hand. It looks like an open-and-shut suicide case for Inspector Holt. Just as he's about to leave the scene, the phone rings. Holt's constable answers: it's the victim's niece. The victim, it turns out, was *left*-handed! Murder! It's a race to the family house to stop the killer striking again. But too late! Another family member has been offed. Holt assembles the suspects and hears their stories.

After fifteen minutes of this, Holt and company fade from the screen, replaced by the gently smiling face of continuity announcer Elizabeth Cowell: 'Well, who *did* do the murder? Viewers have now all the evidence necessary to detect the criminal.' There follows a few moments' reflective pause for the audience to flex their minds, then it's back to the house for a rapid denouement.

The guess-the-culprit interval was an early bit of audience participation that didn't last the pace (although it was revived for Jeremy Lloyd and Lance Percival's 1972 panel game *Whodunnit?*). The rest of *Tele-crime*, though, set the mould for the detective series, the backbone of popular TV drama ever since.

The crime thriller, like most genres, is a self-concealing art: done well, the writing and direction are taken for granted; done badly, they're sitting ducks. 'In an affair of this kind,' observed Wyndham

Goldie, 'nobody expects any depth or subtle characterisation, but the people in the story must be made just sufficiently interesting for us to care which of them is hanged.'[13] Television evolves not with quantum leaps of genius, but by continuous tinkering. *Tele-crime* may have long vanished into thin air, but look at the foundations of any current drama series and you might just glimpse the smudgy, over-lit face of Inspector Holt.

COOKERY (1946–51)
BBC

The first celebrity chef.

THE FIRST PERSON TO sling a skillet in the studio was French restaurateur, novelist and boulevardier Xavier Marcel Boulestin. He essayed suave hob-side demonstrations wearing a double-breasted suit during the BBC's 1930s infancy in programmes like *Bee for Boulestin* and *Blind Man's Buffet*. However, the cult of the celebrity chef – the omnipresent gastronome as relaxed in front of the camera as at the oven door – began with Philip Harben.

Rotund, neatly bearded and rarely seen out of an apron, Harben emerged from the post-war landscape of ration coupons and meat queues to become an ever-present face on TV via his first series, the sensibly-titled *Cookery*. Harben rustled up austerity lobster vol-au-vents and welfare soufflés for the vicarious pleasure of families struggling on one slice of condemned corned beef a week, but few recognise just how many aspects of the twenty-first century tele-cookery landscape owe him their existence. Without Harben, we may never have witnessed these culinary devices:

THEATRICALITY – The son of film actors, Harben knew how to put his recipes, and himself, across to best effect in the muffled turmoil of early television, keeping the stream of patter going as the sheets of flame leapt from his flambé pan. 'He stands almost alone,' remarked an awed Reginald Pound, 'a precision instrument of self-expression.' [14]

MERCHANDISE – Not content with putting his grinning, bearded face on jars of Heinz pickle and packs of Norfolk stuffing, Harben supplemented his meagre BBC salary with the launch of Harbenware, heavy gauge saucepans with a special 'Harbenized' non-stick coating, bearing labels festooned with his grinning, bearded face.

BACK TO BASICS – The ridicule endured by Delia Smith for demonstrating how to boil an egg was nothing new to Harben, who devoted the lion's share of one programme to making a cup of tea. Pot-warming temperatures, infusion times, even the height from which to pour the water onto the leaves were discussed at rigorous length.

NATIONAL AND INTERNATIONAL DISHES – Harben got away from the standard Mayfair dinner party aspirations of TV cookery to celebrate Britain's regional food in 1951's *Country Dishes*, rustling up everything from Cornish pasties to jellied eels. If technology had allowed him a global culinary excursion he'd have made one – instead he brought the resident chef from NBC's *Home* show to the UK for a national dish swapping session in 1955's *Transatlantic Exchange*.

SLUTTY INGREDIENTS SCANDAL – Delia's controversial dalliance with frozen mash and other timesavers was pre-empted in 1954 when Harben rustled up *sole bonne femme* using haddock and milk instead of the traditional Dover sole and wine. An outraged telegram from catering students at Blackpool Technical College reached the Director General within hours. 'The BBC permits Harben to clown with classical French dishes in a way which exposes the British kitchen to a justifiable scorn,' [15] they raged. Whatever, they demanded, would the Americans think if this got out?

NUTRITIONAL CRUSADE – Getting the nation eating properly was another Harben innovation. This being 1949, however, the problem was that folk weren't eating enough. Specifically, Harben attacked the 'sparrow-sized breakfasts' of Britain's working men. 'We cannot stay a first-class power if we give up eating a first-class breakfast,'[16] he told the press, encouraging British men to get up earlier and fry their own bacon if necessary. Harben's Great British Breakfast was possibly unique in food campaigns for also recommending a few post-prandial minutes with a newspaper and a cigarette.

PRIMADONNA ANTICS – Every great TV chef must exhibit a total lack of humour at a crucial moment. Harben set the template in 1957 on the set of *The Benny Hill Show*. He'd sportingly played the stooge before to the chaotic Mr Pastry and rebarbative Fred Emney, but Hill took a step too far. 'They submitted a sketch to me which I considered degrading. The whole thing indicated that I couldn't cook. That's no joke to me.'[17]

MOLECULAR GASTRONOMY – Beating Heston Blumenthal by over forty years, Harben stocked up on microscopes, slide rules and calculus tables for his 1964 ITV series *The Grammar of Cookery*. With technical advice from microbiologist A. L. Bacharach and editions called 'The Three Faces of Meringue' and 'Egg Liaison', he took cookery to new heights of sophistication. 'If you are a great cook, madam,' he claimed, 'you are a singer of songs, a poet, an actress, a painter, a pianist. You are Maria Callas, you are Cilla Black, you are Vanessa Redgrave all rolled into one. And the world is at your feet.'[18]

CAVALCADE OF STARS (1949–52)
DuMont (Drugstore Television)
Vaudeville begets the sitcom.

As TELEVISION PROGRESSED FROM esoteric technology to world-wide medium-in-waiting, one question dominated: what the hell are we going to put on it? The *Manchester Guardian* held a competition asking just that in 1934. Winning suggestions ranged from high mass at St Peter's to a chimps' tea party, 'MPs trying to buy bananas after hours', and 'Mr Aldous Huxley enjoying something'.[19]

In America, such wild fancies became real. There was the 1944 show that led one critic to gush, 'This removes all doubt as to television's future. This is television.'[20] 'This' was *Missus Goes A-Shopping*, a distant ancestor of *Supermarket Sweep*. A more solid solution to the content problem was sport. Entire evenings in the late 1940s consisted of the sports that were easiest to cover with the new stations' primitive equipment: mainly boxing and wrestling. On the other hand, figured New York-based programmers, there was a whole breed of people who were past masters at filling an evening with entertainment off their own bat. They were just a few blocks away, doing six nights a week for peanuts.

Vaudeville stars like the Marx Brothers had dominated pre-war cinema comedy, touring a stage version of each film across America to polish every line and perfect every pratfall before they hit the studio. Television wanted vaudevillians for the opposite quality: bounteous spontaneity. The big, big shows began with NBC's *Texaco*

Star Theatre, hosted by Milton Berle. Through a mess of broad slapstick, elephantine cross-dressing and taboo-nudging ad libs, Berle became the first of television's original stars, with his loud and hectic shtick penetrating the fog of the early TV screen like bawdy semaphore from the deck of an oncoming battleship. No marks for élan, but plenty for chutzpah.

Other broadcasters followed suit, including DuMont. The odd one out of the networks, DuMont originated from TV manufacturing rather than broadcast radio, so had to search harder to find celebrities, and struggled to keep them. *Cavalcade of Stars*, their Saturday night shebang, was a case in point. It was originally hosted by former *Texaco* stand-in Jack Carter, then Jerry Lester, both of whom were poached by NBC as they became popular. Desperation was setting in when they came to Jackie Gleason. Gleason, having bombed in Hollywood, was working through the purgatory of Newark's club circuit when DuMont offered him a two-week test contract. Gleason had worked in TV before, starring in a lacklustre adaptation of barnstorming radio sitcom *Life of Riley*, so had his reasons to be wary. But that was someone else's script. *Cavalcade* was 100% Jackie.

Every show needed a sponsor. *Cavalcade*, lacking the might to pull in big time petroleum funds, was sponsored by Whelan's drugstore chain. Each edition was preceded by a strident, close-harmony paean to the delights of the corner pharmacy, under the bold caption 'QUALITY DRUGS'. Then on came The Great One in imperial splendour with a retinue of his 'personally-auditioned' Glea Girls. Often he'd daintily sip from a coffee cup, roll his eyes and croon 'Ah, how sweet it is!', his public chuckling in the know-ledge that the cup wasn't holding coffee. After his opening mono-logue – a combination of double-takes, reactions and slow-burns as much as a string of verbal gags – he'd request 'a little travellin' music' from his orchestra, and to the resulting snatch of middle eastern burlesque, he slunk around the stage in a possessed belly-cum-go-go dance before freezing stock still and uttering the immortal line, 'And awaaaaay we goooo!' After all that, the programme actually started.

This indulgently whimsical ceremony wasn't unique to *Cavalcade*, but on Gleason's watch it grew into a kind of baroque mass, initiating the audience into his comic realm. The logic of replicating the communal aspect of stage variety on such a private, domestic medium seems odd today, but a large proportion of Gleason's working class audience, unable to afford their own TVs, watched *en masse* in the bars and taverns of the Union's major cities (DuMont's limited coverage never reached the small towns), creating their own mini-crowds who joined in with gusto. Vaudeville's voodoo link with the audience could cross the country this way. Performer and punter were in cahoots.

Cavalcade wasn't all Pavlovian faff. The main body of the show boasted as much meat as that of its star. Dance numbers and musical guests were interspersed with extended character sketches taken from life – Gleason's life. At one end of his one-man cross-section of society was playboy Reggie Van Gleason III. At the other, Chaplinesque hobo The Poor Soul. Somewhere in between came serial odd job failure Fenwick Babbitt and The Bachelor, a pathos-laden mime act in which Gleason would prepare breakfast or dress for dinner with all the grace and finesse you'd expect from a long-term single man, to the melodious, mocking strains of 'Somebody Loves Me'. Hobo aside, Gleason had lived them all.

Gleason's fullest tribute to his Bushwick roots was the warring couple skit that became known as 'The Honeymooners'. Gleason played Ralph Kramden, a short-fused temper bomb of the old-fashioned, spherical kind; a scheming bus driver with ideas beyond his terminus. He lived with his more grounded wife Alice in a cramped, walk-up apartment at 328 Chauncey Street, a genuine former address of Gleason's and possibly the most accurate recreation of breadline accommodation in TV comedy. In this washboard-in-the-sink, holler-up-the-fire-escape poverty, Kramden and his unassuming sewage worker neighbour Ed Norton (Art Carney) sparred, plotted and generally goofed around. The working-class-boy-made-good was talking directly to his peers about life as they knew it, as surely as if they were sat at the same bar. The aristocracy of executives and sponsors that made it technically possible didn't figure in the exchange at all. They delivered the star, and then made themselves scarce until the first commercial break. It would be television comedy's struggle to preserve this desirable set-up against tide after tide of neurotic, censorious meddling from above.

Cavalcade of Stars became DuMont's biggest show. Naturally, this meant Gleason was snapped up by CBS within two years. His fame doubled, and that of 'The Honeymooners' trebled. It broke out to become a sitcom in its own right, but oddly never achieved quite the same level of success outside its variety habitat. Meanwhile Sid Caesar, Imogene Coca and a stable of future comedy writing titans seized the vaudeville crown with NBC's *Your Show of Shows*.

Gleason himself wasn't immune to the odd misstep. In 1961 he hosted the high-concept panel game *You're in the Picture*, in which stars stuck their heads through holes in paintings and tried to determine what they depicted. The première bombed so hard that week two consisted entirely of Gleason, in a bare studio with trusty coffee cup to hand, apologising profusely for the previous week. He was reckless, chaotic and hopelessly self-indulgent, but he instinctively knew when he'd failed to entertain. He was also relentlessly determined, signing off his marathon *mea culpa* with a forthright, 'I don't know what we'll do, but I'll be back.' Television couldn't wish for a better motto.

CRUSADER RABBIT (1950–1)

NBC (Television Arts Productions)

TV's first bespoke cartoon.

AMERICAN CARTOONS DOMINATED FORTIES cinema. The heart-on-sleeve perfectionism of Disney and the demolition ballets of Warner Brothers were known, loved and merchandised throughout the world. But when television began to look like a viable proposition, the animation giants kept their distance: too small the screen, too monochrome, and most important, too cheap the going rate. It might be good for the odd commercial or as a place to dump black-and-white shorts even the dankest fleapit would no longer touch, but cartoons made especially for TV? The idea might have seemed a joke to the main animation studios, but there was a gap in the media market waiting to be filled. This one snugly accommodated an adventurous animal.

Crusader Rabbit and his faithful sidekick Ragland T 'Rags' Tiger were a pairing in the short-smart/big-dumb cartoon tradition that had its origins in Steinbeck's *Of Mice and Men*. Their creator was Alex Anderson, nephew of the self-styled Woolworth of cinema animation, Paul Terry. Anderson reduced his uncle's cheap and cheerful formula even further, basing his methods on a sequence in Disney's behind-the-scenes cartoon feature *The Reluctant Dragon* which showed an embryonic cartoon in animated storyboard form – simple cuts from one still drawing to the next, smartly timed to the soundtrack. Anderson took the idea and applied it to a finished series.[21]

Together with old friend Jay Ward handling production duties, Anderson formed Television Arts Productions. Equipped with an army surplus Kodak film camera and several veteran draughtsmen, TAP began production, leaving no corner uncut. Single poses lasted on screen for anything from one to fifteen seconds, and loops of motion were reused with shameless regularity. Verbal gags did most of the work, but mouth movements were minimal – in the pilot, a fast-talking radio announcer blatantly hides his behind a sheet of paper.

The pilot impressed NBC enough to commission a series, at $2,500 per episode – in the labour-intensive animation world, about as cheap as you could get. *Crusader Rabbit* rode out, sponsored by that great friend of early TV innovation, Carnation Evaporated Milk, at 6 p.m. on 1 August 1950. The show aired every weekday for the best part of a year, pitting the tenacious pair against adversaries Dudley Nightshade, Whetstone Whiplash and Achilles the Heel.

As production stepped up, Ward's talent came to the fore. While Anderson supervised the visuals, Ward took charge of the dialogue recording sessions, coaching the voice talent and editing to keep things as snappy and fast-moving as possible. This was a practical necessity – with budgets this tight, editing in sound only made economic sense – but it gave a quickfire ebullience to the otherwise static show, emphasising verbal gags in a way which would shape Ward's later output and TV animation in general.

It also instigated a less happy animation tradition. Jerry Fairbanks, Television Arts' commercial partner in the *Crusader Rabbit* venture, turned out not to be as financially secure as he claimed. An uneasy NBC sequestered all 195 *Crusader Rabbit* cartoons as collateral.[22] Ward and Anderson found themselves without a franchise, their stake in the original and rights to the characters having been legally spirited away. This sort of custody battle, with the creators forever on the losing side, would become a feature of TV cartooning, where the bottom line drags heavily. *Crusader Rabbit* would eventually be reborn, via other hands, in 1957.

Ward started afresh, in tandem with cartoon veteran Bill Scott, to create a plethora of wisecracking properties that took *Crusader Rabbit*'s chattering statue model and upped the wit, tempo and volume. This began with a blockbuster that aped its progenitor's character template – *The Adventures of Rocky and Bullwinkle*. Meanwhile William Hanna and Joseph Barbera, ex-MGM animators who brought *Tom and Jerry* to life and were briefly engaged by Ward for a legally embargoed *Crusader Rabbit* revival, borrowed the limited animation style for their own work. *The Ruff and Reddy Show*, in which a smart little cat and a big stupid dog engaged in pose-to-pose capers, was followed by *Huckleberry Hound*, *Yogi Bear* and flatly coloured, ever-blinking cartoon versions of sitcoms like *The Honeymooners* (*The Flintstones*) and *Bilko* (*Top Cat*). Even Uncle Paul Terry was lured to the small screen for, among others, *Deputy Dawg*. Vast empires of severely restricted motion conquered television with phenomenal speed – sideways on, with feet reduced to a circular blur, passing the same three items of street furniture every five seconds.

THE BURNS AND ALLEN SHOW (1950–8)

CBS

Still in its infancy, the sitcom goes postmodern.

You know, if you saw a plot like this on television you'd never believe it. But here it is happening in real life.

George Burns

THE COMEDIAN WILL ALWAYS beat the philosopher in a race – he's the one who knows all the short cuts. In the case of postmodernism, that enigmatic doctrine of shifting symbols and authorless texts, the race was over before half the field reached the stadium.

George Burns and Gracie Allen were a dedicated vaudevillian couple. In 1929, the year before father of deconstruction Jacques Derrida was born, they were making short films that began by looking for the audience in cupboards and ended by admitting they'd run out of material too soon. While Roland Barthes was studying at the Sorbonne, Gracie Allen was enlisting the people of America to help look for her non-existent missing brother. A decade before John Cage's notorious silent composition *4'33"*, Gracie performed her *Piano Concerto for Index Finger*. And a few years after the word postmodernism first appeared in print, Burns and Allen were on America's television screens embodying it.

The Burns and Allen Show began on CBS four years after the BBC inaugurated the sitcom with *Pinwright's Progress*. In that time

22

very little progress had been made. Performances were live and studio-bound. Gag followed gag followed some business with a hat, and the settings were drawing rooms straight from the funny papers. Burns and Allen's set looked more like a technical cross section: the front doors of their house and that of neighbours the Mortons led into rooms visible from outside due to gaping holes in the brickwork. The fourth wall literally broken, George (and only George) could pop through the hole at will to confer with the audience. If anyone else left via the void they were swiftly reminded to use the front door. 'You see,' George explained to the viewers, 'we've got to keep this believable.'

While Burns muttered asides from the edge of the stage, Allen stalked the set like a wide-eyed Wittgenstein, challenging anyone in her path to a fragmented war of words. From basic malapropisms to logical inversions some of the audience had to unpick on the bus going home, Gracie would innocently get everything wrong in exactly the right way. She sent her mother an empty envelope to cheer her up, on the grounds that 'no news is good news'. She engaged hapless visitors in conversation with her own, unique, logic ('Are you Mrs Burns?' 'Oh, yes. Mr Burns is much taller!'). Gracie was, admittedly, a Ditzy Woman, but this was the style in comedy at the time – Lucille Ball played a Ditzy Woman, and she co-owned the production company. Besides, Gracie's vacuity could be perversely powerful – she was frequently the only one who seemed sure of herself. In her eyes she ranked with the great women of history ('They laughed at Joan of Arc, but she went right ahead and built it!').

While Gracie defied logic, George, in his mid-fifties but already the butt of endless old man gags, defied time and space. With a word and a gesture, he could halt the action and fill the audience in on the finer points of the story while Allen and company gamely froze like statues behind him. During Burns's front-of-cloth confabs the viewer's opinion was solicited, bets on the action were taken, and backstage reality elbowed its way up front. The story's authorship was debated mid-show: 'George S. Kaufman is responsible for tonight's plot. I asked him to write it and he said no, so I had to do it.' When a new actor was cast as Harry Morton, Burns introduced him on screen to Bea Benaderet (who played his wife Blanche), pronounced them man and wife, and the show carried on as usual. On another occasion, George broached the curtain to apologetically admit that the writers simply hadn't come up with an ending for tonight's programme, so goodnight folks.

Even the obligatory 'word from the sponsor' entered the fun. The show's announcer was made a regular character: a TV announcer pathologically obsessed with Carnation Evaporated Milk, 'the milk from contented cows'. These interludes, knocked out by an ad rep but fitting snugly within the framework provided by the show's regular writers, exposed the strangeness of the integrated sponsor spot by embracing it. The show kept on top of the sponsor, and the sponsor became a star of the show – a very sophisticated symbiosis.

In October 1956, Burns gained a TV set which enabled him to watch the show – the one which, to him, was real life (the Burns and Allen played by Burns and Allen in *The Burns and Allen Show* were the stars of a show of their own, the content of which remained a mystery). He could sow mischief, retire to the set, and watch trouble unfold at his leisure. When he tired of that, he could switch channels and spy on Jack Benny. Burns's fluctuating relationship to audience and plot (of which, he said, there was more than in a variety show, but less than in a wrestling match) was a deconstructionist triumph.

Ken Dodd questioned Freud's theories of comedy, noting the great psychoanalyst 'never had to play second house at the Glasgow Empire'. Burns and Allen, graduates of vaudeville, would have agreed. The self-awareness that high art lauds as sophisticated was part of the DNA of popular entertainment from the year dot – that is, about a day after George Burns was born.

THE ERNIE KOVACS SHOW (1952–61)
DuMont/NBC/ABC

TV's visual gag pioneer.

MOST MODERN COMEDIANS APPEAR on TV. Very few use it. In Britain there have been Spike Milligan, the Pythons, Kenny Everett and Chris Morris. America boasted George Burns, the *Laugh-In* crowd, David Letterman and Garry Shandling. But most of all it had the quintessential TV comedian: the cigar-sucking, second generation Hungarian Ernie Kovacs.

Like many TV comics, Kovacs began as a nonconformist local radio DJ, before becoming a continuity announcer on Pennsylvania's regional NBC affiliate station. His first on-screen stint came in 1950 as eleventh hour stand-in on cookery show *Deadline for Dinner*, where a talent for off-the-cuff wisecracks impressed management enough to give him the blank canvas of a ninety-minute morning programme. In 1950, the 7.30-to-9.00 a.m. weekday slot was uncharted terrain, so Kovacs had free rein to improvise as he wished. He goofed around to music, toyed with random props and chatted calmly to the viewers, seemingly unaware of a live panther squatting on his back. At a time when comedy was ruled by repetition and ritual, Kovacs insisted on constant innovation.

The Ernie Kovacs Show proper first appeared on the DuMont network, in front of an audience of 'twenty-three passing strangers'. Kovacs preferred to work without a full studio audience for one very good reason – he was determined to use the medium in every way possible, so a lot of his gags only worked on the screen. Atmosphere came from the camera crew, who could laugh (and heckle) as heartily as anyone.

He exploited the basic video effects of the day – wipes, super-impositions and picture flips – to make characters fly off screen, expose the contents of his head or superimpose it onto a small dog. He would walk off the edge of the set and give viewers an impromptu guided tour of the studio paraphernalia. With his technicians he made an inverting lens from mirrors and soup cans, built a cheap upside-down set and walked on the ceiling. Or he simply stuck a child's kaleidoscope in front of the camera, accompanied by some music. In an unexplored medium he broke ground with every step – usually accompanied by a discordant sound effect. His work is most often compared to Kenny Everett's, but he pre-empted others. His interest in the personalities of puppet animals is reminiscent of early Vic Reeves (sample stage direction: 'Trevor the stuffed deer is vacuumed – laughs.'[23])

After the DuMont network collapsed, Kovacs returned to NBC to occupy a variety of slots, culminating in his first prime-time gig, an 8 p.m. Monday night spectacular from a real theatre, with a real audience. The show also came with a real budget that Kovacs didn't hesitate to spend with alarming profligacy: huge song-and-dance numbers were choreographed, incorporating giant flights of collapsible stairs; Boris Karloff was paid top dollar to recite the alphabet. The transition from backroom 'improv' to gargantuan showcase came surprisingly easily to him.

One sketch from these shows was far ahead of its time. To the thunderous accompaniment of drum rolls and the clatter of tele-printers, Kovacs appeared as a self-important newsreader, employing primitive in-camera effects to lampoon the already excessive presentation of TV news decades before the likes of Chris Morris. One sketch, 'News Analyst', is uncannily modern in its approach:

KOVACS: Good morning. This is Leroy L. Bascombe McFinister . . .

[Picture is wiped inward, leaving tiny vertical slit in middle through which we glimpse Ernie.]
KOVACS: . . . with the news.
[Wipe widens to full set.]
KOVACS: Behind the news.
[Picture tilts right.]
KOVACS: News flashes and news highlights.
[Tilts upside down.]
KOVACS: Events of the day and events of the night.
[Picture spins 360 degrees to left.]
KOVACS: Brought to you . . .
[Picture spins to right, ends upside down.]
KOVACS: . . . as they happen . . .
[Picture spins upright.]
KOVACS: . . . when they happen.
[Tilts to right, then back.]
KOVACS: News!
[Tilts to left, then back.]
KOVACS: From all over!
[Shot of spinning world globe – hand reaches in and stops globe.][24]

(This complex, frenetic high-tech skit was, astoundingly, performed live.) The final NBC Kovacs show climaxed with a dance number that had close to 100 people and animals on stage, ending with the destruction of the set as the credits rolled, while perspiring executives picked up the tab.

Kovacs simultaneously subbed for Steve Allen, hosting the Monday and Tuesday editions of *Tonight*. His effects-heavy fantasies didn't sit well in a show built around talk and the expense of the more elaborate gags made his tenure brief. But it did incubate two of his most famous routines: Eugene, a featherweight tenderfoot whose every action caused loud, incongruous sound effects; and the tilted room, a set built on a slant which a prism lens restored to the vertical, rendering everything from olives to milk prone to hare off in bizarre directions as the hapless Eugene looked askance.

In January 1957 Kovacs was parachuted into a prime-time slot following a much-publicised Jerry Lewis special. Spotting a potential big break, he put everything into devising a speech-free showcase of his very best material. The 'No Dialogue' show was meticulously executed, including a perfected and expanded tilted room sketch. This was crafted comedy in the fullest sense, and won plaudits galore. Another equally precise special, *Kovacs on Music*, featured the comedy debut of André Previn. Kovacs had finally made the big time, but his pinnacle was precarious. The early experimental spirit of US TV was being rapidly eroded as big money entered the equation, and ratings became the only thing that mattered.

Kovacs was obliged to switch again, to ABC, for a series of specials and a quiz show, *Take a Good Look*. The quiz show featured his most expensive gag of all – as a used car salesman slaps a car on the bonnet, it falls through a hole in the ground, creating a bill of thousands of dollars for a thirty-second quickie. The specials were recorded with a dedicated crew in marathon all-weekend studio lock-ins. Alongside familiar routines, he created elaborate and rather elegant musical ballets of office equipment and other inanimate objects. His disdain for network top brass made itself felt in satirically amended end credits.('Associate Producer (That's like STEALING money!)')

These shows won Kovacs his only Emmy, for 'outstanding achievement in electronic camerawork'. He died in a car accident shortly after recording the eighth, which was shown in tribute a fortnight later. Like the experimenters who followed him, Kovacs remained on the fringes of television, mistrustful of its grandees and eager to undermine and mock them at every opportunity, finding door after door slammed in his face as a result. As a career model for fame-hungry comics, he was as lousy as they came. As a master craftsman, he was among the greatest.

THE PHILCO-GOODYEAR TELEVISION PLAYHOUSE: MARTY (1953)

NBC (Showcase)

TV drama mines the mundane.

I am just now becoming aware of this marvellous world of the ordinary. This is an age of savage introspection, and television is the dramatic medium through which to expose our new insights into ourselves.

Paddy Chayefsky, 1956

As TELEVISION BEGAN COLONISING the lounges of urban America, Hollywood started to panic. Playing to their strengths, the big studios began turning out product that emphasised the things TV couldn't provide: colour, star power, and most of all, size. The big screen was filled with big names in big adventures; pageants, epics and melodramas in which the safety of lives, societies, even the world hung in the balance. The challenge was made: fit that lot into your ten inches of bulbous glass.

Many programmes valiantly, if foolishly, tried to compete. Wiser heads moved in the opposite direction. Paddy Chayefsky, scion of a Russian Jewish family in the Bronx, was one of the first and best writers to size up what the small screen could and couldn't show. A moderately successful playwright, he moved into television in

1952 when the US government lifted restrictions on new TV stations, causing audiences to rocket. As Chayefsky saw it, 'television, the scorned stepchild of drama, may well be the basic theatre of our century.'[25]

TV imitations of cinema condemned themselves to a lazy, second rate status, the lack of resources perpetually showing them up. 'You cannot handle comfortably more than four people on the screen at the same time,' he wrote. 'The efforts of enterprising directors to capture the effect of five thousand people by using ten actors are pathetic.'[26] From his very first TV efforts, Chayefsky took a clear look at how life could convincingly be crammed into that tiny box.

It was during the rehearsals for *The Reluctant Citizen*, a play about an elderly Jewish immigrant, that Chayefsky found the scenario for his greatest TV work. Due to the cost of Manhattan real estate, NBC augmented their rehearsal studios at 30 Rock with any spare bit of space going in the city. Hotel ballrooms in daylight hours were a prime source. While mooching around one of these during a break, Chayefsky's eye fell on a sign put up for a singles night: 'Girls, please dance with the man who asks you. Remember, men have feelings too.' This intimation of painful male shyness caught Chayefsky's imagination, and he soon began writing 'the most ordinary love story in the world.'[27]

Rod Steiger played the title role, a good-natured but reticent Italian-American butcher in the Bronx shamed by friends, family and customers for his enduring single status at thirty-six. ('I'm a fat, ugly little guy and the girls don't go for me, that's all.') One night he's all but forced into going to a singles dance by his domineering mother. ('Why don't you go to the Waverley Ballroom? It's loaded with tomatoes!') The evening looks like being yet another slog of rejection and heartache, until a lairy guy offers him five bucks to take 'a real dog' off his hands. Marty is disgusted by the idea, but finds the girl in question, Clara. He asks her, genuinely, for a dance and they bond over their shared misfortunes. ('You don't get to be good-hearted by accident. You gotta be kicked around long enough and hard enough, then you get to be like a real . . . a professor of pain, you know?')

The rough, natural dialogue with its repetitive, drowsy poetry was a revelation. The final scene, in which Marty finally plucks up courage to spurn his deadbeat pals, phone Clara and ask her out, was partly improvised by Steiger when the real dialogue slipped out of his head on the night. It fitted in seamlessly. His performance impressed director Elia Kazan enough to land him a part on *On the Waterfront*, and a star was born. Cinema may have had TV looking over its shoulder, but 'movie star' remained the top job.

'The basic limitation of television is time,' thought Chayefsky. 'Television cannot take a thick, fully woven fabric of drama. It can only handle simple lines of movement and consequently smaller amounts of crisis.'[28] That said, *Marty* packed a great deal into well under an hour. Its wonderfully minimal effects included an exterior shot of the ballroom made from cardboard and light bulbs. When Marty followed the distraught Clara out onto the ballroom fire escape and asked her to dance, the tender moment was undercut by some incidental laughter from elsewhere in the building. *Marty* was a basic affair, but basic didn't mean simple.

Two years later *Marty* became the first TV drama to be remade for the big screen. With Ernest Borgnine in the lead, real Bronx locations and an expansion of the 'cantankerous aunt' subplot, it was a mighty success and took several Oscars, including Best Picture and Screenplay. Chayefsky had achieved that rarest of fames: the TV writer as household name. In a Nat Hiken comedy sketch, Phil Silvers played one half of a pretentious theatregoing couple who mistake the apartment of a dysfunctional, blue collar family for an off-off-Broadway venue. As they settle on the sofa, the nonplussed residents start squabbling at top volume. Silvers knowingly remarks to his wife, 'obviously by Paddy Chayefsky'.

The TV networks moved their centres of production across country to Hollywood, and Chayefsky fell out of love with the medium he'd championed. The easy, trusting commissions he'd had in the early years gave way to the business-driven pseudo-science of corporation men, with whose ideas the writer was expected to compromise willingly. Many of Chayefsky's pitches got no further than the pilot stage, including a 1965 sitcom version of *Marty* starring Tom Bosley.

Another grounded project was *The Man Who Beat Ed Sullivan*, about a hick Ohio entertainer whose marathon variety show becomes a national sensation. (Chayefsky didn't help his case by insisting that the variety show within the play should actually be a full-on, three-hour spectacular in itself.) It wasn't until 1974 that Chayefsky arranged his televisual disaffection into a film script about a suicidal newsreader, a power-crazed producer and a corporate conspiracy: his valedictory masterpiece, the cellar-dark satire *Network*. It was a damning testimony against the medium's worst excesses by one of its pre-eminent craftsmen; television's finest humane miniaturist denouncing its increasingly inhuman gigantism. Promoting the film, Chayefsky had three sad words for his *alma mater*: 'Television? Forget it.'[29]

SMALL TIME (1955–66)
ITV (Associated-Rediffusion)
Giants of children's television assemble.

CHILDREN HAVE ENJOYED A special relationship with television since the very first transmissions. The BBC gave them their own playground in the schedules with *Watch with Mother*, in 1950, where they could enjoy the company of clattering puppet mules, unintelligible folk assembled from garden implements and the very biggest spotty dog you ever did see – all chaperoned by jolly matriarchs dispensing orotund vowels through shatterproof smiles. With its sailor suits and spinning tops and crumpets on the trolley, it was childhood as the Edwardians would have recognised it: the childhood, more or less, of the programme makers, handed down like a careworn teddy bear. When ITV arrived a few years later, its TV crèche was decorated in unmistakeably bolder, more modern style.

Beginning as a fifteen minute segment in Associated-Rediffusion's weekday *Morning Magazine* line-up, *Small Time* soon gravitated towards its natural teatime home, and grew into a proving ground for a vast swathe of children's TV talent. Many of the segments – *Booty Mole, Snoozy the Sea Lion, Gorki the Straw Goat* to name a few – would live on only in a few very keen baby-boomer memories. A few, though, added up to as great a legacy as one TV slot could hope to spawn.

The Adventures of Twizzle starred a Pinocchio-esque boy puppet who could extend his limbs at will. The stories, from the pen of Roberta Leigh, were brought to life by puppeteer Joy Laurey, but of more historic note was the show's producer, future 'Supermarionation' chief Gerry Anderson. Another artificial lad, *Torchy the Battery Boy*, arrived a few years later courtesy of the same team. The results could only be described as 'sub-marionation': strings were thick as mooring cables, movements spasmodic. But this was the style, or lack of style, of the times. 'Production values' existed neither as jargon, nor as values. The job was done with the means to hand: nothing more and nothing less.

Puppets of the glove variety formed the second line of teatime attack. These were several degrees sprightlier, and occasionally wittier, than their dangling cohorts. Pussycat Willum, a doe-eyed kitten, became *Small Time*'s eager, if slightly mawkish, figurehead. But the strand's undoubted star turns were Ollie Beak and Fred Barker. This portly owl and calcified dish mop of a cockney dog were the creations of Peter Firmin, operated by Wally Whyton and Ivan Owen respectively. Their main human foil was Muriel Young, announcer on Rediffusion's opening night and a primly tolerant foil for the duo's impromptu shenanigans. More raucous yet were *The Three Scampis*: Bert Scampi (operator Howard Williams) and his animal pals, hedgehog Spike McPike (Wally Whyton) and aristocratic fox Basil Brush (Ivan Owen). Again, Firmin was the man behind the sewing machine.

Firmin had been introduced to television by Rediffusion's young stage manager and part-time prop maker, Oliver Postgate. In 1958 Postgate, tiring of organising other people's programmes, created one of his own. *Alexander the Mouse* was a whimsical tale of a rodent with royal aspirations, set behind the skirting board of an old house, the first of what would be a long line of wistfully remote Postgate worlds. Firmin painted the characters and sets, which were stuck to metal strips and 'animated' live on air by dragging magnets about under the table. This attempt to undercut even the ultra-cheap *Crusader Rabbit* production technique had the catch that, according to Postgate, 'hardly a programme went out without . . . a hand coming into shot or a mouse coming adrift.'[30]

Postgate's next attempt, the Willow Patterned *Journey of Master*

Ho, took a more conventional approach to movement. Cut-out figures were manipulated in stop motion in a makeshift studio in Postgate's North Finchley back bedroom, shot and edited on a 16mm film rig made of Meccano and string for £175 per ten minute episode. In 1959 he reunited with Firmin to create their first classic story. *Ivor the Engine* was a gloriously melancholy tale of the sole locomotive of the idyllic Merioneth and Llantisilly Rail Traction Company Limited. Firmin's watercolour evocations of the Welsh mountains were exquisite, but the tone Postgate's narration took, hitting a plaintive, nostalgic note halfway between John Betjeman and Dylan Thomas, was the greatest innovation. Moving away from the stiff-backed, once-upon-a-time scene-setting of previous children's programmes, Postgate injected poetry and personality, trusting small children to engage with something more than a bland narrative of mild peril that ended in time for supper.

As the sixties ran on, *Small Time*'s big talents slowly dispersed to the four corners of television: Anderson and company to forge a puppet dynasty, Postgate and Firmin to carve a homely niche in animation, Brush to Saturday night ubiquity, and Young to produce acres of glam rock television. The strand's last significant signing was Pippy the Tellyphant, a pantomime elephant operated by husband-and-wife team Jimmy and June Kidd, which cost an unprecedented £300 to construct. Pippy provokes few nostalgic reveries these days, while her cheaper, humbler companions, strapped for cash but bursting with ideas, have taken their place in the TV annals. The hearts and minds of millions were won over with cardboard and felt.

THE PHIL SILVERS
SHOW (1955–9)
CBS

Sitcom comes of age.

*'Andrew Armstrong, Tree Surgeon'? That's a television idea? Well,
who knows. Look what they did with a fat bus driver.*
Bilko's Television Idea, 12 February 1957

BY THE MID-1950S, SITCOM was already being dismissed by
critics as a fad on the wane. It had come a long way in the few
short years since its simple beginnings, from the down-to-Earth
compactness of *The Honeymooners* to George Burns hurdling the
fourth wall and Lucille Ball's international stardom with *I Love
Lucy*. Despite this tide of invention, or perhaps because of it, when
inspiration began to flag for so much as a season, critics sprang
up to predict the death of the American sitcom. The trouble was,
as John Crosby observed when hailing *The Phil Silvers Show*, 'every
time you start to count out situation comedy as a dead duck,
something comes along.'[31]

Master Sergeant Ernest G. Bilko was a new kind of sitcom hero,
eight times smarter than the average viewer could hope to be, and
a thousandth as honest and hardworking as they claimed to be.
Bilko's essential good nature, fatherly love of his reprobate army
platoon, and Phil Silvers' winning smile were all trotted out as
redemptive justifications for the popularity of this good-for-nothing

snake, but it was simpler than that. The double-crossing, dissembling, greedy slacker had the American dream down pat – his country was the one serving him.

Though it was, like all sitcoms, an ensemble effort, Bilko had two major creative forces. The fast-talking vaudeville comic Phil Silvers had steadily built up a solid but unspectacular profile since the war, specialising in sketches that showcased his knack for speedy patter and swift ad-libs, usually playing against a taciturn and bewildered stooge. He was paired by CBS executive Hubbell Robinson with writer Nat Hiken, who had moved from local radio comedies to TV variety sketch shows. Steeped in the desperately inventive chicanery of the Broadway milieu, especially its notoriously disingenuous press agents, Hiken saw Silvers in a similarly underhand role. After considering set-ups ranging from baseball team manager to stockbroker to Turkish bath attendant, they settled on the immortal master sergeant.[32]

Initially titled *You'll Never Get Rich* after the lyric from the song 'You're In the Army Now', Hiken's creation was to its rival sitcoms what Bilko was to his rival sergeants. Previously, one plot reversal had been considered quite enough for the average sitcom's twenty-four minutes. Hiken put in at least one more, sometimes two or three. Hitherto simple plots of swindling and misapprehension doubled and quadrupled before the viewer's eyes, finally to be snapped shut again by some spectacularly deft sewing up of strands in the closing seconds. At script meetings, Hiken had a compulsive habit of creating little origami animals as he outlined a plot.[33] Whether it was incidents at an army post or scrap paper, the skill was the same – artfully precise manipulation.

The cast ranged in experience from seasoned actor Paul Ford as Bilko's just-dumb-enough colonel, to complete non-professionals – filthy nightclub comic Joe E. Ross played childlike Mess Sergeant Rupert Ritzik, and hopeless slob Maurice Gosfield played hopeless slob Private Duane Doberman. The bulk of the lines inevitably went to Silvers, but there was a fine balance at work here: Bilko's corporals Henshaw and Barbella oscillated between willing henchmen and disapproving moralists; the excitable Private Paparelli could often out-talk his sergeant; the chorus of rival sergeants occasionally got one over on their nemesis. The scenes when Bilko and Colonel Hall were alone together remain among the best in sitcom, a perspicacious fox inexorably pulling the wool over the eyes of a sappy bloodhound.

Hiken assembled a crack team of writers around him, including a young Neil Simon, but his obsessive nature meant he could never leave a script alone, often rewriting it into a completely new show. The Writers Guild, suspicious of the prevalence of Hiken's name on the credits, tried to lobby for the other writers, only to be told by those writers that he really did have significant input to almost every programme.[34] Hiken also made regular appearances on the studio floor to fiddle with minuscule details of staging. With so much depending on one man, it was inevitable that later seasons began to slip from the early stratospheric heights.

The decline showed in the increasing use of guest stars. Where previously celebrities would be satirical inventions like inane comedian Buddy Bickford or rock 'n' roll sensation Elvin Pelvin, now the real-life likes of Ed Sullivan, Mickey Rooney and Kay Kendall would turn up. Setting the pattern for countless comedies hence, it began as a display of the show's popularity and became a sign of flagging inspiration. The quality level remained high, but the platoon's move for its final season from Fort Baxter, Kansas to the Californian heat of Camp Fremont held a sad irony.

US television's big east-to-west move would affect sitcom as much as drama. Though set in Kansas, Bilko was really a New York show, drawn from the Broadway melting pot, infused with Jewish humour and recorded at the old DuMont studios. Over the next few years sitcoms would become slower, simpler and sillier. The dialogue was less snappy and the characters less smart as network bosses sought to woo Middle America. *The Phil Silvers Show* merely opened with a cartoon; shows like *Gilligan's Island* and *Mr Ed* (the latter backed by George Burns) were cartoons themselves, often not particularly good ones. Add a plethora of

Hollywood-produced 'adult' western shows and the cosy croon of Perry Como to the evening schedules, and the televisual tide was decisively turning from Hiken's satirical high water mark. Those critical jeers began to look less precious and more prophetic with each new season. Bilko could outsmart anyone, but he couldn't cope with being out-dumbed.

A SHOW CALLED FRED (1956)

ITV (Associated-Rediffusion)

Television comedy explodes.

TV isn't like films, radio or the stage. It has bits of all three in it, of course. But it is something demanding a new approach.
Terry-Thomas, *Answers*, 6 October 1951

COMIC GENIUS HAS THE habit of springing up in several places at once. About the time Ernie Kovacs was conducting his early Pennsylvanian experiments, Terry-Thomas, the gentleman's gentleman comic, was regaling BBC audiences with *How Do You View?* Written by Sid Colin and Talbot Rothwell, this loose assemblage of sketches and monologues pioneered countless bits of televisual business: the deadpan nonsense interview (conducted by linkmen Leslie Mitchell and Brian Johnston); mock home movies; the constantly-interrupted speech; and the random foray off the set and around the cameras, booths and assorted detritus of the studio, just for the hell of it. Its success in those sparse early days was considerable, although critics were snooty. 'I should not care to say,' ventured a confused C. A. Lejeune, 'whether the presentation is more formless or the material more inept.'[35]

While 'T-T' was in his pomp on TV, the BBC Home Service was plagued by an infestation of nits. *The Goon Show* didn't so much break the rules of radio comedy as blithely caper on to the air in complete ignorance that any existed in the first place. With its cast of vocal grotesques and relaxed approach to the laws of cause and effect, it became an unhinged institution to a nation still recovering from the similarly lunatic privations of war. Two Goons – writer Spike Milligan and voice-of-them-all Peter Sellers – joined forces with young American director Richard Lester to translate their formula to independent television, in the form of *The Idiot Weekly, Price 2d.*

The fusty periodical of the title, inspired by the florid world of *Daily Express* humorist Beachcomber, provided an extremely tenuous jumping-off point for a bewildering array of skits, with Sellers playing Edwardian schoolmasters and gentleman boxers, 'Footo, the Wonderboot explorer' and even much-loved Goon character Bluebottle. Blackout gags included an expectant audience sat before a curtain, which was raised to reveal another audience, facing them. Singers like Patti Lewis got a custard pie in the face. This time, the critics had caught up with the viewers: even the *Daily Mail* dug this 'bubble of nonsense which stayed miles above the surface of reality.'[36]

A few months later the same gang made *A Show Called Fred*, which scrapped the magazine trappings and intensified the lunacy. As the *Daily Mail* noted, *The Idiot Weekly* 'made a few grudging concessions to the audience, in as much as it was possible to follow the jokes by the ordinary, accepted sense of humour. *Fred* makes no concessions at all.'[37]

A typical edition of *Fred* began with Spike, dressed in rags, mooching around the Associated-Rediffusion studio corridors: a parody of the Rank Films gong (which Terry-Thomas also lampooned) and credits for 'the well-known Thespian actors' Kenneth Connor and Valentine Dyall (usually clad in bow tie, dinner jacket and no shirt). There would be mock interviews with insane individuals, often called Hugh Jampton, commercials for 'Muc, the wonder deterrent', and viewer query slot 'Idiots' Postbag', presented in front of a projected backdrop of open sea, or a burning building. ('Dear sir, do you know what horse won the Derby in 1936?' 'Yes, Mr Smith, I do.')

Even by the primitive standards of the day, the thing was hero-ically shoddy. Backdrops wobbled and frayed at the edges, costumes were either half-complete or non-existent, and in the frequent pull-out shots to take in backstage crew and chunky EMI cameras, the floor was visibly covered in studio junk. As with Kovacs's shows, laughter came from the camera crew rather than an audience. *Fred* ended with an extended parody of the various po-faced dramas with which it shared the schedules. Soap opera *The Grove Family* became 'The Lime Grove Family': 'Mum' cooked roast peacocks' tongues on baked mangoes in the piano, whereupon 'son' hit her with a club, and was reprimanded by 'dad', saying, 'You mustn't hit your mother like that. You must hit her like *this* . . .' Their version of *The Count of Monte Cristo* featured the first appearance of the famous coconut-halves-for-horses'-hooves sight gag and ended with the destruction of the already threadbare set, a rousing chorus of 'Riding Along On the Crest of a Wave', and Valentine Dyall doing the dishes in the studio's self-service canteen.

Descriptions like this are hopelessly inadequate. As Bernard Levin put it, 'if you do not think that is funny it is either because I have failed to convey its essence or because there is something wrong with you.'[38] Peter Black agreed: 'This show has built up in three weeks a following that has gone beyond enthusiasm. It is an addiction.'[39] Critical credentials notwithstanding, these men were television comedy's first fanboys.

When stuff like *Fred* appeared on the continent, it was Absurdist theatre, afforded its rightful place in the cultural pantheon. Over here it was just British rubbish. Bernard Levin tried to redress matters, asserting that the *Fred* team 'have done television a service comparable to that rendered by Gluck to opera, or Newton to mathematics.'[40] Philip Purser claimed *Fred* was 'roughly equivalent to the revolution in the theatre promoted by Bertolt Brecht; and not entirely dissimilar.'[41] It certainly created its own version of Brecht's Alienation Effect. 'I had to make a very real effort of will on Wednesday,' recounted Levin of trying to watch *Gun-Law*, the bog-standard western which followed *Fred*, 'to convince myself that this was not meant to be funny. For a long time I could not stop expecting Mr Spike Milligan to put his mad, bearded head round the corner of the screen with some devastating remark about the shape of Sheriff Dillon's face.'[42]

Milligan's TV year ended with *Son of Fred*, available for the first time in the north, with cartoons by Bob Godfrey's Biographic Films, mocked up technical breakdowns and Gilbert Harding's Uncle Cuthbert playing the contra-bassoon while suspended from wires in a wheelchair. ('Kind of an aerial fairy,' he explained.) It also inaugurated the grand tradition of putting jokes in the *TV Times* listings. ('Frisby Spoon appears without permission.') In 1963 a compilation, *The Best of Fred*, was presented to a public that, claimed ITV, had now 'caught up' with Milligan's anarchic humour, with Milligan and Dyall reminiscing over the show's distant heyday in between clips. Innovation had become nostalgia.

Lester would go on to give the Beatles silly things to do on film. Milligan inaugurated the *Q* series in 1969, which took his illogical methods down increasingly strange paths. Meanwhile his former co-Goon Michael Bentine cooked up a more technically elaborate version of the same mayhem for the BBC's *It's a Square World*. But *Fred*'s place in history would be secured by countless other hands. All around the country, short-trousered future members of *Python, The Goodies* and other anarcho-comic collectives were watching closely and making mental notes. As Peter Cook would later note, Milligan 'opened the gate into the field where we now all frolic.'[43]

MY WILDEST DREAM (1956–7)
ITV (Granada)

The comedy panel show outstays its welcome

A panel of celebrities, of one kind or another, are asked in turn to identify somebody they have met in the past. One of the particular eccentricities of television was shown up in this programme – the choosing of a 'celebrity' for the panel with no qualification or aptitude.

Review of *Place the Face*,
Manchester Guardian, 9 July 1957

THE PANEL SHOW WAS a mainstay of television right from the beginning, for reasons both cultural and commercial. The cultural: since the nineteenth century the parlour game, a relaxed after-dinner orgy of banter and one-upmanship, was the icing on the middle class party cake, a civilised letting-down of the hair. The commercial: it's cheap. It's wit without a script, drama without a set, sport kept safely indoors. A prestigious panel show will have the country's greatest two-dozen raconteurs fighting to appear on it. For a less prestigious one, a hundred dim bulbs will tear each other to pieces. Get the initial ingredients right, and it keeps itself afloat with minimal effort – it's the perpetual motion format.

The cosy, chatty panel game established itself as a national comfort blanket on radio during the war. The BBC Home Service's

Brains Trust, in which clubbable eggheads like Kenneth Clark and Jacob Bronowski debated esoteric enquiries sent in by the public, reached nearly a third of Britons and made highbrows into stars. At the same time, the ease of it all bred suspicion. In 1942, questions were asked in the Commons on whether the *Trust* participants' fees of £20 per session 'for attempting to answer very simple questions' was public money for old rope.[44] It was certainly valuable old rope: in 1954, *One Minute Please*, predecessor to the long-running *Just a Minute*, became the first BBC panel format sold to the USA when Dumont bought the TV rights for $104,000.[45]

On television, two shows dominated. Vocational guessing game *What's My Line?* began on CBS in 1950 and hit the BBC the following year, augmenting the elitist 'wits' enclave' with a celebration of honest (but preferably amusingly odd) everyday work. In 1956 Princess Margaret attended an edition, watching from a special 'royal box' rigged up in the stalls. Then there was the loftier *Animal, Vegetable, Mineral?* This was an archaeological quiz that challenged academics to identify cuttlefish beaks and Tibetan prayer wheels, employed a young David Attenborough on its production team and invited viewers 'to follow the fluctuating course of the contest as the experts grope towards the right solution, and perhaps enjoy a nice cosy feeling of superiority meanwhile.'[46]

Its star turn was archaeologist Sir Mortimer Wheeler, whose powers of observational deduction were second to none, though this wasn't what made him such a draw. With a florid, expressive face, aided by an atavistic moustache made for twirling, he'd frown intensely at a flint axe or quern – hum, ha, squint, peer – then, in a cartoonish light bulb moment, all but leap in the air as the penny dropped. This showmanship was aided by the custom of lunching the panel, together with chairman Glyn Daniel, at a Kensington restaurant prior to live transmission. Occasionally, the team lunched too well: Daniel on one occasion lost complete track of the scores, decided nobody really cared anyway, and later, staring down the camera lens, used one of the objects – an Aboriginal charm – to put a hex on 'the viewer who sent me a very silly letter.'[47]

This element of risk cast a long shadow over the format's early days. Panel regular Gilbert Harding built a reputation for rudeness that frequently tipped over into outright disdain, such as his notorious claim to a *What's My Line?* contestant that 'I'm tired of looking at you.' In 1954 the BBC, in a fit of panel game mania, commissioned several shows based on viewers' ideas. Results included *Change Partners*, in which the panel had to sort eight married challengers into their constituent couples, working out who was shacking up with whom by asking them to recall marriage proposals, ruffle each others' hair in an affectionate manner, etc. A year later they apologetically axed all their panel shows, except *What's My Line?* [48]

ITV rushed in where the Beeb now feared to tread. In 1956 Granada converted an old BBC radio format into a prospective early evening panel hit. The panel took its cue from *Does the Team Think?*, Jimmy Edwards's pastiche of *The Brains Trust*, which consisted of four comedians battling to out-gag and upstage each other. For *My Wildest Dream* the urbane Terry-Thomas led the panel, with his three 'dreaming partners' Tommy Trinder, David Nixon and Alfred Marks. Acting as 'peacemaker' was Kenneth MacLeod. It's worth taking a close look at this particular programme, which handily features all the symptoms of lazy thinking, over-egged whimsy and misplaced trust in star power that marked out the format at its worst.

The panel's objective was to determine, by diligent questioning, the secret fantasies of the humble folk wheeled before them. Inevitably, since most people's fantasies tended towards the predictable ('win the pools', 'go out with Marilyn Monroe'), a bit of creative bending of the rules crept in. Hence a woman appeared claiming she wanted more than anything to put a mouse in a guardsman's boot, while another contestant longed to tickle a point duty policeman under the arms. Such bewildering dollops of 'unbelievably fatuous' [49] whimsy would, the producers hoped, be spun into comedy gold by the dreaming partners.

This turned out to be optimistic. What happened was that four comic minds, all too aware of the humourlessness of the situation, trod water ever more frantically until panic set in. One reviewer captured the mood of an early edition. 'Last night there were intolerable bouts of shouting by all four of the panel and the chairman, and one at least of the challengers was made the butt of what could hardly be called humour. It did remain a little doubtful whether some of the quarrelling was genuine or faked because it seems to come to a peak each time before a break for advertisement.'[50] Shouting, bullying, artifice: these vices would prove hard to suppress. *My Wildest Dream* was 'not merely negatively silly but is positively revolting.'[51] It started to appear later and later in the evening schedule, and the panel calmed down a bit, but the brickbats continued to the bitter end. ('The most actively unpleasant panel show in commercial television.'[52])

A second wave of panel shows in the seventies was more self-consciously refined. BBC2 games like *Face the Music* and *Call My Bluff* were all drawing room erudition and cravatted anecdote. Once again many entries were wireless in origin (in this case Radio 4), but the TV transfer brought certain behavioural tics to the fore. 'On *Face the Music*,' noted Clive James, 'Bernard Levin takes a sip of water after getting the right answer. It is meant to look humble but screams conceit.'[53] This extra level of gamesmanship was often in danger of edging the nominal subject of the programme out of the frame entirely.

The third wave began in the nineties with *Have I Got News for You* and its many derivatives, and this time it stuck. A few years' craze became several decades' industry. Where once strutted eccentrics who'd fallen into the role (Gilbert Harding, Nancy Spain, Lady Isobel Barnett), 'panel show contestant' was now a fully furnished vocation for comedians with the right voice, cultural references and agent representation. Precious little else had changed, though. In 2014, BBC Director of Television Danny Cohen tried to redress the archaic gender balance of the genre by outlawing all-male editions. Bow ties became polo shirts, but the panel show remained essentially a gentlemen's club.

OPPORTUNITY KNOCKS (1956–78)

ITV (Associated-Rediffusion/ ABC/Thames)

The talent show girdles the globe.

THE HARD-BITTEN, SELF-MOTIVATING MEN and women who work the reality talent contests would have no need of anything as mimsy as a patron saint, but come the Judgement Day Live Final they'd be granted the protective arm-round-the-shoulder, whether they wanted it or not, of Hughie Green.

A juvenile song-and-dance man turned compère, stunt pilot and international aerospace hardware salesman, Green created radio talent show *Opportunity Knocks* in 1949 for the BBC Light Programme, though its brash tone proved too gamey for Broadcasting House. Sensing foul play in the cancellation, Green expensively sued the BBC, lost, and took the format to Radio Luxembourg for a two-and-a-half-year stint, before presenting a TV version to Associated-Rediffusion, where he presented a trial run in the summer of 1956, during which time he was declared bankrupt. The motley assortment of talent he initially offered was summed up by Bernard Levin: 'Nobody on the edition I saw actually made a model of Wembley Stadium out of butter, but there was a man who spent his entire time hopping.'[54]

The following January, at the height of its Reithian pomp, the BBC broadcast *It's Up To You*, a fortnightly talent parade from their northern studio. A panel of judges poured praise and scorn on a line-up of eccentric amateurs including, in the first edition, a man from St Helens who tied his braces round his neck and sported a lemon in his left ear, leaving the panel bewildered. 'The thing I found distracting about this man,' complained one judge, 'was the lemon in his ear.'[55]

Over on the commercial channel, Hughie was permitted to take show business as seriously as he liked. His contestants were no half-daft party tricks but honest folk with an honest hunger for fame and, on occasion, the talent to honestly acquire it. Success was determined by a postal vote, with a touch of immediacy provided by the mysterious 'clapometer', which purported to measure the level of the studio audience's applause. Green's default mode of address was a transatlantic unction so treacly its hapless recipients found themselves bogged down to the point of immobility. As one critic remarked, the effect of the Green charm offensive was to leave 'you feeling – for all the smooth assurances that we were watching new talent get its biggest break – that it was the impresario we were expected to admire'.[56] The pattern was set for *New Faces* and its twenty-first century descendants. Many contestants went on to carve decent careers for themselves (Les Dawson, Pam Ayers, Paul Daniels, Su Pollard, Lena Zavaroni and Freddie Starr among them) but the acts were increasingly a means to an end – that end being the furthering of the talent show brand and those behind it.

A man of colossal ambition, Green found national dominance unsatisfactory. In 1970, after two successful international editions of the show with Norway, Sweden and Denmark joining the UK via crackly satellite feeds, he announced his determination to tackle 'probably the biggest challenge television light entertainment has had to face': the creation of a global TV talent show. 'A communication satellite would mother a world star,' he predicted, biblically. On New Year's Eve 1973 he hosted the *Opportunity Knocks Concorde Special* from the flight deck of the supersonic craft as it zipped over the Bay of Biscay, though the acts themselves were, disappointingly, located in the usual studio.

The following year megalomania set in for keeps, as Green commandeered his own show to deliver an unbalanced anti-union rant, pushing the boundaries of celebrity privilege out of sight. It was only natural that Hughie's global stardom should peak with 'a 13,500 mile link-up via the Indian ocean satellite'[57] as OppKnox HQ, London joined its newly-created sister franchise at the Channel 7 studios in Sydney, and Hughie's Aussie counterpart Johnnie Farnham (like Hughie, a former cabaret man with national smash hit 'Sadie the Cleaning Lady' under his belt).

With a studio complete with audience and full orchestra apiece, Hughie and Johnnie batted the banter back and forth across the heavenly void, with plenty of well-wrangled applause to cover the time delay. Five previously successful contestants from each country, including Pam Ayers and Frank Carson for the Brits, competed for the special Satellite Trophy. A brave new world beckoned, a globe unified in the name of talent. Nation shall mark spinning plates out of ten unto nation.

Within two years, all the gimmicks used up, *Opportunity Knocks* came to an end. (A BBC revival in the late '80s featured Bob Monkhouse as compère and introduced the telephone voting system.) Green didn't stay down for long, though. He returned in 1980 as 'adviser' to London Independent Television, one of the many consortia tendering bids for the 1982 ITV regional franchise renewal. LIT's typically immodest bid – it was planning to replace both Thames and London Weekend – included *Crossroads* five days a week, a breakfast programme, *Good Morning London*, and a familiar-sounding entertainment programme called *Talent Scouts*, identity of host to be confirmed. Today's TV talent magnates, powerful as they are, remain little more than tribute acts to the great Hughie.

THE SINGING RINGING TREE (1957)
BBC1 (DEFA)

The garish Euro-fable that haunted a generation.

CHILDREN'S ENTERTAINMENT CARRIES TWO schools of thought. The first, which dominates thinking in Britain and the United States, exalts the carefree state of childhood above all else. Fun, jokes, songs and slapstick are the order of the day – kids will have enough time to learn the dry reality of life when they grow up. Let's name this school after one of its early popular manifestations, a manically droll panto caper initiated by the BBC in 1955: the School of *Crackerjack*. Its opposite number takes the view that life can be harsh, and children need to be prepared for that. Fantasy is good, but always tinged with a melancholy, even morbid, edge. This school was represented in Britain by Oliver Postgate's thoughtful stop motion tales, but was mainly prevalent in Europe, especially the part near the Iron Curtain: the *Singing Ringing Tree* Movement.

Das Singende Klingende Bäumchen was a film made by DEFA, the state film studio of the German Democratic Republic in Potsdam, a loose adaptation of the Brothers Grimm fairy tale *The Singing Springing Lark*, packed with spoilt princesses, dashing princes, evil dwarves and supernatural inter-species transformations. Appropriately enough, it looked like nothing on Earth. Magical forests were rendered in those am-dram materials, papier mâché and plywood. Rustic architecture bulged, twisted and kinked as if

51

grown from seed, and floral forms rippled with a coating of fresh porridge. Lawns had the feel of a grocer's window display, flames were unapologetically papery and those distant hills it took the prince three days on horseback to reach were nevertheless eclipsed by his shadow – or rather one of his four shadows. Then there was the musical score, which began in syrupy orchestral mode but soon veered off into grating organ leitmotifs that would have had members of Throbbing Gristle asking for the night light to be left on.

Even if they couldn't put it into words, kids could sense the wrongness of this world. For many, it added to the appeal, the laissez-faire approach to storytelling mimicking their own, ever-changing, playground adventures. For others, the claustro-phobic kingdom, rendered in a queasy palate of jade greens, sunburst yellows and atomic puce gave the nightmare fable a feverish sheen as enervating as it was compelling. But whether you willingly dived into this bumper colouring book, or warily regarded it through a glass of Lucozade darkly, you were, in the old-fashioned, malevolent sense of the word, enchanted.

Despite jeers from the state's Marxist-Leninist film critics, who deplored its 'positive depiction of a reactionary society', it became one of DEFA's biggest successes in its native country. It would have stayed there if it hadn't been for the BBC's progressive yet cash-strapped children's department, recently rechristened 'family programming' and which by 1964 was scouring the continent for schedule fillers more affordable than the USA's premium product. Heavily subsidised and going for a song, *The Singing Ringing Tree* fitted the bill perfectly. Peggy Miller sliced it into three twenty-minute segments with an overdubbed storybook narration read by *Late Night Line-Up* presenter Tony Bilbow, whose measured tones faded in and out over the forthright declamation of the German actors, a reassuring presence in a world of antlered horses and giant ice-bound goldfish.

While other imports had their fans, like the cheery *Heidi* and wistful *The Boy Who Loved Horses*, nothing came close to *The Singing*

Ringing Tree's high contrast discomfiture. It returned to the BBC every couple of years under the tenure of children's department head Monica Sims, who consulted child psychologists to help determine the limits of child-frightening television. She concluded that 'sometimes quite frightening experiences in fantasy programmes are far enough divorced from their own surroundings not to frighten them too badly . . . they get a frisson from it, but they know it isn't actually happening here.'[58] The Ruritanian cake-in-the-rain trappings of *The Singing Ringing Tree* certainly passed the anti-realism test, and the three-part wonder remained a fixture until 1980.

Along the way, it picked up many companions. From Yugoslavia came equine romance *White Horses*, with a Jackie Lee theme song that made the top ten. France provided the more boyish contingent with overcast swashbuckler *The Flashing Blade*. Some series played up to national stereotype: West Germany's *The Legends of Tim Tyler* was a mordant modern fable about a boy who traded his laugh with a sinister millionaire, while the Dutch *Children of Totem Town* concerned an experimental hippie commune for kids. Towards the end, they were just insane, like Spain's *Oscar, Kina and the Laser*, in which a boy genius invents a talking laser, then flees with it and his pet goose in tow. But perhaps the most potent was Czechoslovakian parable *The Secret of Steel City*, a tale of two rival kingdoms, one democratic and peaceful, the other totalitarian, heavily industrialised in High Victorian manner, and preparing a super freeze weapon to conquer their neighbours. Even its knee-high audience could see through the feathered hats and Jules Verne steamship paraphernalia to the Cold War allegory beneath. The garnish of fantasy could let you slip subversive education to the kids, as well as scare them witless.

SIX-FIVE SPECIAL (1957–8)

BBC

TV's first rock 'n' roll smash hit.

I knew we were in for some laughs when, at our first recording session, we were instructed to play out of tune because, in the words of Mr Good, 'it doesn't sound fascist enough'.
Benny Green recalls his tenure in Lord Rockingham's XI,
Daily Mirror, 27 January 1979

HERE'S AN INSTRUCTIVE EPISODE in the history of media hiring practice. Back in the mid-1950s when he undertook the BBC training course for junior producers, Jack Good made a bizarre mock advertisement as his graduation piece: a promotional spot for luxury coffins, which featured boxer Freddie Mills throwing Chelsea pensioners off the cliffs at Beachy Head.

Anyone exhibiting such jubilant bad taste these days (and allowing for the moral inflation of the last sixty years, its contemporary equivalent would have to be quite something) would be shown the door by the men from compliance. Instead, Good was given a free pass to create a sizeable chunk of youth TV, in the same casual manner. 'These fat guys at the BBC said, "You look like a young chap, put something together with mountain climbing, fashion for girls, that sort of thing,"' Good recalled. 'I thought, I'll put rock 'n' roll on.'[59]

The *Six-Five Special*'s arrival was fortuitously timed. Not only did it coincide with Bill Haley's first, epochal tour of the UK, it got first dibs on the brand new teatime slot. The 6–7 p.m. hour was previously a televisual dead zone by government decree, to allow parents to get younger children to bed, and older ones to do their homework. Into this oasis of orderly sobriety, Good brought unbridled anarchy.

'This is basically a programme for young people,' admitted the *Radio Times*, 'but the term is relative. Rock 'n' rolling grandmothers and washboard-playing grandfathers are welcome aboard the "*Special*".'[60] The Beeb intended rock 'n' roll to be just one element of a varied magazine programme featuring sports coverage and other healthy outdoor activities, but Good knew the kids just wanted music.

For the first edition, conventional sets were built in Hammersmith's Riverside Studios. Shortly before the live transmission, Good had the sets dismantled, leaving a bare studio in which guest stars, house band The Frantic Five and presenters Josephine Douglas and Pete Murray mingled informally with the audience of jiving teenagers. ('A hundred cats are jumping here!') The cameras lingered on the exuberant dancers as much as on the acts, and prizes were offered to couples who 'cut the cutest capers'.

Square folks were aghast. 'I feel thoroughly disgusted that the powers-that-be give time to exhibitions such as this. I cannot imagine that any decent-minded girl would permit herself to be pulled around in such a way, even to the extent of allowing herself to be thrown at times over the shoulders of the males taking part,' fumed an outraged citizen of Penarth.[61] Success was assured.

Early editions established the format, with Tommy Steele a regular draw. Ten shows in, shaggy-haired, surly 'Six-Five Specialist' Jim Dale arrived, graduating from warm-up man to main attraction. Uneasy with what he saw as the forced adulation the audience lavished upon him, he adopted a serious, unsmiling countenance as a defence mechanism. The twelve-million-strong audience, seeing their own youthful sullenness transformed by the cameras into cool belligerence, adored him even more, and television began following the movies in turning previously mortifying awkwardness into an alluring detachment.

Good soon became restless, feeling restricted by the 'jolly, hearty' element imposed on his programme (Freddie Mills's 'healthy activity' spot was fine, but ramrod-backed guests such as Regimental Sergeant-Major Ron 'Tibby' Brittain quashed the groovy mood somewhat). The nugatory wage the BBC paid him didn't help matters either. He upped sticks in 1958 for the more indulgent, independent pastures of ABC, the weekend-only independent broadcaster for the midlands and the north. 'I want to bring a breath of excitement to television,' he claimed in the publicity for *Oh Boy!*, 'the fastest, most exciting show to hit TV' which launched directly opposite the *Special* in June of that year.

Escaping the Beeb's square tendency, Good made *Oh Boy!* about the music only – up to eighteen numbers in forty minutes with minimal fluff in between, accompanied by a wilder house band, Lord Rockingham's XI. Thirteen weeks in, it was netting five million viewers, helped by hot footage of Cliff Richard that was condemned in the press. 'His violent hip-swinging during an obvious attempt to copy Elvis Presley was revolting – hardly the kind of performance any parent could wish their children to witness,' raged, of all institutions, the *NME*. 'Remember, Tommy Steele became Britain's teenage idol without resorting to this form of indecency.'[62]

Most of *Oh Boy!*'s viewers were poached from *Six-Five*. Good played up the inter-channel rivalry wherever he could, issuing dire warnings of industrial espionage: 'Remember that spies are every-where – ours as well as theirs – and a source of leakage will not remain hidden for long.'[63] The *Special* rattled on without Good on the footplate, but the strain was beginning to show. A hasty September revamp went for all-out, show-stopping gigantism. A lavish new set – 'the biggest in European TV' – was built. Three new house bands were hired. Six female hosts – the '*Six-Five* Dates' – shared presentation duties. Rock and skiffle were jettisoned in favour of beat music. It was all to no avail, and the *Special*'s journey ended on relatively desultory ratings of four and a half million.

Good's innovations continued on the other side with *Boy Meets Girls*, featuring Marty Wilde and the sixteen Vernons Girls in a setting Good promised was 'less frantic and less noisy than *Oh Boy!*' The show's main historical claim was the British debut of Gene Vincent, in a career doldrums after 'Be-Bop-A-Lula', whom Good remodelled in a leather-and-medallion rebel biker image, even, according to legend, egging him on to accentuate his motor-bike injury with the off-stage exhortation, 'Limp, you bugger, limp!'

When he tired of that, he went off in the opposite direction with *Wham!*, introducing 'The Fat Noise', a gargantuan house band which produced 'the fattest, roundest sound that has ever come to television.' But nothing was working, and Good departed for the USA, to finally hit real paydirt at the ABC network with *Shindig!* and set The Monkees on their path to self-destruction with the chaotic TV special *33 1/3 Revolutions Per Monkee*.

Good returned to the UK sporadically throughout the next few decades, engineering various *Oh Boy!* revivals to put a spring in the step of middle-aged Teds, but he became increasingly estranged from contemporary pop with every slight return. Finally, in 1992, Jack Good left the music television business he'd been instrumental in creating, in as unexpected a way as he'd entered it – he joined a Carmelite hermitage in Texas.

THE STRANGE WORLD OF GURNEY SLADE (1960)
ITV (ATV)

The sitcom eats itself.

Who and what is Anthony Newley? . . . This brown-haired, blue-eyed searcher after truth hovers and flits in and around and above the world of show business like a creative helicopter.

Radio Times, 9 November 1961

THOUGH IT STILL HANDLED rock 'n' roll with all the aplomb of Stan Laurel taming a cobra, television did as much as cinema and radio combined to bring big, brash all-round American entertainment to the chilly front rooms of ration-squeezed Britain. The size, confidence and polish of those variety showcases were swiftly imitated by home-grown entertainers who got their suits reupholstered, their smiles re-pointed and their accents suspended somewhere between New England and the Old Kent Road. The alien sheen of these imitation Yanks – the brittle charm of Brucie, the oily palms of Michael Miles, the messianic humility of Hughie Green – caused amusement and unease among viewers accustomed to the polite cough and the if-you-please of English stage tradition.

Comic and singer Anthony Newley, from out of the Hackney Marshes via the Italia Conti stage school, acknowledged the incongruity of the transatlantic manner. He developed a penchant for running a self-deprecating commentary on his own act. On a UK tour to promote his film *Idol on Parade*, he stood by the screen as the opening credits rolled, talking them down, one by one. ('"Directed?" The director couldn't direct traffic! "Photographed by?" He nipped out to Boots the chemist . . .'[64]) Television, the most self-referential medium yet hatched, snapped him up.

Newley's TV accomplices were writers Sid Green and Dick Hills, who had constructed specials for Sid James, Roy Castle and, disastrously, Eamonn Andrews. Initially billing themselves as the grand 'SC Green and RM Hills', they soon relaxed into 'Sid and Dick', names more appropriate to their modern, laid-back writing style. 'They admit cheerfully that they belong with the coffee shop and back-of-the-envelope script writers,' reported the *Mail*, 'rather than the agonised pacers around kidney-shaped desks in grey flanelled rooms.'[65]

Newley's attitude to comedy writing was similarly easygoing. 'How do I define humour?' he pondered at the behest of the *TV Times*. 'I don't. I wouldn't dare.'[66] After two reasonably successful *Saturday Spectaculars* for Lew Grade's ATV in early 1960 – one featuring copious amounts of Peter Sellers – Newley, Hills and Green tackled the still maturing world of the sitcom, applying their skills in the same sideways-on manner. Given carte blanche to fill six half-hours how they fancied, they wrote, designed and shot the whole series in seven weeks. Newley was keen to point up the trio's ground-breaking intent. 'We hope to achieve humour without setting out to be deliberately funny.'[67]

An estimated twelve million viewers settled down at 8.35 p.m. on 22 October for the first episode of *The Strange World of Gurney Slade*. What they saw went roughly like this. We open on the front room of a terraced house, wherein Gurney Slade (Newley) is an unwilling participant in a *Grove Family*-style domestic soap with the feeblest acting and script known to man, all hurriedly-discharged paragraphs of backstory and leaden lines of chirpy banter. When the cue finally arrives for him to speak ('Will you have an egg, Albert?') he silently gets up, puts on his coat, moodily strutting past the floor manager and off the set, leaving the other actors mugging desperately. There's even a cartoon sound effect as he smashes through the fourth wall.

The liberated Gurney wanders the streets aimlessly for the next twenty minutes. He despairs of the state of the medium. ('"How'd you like your egg done, dear?" The Golden Years of British Entertainment! So much for Shakespeare and Sophocles.') He reads minds. He chats to animals and the inanimate. He has conversations in invented languages. ('Flangewick?' 'Clittervice!' 'Hendalcraw!' 'Mandelso!') He frolics in the park with Una Stubbs and unsuccessfully tries to dump a vacuum cleaner. Finally, wearying of his constant presence on the television screen ('I'm like a gold-fish in a bowl. I'm a poor squirming squingle under a microscope!') he begs the viewer to switch off the set and put him out of his misery.

The next few episodes were variations on the theme. Episode two in particular was a delightful romantic fantasy set on a disused airfield. Unfortunately it played out in front of an audience a good four million smaller than the opening show. ITV had a flop on their hands. Critics and punters, confused and bothered by this sullying of honest Saturday night fun with existential folderol, jeered as it all came crashing down. As one wag had it, 'Is your Gurney really necessary?'[68] Subsequent episodes were relegated to the depths of the night, where they could do less damage.

This turned out to be good timing, as things promptly became even stranger. Filmed well before the ratings nosedive, episode four swapped the bucolic exterior wanderings for the black-walled studio limbo of the avant-garde, presenting the trial of Gurney, before a Lewis Carroll kangaroo court, on the charge of having no sense of humour. ('I did a television show recently and they didn't think it was very funny.')

The fitful attempts of Gurney to win over the hostile opinions of the eternally perplexed Average-Viewer family, a jury of cloth-capped everymen and a dead-eyed manufacturer of countersunk screws, went about as well as the real world defence of the series. 'We have so much confidence in this progressive type of humour,' insisted ATV, 'that we are negotiating with Anthony Newley for another series in the new year. But not,' they judiciously added, 'necessarily *Gurney Slade*.'[69]

The sixth and final episode was further out still, being a formal deconstruction of the sitcom years before the concept made its academic debut. First a party of bowler-hatted bigwigs are shown the elements of a TV production, from cameras and microphones to The Performer ('it goes through various motions which are calculated to entertain or amuse the viewers'). Then assorted incidental characters from previous episodes reappear, and round on Gurney for giving them inadequately detailed backgrounds, leaving them in a hazily-defined state of limbo after their moment on screen. Finally Anthony Newley appears as Anthony Newley, Gurney Slade grotesquely turns into a ventriloquist's doll of himself, and Newley carries him off into the night.

At this point, the television sitcom was all of thirteen years old. When it was three, George Burns had given it the gift of self-consciousness. As it hit its teenage years, Newley granted it self-destruction. At the time it looked like just another odd little failed experiment; unlike *A Show Called Fred*, *Gurney Slade* had no Bernard Levin, no intellectual cheerleader, to trumpet its glory from the rooftops. It didn't entirely lack a legacy, though: young Newley fan David Bowie was transfixed by the programme, and started swanning about the streets of Bromley in a Gurney-esque off-white mackintosh.[70]

Green and Hills moved into firmer show business territory, helping to resurrect the television fortunes of floundering double act Morecambe and Wise. Newley carried on his own meandering course, majoring in high concept musicals, but returning to television to guest on everything from the Miss World pageant to *The Smothers Brothers Comedy Hour*. His later opinion of *Gurney Slade* was typically equivocal. 'I think it proved something,' he concluded, 'even if I'm not sure what.'[71]

ARMCHAIR THEATRE: A NIGHT OUT (1960)
ITV (ABC)

The theatrical revolution reaches the front room.

I've read your bloody play and I haven't had a wink of sleep for four nights. Well, I suppose we'd better do it.

Peter Willes commissions
Harold Pinter's *The Birthday Party*
for Associated-Rediffusion, 1959[72]

LEGEND HAS IT THAT John Osborne's *Look Back in Anger* transformed British theatre overnight from a staid world of French window farces and solemn verse epics into a fiercely committed force for social change. It didn't quite do that, but it did perform one useful service: getting the under-thirties into the stalls. This demographic shift was helped by the transmission of one of the play's cleaner passages as a BBC television 'Theatre Flash', alerting the chattering youth to the presence of something other than genteel matinees for scone-munching Aunt Ednas. A long and fruitful alliance between TV and the modern stage was born.

Another TV beneficiary was *The Birthday Party*, a drama of nameless persecution in a south coast bed and breakfast, written by jobbing actor Harold Pinter during a 1957 tour of *Doctor in the House.* Disastrous notices on its London debut threatened it with early closure until the *Sunday Times* praised it to the skies, but it took a production directed by Joan Kemp-Welch on peaktime ITV for it to reach ten million viewers. Many viewers took against its obscurity ('We are still wondering what it was all about and why we didn't switch it off').[73] Others had their eyes opened to 'a Picasso in words', something new and wonderfully different from the usual tea-table crosstalk. While many found it disturbing, one viewer reported 'loving every word . . . of the author's uproarious nonsense'.[74] After transmission, the everhelpful press department of the Tyne-Tees region became so overwhelmed by inquiries it issued a fact-sheet offering a 'reasonable and interesting interpretation' of the play. Existential drama had joined the mainstream.

ITV's main dramatic showcase at the time was *Armchair Theatre*. Initially a ragbag of classics and light comedies, it was remoulded by incoming Canadian producer Sydney Newman in 1958 to reflect the new theatrical mood of contemporary social engagement. (Newman's archetypal idea of an armchair play involved a small-time grocer threatened by a new supermarket.)[75] Many new writing talents would be discovered or nurtured by Newman, and Pinter joined their ranks on 24 April 1960 with his first original television work, *A Night Out*.

The nocturnal jaunt is made by diffident office worker Albert Stokes (Tom Bell) escaping from the home of his pathetically possessive widowed mother. The works do he attends ends in disaster when he's mischievously accused of groping a secretary. He flees, ending up in a deeply uncomfortable encounter with a hooker (Pinter's then wife, Vivien Merchant), who affects a cartoon poshness. ('You've not got any cigarettes on you? I'm very fond of a smoke. After dinner with a glass of wine. Or *before* dinner . . . with sherry.') They almost start to bond over their shared tragic isolation, but when she asks him too many questions, in a manner too like his own mum, Stokes spectacularly falls apart. With nothing in his social armoury between taciturn gaucheness and inarticulate rage, Stokes proves himself completely incapable of starting a life outside the suffocating maternal evenings of gin rummy and shepherd's pie: not so much Angry Young Man as Awkward Old Boy. Osborne's threatened men ranted with theatrical garrulousness. More appropriately for the small screen, Pinter's Stokes agonises in silent close-up.

The mysterious, spectral characters that were Pinter's trademark were perhaps unsuited to *Armchair Theatre*'s bread-'n'-scrape naturalism. (Stokes certainly shows none of the buried redeeming features a social realist anti-hero usually possesses.) But his sheepishly combative dialogue fitted perfectly with Newman's mission statement, sketching a repressed lower-middle-class claustrophobia heightened by director Philip Saville's endlessly burrowing cameras. For extra realism, the coffee stall where Stokes meets his workmates was John Johnson's famous all-night concession, normally found outside the Old Vic but shifted to the studio for the occasion.[76]

Though it wasn't Pinter's greatest work, *A Night Out* was a solid hit, reaching 6.38 million. Three days after it aired, Pinter joined the theatrical aristocracy as *The Caretaker* opened to prodigious acclaim, but he calculated that the play would have to run at the Duchess Theatre until 1990 to get the exposure *A Night Out* caught in one go.[77] As well as plays, Pinter's subsequent TV work spanned everything from *The Dick Emery Show* to *Pinter People*, a collection of sketches animated by *Sesame Street* alumnus Gerald Potterton. This was for the psychedelic series *NBC Experiment in Television*, which gave US network time over to the imaginations of everyone from Tom Stoppard to Jim Henson.

By the end of 1960 the all-purpose avant-garde TV play had become such a part of the broadcasting landscape it was ripe for parody. The writer hero of Joan Morgan's *Square Dance* toiled away at a modishly obscure drama called *Ending's No End*, featuring a Greek chorus of Teddy boys and the cast turning radioactive in the final act.[78] The joke relied on every viewer having at one time switched off something by Pinter or his contemporaries in confusion and disgust. What it ignored was the significant portion who kept watching.

HANCOCK: THE BEDSITTER (1961)
BBC

**One man, one room, twenty-five minutes –
comedy stripped bare.**

COMEDY HAS TWO POLES: far-out fantasy and close-up reality.
Both have their problems and rewards, but only one almost guarantees critical esteem by its mere presence. Possibly because of its
superficial kinship with drama, the realistic sitcom is often regarded
as the superior comic format. No-one became more thoroughly
wrapped up in this dogma than Tony Hancock.

On the radio, *Hancock's Half-Hour* distinguished itself by playing
to Hancock's strengths as a reactive, deadpan performer, as opposed
to the standard issue, wisecracking clown. Writers Ray Galton and
Alan Simpson gradually moulded the programme to fit Hancock's
sullen, defeated spirit, relying less on cohort Sid James's zany
schemes and more on the mundane frustrations of real life. The
less Hancock did, the funnier he got. The radio show's zenith was
the episode *Sunday Afternoon at Home*: the dreariness of a wet,
post-war Sabbath distilled into a litany of bored sighs, circular
conversations and desperate inanities. The farce of a life going off
the rails was replaced by the tragicomedy of a life waiting to start.

Hancock's television life was equally motionless. Ray Galton
admitted the only concession they made to the visual was that
'instead of saying "pick up that bucket", we'd say "pick that
up".'[79] What was new was Hancock's face. Framed by a heavy

Astrakhan collared coat and homburg hat, by turns boyishly jovial and froggishly depressed, its athletic malleability perfectly augmented Hancock's innate sense of comic timing. For once the weather-beaten putty features of Sid James were not the centre of attention.

For his seventh (and final) BBC television series, Hancock rationalised even further, dropping Sid and moving from East Cheam to an Earl's Court bedsitter. The new series, titled simply *Hancock*, was presented as a break with the old style. 'Ah yes, it's goodbye to all that black homburg and Astrakhan collar rubbish,' he confided to the *Radio Times*. 'Knowledge and self advancement are the things.'[80] The new Hancock was introduced with the creative bar set higher than ever.

The two-hander, an entire episode featuring just two characters confined to one set, is often seen as the hallmark of sophisticated character comedy, a rite of passage for 'quality' sitcoms. This tradition began on ITV in October 1960. *Bootsie and Snudge: A Day Off* by Marty Feldman and Barry Took saw the eponymous gentleman's club lackeys aimlessly passing the time on, again, a Sunday afternoon. (That pious ennui remains Christianity's lasting contribution to comedy.) Despite constantly making plans, they never left their shared dormitory, encountering no-one else save a rogue pigeon. Seven months later, *The Bedsitter* also centred on entertainment endlessly deferred, going one better, and one fewer.

The premise was simple: Hancock, gay bachelor in bedsit-land, idles his way through a wet afternoon (weekday unspecified), tries and fails to improve himself, accidentally secures then loses a hot date, and generally mucks about. Keeping a solo Hancock funny for 25 minutes was a tall order (aside from fleeting glimpses of Michael Aspel on Tone's dodgy telly, no-one else appears), but the mature Hancock persona was more than rich enough to fill the space – Galton and Simpson's first draft ran twenty minutes too long.[81]

The logistics of filming one man alone were intricately worked out by director Duncan Wood and designer Malcolm Goulding, ensuring the cameras could follow Hancock wherever he wandered.[82] Hancock himself became increasingly keen to exert his influence on the show beyond performance, and persuaded a grudging Wood to let him direct a handful of shots per show himself.[83] Rehearsals were rigorous, and by the time of recording Hancock was on rare word-perfect form. From Noel Coward impersonations to an elaborate TV reception ballet, he barely put a foot wrong.

At times in his frivolous soliloquy Hancock almost – but not quite – catches the camera's eye. There must have been a temptation to break the fourth wall in this episode, but the dedication to realism stopped it going down the *Burns and Allen* route (an episode of which followed *Hancock* at 9.25 p.m.). The early TV *Half-Hours* were awash with self-reference. In the very first, a couple watching Hancock's television debut annoy him so much with their snide comments he leaves the studio and enters their front room, smashing up their set, and finding himself doing the rest of the show live from a hospital bed. It wasn't a classic, and such gags were soon dumped.

A few episodes after *The Bedsitter*, a serious car accident started Hancock's well-documented decline. Galton and Simpson went on to take the two-hander to ever greater heights with *Steptoe and Son*, and the minimalist format remained a sitcom goal, attained by shows as diverse as *Porridge* and *Benson*. The solo feat has never been equalled, not even by the lad himself – ATV's lacklustre 1963 *Hancock* series tried to ape the formula in *The Early Call*, in which Hancock booked a wake-up call and fretted about it for the entire night. But the star was in the descendent and the script was second rate – in place of Tone's epic struggle with Bertrand Russell's *Human Knowledge: Its Scope and Limits*, we got some uninspired business with a chest expander. The closest contender is perhaps a 1973 episode of *All In the Family*, Norman Lear's reupholstering of Johnny Speight's *Till Death Us Do Part*, which locked central character Archie Bunker in the cellar for a night of drunken self-loathing, with only token appearances by other characters.

The cult of the one- and two-hander holds more weight with

writers than audiences, but its role in sitcom craft is considerable. The cult of realism is more problematic. Hancock's obsessive pursuit of it began with him shedding the unnecessary (trad jokes, wacky situations) and ended with him dropping the necessary (Galton, Simpson). He was not the last performer to lose his comic perspective chasing after a phantom seriousness – conversely, lesser talents have used ostentatious naturalism to bolster feeble scripts. A reviewer in 1960 observed, 'Mr Hancock teeters on the verge of tragedy: it is only his fine sense of the ridiculous that holds him . . . on the narrow path of sanity.'[84] In the quest for realism, that sense can be fatally neglected.

KINGSLEY AMIS GOES POP (1962)
ITV (Associated-Rediffusion)

TV's introduces pop to high culture.

I'm looking forward to doing this programme enormously. I'm going to have fun even if nobody else does.
                                    Kingsley Amis, *TV Times*, 14 October 1962

BY THE 1960s, TV had accepted the necessity of covering pop music, but remained confused as to exactly how to do it. Clueless but game, they tried everything. Ken Dodd flaunted his hip Liverpool connections in *Doddy's Music Box*, promising a 'psychediddylic' experience for all. BBC2 floated the unforgettably named *Gadzooks! It's All Happening!*, which became *Gadzooks! It's the In Crowd!* before sanity prevailed, and the title was rationalised to just plain *Gadzooks!* Producers were not so much going to the hop as caught on it.

In one grand misjudgement, BBC1 replaced its long-running *Juke Box Jury* with Alan 'Fluff' Freeman vehicle *All Systems Freeman*, which placed Fluff behind a gigantic space age console, sporting headphones (both to make the link with his radio DJ role, and to craftily relay producer's instructions in pre-earpiece days). 'I shall be sitting at a control panel,' he said, 'and not just for the glamour of it, either! If I press a button or throw a switch to bring in tape, film or disc, and nothing happens, I'm going to look a right idiot.'[85] It may have been a vestigial memory of Fluff fading in pop acts with his mighty right hand that influenced the world of Harry Enfield and Paul Whitehouse's Smashie and Nicey creations decades later.

These were sober affairs alongside Associated-Rediffusion's decision to hire a literary *enfant terrible* to cover the scene. *Kingsley Amis Goes Pop* ('a title which is still amusing him') was a fifteen-minute wheeze knocked out after the evening news in which the *Lucky Jim* author and fellow of Peterhouse College, Cambridge interrogated pop stars in a bewildered and mildly grumpy manner. Amis was no cultural snob – he would go on to write scripts for *Z-Cars* spin-off *Softly, Softly*, and in his later years described *Terminator 2: Judgment Day* as a 'flawless masterpiece'[86] – but rock 'n' roll was a blind spot. 'The pop music business is still pretty much a closed book to me,' Amis admitted. An accredited jazzer, he had little time for rock 'n' roll's 'vapid, monotonous, blaring'[87] asininity. ('Oh fuck the Beatles,' he once told Philip Larkin. 'I'd like to push my bum into John L[ennon]'s face for forty-eight hours or so.'[88])

Fortunately Amis had the help of his pop-loving teenage sons, Philip and Martin. 'Some of their records interest me and I have to ask, "Who's that?"' He also looked to his offspring for sartorial tips. On their advice, he hosted the show wearing the clothes he arrived in off the street – Terylene, head to toe. This brought a tie-in ad campaign. ('"My Terylene trousers are **** great!" says Kingsley Amis.') Thus clad, he began his pop quest in high spirits. 'Quite honestly, I welcome the chance of meeting these extraordinary pop-singer people.'[89]

The show started well enough. Cleo Laine was asked about the gulf between jazz and the hit parade, Bernard Cribbins dropped by to explain the craft of the comedy song, and dancehall tycoon Eric Morley explained how a dance craze could be promoted nationwide, before Amis flexed his Terylene slacks for a crack at Morley's latest fad, the New Madison.

All very amiable, but according to critic Peter Black, Amis the awkwardly groovy dad fell between two stools. 'Either you go along with pop, getting as much empty unquestioning fun from it as you can,' he reasoned, 'or you put up a critic and let him sink his teeth deeply into the rubbish. Mr Amis's teeth have apparently been drawn and he sits there like a vicar at an orgy.'[90] Maybe Amis took this to heart, or maybe he just became bored, but later shows were altogether more frosty affairs. 'Rubber Ball' singer Bobby Vee underwent a curmudgeonly grilling. A meeting with Rolf Harris found the 'Sun Arise' singer reveal his previously unseen prickly, sarcastic mode. '[Amis] must allow for everybody's taste,' complained one fan, 'not embarrass everybody concerned.'[91] By the final edition – a chat with Alan Freeman – the gloves were already off in the programme billing. ('Have DJs too much power in the pop world? Do they encourage "trash"?')

Television's first attempt to mix pop and high culture produced intellectual fireworks of the indoor variety. The series was broadcast to Londoners only, and only lasted eight editions of a planned twelve, shown at an ever-later hour of the day. Memoirs and biographies tactfully skirt its very existence. But it could easily have become a family tradition: as Frankie Goes to Hollywood's career stalled in the mid-1980s, their marketing strategist Paul Morley could have conceived a postmodern film as their swansong along the lines of *The Great Rock 'n' Roll Swindle* – to be scripted by Martin Amis.[92]

THAT WAS THE WEEK THAT WAS (1962–3)

BBC

The establishment-shaking show that used the word 'bum' a lot.

Come 6.30, four hours to go before the soft underbelly of society was to be obligingly exposed to the watching millions, and as yet nothing in the quiver save three outrageous puns and a joke about knickers.

Alan Bennett on writing topical comedy,
5 October 1967

THE REVUE THAT HAD led Bennett to that quiet teatime desperation, *Beyond the Fringe*, is one of the landmarks of twentieth century comedy. As Bennett, Dudley Moore, Jonathan Miller and Peter Cook laid into Macmillan, Churchill and one-legged stuntmen in an apocalyptic basement set, the idea of comedy as a cleansing, angry, youthful force got its first British airing for decades. Many of the older generation hated it, but a surprising number applauded. Even staunch conservative T. S. Eliot gave praise. 'An amazingly vigorous quartet of young men: their show well produced and fast moving, a mixture of brilliance, juvenility and bad taste,' he wrote. In spite of reservations, 'it is pleasant to see this *type* of entertainment so successful.'[93]

Success piled on success. The show conquered the country, then

73

the USA. Cook opened a nightclub, The Establishment, to show-case the best British and American insurgent entertainment in an atmosphere redolent of Weimar Germany. Scurrilous, bedroom-built magazine *Private Eye*, when it wasn't facing imminent legal destruction, thrived. The steady, apolitical 'progress' of the fifties transformed into urgent, questioning rebellion. Television, the medium of the hour, just had to be invaded.

And it was, on 25 October 1962. 'For the first time on television,' promised the publicity, 'a critical, funny, adult, non-singing, non-dancing show about current events.' This 'weekly dose of virulent, unrestrained satire' promised to take an unflinching look at 'people from a race-rioter to the PM, at subjects from the Common Market to the Space Race.' Its crack team of young Turks would 'be seeking pomposity – when they find it they will attack and deflate.'[94]

This crocodile of clichés described *What the Public Wants?*, a hastily assembled late-night sketch show from Associated-Rediffusion, which featured such incendiary concepts as Father Christmas's sleigh being mistaken for a UFO and shot down by the RAF. It was, said *The Times*, 'a feeble and irritating little show that suffers from the callow superciliousness of undergraduate revue'.[95] By the end of the year it was gone, with another, Granada's *Man Bites Dog*, scrapped in pre-production.

If the irresponsible commercial channel couldn't raise a decent satire, what chance the regulation-bound BBC? John Bird, a colleague of Cook, took the concept of 'Establishment TV' to young BBC producer Ned Sherrin, who moulded it into a hip end-of-the-week compendium of sketch, song, cartoon and political barb. The studio would be coolly stripped down, showing its busy internal workings and louche audience of wine-bibbing hangers-on. The pace would be relentless, the cast impeccable: improv singer Millicent Martin, *Private Eye* alumnus Willie Rushton, Joan Littlewood alumnus Roy Kinnear and 'calypsologist' Lance Percival among them. The host would be not Bird or Cook, but David Frost.

This decision raised eyebrows, and a few hackles. Regarded,

rather snobbishly, in his Cambridge years as a hyper-ambitious hack, Frost had already earned Cook's disapproval for performing highly derivative 'homages' to his material. His greatest television achievement to date was fronting Rediffusion's dance craze schedule filler *Let's Twist on the Riviera*. Sherrin ignored these concerns and launched one of television's most prodigious careers.

On 24 November, *That Was the Week That Was* played out in a welter of fluffed cues and missed cameras. The army, the police and composer Norrie Paramor were among the targets. Bernard Levin ('the most detestable smarty-boots on television') hosted an adversarial discussion with public relations workers in a debate disarmingly titled 'Invective'. The stand out sketch, a parody of ITV's shameless 'ad-mag' programme *Jim's Inn*, was a refugee from Cook's *Beyond the Fringe* days. 'Anyone who stayed up in the hope of enjoying some ripe topical savagery, continental-style, was doomed to disappointment,' wrote Peter Green in the *Listener*. 'I hope future editions will get some real bite in them, and shed that air of daring cosiness which bedevils British satire at its very roots.'[96]

Fortunately, *TW3* rapidly grew teeth. The third edition achieved Sherrin's dream of transition from the review pages to the headlines, thanks to comically edited footage of Macmillan talking cobblers and Levin putting the boot into hotel magnate Charles Forte. '*Private Eye* may lash out in all directions and provoke nothing more than a chorus of bland coo-ings,' observed *The Times*, 'but let the BBC do something similar . . . and they arouse the public to close on a thousand telephone calls and a threat of legal action.'[97] Anthony Burgess summed up its winning naivety: 'Its special virtue is its genuine innocence, a sort of schoolboy surprise that the adult world should behave as it does. A very nice little programme at which only a boor could take offence. Wholesome, high-spirited, unpretentious, humanly unbuttoned, often shrewd, amusing and – above all – totally lacking in malice.'[98] Even Peter Green was now sold. '[*TW3*] has acquired that *sine qua non* of satire, a firm moral stance. "We mustn't make fun of Mr Macmillan, we mustn't be rude about British catering" – the terrifying thing is that the views of these witless subtopian boot-lickers command attention. Why, in heaven's name?'[99]

Old and young, subtopian and cosmopolitan, reactionary and progressive – all went head to head last thing on a Saturday night, the latter always getting the final word. And what words they were, from a writers' roster that gathered illustrious names of the past, present and future: Dennis Potter, David Nobbs, Bill Oddie, Kenneth Tynan, John Betjeman, John Cleese, Roald Dahl and many more fed Frost and friends killer lines. For Green, and many others, *TW3* became unimpeachable, mainly because 'it carries a bigger moral punch than all of its critics combined, and the day it is bullied or snivelled out of existence will be a poor one for British television.'[100]

That day was close at hand. When a second series began in 1963, the blaze of triumphant pre-publicity soon faded into critical murmurings of a loss of purpose. 'There is less specific emphasis on politics, and a marked swing towards mildly risqué intimate revue.'[101] Sketches about open flies, and liberal sprink-lings of outré words like 'bum' and 'poo', had a habit of taking over the more considered (and considerably harder to knock out) political material. This smutty path of least resistance would dog topical comedy shows ever after.

The heavyweight stuff did continue, though, and proved to be the show's undoing. When Macmillan was replaced by the ques-tionable choice of Sir Alec Douglas-Home, *TW3* pounced, dressing Frost in Disraeli gear to deliver a politely damning 'in character' summary of Douglas-Home's unique attributes. What with this, a sketch mocking another Tory hero, Baden-Powell, and the continuing stream of 'racy' material, many formerly indulgent cham-pions of the show reached their limits of tolerance, and called for cancellation.

The Director General, Hugh Carleton Greene, felt *TW3* was becoming an albatross for the Corporation, monopolising staff time and detracting from his achievements in the more serious depart-ments of drama and current affairs. With a general election looming the following year, he curtailed its run at the end of 1963. *Private Eye*, the relatively low profile satirical survivor, summed up popular reaction to *TW3*'s sacrifice by having 'Greene' confess: 'What I really wanted was something reminiscent of Berlin in the 1930s; now that I've stopped it, I feel that I have at last recreated that atmosphere.'[102]

THE SUNDAY-NIGHT PLAY: A SUITABLE CASE FOR TREATMENT (1962)

BBC

Drama drops out.

Dear David Mercer, can you please explain why all your plays are about David Mercer?

A student writes to David Mercer, c. 1972

IN CINEMA, THE HIERARCHY was always plain. Stars first, then director, and bringing up the rear, if they're even mentioned at all, the writer. In the 1960s, television – smaller, more flexible and less glamorous – had a more variable pecking order. Thanks to ever-closer ties with the theatrical revolution, the writer could occasionally, and not always reluctantly, become the star of their own show.

David Mercer was one of many post-war playwrights who had risen from the provincial working class through state and self-education. Born into a Wakefield mining family, he spent four years with the Navy before moving to Paris to work as first a struggling painter, then a struggling novelist. Realising the 'abstract cul-de-sac'[103] he'd backed himself into, he turned to drama,

78

specifically the drama of his own experience. His first play, *Where the Difference Begins*, was intended for the stage but found a home on the BBC. It dealt with the culture gap between a working class artist and his suspicious kinfolk in an honest and very straightforward way. Mercer would later describe it as 'one of the dreariest plays ever written by me, or anyone else, for that matter.'[104] He seemed to be cultivating an oeuvre every bit as unforgiving as his resting expression of intense concern.

Then, in 1962, the usually methodical Mercer made a breakthrough, written 'in an absolute kind of trance for three weeks'.[105] When director Don Taylor, Mercer's main early creative collaborator, asked about it, he found his colleague's usual intense frown replaced by 'a large, round-faced Yorkshire grin'.[106] *A Suitable Case for Treatment* left the old straight track of social realism and hiked off into the unknown.

Morgan Delt, disillusioned thirtysomething man for whom 'life became baffling as soon as it became comprehensible', is in the process of being divorced from his wife Leonie. He sleeps in his car and spends his days railing against society like an Angry Brigade Hamlet, or palling around with Guy the Gorilla at London Zoo. Otherwise he keeps himself occupied by pestering his ex-wife, pinning offensive posters in her flat, shaving a hammer and sickle into her poodle's back, hanging her stuffed toys on a small portable gallows and blowing up her mother. A few years before the screen would fill with them, Morgan was its first drop-out hero.

Appropriately, the play didn't conform to the standard two act shape. Scenes fragmented and were interrupted by clips of films from *Battleship Potemkin* to *Tarzan*. Dream sequences were not the usual gauzy, slow motion affairs but stark skits in a black limbo with Morgan's mum in secret police uniform. Don Taylor somehow crammed it all into an hour – a pre-recorded and edited hour, the thing being far too complex to transmit live, as most drama still was.

These technical innovations would have meant nothing without Mercer's increasingly sharp dialogue. Morgan's cockney Trot mum, played to the hilt by Anna Wing, had some beautifully turned lines worthy of *Hancock*: 'Your dad wanted to shoot the royal family, abolish marriage and put everybody who'd been to public school in a chain gang. He was an idealist, was your dad.' But the main event was Ian Hendry's Morgan, manic in all emotional directions. 'I'm a bad son,' he mused. 'Is it the chromosomes, or is it England?' He castigated Leonie's suave new suitor, saying, 'He slid into our lives like a boa constrictor. You've never seen him with her – he undulates. Turned my back one day and he gulped her down like a rabbit.'

This unprecedented play left critics straining for parallels. The slapstick incursions and head-banging philosophy put many critics in mind of Spike Milligan. 'Like Milligan, Morgan Delt was either a thousand years ahead of his time or, more likely, probably an essential antidote *for* his time,' judged Derek Hill, approving what was 'less a play than a welcome disturbance of the peace.'[107] Michael Overton applauded what he saw as a long overdue BBC response to the dominance of *Armchair Theatre*. 'The BBC has been steadily playing safe and countering ABC-TV's adventurousness with dull doldrum plays unimaginatively directed and indifferently acted. David Mercer's play must have shaken the antimacassars in the most staid middle-class homes, and made the majority switch straight back to *Sunday Night at the London Palladium*.'[108]

Scheduled after Mercer was a repeat of Anthony Newley's *The Johnny Darling Show*, a pseudo-sequel to *Gurney Slade* in which the eponymous teen idol senses the end of the world and embarks on a philosophical fantasy journey of social and spiritual Armageddon, with songs by Leslie Bricusse. For some viewers, a whole evening of visual experiment and existential despair was too much, and in the following edition of *Points of View* many antimacassars were shaken at the Beeb, and Mercer especially.

Mercer's protagonists were not so much off the beaten track as frolicking in the tall grass several fields away: a young man who takes an axe to a middle-class Sunday tea party; a leather-clad septuagenarian vicar biker; a childlike pair of zookeepers who fill a disused swimming pool with inflatable animals and trapezes. 'Mercer is not just a nonconformist,' reckoned Don Taylor, 'he is a nonconformist nonconformist, for whom a beard and a guitar are as square as a dark suit and rolled umbrella. He is his own strange self.'[109] *A Suitable Case . . .* became a film, *Morgan!*, in 1966, adapted by Mercer but sweetened, he felt, too much by director Karel Reisz into a poppy tale of swinging outsiderism. 'Dropping out' was now a cultural buzzword, on its way to becoming a mini-industry. Only conformist nonconformists need apply.

For a confirmed outsider, Mercer was gregarious to a fault. Joan Bakewell recalls the 'hotbed of neo-Marxism'[110] he presided over in Maida Vale, where she would dash after presenting *Late Night Line-Up* to hobnob with Pinter, Kenneth Tynan and company. He was the most visible of the new TV playwrights, interviewed by everyone from Melvyn Bragg to David Coleman. His goatee and polo neck became familiar enough for Michael Palin to impersonate him on *Monty Python*, chain-smoking behind a typewriter, captioned simply: 'A Very Good Playwright'.

Mercer's TV output declined in the seventies. Despite quirky successes like the half-hour *Me and You and Him* – a triumph of videotape editing in which three Peter Vaughans conduct a psychiatric slanging match – his style was sidelined in the push toward naturalism. Even the introduction of high-definition colour seemed set against him. In 1972's *The Bankrupt*, a crisis-hit Joss Ackland experiences the same kind of black limbo dreams as Morgan Delt, though where the original monochrome abyss sold the hallucination, the colour camera merely highlighted what Kenneth Tynan once dismissed as 'the platitudinous void, with its single message: "Background of evil, get it?"'[111]

And anyway, argued critics, TV had moved on from this sort of experimental tinkering, hadn't it? 'I'm afraid this kind of crossword-puzzle drama may find a place in the so-called "intellectual" theatre,' opined John Russell Taylor, 'but it cannot make much sense to the average television viewer.'[112] Clive James thought *The Bankrupt* showed a writer losing his way: 'Mercer, like John

Hopkins, is likely to eke out a half-imagined idea by double-crossing his own talent and piling on precisely the undergrad-type tricksiness his sense of realism exists to discredit.'[113]

Mercer died in 1980, firmly out of step with the timid TV mainstream, which duly gave him a retrospective but otherwise continued to mistrust the risky and remarkable. Mercer set the template for the bold, confessional playwright who was as at home appearing on television as writing for it. His more concrete, if less eye-catching, quality was noted by Mervyn Johns: 'A television writer who cares, and is encouraged to care, about words is a rarity; without Mercer's example, that rarity may become an extinct species.'[114]

THE TONIGHT SHOW STARRING JOHNNY CARSON (1962–92)

NBC

The king of chat show kings.

TV excels in two areas – sports and Carson.

David Brenner, comedian
and frequent Carson guest, 1971

THE CULTURE OF THE United States tends to treat any new field of endeavour like the Wild West – a vast wilderness to be colonised and tamed. The TV schedules were no different – beyond the evening hours lay the call of the untamed daytime slots in one direction, and in the other the heart of late-night darkness. NBC launched a daytime expedition in 1952, beginning with early morning chat-in *Today*. Two years later came a companion trek into the late-night zone, which opened up a lucrative and fiercely contested new territory.

Tonight! was shaped by its first host, Steve Allen. A classic vaudevillian drifter who fell into TV comedy after a subversive stint on local radio, Allen turned what was planned as a fairly straight talk-show-plus-sketch format into a self-contained world – a club with its own rules and customs that made the viewers feel part of something wonderfully mad. He'd arrange complex one-shot gags such as being dunked into hot water wearing a suit festooned with teabags, but most of his comedy was cheaply improvised. Regular stunts included walking out into the New York streets in police uniform and stopping motorists for various bizarre reasons, or just pointing a camera at the passing street life and reeling off an impromptu commentary on its comings and goings. Late night was established as a freewheeling refuge from the daily schedule grind.

Allen moved on to Sunday prime time after an unsuccessful splitting of *Tonight!* duties with Ernie Kovacs. Reverting to the chat format, the show gained a new, more earnest host. Jack Paar gathered a round table of fellow wits (including token Brit Hermione Gingold), welcomed heavyweight guests from JFK to Castro, and put his own thin-skinned personality centre stage. A fragile star, Paar would fight the network on-screen, most famously calling out their censorship of a whimsical gag based on misinterpretation of the initials 'WC'.

Paar's successor couldn't have more temperamentally different. Johnny Carson boasted the ultimate down-home American background, having grown up in a backwater of Nebraska. His first TV success was the unpromising daytime game show *Who Do You Trust?* (formerly *Do You Trust Your Wife?*) where he built up the introductory banter with the contestants into a lengthy and often, for the time slot, bawdy art. He was also united with long-suffering *Tonight* second banana and announcer Ed McMahon.

Carson first appeared on *Tonight!* as a guest of Steve Allen, making a prank phone call to Jack Paar. (Paar rumbled the pair within seconds.) As host, he steered a steady course between the hyperactive pranking of Allen and Paar's earnest inquiry. Whether delivering the opening monologue in front of theatrical curtains or sat at his desk in front of a mural of imposing Midwest scenery, idly tossing cue cards full of failing gags over his shoulder, he exuded a comfortingly straight-up bonhomie in increasingly fractious times. The wit was bolstered by a platoon of star writers, and the lurid sports jackets were from his own line of dresswear, but the easy manner and genuine interest in what his subjects had to say were all Carson's own. The show soon became Carson's, incorporating his name into its title and eventually relocating with him from New York to beautiful downtown Burbank.

Teetotal and averse to showbiz parties, Carson was a reluctant off-duty celebrity, becoming a star only after he'd parted the stage curtains following McMahon's preparatory crescendo of 'Heeeeere's Johnny!' Under the lights, he could converse with the cream of Hollywood and hold his own with New York's literati. Long-standing tit-for-tat feuds, especially with actor and compulsive put-down merchant Don Rickles, escalated with each meeting into the realms of obsession; both men walking a fine line between the all-in-fun wink for the audience and all-too-convincing mutual animosity.

When the show ran out of stars, it made its own. Tiny Tim, a towering, baleful oddball who sang 'Tiptoe Through the Tulips' in an unearthly falsetto, was discovered by *Tonight* and became a regular, even marrying his beau in mock-Georgian splendour on a special edition of the programme, with McMahon as chief usher: 'We cordially request the pleasure of your company at the marriage of Tiny Tim and Miss Vicki right here on *The Tonight Show*. But right now here are some words of wisdom from Pepto-Bismol tablets.'[115]

Away from the star circuit, Carson invited 'ordinary folk with a story to tell', especially pensioners such as a 103-year-old woman who still drove regularly, whom he handled with warmth and a total absence of condescension. Folk with odd obsessions were another rich vein: Carson was the first to televise the subsequently worldwide craze for domino toppling, inviting Robert Speca into the studio to knock down 6,999 pieces. All civilians were treated the same as the stars: Carson gave them all their due, resorting to his trademark conspiratorial sidelong glance to camera only if the subject was really asking for it. A tangible link between celebrity and public decades before social media, Johnny Carson sat at the fulcrum of American popular culture.

His unaffected largesse prompted generosity in his guests. When Alex Haley appeared on the show to promote the mini-series *Roots*, he brought with him a leather-bound book entitled *Roots of Johnny Carson*, a 400-page, intensively researched trawl of the Carson family tree reaching back to sixteenth century Essex. It was, of course, the perfect all-American heritage, another piece of the Average Guy legend.

Other chat shows filed up alongside Carson. On ABC, Dick Cavett creamed off the intellectual crowd for whom Carson felt too safe. For CBS, Merv Griffin tackled Carson's populism head-on. From 1982, David Letterman followed Carson in the NBC schedules, triumphantly reactivating Steve Allen's intricate horse-play (including the teabag suit) in an hour produced, as part of Carson's uniquely favourable contract, by Carson's own people. Carson's stature was not so much presidential as kingly. Though Kermit the Frog was briefly mooted as a replacement in the late 1970s, the thought of Carson yielding his desk to anyone else remained taboo.

When Carson abdicated at the age of 66, the effect was of a long-peaceful kingdom plunged into civil war. Letterman, long seen as heir apparent, lost out to the less admired Jay Leno, and decamped to CBS, to be replaced by Conan O'Brien. Rivals, including Tom Snyder and Jimmy Kimmel, proliferated. Machinations behind the desks became as much a public spectacle as the encounters over them. The unholy viewing hour remained exceptionally popular, but it never regained the stature of the man whose one job was to introduce America to itself. Carson himself summed it up, when pausing for breath after an innocuous bit of business spun gloriously out of hand, climaxing in tearful laughter, trademark karate chops and cries of 'Hi-yooo!' 'That,' said the exhausted host, 'is what makes this job what it is.' 'What is it?' asked McMahon. Carson thought hard for a second, and eventually answered, 'I don't know.'[116]

WORLD IN ACTION (1963–98)
ITV (Granada)

Current affairs go commando.

IN 1963 CURRENT AFFAIRS reached critical mass. In the summer, Britain's press enjoyed unprecedented levels of political influence when they published the indiscretions of John Profumo. The shaming of a British minister was followed by the death of a US President. For four days in November, from the first, breathless, interruption of an episode of soap opera *As the World Turns*, through the assassination of Oswald and the state funeral on the twenty-fifth, the USA turned to television for information and support, specifically to Walter Cronkite of *CBS News*. A programme that combined the fearlessness of an investigative tabloid with television's immediate visual impact had to be made, and it was.

The current affairs feature began with BBC's *Special Enquiry* in 1952 and, the following year, its flagship *Panorama*. ITV returned volley with *This Week* and *Searchlight*. The latter, edited by Australian ex-tabloid editor Tim Hewat, caused such regular controversy it devoted one edition to scrutinising itself. When the Television Act finally caught up with *Searchlight's* insufficient impartiality, Hewat reassigned his men the banner of *World in Action*, a 'Northern *Panorama'* that would fundamentally change the look of TV documentary.

Hewat created *World in Action* to cover a single subject each week. On-screen reporters were replaced by voice-overs including that of James Burke, leaving the screen filled with the matter in hand. The matter was often visualised with shamelessly unsubtle tabloid stunts, such as staging a mass funeral in a Salford street to introduce a report on bronchitis. These were organised by the show's team of fixers, who also arranged everything from foreign currency to access to closed borders. Tactics like this helped *World in Action*'s audience rise to twice *Panorama*'s.[117]

World in Action also introduced the 16mm film camera. Several times less bulky than the usual 35mm Arriflex, the smaller gauge apparatus cut the size of a location crew from twelve to six, giving the team greater manoeuvrability. Where before events were brought in front of the camera, now the camera could dive straight into the situation. The consequent grainy smutch of those early guerilla reports was a badge of honour; Hewat upbraided one fastidious producer's suspiciously immaculate African footage as a screen full of 'bloody back-lit begging bowls!'[118]

When a huge story broke at an inconsiderately late point in the week, the leaner team could put an emergency programme together in under three days. All-nighters pulled to cover breaking scoops like the collapse of the John Bloom business empire were celebrated in hard-bitten Fleet Street tones. 'We have to do a week's work in two days. It's impossible, but sometimes it gets done,' editor Alex Valentine told *TV Times*, adding wistfully, 'I've never seen so many dawns in my life, I don't mind telling you.'[119]

Tabloid clichés in the publicity material were fine. Tabloid clichés in the content were signs of slackness. As the same subjects came round again each season, the show's style atrophied. Anything that worked, like the Salford stunt, was recycled when time and inspiration went. '*World in Action* is sometimes in danger of becoming a victim of its own form,' wrote Peter Hillmore, lamenting its use of picture postcard scene setting – canals to introduce Amsterdam, or a politician's view preceded by the Houses of Parliament from the Thames. 'I know the team has to fill thirty minutes with film, but it doesn't always have to look so desperate about it.'[120]

When all parts of the *World in Action* team pulled together, the results were unbeatable. Its many torture investigations of the early 1970s brought horrific news of every regime's actions from Zanzibar to Turkey to Ulster. It risked a great deal more than its reputation to demonstrate how simple it was to smuggle car parts into sanctioned Rhodesia, and arms to war-torn Biafra. It pioneered mass election debate with 'The Granada 500', a panel of pundits bussed in from bellwether constituency Preston East to grill the party leaders. The edition with perhaps the greatest impact, 'The Rise and Fall of John Poulson', didn't unearth much in the way of new material on the corrupt property developer, but did set out the available evidence in a clearer way than anyone had managed before, laying bare the dense web of connections. The film was still incendiary enough to be temporarily blocked by the IBA, which led to accusations of a conflict of interest among ITV grandees – T. Dan Smith, one of the main accused, had been until very recently a director of Tyne Tees Television. (Later, while in jail for corruption, Smith encouraged fellow inmate Leslie Grantham to take up professional acting, and a future star of *EastEnders* was born.)[121]

Occasionally the programme went too far. Covering anti-Sony factory protests in 1977, its team hunted America to film the rumoured gatherings of people in T-shirts claiming, 'Sony – from the people who gave you Pearl Harbor'. Not finding any such shirts, they printed a few off themselves.[122] 'Born Losers', shown in 1967, was a compassionate study of a nine-child family living on £16 a week; it got its message across to many viewers, but broadcasting the Walshes' intimate details came close to destroying the family itself.[123] From then the team were wary of putting members of the public quite so brazenly on show – a consideration regarded as optional by other programmes.

The emergent youth culture demanded coverage. Young producer John Birt's idea of helicoptering Mick Jagger into the grounds of a stately home to chat with the Bishop of Woolwich was a success, in publicity terms at least. ('We should aim to transmit at least one outrageous and improbable programme each year,' demanded long-serving editor Ray Fitzwalter.[124]) But most youth culture stories, from the Mod revival to acid house, tended towards prudishness. 'No speed party is complete without a joint of grass,' vouchsafed the authoritatively prurient narrator of Haight-Ashbury examination, 'Alas, Poor Hippies, Love is Dead'.

News technology progressed apace. Through the late 1970s, the old film crews were steadily replaced by 'creepy-peepies': lightweight video cameras far more convenient even than 16mm. A generation of cameramen were left feeling, in the words of one ACTT member, 'like wheeltappers at a hovercraft rally'.[125] Even the BBC's *Panorama* started to catch up with the times: a 1981 documentary on German rocket makers OTRAG used a blizzard of electronic effects to enliven the presentation of its great mountain of paper evidence. 'The days of pointing a camera at a newspaper cutting are threatened at last,' predicted Peter Fiddick. 'If you can't read it, they'll flash it, colour it and creep it across the screen . . . until you're blinded into literacy.'[126] The Richard Dimbleby generation of current affairs gave way to Hewat's boys across the board.

World in Action wasn't killed off by IBA ruling or legal challenge, but a soap opera. In 1994 *EastEnders* went thrice-weekly, ruining ITV's Monday night. The 1990 Broadcasting Act had already loosened the third channel's current affairs commitments. *World in Action*, now reaching as little as five million viewers,[127] was promptly shifted up against the soap as a sacrifice. It lasted a little over three years. Granada won the bid to replace its old show: 'Whether by performance, image, heritage or perception, all agree on the value of *World in Action*,'[128] it admitted in the tender, but 'we need to make current affairs less threatening to younger viewers.' Its solution, based on CBS's *60 Minutes* model, became *Tonight with Trevor McDonald*. Broadsheet pundits began making merry with the freshly imported phrase 'dumbing down'.

PLAY SCHOOL
(1964–88)

BBC2

The BBC loosens its old pre-school tie.

*Anyone can fill time with pap and the kids will watch it. It's
safe and it's easy. We are trying to break away from that.*
                    Joy Whitby, *Play School* executive producer, 1966

THE BBC'S EARLY CHILDREN'S television was a fortress of twee.
Amiable (if slightly grotesque) puppets would get into a jolly old
fix, patrician ladies would trill nursery rhymes in strident falsetto,
and improving fables would be slowly read out of leather-bound
books the size of shed roofs. When Doreen Stephens took charge
of the BBC's family programmes in 1963, this had been the case
for rather too long. She found a 'demoralised, miserable children's
department'[129] plodding along with the same *Andy Pandy* mindset
that harked back to before the Suez Crisis. Her initial desire to
scrap Andy, Bill and Ben outright was countermanded by an early
manifestation of popular nostalgia, but she did gradually phase
them out in favour of *The Magic Roundabout, Camberwick Green*
and a new daily morning programme for the under-fives.

Stephens employed Joy Whitby to edit *Play School*. With two
presenters, a tiny studio, a clock for telling the time and an initial
weekly budget of £120,[130] Whitby concocted a feast of ideas, songs,
rhymes and (very basic) documentary films designed to stimulate

91

toddlers' imaginations. The fustiness of old gave way to bold designs and plush soft toy companions (though Hamble, a grotesque china doll, was the one anomalous throwback to morbid Victoriana and suffered chronic abuse from presenters and technical staff as a result, before being replaced in 1986 by the marginally less creepy Poppy). In a reversal of the usual metrics, the programme was judged a success by its makers if children abandoned the show half way through to go outside and do a wobbly dance or search for round things.[131]

If this sounded like a tepid bath of liberal unction, the third woman involved in *Play School*'s inception, series producer Cynthia Felgate, added a tougher note. 'Talking down is really based on the assumption that you are being liked by the child,' she reasoned. 'But if you imagine a tough little boy of four looking in, you soon take the silly smile off your face.'[132] As a former actor with a theatrical troupe specialising in that toughest of gigs, the in-school educational performance, she knew whereof she spoke.

An experienced general, Felgate recruited troops from the ranks of repertory, with a sharp eye for nascent talent. *Play School* staff would take roles in countless other children's programmes after their toil at the clock-face. They included musicians, from the classically trained Jonathan Cohen to the folk-schooled Toni Arthur and the downright countercultural Rick Jones. The show also pioneered, in its own quiet way, the employment of non-white hosts, beginning in 1965 with Paul Danquah, fresh from filming *A Taste of Honey*. Humour played a huge part in proceedings, courtesy of Fred Harris (who graduated to adult comedy when radio producer Simon Brett chanced upon his work while, appropriately, off sick), Johnny Ball (soon to launch his own one-man science-and-puns initiative *Think of a Number*), Phyllida Law (sharing the arch eccentricity of her husband Eric Thompson, *Magic Roundabout* narrator and fellow *School* player), and virtuoso mime Derek Griffiths. Add to this a roster of guest storytellers from Roy Castle to Richard Baker, George Melly to Spike Milligan, and you had a clubhouse of wits in the front room daily: the Algonquin Round Window.

Play School was born with the BBC's second channel, the first scripted programme the morning after BBC Two's notoriously blackout-blighted launch. It became such a fixture that households equipped with sets new enough to receive the new UHF channel were often invaded by the children of less well-off neighbours round about eleven o'clock. Camera operators, who suffered previous *Watch with Mother* efforts under duress, actively fought over the chance to cover *Play School.*[133]

In 1971 there came a spin-off, the altogether less restrained *Play Away.* Eminent *Play School* old boy Brian Cant, 'merry as a stoned scoutmaster'[134] in one critic's memorable description, led cohorts including Jeremy Irons, Tony Robinson and Julie Covington through groansome puns, venerable slapstick routines and jolly songs which could, like the catalogue of gargantuan consumer goods 'Shopaway', become mildly satirical. This all-year panto became big enough to transfer to the Old Vic in 1976.

Play Away's high standards drew high expectations from its audience. George Melly observed that while children never questioned the knocked-off likes of *Pinky and Perky* (rudimentary puppets jerking up and down to grating pitch-shifted covers of pop hits), when faced with the higher craft of *Play School* they 'become almost Leavisite in the severity of their criticism'.[135] The ability to spot quality among the dross was learned at an early age.

A few years in, the *School* started to expand. By 1970 it was playing, in recast local versions, everywhere from Switzerland to Australia, with the use of a specially assembled '*Play School* kit'. Most of the toys made the transition to other cultures more or less intact: Humpty, for instance, became 'Testa D'Uovo' – Egghead – in Italian. Unlike the conquering franchises of children's television to come, *Play School* established more of a commonwealth than an empire, importing songs from Israel and films of Roman ice cream factories as it exported Norwegian translations of *The Sun Has Got His Hat On.* (The Scandinavian connection, which culminated in a joint TV special between the UK and Norwegian *Play Away* franchises, highlighted an interesting difference in approaches to children's television. A 1973 Danish seminar on kids' TV produced a twelve-point list of good practice, a copy of which was pinned up in the BBC children's department in Television Centre's bleak East Tower. Alongside the expected exhortations to honesty and clarity was the suggestion: 'When you want to tell an exciting story, try to relate its conflict to the central conflict in society between labour and capital.'[136] If this particular directive was acted upon at the Beeb, it was well disguised.)

Like all timeless children's programmes, *Play School* became a slave to adult fashion. A much-publicised 'moving house' in 1983 altered the theme tune, redesigned the studio and replaced the magic windows with 'shapes', to the horror of many parents who'd grown up with the old show themselves. Five years after that the school was closed for good, replaced by *Playbus*, made by the newly independent Felgate Productions, which was 'more attuned to the needs of today's children' and featured children in the studio – one of the original *Play School*'s prime taboos. The intuition of a handful of creative producers was replaced by a squadron of educational advisers and child psychologists. No longer would British kids have their formative years soundtracked by vintage songs such as *Little Ted Bear From Nowhere in Particular* and *Ten Chimney Pots All In a Row (When Along Came a Fussy Old Crow)*. There's progress, and there's progress.

CROSSROADS (1964–88)
ITV (ATV/Central)

'Soap' becomes a four-letter word.

Crossroads *is not a programme, it is a vacuum. A hole in the air, abhorrent to nature.*

Nancy Banks-Smith, 1971

IF YOU WANT TO explore the fundamental differences between two cultures, take a look at how they handle their low entertainment. The soap opera, for instance. Its early American incarnation carried titles which were expansive, portentous, quasi-Biblical: *Days of Our Lives, The Bold and the Beautiful, The Guiding Light.* British afternoon serials, meanwhile, got the most humbly domestic of names: *Honey Lane, Castle Haven* and, most utilitarian of all, *Crossroads.*

An attempt by ATV to move into US-style daily serial territory, *Crossroads* was the culmination of Reg Watson's quest to find a solid vehicle for his daytime star Noele Gordon. Hazel Adair and Peter Ling were hired to fashion a genteel Midlands milieu set in the fictional Warwickshire village of King's Oak, paying special attention to the nearby Crossroads motel. Gordon was the motel's widowed owner Meg Richardson, the head of a tiny dynasty including her son Sandy and hapless daughter Jill, and assorted managerial staff. Beneath the matinee idol leads were the Dickensian comic foils, led by line-fluffing cleaner Amy Turtle, later joined by short order cook Shughie McFee and simpleton handyman Benny Hawkins. Cast regulars and intransigent guests conspired to commit adultery, grand theft, murder, suicide – just about every mis-demeanour aside from smoking, which was beyond the pale for a teatime slot.

Dispensing with ITV's standard twice-a-week soap model, *Crossroads* went daily, its production team ripping through five twenty-minute episodes a week. (From 1967 they got Mondays off.) With such a punishing itinerary, the scripts – production line affairs under the guidance of a supervising story editor – were of necessity thriftily furnished with off-the-peg dialogue. 'The sheer volume,' admitted producer Phillip Bowman, 'precludes excel-lence.'[137] The odd *Coronation Street*-style gag still managed to appear amid the expository tundra. ('What's that? "Goulash Budapest"? Looks like "Shepherd's Pie Walsall East" to me.')

Then there were the plywood sets and the under-rehearsed acting. Props were mislaid, eyelines unmet, extras (literally, on the first transmission) prodded into life with sticks. In Nancy Banks-Smith's opinion, 'The Acocks Green Wavy Line Drama Group could prob-ably put on a preferable performance.'[138] There was also Tony Hatch's strange theme tune, in which an electric guitar imperson-ates a doorbell, accompanied by a perfectly mismatched quartet of piano, harp, oboe and drums. And there was the odd inexplicable directorial flourish, such as the decision to open episodes with a prolonged close-up of a telephone, a half-eaten cucumber sandwich, or, on one Burns Night, a huge pile of sheep offal. This jumble of eccentricity gave the constant sense of a production obliviously strutting around with its flies undone.

The torrent of critical vitriol had no effect on *Crossroads*' march from regional curio to national mainstay. In 1972, the recalcitrant northern ITV regions finally took the soap. By 1974, it matched and occasionally outflanked *Coronation Street* in ratings terms, peaking at roughly fifteen million viewers, with the Queen Mother and Harold Wilson's wife Mary among its noted fans. It became a truly national programme on 1 April 1975, when the assorted regional stations synchronised their transmissions. ATV made special 'catch-up' programmes for the likes of Granada and Thames, who'd snootily let their screenings of the soap lag by the best part of a year.

With the entire country occupying the same time-zone, Meg Richardson and Hugh Mortimer had their marriage blessed in Birmingham Cathedral. This wasn't the normal soap wedding, with forgotten rings, catering panics and a ghost from the past interrupting the 'speak now's. This was a full mock ceremony, shot as an outside broadcast, not a million miles from Princess Anne's nuptial coverage a couple of years earlier. Soap royalty ruled for a day. A *TV Times* commemorative wedding brochure sold half a million copies.

Merchandise multiplied. In 1976, *Crossroads* became the first British TV show to have its own regular magazine: *Crossroads Monthly* was published by Felix Dennis of *OZ* infamy, with star profiles, a cookery column and a gatefold pin-up of Gordon. A roaring trade was also established around reproductions of a still life that hung on the wall of Meg's bedroom.

One spin-off had dire repercussions. Paul McCartney, another star fan, recorded a keening stadium rock version of the Tony Hatch theme. Jack Barton, then series producer, decided it was good enough to replace the original in the programme proper. Huge mistake. 'The *Crossroads* theme was bright and happy,' fumed Martyn Finch of Croydon to *TV Times*. 'Now it has plunged into insignificance. The rhythm has gone and the roll of the credits no longer fits the music.' This was perceptive; the famous crossover credit rollers did indeed come and go in reasonably good time with the old doorbell theme, and McCartney's theme upset the balance. After a few weeks of mass grievance, Hatch's original made a triumphant return, with Macca reserved, as Barton explained, 'for downbeat and dramatic, cliffhanging endings. I am hoping that Paul McCartney will write us another, more up-tempo, version of the *Crossroads* theme,' he added hopefully.

In 1981, the glory faded with the termination of Noele Gordon's contract: programme controller Charles Denton found the resulting correspondence 'ranged from abuse to lumps of foreign matter'.[139] On 11 November, after narrowly escaping death ('Oh, my God! The motel! It's on fire!'), Meg Richardson took her final bow in the *QEII*'s Queen Mary suite. Fans were beside themselves: 'The girls on the switchboard have been trying to sympathise,' reassured an ATV representative, 'and have been telling them not to give up hope.'[140]

Crossroads soldiered on for another six and a half years, but successive revamps and tinkerings with the theme tune couldn't stop its ultimate slide to an audience of a then paltry twelve million. It inspired few words but generated huge numbers. In a time before the posh papers found they could cheaply fill space by grabbing any piece of low culture that toddled along and hugging it to death in a giant set of inverted commas, *Crossroads* had a tremendous reach that was all but invisible to the media at large – the media still being dedicated, in Tom Stoppard's words, to 'preserving the distinction between serious work and carpentry.'[141] But as Stoppard would have admitted, there'll always be a market for stools.

LE MANÈGE ENCHANTÉ (1964–1971)

THE MAGIC ROUNDABOUT (1965–1977)

ORTF/BBC One (Danot Films/BBC)

The original cult children's programme.

ANIMATION IS THE MOST meticulously planned form of film-making in front of the camera. Behind the camera, it can be more chaotic than anything else. Serge Danot was a young technical assistant for French producers Cinéastes Associés, working on stop-motion animation for commercials and television effects under Leeds-born animator Ivor Wood. A keen and quick learner, Danot began regaling Wood with ideas for children's entertainments he'd come up with. One, based around the slapstick adventures of various people and animals who lived near an enchanted merry-go-round, was deemed strong enough to go into production in 1964.

Danot and Wood made the first thirteen five-minute films in a small back room in Danot's suburban Paris flat, which had to be periodically abandoned to allow the lighting equipment to cool off. A deal was made for French state television to broadcast them, due as much to the engaging character design and minimalist white scenery as the overt 'Frenchness' of the cast. Each character paid vocal homage to a different French region with the exception of Pollux – an initially incidental long-haired dog who, inspired by Wood, spoke broken French in an English accent.

Domestic success made the show a candidate for the international market, and the first thirty-nine films were bought by the BBC in 1965. Crucially, the means to translate the original dialogue from the French was not forthcoming, so it fell to Play School presenter Eric Thompson, hired to provide the English narration, to also provide the English translation. Unfortunately he hadn't a word of French, so he watched the silent episodes reel-by-reel and started scripting from scratch. Without even a character guide to hand, Thompson looked to his family and the pupils of nearby Ardentinny primary school in Strathclyde for personality types.

Azalea the cow became Ermintrude, Ambrose the snail became Brian, Father Peony became Mr Rusty, and Pollux the dog was rechristened Dougal. Zebulon's mystical incantation *'Tournicoti Tounicoton!'* was now Zebedee's thoroughly agreeable 'Time for bed!' Thompson's contributions are famous for turning the original knockabout cartoon into something subtler, even – in a very broad sense of the word – subversive. This stemmed from an attitude that would logically have debarred him from working on the show. 'I don't actually believe children exist,' he claimed, 'except as part of the adult imagination. When I started to write, I wrote for people, since I think that's what children are – people who haven't lived very long.'[142]

A professional children's writer would have diligently kept esoteric references to Ken Russell and trade unions well out of it. Thompson kept them in, like an inexperienced but eager dad reading a bedtime story and periodically drifting back into the workaday world, using 'long words, intricate phrases . . . if I could find a long word where a short one would do, I used it because children want the real thing.' Occasionally Thompson, by his own estimation, overdid the knowing asides. When Dylan the laid-back rabbit is introduced, Dougal remarks that for a rabbit he doesn't hop about much. Dylan's reply: 'We're re-thinking the image.' Thompson confessed, 'children couldn't really get hold of an idea like that'.[143]

The new narration had the side effect of quietening things down: the adversarial shouts of the French soundtrack were replaced with Thompson's more modulated table talk. This was easier on parental ears than the standard full-throated cartoon declamation, so child-minding adults were more predisposed to listen, catch Thompson's politely skewed monologue, and get hooked. Viewing figures leapt towards eight million, an extraordinary figure for an afternoon slot, equally split between adults and kids, united in their fervent love of Dougal. When the BBC moved it from 5.50 p.m. to 4.55 p.m. in 1966, as a spoiler against ITV's successful *Playtime*, the outcry was colossal. One letter to the *Guardian* complained that 'Mothers everywhere now clock-watch and switch from channel to channel in order not to miss the Roundabout and usually end up by spoiling both.'[144] It swiftly returned to its old slot just before the evening news. Further uproar occurred in February 1971, when it was decided the slot would be more profitably filled by currency aware-ness series *Decimal Five*. Once again, parents and children united in a national tantrum.

From Australia to Mozambique, *Magic Roundabout*'s staggering international success meant the programme was a perfect target for merchandising. A range of Pelham puppets were ready for Christmas 1967. The following December the *Roundabout* was the theme for Selfridges' window display. Along with the expected books and records, an unprecedented variety of trinkets rolled off production lines worldwide: Corgi cars, stationery, duvet covers, lampshades and wallpaper included. Anything with a printable surface or malle-able constitution became a facsimile of Danot and Wood's creation. Canny licensing deals made it all highly lucrative: when, say, a Canadian dog food manufacturer used Dougal on their packaging, Danot and the BBC received one per cent each of gross sales.[145]

From this point on, children's television animation was big business, and, inevitably, high risk. The fledgling London Weekend Television offered Danot £250,000 for UK rights to his follow-up *Les Poucetofs*, about a bunch of elves who live in a world reached via a hollow tree, to be screened in autumn 1969.[146] Unfortunately this coincided with LWT's near financial collapse, so British children thrilled instead to the more rough-hewn adventures of Dutch creation *Paulus the Wood Gnome*. Ivor Wood, meanwhile, set up on his own to animate a string of merchandisable hits for the BBC including *The Herbs*, *The Wombles* and *Paddington Bear*.

After around 500 episodes and a feature film, the original *Roundabout* stopped. Subsequent revivals have met with varied success, the most notable being 1992's affectionate update for breakfast show *The Channel Four Daily*, with Nigel Planer more than adequately filling the Thompson role. But there's never been a chance of recapturing the essential ingredient of the original adult/child TV cult: pure accident.

WORLD OF SPORT
(1965–85)
ITV (ABC/LWT)

The sports magazine that preached the three Rs: racing, wrestling, results.

TV SPORT RELIES UPON technology and scale. From 1937's momentous fifteen-minute spectacular *Football at the Arsenal* to the live worldwide televising of the 1964 Tokyo Olympics via the Syncom III satellite, early sports broadcasting went hand in hand with technical innovation and huge production armies: the broadcasters, like their subjects, pushing the limits of human endeavour each season. Just as sport is as much about skill as raw power, so its transmission isn't just a matter of throwing hardware and men at the pitch. Editorial cunning takes precedence over machinery and manpower, especially when the budget is tight.

The BBC, pioneers of the outside broadcast with a fast-growing national network at their disposal, took an early and seemingly unassailable lead. In 1958 it rolled out the Saturday afternoon miscellany *Grandstand*, which dipped into three or four sporting events from around the country, mixed in a bit of studio punditry and rounded things off with a frenzied dash to the football results – the dumpy, battleship grey teleprinter drowning out presenter David Coleman with its metallic clatter as the no-score draws piled up.

This simple format was immensely popular. By 1961 *Grandstand's* four hour stretch was the only time the BBC outstripped the otherwise triumphant ITV in viewing figures.[147] It was also morally upstanding, refusing to show film of major boxing title fights as 'the programme audience includes many young viewers'.[148] The lack of time did rankle with fans – one viewer branded it a 'flibberti-gibbet lucky dip . . . which ensures that no sooner has the follower of one particular event got interested and involved than he or she is at once whisked away into something quite different, usually horse racing.'[149]

The independent channel, with no dedicated sports unit of its own, couldn't compete with that. For inspiration ABC, the weekend-only ITV company, looked to its state-side namesake. The third US network, still regarded as the runt of the TV litter, had since 1961 enjoyed modest success with its magazine show *Wide World of Sports*. While NBC had the money to snaffle the rights to major events, ABC looked outside the headlines – even outside the USA – at what else was going on in the name of sport. So instead of baseball and the NFL, it gave viewers pelota, lacrosse, sundry motorsports, competitive fire fighting, assorted kooky stunt challenges and the ever-popular cliff diving from Acapulco. It even introduced America to something called the Wimbledon Tennis Championships.

Dropping the transatlantic plural, the British *World of Sport* made up for lack of coverage with urgent pizzazz. *Grandstand*'s bare studio was replaced with a bustling typing pool. 'With a battery of tape machines, backed by a staff of Fleet Street sub-editors, *World of Sport* will bring all the glamour and thrills of Saturday afternoon sport right into your living room.'[150] Like *TW3*, *WoS* flaunted its workings, making the process of getting sport onto the screen part of the show itself. 'Film of outstanding sporting events of the day will be rushed onto waiting aircraft,' panted the publicity, cannily avoiding mention of what those events might actually be.

Sat in front of the typists was presenter Eamonn Andrews. A former boxing commentator, Andrews had been lured over from hosting *What's My Line?* on the Beeb with a rumoured £120,000 three-year contract. Viewers of his chat show often paused to wonder why. In 1968, as London Weekend gained control of *WoS*, he was replaced by infinitely more affable former cruise ship entertainer Richard 'Dickie' Davies, whose two-tone bouffant became as much a part of the show as the typists, the aeroplane banners bearing the programme titles, and the four sporting pillars of its afternoon line-up.

First, and in some ways least, was football. Even though *WoS*'s advent coincided with the deployment of the Ampex HS-100 video-disc recorder and the dawn of the action replay, full match coverage was beyond its remit. Instead the programme kicked off with 'On the Ball', in which Pete Lorenzo or Brian Moore rounded up the week's goals, knocked out a write-in postcard competition, and let LWT's Head of Sport, 'Jimmy Hill, the crusading ex-soccerman', pontificate at length on the state of the game. Similarly at large was champion cricketer Fred Trueman, who did pretty much whatever he fancied. 'Freddie has a roving commission with *World of Sport*. Might pop up at a rugby league match . . . or a gentle ladies' croquet meeting!'[151]

Next came racing. Weather permitting, *WoS* covered two meetings each week, the various races punctuating the programme as part of The ITV Seven, which for those of a betting disposition had a potentially lucrative accumulator attached to it. It was altogether more populist than the Beeb's blue-blooded coverage, though it was overseen by the gracious, trilby-sporting John Rickman. The Seven was 'a streamlined, more crisp, horse-racing service', in which hand-scrawled betting odds flashed on screen and 'an attractive girl' was nominated to give tips – a touch of ritzy glamour amongst the sheepskins and Woodbines.

'International Sports Special' usually followed, which was either the bought-in item from the US ABC show – truck racing, clown diving, bus jumping *et al* – or a useful boost for unsung pastimes like darts, bowls and table tennis, or the extraordinarily popular speedway. But the programme's main attraction was professional wrestling. ITV took the ancient art's modern equivalent to its bosom, helping it bloom into the loud and sweaty suspension of disbelief in leotards that drove eight and eighty-year-olds mad with pantomime rage. In drill halls across the land, slow-mo karate chops and well-rehearsed somersaults were executed by barrel-chested athletes with stage names steeped in bathos: 'Gentleman' Chris Adams, 'Mammoth' Ian Campbell, 'Cyanide' Sid Cooper, 'Gaylord' Steve Peacock. Everyone knew this wasn't a sport, but nobody gave two hoots.

Even this made-for-telly spectacle lost impact in translation – the wet slap of belly on canvas and the perspiration-drenched singlets fell, perhaps thankfully, outside the scope of UHF transmission. Atmosphere was replenished by commentator Kent Walton, host of ITV's earlier *Cavalcade of Sport* and the man who'd beaten Jack Good to the punch by hosting the UK's first rock 'n' roll TV show *Cool for Cats* in 1956 – thus knowing all about scream-worthy spectacle. 'You tell me where else a nice, demure young lady can scream or shout her head off,' demanded wrestling's star villain Mick McManus. 'It doesn't matter how sophisticated you are normally, you can become a fishwife for half an hour and then go home all relaxed.'[152] After that climax there was nothing for it but to read out the football results, 'presented in a slick, new, easy-to-follow method' with plenty of emphasis on the pools dividend forecast.

The sports magazine was a stopgap format, a compromise that had to do until there were sufficient channels to give sports of all kinds enough space – and the means to charge premium rates for the privilege. Good news for the major sports, but aside from darts, which *WoS* helped popularise, the also-rans faded from view. Without Uncle Dickie to guide them, generations grew up knowing nothing of the Wisconsin World Lumberjacking Championships.

TALKING TO A STRANGER (1966)

BBC Two

Television's 'first masterpiece'.

It is wrong for all television programmes to be immediately understood . . . and forgotten. There must be some which nag the mind.

John Hopkins, 29 October 1966

UNIVERSALLY FAMILIAR AND CHEAP to stage, packed with paranoia, resentment, barely concealed animosity and subtly devastating mind games – the family should be the most fruitful subject for the TV dramatist. For many years, however, the lid remained firmly on the familial study, and net-curtained nothings prevailed. Pull apart the family and you unnerve society, as Henrik Ibsen discovered when *Ghosts*, his destruction of Scandinavian moral hypocrisy, practically made him a theatrical pariah.

The respectable British stage recoiled from this dangerous filth and embraced what Kenneth Tynan called the 'Loamshire' play: the harmless, pointless minor mishaps of well-bred Home Counties model families. 'Loamshire is a glibly codified fairy tale world,' he wrote, 'of no more use to the student of life than a doll's house would be to a student of town planning . . . its inhabitants belong to a social class derived partly from romantic novels and partly from the playwright's vision of the leisured life he will lead after the play is a success.'[153] Loamshire is a resilient construction – turn on Radio Four of a weekday and you'll find it alive and well, dusted with a few contemporary references. Media spoof *On the Hour* perfectly captured its recycled angst with a twenty-four-hour rolling drama service, spewing an unbroken stream of over-emoted suburban boilerplate into the indifferent afternoon sky. ('She's my WIFE!' 'You OWE it to yourself, George!') Back in 1965, television drama was up to its aerial in Loamshire, and discerning observers prayed for a small screen Ibsen.

Despite working as a producer for BBC radio at the time, John Hopkins got his first written work televised, as so many first generation TV writers did, by Granada. The Beeb soon became his main source of work, largely via *Z-Cars*, Troy Kennedy Martin's northern police serial which startled audiences on its 1962 debut with a determinedly hard-edged realism that made Paddy Chayefsky look like Noel Coward. Sitting diligently down to work from nine thirty in the morning until the end of *Housewives' Choice*, Hopkins completed nearly twenty-four hours of *Z-Cars* material over two and a half years, which he came to regard not so much as a serial but 'the longest play anyone ever wrote'.[154] This regular grind contrasted with the drawn out creation of his magnum opus *Talking to a Stranger*, a four-part study of one fatal Sunday gathering of a fractious adult family.

The year 1966 was a peak one for bold British drama. In November *Cathy Come Home*, a docudrama dealing squarely with homelessness, stopped a good portion of the country in its tracks and set new standards for dramatic realism and journalistic fortitude. At the other extreme, Jonathan Miller served up his psychedelic, Orientalist *Alice in Wonderland* to a nation rendered powerless by the Christmas festivities. Hopkins, however, got in before both these milestones with what George Melly called 'the first authentic masterpiece written directly for television.'[155]

Melly credited Hopkins with being the first serious TV dramatist to read 'the cliché-ridden runes of the semi-detached petit-bourgeois.'[156] From these he created the Stevenses, an outwardly unremarkable lower-middle-class family: Ted and Sarah the ageing, unspeaking parents; Alan the son with a family and a business opportunity in Australia; Terry the headstrong, flippantly wayward daughter with a surprise baby on the way. Over six hours of television, Hopkins looked at their final get together from the perspective of each family member in turn, clarifying details and altering perspective as it unravelled. This was not just a TV novel, it was a modernist TV novel, shuffling time, juggling styles and occupying minds.

Psychologically speaking, the Stevenses had got the lot. This made the plays a slog in some ways but, as the lighter end of family television used to boast, there was something for everyone: a taciturn father, wanton teenage antagonism, unplanned pregnancy, miscegenation and parent-child relations that seemed to have stalled at the latter's twelfth birthday. Jam the lot into a now tiny-looking ancestral house and douse liberally with the pervading misery of an old school, full-fat Christian Sunday, and you have the modern British human condition in all its shameful ignominy – quietly having a nervous breakdown as it dodges into the kitchen and pretends to busy itself with the tea things.

It was tough going, starting off as suburban Ibsen and concluding, with the mother's tragic story, in the abyss-gazing manner of Eugene O'Neill. Like a good modernist, Hopkins incorporated phrases and words from pop culture into his script. 'Everything is relevant. I'm not in the market for polished sentences.'[157] The title of Ted's episode, 'No Skill or Special Knowledge is Required', came from an overheard ad on Radio Caroline.

It was heralded as Big Television, but reviews were thoroughly mixed. The scale of the piece baffled some. 'The dramatist, I am certain, could have expressed in sixty minutes all that was essential, and it would have been a much better, more compelling work.'[158] Some praised the restrained direction of Christopher Morahan, though many disliked what they saw as tricksy flashbacks indicated by 'meat safe mottling on the screen'.[159] Even those who longed for Loamshire gave the actors due credit, particularly Margery Mason as the mother and Judi Dench as Terry. J. C. Trewin, though no fan, captured its texture: 'a medley of half-sentences, choked emotions, sudden outbursts, hopeless realisations; in fact it was very much like life, in its drearier repetitions.'[160]

The BBC believed in the play, and gave it an unprecedented two repeats in eighteen months. It was granted a detailed, shot-by-shot analysis on arts programme *Late Night Line-Up*, the first in-depth technical criticism of TV on TV. Hopkins had cleared the way for complex, allusive, emotionally honest television drama.

He had also opened the doors to a flood of overwrought obscurity, with some of the most obscure stuff coming from his own typewriter. On two consecutive nights in 1972, the BBC screened *That Quiet Earth* and *Walk Into the Dark* – heavily symbolic studies of modern society and mental disturbance, directed by Hopkins himself and starring his wife Shirley Knight. They didn't go well. 'Drained of life-blood and injected up to the hilt with portent,' observed Clive James, 'each line is guaranteed to win from an actor the most face-wrenching trick in his book – abstract significance.'[161] Nancy Banks-Smith whittled her dismissal down to eight syllables: 'primeval mulligatawny'.[162] A wounded Hopkins bit back. 'Critics come to a play like a football match,' he complained, 'they are not prepared to work at it. It's almost like a conspiracy to stop me writing.'[163] TV gave Hopkins valuable early freedom, but as a mass medium it demanded in return a degree of artistic compromise. And as Ibsen said, 'the Devil is compromise'.

THE SMOTHERS BROTHERS COMEDY HOUR (1967–9)

CBS (Comedic Productions)

Variety drops out.

This is my electric cigar. I plug it in, smoke it . . . and it turns me on.

George Burns guests on the third
Smothers Brothers Comedy Hour, 19 February 1967

THE COUNTERCULTURE HIT NETWORK TV like an ink dart in the back of a teacher's neck. While music could change its garb in a week and cinema created its own underground movements, TV was beholden to the conservative strictures of its sponsors and had the cultural flexibility and grace of an oil tanker. The television networks eyed up the long-haired dropouts, and vowed never to let their fragile offspring out to play with them. Until one day, when two nicely-barbered brothers came knocking.

Tom and Dick Smothers were a whimsical duo who rose through the US café scene during the early sixties folk revival. Not being virtuoso players of the guitar and double bass respectively, they gradually ramped up the sibling cross-talk in their act until their LPs were less a collection of toothsome ditties than one long tit-for-tat tantrum. Seeing TV potential, CBS snapped them up, and promptly wasted them on *The Smothers Brothers Show*, a cookie-cutter sitcom in the *I Dream of Jeannie* mould. It cast Tom as Dick's deceased brother, a bungling apprentice angel; appropriately, it stiffed.

The brothers were given creative control of their next show, a traditional comedy-variety hour. With a wacky toy town military band opening and Tiffany stage trappings, the early shows were safe, homely fare, and even admitted as much. ('We're going to present some pungent social comment on the pressing issues of the day.' 'Tommy, we're not going to do anything of the sort!') When George Burns and Jack Benny turned up to indulge in scripted horseplay, a coded marijuana gag delivered by Burns was as dangerous as things got. CBS were content with what they saw as a likeable, clean-cut duo gently but respectfully guying their star guests. It didn't hurt that they soon overtook NBC's behemoth *Bonanza* in the Sunday night ratings.

With Tom as the mainspring, the show evolved into something sharper than the networks had ever seen. The writing team, including Mason 'Classical Gas' Williams and, later, Steve Martin, began exploring the acceptable limits laid down by CBS's forbidding Department of Program Practices. These limits were tight indeed. Guest comedian Elaine May supplied a sketch about film censors which was itself censored for pivotal use of the word 'breast'. The brothers eventually got the sketch on TV – by holding up the pages to camera. While the Vietnam War and erosion of democracy on the home front became the show's main satirical targets, there was just as much risk in their taunting of CBS, its ultra-conservative affiliate stations and, most audaciously of all, the Nielsen ratings system. After several decades of uneasy coexistence, comedy had formally declared war on television.

Musical guests were initially as tame as the brothers themselves – the show introduced Glenn Campbell to the world. But the bookings became more esoteric, and so did the presentation. Jefferson Airplane were superimposed over the live psychedelic ink swirls of Glenn McKay. (For this and other videotape experiments, the show won the 3M company's inaugural award for 'Excellence in Electography'.) The Who overloaded a cannon in Keith Moon's bass drum, scaring the audience to death, singeing Pete Townshend's hair and, according to Roger Daltrey, causing guest star Bette Davis, watching in the wings dressed as Elizabeth I, to faint clean away.[164] But the greatest musical triumph was the reappearance, after seventeen years in the wilderness, of blacklisted folk pioneer Pete Seeger, performing an impassioned rendition of his anti-war song 'Waste Deep in the Big Muddy' to euphoric applause.

The show amassed a gallery of resident freaks. Leigh French appeared from the audience, seemingly unbidden, as flower-haired hippy child Goldie, firing off a dreamy stream of countercultural innuendo with wide-pupilled innocence. Writer Bob Einstein's Officer Judy, a motorcycle cop with a storm trooper's attitude to community policing, broke up sketches and threatened the hosts. Most of all, though, there was the numb and knackered Pat Paulsen, whose hapless disinterest and tenuous grasp of English made him the ideal candidate to run for the 1968 presidential elections. Following in the steps of Gracie Allen some twenty-eight years previously, Paulsen toured the country on a completely non-committal ticket. He laid into his opponents while getting their names wrong. He adopted a free jazz approach to policymaking. He conferred with Bobby Kennedy. He promised precisely nothing. He even defended the network censors. ('The Bill of Rights says nothing about freedom of hearing.') His vote collapsed, but he did much to dislodge presidential office from its lofty plateau. (His victorious rival Richard Nixon would soon finish the job for him.)

In 1968, the brothers lost their unique position in the affection of the youth audience as *Rowan & Martin's Laugh-In* debuted on NBC. *Laugh-In* was quick-fire, catchphrase-strewn and while superficially just as hip as the Smothers brothers, lacked their moral mission. Nixon kept close tabs on what the brothers said about him; *Laugh-In* welcomed him as guest star.

The third season of *Comedy Hour* opened with a statement of intent on the brothers' top lips. Moustaches, long considered a major viewer turn-off in the Midwest, were just the beginning. Guest Harry Belafonte sang a re-worded version of 'Don't Stop the Carnival', superimposed over footage of violent disorder at the recent, disastrous National Democratic Convention in Chicago. Program Practices snipped that out the instant they saw it. As compensation one sketch that did get through, parodying *Bonanza*, beat *Star Trek* to the first networked interracial kiss by a month – and this kiss was between Mama Cass and macramé-loving former LA Rams footballer Rosey Grier, both in drag.

These stunts riled the affiliates, who in turn riled Tom Smothers, creating an escalating atmosphere of mutual mistrust between show and network. It was made clear by CBS that the majority of Americans were not about to 'turn on' any time soon. 'In the Thirty Cities ratings the Smothers clan does well,' wrote Harlan Ellison, 'but in the outlying regions, where most of the soap-suds are bought, they die.'[165] Midway through the season, insurrection peaked. Joan Baez dedicated a song to her husband, in prison for protesting against the draft. Dan Rowan turned up to award a *Laugh-In* Flying Fickle Finger of Fate award to Smothers nemesis Senator John Pastore. David Steinberg delivered a comic sermon observing, with appropriate hand gestures, that Christian scholars 'literally grab the Jews by the Old Testament'. All three incidents were butchered in the edit.

Today, as Steinberg admits of his own bits, 'you look at these things and they're tame, they're just . . . *okay*.'[166] But at the time, combined with the crusading zeal of Tom Smothers, they created a national scandal and precipitated the firing of the duo. Adding inbreds to injury, *Comedy Hour* was replaced with *Hee Haw*, a backwoods *Laugh-In* clone that linked bluegrass numbers with cornball gags in a stream of Bible-belt-friendly inanity. This hayseed hooey would soon be swept away by incoming CBS vice president Fred Silverman, but for now it was a great stride backward for US TV. Still, the Smothers had unquestionably made their mark. Elvis Presley, who had recently used TV to great effect in NBC's stripped down comeback special *Elvis*, named the brothers in his 1970 meeting with the FBI as people who 'have a lot to answer for in the hereafter for the way they have poisoned young minds'.[167] After the Smothers brothers, television was no longer rock 'n' roll's square uncle. It was now its goofy younger cousin with a 1910 Fruitgum Company LP and subscription to *Tiger Beat*. Still, that was better than nothing.

THE PRISONER: FALL OUT (1968)
ITV (ITC/Everyman Films)

TV collapses under the weight of its own splendid folly.

When The Prisoner finally got upstairs and tore off the mask in the end, who would Number One turn out to be? We knew it couldn't be an anti-climax and we knew on the other hand it couldn't be a climax . . . Well, one day I turned to Pat and said, 'I know! You pull the mask off . . . and it's Lew Grade.'

Alexis Kanner

THE RULE'S AS OLD as the medium itself: the more idiosyncratic the drama, the more rarefied the audience. Personal visions and big ratings don't mix. As an immutable law it only has one drawback: in 1968 it was not just flouted but comprehensively repealed by Patrick McGoohan.

When Lew Grade, ruler of the ITC production empire, offered McGoohan the lead in espionage thriller *Danger Man*, McGoohan did more than just turn up and read the lines: he made sweeping changes. He vetoed the 'contrived romantic liaisons and excessive violence . . . the corny show-business formula, the publicity machine grinding away,'[168] in favour of psychological complexity and character depth. Then, when he tired of the whole thing – the whole multi-million pound, salary of two grand a week, sold to over sixty countries thing – he quit. He was offered countless more action roles but turned them down flat, just as he'd refused James Bond a few years before.

In an early morning private meeting with Grade, McGoohan expounded an idea he'd been toying with since about the same time Anthony Newley – another leading man who couldn't abide the path of fame down which he was herded – came up with *Gurney Slade*. Grade couldn't make head nor tail of the pitch, but McGoohan's ambition, and the charming images of Portmeirion – his location of choice, previously used in an episode of *Danger Man* – sold it.

McGoohan's nameless hero was a high-ranking secret agent, similar to *Danger Man*'s John Drake, who quits his post on a point of principle, is subsequently abducted by forces unknown and sequestered in an inescapable 'village' of wedding cake architecture, English country manners and high-tech totalitarian surveillance. Re-designated 'Number Six', he first makes fruitless attempts to escape, then tries to break the security surrounding the Village authorities, never getting higher up the pecking order than the constantly changing 'Number Two'. Each self-contained adventure was also a baroque satire on modern concerns: technology, education, politics and defence were among the big topics allegorically served up at seven thirty on a Sunday evening.

The Prisoner's look, masterminded by Jack Shampan, started from the same end of the Kings Road as *The Avengers*, before veering off into the films of Federico Fellini, with their incongruously costumed figures performing mysterious rites in remote landscapes. The plot similarly began with the standard ITC adventure serial, a rough and ready style known in the trade as 'kick, bollock and scramble', and added a dollop of colour supplement conspiracy from Hollywood paranoia trips like *Seconds* and *The President's Analyst*, where extravagantly sinister secret societies pursue our dauntless hero through a forest of sliding panels.

While *The Prisoner* operated in the familiar pulp world of sharp tailoring, bloodless gunfights and the single knockout punch to the head, there were hints at something more grown-up, perhaps even revelatory, behind it all, to do with society, identity and authoritarian control. Some found this blending of low- and high-brow hard to take. '[Is it] meant to be taken seriously,' asked T. C. Worsley, 'or is it a spoof? If the latter, it lacks edge; if the former, conviction.'[169]

It collected many respectable fans, including Anthony Burgess, who declared himself 'thoroughly hooked' on a series he likened to 'the old picaresque novel, [producing] characters and adventures of a Cervantes-like richness.'[170] A generation weaned on old-fashioned heroics, now maturing to the accompaniment of progressive pop, turned-on cinema and arch fashion, got McGoohan's creation instantly. Or at least, they were willing to go along for the ride without checking the destination first.

Lew Grade, while appreciative of the episodes he previewed, was enough of a traditional showman to voice concerns over where it was all leading. By now *The Prisoner*'s mix of High Englishness and international glamour had sold to the US, Canada, much of Europe, Australia, Latin America and Japan – no pressure. As the final episode approached, McGoohan finally came clean: he didn't have an ending. 'I thought it was very nice of him,' recalled Grade, reflecting in tranquillity some years later, 'to come straight out with me and admit it.'[171] But great things had come out of thin air before: the infamous Rover, a white, seemingly sentient balloon which menaced, chased and captured would-be Village defectors, was a last minute, desperate on-set replacement hurriedly deployed when the original prop robot failed. Grade gave McGoohan the benefit of a great deal of doubt.

In the final four episodes, the show's tics grew to excess: scripts that got bored with themselves before the ink was dry; the dressing-up-box approach to narrative continuity; the general atmosphere of a radicalised edition of *Play School*. The multifarious possibilities of Portmeirion having been exhausted, the show went on a metaphysical tour. A western episode was followed by a dialogue-free bedtime story that mixed *Mission: Impossible* and Roadrunner cartoons, with a crafty swipe at petty nationalism along the way. It went from a cricket match to Kenneth Griffith dressed as Napoleon in an exploding lighthouse without a pause – a parodic distillation of the camp action format the series had decisively outgrown.

The next episode, by contrast, was a minimalist fever dream. Locked for a week into a black-walled chamber, McGoohan and the final Number Two, Leo McKern, rounded on each other in a series of make-believe mental battles pitched somewhere between psychological torture and a fringe theatre party piece. Childhoods were relived, nursery rhymes chanted and brandy knocked back. Prop master Mickey O'Toole openly slagged off the abstruse script on set, unaware it was written, in one draft, by a pseudonymous McGoohan. The two-hander was so intense, it came close to killing McKern. The show was behaving like a cult before it was even broadcast.

McGoohan also wrote *Fall Out*, the anti-denouement: Number Six's enthronement in a Bond villain bunker, promising gobsmacking revelations to a Beatles soundtrack. Kenneth Griffith, in full-bottomed wig, presided over a court of symbolic, hooded and masked officials. (This was acute symbolism, the symbols being handily written down on nameplates, like a live action newspaper cartoon.) McKern was brought back from the (fictional) dead and given a shave. Alexis Kanner played a Revolting Youth, singing and capering like Anthony Newley. It was pompous, funny, insane, fascinating, boring: the most deranged thing ever to infiltrate peak time commercial television.

It was also, in conventional TV terms, cheating. The sets, speeches and mind games were like magician's props, patter and ceremony: an awesomely elaborate way of guarding an empty box. So Number One was . . . a *Morgan*-style gorilla? McGoohan himself? What kind of a punchline was that? Front rooms and pubs fell silent as the credits rolled, then erupted with the terrible rage of the insufficiently entertained. 'The whole tumulus of the series rested on jelly; the crash was frightful,' wrote Anthony Burgess. 'I will never again hope [for] too much from television.'[172] McGoohan later admitted, 'I had to go and hide myself in case I got killed.' [173]

But among the mob, many appreciated this new way of doing serial business, seeing speculative possibilities in the untied loose ends. One viewer neatly killed two televisual birds with one stone: 'I have come to the conclusion that it was part two of the *Magical Mystery Tour*.'[174] (McGoohan was the Fab Four's prime candidate to direct a planned follow-up to that notorious Boxing Day indulgence.)

That promise of enlightenment, those unanswered questions, kept the show alive in many viewers' minds. The temptation to explore its self-contained world further than its creators had ever dared proved enormous. McGoohan, always coyly tight-lipped, refused to explain his 'allegorical conundrum', so amateur sleuths went to work.[175] A fan club formed in 1977, holding its first convention the year after, complete with screenings, seminars and home-made Village blazers. The hobby of filling in the show's many gaps became a vocation, at once knowingly frivolous and deadly earnest, giving *The Prisoner* an afterlife even more fruitful than its twelve-million-rating British heyday. Since then, cultdom has been the Holy Grail for the genre drama series, though few attain it and those that actively try to foster it often die an anonymous death. Almost half a century on, the formula for cult success remains as elusive as Number One.

IF THERE WEREN'T ANY BLACKS, YOU'D HAVE TO INVENT THEM (1968, 1973)

ITV (LWT)

Alf Garnett's creator takes the race issue to its absurd conclusion.

> *JOHNNY SPEIGHT: I'm a Chekhov character, that's what I am*
> *– right out of* The Cherry Orchard . . . *I want to write a play.*
> *MRS SPEIGHT: I want to finish this ironing without a lot of*
> *aggro.*
>
> Dialogue in the Speight household, c. 1960[176]

JUDGING THE SOCIAL ATTITUDES of cultural artefacts from the past is always a fun sport, particularly if you get to feel smug about your own era in the process. Any TV programme of old that deals with race, sex or class is bound to look crass, bigoted or quaint to modern eyes. Something would be badly wrong if it didn't. The consensus is of a steady upward progression from antediluvian ignorance to modern inclusiveness, and this is often true. To complicate matters, however, many aspects of society and its entertainment have become more divisive. One notorious 1960s comedy play is an example of both cases.

A son of toil from Canning Town, Johnny Speight made his early fame writing comedy sketches for Arthur Haynes, whose gentleman tramp character achieved national recognition in the late 1950s. In 1962, the Arts Theatre Club launched a season of controversial, censor-baiting plays with *The Knacker's Yard*, Speight's tale of the sinister resident of a boarding house, a violent nihilist muttering 'Frozen peas and the H-bomb, that's the menu for this century.' Its combination of broad comedy and unrelentingly grim symbolism was tough on even the strongest critical stomachs.

Speight owed a debt to Pinter (who was no stranger to sketch comedy himself, writing spot pieces for Dick Emery in between 'legitimate' appointments), but overlaid the unease with a plethora of traditionally crafted one-liners. The end result was frightening and familiar at once: the continental Theatre of the Absurd passed several times through the music hall mangle. When Spike Milligan's post-holocaust phantasmagoria *The Bed-Sitting Room* arrived at the Mermaid Theatre the following year, the genre had acquired a reassuringly cosy name: British Rubbish. The nation's theatrical establishment was starting to give the avant-garde its due, but not if it was going to stoop to cracking jokes.

In 1964, Speight wrote *If There Weren't Any Blacks, You'd Have to Invent Them* – a knockabout *reductio ad absurdum* of racism, liberal guilt and entrenched bigotry for Sidney Newman's BBC Drama Unit. It was turned down in short order as being, in a typically vague description, 'unsuitable'. Speight put on a brave face by reflecting that he made more money by having it turned down, as he could then sell it to independent station Associated-Rediffusion. In the meantime the RSC performed a twenty-minute chunk on stage and Speight created his most enduring and problematic character: the East End bigot Alf Garnett. *Blacks* then sat on Rediffusion's shelf a while longer before finally becoming the first drama production of the new London Weekend Television.

The play takes place in a graveyard, presided over by an upright undertaker, two priests (Catholic and C of E, who squabble over particulars but back each other up in the face of secular threats) and a bolshie, salt-of-the-earth sexton. The latter tolls the bell and buries the dead till his joints give out and is the only character who manages the odd Brechtian aside to camera, rousing the workers and calling for 'council house bishops'.

Into this macabre plot stumbles a sickly young mother's boy with a morbid fear of 'postal diseases'. He falls foul of a bigoted blind man straight out of Beckett, who leads his constant companion everywhere, a *bien pensant* liberal who can see perfectly well but prefers to keep his eyes shut, and walk backwards. ('What the eye don't see the heart don't grieve over.') Between the two of them, they come to the conclusion that the young man must be black – or if he isn't, he ought to be. Gradually everyone else in the cemetery, including a doctor, military officer and judge, identify the boy as the weakest in the graveyard, and best done away with. ('Don't want your sort hanging round, lowering our land values, do we?') The gang swells via a mixture of unfocussed hate and circular logic, into a lynch mob. One more grave for the sexton to fill. Innit marvellous?

Speight's play may not add up to more than a selection of interlocking sketches, but he pinpoints origins of racism in social panic: 'they might be different, but you don't know until the damage is done, do you?' There are some grand acts of audience provocation, like the opening image after the commercial break of a 'Keep Heaven White' church poster in full close-up. Fine actors filled the cast, from Frank Thornton's stiff Undertaker to the rugged Leslie Sands's deeply sinister Blind Man and his cheerfully ignorant partner, played by Jimmy Hanley, best known to ITV viewers for hawking products in his pretend pub for advertising magazine *Jim's Inn*. The 1968 production, directed by Charles Jarrott with not too much gimmickry, was received with mixed critical enthusiasm. Tom Stoppard liked it, but felt its moment had passed: 'a bit too close to the post-*Bedsitting Room* period.'[177] Robert Pitman just let out a loud yawn: 'We were warned it would be oh, so controversial.'[178] Robin Thornber treated a stage revival a year later with more zeal – 'a Goon Show dictated by Alf Garnett to a drunken Ionesco.'[179]

Then in 1973 it received the rarest of all accolades for a television play: a revival. Big names were cast – Leonard Rossiter as the Blind Man, Richard Beckinsale as the young victim, Bob Hoskins as the sexton, now attired as a ragged ex-Teddy Boy. (Neither production cast any black actors, although that was at least partly the point.) The cemetery was now a stylised apocalyptic wreck of Cadillacs and Rita Hayworth hoardings, reminiscent of Fernando Arrabal's 1958 play *The Automobile Graveyard*. Directing, Bill Hays pushed the cast towards belly-laugh territory, and added rather intrusive comedy trombone interludes. Not so much the Theatre of the Absurd as the Plain Daft.

What had happened was that history had overtaken fiction. Enoch Powell had made his notorious 'Rivers of Blood' address while the original production was in progress, and in the intervening years had soared in public esteem to become pretty much the nation's most admired politician. In the meantime, *Love Thy Neighbour*, an ITV sitcom about a white bigot with black neighbours which treated the race issue in much the same way as Derek Nimmo's *All Gas and Gaiters* approached the deeper questions of theology, had become more popular than Speight ever dreamed. What had been a peripheral issue was now central to British politics, to a dangerous extent. LWT's answer was to camp the whole thing up. 'It is almost pantomime,' admitted producer Rex Firkin, 'although the underlying tone is still there.'[180]

Tastes would shortly change again, and not in ways of which Speight approved. 'Alternative comedy,' he mused, 'as far as I can see, sets out, not only not to attack our appalling prejudices and awful bigotry, but to assuage our prim national propriety by declining to notice them.'[181] An unfair generalisation maybe – Rik Mayall's congenitally hypocritical Rick the Poet alone refutes it – but a decade after *Blacks* was first broadcast, TV comedy increasingly segregated working class humour from its collegiate counterpart, and that gulf would only widen with time, leading to the marginalisation of the former and the distortion of both. The brief days when a factory worker, self-educated on volumes of Bernard Shaw at the local library, could get an absurdist satire on middle-class attitudes to race relations broadcast at peak time on a commercial channel on a Sunday night had gone for good.

SESAME STREET
(1969–)

WNET/PBS (Children's Television Workshop)

The awakening of public service broadcasting produces monsters.

PUBLIC SERVICE BROADCASTING, EDUCATIONAL television, non-commercial programming: in Britain, Canada and many European countries, TV funded by various means from the public purse with the sole intent of improving the cultural lot of the people was a familiar, sometimes dominant, part of the entertainment landscape. The USA, raised on a commercial system since the early days of radio, lacked a free, unsponsored national network.

One service, however, has somehow managed to keep going since 1952. Kick-started by a grant from the Ford Foundation and bearing several titles before settling on National Educational Television in 1963, it aimed to grow into a fourth network of intelligent, edifying material. In reality it had a job staying on air. Funding crises, government intervention and, in the late 1960s, fallout from controversial documentaries including *The Poor Pay More* and *Black Like Me*, threatened its very existence. In 1970, it was radically restructured into the Public Broadcasting Service (PBS), with over half its funding coming from private donations. A year before that, it inaugurated its greatest asset: the first global children's television programme.

Sesame Street was a colourful, inclusive, charming, laid-back and endlessly inventive jamboree, as far from the staid educational stereotype as anyone – and in particular Jim Henson – could imagine. Lloyd Morrisett, educational psychologist and vice president of philanthropic institute the Carnegie Corporation, concocted a pre-school programme with Joan Ganz Cooney, producer of some of those troubling NET documentaries. The show had to combine formal and social education, and be snappy enough to hold its own against the hit-and-run competition of the commercial channels' output, especially the commercials themselves, which Morrisett noticed had the knack of embedding themselves in the memories of small kids. The Children's Television Workshop was born, and two years of research and development, estimated at $8 million, went into honing a mixture of dramatised learning, puppetry and animation. The result was a programme that caught the attention of around ninety per cent of three-to-six-year-olds, as opposed to sixty-five per cent for traditional educational shows.[182]

These were forbidding figures, but in this case laboratory tested didn't mean sterile. Sesame Street itself – a partially idealised suburban set, complete with brownstone stoops and fire hydrants – was a more realistic take on another NET children's property, *Mr Rogers' Neighbourhood*. Initially, the street was populated by four adults – amiable musician Bob, married couple Gordon and Susan, and convenience store owner Mr Hooper – a rolling cast of children, and a repertory of monsters ranging from one to eight feet in height.

The monsters sold the show. Jim Henson had been plying his own style of puppetry – foam and fabric glove puppets with rod-operated marionette limbs – since the mid 1950s, on local Washington show *Sam and Friends* (featuring an embryonic Kermit the Frog) and a string of surreal commercials. Some puppets, like overstuffed greenhorn canary Big Bird, were overtly childlike, slightly cloying characters in the baby-talk tradition of children's entertainment. Others, most of them voiced and operated by Henson and master puppeteer Frank Oz, were a new breed: witty, sharp and gambolling on the borders of sanity.

There was Oscar the Grouch, a dyspeptic Diogenes who skulked in a trashcan and railed against such cissy activities as helping people and joining in. The Wheel Stealer, a boggle-eyed, shark-toothed monster who pilfered corn snack wheels in 1960s commercials, lost the teeth and became biscuit-revering buffoon the Cookie Monster. Ernie and Bert, a live-in couple with the personality dynamics of Henson and Oz allied to the crosstalk of Abbott and Costello, were the only good thing in the original pilot. Their touching co-dependence of wide-eyed wonder and obsessive worry become the show's internationally recognised backbone.

Two highly versatile puppets provided the best of the sketches. Henson's Kermit evolved into a crack roving reporter, covering historical events and fairy tales in an eager but increasingly bemused manner. He was on the spot when Don Music, precious composer of everything from 'Mary Had a Little Lamb' to 'Humpty Dumpty', stumbled over a crucial rhyme ('I'll never get it!') and slammed his face into the keyboard with artistic angst. ('You'll hurt yourself in the head there, Don.') Then there was Oz's Grover, an exhaustingly keen inhabitant of alter egos ranging from superhero to eccentric waiter at Charlie's Restaurant, where he forever wound up his fat, blue-headed customer by muddling orders ('Listen carefully . . . ' 'All right, speak carefully!') before promising a dramatic break-through in comprehension. ('Hold everything! Lock the doors, I've got it!') Through a mixture of breakneck scripting and grown-up (but never off-colour) ad-libbing, Kermit and Grover crammed basic life skills into young heads without a sniff of educational bromide.

As well as news reports, the team commandeered game shows, documentaries and dramas as clandestine vehicles of learning. Other PBS shows came in for parody, most notably the British heritage dramas shown under the umbrella title *Masterpiece Theatre*. Resplendent in velvet smoking jacket and pipe, 'Alistair Cookie' introduced 'Monsterpiece Theatre', 'home of classy drama' such as 'The Postman Always Rings Twice' ('famous drama of suspense and lots of waiting around'); 'Twin Beaks' (featuring David Finch) and 'Me, Claudius'. Truffaut's *The 400 Blows* became Grover's epic attempt to blow out the candles on his birthday cake. *One Flew Over the Cuckoo's Nest* was mistakenly translated as 'Two Flew Over the Chicken Coop'. ('Very beautiful, very moving . . . very silly.') Even Samuel Beckett appeared, with 'Waiting for Elmo'. ('A play so modern and so brilliant it makes absolutely no sense to anybody.')

Nobody at CTW was wringing their hands over how much of this would alienate your average Bronx toddler – meddling middle management was a luxury they couldn't afford – and kids accepted the fact that a blue monster could conduct a lightning verbal exchange one minute and be anxious about getting a haircut the next. The monsters were both kids and adults, bridging the gap between the two rather than seeking to preserve a sentimental innocence.

Less vaudevillian and more abstract were the musical cartoon interludes. The use of songs to drum in educational concepts was old news, but *Sesame Street* had no time for the traditional marching-on-the-spot with piano accompaniment. In the early years Joe Raposo composed the bulk of the songs, from the jaunty theme tune to esoterically specific numbers like 'Caterpillars Never Wear Brown Boots'. His speciality was pastiche: everything from country and western ballads about sharing to dirty funk workouts based around the number six sounded note perfect. A retouching of Talking Heads' 'And She Was' filled the viewer in on the Aristotelian concept of storytelling, while Otis Redding's '(Sittin' On) The Dock of the Bay' instructed children in the art of lake recognition. ('If you don't know by now, then you oughta/That a lake is a body of water.') Best of all, the Pointer Sisters sang a jazz-funk anthem counting groovily to twelve, accompanied by a psychedelic animated pinball machine. While the visuals beguiled, the lyrics sank in as surely and as permanently as any frozen food ditty. Those pesky liberal do-gooders could out-Man the Man.

The *Street*'s decadent methods drew a wave of scholarly fire. The journal *Childhood Education* demanded to know why the Workshop thought it could 'debase the art form of teaching with phony pedagogy, vulgar sideshows, bad acting [and] animated cartoons, in rapid tachistoscopic style with an obbligato of juicy jingles.'[183] Britain was even more suspicious. The BBC turned it down flat, and some ITV regions only showed it sporadically, but it did precipitate a new style of home-grown pre-school programmes, from *Rainbow* to *Pipkins*, less schoolmarmish than *Watch With Mother*.

By the end of 1971, *Sesame Street* was showing in fifty countries, and would eventually reach over one hundred and twenty. '*Sesame Street* is an idea which has swept the world,' said Cooney. 'I liken it to a Tiffany jewel.'[184] Grand words for a kids' show, but they had shown that for children's TV to be taken seriously by its audience, it had to take its audience seriously, as minds to be entertained for their own benefit, not back doors to their parents' bank accounts.

THE OWL SERVICE (1969)

ITV (Granada)

Children's drama reaches a whole new plane.

THERE ARE TWO WAYS to write for children. One is the self-conscious arm's-length approach, addressing the young audience with all the easy charm of a Tory minister kissing a baby in a covered market. The other is to forget the age gap and just write something that will entertain you and children alike. The latter being a rare skill, the former takes precedence in commercial entertainment, grasping nervously at tried and tested stories and formats, disgorging a parade of suspiciously uniform-looking product. Once you and your fearless dog have nabbed one gang of swarthy smugglers, you've nabbed them all.

Alan Garner, 'a cheerful egotist from Cheshire,'[185] had since the late 1950s been writing children's fiction – books that seemed to sell mainly to children, at any rate. Though they were steeped in historic fantasy and a soup of ancient mythology, Garner felt that his stories had to be anchored in actual places – 'everywhere I mentioned could be touched.'[186] The strange forces and mysteries were carefully tied to existing parts of the country, mainly Garner's childhood and adult home of Alderley Edge. For a fantasist, he kept it real.

Garner's profile broached the kids' ghetto with the publication in 1967 of *The Owl Service*, which put a fragile, re-married middle class couple and their new, combined family into rural Wales and at the mercy of ancient energy. Alison, the more sensitive of the two teenagers, takes refuge from family trauma in a weird owl patterned dinner service she finds in the attic of their inherited holiday cottage. Her tracing of the design was Garner's childhood method of creation – a sickly boy, he spent weeks on end confined to bed, with only a crazed, half-timbered ceiling for entertainment, which eventually became a whole obsessively imagined world.

Finding creativity by the back door, Garner dodged the clichés and hang-ups of mainstream juvenile fiction to make something unique and direct. As the poet Robert Nye put it, he 'starts up rhythms which haunt the memory'.[187] His publisher, William Collins and Sons, duly clad *The Owl Service* not in child-friendly watercolours, but 'a plain wrapper and no pictures because it mustn't be put too emphatically in the "children only" category.'[188]

Granada snapped up the TV rights, and set about adapting Garner's dense mass of allusions and apparitions into something that would fit into the children's drama landscape of rollicking adventure stories and lavender-scented period romps. The result, overseen by Garner and producer Peter Plummer, instead warped the habits of children's TV to fit its own landscape, the Welsh valleys. Garner had his own picture of the British countryside to paint, and bucolic didn't come into it.

There are no kindly adults in Garner's story. The father was haughty, the locals sinister and suspicious. Only Alison and house-keeper's son Gwyn started out remotely likeable, and they had their fractious side exposed soon and often enough. Old oppressed young, boys sulked from girls, common Celts squared up to silver spoon Anglo-Saxons – this was a farmhouse holiday without a drop of cold comfort. Shifting between petulant moping and baffled intrigue, the kids stumbled through a hormonally charged passion play, deftly played by the teen leads, especially Gillian Hills as Alison, taking a break between cavorting in *Blow-Up* and humping Malcolm McDowell Keystone Kops-style in *A Clockwork Orange* to work on some genuinely sensual material. When the fantasy arrived, it wasn't an escapist fairyland, but a dissonant, looming valley of patterns, objects and myths, half-glimpsed and semi-understood but totally mesmerising and utterly inescapable.

Plummer's camera lingered at the extremes too – either freakishly wide-angled to cram the landscapes and buildings into claustrophobic master shots or zooming in to patterns and photographs with a desperate curiosity. Topped with an impressionistic title sequence and theme 'tune' consisting of harp, creaking leather and an emptying bath, and you were looking at the most radical departure from the accepted way of doing things that children's entertainment could hold. There was no mistaking this for the standard frock-coated lark. Viewers lapped it up as they did the books; the children's department loosened its corset and youth drama came of age.

The Owl Service was shot on colour negative by cameraman David Wood, but only seen in black and white on its original transmission. After Wood's early death in 1978, it was given a Sunday repeat in colour as a tribute, along with some slightly grim publicity concerning a 'curse' on the series, referring to the murder of Michael Holden (Gwyn) in a Piccadilly pub the previous year, along with a few apocryphal stories of cursed editions of the real life crockery set on which Garner modelled the owl service in the book.[189] Tracing superstitious patterns could work in the publicity trade, too.

NATIONWIDE
(1969–83)
BBC One

Television news lightens up – and never quite comes back down again.

A programme to be swallowed effortlessly between filling the children with beans and popping the old man's dinner in the oven.

Richard North, *Listener*, 30 September 1976

IN 1957, THE BRITISH government relaxed the broadcasting restriction that shut down television entirely from 6 to 7 p.m., so that parents could pack young children off to bed with the minimum of distraction. The new slot gave the teenagers *Six-Five Special*. For the rest of the family there was *Tonight*, a stepping stone from the daily grind to the light entertainment pantomime, a removal of tight shoes via the medium of the whimsically extrapolated current affair. Cliff Michelmore linked quirky stories in the manner of an uncle extracting a shilling from behind the viewer's earlobe. *Tonight*'s reporters cultivated signature styles – Fyffe Robertson's arch confusion with the modern world, Alan Whicker with the levelled gaze and level drone of the man of experience running through that anecdote one more time – but the attitude was always gentleman amateur, and the humour agreeably hearty. This was a clubhouse of the air.

In 1969 Derrick Amoore, assistant head of current affairs, mixed *Tonight*'s spirit with the evening news proper. Tentatively titled *Britain at Six*, this truly national magazine would use telecommunications technology to link regional studios 'the length and breadth of the land' with Lime Grove mission control. Local representatives would fall in on a phalanx of monitors behind Amoore's chosen captain, Michael Barratt. A reporter of the sports jacket and sheepskin school, Barratt tempered his world-weary brashness with a raffish geniality, the embodiment of senior journalism in repose.

After several try-outs that rapidly fell apart while Barratt brushed up his apologetic twinkle to camera, *Nationwide* went live on 9 September 1969 with no major mishaps to report. Twenty minutes of regional news gave way to the national confab without a hiccup. Items including an investigation into Belfast's sectarian schools were capably carried off. 'Technically it was a good, clean, professional job,' thought Peter Black. 'In content it was dullish. Amoore's chief difficulty will be to inject some fun into it.'[190]

All was set fair for the second edition. Barratt began the national section with confidence, following on from one regional story – the end of a brewery strike in Glasgow – with a light item starring their first guest eccentric, 'Mr George MacRae of Hackney, who drinks twenty-one pints a night!' The camera cut, not to MacRae, but a confused-looking chief constable in charge of security at Heathrow Airport. Back in the studio, a now flustered Barratt suggested we instead go over to David Coleman in Belfast, to see 'if they're at half-time'. But Coleman came there none. Barratt picked up the phone on his desk and began one of those achingly long conversations with the production gallery. 'I'm sorry about that mix-up. We're lucky it didn't happen on the first night!' The rest of the show, now firmly jinxed, stumbled through its main item ('Gypsies') in the same haphazard manner, before ending with the now located MacRae downing pints over the closing credits as the crew chanted 'Drink! Drink! Drink!'

From such misfortunes are reputations made. 'The Michael Barratt *Nationwide* comedy show is off to a grand start!'[191] chuckled the *Daily Express*. 'The danger with technical gimmicks,' wrote William Hardcastle, 'is that the news is bent out of shape to fit them.' The glitches that dogged *Nationwide's* first year were gradually tamed, but the damage had been done. The laughter would always be as much at the programme as with it.

Calamity notwithstanding, *Nationwide* established itself both as family viewing and as a family in itself. Barratt was head of the clan. Eldest son was Bob Wellings, the South East's linkman promoted to national status, a move that seemed to puzzle him more than anyone else. ('Wellings breaks the gloss barrier. His manner is of inspired muddle, a sort of highly-tuned bewilderment.'[192]) Under the editorship of Michael Bunce, Wellings was joined in 1972 by Sue Lawley ('drips competence and breeding'[193]), Esther Rantzen and the cheerfully reassuring Frank Bough, sports department graduate and natural heir to Barratt's comfy, reclining throne.

December 1972 also saw the founding of the Consumer Unit. Just as the increasing polarisation of mainstream politics was putting fresh heat into studio debates, so the inflation-stoked national preoccupation with 'prices' gave this normally dreary form of television crusade a sudden urgency. Nearly two years before Shirley Williams was made Minister of Prices to enshrine the obsession in government, Valerie Singleton was created 'high street ombudswoman', rescuing the realm from stagflation, dodgy retailers and lipstick made out of 'soot, chalk, whales' innards and civets' naughty bits'.

Consumer Unit producer David Graham understood that consumer affairs were never going to be Pulitzer material and so let the unit wear its investigative muscle lightly. The detective theme was played for laughs: an anonymous local authority informant was dubbed, Watergate-style, 'Shallow Larynx'. Richard Stilgoe turned viewers' consumptive woes into droll musical routines. Composing elegantly witty squibs about the Supply of Goods (Implied Terms) Act was an esoteric skill, and Stilgoe was its singular master. His finest three-and-a-half minutes came on New Year's Eve, 1974. Tasked with detailing the various professions possessing a statutory right of entry to your home, he recorded a full explanatory song and dance number, performed by seven electronic duplications of himself. With just forty-five minutes in a blue screen studio to tape the various elements, Stilgoe over-fulfilled his brief by a mile, crossing in front of and manoeuvring around 'himselves' in a technical *tour de force* that was reprised by popular demand several times. It was froth, but precision-tooled froth.

By 1975 *Nationwide* was a genre in itself. New editor John Gau helped it become a law unto itself. The tone lightened and the coffers expanded. Barratt's hub was shifted for a week from London to Newcastle in the first of several stabs at increasing regional appeal. Likewise, local mainstays did duty in the capital. ('Mike Neville did get quite larky.'[194]) After an item on package holidays featuring the music from *Colditz* led to a tour firm successfully suing the Consumer Unit for 'unjust ridicule', Stilgoe was moved to the lighter 'Pigeonhole'. His mission, to 'reflect ideas from the *Nationwide* postbag', started as it meant to go on with a man who'd spent sixty-five consecutive summers in a tent. *Nationwide* was the country's showroom for harmlessly aberrant behaviour: if you'd taught a duck to skateboard, could impersonate a Trimphone or hatched an adder's egg in your late husband's trilby, an audience of ten million was a phone call away.

There was a great deal of serious reportage as well, like 'Inside Parliament', 'On the Mersey Beat' and Tom Hodgkinson's famous retread of Orwell's footsteps through London's hostels in 'Down and Out'. But the show's image was formed by the daft stuff. Rival current affairs producers like *This Week*'s David Elstein jeered at the Corporation flagship's pedalo trimmings. But one man's inanity is another child's stepping stone into the forbidding world of grown-up affairs. *Nationwide*'s large youthful following showed they were giving plenty of otherwise uninterested kids a taste for keeping up with the news.

The programme slowly became more self-indulgent. During Silver Jubilee year, television went nuts by royal appointment. *Nationwide* expanded accordingly, beginning at nine forty-five on the morning of the big day with the entire studio dancing a commemorative Jubilee Rumba. This was nothing compared to the self-regard of July's *Nationwide InterCity*. To mark Barratt's retirement, the BBC chartered British Rail's conference train, fitted it with an OB studio and sent it to towns with 'special emotional resonance' for Barratt. Here he would meet old faces, greet local nutters, and generally reminisce to his Boswell, Valerie Singleton ('who looks only slightly sickened by it all'[195]).

In Bournemouth, Barratt enjoyed community singing led by Arthur Askey while a man threw himself off a sixty-foot building. In Leeds, he discovered his birthplace was now an NCP car park. The tour wound up at Saltburn-by-the-Sea in a hubbub of vintage cars, Denis Healey, and regional presenters towing a tractor with their teeth. 'If there is a lesson here,' wrote John Naughton, 'it is that media planners should be more sceptical about the myth of their omnipotence.'[196] With Frank Bough now presiding over the family, this year of indulgence culminated in the *Nationwide* pantomime, one of those end-of-term shows of compulsory jollity with which the humourless let down their hair. Hence, perhaps, the willing involvement of Healey, Norman St John Stevas and several trade union bosses, all paid the standard appearance fee of ten pounds.

Things were never the same after that. A 1982 reshuffle made Roger Bolton editor, David Dimbleby anchorman, and gravity the new watchword. ('Light Entertainment is not my job,' said Bolton. 'I'm not interested in custard pies.'[197]) Inevitably, fans protested ('return the chubby chap to "Miserama" and give us back Frank and Sue!') but points were scored. In a 1983 'On the Spot' election interview, schoolteacher Diana Gould cornered Margaret Thatcher on the sinking of the *Belgrano*, affording a rare glimpse of sheer panic in the PM's eyes. But it was both too little too late and too much too soon. For the final edition in 1983 Bough was restored to the throne and presented with a cake 'passed' from presenter to presenter across the regional studios. *Nationwide*, like all British institutions, retained its pomp and ceremony to the bitterly jolly end.

THE MARY TYLER MOORE SHOW (1970–7)

CBS (MTM Enterprises)

Women liberate the sitcom – a bit.

LAUGHTER IS A REACTION, and comedy naturally tends toward the reactionary. Television's first female comedy star embodied this dilemma. While the off-screen Lucille Ball was one of the most powerful people in the 1950s television landscape, co-owning what became a giant production company, the on-screen Lucy Ricardo was as flaky as they came – a wide-eyed, wide-mouthed grasper of the wrong end of the weekly stick, deferring to the men in her life to sort out her many self-authored disasters. Nevertheless, Ball's achievements changed the comedy game, clearing the ground for the next woman to make significant inroads.

Mary Tyler Moore had certainly risen through the pecking order. Her first regular gig was as David Janssen's receptionist in 1959 detective drama *Richard Diamond*, taking no screen credit and being mainly shot from the shoulders down. It was a slow slog from there to her star-making role. *The Dick Van Dyke Show* had been a rare gem in the 1960s, a far from vintage decade for American sitcoms. Moore's character, Laura Petrie, was significantly truer than the doting waifs in floral prints who rose from the Midwest's collective psyche to sigh with affectionate tolerance at their quarrelsome broods. More active by far, and smarter too, Laura was often the one explaining the world to her Milquetoast husband (though more often still, she burst into tears or got her toe stuck in the bath tap).

By the end of the 1960s, Moore was treading water on Broadway. CBS offered her a series of her own after reunion variety special *Dick Van Dyke and the Other Woman* reminded both the public and Moore what they'd been missing. With husband Grant Tinker, then head of 20th Century Fox Television, she formed MTM Enterprises and hired an unlikely duo to produce the as-yet nebulous show: James L. Brooks had a background in documentary; Allan Burns cut his writing teeth at Jay Ward's cartoon studio, and was half the brains behind archetypal dumb sixties sitcom *My Mother the Car*. Together they'd made *Room 222*, the story of an African-American high school teacher that took situation comedy closer to serious drama than was previously thought sane or decent. Somewhere between those two poles, reckoned Tinker, was Mary's show.

In Brooks and Burns's concept, Moore's character Mary Richards was a thirty-something divorcee, moving to Minneapolis to start a new life and job at the local TV newsroom. CBS had a problem with that, their audience research team protesting that divorce was one of America's great viewer turn-offs, just behind 'moustaches, New Yorkers and Jews'.[198] They eventually downgraded Richards to just single. If the premise was tamed, the scripts themselves would be more progressive, with Brooks and Burns hiring women writers (most notably Treva Silverman) in an acutely male field.

Despite the star's name in the title, this was an ensemble piece. 'At one time in television Jackie Gleason could sit out there and practically do it all by himself,' explained Tinker. 'But by the 1970s the attention spans of viewers had shortened . . . you had to come at them in all directions.'[199] Mary Richards may have shambled through the days in a jumble of berets, scarves and assorted floor-length static generators, but her life took on a sharp symmetry. In her one-room, split-level, shag-pile-and-distressed-brickwork home, she was suspended between kvetching single neighbour

Rhoda Morgenstern and antsy family woman Phyllis Lindstrom. At work Mary clashed with a full spectrum of male personality disorders, from writer Murray Slaughter's lofty sarcasm, through newsreader Ted Knight's idiot dignity to editor Lou Grant's defensive machismo. Though the cast wasn't intended as a diagram, this bunch of arrogant stumblebums were a shorthand for society.

The show inaugurated or developed a range of modern sitcom techniques. Mary and Rhoda were the prototype single girl survival pact, equal parts heart-on-sleeve emotional support and two-fingered defiance to the world at large. The newsroom milieu launched the modern workplace comedy that James Brooks's *Taxi* would make into a thriving sub genre with its web of alliances, rivalries, insults and in-jokes. Crucially, the show wasn't afraid to cut through a life-affirming resolution or heart-warming bonding session with an acerbic aside. Later the comedy of sexual one-up-manship arrived in the form of waspish, horny 'Happy Homemaker' Sue Ann Nivens, played by Betty White, who judged her character 'a very lonely, frightened lady'.[200]

The show's advances in character development were, on the face of it, absurdly elementary, but hardly anyone had applied them before. Simple addition of basic traits multiplied depth and possibility. In a typical 1960s sitcom, Lou Grant would distrust Mary simply because she was a woman in his rightful domain and all plots involving them would flow from there. Here, Lou actually distrusted Mary because her mixture of cocksureness and honest empathy both mocked his aggression and teased out his insecurities, meaning he was often in her debt, which he hated more than anything. There was almost no limit to where you could go with that.

There was texture in the cast as well. Straight actor Ed Asner gave Lou Grant more of an edge to his rage than broad tradition dictated, which meant he could crumple into a desperate, vulnerable heap that bit more credibly. As Bronx Jewish Rhoda, Valerie Harper avoided the obvious burlesque delivery, perfecting instead the fine art of throwing away prize zingers, and doubling the laughter in the process. Cloris Leachman, meanwhile, inhabited the restless Phyllis with Method levels of status-mad tetchiness. All three would eventually get their own shows.

The first series gathered less than stratospheric audiences. If it had arrived a year or so earlier, it might have been swiftly dumped, but in the meantime Nielsen, the TV rating yardstick of choice, had added demographic information to their equations. Suddenly a show needn't pull in huge numbers if it was doing especially well with young, educated urbanites with income to burn – the people who bought a disproportionately large amount of the luxury goods advertisers hawked in and around the action. From now on, TV in America (and, slightly later and to a lesser extent, elsewhere) would follow their tastes. This wouldn't always be to TV's benefit, but for now CBS knew these folk liked their sitcoms enlightened and classy. Talking cars were out, head-scarfed professional women in.

The Mary Tyler Moore Show was the first of a series of intelligent, honest sitcoms that placed adult life centre stage. The following year saw Norman Lear and Bud Yorkin's Alf Garnett-inspired *All in the Family*, with film spin-off *M*A*S*H* the year after that. Of these three, Mary Richards's world was the most reserved, and these days provokes little beyond a marshmallow feeling of nostalgia, but it was an entirely original creation, and deserves immortality for its impact behind the cameras.

Moore herself tried several unsuccessful further combinations of comedy and variety, many referring back to her previous sitcom roles with increasing archness, one featuring David Letterman in full dance. The blow-out came with *Mary's Incredible Dream*, an all-singing, all-dancing trawl through the Bible, with Jack Good at the controls. This $900,000 affair soon became known as *Mary's Indelible Nightmare*. MTM the star had peaked. MTM the production house was just getting started.

MISS WORLD (1970)
BBC One

The year the beauty contest fell apart as the world watched.

MANY OLD TELEVISION CUSTOMS are unfathomable to the modern viewer. American hosts suddenly breaking character to recite short eulogies to orange juice and Spam without missing a beat hail from a world simultaneously more innocent and cynical than our own. The Great British closedown, with its spiritual poem, blast of national anthem and screaming point of light, could only be the last broadcast of a dying alien civilisation two billion light years away. And what uncharted Dark Age could have produced the annual contest in which women from all over the world, aged seventeen to twenty-five, were lined up in glittery formality and judged on the condition of their teeth, hair, legs and torso measurements, the possessor of the best being crowned by the owners of a ballroom and bingo empire?

Miss World's formula was set in stone from the start. All the girls paraded before the audience in 'national dress' (lace bonnets and frumpy frocks for northern Europe, bare midriffs and/or neck-straining head ornaments for most territories south of the equator). Then a classy judging panel whittled the numbers down, and the remainder paraded once more in evening gowns. More whittling, and the final group trooped out once more in swimwear, and were engaged in famously fragmentary chat by the host.

This gesture towards intellectual appreciation was swiftly undercut by the final humiliation, in which the finalists lined up and, at the organiser's shout of 'Turn!', made a military about-face. ('And there they are,' wrote Ian Hamilton, 'for Everyman, a screen full of silken bums to choose from.'[201]) Then a stretched out snatch of hushed tension before the part where, as Nancy Banks-Smith described it, 'Reg handed up the results and Thingy was It.'[202] In a final flourish of ersatz pomp, the newly-crowned Miss World ascended to a golden throne and was helped into a silk cape by two periwigged footmen.

The contest was inaugurated in 1951, and the BBC first televised it in 1955, with a short after-ceremony meet-and-greet for the winner and runners-up. The following year they lavished half an hour of peak time on the ceremony's final half-hour, 'organised by Mecca Dancing in association with the *Sunday Dispatch*'. It pulled the crowds, but some were already noting how the 'far from flawless presentation arrangements made it sometimes hard to suppress the ribald mood, especially when the chosen beauty's crown slipped down over her right ear.'[203]

It wasn't to everyone's taste. The poet Hilary Corke (Mr) was confused as to the judging criteria. On what grounds, he demanded in 1954, were the hopefuls whittled? 'Of abstract beauty? Of charm? Of "personality"? . . . Or what was presumably in all our male minds but the promoters agreed to pretend wasn't?'[204] He also noted all non-white contestants 'were eliminated without question on the first sitting . . . on the next, out went all the non-Teutonics.'[205] But wilful detachment from the real world was exactly what its audience wanted. Whether commentators thought it a 'human Smithfield' or 'as meaningless as a beautiful baby contest at a West Hartlepool church fête,' by 1962 *Miss World* was ensnaring a reasonably healthy seventeen million viewers globally.

Dissent became serious in 1969, with feminist protests outside the Albert Hall and a telephoned bomb threat during the ceremony. But this was just a practice drill. At 9.20 p.m. on 20 November 1970, as the Lionel Blair Dancers ran through a desultory opening routine, it looked like business as usual, with the biggest upset of the evening likely to be Miss Yugoslavia almost toppling down the stairs in the evening wear round. While in London, Miss Brazil professed her desire to 'get to know the manifestations and faces of one of the basic civilisations of the world,' while Miss Hong Kong wanted to meet Cliff Richard. Among the expected tide of models and mannequins (a seemingly important distinction), the Gibraltarian contestant presented the local franchise of children's programme *Romper Room*, while Miss Malaysia was 'a colour consultant'.

The set combined classical kitsch with modernist glitz: Corinthian columns and polystyrene Venuses de Milo populated a disco causeway of glitter-encrusted hexagons. The judges represented the cheesily lavish realm where show business meets diplomacy, as Joan Collins and Glen Campbell shared a joke with The Maharajah of Baroda. The hosts poured forth a stream of calcified patter. 'Sweet and petite, Miss Japan!' chortled Michael Aspel. 'Quite a character, is Miss Tunisia!' vouchsafed 'second lucky man' Keith Fordyce, tantalisingly declining to elaborate further.

At the halfway mark came the star turn, a languorous Bob Hope, unashamedly reading third-string gags from idiot boards. ('I'm very happy to be at this cattle market tonight . . . I've been back there checking calves!') After a few minutes, he was interrupted by a squall of whistles and rattles, as members of the Women's Liberation Workshop stormed the hexagons with flour bags, stink bombs, rotten tomatoes and a water pistol filled with blue ink, chanting, 'We're not beautiful, we're not ugly, we're angry!'

Though the activists never came into shot, viewers were treated to the heady spectacle of live television completely breaking down. The Albert Hall swam and shook on the screen. A halting voice-over tried to hold the fort: 'Not entirely unexpected . . . the security here has been extremely tight . . .' After about five minutes of pictures of the floor and backs of bewildered men's heads, a visibly shaken Hope remounted the causeway: 'For a minute there I thought I was back in vaudeville!' Last year's winner was bustled on for a stilted time-filling chat. 'Sooner or later, these people have to get paid off,' Hope muttered conspiratorially to a nonplussed

Miss Ruber-Staier. 'There's someone upstairs who takes care of that.'

Slowly things got back on track. Places were found ('Can you just stand on where that cross used to be?' asked Aspel of one contestant). Cameras resumed pointing in purposeful directions. Men in headphones stopped darting in and out of holes in the set like meerkats at war. On went the swimming costume round, introduced by Aspel as 'lock-the-husband-in-the-coal-house time', and then the meet-and-greet: 'the part where I say "Is this your first time in London?" and they answer "Steve McQueen".' Protesters were still in the building – one was just stopped from letting off a smoke bomb during the crowning – but aside from a residual unease, ceremonial normality was restored. Miss Grenada won, and came out, unsurprisingly, against the militants. 'I do not think women should ever achieve complete equal rights . . . I still like a gentleman to hold my chair back for me.'[206]

Five protesters were arrested, and turned their magistrate's court appearance into an interrogation of witnesses on their attitudes to women's rights, with some success. Their actions became a media chattering point for months. Many censured, some supported. Germaine Greer reckoned they got it all wrong. 'Women should buy tickets,' she suggested, 'and just take off all their clothes, so that all these extraordinary dolls were surrounded by real people, and you could suddenly see what kind of fantasy the whole thing was, and the bottom would drop out of it.'[207]

As it was, the bottom remained in place for a long time. The next year protesters were kept firmly outside the Hall, staging their own 'Miss Used' mock contest. Thames Television snatched the rights in 1980 and retained them until its dissolution in 1988. It remains a big deal in many countries, but in its nation of origin it can now only be watched via a corner of the Internet, a genteel flash of thigh in a liberated hardcore supermarket, a relic of times more innocent – or at least differently guilty – than our own.

COLUMBO
(1971–8/1989–2003)
NBC/ABC

A shabby revolution in crime.

LIKE SOLAR SYSTEMS LIGHT years distant, TV action series sometimes need sensitive probing to discern signs of intelligent life. While many have exploited the infinite possibilities of the format for thrilling, ingenious plotting and gleeful absurdity, many more are mere snap-together schedule fillers with the sole ambition of detaining a few million teenagers in the living room long enough to clock the sponsor's merchandise. When John Boorman described filmmaking as the process of turning money into light, he meant to invoke the mysterious art of creative alchemy. The average network drama series preferred to just pump in the coins and pull the lever.

The action production line couldn't expunge wit entirely. In 1957 producer Roy Huggins, tasked with lashing together a western series for Warner Television, created *Maverick*, an inveterate gambler played by James Garner, who cut a louche, non-heroic figure in a land full to brimming with noble white hats. A show already retreating at speed from sombre tradition was tipped into outright comedy when Huggins's collaborator Marion Hargrove caught herself typing the cornball line, 'MAVERICK LOOKS AT HIM WITH HIS BEADY LITTLE EYES'.[208] Like a painted desert backdrop, the façade slipped to the floor. Neither writers, producer or star could look at a stagecoach or saloon pianola with a straight face again. *Maverick* was TV's first self-aware outlaw, and the American action series developed a sly wink to go with its right hook.

Despite this playfulness, dumb sincerity largely prevailed. Nothing was more sincere than a Quinn Martin production. Beginning with melodramatic prohibition procedural *The Untouchables*, Martin set the standard for breathlessly serious tales of high drama. With title and cast formally announced by an urgent, authoritarian voice, and the hour divided into three 'acts', plus an 'epilog'[sic], Martin took the structural divisions imposed by commercial breaks and fashioned them into the stone-tablet gravitas of hard literature. *The Fugitive*, *Cannon* and *The Streets of San Francisco* were but three series that shook to Martin's thunderous end-of-days treatment.

Martin made solidly popular shows, but there was something about the totally solemn adventure that paradoxically made it less of a serious dramatic proposition. With their brass-driven theme tunes, off-the-peg plots, actors gamely frowning their way down endless corridors of explanatory dialogue and flop falls from fire escapes onto concealed mattresses, the mid-evening dramas of the sixties and seventies became increasingly hard to tell apart.

NBC, who'd resisted Martin, changed the emphasis of the action slot with *Mystery Movie*, a rotating bill of (initially) three maverick detective stories rich in humour and personality. Dennis Weaver, when he wasn't taking advantage of a gap in the shooting schedule to star in Spielberg's *Duel*, was *McCloud*, a New Mexico sheriff at large in the Big Apple using frontier methods to round up dope dealers. The premise was a straight rehash of Clint Eastwood film *Coogan's Bluff*, and the second *Mystery Movie* strand was similarly derivative. *McMillan and Wife* cast Rock Hudson and Susan Saint James as a sophisticated crime-solving couple very much in the mould of the *Thin Man* films of the 1930s. Not so much 'mystery movies' as 'mystery re-sprays', but at least they weren't stiff.

The third story was far less blatantly derivative. Lieutenant Frank Columbo, the brilliant detective in the dull mackintosh, was one of TV's enduring cops, even holding his own against megastar confectionery addict *Kojak*. The creation of William Link and Richard Levinson, he first appeared in *The Chevy Mystery Show* in 1960, played by the thick set Bert Freed. This decrepit gumshoe, extracting a confession by sheer dogged pestering alone, stood out from the identikit mob. A dedicated Columbo special, *Prescription: Murder*, was commissioned as a vehicle for Bing Crosby. It was probably fortunate that the casting changed. Peter Falk, the eventual occupant of the celebrated raincoat, had previously appeared in *The Trials of O'Brien*, the comic adventures of a down-at-heel lawyer with a trash-strewn office and a wily way with an argument. He shifted those low qualities onto *Columbo*, along with an array of brow-clutching mannerisms and a casual slyness to his delivery of the dreaded, arrest-heralding phrase, 'just one more thing . . .'

Columbo was fresh because Levinson and Link looked beyond detective shows for inspiration. A major inspiration was Porfiry Petrovich, the sly, unassuming magistrate in Dostoyevsky's *Crime and Punishment* who interrogates the suspect Raskolnikov in unorthodox but effective style. When we first meet him, he's 'wearing a dressing-gown . . . and trodden-down slippers . . . His soft, round, rather snub-nosed face was of a sickly yellowish colour, but had a vigorous and rather ironical expression. It would have been good-natured except for a look in the eyes, which shone with watery, mawkish light.'[209] These could almost be *Columbo* stage directions. They certainly beat 'beady little eyes'.

Columbo's raincoat was the nearest thing in mainstream American TV to a class signifier, allowing him to slip under security cordons, get mistaken for night-watchmen and worse by haughty suspects, and produce hard-boiled eggs miraculously from the pockets *à la* Harpo Marx. A constantly amused outsider of low birth, he brought down well-connected killers as a flea might make a bear collapse in ticklish agony. Action had been stripped out, replaced with a series of intense one-to-one conversations as Columbo slowly homed in on the suspect's motive and method. These were punctuated by moments of high-octane excitement where Columbo would bend down to inspect a discarded tie clip. It was talk, talk, talk – but what talk!

The programme's quality reputation established, talent beat a path to *Columbo*'s door. From Faye Dunaway to Janet Leigh, John Cassavetes to Johnny Cash, special guest villains gladly submitted to sweaty inquisition. Patrick McGoohan was a serial guest murderer, often directing his episodes himself. The scruffy upstart hassled the best in the business.

Columbo didn't take the business of murder too seriously. The killings could get ridiculously convoluted, involving subliminal advertising and Heath Robinson contraptions wired up to record players, but all that was deposited in the opening reel to make way for the good stuff: Falk and defendant facing off in lush locations. Falk would freshen up long production runs by ad-libbing around the script in an attempt to catch his co-stars off-guard. There was a spirit about the show, beginning with Falk and spreading in all directions, that Quinn Martin would never achieve with all the concerned frowns in Christendom. The sincere-but-stupid crime series had been on the case too long; in all senses but the sartorial, *Columbo* smartened it up.

THE LARGEST THEATRE IN THE WORLD: THE RAINBIRDS (1971)

BBC One

Drama goes off the rails.

I have not been impressed by BBC One's Play for Today *series – there have been too many weirdies, too much self-indulgence by the producers.*

James Thomas, *Daily Express*, 11 February 1971

WEIRDNESS IS IN THE eye of the reviewer. Some of the 'weirdies' in BBC One's flagship single drama slot had recently included a study of teenage existentialism with added pot smoking and underage gay sex, an everyday tale of ritual human sacrifice in a Black Country village, and a mid-life crisis told through the medium of the saucy seaside postcard. But James Thomas hoped that night's offering, in which a young man throws himself out of a window, goes into a coma and hallucinates nightmarish visions of his oppressive family, wouldn't fall into the weird basket. It was by Clive Exton, whose 'name on the titles usually spells an interesting piece'.

Exton was one of the most lauded of early TV dramatists. Turning from acting to writing in his twenties, he made his name at Granada with *No Fixed Abode*, a terse encounter between various reprobates in a lodging house. Hard-bitten realism gave way to something headier in 1962 with *The Big Eat*, a satire on consumerism in which a food company organises a television eating contest, complete with smarmy compère (Peter Sallis), rock 'n' roll interludes and gluttonous contestants (including Arthur Mullard) sat in high chairs suspended on giant scales. The results are loud, crass, and fatal. Exton wrote it for ABC, but the commercial channel found a satire of commercialism too hot to handle, and it went to the BBC. On the night, thirty-six viewers phoned Television Centre in outrage.

The Trial of Dr Fancy depicted a court case which uncovers a conspiracy between a psychiatrist, a surgeon and a gent's outfitter to induce a complex in tall men about their height, leading them to seek amputation of their legs. It was made by ABC in 1962 and then sat on for two years for fear of offence. A fortnight after *Dr Fancy* finally went out, the BBC were to show Exton's *The Bone Yard*, about a slightly dim police constable who thinks he can talk to Christ, though he may just be being set up by his randy, tap-dancing chief inspector who's having it away with his wife ('as nice a piece of knitting as I've laid eyes on!') while he hangs around graveyards at night. Unfortunately it coincided with the trial of Harold Challenor, a delusional flying squad detective prone to fitting up suspects in the most blatant manner, and was pulled for fifteen months.

Understandably nonplussed by this treatment, Exton moved into films, writing screenplays for *10 Rillington Place* and Joe Orton's *Entertaining Mr Sloane*. The BBC tempted him back in 1970 with the most prestigious slot they could muster. In 1962, the European Broadcasting Union decided to augment their already ridiculed annual Song Contest with a regular exchange of new drama between its thirteen member states. *The Largest Theatre in the World* employed big names like Terence Rattigan and Ingmar Bergman to write a play which each country's public service station would then produce as they saw fit. The attractions were obvious: a vast potential audience, strewn across the cradle of western culture, the prestige of the art-house with the scope of a blockbuster.

Exton gave Europe the mother of all satires. The family, the military, the medical profession, Christianity, television, the monarchy and any class you cared to mention were thrown up as distorted vignettes within the comatose brain of John Rainbird. His parents, oddly demoted half a class from genteel reality, become monsters obsessed with 'testing' him in combat. He's signed up to the army, strung up in an abattoir, and repeatedly finds himself in a white limo that keeps crashing. In the real world, his mother is encouraged to accept a dangerous operation which will bring him out of his coma while knocking his IQ down a hundred points. With the prickly young man reduced to a mooing infant, the fractious family unit is saved.

Who could direct this heady brew? Exton had reservations about the way *The Bone Yard* was played up for panto laughs by James MacTaggart. *The Rainbirds* was given to Philip Saville. His portfolio veering between a sombre *Hamlet* shot on location at Elsinore and a comedy about Victorian prostitution written by Denis Norden, Saville had come a long way since the days of *Armchair Theatre*'s kitchen sink. The kitchen sink is what he threw into this already well-stuffed play. Observing theatre's total liberation with the arrival of the anarchic 'Happenings' in the late 1960s, Peter Brook observed, 'give a child a paintbox, and if he mixes all the colours together the result is always the same muddy browny grey.'[210] With TV drama hitting similar all-bets-off territory, the evening schedules were daubed in many shades of experimental taupe.

Shooting colour film entirely on location, Saville was given *carte blanche*. With no chance of executives idly patching into the closed circuit to see what he was up to – the bane of directors working in studios – he was free to augment Exton's already baroque script with cigar-smoking male nuns, S&M nurses, inflatable fish and yards of graphic Vietnam footage. This last had become a radical TV mainstay since Tony Palmer stuck clips of napalm victims in between scenes of The Who and Hendrix in concert for his 1968 pop documentary *All My Loving*. The TV director was starting to catch the writer up in the production pecking order, with Saville as frontrunner. Exton's hopes for a sober treatment went out of the window.

The critics didn't know where to begin, but generally agreed on where to end. 'Surely it would be churlish to be disappointed,' pre-empted *The Times*. 'It was a virtuoso piece, using all the tricks of the medium.'[211] There were plenty of churls about, though. *The Observer* reckoned the dream sequences suggested John Rainbird 'had spent far too much time watching fashionable television plays,' adding that 'they do these things much more amusingly (and imaginatively) on *Monty Python*.'[212] In the *FT*, the venerable T. C. Worsley had trouble believing this was the work of men in their forties: 'Surely the mature Exton wouldn't be naïve enough to expend such a waste of spirit on the simple psychological truism that over-mothered boys risk emasculation? If it was therapy for him, it was a pain in the psyche for us, and I still cannot imagine how it ever got on.'[213] Neither could the *Daily Mail*: 'I imagine very few viewers will have stayed longer than ten minutes . . . nothing but the worst was good enough.'[214] Nancy Banks-Smith in the *Guardian* just exclaimed, 'I feel rather as if I had been run over by a bus.'[215]

After the fallout subsided, Exton quietly switched to lighter fare like *The Crezz*, a valiant attempt to create a middle-class soap opera set in west London. After a fruitless dalliance with Hollywood in the early 1980s, tinkering with stillborn dreck like *Red Sonja*, he scored a solid hit with Granada's Fry and Laurie period caper *Jeeves and Wooster*. His deft translation of P. G. Wodehouse's comic rhythms to the screen might seem the antithesis of the crazed sprawl of *The Rainbirds*, but a keen ear for snappy lunacy had always been in his work. (Even his contributions to dour apocalypse adventure *Survivors* were made under the pseudonym M. K. Jeeves, as previously used by W. C. Fields.) Exton's last big project was 'gardening detective' series *Rosemary & Thyme*, a distillation of the British Sunday evening tea-and-crumpet murder mystery that took cosiness to new heights. It's tempting to see his leap from extreme bad to extreme good taste as symbolic of TV drama's rapid retreat from the avant garde, but Exton was no hack. He just appreciated that the highly regulated televisual climate where ambitious TV writers could make a living from their esoteric visions alone was devolving into a much less forgiving environment. The 'weirdies' would have to pay their way.

DUEL (1971)
ABC (Universal Television)

The TV movie beats the big screen.

'TV MOVIE' IS THE perfect oxymoron. The words don't just repel each other, as in 'rock opera', they actively cancel each other out. It's a zero-sum phrase, holding no promise and reeking of shame, like 'government initiative'.

Despite their similarities, the two media work in completely different ways. Most cinema films make a loss, but the potential is there for amassing a fortune, hence the fevered speculation and constantly inflating budgets. Television operates on limited stakes – the best you can hope for is to fill the full complement of advertising slots, with the promise of syndication a distant incentive. The life-blood of television is the series, the franchise, the rolling cash generator. Stuffing a one-shot TV movie with millions of dollars makes no sense – it's a sure way to turn a king's ransom into a tramp's pension. TV movie directors have to add ingenious thrift to their armoury. They often treat it as a means to get noticed by Hollywood, but in the process they can learn a great deal.

One of the better TV movie slots in the early 1970s was the *ABC Movie of the Week*, an anthology of seventy-five-minute dramas ranging from series pilots like *Alias Smith and Jones* to continuations of the cutesy 1960s *Gidget* franchise, wrapped up in a title sequence that was half *2001*, half Pearl & Dean. Some were fine, some were lousy, but their artistic ambition generally lay no higher than tempting a significant chunk of Tuesday night's audience away from the charms of *Hawaii Five-0* on CBS.

Duel (1971)

Universal Television had started the made-for-TV game with 1964's kids-and-criminals adventure *See How They Run*, for NBC. By 1971 their allegiance had switched to ABC and staff writer Steven Bochco was engaged in turning up material for *Movie of the Week* when he found *Duel*, a Richard Matheson story, in an issue of *Playboy*. The minimalist tale of an average guy in the Californian desert menaced, for no reason, by a battered articulated tanker with an unseen driver gripped Bochco. Matheson, whose novels *I Am Legend* and *The Shrinking Man* had been filmed with varying results, and had written the odd TV script himself (most significantly classic *Twilight Zone* story 'Nightmare at 20,000 Feet'), tried to sell *Duel* as a TV episode idea, but was told it lacked enough meat for a whole hour's drama. When Universal accepted it as *Movie of the Week* fodder, he was understandably sceptical, especially when he got wind of the appointed director.

Awarded a seven-year contract by Universal head Sid Sheinberg on the strength of a twenty-minute home movie project, Steven Spielberg was warily regarded by his colleagues. He was wet behind the ears, he was self-important, he couldn't handle actors, he wasted time setting up tricksy shots – he was every inch the irksome tyro. He'd steered some decent TV through production, though, most notably the Bochco-written *Columbo* episode 'Murder By the Book'. He had big ideas for *Duel*.

Spielberg imposed his will on the producers from the start. A less committed director would have caved in to the studio's insistence on filming most of the in-car close-ups indoors, with back-projected desert. Spielberg knew how cheap this would look, and insisted on a full location shoot. He also demanded as little speech as possible. The studio wanted chunks of the protagonist's explanatory interior monologue in voice-over. Spielberg cut them down as far as he could. But he couldn't do much about the budget and schedule: $750,000 and two weeks' shooting in the San Fernando valley would test his creative generalship to the limit.[216]

TV production schedules militate against creativity. A good director is one who can shoot the most footage in the shortest time. Spielberg put in the cost-cutting work, varying camera angles to help the same car travelling round the same bend work in a dozen separate scenes.[217] Everything else from the TV directing rulebook he ignored. Hating the preponderance of close-ups on TV – a hangover from its low-definition origins – Spielberg favoured the wide angle, deep focus shot. An anxious interlude in which Dennis Weaver's petrified hero stumbles, dazed, through a remote diner was shot in one three-minute, hand-held take. The final collision between Weaver's car and the truck, due to good planning, great stunt work and a massive dose of luck, similarly came in one long, slow motion chunk.

Spielberg's balance of compromise and vision was perfectly judged. Marshalling his limited resources to the best possible end, he and his team injected a hitherto routine format with atmosphere and visual excitement. *Duel* was an instant hit, attracted lustrous reviews, and got the most out of its mayfly spell in the limelight. An extended cinema version was released theatrically in Europe. Its central conceit was blatantly ripped off by third string efforts like *Killdozer* and *The Car*. Finally, its many gorgeous vehicle shots were recycled as stock footage in cheap action series like *The Incredible Hulk*.[218] The odd late night rerun aside, such is the legacy of the made-for-TV masterpiece.

Small wonder, then, that Spielberg, after a couple more TV pictures, including rakishly shot paranormal oddity *Something Evil*, ran off to the cinema and rarely looked back. The TV movie, once more starved of hungry geniuses, slipped back into its cycle of cop show try-outs, bleary alcoholics and 'Disease of the Week' tear-jerkers, begging for the more financially viable format of the mini-series to come along and put it out of its misery. Spielberg, though, had proved this most workmanlike of formats could be dragged in the direction of art. Even cultural deserts can harbour the odd breathtaking explosion.

THE SPECIAL LONDON BRIDGE SPECIAL (1972)

NBC/BBC One
(Winters Hollywood)

Big time variety makes a
transatlantic trip – by bus.

SMALL AS IT WAS and shoved in a corner, television always struggled with the spectacular. Fuzzy pictures of the moon landing had the weight of history behind them, but live coverage of a circus just made an immersive experience tiny and distant. This didn't stop the late 1960s wave of international variety spectaculars: latter day Busby Berkeley musicals shrunk to a square foot of phosphor. The hidden motive was to make the squinting viewer upgrade their set, but a twenty-four-inch colour screen was still a dream for most. They thrived nonetheless, simultaneously monolithically self-assured and gawkily ingratiating: visually a knockout, verbally a coma.

One of its chief architects was steeped in television. David Winters began as a dancer on Jack Good's *Shindig!*, then graduated through choreography (mentoring Toni Basil among others) to produce the sort of jet-setting musical TV specials that were the inevitable result of the perennial network demand: 'We need something for our very expensive talent to do, and fast.' First came *Lucy in London*, CBS's contract-renewal sweetener for Lucille Ball in 1966, sending the red-haired ditz on a breakneck trip through the swinging capital in a motorcycle-sidecar combination driven by

Anthony Newley. The formula was simple: a bare bones storyline, camped up and semi-acted by the star, is unceremoniously stuffed with musical guests (in this case the Dave Clark Five) and character actors (James Robertson Justice). What it lacked in art it more than made up for in sheer all-singing, all-dancing, all-Rolodex-consulting effort.

In 1970, Winters took full creative control of *Raquel!*, a gossamer-thin vehicle for Raquel Welch to hop across the globe in assorted tiny outfits of scalloped Bacofoil. She sang numbers from *Hair!* on the slopes of an Aztec pyramid accompanied by twelve dancers in costumes half Zodiac sign, half genetically engineered football mascot. She teamed up with Bob Hope to sing – and, in a cack-handed way, act out – the Beatles' 'Rocky Raccoon'. With some judicious manipulation of microphone levels, she duetted with Tom Jones on a medley of rock 'n' roll standards. Welch's indeterminate song-and-dance skills were ameliorated by Winters's production, a high camp jamboree in which Broadway reached out to Haight-Ashbury in entirely the wrong direction, settling somewhere between Cairo and Cape Canaveral.

Jones the Voice acquitted himself well enough to earn the Winters treatment two years later. Tom, being a more heavyweight talent than Raquel, was going to require a more substantial vehicle: less your standard featherweight rump-shaker, more a modern opera. 'Tom has a proper acting role in *London Bridge*,' insisted Winters. 'He has seven songs, but they arise from the story.'[219] He was suitably vague on what this story involved.

On transmission, all became clear. Tom, having toured the capital's overcast tourist spots while singing an ode to 'cockney champagne' called, indisputably, *London Is London*, boards a bus conducted by Hermione Gingold. Gingold is in full Grand Dame mode, with, in Philip Hope-Wallace's phrase, 'her voice swooping campingly through a whole two octaves of sneer.'[220] Tom is gobsmacked when the bus is spirited to the Arizona tourist resort where the original London Bridge has been relocated piece by piece, thus conveniently aligning him with a galaxy of Hollywood stars and sealing a lucrative sponsorship deal with the resort's proprietors in the process. This was screened the night before the Queen opened the relocated bridge for real, with live coverage of the snip to a Tom Mangold commentary.

Having retrospectively funded his own TV special by magic, Tom finds no showbiz feat beyond him, and demonstrates his new acting chops by reciting lines of the script while a) smiling, and b) not looking into the camera. There's almost a plot in which Jones has a desultory romance with Jennifer O'Neill, which consists mainly of longingly reciting chunks of the Lake Havasu City guidebook at each other. The resort's non-bridge attractions are highlighted by having The Carpenters sing on top of them, Charlton Heston play tennis in them, and Kirk Douglas shoot Lorne Greene off their roofs.

The weird US/UK hybrid theme is kept up at all times: 'Consider Yourself' becomes a hoedown. For the connoisseur, art is provided by a gratuitous ballet interlude with Rudolf Nureyev. It comes as a relief when Tom finds the whole thing's been a dream, and Terry-Thomas sticks his head into shot to deny that he's Terry-Thomas, presumably for tax purposes. As with all these specials, there's some solid musical talent at the root of it – here co-ordinated by Marvin Hamlisch – but what defines the genre, for better or worse, is the half-ton of ludicrous icing under which it's buried.

Such chaotic exorbitance suggests the variety spectacular was in rude health, but a long decline was just beginning. The insane amount of money required to hire, co-ordinate and film all that talent, let alone fly it round the world, was running out. The feeble gags which held the numbers together were never fresh, but in an increasingly sophisticated comedy environment they began to look less like an indulgent groan and more like an insult. Most devastatingly of all, music itself was moving on, and decisively away from the shiny studio floor. Showcases for Doris Day and Cilla Black were the rearguard of an entertainment force that had flattened the competition when Perry Como first stretched his lungs on behalf of Chesterfield Cigarettes in the early 1950s.

The name-in-title series slowly thinned out, replaced by the once-in-a-blue-moon special. In the US the genre went right back to its roots, with Perry Como shepherding holiday audiences through songs and sketches into the late 1980s. Its British cousin tended instead toward the humble environs of the holiday camp. *Hi Summer!* and *Summertime Special* toured the country's holiday destinations for tunes, jokes and – weather permitting – displays of formation dancing to increasingly inappropriate current hits. Out of time they certainly were, but only a cynic wouldn't regret the loss of the most audacious TV confections ever baked.

UN, DOS, TRES . . .
(1972–2004)
TVE1

TV's first political allegory with cash prizes.

Uruguayan writer-director Narciso Ibáñez Serrador holds a singular place in the history of Spanish – and through one programme, world – television. A pioneer of dramatic anthologies, he made the horror story a crucial part of Spain's early television drama with series like *Historias Para No Dormir* (Stories to Keep You Awake), which ran from 1965 to 1982. His major legacy, however, was in an entirely different field.

On 24 April 1972, Serrador's game show *Un, Dos, Tres . . . Responda Otra Vez* (One, Two, Three . . . Answer Again) opened its doors with cartoon ceremony, making as colourful an entry as Spain's monochrome state television service permitted. Sprawling over ninety minutes of Monday evening television, the contest was interspersed with musical, comedy and variety guest turns, a game show version of the mammoth variety spectaculars that filled entire evenings of European television.

Each edition had a broad theme: horror, the circus, ancient Greece, and so forth. It was formed of three stages, corresponding to Serrador's theory of the three basic types of contest: a test of knowledge, a challenge of skill and good old fashioned gambling. In the first round, four pairs of contestants competed to name as many things in a given category as possible. They had forty-five seconds to itemise 'famous Greeks', say, 'parts of a rocket' or 'reasons for a car accident'. There followed an elimination round based around party-game physical challenges like walking a tightrope or passing eggs around without using the hands. The remaining pair of contestants had the long final round, the auction, all to themselves. Assorted variety turns appeared, leaving cryptic clues to one of the prizes. The contestants had to eliminate the inferior prizes, ideally retaining the star prize – a car, a holiday, 100,000 pesetas – and avoiding the duff booby traps.

Serrador the game show deviser had created an original, if unspectacular, format. Serrador the writer added the crucial twist. Looking at the quiz as a dramatic situation, he reasoned that everyone on set needed a role – either for or against the contestants. Support came from the genial host (initially Peruvian actor Kiko Ledgard) and six 'secretaries' in outsize glasses who chaperoned the contestants and wheeled prizes on and off-stage. Against them were the 'Downside': three ashen-faced, long-bearded men dressed like Victorian undertakers in frock coats and stove-pipe hats, led by one 'Don Cicuta' ('Hemlock'). These miseries held the purse strings, operated the stopwatches and generally radiated bad vibes from the sidelines, heckling successful contestants and relishing wrong answers.

The Don was more than just a pantomime novelty. He was, according to Serrador, 'an image of the Censor', symbolic of the spooks of Franco's late-period dictatorship who repressed anything lively and progressive, enforcing the resentful austerity of 'black conservatism'.[221] This Franklin Mint Franco stalked a Spain-in-miniature, the fictional community of Tacañón del Todo (roughly: 'misers of everything'), a society crushed by puritanical bureaucracy.

When Un, Dos, Tres . . . launched, Spain was preoccupied with what would happen after its ailing dictator finally passed on. With various factions of the ruling elite jockeying for position, and ETA's bombing campaign on the rise, the heartening prospect of an end to decades of repression was tempered with fear and uncertainty. This wasn't, of course, the kind of thing that could be openly aired while Franco still drew breath, but under cover of a harmless game show, a little of that unease could be relieved. Kiko and his Secretaries were performing a unique public service.

After Franco, *Un, Dos, Tres . . .* evolved elaborate new features. When Valentin Tornos, the veteran actor playing Don Cicuta, retired in 1976 through ill health, his role was split three ways, creating the Tacañones: Don Slacker, Don Strait and Professor Pencil; a miser, a prude and a pedant respectively. In the eighties, three distaff Tacañonas took over: Mary Immaculate, Mari-Puri and the Little Widow, as cheerless and sombre as ever. Over the next two decades more changes were made to the show's burgeoning mythology, including the introduction of two-faced Secretaries who could suddenly turn against contestants. The original bold anti-fascist statement faded from the collective memory, but the simpler advocacy of hedonism over inhibition remained. For once, the epithet 'national institution' seems genuinely deserved.

The format was adapted all over Europe, most notably in the UK as Yorkshire Television's *3-2-1*, commissioned as a rival to the BBC's big couples contest *The Generation Game* (itself an import from the Netherlands). Despite Britain picking up the show just as it was entering its own long period of political repression, the allegorical elements were the first to be dropped. Ted Rogers compèred a simple variety quiz, half the length of the original, with two new ingredients: Rogers's high speed hand jive illustrating the show's title (which was later re-assimilated into the Spanish show), and Dusty Bin, a remote-controlled ash-can clown acting as programme mascot and booby prize signifier (which wasn't). It didn't give any Catholic military autocrats a metaphorical poke in the eye, but it did send a young married couple back to Gateshead with a forty-four-piece canteen of sterling silver cutlery.

INIGO PIPKIN/PIPKINS
(1973–81)
ITV (ATV)

The puppet show that pulled strings but no punches.

PUPPET SHOWS ARE POPULAR with children's programme makers of a subversive bent, being great decoys for smuggling all types of mischievous business onto the screen. They're equally popular with TV stations being, as they are, phenomenally cheap to make. Children, naturally, can't get enough of them. With such universal appeal, puppetry has enjoyed a long and lunatic tenure on television. The odd professionally outraged moral guardian aside, everyone's happy.

Hand-operated sedition featured in one of the first regular children's shows, *Time for Beany*. Broadcast on America's short-lived Paramount Network from 1949, it was the brainchild of Bob Clampett, the most energetic and surreal of Warner Brothers' golden age cartoon directors. In the few years before the intro-duction of the Television Code in 1951, *Time for Beany* frequently pushed the boundaries – and its luck – with randy puppet wolves chasing after nubile blonde actresses, and demented puppet sea serpents singing jazz standards accompanied by President Truman on the piano.

In Britain, puppetry could be relied upon for teatime smut (Basil Brush's not-so-cryptic monologues about 'Dirty Gertie at number thirty') and afternoon terror (the nightmarish marionettes of *Rupert the Bear* and *Paulus the Woodgnome*). One puppet show, however, stuck its stubby plush paws into more subtle areas.

Inigo Pipkin was one of several children's programmes (*Rainbow* was another) that arrived on ITV in the wake of two major changes. The first was the permission given to TV companies to disport themselves on the previously protected weekday afternoons by the Minister of Posts and Telecommunications, who offered a vague hope the extra hours could provide 'more time for experimental programmes . . . perhaps'.[222] The other was the shadow cast over British children's programmes by *Sesame Street,* which generated earnest pedagogic debate by the yard. Parents and kids loved it, while many educationalists 'abhor it for possibly corrupting educational objectives'.[223] *Sesame Street* was for several years only shown in small pockets of the UK, but the new home-grown pre-school programmes carried its influence nationwide.

Inigo Pipkin was instigated by Michael Jeans, who had curated some potent schools programmes for ITV. Graphic social justice primer *Law and Order* was denounced by Mary Whitehouse as 'brutal, despicable and a very bad example to children'.[224] *Rules That Are Not to Be Accepted* imagined an Orwellian future Britain where smoking is a prison offence, leading to bursting jails, overrun police and the rise of lighting up in public as the ultimate rebellious act. This new programme, about a lovable old puppet maker whose creations come to life, with a catchy theme sung by Jackie Lee of *Rupert* and *White Horses* fame, was going to be altogether more wholesome, though, wasn't it?

Up to a point. Jeans was keen to escape from the restrictive pre-school template of the time, where a responsible, omniscient adult leads a group of inquisitive child-surrogates on a journey to discover where biscuits come from. He still had the responsible adult (George Woodbridge, veteran comic actor and rare survivor of John Gielgud's ill-fated production of *Macbeth*) and the child-surrogates (expertly manipulated by Heather Tobias and Nigel Plaskitt), but their concerns went beyond the genesis of baked goods.

Though they were full of life, Hartley Hare (fey, mischievous), Topov the monkey (childlike, curious), Pig (sarky, omnivorous) and Tortoise (mature, avaricious) were manifestly puppets. Their manufactured nature was emphasised by showing Pipkin making new companions in early episodes, to the confusion and concern of Hartley. This was existentialism with stabilisers, but it all related to real life – main writer Susan Pleat, a *Coronation Street* graduate, treated the show as 'a soap opera for the under-fives' that aimed to 'take small children seriously'.[225] Hence Hartley's ignoble reaction to the creation of new puppets: he was only reacting as many viewers would to a new baby in the family. Tackling the issue indirectly, the script achieved honesty and avoided sentimentality. It was metaphor, not euphemism.

A more head-on approach was adopted after Woodbridge died. Jeans made the decision to address the actor's death in the series (now called simply *Pipkins*), having Pipkin die, and the puppet shop carry on under his assistant Johnny. Suddenly children's lunchtimes were awash with grief, confusion and insecurity (Johnny, being a novice craftsman, was unlikely to keep the gang solvent). Despite complaints (usually from adults acting unilaterally on the children's behalf) Jeans and co. stuck to their guns, confronting eternity once more when a pet goldfish died. This episode, written by former *Siege of Golden Hill* star Billy Hamon, captured the frightened, shapeless worry of the underage mind, as Topov asked Johnny if they were going to die too, and Johnny admitted that yes, they were. This was strong medicine, outpacing even *Sesame Street*, which wouldn't tackle death until 1983, after cast member Will Lee passed on.

In terms of content, *Pipkins* was audacious. (It only rarely capitulated to censorship, such as when a Johnny Morris story about a cow trying to achieve herd domination by braving an electric fence was nixed by the British Safety Council.) Visually, *Pipkins* was no kaleidoscopic sugar dream. The gang's headquarters was located at ATV's Elstree studios, adjacent to *The Muppet Show* (which had a habit of pulling rank over its neighbour, often commandeering the platforms which raised the human actors above the puppeteers),[226] but had the fly-blown, cluttered look of a genuine backstreet emporium. The puppets were similarly ragged, though expertly made by Jane Tyson, who went right back to the BBC's *Andy Pandy*. *Pipkins*'s dilapidation was precisely crafted.

Jeans's pensive innovations and flea-bitten aesthetics didn't make a great impact. As *Pipkins* ended, a new ethos emerged in children's programming, filled with dreams of international markets, easily merchandised designs, primary colours and relentless exuberance. There was no place for questions of mortality in the new, heavily monetised, no-risk set-up – it was back to happy songs and biscuit nativities. The moral of today's story: mindful melancholy may help a child's development, but it's crap at shifting pencil cases.

THE INDOOR LEAGUE (1973–8)

ITV (Yorkshire)

TV sport in its cups.

It is a rather pathetic idea to think of people, in the sort of ghastly modern pubs which have television, standing there watching traditional olde worlde pub games on television.

Stanley Reynolds, *The Times*, 6 April 1973

FOR THE BETTER PART of half a century, British independent television was a cluster of cantons. The larger ones provided output for the nation: London's timesharing duo, Granada's titan of arts and current affairs, and Lew Grade's entertainment palace ATV, based in the Midlands but prone to 'nip up' to the capital on frequent away days.

Regions too thinly populated to raise enough cash for regular national programming found their niches. Rural Anglia and Southern brought their rolling acres to metropolitan viewers via nature documentaries such as *Survival* and hymns to country crafts like Jack Hargreaves' *Out of Town*. Welsh and Scottish stations promoted their native culture and language. But it took Yorkshire to curate a sporting tournament that was the very essence of the locale, distilled into twenty-five minutes of parsimonious broad-casting.

The Indoor League was a simple knockout pub games tournament, brought to the nation from Leeds's Queens Hotel (later upgrading to the more spacious Irish Centre) by illustrious England cricket captain Fred Trueman. Pint in one hand and pipe in the other, Fiery Fred burst onto the afternoon schedules to open jaded eyes to the pseudo-athletic prodigies loitering by the pickled eggs.

With the action on such a small scale, the commentary obligingly thickened to compensate. Fred, mindful of his sport's tradition of sumptuous prose embodied by the likes of C. L. R. James and Neville Cardus, waxed lyrical over the Old Peculier. 'We openly and humbly salute the wizards of the taproom,' he intoned, anticipating 'the biggest bonanza of sporting skill I've ever clapped eyes on.'

Initially, five games were covered: bar billiards ('snooker with bunkers'), table skittles ('the Devil among the tailors'), table football ('very popular in the technical colleges'), shove ha'penny and darts. ('That's real darts on a Yorkshire board, with no trebles and no flukey shots.') Further series added pool and, notably, arm wrestling, precipitating a national revival of the contest supposedly invented by Genghis Khan, thanks to the runaway success of a southerner, Don 'Buster' Whitney, Kent's Ace of Armlock.

Darts would prove to be the show's big draw. In the past decade it had grown from pub game to spectator sport, but while tabloids sponsored well-attended tournaments, TV coverage remained sporadic. Three weeks after its *League* debut, the game was televised in earnest as the *News of the World* Championship took up residence on *World of Sport*. For now, though, the arrows lined up among the other tavern pastimes for a top prize of £100. 'Let's see how they go on with the smell of money up their nostrils!' said Fred. 'Just how tense are these lads when the money's on their arrows? Are they cocky, or quivering? Who's your money on? I'm saying nowt.'

Much of this sonorous hyperbole was the work of producer Sid Waddell who, on his way from the mines of Northumberland to a history degree at Cambridge, had picked up a few tips for embellishing introductory speeches. Shove ha'penny players became 'stars of the sliding small change,' exhibiting a flair to 'match the delic-ateness and the dexterity of the miniature portrait painter'. Leaning on the skittles table like Dr Bronowski on a lectern, rolling every 'r' within reach, Fred eulogised, 'what's probably the oldest pub game in England. I hear Henry VIII used to knock the old shove ha'pennies about a bit – when he weren't bashing t'missus. Well, I don't know how Barry Stones or Alan Brown of Durham treat their missuses, but they certainly can nudge a crafty ha'penny!'

Aside from the sport's 'wild characters' like 'Buffalo Bill' of Scunthorpe (who shoved ha'pennies while wearing a ten-gallon hat), Fred drew tantalising sketches of the contestants, giving each one an intriguing *nom de guerre*: 'Charles Ellis, the Dark Horse . . . he's got five kids, and he takes his arrows seriously and all'; 'Dennis Jones, the Lad Who Crouches to Swing, owns a chip shop, and is going a bit thin on top.' These portentous vignettes were often brutally undercut when he interviewed the man in question, with thoroughly prosaic results. 'You weren't as consistent as you usually are today.' 'No Fred, I forgot me darts. I left them in the pub and had to borrow some.' Occasionally the programme unearthed a snug bar Muhammad Ali, like 'King Ben' Bootham of Keighley, who proudly declared, 'I can ride a unicycle after downing ten pints!' Supermen all.

The commentators varied in style as much as the players. Neil Cleminson filled the layman in on arcane technical matters. 'He knocks off that chalk in the bay, but still has two required in the first bay. So this means he has six to get in the top, and two in the bottom, so it's twenty chalks already in, seven to get, and the break ends.' Dave Lanning, meanwhile, hyped them up for all they were worth. 'Ooh, shiver me timbers! The drama! The stark naked drama of table skittles! He got two successive floppers . . . Now, can he get all twenty-seven? No, he can't.'

The Indoor League is one of those programmes that gets dragged out today as an example of the screamingly parochial – a room-size remnant of a fag-packet world long since gentrified to oblivion. Such easy mockery conveniently ignores the fun Fred and company had at their own expense. It's not immediately obvious – it is, admittedly, a very Yorkshire kind of fun – but it's there.

The 2012 Olympic Games, legend goes, saw the UK shed its entrenched mardiness and become a nation of grudgeless, classless joiners-in. But *The Indoor League*'s combination of domesticated superlatives and floor-gazing trophy exchanges points to a more nuanced form of support. Pulling in two directions at once, local pride is elegantly cantilevered; like a Playtex bra, it lifts as it deprecates. *The Indoor League* was a monument to human endeavour that never got too peas-above-sticks, a tongue-in-cheek thumbs-up, a lavishly tooled tin medal. It hailed its saloon bar heroes with a beautifully muted fanfare that seemed all the more genuine for its sardonic undercurrent. In Dave Lanning's immortally moderate words, 'The hundred pounds is in his back pocket and the beer will be flowing tonight I am sure!'

WHATEVER HAPPENED TO THE LIKELY LADS? (1973–4)

BBC One

The sitcom sequel that outdid its original.

COMEDY HISTORY IS LITTERED with legends of executives bumping into canteen staff and commissioning six episodes of a national institution from them on the spot. Such stories are often romanticised – John Sullivan was less a scene shifter who happened to have written *Citizen Smith* than a sitcom writer who happened to realise the best way to collar producers was to get a job on the studio floor – but many great comedies have had the most ad hoc conceptions.

At the start of the 1960s in Notting Hill's Uxbridge Arms[227] Dick Clement, a young radio producer for the BBC's African service, and drinking pal Ian La Frenais wrote 'Double Date', a conversation between two idle, sarky and randy lads, for the off-duty amusement of the BBC staff drama society.[228] When Clement took a TV directing course and was given one day, £100 and the Corporation's tiniest studio with which to make broadcastable television, the trenchant two-hander seemed obvious material. The result was deemed good enough for the consideration of Head of Comedy Frank Muir, who was advised, 'it won't do anything, but at least it's cheap'.[229]

The Likely Lads debuted on the fledgling BBC Two in 1964,

with twenty-something Tyneside mates Bob Ferris (Rodney Bewes) and Terry Collier (James Bolam) returning from holiday to their mundane world of dominoes, electrical repairs and largely fruitless wooing of the local talent. You couldn't hope for a less remarkable premise, but from this barren plot grew some of television's ripest comedy.

Naturally funny dialogue had already been cultivated by Ray Galton and Alan Simpson in *Hancock* and *Steptoe and Son*, but these shows retained an element of the grotesque, be it Hancock's surreal delusions of adequacy or Steptoe's operatic filial resentment. Bob and Terry weren't oddballs or outcasts. Their ordinariness was absolute; it was the writers' genius to locate the rich comic seams in the workaday landscape. The lads transferred to the BBC's main channel via a sketch on 1964's *Christmas Night with the Stars*, in which dewy reminiscence over old Rupert Bear annuals turned into a full-blown duel of competitive nostalgia. The most prosaic subject matter became comic poetry.

The duo's regrouping a decade on was something else entirely. Bob and Terry have grown from their original broad types into those rare birds – fully-rounded sitcom characters. Bob, once meek, naïve and apologetically gauche, has thrown in his lot with the newly rampant middle class. With one foot in the badminton club and an eye on the Rotary, he clings to the suburban greasy pole for all he's worth – not because he relishes its rituals, but more out of sheer relief that others are prepared to do the hard work of ordering his life for him.

Terry, once brash, ignorant and unrepentantly rude, has been hardened by a dud marriage and a singularly humdrum tour of duty into a shambling, shiftless professional prole, half Orwellian autodidact (thanks to such crucial texts as the Open University's *Metamorphosis of the Frog*), and half northern Nietzsche, foretelling imminent doom for those above him on the social ladder, and an imminent thick ear for those in front of him in the bus queue. The small things that differentiated the pair in youth have grown into an unbridgeable social chasm. Naturally, this makes them closer than ever. Apart, they're the two poles of male hopelessness incarnate. Together they're a complete fool.

Wedged disconsolately between them is Bob's fiancée Thelma Chambers (Brigit Forsyth), chief architect of the Ferris renaissance and congenitally deaf to the Collier repartee. While Terry stews in his ancestral back-to-back, Bob and Thelma are snug in their Arcadian bolt-hole on the Elm Lodge Estate. Inside it's all melamine serving hatches, heliotrope cookware and pottery owls in self-assembly nooks. Outside the anaemic brick terraces are fringed with a front garden of blasted tundra and the milkman does double duty as a John Pilger of inter-mews gossip. When Terry tells Bob he'll need to give his house a name otherwise he'd never be able to find it again his words have weight, or at least they would if he wasn't kipping on Bob's sofa-bed at the time.

If *Whatever . . .* were a drama series, it would be renowned for the way it compresses the grit of quotidian domestic experience and working class male angst into crystal-clear speech. Sadly for posterity's sake, the writers had to go and make it funny as well. Drama is the minutes of life's meeting taken down in exquisite copperplate. Sitcom is the conversation in the pub afterwards copied in Teeline shorthand onto a fag packet. *Whatever . . .* is a parade of observations so deadly accurate as to give the illusion of a fully-fitted history. Characters like Lugless Douglas and the infamous Sylvia Braithwaite, legendary hang-outs like the Go-Go Rock Club ('the north's premier music Mecca') exist only as a few lines of bitty recollection, but are all the more vivid for it. Each word has a job to do, and every word counts.

Clement and La Frenais give all their characters due sympathy. Even Thelma, who initially lived up to her Medusan reputation in the lads' Park Junior School mythology ('We tried not to make her a monster,' said Clement, 'but I'm afraid we failed'[230]) was gradually rounded out as Bob's true other half: equally neurotic, but emotionally practical (unlike Terry, who's free of neuroses but cooks chops in the toaster). This was partly due to Forsyth's skill in humanising the authors' rough model, just as Bolam and Bewes's on-set back-and-forth enriched the original scripts to create, in less than fourteen hours of television, three of the most solid, believable characters of any genre.

It sounds odd to describe such a downbeat show as revolutionary, but *Whatever . . .*'s realism made a great impression on the brightest of its successors. Sitcom talk dropped the last vestiges of the old punchline set-ups for the rattle and roll of real speech. Characters occupied the same readily recognisable world as their viewers. The dialogue was littered with cultural ephemera. Once established, all these traits, especially the last one, could be grossly overused by writers looking for a shortcut to 'quality' comedy. They forgot to purloin the trick *Whatever . . .* didn't invent, but helped to perfect: a script which, by judicious craftsmanship, is perfectly balanced, even – especially – when the situation goes haywire. Towards the end of the last series, various confusions lead Terry and Thelma to charge into the kitchen and pull Bob out from what looks like a gas oven suicide attempt. The concluding tableau, straight out of stock melodrama, with the three of them sprawled tearfully on the kitchen floor, is capped by Bob's plaintive cry to a distraught Thelma: 'You'll get Ovenstick all over your blouse!' Advantage: sitcom.

THRILLER (1973–6)
ITV/ABC (ATV)

The deluxe crime anthology.

The perfect murder, like the perpetual motion machine, has often engaged the attention of the whimsical. And, as parlour games go, both are better than snakes and ladders. It is as harmless as a bug in boiling water. Even the corpses appear to wink!
Dennis Potter, *Daily Herald*, 12 May 1964

THE CRIME DRAMA IS as much sport as art. While a football match only has so many different outcomes, there are infinite ways to reach a no-score draw, some more thrilling than others. A murder yarn also sets its field at kick-off – playing the young married couple freshly moved into an old cottage up front, putting the stranger who may not be all he seems on the wing, keeping the recently escaped serial killer on the subs bench. The joy's in the journey, the masterly variations and wrong-footings wrought from these familiar scenarios.

By the early 1970s Brian Clemens was one of British television's most successful scriptwriters, with a hand in creating many of the big Golden Age action hits, from *The Avengers* to *The Persuaders*. He learnt his craft in the distinctly un-flashy B-movie trade of the 1950s. Quota producers like the Danziger Brothers inherited some random sets from major films and Clemens ran up a script that somehow tied together the Old Bailey, a Georgian street and the bridge of a nuclear submarine. It was this artisan dexterity that he most prized. 'Any fool can do a good job given £10 million and a hired army to stage the Battle of Waterloo,' Clemens reasoned. 'But it takes real ingenuity to do it with two soldiers.'[231] Lew Grade gave him the ideal opportunity to showcase his prudent knack when he commissioned one of Clemens's long-cherished ideas: a thriller anthology.

The anthology series was a familiar feature of the 1970s schedule. Ratings-conscious channel controllers saw how conveniently they combined the benefits of the long-running series (which made the money, but caused a lot of damage when they crashed) and the single play (which won the accolades, but was already lost to posterity as the end credits rolled). All the stories had in common was a loose theme or genre, but add in a snappy theme and stylish introduction, and a bunch of light dramas became a scheduling fixture. *The Wednesday Play* and the *Philco-Goodyear Playhouse* reclined at the posh end of the form, while peak time mustered Rod Serling's *The Twilight Zone* and Roald Dahl's *Tales of the Unexpected*. (The anthology was just about the only TV format in which a writer could get his name billed above the title.)

Thriller wasn't monogrammed with Clemens's name, but his fingerprints were all over it. Out of forty-three episodes, he wrote over thirty and provided detailed story outlines for the rest. His building blocks were life's mundane panics: the front door creaking after midnight, the shifty stalker in the crowd, the boarding house full of ominously frosty tenants. His narrative tools were unabashed cliché. Characters entered living rooms refracted in crystal decanters placed just so on an occasional table in the foreground. Anonymous black-gloved hands picked up telephone receivers and slowly dialled very long numbers. Flashy TR7s would gravel-crunch up driveways of well-appointed country houses, arousing the mutton-chopped gardener's suspicion. Blonde Americans in trouser suits merrily announced they were 'new in town' to public bars full of ruddy and watchful character actors.

The budgets were boosted by a deal with US network ABC, who insisted on two alterations in return. First, they wanted each episode to cover ninety minutes of American evening, which worked out at seventy-two minutes of programme content. This turned out to be a boon for Clemens, who could use those extra twelve minutes over the hour to build suspense in long, largely silent takes, helped immensely by the bespoke incidental music of Laurie Johnston (standard procedure at the time was to slap on a slice of 'Eerie Oboe' from the music library every time the killer wandered on set). Second, a high proportion of the tales had to include, some-where near the top of the billing, either an American actress with a first name for a surname, or an American actor with a surname for a first name.

Research was not Clemens's bag. He wrote a police procedural or court case as he imagined it, only running a cursory check against the facts on completion. He claimed that ninety-nine per cent of the time he didn't have to alter anything, although one notable feature of the series is the high incidence of walk-on desk sergeants who comment darkly on the 'highly irregular' methods of the detect-ive in charge. The production schedule was tight: ten days' rehearsal in a draughty Masonic hall, a four-day shoot in ATV's Elstree studios (plus a few exterior shots, often just a silent trudge from front door to Ford Granada) and three days for editing.[232]

All this suggests the worst kind of slapdash stab-'n'-scream farc: Primark Hitchcock shot by the yard. Clemens's writing raised the game. While characterisation never rose above broad types and the dialogue largely stuck to unvarnished exposition, Clemens marshalled the familiar, the expected and the done-to-death into flamboyant new combinations. Twists were second-guessed, undercut and double-crossed. The rug was pulled out from under the viewer, often taking several square feet of parquet flooring with it. The giddy feeling of a murder case folding in on itself like deadly origami enhanced the already giddy feeling of sumptuous 1970s interiors peopled with famous murder suspects clad in vibrant artificial fibres. Sometimes the detective schlepped more satin than the kidnapped heiress. Everything on screen was arch contrivance. Subtlety got you nowhere.

Take 1975 episode, 'The Double Kill'. Ingredients: one desperate, psychopathic cat burglar; one loud-mouth Yank hubby of a wealthy heiress; and one suavely unorthodox detective played by a pinstriped Peter Bowles. The three men confront, dodge and bluff each other as clues and events pile up. A botched burglary, a murder contract, a giveaway pair of blood-stained kid gloves – championship games of Cluedo have unfolded in less ceremonial fashion. Blackmail leads to counter-blackmail, murder weapons appear and vanish, a Wodehousian dipsomaniac stumbles in with crucial evidence, and copper and suspect size each other up via protracted sidelong glances across the crime scene. But while the screen overflows with old chestnuts, the plot keeps throwing curveballs up until the closing lines, and the players visibly relish every minute.

This is after-dinner crime: murder as party piece. Future generations would delight in this florid overkill, but it was considered outrageously camp even at the time. It was TV's equivalent of Victorian melodrama, and like that much derided genre its job, according to Eric Bentley, was 'not to tumble into absurdity by accident but to revel in it on purpose'.[233] Unspeakable evil and outrageous coincidence reigned supreme. Sir Arthur Conan Doyle, priding himself on the insoluble nature of his Sherlock Holmes plots, 'positively bet his wife a shilling that she would not guess the true solution of it until she got to the end of the chapter'.[234] *Thriller* pushed the limits of credulity in all directions. Its closest thing to a recurring character, private detective Matthew Earp, played with Noel Coward levels of fanciful abandon by Dinsdale Landen, was prone to prefacing revelations with 'fasten your seatbelts!' Writer, director, cast and even the characters they played were having a lark. The game show was afoot.

When a TV format accumulates this much froufrou garnish, diagnosis of decadence is never far away. *Thriller* and its contemporaries engendered a backlash and a thirst for realism. Crime in the cinema was starting to get very bloody. TV couldn't be that explicit, but its locations slowly became back alleys rather than front parlours, and murders shattered whole families instead of just altering wills. The detective was just as likely to be an amoral thug himself rather than an omniscient savant with a passion for real tennis. But this messier, less reassuring thriller wasn't always more real. Take *The Professionals* – top-level criminal intelligence operations performed by a Ford Capri-skidding, semi-automatic firing pair of dolly boys with an eye for the birds and a morbid fear of car door handles. Bodie and Doyle set new standards for unflinching depiction of mob violence and terrorism, but with all the documentary realism of a school playground reconstruction of *Diamonds Are Forever*. For this, they could thank their creator: Brian Clemens.

TISWAS (1974–82)
ITV (ATV)

Television gets the kids right.

Surrealism is an almost impossibly demanding aesthetic, since only a genius can be free without restrictions. Tiswas *is a surrealist television programme. It ought to be a flop. Happily it is quite the opposite.*

Clive James, 'The True Artists',
Observer, 18 February 1979

SOME GREAT TELEVISION PROGRAMMES are painstakingly constructed. Others achieve success through trial and error. A tiny few are the product of one brief flash of inspiration. Perhaps the rarest category of all, though, is the kind of programme which spontaneously crops up, often unplanned and beneath the radar of both executive and critic, in the gaps between other programmes: televisual weeds.

Saturday mornings in the early seventies remained one of British television's many uncultivated waste grounds. If ITV bothered to stir at all before *World of Sport*, it was for a hotchpotch of children's reruns like *Thunderbirds* and adult education series on DIY or bridge playing. Gradually the kids' stuff won out, and the couple of hours before noon became the new teatime.

On 5 January 1974, in the tiny presentation studio at ATV's Birmingham headquarters, the regional links between the old shows were billed as an umbrella programme, tentatively titled *Today is*

Saturday, or the Tis-Was Show. Gags, competitions and 'fun facts' festooned the spaces between old episodes of *Tarzan*, providing a bit of conceptual glue and cutting drastically down on costs. In charge, at least nominally, were the '*Tiswas* Twins', John Asher and Chris 'Strawhead' Tarrant, administering ad-hoc bits of business that were half written in the pub the night before, half pulled out of thin air before your very eyes.

It was, as the *TV Times* quietly allowed, 'informal and experimental in a modest way,'[235] but nobody, the Twins included, realised how big it would become in its first eleven-week run. Producer Peter 'Poochie' Tomlinson and sports presenter 'Me, Myself, Yours Truly' Trevor East were enlisted to make up the show's original back-seat-of-the-coach crew. Gradually the inter-programme chaos began to take over from the pre-recorded stuff it was supposed to be linking. Confidence grew, and with it, chaos. It moved into the significantly larger Studio Three, where an important discovery was made: water and other substances could be thrown around without fear of electrocution. The plot thickened.

Week by week, almost imperceptibly, a new show formed, concerned less with back-announcing the exploits of *Arthur, King of the Britons* and illustrated lectures on the life cycle of the moth, and more with ramshackle, off-the-cuff parodies of current films, TV shows and celebrities, which began with a chorus of barely suppressed giggles and rapidly descended (or rather ascended) into a maelstrom of airborne fluorescent treacle. Then, as the typhoon wore itself out, Tarrant, gasping for breath as the last empty bucket careened off the woodwork behind him, hastily looked for the working camera and panted the introduction to an ancient Roadrunner cartoon; after which, the fury would start up all over again. Veteran supervisors of Tartrazine-fuelled children's parties recognised the pattern.

Tiswas's most significant contemporary, *Saturday Scene*, grew out of programme links in the same way, moulded by London Weekend's head of presentation Warren Breach around repeats of *The Bionic Woman*. Its most popular segment was a quarter-hour pop slot, in which David Essex and the Bay City Rollers were interviewed by actress Sally James. By early 1977 *Tiswas* had become big enough to poach Sal from the metropolis to conduct her patent Almost Legendary Pop Interviews. Genuine star guests were augmented by Tarrant and East impersonating names too big to hit the Midlands, donning outsize cardboard grins as Donny and Marie Osmond. In the days when pop music was still presented with wooden mock enthusiasm across the board, this implicit mickey-taking was a welcome corrective to the 'teenybop' ritual, earning the respect of many post-punk acts. The Clash boycotted *Top of the Pops* outright, but had no objections to a quick chat with Sal.

For the rest of the decade the show retained its rough format, though personnel changed around it. Out went Tomlinson and East. In came ex-Scaffold member John Gorman (specialities: tramps, military types, high-concept mucking about); Bob Carolgees (dim escapologists, phlegmatic pets) and Lenny Henry (moustachioed newsreaders, bearded botanists, reggae artistes with exacting dietary requirements). And in all directions, the constant chorus of kids, often holding up jokes on placards like a cracker factory picket line, alternately cheering and jeering the adults, sometimes both simultaneously.

The show slowly smothered the country in its Wunda-Gloo. First Wales, then the North West and Scotland fell. By 1979 only the Southern and Tyne-Tees areas held out with their own brave but inferior stabs at a rival, leading geographically deprived youngsters to hit the black-and-white portable set in an attempt to catch some fuzzily fading remnants of the Midlands signal. By 1980, it was finally a true national programme, and a considerable threat to the BBC. Edward Barnes, head of the BBC children's department, labelled it 'indigestible candyfloss with no intellectual grit',[236] as opposed to his own stately rival, *Multi-Coloured Swap Shop*, with mugs of tea, a cosy club atmosphere and an initial theme of diligent collecting (admittedly soon abandoned in favour of pop guests). Everyone had a preference, but the idea of the rival shows dividing the nation's youth along tribal lines was largely a myth: both had peaks and lulls, and many kids energetically switched between the two.

This made ratings very difficult to measure, but relatively modest estimates of between two and three million for turn-of-the-decade *Tiswas* still constituted a solid achievement for those who remembered when this part of the schedule was all farming bulletins. The ATV mailbags were gargantuan. The show got through fifty cans of custard pie foam a week, supplied by local joke shop proprietor David Lynex. Tarrant, James, Carolgees and Gorman formed the Four Bucketeers, had a hit record and did a national tour of rock venues.

National glory latest barely a year. Tarrant, Carolgees and Henry left the show in mid-1981 to found *OTT*, Tarrant's vision of an 'adult' *Tiswas* at the other end of the Saturday schedule, which introduced the comedy of Alexei Sayle, and stirred up plenty of froth in the press, but never quite got its round in. Under the quieter reign of Gordon Astley and Den Hegarty from doo-wop revivalists Darts, *Tiswas* carried on until Central Television, new holders of the Midlands ITV franchise, put it to bed.

Central's replacement, *The Saturday Show*, showed how much work really did go into keeping *Tiswas* running, by letting the chaos overwhelm the hosts. Cues were fluffed, cameras lost, and microphones flooded with crowd chatter, resulting in a blob of grey un-television with all the party ambience of a fire assembly point. They really did just throw that show together, and it showed. Later Saturday morning affairs were better than that, but rarely touched *Tiswas* for spontaneity that sparked.

Tiswas's greatest innovation took time to become apparent. The adults allowed themselves to be witty in a way which belonged to the world at large rather than the imagined world of children, giving the kids the benefit of the doubt. By not giving two hoots about responsibly preparing its young charges for adult life, *Tiswas* gave kids perhaps the most appealing and honest advice about what lay ahead for them: it's all just a big, ridiculous mess anyway, so get stuck in.

DON'T ASK ME
(1974–8)
ITV (Yorkshire)

TV science goes populist in a big way.

In this state of unselfconsciousness, it seemed that, to emphasise what I was saying, I made certain characteristic gestures.

Magnus Pyke

FOR DECADES, SCIENCE ON television commanded reverential restraint. Straight dissemination of the known facts with a bare minimum of visual garnish gave broadcasts plenty of sombre purposefulness, but minimal entertainment value. When heavyweight presenters were replaced by laymen things relaxed slightly, though critics often bridled. *Meet Mr Marvel*, co-hosted by Muriel Young, was dismissed in 1956 as 'an extraordinary farrago of pseudo-scientific demonstrations at nursery level and facetious backchat.'[237] But it took one of the country's top nutritional biochemists to turn science into full-blown cabaret.

Dr Magnus Pyke began his unique broadcasting career at the age of sixty-three, when a graphic lecture on synthetic foodstuffs he delivered to the Royal Society led Yorkshire Television to employ him for *Magnus and the Beansteak*, a premonition of the imminent future of texturised vegetable protein with everything. Pyke's gambolling analysis caught the eye of producer Duncan Dallas, who hired him for the new popular science show he was putting together. Pyke joined lisping, booming, bearded botanist David Bellamy and personable pharmaceutical magnate Miriam Stoppard, both equally new to the cameras. 'We decided that authority and enthusiasm were more important than slick television technique,' explained Dallas.[238]

The chasm between the scientists and lay public was bridged by a down-to-earth interlocutor, initially actress Adrienne Posta, latterly future MP Austin Mitchell, *Play School*'s Derek Griffiths and ex-wrestler Brian Glover. With friendly in-the-round presentation, a firm focus on science's place in the everyday world, and a bevy of decorative young women in *Don't Ask Me* T-shirts, the show was unashamedly targeted at what Pyke called 'the great, multitudinous *Sun*-reading backbone of the nation'.[239]

Pyke stole the first show with a demonstration of the Coriolis effect: the old saw that bathwater drains in opposite directions on each side of the equator. To this end he pulled the plug from a bath in the studio, while acrobatically referring to a six-foot model globe and simultaneously holding long-distance telephone conversations with bath-watching scientists in New York and Sydney, as well as cueing in some film of a similar set up bang on the equator in Kenya. After a tenuous moment when it looked like the props department's little balsa wood raft would turn obstinately in the wrong direction, it miraculously corrected itself, and the yelp of joy emanating from Magnus's direction sealed his fate as the nation's favourite hysterical boffin. The fact that the Earth's rotation actually has little or no effect on bathwater direction was neither here nor there – a star was born.

Pyke's windmilling gestural ballet, swooping here, grasping there and ducking behind his own shoulders as if he was trying to capture the Higgs Boson with his bare hands, was eminently imitable. In a decade where impressionists sat at the peak of light entertainment, his rise to fame was almost instant. Dallas instructed his cameramen to always hold Pyke in a wide shot, lest he bound out of frame. With all this energy directed to the extremities, sometimes the words went awry: reference to rump steak came out as 'ox bum';

'My Uncle Harry,' he once found himself expounding, 'is older than I am, because he is dead – though that doesn't necessarily follow . . .'

Fame didn't lead Pyke to give up his day job as chairman of the British Association, so the inevitable flood of showbiz opportunities had to be managed with a discerning eye. Offers of Penguin biscuit ads and panto in Norwich were regretfully turned down, as was the suggestion made by the *Parkinson* chat show that he team up with Bellamy and the BBC's own crazed boffin Patrick Moore for a full drag rendition of 'Three Little Maids from School'. He did, however, join Moore in a full dance rendition of 'Tiptoe Through the Tulips' for *The Lennie and Jerry Show*, and accepted invitations from nightclubs to stand on a podium and answer the kids' hastily scribbled scientific posers between records. His attitude to all this was somewhere between modestly grateful and loftily ambivalent – he reflected that his turn on *Celebrity Squares* 'was, I suppose, of some sociological significance, if nothing else.'[240]

As *Don't Ask Me* continued, the stunts got bigger and bolder, and so did the cock-ups. In 1978, new recruit Rob Buckman presided over the firing of a nineteen-year-old woman from a circus cannon, to answer the vexed question of whether human cannonballs lose height during the flight. Sadly she fell short of the safety net and suffered injuries serious enough for that particular theory to remain untested.[241] The following year, with Pyke and Bellamy now familiar enough to television for the 'common man' presenter to be made redundant, it relaunched as the equally frenetic *Don't Just Sit There!* Subsequent science shows would clone the approachable question-and-answer formula, but none managed to dig up a host that could match Pyke in what he daintily identified as 'the element of unselfconscious loquacity in my make-up'.

SUPERSONIC (1975–7)
ITV (Thames)

The glitter-strewn apotheosis of pop TV.

Don't stare at the monitors and say, 'We're on now, Sylvia, ooh,'
that's a terrible drag. And do watch the cameras . . . they go
zooming around and if one hits you you'll know all about it.
Make some sort of motion to the record, don't stand gawping, or
chewing or nattering. If I catch anyone hanging round the side
there'll be a quick one up the backside.
Assistant producer to audience, *Top of the Pops* recording,
Lime Grove studios, 27 October 1966

THE STORY OF *Top of the Pops* is long, well-rehearsed and in
places deeply disturbing. Though it had longevity and star power
on its side, as television it was tame. In the mid 1970s its production values were still making Jack Good seem radical. '*TOTP*
mummifies rock in a middle-aged, pop casket,' wrote Bart Mills.
"'All right, kiddies," says the BBC, holding its nose. "Unfortunately,
you exist, and I'm told there are millions of you. We must give
you something. Here, take this. I think I'm going to be sick."'[242]
The pop audience was getting younger every year. *TOTP*'s core
constituency became pre-teen, though it still provided thrills for
older kids when the right acts were on, but usually in spite of the
surrounding show.

There was a more dynamic pop TV producer at large. Mike
Mansfield was an ambitious, technically adept gallery controller

who cut a distinctive figure in Southern Television's Southampton studios in the late 1960s with his coiffured hair, Aztec-patterned knitwear and huge 'M'-shaped medallion. His early works included *As You Like It*, a lavish pop request show in which Adam Faith solicited viewers' requests from a different novelty location each week, and *Time For Blackburn*, a spoiler scheduled against the BBC's *All Systems Freeman*. Tony Blackburn was an affable host, but the real star was up in the gallery.

Denied Fluff's lavish gimmickry, Mansfield got creative in the control room, getting the most out of the studio basics – three cameras and a vision mixer. When The Who turned up to perform a tumultuous version of 'Magic Bus', Mansfield instructed his mixer to switch cameras with psychedelic abandon, practically on every beat, resulting in a blizzard of images of Daltrey and Moon flashing before the unwary audience as they had their Saturday tea, and doubtless playing hell with a few poorly-adjusted vertical holds. Southern's viewers blinked, and so did the Beeb. *All Systems Freeman* was off the air within two months.

Mansfield moved to London Weekend Television, and seizing two exciting new developments – colour and glam rock – instigated *Supersonic*, his own musical attempt 'to beat the Depression'. Gurning presenters were out; silver-maned producers were in. From the gallery, Mansfield himself linked acts with manic techno-chat. 'Lights, standby studio, going to you, three . . . and cue Gilbert O'Sullivan!' The studio proper was worlds away from *Top of the Pops*. The audience, though seated, was visibly enthusiastic. Cameras glided shamelessly into shot, often with flashing police lights on top. The glam rock acts of the day performed on an appropriately glittering set – a multi-level glass and steel construction which seemed only just capable of supporting the full weight of the Rubettes. Mansfield deployed a battery of technology: fish-eye lenses, mole cranes ploughing into swarms of descending balloons and drum kits going up and down on the pallet of a fork lift truck.

'I was sick of seeing groups who seemed rooted in concrete,'

Mansfield explained. 'Any director can shoot that standing on his eyelashes. I wanted to contribute something visually . . . People love our machinery and our ironmongery. The success of the show is that it proves pop is fun.'[243] Such was *Supersonic*'s level of innovation that even the *Listener* grudgingly approved. '*Supersonic* does, at least, present its rubbish with panache,' it mused. 'The cameras swoop and soar. The props glitter and flicker. The audience seems wakeful. There is no Jimmy Savile. At one point, I thought Mike Mansfield was going to direct one of his cameras into a fifty-foot dive through a hoop of fire. Maybe, next week, this bricks-without-straw craftsman will find a way to do that.'[244]

Mansfield didn't have independent pop TV to himself. Muriel Young shared the channel with him, offering her more conventional takes on underage rock, *Lift Off with Ayshea* and *45*, the latter hosted by ex-Radio Luxembourg DJ David 'Kid' Jensen from the Hardrock Disco, Manchester. Young's attitude to pop was perhaps less wholehearted than Mansfield's. 'My work fills a gap between baby and adult music,' she said, adding hopefully, 'pop music brings them to progressive jazz.' Visually, she had predictably firm views. Mentioning no names, she railed against the 'mind-battering camera antics and lightning changes of shot' of other producers. 'It's not fair to the artists and children don't specially like it.' Smoke machines were also out: 'it makes the singers cough.' Instead, she favoured 'lighting effects and abstract graphics' which 'take a week to do and last eight seconds on the screen.' Both Mansfield's and Young's gimmicks were quietly co-opted by *Top of the Pops* over the years.

The unsettling phenomenon of the Bay City Rollers proved a strong enough force to unite Young and Mansfield for scarf-waving scream-in *Shang-A-Lang*, with Young producing and Mansfield calling the shots. Though the show came from a tiny studio, it generated mass hysteria. Fans hid in bins and smashed windows in attempts to broach Granada's hastily erected ring of steel and touch the hems of the Rollers' sainted tartan 'trews'. Inside, the mania was beyond even Auntie Mu's control. 'I once screamed

"Shut up or I'll kill you all!" at them,' she admitted. 'I think they were quiet for about six seconds that time.'[245]

The Rollers were big time, but *Shang-A-Lang*'s budget was small beans. This frustrated Mansfield, who soon left the programme. 'There's a prejudice against pop,' he complained. 'Whenever they put pop on TV they do it on a shoestring.' Young was more sanguine. 'I work on minimums and imagination . . . I think I'd be embarrassed if someone gave me an enormous budget. I wouldn't know how to behave.'[246] *Supersonic* came to an end in 1977, and after an abortive attempt at a more 'adult' sequel, *Blast Off!*, presented by Michael Aspel, Mansfield moved into pop promos.

In 1983, he made a return to broadcast television with a *Supersonic* special for Channel Four, keeping the original format, with some new-fangled Quantel visual effects on top. His other work for the channel was more controversial. In the summer of 1982, nationwide auditions were held at theatres, schools and youth clubs for a pre-teen musical talent show. As the tots gamely trilled to an accompanying pianist, all seemed innocuous enough. The programme was the creation of Martin Wyatt, who'd had a success with an LP of kids performing popular songs in a winsome manner. 'Don't forget,' he reassured the *Mirror*, 'they're all twelve and under. When they get older than that I have to say, that's it.'[247]

When the *Minipops* arrived on screen, togged up in appropriate (or perhaps inappropriate) costumes, given the full-on glamour treatment by Mansfield and mouthing lyrics with, albeit fairly mild, sexual content, the press grabbed at the stick Channel Four had lovingly crafted to beat them with. The confusion and unease this 'shop window of junior jailbait' engendered was best summarised by Julian Barnes. 'Is it merely priggish to feel queasy at the sight of primary school minxes with rouged cheeks?' he pondered. 'Does the show thrust premature sexual awareness onto its wide-eyed performers? I don't know.'[248] To which a waggish reader responded, 'Since paedophiles are a minority in this country, it's only right they should get their own show on Channel Four.'[249] Rock 'n' roll's wilful blurring of the age of consent had by now become an established tradition, but misgivings were starting to be voiced – albeit mainly directed at the less coolly aloof, old-school showbiz end of operations. It would take another few decades for the activities of certain *Top of the Pops* presenters to really get out. Which is, unfortunately, where we came in.

THE THRILLA IN MANILA (1974)

HBO (United Artists-Columbia)

The dawn of pay-per-view sport.

TELEVISION WAS MADE FOR boxing. In the years after the war, the USA's fledgling networks would fill whole evenings with an extended programme of prizefighting live from New York's Madison Square Garden or Jamaica Arena. Viewers gathered round sets in bars, just as they did for the big variety specials, and created their own crowds in miniature. Through the '50s and '60s however, boxing's network popularity dwindled. An over-reliance on the sport and increasingly blatant match fixing played their part, but the writing was on the wall after the 1962 bout in which Emile Griffith pounded Benny 'The Kid' Paret into a coma from which he would die ten days later. ABC carried the scenes live to the nation's living rooms. This was not the kind of event television they wanted on their books.

Fights became increasingly scarce on the networks after that, but a different way of viewing was on the rise: the closed circuit show. Theatres, sports halls, and even real boxing venues like Madison Square Garden were fitted out with a huge projection screen and had distant fights cabled in to hundreds, maybe thousands of paying punters. The coverage was a fraction of what the network would bring, but with customers willing to pay as much as five dollars per fight, business boomed once more. But there was a third television technology, then still in its early days, that would slowly gain momentum over the next couple of decades to become the default televising method for big name prizefights. It was pay-per-view cable, and it appeared on the scene during one of the most famous and mythologised boxing matches of all time.

No single sportsman has ever revitalised the fortunes of his game as much as Muhammad Ali. In the 1960s as Cassius Clay, he had perfected something rare in the sports world, a magnetic personality, by turns witty and pugnacious, charismatic and belligerent. His garrulous confidence took some getting used to on the part of his interviewers – he walked out on a live edition of the BBC's *Sportsview* after David Coleman complained that he 'talked too much'[250] – but they quickly realised that an articulate, funny champion was the best asset a sport could possess, and played along. His name-changing affiliation with the Nation of Islam made things difficult all over again, especially when he came out against American involvement in Vietnam. His refusal to fight the Viet Cong earned him, with no small irony, a three-year suspension from fighting in the ring.

Ali's eventual return marked the beginning of a new phase of both his career and the sport in general. While Ali was kicking his heels, Smokin' Joe Frazier had risen to prominence. With Ali back in action, their first bout in 1971, nicknamed 'The Fight of the Century', ended in a win on points for Frazier and a ratings triumph for ABC. A disappointing rematch followed in 1974 which Ali won, but the most memorable punches were thrown outside the ring, when the pair, invited to talk over the fight on ABC's *Wide World of Sports*, came to blows in the studio after Ali taunted Frazier for being 'ignorant'. As the two suited heavyweights sprawled on the floor surrounded by their respective entourages, the familiar nasal tones of presenter Howard Cosell chimed in. 'Well, we're having a scene, as you can see,' he observed. 'It's hard to tell whether it's clowning or for real.' At that moment Frazier really let fly, and Cosell changed tack. 'It's a bad and an ugly scene, and it's unfortunate I think that it's happened.' It also happened to set the stage beautifully for a third fight.

The next development was the arrival of promoter Don King. Relatively new to high-end boxing but with a canny eye for the main chance, King raised a $5 million prize purse for a fight between Ali and undefeated champion George Foreman by staging it in Kinshasa, capital city of the then African dictatorship of Zaire (now the Democratic Republic of the Congo). The bombastically titled 'Rumble in the Jungle' of 1974 set new standards for big name fight promotion. The controversial 'rope-a-dope' methods Ali employed to seal his victory were of a piece with the intensely theatrical nature of the bout and its build-up. King immediately set about planning a similarly grandiose match between Ali and Frazier. For this he picked another third world country keen for good publicity – this time Ferdinand Marcos's Philippines, then under martial law – and ran up another memorable rhyming title: 'The Thrilla in Manila'.

The fight was scheduled for 10 a.m. local time to maximise American ratings, but unlike previous fights, it was not to be networked. Many viewers watched it in the old closed circuit style, in 276 locations across the USA.[251] Some viewers had another option, courtesy of the struggling early cable provider Home Box Office. One of the cable pioneers, HBO had been around since the mid-1950s when, as Box Office Television, it organised closed circuit broadcasts of sport and Broadway plays, with financial backing from comedian Sid Caesar, among others. Two decades on, cable was steadfastly refusing to take off, but it retained a foothold in rural parts where conventional TV signals were weak. Vice president Bob Rosencrans took the plunge and bought the rights to transmit the fight on a pay-per-view basis.

The gamble paid off. The satellite broadcast, even after a transfer from ground station to cable, was crisp and clear. 'When you looked at the close-ups,' claimed Rosencrans, 'the fighters looked like they were in the next room, the picture quality was that extraordinary.'[252] The threats of closure HBO had been facing receded, and the painfully slow progress of cable television in the USA turned into a gold rush, propelled mainly by big sporting events. A fully-fledged cable service delivering satellite-transmitted events from around the world, the Madison Square Garden-affiliated MSG Sports Network, launched in 1977; many more would follow. The decisive step from television being a mass, communally viewed medium to a fragmented cornucopia of enter-tainment options had been taken. Oh, and Ali won, of course.

THE NORMAN GUNSTON SHOW (1975–9)

ABC/ Seven/ BBC Two

The spoof interviewer arrives in the form of a little Aussie bleeder.

'Let's get on with the in depth questions and get out of here real quick.'

Norman Gunston interviews Sally Struthers, 1975

ONE OF THE DEFINING moments in Australian culture was Gough Whitlam's brief but busy reign as Labour prime minister in the early 1970s. Before then, national culture was safeguarded by men like Adelaide's Detective Inspector Vogelsang, who impounded poetry books for containing the word 'incestuous' while freely admitting he didn't know what it meant.[253] Once the cultural shackles were loosened, there was a lot of ground to make up.

Those impounded poems turned out to be spoofs, and parody thrived in the newly permissive environment. Barry Humphries was the foremost exponent, already long adept at skewering Melbourne's suburbanites through characters like time-stopping convalescent Sandy Stone and as-yet-untitled denizen of Moonee Ponds, Edna Everage. Edna's nephew Barry MacKenzie epitomised a whole sub-genre of Akubra hat-sporting, Fosters-chugging,

Technicolor yawning 'ocker' humour, which was founded back under the old regime on *TW3* clone *The Mavis Bramston Show*, and moulded into a global industry by Paul Hogan. Elsewhere there was untrammelled sauce, in the form of Graham Blundell's *Alvin Purple*, close relative of the *Confessions* films' Timothy Lea who brought full frontal nudity to network television screens. 'Making *Alvin Purple* without frontal nudity,' claimed ABC's Head of Light Entertainment, Maurice Murphy, 'is as ludicrous as it would have been to ask Edward G. Robinson to play Shirley Temple.'[254]

Another of Murphy's commissions was *The Aunty Jack Show*, a knockabout pantomime with overtones of *The Goodies* that racked up a healthy tally of complaints for swearing and violence. One of the *Aunty Jack* troupe, Garry McDonald, featured in a recurring sketch called 'What's on Wollongong'. In the guise of anaemic reporter Norman Gunston, he covered local events from a grotty bedsit in the eponymous Sydney suburb, or promoted sophisticated new perfume 'Après-Midi in Port Kembla'.

The hopeless but keen would-be star had been a comedy staple since Horace Kenney toured British music halls in the 1930s as a whey-faced weakling, nervously dragging himself through a singing fireman act by the power of totally misplaced self-belief.[255] McDonald, who shared Kenney's sickly appearance, shaped Gunston into a similarly overconfident 'feeb': nervous and mal-adroit, but with a mile wide narcissistic streak, convinced of his destiny as a star of titanic renown.

Gunston's showbiz origins lay in the interminable evening chat shows Australian TV would put on in the late 1960s to fill space on the cheap, and have McDonald and his mates 'falling about laughing at them'. Their deadly combination of tenacity and inepti-tude was poured into Gunston, who was recast as a walking cultural cringe, forcing his crass ignorance on assorted visiting stars, begin-ning with Joe Frazier, preparing for the Thrilla in Manila and snared by Gunston for ABC's *Sports Scene*. Gunston's intrusion into the 'real' world brought him alive. Mock interviews were nothing new – San Franciscan duo Coyle and Sharpe were bamboozling the man in the street with questions about hockey puck shortages in the early 1960s – but here they were part of a frontal assault on the showbiz system itself.

With a gigantic 'Press' badge on the lapel of his shop-worn jacket, thinning strands of hair slicked over his shiny pate, chin festooned with shaving wounds and clutching a Qantas holdall for dear life, Gunston crouched at the feet of the showbiz elite, showering them with backhanded compliments and befuddled platitudes. Crashing press conferences guerilla-style, he left touring stars including Burt Reynolds ('How's your mum, Debbie?'), Warren Beatty ('Did Carly Simon write that song about you, "The Impossible Dream?"') and Kiss ('Which one of you is the construction worker?') bewildered. Tame stuff by modern standards perhaps, but the po-faced ceremony of the showbiz press conference had never before been subjected to such mongrel disrespect.

Through two series for ABC, Gunston, guided by the show's chief writer Bill Harding, developed from basket case to perversely dominant personality, fronting 'half an hour of packed entertainment with the slow learner in mind'.[256] His technique even filtered into the legitimate chat circuit, as hosts like Paul Makin began playing the innocent to spice up otherwise deadly dull interviews with low wattage celebs like Leif Garrett. In retaliation, Gunston took to introducing himself as 'the thinking man's Paul Makin'. The second series took him to the UK, where he requested the pleasure of an interview with the Queen, Edward Heath and Harold Wilson, though after their respective offices found out the nature of the man from Australia House, they wisely backed out.

After years of pining for a Gold Logie – the greatest prize in Australian television – Gunston was finally awarded one, and accepted in character. 'When you do an excellent programme like mine, it's not just you up there on the screen – there are many other people behind the scenes that you have to carry as well.' Flipping between parochial naivety and grandiose gracelessness in a second, Gunston laid out the form for every fake interlocutor thereafter.

In November 1975, Gough Whitlam was controversially dismissed from office by the Governor-General. Appropriately enough, Gunston was in Canberra, soliciting views, congratulating incoming PM Malcolm Fraser on being nominated 'Father of the Year', and all but upstaging Whitlam himself as he addressed the crowds outside parliament, many cheering 'Gunston for Governor-General!' One bystander added, 'Norman, you're the only true Australian!' A sobering thought.

PLAY FOR TODAY: DOUBLE DARE (1976)

BBC One

Dennis Potter writes himself into a corner.

By 1976, DENNIS POTTER was ready to quit television. In just over a decade, he'd graduated from co-writing quick squibs for *TW3* to being television's most prominent, and certainly most identifiable, playwright. But censorship, executive timidity and the sheer frustration of pushing ideas through the production mill became wearying. 'I think the days of the television play are numbered,' he told the nation in the publicity for his valedictory work, 'but before it ends I want to make a few defiant noises.'[257]

Before his dramatic career, Potter spent the early sixties as chief TV critic at the *Daily Herald,* cataloguing his television likes and dislikes. Into the 'hate' pile went ecclesiastical sitcoms ('as predictable as the epilogue, but considerably less amusing'[258]) and humorous panel games ('this rather coy, ponderous, often excruciatingly twee sort of comedy is as depressingly English as fried eggs and thumb-thick chips'[259]). Conversely, he was a champion of 'the rather shrill, often overblown journalism of *World in Action*,'[260] shed a nostalgic tear for *Children's Hour* ('the thing [the BBC] has slaughtered so wantonly'[261]), and declared a fondness for the weird, semi-abstract animation then colonising British TV from Canada and Eastern Europe, with its 'tipsy triangles and pompous oblongs, depressed squares and bad-tempered rectangles . . . an exuberant delight.'[262]

On the one hand, he wanted sexual frankness on the box: 'A lot of prigs seem to get very hot under the collar when contemplating something as harmless and pleasant as an unclad breast.'[263] On the other, his squeamish inner censor occasionally showed its head, most often when confronted with bloody operation footage on programmes like *Your Life in Their Hands*. 'I was left wondering whether the BBC . . . had gone too far in permitting pictures of the kind we saw.'[264]

His opinions on drama were naturally forthright. He had a sharp eye, spotting even in 1964 a fall-off in the quality of revolutionary police serial *Z-Cars*. ('The mannerisms of the actors have replaced characterisation. The tiny bursts of automatic dialogue squirt onto the screen without producing truth.'[265]) While not a massive fan of American crowd-pleasers like *Dr Kildare* and *77 Sunset Strip*, he admired their energy, lamenting 'I've always wished this compelling know-how could be transferred to our so-called "serious" TV.'[266] It was 'serious' drama he craved the most, the sort of stuff that exposed 'something rotting and horrible beneath even the most placid surface,'[267] and got under its characters' skin. ('Plays that prowl around inside the head can be even more exciting than those which deal only with external actions.'[268]) After he left the *Herald* in 1964, he put this manifesto into action.

Some plays betrayed his critical origins. *Paper Roses*, set in a flea-bitten Fleet Street tabloid office, was periodically interrupted by a cantankerous TV critic moaning to himself about the play's shortcomings – an arch, self-exonerating gag. *Follow the Yellow Brick Road* gave Denholm Elliott's cuckolded misogynist actor a paranoid suspicion that his whole life was a television play – a cheap, badly-scripted one, at that. *Double Dare* was a further inversion: creatively exhausted playwright Martin Ellis (Alan Dobie) organises a 'date' with an actress (Kika Markham) in a London hotel to kick-start inspiration for what, he says, will be his last ever television play. Nearby, a seedy businessman has a baleful meeting with a hooker (Markham again) which eerily starts to resemble Ellis's work in progress. Either his characters are becoming real people, or he is turning into a fiction himself. The writer's conflicting senses of power and helplessness, stirred up by his fear and mistrust of women, intensify as the evening progresses, and it's clear the actress – both of her – will be the victim.

Often the phrase 'fiction becomes fact' is a warning sign of writerly indulgence ahead, a respectable version of the lazy child's 'it was all a dream' essay, but *Double Dare* is no soft play fantasy. Potter prepared for the play by . . . meeting Kika Markham at a hotel. Markham has claimed whole chunks of the conversation they had there are quoted, almost verbatim, in the finished work. Discussing acting and writing, the actress muses 'we both fall headlong into other people's dreams,' a sentence Ellis had written on the back of an envelope that morning. Unsure if he's psychic or delusional, Ellis is gripped by a morbid apprehension: 'Someone's going to get hurt.'

Ellis is bitterly misogynist, but his attempts at verbal connection with Markham's character are painfully universal examples of male hopelessness: awkward and aggressive, nervously choking back sentences for fear of offence, then ploughing ahead in another, equally obnoxious, direction. Likewise, Markham's actress has increasing trouble keeping up the headstrong assurance she feels obliged to project to stay one step ahead of her 'puppet-master', and bristles when her work on a blatantly pornographic ad for 'Fraggie' chocolate bars is brought up. Potter denies the viewer any moral high ground, even when events turn monstrous. The vile businessman and the cheap whore are caricatured Aunt Sallys to help excuse our own flaws. *Double Dare* shows the dangers of this sort of detachment.

The middle-market hotel, fully recreated on an Ealing sound stage, is a sumptuously artificial, Muzak-backed and air-conditioned pocket of potted palm unreality – just the place for fact and fiction to lose their distinction. The world claustrophobically closes in on Ellis as Klaus Wunderlich performs a jaunty rendition of 'Magic Moments' on the Hammond organ. John Mackenzie directs the ensuing collapse with an adept deployment of uncomfortable close-ups and vignettes of tacky detail. It's the visual equivalent of a clammy handshake that won't let go.

Predictably, breast-fearing prigs got hot under the collar. 'Some authors,' wrote Mrs Joan M. Cutts admonishingly to the *Radio Times*, 'seem to have as little sense of responsibility as the peculiar, unreal people they write about,' suggesting some elements of the play had completely escaped her.[269] Professional critics also felt stung. Richard North thought Potter's plays were 'a propaganda exercise in a private crusade . . . that I wish was either more out in the open, or which he would grow beyond. I'm beginning to feel got at.'[270] This was Potter's main distinction from other writers – he was so overwhelmingly present in his work, in many ways, that the viewer felt they weren't so much being entertained, or even lectured, as entering a personal confrontation. Critics were always calling for greater intimacy in TV drama, but Potter got too close for comfort.

PAULINE'S QUIRKES (1976)
ITV (Thames)

The foul-mouthed teatime scandal that pre-dated the Sex Pistols.

I'm sorry if I offended anyone. I believe I did say 'get 'em off'
several times.

Pauline Quirke, 1 December 1976

CHILDREN'S COMEDY WAS, FOR much of television's early life, one long pantomime. Variety stars delivered knowingly corny gags and well-aimed custard pies with a mannered 'kindly leave the stage' flourish as an audience of cub scouts groaned theatrically. When pop was allowed to intrude on this hermetic world, it didn't quite fit. The prime example was *Crackerjack*, which featured a long, rambling sketch performed by the show's regulars, ending in a maladroit segue into a rendition of a hit parade tune. As the programme got further from its 1950s roots, the discrepancy between the songs and the ability of ageing entertainers Peter Glaze and Don McLean to get a handle on them increased to absurd proportions. The comedy/rock generation gap was perfectly illustrated.

Enter Roger Price, a children's producer at Thames Television who, in 1973, had been the driving force behind *The Tomorrow People*, a science fiction serial that melded the tribulations of adolescence with the Nietzschean concept – brought into pop culture by David Bowie – of the *homo superior*. Price treated the kids and their concerns in an honest, unpatronising way which sealed the programme's popularity. Two years later he turned his attention to comedy, assembling a group of child actors, including brassy London teenage chums Pauline Quirke and Linda Robson, for *You Must Be Joking!*, a raucous sketch show featuring material sourced partly from the juvenile cast. Unsurprisingly, the results were rather less innocent than the adult-administered groaners of *Crackerjack*. As the theme tune put it: 'Even Mary Whitehouse can't touch you for it!'

The following year, Price gave Quirke the starring role in an even more outlandish comedy. *Pauline's Quirkes* cast the seventeen-year-old as bolshie mistress of ceremonies, obsessed with Flintlock, the house band featuring Mike Holloway, who also starred in *The Tomorrow People*. Modelled on the Bay City Rollers, Flintlock inspired similar levels of randy delirium in young girls, as the *TV Times* discovered when their reporter trailed a gang of stalkers camping outside their houses. ('I think I can safely say that is Mike Holloway's underwear hanging on the clothes line.') Price, amused and concerned by the slavish adoration such ordinary lads could command, mined the fandom for subversive giggles.

Sketches included Quirke and Robson buying and selling Flintlock members as slaves, complete with chains and leather accessories ('I'll 'ave 'im!'), and an odd gender reversal number wherein the girls tried to look up the skirt of a cross-dressing Flintlocker climbing a ladder in a library. Then there was Quirke's continuing quest to get hold of a rumoured nude poster of the boys, whipping the under-sixteen female studio audience into a lustful frenzy with the rallying cry 'Get 'em off!' Eventually, Flintlock appeared nude – albeit with their groins rendered completely transparent by Chroma keyed swimming trunks, leaving Quirke crestfallen that they literally had 'nothing down there'.

The kids might have gotten away with it, if it hadn't been for Alan Coren. The normally unflappable humorist, then TV critic of *The Times*, happened to see the second edition, and felt duty bound to inform his readers of the filth their children were imbibing while they were hard at work. It was 'the endorsement of ignorance, the celebration of vulgarity, the apotheosis of trash,' he fumed. 'I really do not know which I most hate: the ruining of the language, the pandering to the lowest levels of intelligence . . . or the smut. All I know is, I hate.'[271] The tabloids picked up the story, eliciting a sheepish apology from Quirke at her Stoke Newington home, while mum looked disapprovingly on. Anglia became the first ITV region to drop the show, replacing it with the more wholesome *Spiderman*.

Two days later, the Sex Pistols were invited to fill up the very tail end of Thames TV's teatime magazine *Today*, as an 'if wet' replacement for Queen, and promptly outed host Bill Grundy as a 'rotter'. Only Londoners who'd knocked off work early actually saw the offending item compared to Pauline's national audience, but a slew of press coverage followed, some stories linking Johnny Rotten and Pauline Quirke as twin figureheads of feral youth.

Price defended the programme's satirical content. 'The programme was made exclusively for partially-literate teenage girls, the sort you see hanging around pop groups, prostrating themselves in blind worship,' he explained. 'We want to show them that they don't need to behave in that sort of way.' He also impishly suggested that Coren 'was giving vent to suppressed male chauvinism.'[272] These remarks cut little ice with the offended, who took exception more than anything else to the autonomous nature of the unchaperoned revels, with Quirke as *de facto* Lady, in all senses, of the Flies. It's precisely this quality that seems winning today. In a world where teenagers are given ludicrously airbrushed sexual ideals to live up to, these sketches have an authentic ring of panicky teenage curiosity about the opposite gender, with awkward eye contact and sarcastic jibes deployed to deflate the sexual tension. The show had one adult champion in the *Guardian*'s Nancy Banks-Smith, who judged it a 'cheap, cheerful pop show,' lavishing special praise on Quirke as 'a Janet Street-Porter whose line-hold has gone.'[273]

Pauline's Quirkes continued, in most regions, to the end of the year, introducing Pauline's all-girl rival group, The Flintarts, throwing themselves at then Radio 210 DJs Mike Read and Steve Wright, and forewarning viewers with mischievous 'clarifications' in the *TV Times*. ('All the times Derek wears dresses or cuddles up to Bill in a sketch, they're not doing it because they're kinky, but because it's in the script. Who is the kinky scriptwriter?') Dodgy moments aside, *Pauline's Quirkes* still comes across as a genuine, if often slightly corny, attempt to get modern adolescence onto the small screen, with a minimum of adult prudery. Even Coren's heart would have melted in the final edition, as Flintlock presented Pauline with end-of-series gifts, prompting a bit of *X Factor*-style emotional journeying: 'I expect now I'll be able to move me, me mum and me little brother Shaun into a flat with a bathroom!'

I, CLAUDIUS (1976)
BBC Two (BBC/London Films)

The imperial phase of period drama.

FOR ALL SOCIETY HAS progressed in the past couple of millennia, superstition seems as rife as ever. People still fall for a good curse. In 1937 cinematic potentate Alexander Korda began film production at his brand new Denham studio complex. *I, Claudius* was adapted from Robert Graves's two bestselling volumes of mock autobiography detailing the accidental rise and largely benevolent rule of the third emperor of ancient Rome. The books had everything: epic sweep, carnality, and the fairy-tale transformation of a lame stammerer into – however briefly – a deity on Earth.

Korda's *Claudius,* directed by Josef von Sternberg in riding breeches and Javanese turban, was colossal, and modishly with-it; the *Daily Mirror* discovered the makers had 'psycho-analysed the character of Messalina to find out why she was such a lurid lass'.[274] The actress in that role, Merle Oberon, was put out of action in a serious car accident. With no replacement found, the £100,000 picture was abandoned. The curse had descended.

Nearly four decades later, the BBC had a go. A painful rights deal was extracted from Korda's London Films and the budget was set at £750,000 – a big investment for such a 'cursed' project, but comparisons with Korda were briskly warded off. 'Allowing for inflation, it won't cost anywhere near as much,' said producer Martin Lisemore, 'but we do intend to finish it.'[275] Jack Pulman, capable adaptor of Dickens, Tolstoy and Henry James, prepared the screenplay for Herbert Wise, a director with twenty years' experience in the studio.

In front of the cameras, Derek Jacobi's Claudius avoided speech-impaired sentimentality with a performance of confusion, slyness and desperation. Brian Blessed's Augustan thunder was succeeded by John Hurt's pathologically twee, demented Caligula; while Livia, wife of the former and great-grandmother to the latter, was given conniving life by Siân Phillips. There was more group sex, murder, incest and infanticide per square inch than anything previously screened. In one irate viewer's opinion, it was 'far more damaging' to potential teenage viewers than even the dreaded *Pauline's Quirkes*.[276]

The casting of Graves's multitudes summoned actors from the four corners of *Spotlight*. Patrick Stewart commanded the Praetorian Guard. Bernard Hill identified Jacobi as the new emperor. Ian Ogilvy fell off his horse. Peter Bowles was an unusual choice for an ancient British chieftain; Christopher Biggins – soon to appear as Mother Goose at Darlington's Civic Theatre – a surprisingly appropriate Nero. There was even a mini *Z-Cars* reunion as Inspector Barlow (Stratford Johns, aka Gnaeus Calpurnius Piso) was put on trial for treason against the stepson of PC Fancy Smith (Brian Blessed, the Emperor Augustus). Quentin Crisp was assassinated by George and Mildred's uppity next-door neighbour, who in turn was grandson of the Emperor Inspector Wexford. Television's version of the MGM 'cast of thousands' helped audiences follow the story's labyrinthine, genealogical body swerves.

It wasn't an instant hit. In fact, early critical impressions were poor. The chief stumbling block was creating a believable yet intelligible antiquity. Modern parallels helped the makers get a handle on the distant times: Pulman visualised the Empire as a branch of the Mafia; Siân Phillips played scenes as Jewish family comedy.[277] Graves' books described great and lurid events in the flatly chatty, rambling style of the often boring Claudius, but some critics had trouble with Pulman's version of this ironic effect: modern phrases delivered in togas. The *Guardian* complained that 'a Roman lady turning to her threatened husband in the moment of crisis and crying "They're bluffing!" evokes not so much the shades of Plancina, wife of Piso, as of Olivia de Havilland, wife of Stewart Granger.'[278] The reviewer also thought Wise had dished up 'the worst lighting and camera angles since 1925.' (In fact Wise and cameraman Jim Atkinson achieved wonders with intricately choreographed cameras and little more than a dozen extras.)

This initial dismissal was understandable given the Roman pageant's reputation for cinematic lavishness. The Hollywood epics scored zero for historical accuracy, but the sheer bombast of the production values and costumes, combined with the distancing sheen of film, made television's harsh lighting and self-assembly villas look cheap and very recent indeed. Unfair perhaps, but it would soon lead to the abandonment of videotape for period drama, then gradually all drama outside of soap opera. When Simon Langton was preparing to direct Andrew Davies's 1990s version of *Pride and Prejudice* – the one which would finally demolish television's historical inferiority complex – he watched a copy of the BBC's previous version from 1981. As the videotape unspooled, 'my partner's daughter, who was about thirteen or fourteen at the time, just sort of walked through the room and glanced at it and just went, "Ugh!" and I said, "Well, why did you go like that?" and she said, "It's all artificial" – and that's all I got. Then she went out.'[279] Sporting lush 35mm from head to toe, *Pride and Prejudice* would re-conquer the world in the name of British drama.

For those who could look past the lack of sumptuous super-ficialities *I, Claudius* brimmed with restive psychodrama and sharp observation. Clive James noted that, contrary to the videotape gripers, 'the differentness and long-ago-ness were maintained throughout the series, less by trying to prove that the ancient Romans were unlike us than by assuming they were just like us but living under different laws.'[280] That perfectly summed up Pulman's masterstroke, although, James noted, some of the old period vices remained. 'There were numberless Flanagan and Allen routines where pairs of subsidiary characters in tightly gripped togas met behind a convenient column to tell each other what they already knew and so update us on the plot.'[281]

Critical misgivings had little effect on the saga's popularity. *I, Claudius* came to a triumphant end in December after twelve episodes. Like its protagonist, it had proved all those who grossly underestimated its worth hopelessly wrong, although within months of transmission, Lisemore and Pulman both died far too soon, and the press had its 'curse' restored. In 1977, it was show-cased in the USA on Brit-heritage strand *Masterpiece Theatre*, with each episode introduced by Alistair Cooke surrounded by grapes, scrolls and statuary. The critical drubbing started all over again: the *New York Post* called it a 'masterpiece of a bore'[282] and the *Christian Science Monitor* alluded to a '*Monty Python* Royal Academy of Overacting'.[283] Once again, opinions had to be reversed as ratings took hold. *I, Claudius* made popular, quality drama from one of history's most alien, barbaric periods. For boldness and grandiosity, nothing before or since in the pantheon of TV drama can touch it.

THE FALL AND RISE OF REGINALD PERRIN (1976–9)

BBC One

The sitcom's nervous breakdown.

THERE'S SOMETHING ABOUT THE transparent etymology of the word 'sitcom' that encourages waggish critics to pick it apart as they take down one of its less triumphant examples: 'LWT's latest Saturday night offering was all sit and very little com', and so forth. Something about the word suggests a crude sketch of life, with gags bolted on willy-nilly. Only the poorest sitcoms are actually like this, but the inglorious label is hard to shift. One sitcom asked the opposite – what if life was a crass imitation of a sitcom?

The Fall and Rise of Reginald Perrin only became a sitcom by degrees. It began as a contribution David Nobbs made to BBC Pebble Mill's *Second City Firsts* strand of half-hour plays, which would give early breaks to artists as diverse as Mike Leigh and Toyah Willcox. Nobbs had graduated from *TW3* to various sketch shows and sitcoms with writing partner Peter Vincent, including one set in the ultimate minimalist sitcom location, a lighthouse. He gave Pebble Mill the tale of a businessman sent mad by the frantic emptiness of the commercial world. Their curt rejection was, he claimed, the best news he ever received.[284]

Nobbs radically reworked the half-hour play into a comic novel that did pretty well. Ronnie Barker enthused about it on book programmes and it started doing very well. Granada wanted to turn it into a two-part prestige drama with Barker in the title role, but the Beeb weighed in with an offer of a seven-part sitcom starring Leonard Rossiter. Sitcoms and novels were still regarded as mutually incompatible arts. Nobbs's friend Peter Tinniswood was just starting to break the mould with *I Didn't Know You Cared*, based on his mordant Yorkshire family saga *A Touch of Daniel*, but many still nursed memories of the BBC's ill-starred attempt to adapt Evelyn Waugh's *Scoop!* into a vehicle for Harry Worth. Despite the weight of history, Rossiter it was.

Perrin was born from banal fragments: a colour supplement feature on jam marketing, fatuously cosy building society ads, all the asinine trappings of modern life which nobody ever asked for, but were presented as indispensable. The more examples Nobbs amassed of this emetic hokum, the more he wondered who could stand to live and work amongst it. The vision came of a hapless middle-aged dessert pedlar, bored with his job, failing to have a torrid affair with his secretary, suddenly realising he's been sleep-walking his life away, busting out of his confined little world and faking his own suicide on a beach at night. (Soon after Nobbs completed the novel, MP John Stonehouse was coincidentally arrested for turning the same trick.)

In later and more affected times, this plot would be called 'dark'. But *Perrin* was quite the opposite – it was sitcom with the brightness and contrast turned right up. The umbrella-swinging, whisky-swilling, British-Railing repetition of middle class middle age became a gaudy diagram via high-key performances, a litany of catchphrases and Ronnie Hazlehurst's chirpily melancholic incidental music. Elizabeth the patient wife, CJ the pompous boss, the saucy secretary, the drop-out son, the woolly liberal and the pseudo-American go-getter lined up like a demographic identity parade. Boring dinner party followed soul-sapping meeting followed nightmarish in-law visitation with exhausting relentlessness. It was a close thing as to whose nerves would snap first – the viewer's or Reggie's. As only a few dramatists like David Mercer understood, comedy proves a sharper tool than straight drama for conveying the depths of a crack-up.

Creating a sitcom that pulled the clichés of the genre apart as it piled them up was not, of course, Nobbs's intention – he was too smart for all that. When a close reader over-interpreted Sunshine Desserts' corporate tyrant CJ's initials (CJ – JC – Jesus in reverse – the Messiah of Mammon, etc.) Nobbs politely acknowledged the coincidence, but said that if he'd consciously come up with something like that, he'd have nixed it immediately.[285]

He did have serious intentions, though. Reggie's drunken address to the Fruit Association is both funny ('You show me a hero who makes fondue tongs and I'll show you happy man who earns his living perforating lavatory paper') and a sincere anti-capitalist rant ('Man's the only species neurotic enough to need a purpose in life'). It would sit well on *Play for Today*, one of the prime liberal targets on Reggie's half-brother Jimmy's famous hit-list. And for emotionally fraught drama, it's hard to beat the scene where Reggie, having faked his suicide and disguised as a buck-toothed plumber, revisits his 'widow', finds she's remarrying, fails to pluck up courage to reveal himself and politely leaves the house as an agonised scream echoes through his skull. *Perrin* drastically pushed the limits of what you could do in front of a studio audience.

In an eminent cast Rossiter excels, maintaining the shrill authority of a man who knows he's the fixed centre of a capering universe. He addresses professional superiors and family members alike as if they were slow children or *Generation Game* contestants. Impatient to hear their dull conversations, he fills in their replies before they can get them out, reacts to them, and hammers out another half dozen lines before they can muster an 'erm' of protest. Surrounding him is a range of sitcom types, or – different thing – people who've acquiesced into sitcom types, from Geoffrey Palmer's bewildered former major to John Barron's childish sociopath CJ. That Perrin's path to happiness was obstructed by the greatest concentration of loveable berks ever gathered together gave his struggle a redeeming warmth.

The perfection of *Perrin* and its full-circle ending made further series a heavy task, which Nobbs deftly tackled by making the sequel a straight inversion of its predecessor. While the resurrected Reggie alternates between the dole and the piggery, Elizabeth (Pauline Yates, given much more to do this time round) joins Sunshine Desserts, fails to have a torrid affair with CJ at Sunshine Desserts and is sacked from Sunshine Desserts. Together they decide to play one last joke on the world and open Grot, a shop selling all the useless junk made by their berkish friends and relatives. True to form, the parody company becomes a real international success, and Reggie this time is trapped in the unfulfilling drudgery of an ironic millionaire lifestyle. Happiness is thus proved impossible. A third series, concerning a suburban drop-out community, was less successful, merely retreading this theme.

It was still way above average, and several leagues ahead of American adaptation *Reggie*, with *Soap*'s Richard Mulligan in the lead and a mawkish theme song bathetically conflating *Perrin*'s desperate rebellion with the USA's burgeoning self-help industry. A Rossiter-free UK sequel in 1996 and a full remake thirteen years after that were less gruesome, but still little more than footnotes to the original, which generated a very rare and special experience: that giddy feeling of space being warped in the name of laughter. *Perrin* was properly serious comedy, a psychic spring clean that wasn't afraid to rearrange the furniture while it was in there. After *Perrin*, only the most obtuse snobs still considered 'sitcom' a dirty word, however they sliced it.

BBC NINE O'CLOCK NEWS (1976)

BBC One

The year when information went showbiz.

Like the electricity bill and the income tax demand, the revamped
BBC Nine O'Clock News *is a nasty shock in a tasteful, plain*
beige envelope.

Nancy Banks-Smith, *Guardian*, 9 March 1976

NEWS IN PRINT OR speech is a thing of direct simplicity. When
visuals enter the mix, newsmakers can find their attention drifting
away from hard reportage and towards the more superficial matters
that occupy less serious forms of television. For a long time, the
BBC refused to have their television newsreaders appear in front
of the camera. If a disembodied voice was good enough for radio,
it would do for the cathode upstart. (Having said that, radio newsreaders were still obliged to perform for the microphone in full
evening dress. The Corporation's sense of protocol overruled its
austere logic.)

When the independent channel launched its rival news service,
the bare bones ethos was, if anything, amplified. Producer Robert
Tyrrell recalled the dummy bulletins staged in ITN's brand new,
sawdust-strewn Aldwych headquarters before cameras or lights
were installed. The newsreader, lit by an overhead projector, peered
'through a rough wooden frame rather like a gallows, which was

supposed to represent the screen of a television set.'[286] Describing the early years of television news, the last word you'd reach for would be 'glamorous'.

Newsreaders did become household faces, though. American anchormen like Walter Cronkite and Ed Murrow had, in the rough times after JFK's assassination, become sturdy father figures on a national scale, and there was much excited talk of US network bulletins shaping the self-image of the States. British newsreaders, by tradition as well as temperament, settled for a more modest form of fame. 'We're terribly well known to people,' admitted Kenneth Kendall, 'being part of their daily deliveries, along with the milk and bread.' On the other hand, Leonard Parkin observed, 'there's a feeling that it's no job for a grown man.'[287]

Things changed when a woman joined the men's club. A reporter for BBC South West since the sixties, Angela Rippon's sober style and Waterford Crystal diction helped her broach the news's hyper-masculine domain. When she got a regular gig behind the desk on BBC One during 1975, it was promoted as an equality breakthrough, even though she was still referred to as 'the BBC's cover girl'.

She wasn't the first: Nan Winton had a brief stint at the Beeb in 1960, but the country wasn't ready. Inevitably, a female news-reader was watched as much for how she looked as what she was saying. Rippon's sartorial decisions for each bulletin were scrutin-ised in a way Richard Baker's choice of blazer had never been. When, on 12 January 1976, her earring fell off just after she announced the death of Agatha Christie, the country gasped as one, twice.

Angela enthralled the nation and pundits spent a great many words trying to sum up her often contradictory qualities ('a plucked arch of the eyebrow and a sense of steel in the bones' – Peter Fiddick). These descriptions were often physical (Dennis Potter compared the baleful eyes of Rod Hull's Emu to those which Rippon 'keeps for news of the pound'), occasionally patronising ('stern and delicious' – Barry Norman), but always affectionate.

Unless you counted the disgruntled newsroom assistant who complained that Rippon, to maintain her stately, unflustered manner, read the news at twenty words per minute slower than her male colleagues, thus providing less news per bulletin.[288]

On 8 March 1976, the *Nine O'Clock News* was completely overhauled with less clutter, the retirement of the bank manager nameplates on the desk, and a return to a solo newsreader instead of the double act that had prevailed in recent years. Angela would be first on air. She more than rose to the occasion, but that still didn't stop the press concentrating on her clothes. In a surprisingly twenty-first-century-style 'open letter to TV's first lady,' the *Daily Mirror*'s fashion editor implored Rippon, thirty-one, to dress her age and less like a maiden aunt: even though 'we know you get a clothes allowance of only £70 a year.'[289] The 'letter' was accompanied by a month's worth of 'telesnaps' (the old money equivalent of screen grabs) detailing the frosty sartorial parade. ('March 19: paisley blouse, cream jacket.')

Angela wasn't the only source of aesthetic concern. The *Nine*'s new title sequence was a matter of great press interest. To modern eyes it was so basic as to hardly be noticeable at all, but in the days before no self-respecting news source would release so much as a travel alert without a good ten seconds of bombastically somersaulting CGI globes, the very idea of the news having animated titles could still prompt sniggers. 'The trumpeted titivations will come into vision,' wrote Peter Fiddick with mock awe, 'a new opening map of the world, with two hemispheres moving into one before our very eyes.'[290] Another critic reckoned the programme was 'in need of more than a pair of sliding soup plates for starters.'[291]

Then came the set. Incoming news editor Andy Todd had, for the first time, devoted serious thought and research to the question of what Rippon and company should deliver their reports in front of, and the result was . . . beige. Or, to be completely accurate, gamboge. Creating a comforting, warm environment to offset the discomfiting content of economic and foreign bulletins, gamboge was 'a sort of pale yellow, but done on a weave-textured backcloth which replaces the more assertive geometric reliefs we have been used to.'[292] The newsreader's domain was no longer an abstracted military bunker – or if it was, it had been given a lick of paint and a few rolls of hessian wall-weave left over from doing up a nearby unisex hair salon.

Rippon was also at the forefront of the newsreaders' crossover into light entertainment. They'd been popping up in comedy programmes ever since wartime radio announcer Stuart Hibberd was lightly roasted by Arthur Askey, but only started fannying about themselves after Robin Day cracked a public joke about his ITN cohort Reginald Bosanquet, with the result, according to ITN editor Nigel Ryan, that 'people suddenly realised you could be light-hearted without losing authority.'[293] Despite this, comedy and news remained separate TV disciplines, and attempts to generate fun at the end of bulletins often looked woefully misplaced. 'The Newsreader's Joke,' said Jeremy Bulger, 'stands in the dunce's corner of humour.'[294]

Wisely, Angela Rippon's comic debut was largely wordless: a comedy song-and-dance routine on the *Morecambe and Wise Christmas Special*. Unlike Michael Barratt's in-depth interview with Sooty for *The Goodies*, or Richard Baker's appearance on *Monty Python* earnestly enquiring, 'Lemon curry?', this was a media event of the very top rank, garnering acres of jokey pre-publicity. The intended surprise was spoilt by one George Harris, former editor of Rippon's *alma mater* the *South Devon Times*, who obtained some on-set stills of the threesome in mid-prance and promptly flogged them to the *Daily Mirror*. With the floodgates opened, Rippon's male counterparts signed up *en masse* for a *South Pacific* pastiche the following year.

After her Christmas triumph, Rippon became a fully articled celebrity. In 1977 she presented everything from the *Eurovision Song Contest* ('I think we're having a bit of trouble with our score-board again!') to fledgling motoring magazine *Top Gear*, becoming the first British newsreader to employ a personal PR consultant on the way. Margaret Thatcher prepared for government by adapting her hairstyle into a pointedly Ripponesque form. On a purely presentational level, the new News had won over the population.

From now on, visuals and personality would compete with reporting and analysis for the news editor's attention. This was fine, but, as the *Listener* pointed out, BBC news had far more serious problems, namely 'the radical ills of an overgrown and impoverished bureaucracy, whose money troubles at once bind it to cheap coverage of home affairs, and make it particularly sensitive to political pressures on the home front.'[295] It would take more than a new pair of earrings and some gamboge wall-weave to fix that.

BATTLE OF THE NETWORK STARS (1976–88)

STAR GAMES (1978–80)

ABC/ITV (Trans World International)

Celebrities start to be celebrated for what they can't do as much as for what they can.

CELEBRITY IS A STRANGE and confusing state for a human being to inhabit. In the majority of cases (contrary to popular cynicism) a celeb achieves fame via the mastery of a particular skill (singing, cooking, talking and walking simultaneously) to at least a basic level of competence. When their star status exceeds a certain level, though, the system demands they start spreading themselves thinner, branching out from singing to acting, say, or from grilling sardines to descending a staircase while giving a potted history of the fish finger. Perform these new tasks badly, and the brand is irreparably damaged. Unless, that is, the cocking up can be wrangled to show the celeb to be, hey, human just like us after all.

One of the first manifestations of this kind of second-tier

celebrity came via a televised end-of-term sports day. Trans World International was a grand-sounding US media company that began in the late sixties staging exhibition golf tournaments for British TV before landing a hit with *Superstars*, an all-comers gala in which sportsmen at the top of one particular field of physical endeavour gamely fell straight to the bottom of half a dozen others. Then Trans World kingpin Jay Michaels struck on an idea so shamelessly opportunist that its place in television history is assured. Translating the *Superstars* format to the world of TV, Michaels envisioned a grand athletic face-off between the star rosters of the three US network stations. In order to get them to co-operate, he sold a variation on the format to each of them. CBS had *Us Against the World*, in which a US celeb team competed against the rest of the world's stars. NBC were given the self-explanatory *Celebrities Challenge of the Sexes*. ABC, the sportiest, most downmarket and, at the time, most successful network, got the most successful format: *Battle of the Network Stars*.

As befitted a self-confessed 'trash sport', *Battle* was presented with maximum pomp and energy. The three teams were pictured arriving in separate fleets of limos. Esteemed *Monday Night Football* frontman Howard Cosell was MC and commentator, giving earnest appraisals of Loretta Swit's chances in the tug-of-war or Lynda Carter's form in the swimming relay. (If the activities sometimes seemed devised to maximise the exposure of young, tanned celebrity flesh, that's because they were – Michaels himself categorised the tournaments as 'underwear shows'.[296] *Battles* were staged twice a year, give or take, for over a decade.

Two years in, it spawned a British variant, necessitating a certain amount of adaptation to the local climate and customs. Actors, comedians, newsreaders and continuity sundries from 'both sides' divided into teams by occupation to compete at sprinting, swimming, motorcycling, ten-pin bowling and a climactic obstacle relay race direct from Jesus Green, Cambridge. Michael Aspel, the presenter's presenter with an unmatched ability to meet with gravity and trivia, and treat those two impostors just the same, provided what Martin Amis identified as '*Jackanory*-style unctuousness'.[297] Punters slavered at the spectacle of Roy Kinnear sweating through a round of clock golf, Blakey from *On the Buses* floundering in a canoe, and a short-trousered Bonnie Langford and Sandy Gall colliding on the six-a-side pitch. The winning team garnered £15,000 for charity. Boxing Day specials were scheduled. This was event TV.

It wasn't all sweat and grunt. Stars being stars, theatricality and swanning about were never absent for long. Reggie Bosanquet swaggered the length of the mud-churned sports field, resplendent in leather cowboy boots and a tracksuit with 'REGGIE BOSANQUET' emblazoned on the back. Each team was granted a 'non-playing coach', a whimsical ruse which allowed the likes of Magnus Pyke and Frankie Howerd to sling towels round their necks and excitedly organise pep-talks and strategic huddles as the drizzle set in.

The first series was such a hit that two more followed, keeping the formula the same but downgrading the location slightly: first to a Finsbury Park leisure centre and then to a field near High Wycombe. This did not, however, lessen the momentousness of the occasion. The 1979 tournament saw prize signing Captain Mark Phillips called off with flu, to be replaced, somewhat anticlimactically, with Jess Conrad. Princess Anne phoned Mark's team-mates to apologise, but failed to comfort Robin Askwith. ('Our spies told us he was hot stuff in the swimming pool!') Then, when Conrad was put in goal for the six-a-side, rival captain Patrick Mower stormed off the pitch, protesting that Conrad was a ringer, a seasoned custodian of the onion bag. The whole tournament was thrown into chaos. It made the papers. Interesting times.

ROCK FOLLIES (1976–7)
ITV (Thames)

A depression musical for the 1970s.

LIKE ANY OTHER BRANCH of entertainment, television progresses not through the smoothly executed plans of creative masters, but an endless stumble of fudge, calamity and betrayal. Brooklyn-born and Berkeley educated, Howard Schuman spent his youth on New York's off-Broadway circuit, devising experimental musical happenings of varying failure before emigrating to Britain in 1968. Deciding that television was the thing in the UK, he pitched two ideas to Joan Kemp-Welch, now head of drama at Thames Television. *Censored Scenes from King Kong* concerned a frazzled journalist obsessed with the idea of tracking down a missing scene from the 1939 movie featuring graphic ape-Wray congress. This didn't go down too well with the former devotee of *Little Women*.

A second idea, about a marital therapy clinic that used video cameras as tools, enthused Kemp-Welch with the potential of visual tomfoolery, and *Captain Video's Story* was commissioned for the late night half-hour *Armchair 30* series. In addition to that, an hour's worth of *Armchair Theatre* proper had suddenly been freed up, which was promptly filled with another Schuman play, *Verité*. This story of a quiet, middle-class North London couple's life invaded by underground filmmaker Tim Curry and unstoppable tap-dancing Brooklynite Beth Porter went a mile over the top but put Schuman on the map.

Then *Censored Scenes* was picked up for a BBC series of topical plays, which was drastically cut after the 1974 miner's strike necessitated the closedown of all television by 10.30 p.m. It was shot using what power was available, in a budget-beating bare studio plus blue screen inserts, with Beth Porter joined in the cast by Julie Covington as an intellectual cabaret act billed as a cross between John Stuart Mill, Nietzsche and the Andrews Sisters. The production beat the blackout, but failed to get past Head of Plays Christopher Morahan, who took against Schuman's trash aesthetic and canned it indefinitely.

The central idea of smart women being turned into a dumb show business act resurfaced when Schuman and producer Andrew Brown concocted a version of Hollywood's 1930s *Gold Diggers* movies for the new depression of the mid-seventies. The rock music scene was to be the backdrop, or rather the homogenised branch of show business Schuman saw rock as becoming by the middle of the decade. Hapless group the Little Ladies comprised three dissimilar aspiring actresses: Nancy Cunard 'Q' de Longchamps (Rula Lenska), a laid-back Sloane Ranger with a dim-witted surfer boyfriend who dreams of being a 1920s-style 'topping girl'; Anna Ward (Charlotte Cornwell), juggling a thin career on the serious stage with a decaying marriage to a nihilist Eng. Lit. teacher; and Devonia 'Dee' Rhodes (Covington), magician's assistant and increasingly reluctant member of a radical commune that's a tad heavy on the group hugs. It's an obvious cross-section of British class, but Schuman fills out the diagram with living details.

The three meet as auditionees for *Broadway Annie*, a foredoomed 'let's do the show right here' revue of the pre-*TW3* variety. 'A bum script, a nowhere score and a squiffy director,' notes Q. 'All the hallmarks of success.' It crashes in short order, and musical director Derek Huggins promises he can 'mould' the girls into an all-female rock group – reluctantly they agree. 'If I don't have a mystical experience, at least we might get a new boiler out of it.' Cue a dilapidated switchback ride of manipulation, penury, paranoia and appending the definite article to every noun, coming to a desultory end with the Little Ladies, powerless and utterly spent, cynically refitted as a wartime cabaret nostalgia turn.

The fully rehearsed, fully scored, multi-set six part musical drama was made on a swift six-month turnaround in late 1975. It had to be fully written too, which put the free-forming Schuman under intense pressure, leavened only slightly by two timely strikes. Roxy Music's Andy Mackay created the musical numbers, while Rod Stratford and Alex Clarke got round the panic-inducing number of set changes with a spare, stylised look which would serve pop video makers well throughout the following decade. Its 'indoorsy' nature was pointed up in the opening shot, when a panning shot over a tranquil English landscape turns out to be a picture on the wall of a grotty Soho office. It was all, of course, shot on crisp, bright videotape, praised by Schuman as 'a bolder medium which conveys an immediate "presence" that is, paradoxically, far more unreal than film'.[298] The video sheen that some thought cheap-looking in *I, Claudius* was a perfect match for this lurid adventure. Its relative low cost led Thames to agree.

Rock Follies' appeal was broad. The music and the citric burn of the visuals brought in a younger crowd who normally eschewed the worthy, taupe-hued drama of the time. The all-female focus was a refreshing change too, evoking fond memories of the BBC's swinging series *Take Three Girls*. The risqué dialogue – 'As far as I'm concerned, the straight sex brigade are a load of wankers' – sent the press into spasm. A soundtrack album was released and spawned a few minor hits, even though the songs sounded slightly ludicrous away from the cartoonish context of the show itself. Huge audiences and a BAFTA for best drama sealed the triumph.

A sequel quickly followed. *Rock Follies of '77* promised more of the same ('Do you get the feeling that we've only changed the date?' asked one number, knowingly). Finally, tangible success was within reach for the group, moving from grubby digs and flyblown back offices to the pile-carpeted, chrome-trimmed world of the record business proper. They gained a new manager: Beth Porter stealing every scene as the rapacious Kitty Schreiber, 'cray-ZEE' about everyone and everything. A new recruit, Rox (Sue Jones-Davies, late of the Bowles Brothers Band who'd recently shared a studio with the Sex Pistols' TV debut), ruffled group relations, Bob Hoskins played a John Bullish club owner and Tim Curry cameoed as Stevie Streeter, a Kwik Save Springsteen. It was twice as mad and loud as its ancestor, but no less despondent about the moribund state of the business. The shooting schedule was as enervating as before for all concerned, not helped when a strike by female production assistants over pay increases caused a break in transmission of several months.

By 1977, Schuman was convinced society had already moved into the eighties. When the eighties did arrive, so did a nasty shock. Rock Bottom, an all-girl vocal trio formed in the early 1970s under the aegis of composer Don Fraser, claimed they had approached Schuman and Brown with the concept of a series based on their tribulations, starring the three members as themselves.[299] Though the basic idea was nowhere near as refined, the group's stories were eerily familiar: Annabel Leventon had toured her Desdemona around France, just as Anna had 'given her Ophelia' at Preston. Schuman, Brown and Thames were judged in breach of confidence, and settled out of court for a sum reportedly reaching £500,000.[300]

Drama soon moved decisively away from Schuman's kitsch video techniques. One of his last efforts in this mode, 1987's *Up Line*, another semi-musical about desperate ambition with pyramid selling replacing show business, made little impact. '[Schuman's] apparent love for . . . the low-rent side of "the show business",' wrote David Housham, 'rubs uncomfortably against the tougher, satirical edge of his writing, giving it an overall camp, throwaway gloss that makes *Up Line* . . . seem unconvincing and dated.'[301] One minute you're up . . .

TRANS AMERICA ULTRA QUIZ (1977–92)

ULTRA QUIZ (1983–5)

NTV/ ITV (TVS)

The West laughs at those crazy masochistic Japs, then has a go itself.

WHEN DOES A GAME show become a reality show? The simple answer is when it gets beyond a certain size. The longer each edition lasts, the more it has to bring the contestants' personality into the foreground far beyond the usual hurried courtesies exchanged over the buzzer. ('Now Adrian, a little bird tells me you're something of a whiz on the old Rubik's Cube?') The more money a show costs, the more it tends to blot out every other programme on the channel, a monolithic skyscraper leaving well-mannered Neo-Georgian dramas cowering in its mighty shadow. *Ultra Quiz* was one such competitive carbuncle.

For decades, British game shows were held back by the scale of prizes. Remuneration was heavily restricted to avoid the unedifying scenes of naked greed witnessed in America. The Yanks even had a soppy-ugly word for the phenomenon: these weren't quiz shows, they were 'desire' shows. Foreign language, foreign concept. We're made of sterner stuff.

If American techniques were off the menu, what chance had British channels of buying *Trans America Ultra Quiz*, a gargantuan Japanese trivia trail which began with 5,000 contestants and slowly whittled them down in a variety of increasingly cruel ways while touring the beauty spots of the States over many weeks, before packing off the eventual winner with a 'life-changing' lump sum? Even the Americans themselves couldn't stomach their own version, *All-American Ultra Quiz*, hosted by *Laugh-In*'s Dan Rowan and Dick Martin, for more than one season. Such obstacles didn't stop both BBC and ITV representatives sizing up the format when Nippon Television put it up for grabs at the Monte Carlo Festival in 1982. Calculators and napkins were employed to determine the likelihood of bringing an affordable version to our shores. 'Maybe we could run an in-flight quiz to Jersey or the Isle of Man,' mused a BBC buyer. 'I wonder if we could interest Cross-Channel Ferries?'

The show was finally sold to brand new ITV franchise TVS. Keen to distance itself from its regional predecessor, the rural-traditional Southern, TVS aligned itself with the sort of south coast viewer who was more likely to own a yacht than a potting shed, and *Ultra Quiz* was just the sort of big, loud, network-frightening entity which could help propel them into the national consciousness. A few judicious tweaks of the maximum prize fund ruling allowed for a top bounty of £10,000. (Soon afterwards, *The Price is Right* would similarly break the agreed limit, but they used a different tactic: they just didn't tell the IBA.) Glamorous locations were sussed out: planes and boats were chartered; Michael Aspel, Sally James and Jonathan King were hired.

On the morning of Saturday 16 April, 2,000 contestants assembled on Brighton beach for the first round, a mass 'yes or no' marathon to sort the wheat from the chaff. The wheat would then board a ferry to France, answering more questions en route, with only the winners allowed to disembark at the other end. To provide a bit of variety, Eddie Kidd performed impressive stunts, astrologer Russell Grant competed with a 'computer boffin' to predict who would make it to the next stage, Sally James wore a jumpsuit accessorised with a Panama hat, and Jonathan King shouted encouraging things like 'He's got brain power packed in his head!'

Even Aspel's capable hands couldn't mould that into light entertainment. As the quiz ambled from exotic location to exotic location (and, for the final, back home to Southampton), viewers dropped out faster than the contestants, and derision multiplied by the week. Even TVS controller Michael Blakstad had to admit the programme had been 'quite awful'. Stuck with a costly dodo, TVS had a choice: silently bin it in favour of something nice and cheap with Fred Dinenage, or fiddle with the details and launch a second series. Stubbornly determined to prove themselves the equals of Granada and Thames, they went for the latter option.

The 1984 series of *Ultra Quiz* is the one most people tend to remember. Fronted by David Frost ('Hello, good evening, and a thousand welcomes!') and assisted by his *TW3* compadre Willie Rushton, it held together slightly more convincingly than the first incarnation, helped in no small measure by Frost's legendary connections: when the owners of Leeds Castle refused to host the final there, fearing the large-scale silliness might dent its image, Frost secured the use of Arundel Castle instead, by dint of being the son-in-law of its owner.

Despite Frost's mollifying assurance that the UK *Ultra Quiz* was 'as different from the Japanese as karate is from cricket', similarities with the cruel daftness of the original remained. On the beach at Deauville, twenty-eight contestants were buried up to their necks in sand, with balloons attached to strings held between their teeth, the release of which would constitute their answers to questions. Rushton, perhaps not the best choice for a programme that relied on taking stupidity seriously, observed that the losing contestants, when they were dug out of their pit, looked glad to be out of the running.

In Paris, with a characteristic mix of jet-set glamour and party game tomfoolery, the remaining hopefuls were ushered into a high class perfumery, blindfolded, and asked to identify a series of increasingly rancid smells, under the watchful eye of TV production legend (and, appropriately, *It's a Knockout* instigator) Major Barney Colehan. Then came Bruges, a tour of California, and back to Arundel. Ratings this time held up pretty well, but then they had to. With a budget of over £600,000, TVS had a lot more than their fledgling reputation riding on *Ultra Quiz*. So when questions of decency arose, they were ready to tackle them.

Matters came to a head in a debate at the 1984 Edinburgh Television Festival, chaired by one D. Frost. Putting the case that ITV's mania for game shows lowered standards was Jim Moir, BBC Head of Light Entertainment. *Price is Right* producer William G. Stewart put the case for the defence, cannily pointing out that ITV's ratio of quizzes to LE shows was the same in 1984 as it had been in the 'golden age' of 1968. More vocal still was LWT director of programmes John Birt, who unsettled the audience by insisting the anti-game show agenda was a case of middle class snobbery. 'Is the BBC interested in entertaining the working class?' he demanded.[302] The names may have changed, but today's arguments over 'reality' shows run on exactly the same lines as the 'desire' show debate.

Ultra Quiz, meanwhile, plugged away for another year. *Ultra Quiz '85* saw yet another clear-out of personnel. This time the master of ceremonies was Stu Francis, and locations were very much restricted to the UK, a tour of grey beaches and crumbling pier heads more reminiscent of the Radio One Roadshow than a slick globetrotting mental tournament. Gyles Brandreth, roped in to devise puzzles, wondered in his diary what he was doing with his life.

The modern reality juggernaut is run on much tighter lines than *Ultra Quiz* ever was but there's a similar weakness at their heart. The sheer scale of the programmes is forever in danger of being undercut by their inherent absurdity. It takes a great force of will to keep the ship afloat, hence the overbearing seriousness that often pervades the likes of *X Factor*. By treating a random MOR singing contest as if it were a war crimes tribunal, buoyancy is achieved, but only as long as the audience are willing to provide the necessary hot air. Lose them, as *Ultra Quiz* quickly did, and the enterprise comes crashing down under the weight of its own triviality. Today's craft may be capable of longer flights than *Ultra Quiz*, but there's no guarantee they won't end in the same undignified way.

SOAP (1977–81)
ABC (Witt/Thomas/Harris)

The troughs of drama become peaks of comedy.

TV is a business, and you're not allowed to be as adult as I wish you could be and you're not allowed to do things as adult as I wish you were.

Susan Harris,
Toronto Globe and Mail, 8 January 1983

THEY ONLY EXISTED TO sell soap powder. They purveyed dumb stimulation to bored housewives in the days before Quaaludes and Valium. They habitually featured at least one murder, abduction, divorce, suicide attempt, conversion to the priesthood or fatal act of God per episode. They were, according to James Thurber, twelve minutes of dialogue spread between thick slices of advertising.[303] The list of cultural charges against the American daytime soap opera is long and damning.

By the late 1970s, the network soaps were among the last relics of TV's post-war gold rush. *As the World Turns, Search for Tomorrow, The Guiding Light* and their ilk had been around for a quarter of a century. Some were even older, having begun as radio soaps before the war. They drew flak from the beginning, the wireless pioneers accused of hobbling the war effort by unnecessarily adding to their audience's neuroses.[304]

Yet soaps had social purpose. In the early days, they took a strong, moralistic stand on their characters' antics. Bad deeds were punished, familial loyalty and civic duty espoused. They later became a platform for promoting health and psychological issues. The problem was that they did it so crassly. A 1963 episode of *The Guiding Light* illustrated a traumatic birth with a shot from the unborn child's point of view: a leg on each side of the frame and a concerned obstetrician thrusting a giant pair of forceps toward the camera. The cast of *As the World Turns* were menaced by a giant Venus flytrap. This was *Grand Guignol* with pelmets, positively begging for parody.

Susan Harris began her TV career writing drama, but 'it came out funny,'[305] so she joined Norman Lear's new wave of sitcom outrage. For *All in the Family* spin-off *Maude*, she wrote 'Maude's Dilemma', the celebrated two-parter in which Bea Arthur's eponymous middle-aged liberal gets an abortion. Transmitted two months before the Supreme Court's Roe v. Wade decision legalised abortion nationwide, the story was a turning point for Harris. 'It became impossible,' she decided, 'for me to write something that didn't have a point of view, that wasn't about something, that couldn't touch you in some way.'[306]

Harris began creating her own series in partnership with producers Paul Junger Witt and Tony Thomas. Their first effort, divorcee study *Fay*, came and went in short order, so they started again. Instead of reining in *Fay*'s controversial aspects, they cranked them up. The new scenario was deliberately off the daytime peg: sisters Jessica Tate and Mary Campbell married adulterous, wealthy and disturbed, poor men respectively. Affairs, murders, personality disorders and aliens appeared weekly.

Initially, *Soap* wasn't so much a satire of daytime drama as an experiment in form. Harris's main reason for adopting the serial format was liberation from the need to wrap up a tight twenty-three-minute plot each week, freeing more space for 'scenes that were just good talk'.[307] That 'good talk' was the Susan Harris formula, nailed by Martin Cropper as 'social embarrassment punctuated by daggered one-liners'.[308] *Soap* the comedy was soap grown up.

Harris broke the daytime style down into its constituent parts, supersized each one, and crammed them willy-nilly back into the box. The base note was absurd, melodramatic exposition. On top of this came a steady stream of minted witticisms ('What use is algebra? I have never once, in all these years, had to find x'), with a top note of out-of-character meta-commentary. ('I always over-react when the person I love more than anyone else in the world drops dead. I'm sorry.') By bending realism, *Soap* could have its dramatic cake, eat it, and make sarcastic comments about its own rotten table manners all at once.

Trouble began in June 1977 when *Soap* was screened as part of ABC's new season première for critics in San Diego. *Newsweek* wrote of an opening episode packed with filth, including ecclesi-astical sex scenes on consecrated ground, prompting a loose coali-tion of church leaders and right-wing pressure groups to call for a ban, sight unseen. Atlanta's Baptist minister Bob Spencer echoed the sentiments of censors down the ages. 'We don't have to see the show to know it's indecent . . . I believe in the Bible and I don't have to see certain things to know they are wrong.' Nineteen panicking ABC affiliates cancelled *Soap* and twenty more shunted it to the late night slot of doom. It was, claimed Harris, 'the first fatality of the moral majority'.[309]

Why did ABC stick with it? One reason was the tenacity of Fred Silverman, now ABC's head of entertainment after revitalising CBS's comedy roster with *The Mary Tyler Moore Show*, *All in the Family* and *M*A*S*H*. There was another factor more appropriate to the spirit of the show. Beverlee Dean had been hired as 'creative consultant' by network president Fred S. Pierce. She was previously a consultant psychic to Hollywood stars. With stakes so perilously high, a network will rule out nothing to get in front. Dean predicted hit status for both *Soap* and *Taxi*. She even got a visit from a scep-tical Harris. 'As a writer, I'll try almost anything once. She told me *Soap* would become a hit, but then my grandmother said that too.'[310]

In the studio Jay Sandrich, director of *The Mary Tyler Moore Show*'s early years, was in charge, swapping the former's orange-and-brown film of hugs and resolutions for a non-stop nightmare on acid-hued videotape – a striking change of tone and pace. With no pausing for breath, or even sitting down, acting in *Soap* was an equally tough assignment. Moore's sitcom offered lovably flawed role models. *Soap* was a parade of clinical case histories.

The cast, bouncing in and out of melodrama and panto with the odd heavy thump on the fourth wall and the occasional oasis of genuinely touching sentiment, had a gruelling task. As the otherworldly Jessica Tate, Katherine Helmond turned blanket ignorance into a state of grace, like Katharine Hepburn channelling Lamb Chop. At the other end of the scale, Richard Mulligan's Burt Campbell was a full-blown dyspraxic fidget: a startled dinosaur with a separate brain for each limb. Somewhere between, Robert Guillaume made the Tates' butler Benson into a Greek chorus of narrow-eyed, scattergun contempt. Billy Crystal's Jodie Dallas wasn't the first gay sitcom character – ABC's 1972 summer filler *The Corner Bar* was first with rococo set designer Peter Panama – but he did develop from the predictably stereotyped early sex change and suicide storylines into one of the show's few points of relative normality.

Risking her own sanity, Harris wrote the entire first season by herself. The inevitable collapse convinced her to collaborate on the remaining seasons and restrict her future comedy work to creating shows, rather than day-to-day scripting. After *Benson*, a conventional sitcom spin-off relocating Guillaume in governmental service, she tried to repeat the serial pastiche with *Hail to the Chief*, a misfire starring Patti Duke as the first female US president. The shock ante was upped, but by now pensioners contracting herpes and eight-year-old boys complaining of enlarged prostate glands seemed somehow stale. Harris finally reached the top of the sitcom pyramid with *The Golden Girls*, an altogether more empathetic comedy with fully rounded characters and family appeal. A sell-out to respectability in situation terms perhaps, but a quick survey of the Miami quartet's back-chat showed Harris's daggered one-liners had, if anything, been comprehensively sharpened.

ROOTS: THE SAGA OF AN AMERICAN FAMILY (1977)

ABC (David L. Wolper)

Network television's black history week.

You've probably noticed that I was a little late in arriving. I met Alex Haley outside, and I made the mistake of saying, 'Alex, how's your family?'
Jimmy Carter addresses the Congressional Black Caucus
annual dinner, 24 September 1977

WHILE IT WAS YEARS ahead of other countries, early American television struggled to present non-white characters, particularly African-Americans, in a balanced and unpatronising light. Sitcoms led the charge in the 1960s, with Bill Cosby's equal top billing in *I-Spy* and Diahann Carroll's positive lead role in MTM's *Julia* helping banish painful memories of The Kingfish, the eye-rolling get-rich-quick schemer from cartoonish radio and TV coon turn *Amos 'N' Andy*. By comparison drama held back for an unconscionably long time, but when it did broach the subject it was at top volume.

Roots the book was the result of twelve years' genealogical research by Tennessee journalist Alex Haley, sparked by the story his grandmother told of Kunta Kinte, a Gambian youth who was captured by colonialists and put to work on a plantation. The TV rights were bought by producer David L. Wolper, who'd been trying to get a pan-generational saga on screen for years, pitching native American family sagas, police family sagas, blue collar car worker sagas and the like to little network interest.[311] *Roots*, however, already had momentum. It was taken up by ABC, who had pioneered the mini-series format by taking big novels and splitting them into multiple hour-long chunks, beginning with Leon Uris's *QBVII* in 1974 and finding mass success two years later with *Rich Man, Poor Man* by Irwin Shaw. Audience attention spans had been tested by the new format, and passed. *Roots* would assess their stamina in a few more areas.

Its scope was epic, from the Mandinka village of Jufareh in The Gambia in 1750 to Tennessee shortly after the Civil War. Kunta Kinte (played by eighteen-year-old student LeVar Burton) is uprooted from the village and shipped to a Tennessee plantation. His tribulations are followed by those of his daughter Kizzy (Leslie Uggams), who is sold down the river to an even harsher planter. He rapes her, leaving her with a son who becomes skilled in the art of training fighting cocks, earning him the name Chicken George (Ben Vereen) and a sojourn in England breeding birds for his new English owner. Back in Tennessee, George's son Tom Harvey, a plantation blacksmith, faces the Civil War and the rise of the Ku Klux Klan.

Four generations of bondage, rape, violence, poverty, starvation, stillbirth and murder at 9 p.m. was a massive risk. The all-important Midwestern (and predominantly white, conservative) audience was mollified by a raft of big name white stars – Lorne Greene, Lloyd Bridges, Chuck Connors and Ed Asner among them – alongside an encyclopedia of black talent (Scatman Crothers, O. J. Simpson, James Earl Jones, Maya Angelou). They pitched *Roots* as a saga about a family that happened to be black, rather than a black story *per se*, with much talk of Kunta Kinte being a 'universal symbol'. Finally ABC president Fred Silverman decided to strip the show across eight consecutive days in late January. If it flopped hard, it would at least flop fast.

Within a couple of episodes the impact of ABC's strategy was obvious; the country stopped as one when *Roots* aired. Audiences started at nearly twenty-nine million and rose to over thirty-six by day eight. The idea of a huge, diverse nation coming together over a simple story of suffering and injustice was not the whole truth: when Kunta Kinte was hobbled after an attempted escape in episode three, a rise in racially based fights was reported in schools. But it was an education for many in the reality of the West's ignoble past, and chimed with the new, compassionate mood which had got Jimmy Carter into the White House just three days before transmission. It was showered with Emmys and a special Pulitzer, and merely watching the show counted towards academic credit in universities across the States. No television programme had made anything like this impact before, especially with such a short run-up.

Roots was as expansive, solemn and simple as the watercolour montage that opened each episode, straight out of your illustrated family Bible. Some had reservations about the broadbrush approach adopted by Wolper's team. Much of Haley's 700-page book had necessarily been trimmed away and the straightforward, populist style of the series was open to accusations of trivialising slavery by adopting a personal, 'soapy' approach. Richard Schickel in *Time* magazine famously derided it as a 'middlebrow *Mandingo*'.[312] The simple answer to that was that the show's remit was to reach the maximum audience, and you didn't do that by wedging huge tracts of socio-historical analysis into a compelling yarn. Haley was transmitting history 'gut-to-gut' and television was the ideal medium. Others quibbled in the margins over anachronisms. 'It was painful,' wrote Anthony Burgess, 'to watch natives of West Africa who had never been in contact with white society indulge in facial gestures they could have learnt only in sophisticated Manhattan.'[313]

Most damningly, Mark Ottaway of the *Sunday Times* claimed the whole justification of Haley's story was unsound: the Gambian storyteller who told Haley of Kunta Kinte's entrapment being 'a man of notorious unreliability'[314] and telling him what he wanted to hear. Now it was political. Haley dismissed the criticisms. 'For years we've been offered a Tarzan and Jane view of Africa and there was no quarrel with it . . . there are basic vested interests in maintaining the old social order.'[315] Black academics piled on this attempt by the British establishment to distract from the show's central message. 'The English know better than anyone else what black research will lead to,' claimed Professor John Henrik Clarke. 'It will expose that the English were the leaders in slave trade and that they made the greatest profit from it and built an empire on those profits.'[316]

Roots affected the American populace in many ways. Radical African Americans disavowed their 'slave names' in the greatest numbers since the late 1960s, while babies were named Kunta and Kizzy by the score. A craze for genealogical research in general took off, which proved big business for the Mormon Church, owners of a mammoth vault of historical records. Historical tales of family turmoil appeared everywhere, the strongest being NBC's *Holocaust* with Meryl Streep.

Roots established the mini-series above the derided TV movie in the pecking order of American drama for the best part of the next two decades. It wasn't a fail-safe format though, as Wolper found when he finally broadcast his 1984 native American *Roots* series, Sioux saga *The Mystic Warrior*, to mass indifference. Even in the diverse USA, some stories were still a touch too niche.

LEAPFROG (1978–9)
ITV (ATV)

Educational programming goes in at the avant-garde deep end.

MENTION SCHOOLS' TELEVISION AND a dull, half-baked world is evoked of pencils pointing at litmus papers in huge close-up and jobbing actors fluffing lacklustre speeches while dressed unconvincingly as Victorian industrialists. But creativity touched even this arid broadcasting sector, in some very unusual ways.

The BBC made the first broadcasts in 1952 to a handful of London schools equipped with special aerials, but America saw the first regular service two years later, as WQED sent out four hours of educational fodder a week to the folk of West Philadelphia in a pre-breakfast 'sunrise semester'.

The first closed-circuit BBC programme – Leslie Woolf of Hemel Hempstead Grammar doing the old 'electric current through the frog's legs' biology crowd-pleaser – was, like many early programmes, a no-frills lecture.[317] In 1965 ITV explored new areas, techniques and frontmen. In *One World* the young Peter Snow explained contemporary geopolitics. English language lesson *English and Life* was introduced, strangely, by 'Come Outside' singer Mike Sarne.[318] On the wilder shores, *Picture Box* sought to stimulate children's creativity through a range of usually wordless and often psychedelic internationally-sourced short films of the type that could lead to much thoughtful 'topic work'.

ITV was also the first to televise sex education in 1970 with *Living and Growing*. Sex-ed films for cinema distribution caused controversy at the time for their graphic approach, as the director of one, *Growing Up*, explained: 'if you were making a film about cooking, you would photograph an egg.'[319] ITV's effort was an orgy of soft-focus diagrams and deliberately non-Anglo-Saxon terminology, carefully preceded by a late night discussion for anxious parents, chaired by Ludovic Kennedy. This diligent decorum didn't stop Mary Whitehouse lodging a complaint against Granada Television over a mid-morning broadcast of *The Facts Are These: Venereal Disease*.

By now TV was steadily becoming a fixture of school life. Most schools still had one set apiece, usually pushed from class to class on a sturdy trolley. In primary schools children would ritually gather cross-legged on the floor to bask in its instructive glow. This led to spurious health warnings, with one orthopaedic surgeon claiming children's feet could be permanently deformed by the 'TV squat'. But the medium became a scholastic fixture, thanks to the combined attractions of pupils getting to pursue one of their favourite pastimes during school hours and teachers having to do little more than turn the thing on and run a few fact-sheets through the duplicator.

Drama prepared teenagers for life in the real world. Thames's *Viewpoint* encouraged kids to question their elders and betters in the media. (When this list of elders was shown to include several ITV companies, the IBA stepped in and quietly put it to sleep.) Andrew Davies, dramatic champion of the 1980s and 1990s, got an early break chronicling the trials of a working class school leaver in ATV's *The Time of Your Life* (sample episode title: 'I Don't Like Them Hippies'). Even experimental author B. S. Johnson was drafted to create an entire class of 'C-stream' sixteen-year-olds for Thames's *You and the World*. (His original script featured the suicide of the class's old teacher, which was tactfully removed after he took his own life and the show was completed by other hands.[320])

Programmes for primaries reborn as 'active learning' became the new orthodoxy, shifting the emphasis from learning by heart to finding out for yourself, and swapping regimented lines of desks for tables set at jaunty angles and womb-like walls of maroon sugar

paper. It arrived on screen in the shape of BBC literacy fantasy
Sam on Boffs' Island. An innovative bit of whimsy which saw Tony
Robinson transported over his morning cereal to a world of phon-
etically challenged puppets, it combined artwork from Oliver
Postgate and Peter Firmin with a script from Michael Rosen.
Sadly Rosen was soon politely asked to leave the BBC (allegedly
due to his troublesome far-left political sympathies), and the
Corporation's schools' output returned to more conventional styles
soon afterwards.

It was left to ITV to pick up the creative slack, which they did
while wrestling with the thorny problem of interesting the average
seven-year-old in maths. *Figure It Out*, a previously mundane
numbers-and-shapes affair, was refitted in 1974 with a 'magazine'
format comprising characters, sketches and achingly bad puns,
delivered by actor and maths graduate Fred Harris. Harris ('a relaxed
and dashing presenter using a variety of household objects' – the
Listener[321]) combined knowledge with kid-friendly charisma in
ideal proportions to engage the short-trousered masses.

This was revolutionary enough, but *Figure It Out*'s replacement,
Leapfrog, took the most abstruse of primary school subjects into
the outer realms. The Leapfrogs Group were a band of radical
educators led by Dick Tahta, a maths evangelist cited as a great
inspiration by Stephen Hawking. They adapted Egyptian pedagogue
Caleb Gattegno's intuitive teaching methods into a quarter-
hour jamboree of graphics, mime, abstract film and hypnotic
geometrical animations set to the eerie synth-blues of Pink Floyd
collaborator Ron Geesin. Fred remained as a friendly face to guide
the kids through this disjointed, occasionally disturbing fantasia,
helped by others including, appropriately, *Vision On*'s Sylvester
'Sylveste' McCoy.

Not everyone approved of this kind of trendy flimflam. Teachers
who thought innovations like 'circle time' were the work of a
dungaree-clad devil abandoned the series mid-way, and many children proved less receptive than Tahta hoped. Sequels such as *Basic
Maths* slowly added more explanatory chat and moved back towards

the conventional middle ground. Eventually technology would make mainstream educational TV redundant, but for a brief while its ingenuity ranked it among the medium's weirdest and best.

THE BBC TELEVISION SHAKESPEARE (1978–85)

BBC Two/PBS (BBC/WNET/Time-Life)

The last hurrah of prestige single plays.

'O for a highbrow play, that would ascend
The brightest heaven of syndication,
All channels for a stage, big names to act
And billionaires to fund the swelling scene!'
So went the dreams of certain drama chiefs
In times when brows soared high, but funds ran low.
What if the nation's broadcaster took on
The work of history's greatest dramatist?
It couldn't lose! Esteem! Fame! Merchandise!
A credible and creditworthy scheme.
The Bard, the Beeb: a dish fit for the gods
That some called, 'gloriously BBC!'[322]
Cedric Messina, of *Play of the Month*,
Was ministering angel to the plan.
Fond of the grand gesture, he came up with
The idea to produce Shakespeare complete –
No skipping out the likes of *Pericles*,
Nor all those Henrys, nor the one which has

The daft, bathetic cry 'Where is thy head?'
There was to be no short shrift, no foul play,
Just every Bardic drama, soup to nuts.
The single play, though still a 'prestige' form,
Had shed its old contemporary grit
As period pomp brought better sales returns
From overseas. (Despite the sorry sight
Of duds like *Churchill's People*, ill-conceived
Dramatic squibs adapted from the book
That won the ex-PM the Nobel Prize
But on the screen looked stiff, cheap and absurd,
And soon were dashed to pieces by the press.)
The raw, unflinching modern single play
Remained a tricky sell to foreigners,
But antique stuff sold like hot cakes and ale
To lands with anorexic history books.
The Beeb had knocked out Shakespeares all its life,
But thirty-seven plays in just six years
Went way beyond its public-funded means.
The budget shortfall led Messina to
Acquaint himself with strange bedfellows for
Such highbrow entertainment. Even then
The idea of a drama series backed
By Exxon Oil, a huge investment bank
And an insurance company seemed mad,
But there they were, each chipping in a third
Of the outstanding million-and-a-half
Required to get Messina off the ground.
There were conditions that came with the cash,
The main one being, 'Please don't muck about.
Don't do the plays in ersatz modern dress
To make some vague point about Vietnam
Or Ulster, or some made-up fascist state,
And don't go mad with kooky abstract sets
Or kinky costumes. Stay traditional.

Doublet and hose, crossed garters, and the rest.'
The money-men demanded heritage,
And 'maximum acceptability'.[323]
The series was to start with *Much Ado*,
That most agreeable romance of wits
With Penelope Keith and Michael York,
But someone, somewhere, called Messina out
For past injustices (no-one knows what)
And, in the row, the play was quickly binned,
Abandoned as a sacrificial goat
To BBC internal subterfuge.
To kick things off instead, they played it safe
With *Romeo and Juliet*. The leads
Were two unknowns, but big names dwelt
Within the lower body of the cast.
The look of it, though, was another thing.
By taping in the studio, the costs
Were kept down, continuity maintained
And dialogue kept mostly audible.
The problem was that Zeffirelli's film,
Though ten years old, was still definitive
To public taste. The poor old BBC,
With no backlighting, no heavenly beams
And, worst of all, no lush location shots,
Was naff enough to set your teeth on edge.
The old Verona square looked oddly flat,
And Alan Rickman's tights from Woolies bought.
The critics, sniffing mediocrity,
Were minded to dismiss the thing outright,
And household words were tossed Messina's way.
He had successes too, but two years in
He quit, and in his place the station hired
Jonathan Miller, a Renaissance man
In both the modern and Renaissance sense.
A polymath, exceedingly well read,

He looked at Exxon's strict proscriptive list
And, rather than lie low, fought fire with fire.
Taking the period trappings to extremes,
He laid on references with a trowel
To Veronese, Dutch masters and the like,
By recreating their work on the screen
As knowing *cinquecento* allusions.
The budget, just two hundred grand an hour,
Was made to work in new and lateral ways.
The castle walls were still of plywood hewn,
But now, instead of corny painted stones,
The plywood remained plywood, unadorned,
For Miller knew the trick with stylised sets
Was not to ape materials, just the shape.
Though still on tape, it broke the studio curse,
And grew an atmosphere all to itself
For actors to breathe in – that is, when they
Weren't trying bits of business Miller cribbed
From Erving Goffman's books on social gaffes.
(The best examples came when Miller cast
John Cleese as lead in *Taming of the Shrew*.)
It wasn't all about the Miller way.
The new directors whom he took aboard
Had striking visions of their own to stage.
Elijah Moshinsky, an opera man,
Turned off the studio's usual million watts
And lit whole scenes, it seemed, with just one bulb,
Suffusing actors with gold candlelight.
Then, later on, Jane Howell went for broke
With cones and wedges in *The Winter's Tale*,
Creating just the sort of abstract set
The Exxon boys specifically ruled out.
She also organised *Henry VI*,
As three gargantuan games of soldiers, in
A vast, decaying adventure playground.

This wouldn't have done on Messina's watch.
If these were gimmicks, no-one could complain
In light of their success. As Miller said,
'They're only "monkey tricks" if they don't work;
When they come off, they're "strokes of genius".'[324]
The educational cherry on the cake
Was *Shakespeare in Perspective*: lecture films
Presented by big names to warm things up
For each play that was broadcast. So you got
Frank Kermode on *Lear*. *The Winter's Tale*
By Stephen Spender. Clive James did *Hamlet*
In witty fashion, and the *Merry Wives*
They gave to Jilly Cooper – quite a range.
One week Roy Hudd explained *The Comedy*
Of Errors from a music hall in Leeds,
Then Donald Sinden appraised Anne Boleyn
As (his words) 'eminently beddable',
And Dennis Potter savaged *Cymbeline*
While trudging through the dark Forest of Dean.
Something, as linkmen say, for everyone.
The *Shakespeare* was originally pitched
In 1975, when single plays
On BBC TV, across the year,
Filled a hundred and twenty slots, against
A figure less than one-third that when Howell's
Vastly delayed *Titus Andronicus*
(All severed hands and Toyah Willcox Goths)
Stood hairs on end in 1985,
And brought the project to a bloody close.
(By now Shaun Sutton, veteran of the Beeb
Who had directed *Z-Cars* episodes
Some twenty years ago, was at the helm,
Producing the last fourteen of the plays.)
The studio-bound drama, on its own,
Would scarcely make it to the next decade

As TV plays contrived to look like films,
And took their style cues from the cinema.
The long and fruitful exchange of ideas
Between theatre and television was
Cut by the former's slide into a niche
As musicals became its staple fare,
And by the shift of TV's self-image
From national stage to pseudo-Hollywood.
It's bleakly fitting that the Shakespeare plays
Became the curtain call for the old style
Of making drama. While its look and style
And methods swiftly died out, other things
Such as the corporate funding, worldwide sales
And wrangles over star names, would increase
And dominate productions from then on.
Since films cost more than plays, they had to make
More money back, which meant that any risks
Had to be minimised, and 'Play it safe!'
Became the rule. To innovate is to die.
The game was up, and drama on the box,
After this business-related sea change,
Became a lot more rich, but much less strange.

CONNECTIONS (1978)

BBC One/PBS
(BBC/Time Life Films)

The blockbuster science documentary grows too
rich for many people's blood.

Morecambe and Wise on ITV, James Burke on BBC One – who
says the autumn schedules have given us nothing to laugh at?
David Wheeler, *Listener*, 26 October 1978

WHEN EDUCATION IS DISCUSSED, the relative merit of a scientific
versus a literary schooling is guaranteed to bring out the priggish
schoolboy that lurks within even the greatest thinkers. In the
nineteenth century the botanist T. H. Huxley had it out with poet
Matthew Arnold in a relatively civilised duel of words. The quality
of debate went down a notch in 1959 when C. P. Snow, scientist
turned novelist, delivered a lecture lamenting the widening gulf
between the 'two cultures'. F. R. Leavis, self-appointed guardian
of the grand literary tradition, mocked Snow's thesis as biased,
vulgarly written, and told him his novels were rubbish to boot.
Since then, the borderland between the humanities and science
has been a minefield for well-meaning pundits. James Burke stepped
boldly into it with the world watching.

An English graduate, Burke started out as a language teacher
in Bologna before getting into broadcasting almost by accident,
when Granada Television cast about the locality for resident

reporters. Moving to the BBC he fell, equally serendipitously, into science with *Tomorrow's World* and a central role in round-the-clock coverage of the Apollo space launches. With his boundless, electric enthusiasm and his penchant for eye-catching visual aids, including scale models of orbiting craft into which he gleefully clambered, he became TV's technological figurehead.

For Burke, though, space-shots became increasingly monotonous. He dismissed the 1975 Apollo-Soyuz link-up, a political stunt with little technological benefit, as 'crucifyingly boring'. Burke the humanities man was only interested in technology that affected society, and to this end he fashioned *The Burke Special*. Clothed head to toe in black, he dashed through an audience seated in a set decked out in chrome and nylon shag-pile, reeling off informal lectures-cum-demonstrations of everything from body language to biological terrorism. His mission was to explain without being dull or appearing elitist. The presenter, he said, must keep things access-ible: 'if you're bored stiff by the man, you won't listen to what he says.'[325] One critic compared his performance to 'a finely honed conjuring act'.[326] Another, less enthusiastically, lamented his tend-ency 'to dash around from spot to spot, shaking trinkets in people's faces so that they wouldn't notice the nonsense that was being babbled.'[327]

Burke wasn't confined to a studio for long. The US bicentennial celebrations prompted NBC to hook up with the Beeb for *The Inventing of America*, in which every major technological break-through made on American soil was recreated by Raymond Burr while Burke explained what connected them in animated fashion. Dramatic skits, song and dance numbers choreographed by Arlene Phillips, gags and TV parodies crowded into two frenetic hours. Critics reeled from the overload. 'The show's script was so bent on finding ways to say things,' complained Clive James, 'that it hardly got anything said.'[328]

The dissenters couldn't stop him. Burke's next series, tentatively titled *Changes*, was a juggernaut. Ten hours to give an 'alternative view' of technology, taking Burke, now clad in an off-white safari suit, to 150 locations around the globe. The task, as laid out on a mammoth wall chart in Burke's office, was to trace the history of eight key inventions, brought about by accident as much as design. A change of name to *Connections*, a lavish transatlantic budget and the skills of *Ascent of Man* producers David Kennard and Mick Jackson gave Burke an impressive setting from which to ask probing questions like: 'What has the recipe for Chicken Marengo got to do with air conditioning?'

Here, for many, was the problem. The production values suggested seriousness, authority and weight. But Burke's skittish script was never far from a flippant aside: 'When Queen Elizabeth took over the place in 1558, it was national disaster week!'; 'Meanwhile, at the King's palace, it was lead balloon time'; 'Who knows what somebody's doing with a toilet roll right now?' Combine this with a puckish tendency to start a sentence in downtown New York and finish it on a rocky promontory in the Mediterranean, and a certain omniscient smugness was palpable. It grated with Clive James, who diagnosed 'Burke's Smirk – a twitching grin of self-approval at being in on secrets.'[329] For Julian Barnes, 'everything is terribly, terribly clear to Mr Burke, which is a major reason for being suspicious of him'.[330] Brian Winston demanded: 'If he is a reporter, why does he never let anyone else get a word in edgeways? If he is an authority, what exactly is he an authority on, other than talking to the camera?'[331]

Conversely many viewers, mainly the young, were riveted by the gee-whiz visual rhetoric and inspired to discover more for themselves, which was Burke's main goal from the outset. The style wasn't an issue to them then, and the controversy seems distant today, when even world leaders habitually remove ties and preface each obloquy with a chummy, Burkean 'Look . . .'

Connections broke public TV ratings records in the US and was exported to over ninety countries. Two sequels followed: *The Real Thing*, concerning human perception; and *The Day The Universe Changed*, on philosophical perspectives, which ended with Burke delivering an impassioned and prescient speech arguing that a global network of computers might one day democratise all know-ledge, encourage true freedom of ideas and challenge centuries-old systems of repressive government. He did this from the top of a mountain in the Himalayas, of course.

BLANKETY BLANK
(1979-90)
BBC One

The little game show that couldn't.

IN THE EARLY DAYS of American television, the quiz show ruled. The Federal Communications Commission had cracked down on network radio's proliferation of phone-in giveaways in 1949, and the celebrity panel show expanded to fill the gap. Five years later the ban was lifted, and television decided anything radio could do, they could do a thousand times bigger. Never mind *The $64,000 Question*, US quizzes offered prizes all the way up to $250,000 (which was never won) and a genuine Scottish island (before the British government waded in to stop them).[332] The real winners were the networks, as the national press became captivated by the progress of punters up the prize ladder, moving coverage of the shows from the TV section at the back to the headlines at the front.

Producers' desire to control those headlines became the format's undoing. Addicted to front page exposure, they replaced the disappointing, know-little members of the public with ringers groomed to romp to victory week after week. In August 1958 they were called out, when a contestant was found in possession of a book of answers on the set of NBC's *Dotto*, precipitating a federal inquiry which soon became a scandal when the fixing of *Twenty One* came to light. Contestant Herb Stempel revealed how he'd been coerced into crashing his winning streak (pretending not to know *Marty* had won the Best Picture Oscar in 1955) to clear the decks for suave WASP ringer Charles Van Doren. The producers started appearing in the headlines rather than writing them. By the end of the year the big quizzes had been cancelled in favour of comedy and westerns. They would slowly reappear over the next few years, but only as also-rans in the margins, never the day's main draw.

One of the schedule fillers was CBS's *Match Game*, a two-handed word quiz with celebrity trimmings devised by Frank Wayne of 'telepuzzle' behemoths Goodson-Todman Productions. Contestants completed the blank space in host Gene Rayburn's statement with a word or phrase, which was tested against the written guesses of a panel of assorted celebrities. If they matched, points were won. It lasted nearly twenty-two years in its original form, during which American screens captured the rise of the natural born game show contestant, as brash and slick as the compère, miming theatrical concentration when asked the question and gleefully applauding themselves when they got the answer right. Competing on afternoon TV quizzes was the USA's true national sport.

As with all game shows of even moderate fame, the format was sold overseas. Australia's Network Ten, well on the way to becoming a Rupert Murdoch majority interest, took it up in 1977 as *Blankety Blanks*. The host this time was Graham 'Gra-Gra' Kennedy, who'd become one of Australia's first bona fide TV stars via the thirteen-year Johnny Carson-style chat show *In Melbourne Tonight*. Filling the star stalls with his pals from the rather restricted pool of home-grown celebrity, Kennedy made the show less formal, funnier, more relaxed and less and less about the contestants and their tedious task of filling in the blanks. In-jokes proliferated: the hapless stagehand who uncovered the clues from behind a screen was dubbed 'Peter the Phantom Puller', and every drop of potential innuendo arising from the missing words was milked. If all else failed, he just shouted 'bum!' The wholesome *Match Game* had a feeling it wasn't on KOAM-TV Kansas any more.

The British adaptation of Kennedy's adaptation, subtly renamed *Blankety Blank,* was launched by the BBC on 18 January 1979

– the very bottom of the year. The UK was already up to speed with the 'wall of quipping celebs' format, with ITV having adapted *The Hollywood Squares* – a US format that post-dated *Match Game* – into the slick Bob Monkhouse vehicle *Celebrity Squares*. That show stacked its stars in a three-by-three formation, while *Blankety Blank* went for two rows of three. Otherwise there was only one fundamental difference between the two shows, but what a difference it was.

The son of a Limerick grocer, Terry Wogan made his name in Irish radio in the 1960s as a disc jockey and on television replacing Gay Byrne as host of Ireland's first game show, *Jackpot*. When the BBC assimilated elements of the offshore pirate broadcasters into its national radio line-up, Wogan was also inducted, and soon forged a dreamy, chatty manner, heavy on the whimsical non-sequiturs. He amassed over seven and a half million regular listeners to his Radio Two breakfast show, and his commentaries for the Eurovision Song Contest added a welcome layer of homely scepticism to the international MOR tournament. If anyone could make a go of this inane format it was him.

From the opening theme music, the show was seemingly designed to sour the sherry of the BBC governors. Ronnie Hazlehurst, the number one light entertainment composer, turned in a four-note motif that sounded like a cashpoint's nervous breakdown. Wogan, light-suited and brandishing a slim silver microphone (a copy of Gene Rayburn's original) was the only mobile figure on stage. Contestants from central suburban casting (here's Nigel Creffield, who works in the plywood business) came and went via a turntable, not even trusted to negotiate a flight of illuminated stairs. From the first, the tone was one of resigned stoicism: 'You've already met the creatures from the black lagoon . . . let's meet the plain but honest people of England'; 'Lennie Bennett, what are you doing these days, as if anybody cared?' Not for Tel the one-man party atmosphere of the US hosting regime.

Nothing was talked up, least of all the micro-achievement of thinking of the same word as Gary Davies. Even commiserations were barbed: 'It's hard to think in these circumstances, particularly when you're surrounded by eejits.' The hollowness of the enterprise was out there in the open. The American aspirational dream had its wings clipped with a stout pair of British garden shears (which is roughly what a score of fifty blanks would win you). At no point did anyone concerned forget the reality of the situation: nine grown-ups in a television studio doing something inescapably stupid. Only a change of host in 1984 modified the Soviet bread queue vibe. With Les Dawson presenting, it became a wet whist drive in purgatory.

Yet *Blankety Blank* was insanely popular. From a tentative debut it shot up the ratings to third place, just behind *Coronation Street* and *This Is Your Life*.[333] This caused some embarrassment to BBC bosses, keen to paint their channel as the home of quality acts like *Life on Earth* and *The Voyage of Charles Darwin*. 'They regard it as a bit silly,' admitted an insider, 'more the kind of quiz show that ITV puts on.'[334] Reluctantly, 'the most imbecilic programme in the history of the world'[335] was renewed for the autumn season, where it promptly started pulling in nearly twenty-three million viewers, making headlines through the power of pure crapulence.[336] With woks, croquet sets and self-assembly greenhouses as the ultimate reward, any accusations of contest rigging would have been laughed out of court.

Set among the serious entertainment of the 1979 schedule, *Blankety Blank* provided a corrective to the main diet of gut-punching drama and showbiz ostentation. Years later, when plummeting budgets led to a more widespread adoption of its apologetic shrug, the effect was lost. Twenty-first century evenings burst at the seams with cookery contests and celebrity jousts decked out in the knowingly guilty fashion that says 'Yes, we *know* we're better than this, but come on, so are you, and here we both are, eh?' When ironic underachievement becomes the rule rather than the exception, when everything's a guilty pleasure and no-one makes the effort, you're in trouble. 'The only consolation to be derived from this ongoing débâcle,' wrote John Naughton of *Blankety Blank*, 'is the thought that a TV programme can never be worse than its viewers; for the more stupid it is, the more stupid they are to watch it.'[337]

LIFE ON EARTH (1979)
BBC Two (BBC/Warner Brothers/ Reiner Moritz)

The apex of the educational blockbuster.

WHEN TELEVISION STARTED TO educate the people, it looked to the universities for interlocutors. Some made a notably better fist of it than others. An early success, Professor Alan Taylor gave historical lectures which may seem staid by modern standards but at the time were praised as 'mischievous, and his satirical remarks about history have the authentic dig of the irreverent, independent mind.'[338] Charisma was the quality that would sort television's men of intellect from the mumbling, donnish boys.

In the late 1960s, BBC Two controller David Attenborough commissioned Sir Kenneth Clark to produce a history of Western art, with no location too exotic. *Civilisation*, the first of the authored blockbuster documentary series known in the trade as 'sledgehammers', was born. Jacob Bronowski's *Ascent of Man*, also greenlit by Attenborough, concentrated on scientific advancement. The genre soon attracted dissidents, with John Berger's *Ways of Seeing* and James Burke's *Connections* arguing across Clark and Bronowski respectively – all on BBC Two. When he retired from executive office, the man who'd introduced the sledgehammer took charge of one of his own.

The natural history TV film evolved from the basic chimp-on-a-table exhibitions of George Canston's *All About Animals* into two distinct species. The lecture, usually consisting of wildlife footage strung together over a voice track, was simple and respectable. Less so was the explorer's diary, in which flamboyant experts toting pith helmets and snorkels – Armand and Michaela Denis in Africa, Hans and Lotte Hass or Jacques Cousteau in the sea – chronicled their fearless sojourns to the outer reaches, often usurping their zoological quarry as their own central subject.

Attenborough had a foot in both camps, having produced straight lectures like Sir Julian Huxley's *The Pattern of Animals* and hopped into khaki shorts himself to front the massively popular *Zoo Quest*. He built a new type of programme that fused the best of the lecture and the explorer's diary formats, taking the authority of the former and the showmanship of the latter. David Bellamy was already taking the world of botany for an enthusiastic, cactus-hugging ride on ITV. For zoology, Attenborough went much further.

Each of *Life on Earth*'s thirteen editions would deal with one evolutionary step along the archaeological timeline. More than thirty cameramen brought back footage from exploratory South American treks – lugging heavy and fragile equipment deep into rainforests and up to the rims of volcanic craters – to microscopic laboratory work, patiently waiting for a dragonfly to shed its skin or a breeding pair of deadly spiders to start going steady.

Each programme started, in all senses, with a wide view. Attenborough set the scene in aeons past, walking through a prehistoric landscape (often Yellowstone National Park), lifeless rock and sulphurous seas up to the horizon. The landscape presented an evolutionary challenge. The camera zoomed in to a hand-held fossil, mixing into micro-photography from the programme's many laboratory set-ups. (Only rarely did the footage need help from that cop-out of TV nature shows past, the watercolour artist's impression.)

Time was just as easily manipulated: a fern could show a month's worth of growth in ten seconds, and the exquisite mechanics of a beetle's wings were decelerated a hundredfold. A lot of scientific ground was covered, but it never felt like hard work keeping up. The specific case having illustrated the general point, the camera refocused on Attenborough, succinctly wrapping up with a tantalising glimpse of next week's treasures. The grim prospect of waiting a whole seven days was offset by a mid-week repeat, often devoured by eager viewers as a second helping. This wasn't TV made to be casually glanced at – by constantly outdoing itself visually, it challenged you to take your eyes off the screen from one moment to the next. You couldn't miss a frame.

The Pre-Cambrian oddness of the early shows made the series a hard sell internationally. American executives were not overjoyed about the series kicking off with what they anticipated as an hour of green slime.[339] In the end PBS was *Life on Earth*'s only American outlet, with network suggestions of an American alternative narrator – Robert Redford was a favourite candidate – calmly but firmly batted back.

Attenborough somehow managed to flit through time and space, laying down the origins of everything alive while remaining humble. He wore his knowledge lightly, and his enthusiasm like an old sweater over the shoulders. In Attenborough's eyes, if a peacock was a miracle, so was a hagfish. He hymned them all in gentle tones, letting the cameramen do the majority of the work.

Over the next thirty-five years, *Life* . . . became an accidental franchise with ever bigger, more technically advanced, more visually spectacular sequels. It's true that the visuals, more than anything else, have helped this strain of the sledgehammer series to survive in the harsh wastelands of the twenty-first century schedule. There's always a sense of more to be shown. Blue whales look progressively more imposing with every leap in camera technology, while a Caravaggio remains the same Caravaggio. The nature documentary looks like lasting as long as its subject – although as Attenborough's more recent programmes point out, how long that might be is anyone's guess.

MINDER (1979–94)
ITV (Euston Films)

The comedy drama becomes a nice little earner.

THE FIRST FOUR DECADES of British television had little use for the entrepreneur. Between the state-funded BBC monolith and the old-style entertainment palaces of the independent channel, there was little room for the sort of seat-of-the-pants backroom set-up on which much of the nation's cinematic glory had rested. Programmes were made, by and large, by the channels that ran them, and were seldom expected to be seen anywhere else. The chief exception was ITC, Lew Grade's transatlantic action-fantasy partnership, but that always seemed at the mercy of American money and tastes. In the late sixties executives at Thames, a new and forward-thinking independent station, took the plunge and inaugurated a fully home-grown filmed drama unit. Euston Films was born.

Euston eschewed standard TV practice. With no large permanent studio at their disposal, production was entirely location-based. When a major series got underway, London would be scoured for a 'base' – an abandoned public building or disused warehouse – which would serve as production HQ, rehearsal space and home for any regularly occurring sets. Everything else was shot on location, with as slender a crew as possible and maximum efficiency.

The first production, *ITV Playhouse* entry *Suspect*, achieved an authentically dilapidated look thanks to the new method and the experience of its director: *World in Action* graduate Mike Hodges used hand-held cameras for a style later christened 'wobblyscope'.[340]

Directors were valued at Euston – American conveyor belt productions often mutilated a director's intentions in the editing room, but Euston gave Hodges and his cohorts final cut, getting better quality results and attracting greater talent. These aesthetic achievements produced commercial success through two block-buster police series, the violent *Special Branch* and the more soph-isticated *The Sweeney*, creating a crime sub-genre of their own: two-fisted, foul-mouthed and bleary-eyed, with every trace of American cop show glamour ruthlessly expunged. Its unofficial title was 'kick, bollock and scramble'.

Leon Griffiths was a writer with a solid and wide-ranging portfolio stretching back to *The Adventures of Robin Hood*. One of his most notable works was 1965 sitcom *A Slight Case Of . . .*, which starred Roy Kinnear as a shady operator professing to work very high up in a different profession each week – out-manoeuv-ring, swindling and generally one-upping his competitors with high-flying patter and low moral standards. Another was *Dinner at the Sporting Club*, a downbeat *Play for Today* set in the sleazy world of small-time prize-fighting, where dreams were ground into the canvas and the best anyone could hope for was being slipped a fur coat as a backhander or saving enough for 'a down-payment on a bungalow out in Ongar'. When Thames were looking for a replacement flagship series for the freshly decommissioned *Sweeney*, Griffiths gave them a combination of these two shows, placing the comic wide boy into real, inescapable dramatic situations.

Minder was conceived as '*The Magnificent Seven* minus six,'[341] the misadventures of a professional minder operating in the grey area between legitimate business and organised crime. It followed the pattern of *Budgie*, Keith Waterhouse and Willis Hall's under-world sleaze-com from the other end of the decade, with the awkward corners knocked off and less salubrious values thrown into storage. Terry McCann is an ex-boxer who fell into violent crime and now works through a kind of East End purgatory as a hired heavy to various physically vulnerable clients. Griffiths stressed from the outset that Tel was the strong, silent type, more likely to use his nous to prevent a situation flaring up than to wade in with fists flying. The aim was to instil a sense of menace without the 'shattered balsa-wood bannisters' of *The Sweeney*. And lest ITV's moral guardians quail at making heroes of ne'er-do-wells, a simple, transcendent morality ran through the series. 'Although Terry sometimes finds it hard to distinguish between legal right and wrong he is always certain about good and bad.'[342]

Dennis Waterman, junior partner in *The Sweeney*, did the part of Tel justice, neither overplaying the lovable rogue or acting dim for laughs. But for many the real star was Tel's sole agent and confidant Arthur Daley, a borderline respectable conman who knew everyone from East End thugs to Mayfair socialites, yet always had a consignment of gentlemen's literature in his lock-up awaiting shipping. George Cole, former protégé of the great Alastair Sim, was Arfur incarnate from brogues to trilby. A fully certified comic actor, he knew how to turn down the jokey business many straight actors would have wrongly piled on. With a mantle of streetwise confidence sitting on his shoulders as snugly as his camel hair coat, Arfur introduced young Terence to the denizens of the underworld with the wise wit of a Castella-sucking Virgil: 'She caught the old man in bed with the au pair and took him for the national debt'; 'He's got a degree in sociology. He still does the thieving but now he knows why.' Guest star villains were drawn from the cream of the character-acting crop: Kenneth Griffith, Alfie Bass, Max Wall. Script, actors and locale were perfectly matched.

The show took a while to establish itself. The first episode transmitted shortly after the end of a three-month ITV strike, so publicity was practically non-existent – but it soon outstripped expectations. After a couple of series the reason for this success was unearthed: *Minder*, though firmly tucked in after the 9 p.m. watershed, was playing to a family audience. Not the traditional notional family audience, settling down to a Sunday evening period romp with crumpets on the trolley, but an organically grown one of kids allowed to stay up late. One 1983 survey estimated nearly half of

Britain's twelve to fifteen-year-olds were at least semi-regular watchers, fluent in the ways of the Winchester Club.[343]

ITV turned an entirely appropriate blind eye to this transgression, and marketed the programme to kids as much as adults: Waterman and Cole started turning up in character on children's programmes; there was a novelty Christmas single 'What Are We Gonna Get for 'Er Indoors?' and a spin-off computer game enabling kids to trade ballcocks and dirty books for a tidy bundle in their own bedrooms. Eventually this appeal began to affect the quality, as off-the-peg swindling capers swamped the well-observed character work, but most of the time *Minder* was a trans-generational joy, a crafty shandy in the beer garden of TV drama.

NOW GET OUT OF THAT (1981–5)
BBC One

Personal incompetence becomes a spectator sport.

THE HIGH CONCEPT, PRODUCER-LED programmes that form the core of terrestrial broadcasting in the twenty-first century are painted as something new and utterly modern. Their Year Zero was 1999, when *Big Brother* was first transmitted on Dutch TV station Veronica on 16 September. But however achingly fresh the show, it doesn't take much work to dig up some vintage ancestors.

Take the millennial incarnation of *Top Gear*. Did any twentieth century show shamelessly take a blokey, suburban hobby out of the garden shed, pump it full of testosterone, set fire to it and push it into a canyon for laughs? Well, there was BBC Two's 1976 squib *The Fishing Race*, a raucous, semi-scripted pseudo-competition devised by sports writer Ian Wooldridge, pitting three teams against each other for a sixty-hour dash across the UK in specially tooled-up Range Rovers to catch as many species of fish as possible, including stingray in the Thames and piranhas in Essex, slagging and sabotaging their rivals all the while. It was silly, offbeat and over the top, condemned by the National Angling Council for not treating the sport with 'due solemnity'.[344] Unrepentant, the team took to Sweden for a second series, augmented the four-wheeled transport with speedboats and helicopters, and the cast with rugby star Gareth Edwards and a naked woman in a canoe. Though fuelled by Watney's rather than Stella, laddish abandon was present and incorrect.

Channel Four pre-empted their own recent success story *Gogglebox* by nearly thirty years with *Open the Box*, which invited Oxford psychologists to install cameras in the nation's front rooms to observe the public watching television. As with the twenty-first century incarnation, choice epigrams flowed like fine wine. 'She's a lot of use, isn't she,' muttered one Mrs Brown, watching *Dallas*'s Pam Ewing emoting helplessly as husband Bobby was gunned down, 'fucking around like that. Get a bloody ambulance!' In a further twist, the subjects were shown the recordings of themselves watching TV, which they then watched on TV, their reactions in turn recorded for posterity. 'So much self consciousness,' lamented Julian Barnes, 'so little insight.'[345]

Then there's another modern format, which lumps together two teams of self-regarding dimwits, lumbers them with some fiddly task which we can see is plainly beyond their meagre abilities (though they of course must never realise that), and films them bickering, backstabbing and falling on their collective arse while a hired smart Alec rolls his eyes theatrically in the background. This clan is headed by business-oriented sneer-along *The Apprentice*, but it can trace its lineage back to *Now Get Out of That*, BBC One's outdoor puzzle-solving romp launched in the dog days of 1981.

Described by its deviser Derek Smith as an 'open-air action crossword', *Now Get Out of That* sent two teams (initially Oxford vs. Cambridge, latterly Brits against the Yanks) stumbling across overcast hillsides, surviving on badly-cooked rabbit and applying logical brainstorming to such tasks as retrieving a Land Rover from a swamp with nine yards of rope, a milk bottle and a house brick. All rather wholesome, really.

Fortunately, there was Bernard Falk. Blessed with a raised eyebrow of a voice, Falk sat snugly in a presentation studio, watching and reprimanding the contestants' windswept fumblings with all the sarcastic devices of the TV viewer at his disposal. There was the sarcastic riposte. ('Why am I standing in the middle of a river in my swimming costume?' 'You might well ask!') The sarcastic reversal. ('Here's Tony, showing all those qualities of leadership that inspire others to follow without question.' Cue Tony being shouted at while squatting miserably in a stream.) The sarcastic benefit-of-the-doubt. ('Either they like the extra work, or this lot can't measure eight feet properly.')

Stripped across a week of teatimes – then a novel scheduling approach, hitherto restricted to Scottish soap operas and embassy sieges – the show thrived in the only niche it could have hoped to occupy, the frivolous teatime filler slot. It served its humble station perfectly. The *Guardian* called *Now Get Out of That* 'hypnotic viewing, truly terrible but unmissable once you get stuck in. This is as moronic as you could hope for.'[346] Over eight million viewers agreed.

It was all based on army survival games of the type which had lately been adapted by some wily entrepreneurs and flogged to corporations as staff 'team building' exercises. In this way, it was a consummately eighties programme, and more vocational frolics would follow. Various ITV regions aired their own knockout competitions for businesses, typified by Granada's *Flying Start*, though these tended to be the driest game shows imaginable. ('Who's likely to create most jobs – the canvas bag maker from Chester, the Runcorn firm which makes healthy Middle Eastern snacks, or the welders from Winsford?')

What distinguishes *Now Get Out of That*, *The Fishing Race* and countless other proto-reality programmes from their modern descendants is their modest nature. Made on a shoestring for the scheduling wilderness, these shows were never intended as anything more than a bit of close-season tomfoolery to mark time while entertainment's big guns were stripped and reloaded. The idea that they might ever be the main draw, or even come to represent the station in the mind's eye of the nation, would have been laughed out of the boardroom. Whimsical, impromptu fun, yes, but flagship material? What a load of old toot.

ARTEMIS 81 (1981)
BBC One

Christmas holiday viewing doesn't get tougher than this.

IT WAS NO DOUBT near the bottom of their list of priorities, but the incoming Conservative government of 1979 had it in for state subsidised drama, especially the sort that attracted the epithet 'pretentious'. Pretension is a slippery word, one that often says more about the person employing it than their target. It becomes a catch-all synonym for 'ambitious', 'solemn', 'confusing' – anything the critic finds a chore. As hard-headed populism swamped the corridors of power, the P-word was heard more than ever.

From May 1979, the word started appearing a lot more in discussions of subsidised theatre, and especially the BBC. Licence payers' money, it was decreed, shouldn't be frittered away on the impenetrable, obscene outpourings of the beard-and-polo-neck militia. One of the first casualties of the new regime was *Solid Geometry*, Ian McEwan's complex trawl through mathematics and sexuality. Two days before shooting began, the play was summarily canned by Head of Network Production Phil Sidey, who explained his reasoning in concrete terms to David Hare. 'How do you think it would look,' he confided, 'if, just as Margaret Thatcher was about to be elected, we were stupid enough to record a play which featured a twelve-inch penis in a fucking bottle?'[347]

David Rudkin was another prime candidate for the priggish chop. His stage debut *Afore Night Come*, a tense tableau of ritual slaughter among volunteer apple pickers in his native Worcestershire, took its place alongside works by Pinter and Beckett in the early 1960s 'dirty plays' controversy, which precipitated the abolition of stage censorship by the Lord Chamberlain. Given a few drama slots on TV, he emerged as 'a playwright of strange powers, with a capacity to illuminate the dark crannies of the soul'.[348] Despite swimming directly against the mainstream, he scored a big hit in 1974 with *Penda's Fen*, the emotional awakening of a repressed vicar's son in a riot of ancient legends, homoerotic wet dreams, government conspiracies, severed hands and Elgar symphonies.

Summarised, Rudkin sounds distant and humourless, but this wasn't the case. *The Sons of Light*, a sprawling, solemn and portentous epic staged by the RSC in 1977, featured a scene in which the saturnine Dr Nebewohl, overseer of a post-apocalyptic underground mine staffed by zombified slave children, whips off his dark glasses – to reveal another pair of dark glasses underneath. This same gag would turn up – presumably coincidentally – in the comedy film *Airplane!* three years later.

But despite such moments, *The Sons of Light* was heavy going. 'It's as if he had taken a plot from *Doctor Who*,' wrote Michael Billington, 'and rewritten it in the language of the Authorised Version.'[349] A later, even darker stage play, *The Triumph of Death*, was likened by Michael Coveney to 'watching a dramatist topple over the edge then clamber up to the summit only to leap joyously once more into the abyss.'[350]

Rudkin operated from the centre of an impenetrably dense personal mythology. So naturally the BBC, at the word of commissioning editor David Rose, spent half a million pounds[351] on bringing it to the nation's front rooms over the 1981 Christmas holidays.

The result was three hours long and enigmatically titled *Artemis 81*. Director Alastair Reid described it as 'a television Rubik's Cube.'[352] No two plot summaries were the same, and it definitely looked like tough going for those torpid evenings between Boxing Day and New Year's Eve, but the British media were still receptive to ambitious television. Even the red tops offered good will. 'Don't worry about understanding it,' reassured the *Daily Mirror*, 'just relax and enjoy it.'[353]

This was easier said than done. From nine till midnight on Tuesday 29 December, BBC One broadcast one of the most densely symbolic, allusive and obscure pieces of television ever made. (The commercial channel were showing – what else? – Trevor Nunn's production of Chekhov's *Three Sisters*.) Flitting from a North Sea Ferry to Liverpool Cathedral to a laser-festooned slave camp buried under a Welsh mountain to an alien planet with two suns, *Artemis 81* was a thicket of classical Gods, fragmented relics, Hitchcock blondes, dry ice, master organists, trolleybuses full of consumptive Danes, abused jellyfish and mass clinical torture with muzak accompaniment. Low on explanatory dialogue and rich in meditative atmospherics, it was, even by Rudkin's own standards, extraordinary.

Hywel Bennett was the nominal protagonist, a fantasy author who stumbles from one weird piece of the puzzle to the next, sporting an expression of quizzical determination throughout. The name that got the papers excited, though, was Sting. This was a time when rock stars and heavyweight TV drama were in alignment – Sting would next star in the cinema version of Dennis Potter's banned *Brimstone and Treacle*, while David Bowie turned up a couple of months into 1982 playing the title role in Bertolt Brecht's *Baal*. In *Artemis 81*, Sting didn't exactly do much apart from drift moodily across the landscape in a cowl and dangle from a helicopter, but his teen appeal put him top of the publicity pecking order.

As a whole, *Artemis 81* struck a chord with the same thoughtful teenagers who'd fallen for *Penda's Fen* – many of them still shell-shocked from the traumatic finale of space opera *Blake's Seven* the previous week – but adults were less entranced. The reviews weren't nearly as forgiving as the previews. The *Listener*, admirably reluctant to wheel out the P-word, found it 'absorbing, bounteously over-stuffed,'[354] but the general impression was of a large egg painfully laid. 'The tail-end turkey of the year,' snorted the *Express*, 'turned out to be three hours of codswallop.'[355]

It wasn't that, but it was no flawless classic. Half a million quid was extravagant for the time, but it wasn't nearly enough to illustrate the apocalyptic cities, swarms of ravens and mythic alien worlds Rudkin's script demanded, despite some resourceful production shortcuts. Rudkin's preference for long, portentous speeches instead of naturalistic dialogue was another problem, making comparisons with the cheesier end of science fiction inevitable, though Bennett's character's girlfriend got a good speech tearing into the cheap end of the fantasy genre. 'In your stories . . . man is a moral child, because you who tell them are yourself a moral child. Those who so love your books are moral children, too. For them the world's too much.'

For the 1980s, Rudkin was too much. David Rose jumped ship to the new Channel Four, and Rudkin made only two more TV appearances for the rest of the decade. Fearful of getting its fingers burned on such a scale again, the Beeb wound in their commitment to dramatic experiment. Many argued they were throwing out the ambitious baby with the pretentious bathwater, lamenting the loss of 'the right to fail' – a noble mantra that unfortunately just served to drive home that final, four-letter word in the ears of executives who heard it. As time went by, though, even they came to agree that something special had been lost: the sort of television Nancy Banks-Smith once described as 'made with great skill, devotion, beauty . . . and no mercy.'[356]

HILL STREET BLUES (1981–7)
NBC (MTM)

The cop show disintegrates, and reassembles.

No matter how well intentioned you are when you go out to do a cop show, it's almost impossible not to end up with a bag of shit afterward.

Michael Kozoll, co-creator, *Hill Street Blues*

THE GREAT BREAKTHROUGH IN police drama, the one that separates the old world of wisecracking maverick gumshoes from the new world of fallible folk desperately holding the fort, is often depicted as instantaneous. One minute Kojak is inhaling kids' lollipops and shouting for Crocker, the next Captain Frank Furillo is contending with an officer down, a rogue lawyer and pressure from his ambitious junior staff to take early retirement all at once. The gulf between crime on the screen and on the street decisively narrowed overnight. Things were more gradual than that.

Upon his appointment as President of NBC in 1978, Fred Silverman began shopping around for a police programme with grit. Cinematic portrayals of crime-fighting had taken a dive into the seedy and morally dubious over the past few years. Silverman felt this should be reflected with something a few degrees tougher than recent hits like *The Rockford Files* and *Police Woman*. At MTM Productions, Steven Bochco and Michael Kozoll, veteran writers of *Quincy, Columbo* and *Ironside*, envisioned a cop show that worked like a soap opera: one that didn't reset at the end of each episode; where the characters remembered, evolved, became worn down and grew before the viewer's eyes.

In Britain this was nothing new – Troy Kennedy Martin's *Z-Cars* had turned this trick on the BBC nearly twenty years ago – but the American crime drama was firmly cast in self-contained, heroic mode. Bochco and Kozoll looked to other genres. Workplace banter and social unease were there in sitcoms like *M*A*S*H* and *Barney Miller*, which also had an ethnically mixed cast that avoided stereotype, with its liberal ex-Marine and African-American sergeant who wrote memoirs on the side.

To this soft soap they added harsh abrasives. Their previous collaboration, *Delvecchio*, was a routinely episodic story where Judd Hirsch had the guilty banged up by the epilogue. But Delvecchio had compassion. Not the 'tough love' one-liners of the old school 'tecs', staring into the middle distance and musing tritely on the bad hand life had dealt the scum they'd apprehended, before grabbing a Danish and wiping the moral slate clean. This was full-blown liberalism: a constant burden on the conscience of the law, bullishly masked with streetwise gags and worldly cross-talk. In *Hill Street Blues*, this wit was distributed among everyone: cops, gangsters, hookers and Puerto Rican kids alike drew crystal clear epigrams from deep wells of bitter experience. Then, just when it looked like the cast were going to collapse under the weight of their own lay wisdom, they started playing infantile pranks against each other with candy cockroaches and butcher's offal. The creators themselves exhibited an unquenchable thirst for toilet humour, getting scatology into the script as often as Program Practices would allow. This was an indulgence, but it still contributed to reality – the gents' toilet became an unofficial secondary briefing room, much like in a real station.

Much like a real captain, Frank Furillo (Daniel J. Travanti) was besieged on all fronts, taking it from his own men, his superiors and the press as much as from the criminal element. He didn't make things any easier for himself by conducting a dangerous affair with the station's resident public defender. Joyce Davenport (Veronica Hamel) was a new type, the tough but glamorous high-flying professional woman, a role so enticingly fresh it just had to be trodden into cliché by the end of the decade. At the other end of just about every scale, Lt. Howard Hunter was a special weapons zealot who made John Wayne look like Jimmy Carter. A character who could so easily have become a *Police Academy* punchline was redeemed by a writers' campaign of strategic humiliation, from losing an assault tank to impotence and a cancer scare, and an Emmy-nominated performance from James B. Sikking. Even walk-on parts were carefully considered. It was a living, breathing, farting, swearing world.

The most immediately striking thing about *Hill Street Blues* was the way it looked. Much of this was down to line producer Greg Hoblit and director Robert Butler. The network's model for the series was recent Paul Newman vehicle *Fort Apache: The Bronx*, a popular but unspectacular slice of ghetto sleaze that used industrial no man's land locations to good effect, but suffered from banal direction. Butler had a hatred for the traditional visual syntax of establishing shot followed by cuts back and forth between two characters who politely took it in turns to do the talking. It was unreal, lethargic and deadly dull.

Butler's visual bible was *The Police Tapes*, a 1977 PBS documentary covering the same locale as *Fort Apache*, but shot on a smudgy portable video camera, giving a frustratingly messy, chaotic view of street confrontation. To ape this look as closely as possible, Butler suggested black-and-white 16mm film stock full of bobbing and weaving camera moves.[357] The network insisted on full colour 35mm like every other show, but allowed the hand-held work to remain. Like *World in Action*'s Tim Hewat, Butler abhorred polish as the enemy of realism. 'Don't use the stuff once the shot has settled down,' he told his editors. 'Use the bad stuff. It's terrific.'[358] The result was an atmospheric cacophony of muted colour, woozy motion and competitive yammering, plunging the viewer into the urban maelstrom right from the opening moments of Sgt Esterhaus's quick-fire morning roll call. It took more mental effort than *Kojak* demanded, but the rewards were far greater.

Hill Street Blues had a troublesome birth. The first season thrilled the critics and surfed a tidal wave of Emmy nominations, but ratings were dire. It took network goodwill, and not a little creative bartering, to ensure a second run of thirteen episodes. Hoblit reckoned it was 'the lowest-rated renewed show in the history of television.'[359] Even after it became a fixture, things remained dicey. A Writers' Guild strike in 1982 took its toll on the quality of the scripts, as did network insistence that more story strands come to a satisfactory conclusion by the end of each episode. Quality began to decline, and stunts covered the cracks. The seventh and final season didn't even figure in the Emmy nominations for outstanding drama – a flop by the show's lofty standards. But its bold synthesis of difficult elements lasted as long as could be reasonably expected against television's glide into blandness.

The show established a new direction for mainstream drama. Its influence remains tangible, though not all its imitators flatter. Butler's camerawork is probably the most obvious legacy, its ubiquity bordering on infamy. Some time in the late 1990s, hand-held camera became the default visual aesthetic for TV drama. It wasn't restricted to street locations: before long even period drama was dripping with shaky telephoto takes. A generation of hacks discovered a way to add visual interest, even a sense of urgency, with minimal expense and creative effort. The style seeped into sitcoms, game shows, even cheery commercials for bingo websites. A bold directorial risk had grown into a cheap, context-free add-on, as much a part of the optical furniture as the use of close-ups or colour. What began as an augmentation of already highly advanced realism became, at worst, a lazy substitute for it.

Hill Street Blues also pioneered, in its own modest way, another twenty-first century mainstay: online audience interaction. The producers hooked up with *The Source*, a primitive information exchange service used by roughly 17,000 computer users, inviting them to share and discuss their opinions on the series as it played out over the season.[360] *The Source*'s effect on the show might have been minimal, but the willingness to listen to and cater for a discerning, educated and – hopefully – loyal band of fans would, thirty years on, become a priority for TV dramas faced with shrinking budgets and multiplying competitors, finding it all the more important to heed Sgt Esterhaus's motto: 'Let's be careful out there.'

THE OXFORD ROAD
SHOW (1981–5)
BBC Two

When 'youth' TV tried far too hard.

FOLLOWING PUNK'S EXPLOSION OF discord and nasal haber-dashery, questions were asked of television's predilection to douse the kids with non-stop rhythmic licentiousness. *Broadcasting and Youth*, a 1979 report commissioned by various organisations including the BBC and IBA, concluded that 'the 14-21 age group does have needs distinct from the totality of the adult population' not adequately served by TV, which was 'offering "circuses" when what they need is "bread".' For the next decade, the video toaster went into overdrive.

The first specimen, Chris Tarrant's *Kidsworld,* was a magazine programme which aimed to serve the kids' needs by putting them in charge. In a phrase that was to become wearyingly familiar, it was 'a magazine for young people, presented by young people'. *The London Weekend Show* was a spin-off from LWT's Friday news magazine *The Six O'Clock Show,* masterminded by Janet Street-Porter. 'London's fast-moving programme for young people' covered everything from pirate radio to Barry Sheene to 'why more and more children are burning down their schools'.

BBC One's *Something Else* opened with a timely montage of Damned posters and venereal disease leaflets. Its content was decided by a hundred-strong teenage panel, from which its presenters were drawn. A typical edition featured collectively

written and performed sketches interspersed with public information films on what you could legally get up to at the age of fifteen,
and music from Sad Café and Secret Affair (the choice of bands
was also rigorously put to the vote).

Such a doggedly democratic programme could justly claim to
be 'by teenagers for teenagers'. 'What the kids on *Something Else*
have got that TV producers obviously lack,' said the *NME*'s Phill
McNeill, 'is *empathy*. I mean, suppose you forget about technical
wizardry, fancy dress audiences and pristine studios, and just put
a band in a conducive situation in front of a small, genuinely
responsive audience and then *concentrate on getting the best out of
the group!* Y'know, it might just work . . .'[361]

Janet Street-Porter's next LWT venture, *20th Century Box*, was
a programme 'for and about young people' made, in modish black-
and-white, in association with the London Minorities Unit. The
first series tackled an uneven mixture of hobbies and 'issues' from
dog grooming to incest. It stood out in two ways: it boasted a slick
graphical title sequence to the music of John Foxx, and a genuinely
smart and personable presenter, Danny Baker.

The high spot was a look at 'the growth of gang fights in the
towns and villages around Watford and Aylesbury,' which, in its
hilariously bathetic scenes of bored rural skinheads telephoning
desperately around to try and organise a regional rumpus for the
cameras, said more about teenagers' lives than any number of
hard-hitting urban exposés. The *Observer* predicted Baker, with
presumably laudatory intent, would be 'a cockney Parkinson for
the 1990s'.

The mutual suspicion between television and youth was crippling.
Nevertheless, 1981 saw the advent of the longest-lived, and most
reviled, of the right-on youth magazines. Again, The Kids were
consulted at every step. After punk, TV's relationship to youth
culture had gone beyond anthropology and was now in the realm
of quantum experimentation: the very act of observation skewed
the results. When the BBC's *Arena* arts strand made a study of
earnest New Wavers Sham 69, the small hand-held camera they

deployed to cover a gig (operated by Philip Bonham-Carter, brother of Helena) spurred some skinheads to comprehensively break up the place, and helped the band itself implode.

Broadcast from the BBC's Manchester studios on Oxford Road, 'opposite Amigo's Café and just past the faulty traffic lights,' *The Oxford Road Show* promised to be 'a live and lucid look at the week.' Its main presenters were a trifle doddery: Rob Rohrer, ex-*Sunday Times* Insight journalist, and former Cambridge Footlights performer Martin Bergman ('the thinking man's David Frost') lacked Baker's street cred, but were soon joined by the more youthful Jackie Spreckley and Paula Yates.

After a quiet try-out, a rejigged second series, this time with Spreckley and Robert Elms as main presenters, was trumpeted abroad. 'Every Friday there will be 150 people on the set sounding off, questioning, caring and generally carrying on in a way that's bound to upset some older viewers,' reported John Craven. 'Because involvement is what the show is all about, the Manchester switchboard will be open until 9 p.m. after the programme for reactions,' he explained, 'and if they choose to ignore it in their millions they can, in the words of the production team, "belt up about the fact that TV doesn't cater for them or provide a platform for their views".'[362]

This effort to silence derision was doomed, with the hapless enthusiasm of the presenters provoking the worst brickbats. 'Robert Elms poses as the representative for happy vacuity,' sniped Ian Penman. 'When he smiles one fears that his whole face shall disappear between his teeth.'[363] One correspondent attacked the general patronising youth tone in spookily modern terms, bemoaning 'the great levelling-down fever that grips much of the communication industry today'.[364] Clive James identified youth presenters' propensity 'to talk a strenuously classless language from which all consonants have been removed.'[365] All identified a condescending insincerity – a trendy vicar in a studded dog collar.

It wasn't just critics who mocked. In an attempt to leaven the earnest debate, the *Road Show* booked alternative comics including

Ben Elton, Adrian Edmondson and Rik Mayall. They exacted their revenge the following year in the pilot episode of student sitcom *The Young Ones*, creating *Nozin' Aroun'*, a painfully hip programme 'for YOUNG ADULTS, by YOUNG ADULTS'. ('I'm standing up here on this scaffolding because that's what this programme is all about: shock!') After that, the show had a drastic clear-out, putting Radio One veteran Peter Powell in charge of 'TV's electronic magazine', now chummily abbreviated to *ORS*. The final 1985 run went for broke with different celebrity hosts each week and a phone-in Megaquiz captained by Timmy Mallett.

Youth TV soldiered on. BBC2's *Sixteen Up* air-dropped the likes of lawyer Paul Boateng into regional coffee bars with modish names like The Negative Café and Action Space for some heartfelt civil rights chit-chat, 'with interruptions from John Cooper Clarke,' a sort of apocalyptic Ollie Beak. The *Observer* judged it 'remorselessly glum'. Channel Four contributed *Whatever You Want*, the most radical show of all, which lured the kids with the promise of Wham!, and hit them with lengthy political discussions chaired by Keith Allen. Some small infamy was achieved when a vicar stormed out as fringe actors simulated sex on stage. Then Allen made history when, in protest at the butchering of a film on trade unions, he stormed out of his own show.

Such transgressions were the exception for a format that, much as it denied it, had more in common with a church youth club than street-level insurrection. In the late eighties it retreated into precisely that pious mantle, as ex-choirboy Aled Jones interviewed reformed glue sniffers for HTV's *Chatterbox*. When Jonathan Meades visited the set, he discovered a sinister green room containing 'more orange squash than I've ever seen.'[366] Maybe this was what the kids wanted all along.

JANE (1982–4)
BBC Two

The apotheosis of television's flagship special effect.

THE STORY IS TOLD of Andrew Gosling, young and enthusiastic television director with a keen interest in technology, on the set of 1978 Christmas fantasy special *The Light Princess*. His task for the day was to initiate Irene Handl, veteran actress of stage and screen, scion of European aristocracy and obsessive Elvis Presley fan, into the mysteries of Colour Separation Overlay.

'You see,' he began, 'I shall be filming you against this blue screen. Now, at the editing stage, a special electronic device will remove the blue from the picture and replace it with all the wonderful phantasmagoria our animators can dream up, so it will look as if you're standing in the middle of this fantastical realm. All you have to do is . . .'

'I'm sorry, dear,' interrupted Irene, 'you're confusing me . . .'

'Ah. OK, look at it this way, then. The television picture is made up of hundreds of lines . . .'

'No, no,' came the reply. 'I mean, you're confusing me with an actress who gives a fuck.'

So it ever was. CSO (or, for those operating outside the wilfully idiosyncratic BBC's nomenclature, Chroma Key) defined the look of television, be it in dense scientific lectures, experimental dramas or slapstick sketch shows, for a generation. Whenever TV felt the desire to explain the workings of this omnipresent process, however – and it happened a lot, especially on children's programmes – fidgety incomprehension and glazed eyes were the result. But even if they weren't aware of the skill involved, everyone came to know the harsh, acidic fizz which took hold of the screen whenever it was employed.

Technology improved all the time. As well as advances in the 'box of tricks' itself, lights and cameras became ever more powerful and sensitive. Even so, certain problems would always arise. Most noticeably, the electronic gate separating foreground from background was very strict – each pixel was judged to be either one or the other. Hence anything blurred or rough on the outline of your foreground subject – diaphanous clothing, hair, shadows, spectacle lenses, a physics lecturer's beard – had a tendency to fox the electronics, which would allocate it foreground status one instant, and relegate it to the background the next. You had to work hard to avoid the subject breaking up into a feverish swarm of electronic midges.

Other shortcomings required meticulous planning. Unless you had days to spend in the studio lining up sets, actors and background artwork (and you didn't), errors of scale crept in, angles became contorted, and perspective went for a Burton. Despite your best efforts, colours and lighting angles were doomed to clash, giving the effect of a moving collage of random cut-out photographs from colour supplements. To get that blue screen nice and clear, lighting tended toward the over-bright and the flat, limiting dramatic possibilities. And any camera movement was right out.

These issues combined to give the 'Chroma look' to vast swathes of television. Fantasy serials and weather forecasts took on a visual kinship that wasn't necessarily flattering to either. Nevertheless, in the early days of colour television it was the number one new toy, and prone to pop up everywhere. As John Beveridge, videotape editor for *Nationwide* and consequently no stranger to the process, cautioned in 1975, 'it is just a tool of our time. It should be put in a drawer and only used where there is good reason.'

In the view of James MacTaggart, a producer with a strong antipathy to naturalism, drama provided many good reasons. His 1973 adaptation of Voltaire's *Candide* used CSO in every shot, founding the short-lived genre of the blue screen epic. Ian Ogilvy's eponymous delusional optimist tripped gaily from one hand-drawn set-piece to another while Frank Finlay, as Voltaire himself, took charge of the paper environment, at one point literally drawing a discreet veil over a bedroom scene. It was praised as 'the work that took the medium a step nearer its future,'[367] though not everyone was convinced by the technique. 'Maybe irony isn't televisable,' mused John Carey, 'but a firmer substitute for it than these doll's house droolings could surely have been managed.' For him the cartoon backgrounds overwhelmed the foreground, and had an adverse effect on the cast. 'Actors seemed to have been left over from when they cast *Whoops Baghdad*, and to imagine that the same sort of effect would be welcome here.'[368]

The tendency of these dramas towards pantomime was perhaps inevitable – outlandish scenery (which the actors couldn't see anyway) encouraged gigantic performances. MacTaggart's second bite at the blue screen cherry was *Alice in Wonderland*, a more fittingly over the top subject. Piers Haggard picked another appropriate source with his *Chester Mystery Plays*, placing his mumming actors, including Michael Hordern as God, into the warped anti-perspectives of medieval religious paintings (which handily got round the perennial scale problem).

After that, the technique was largely relegated to children's fantasy fare. (Although it remained strong in the gaudier reaches of Italian television, where all-dancing extravaganzas like *Tilt* and *Chromakey Follies* were awash with electrical fizz.) Andrew Gosling did give it one last 'adult' hurrah, however, when the curious decision was made to adapt *Jane* for television. The original wartime *Daily Mirror* comic strip chronicled the misadventures of an accident-prone blonde who habitually found herself behind enemy lines with no clothes on. Simultaneously quaint and creepy, it was such a relic of its time that any revival could only take place under a thick crust of irony. Which is where the blue screen came in.

Gosling and designer Graham McCallum took the comic strip

element literally, boxing Paul Birkbeck's elegant art deco illustrations in tight areas of the screen, and draining the colour from the live action elements (mainly Glynis Barber in assorted camisoles) just enough to mute the usual retina-scorching electronic palate to a more restful wartime sepia. As a ten-minute frippery it more than fulfilled its remit, 'a sprightly bit of nonsense told more delicately than one could have expected.'[369]

Shortly after the sequel, *Jane in the Desert*, digital effects superseded the bare-bones Chroma Key set-up, and the visual aspect of TV moved inexorably closer to unmitigated realism. More recently, though, the coloured screens have made a comeback, as effects overtake location shooting in terms of value for money. Directors are ever more required to brush up their technical chops, and actors can no longer exercise the Handl Defence. The possibilities are endless once more, though only the skill of the writer can decide whether digitally augmented drama will be a flight into the imaginative wilderness or just a flashier heap of doll's house droolings.

BOYS FROM THE BLACKSTUFF (1982)
BBC One

The North rises, again.

'TELEVISION DRAMATIST' MAY BE a legitimate career these days, studied in universities and taught in creative writing courses, but until recently it was more something for writers to fall into on the way to and from other things.

Alan Bleasdale stumbled into drama via the stories he wrote, after sifting through uninspiring published alternatives for the slow learners he taught at a Huyton secondary modern. Franny Scully, the hero of the tales, was a disenfranchised but smart, put-upon yet indefatigable amalgam of his pupils and the near-legendary exploits they relayed to him in class. Bleasdale soon picked up a voice for Scully, a breathing, scheming entity rooted in life, who graduated from hosting his own radio show to infiltrating otherwise misbegotten Saturday morning kids' jamboree *The Mersey Pirate*. Bleasdale would later reflect that latching onto Scully's personality at the start of his career stopped him becoming 'sub-Beckett, sub-Pinter for the rest of my life.'[370]

His voice matured with *The Black Stuff*, the tale of five lads in the building trade whose decision to do a 'foreigner' – a crafty cash-in-hand extra job using their firm's 'borrowed' time and equipment – ends in calamity. The series that grew from there, exploring the subsequent struggles of each of them in the tanking labour market, was depressingly timely. In the decade to 1982 employment in Liverpool fell by nearly a third. Tapping directly into a national fear via a regional crisis, *Boys from the Blackstuff* outgrew its Sunday night slot on BBC Two and was repeated in full fig on the main channel for an audience of up to eight million. Kids who'd developed a palate for this sort of drama via the likes of *Minder* lapped up at least some of its expansive imagery, though its physical manifestation, the playground Yosser Hughes head butt, did little for its educational rep.

The apolitical Bleasdale dropped the baggage of northern drama and struck out on a more personal, simultaneously more and less real, course which perfectly matched the awful absurdity of the state of Merseyside, seemingly abandoned by the rest of the country. Two of the sharpest ears in the business gathered anecdotes, attitudes and patterns of speech fresh from the front, and with plenty of input from the actors, five solid characters emerged from behind the DHSS grilles, from Michael Angelis's slowly drowning Chrissie Todd to Bernard Hill's bricklaying Titanic Yosser Hughes.

The production was almost as strapped for cash as its subjects. Still the default medium for quality drama, film was out of the question for all five shows, with video – the sharp and tacky stuff of soap opera – the only viable alternative. Only Yosser, the most lost of them all, was granted the mythical soft light and grain of film, a fitting atmosphere for his quixotic bouts of violent self-assertion. His cohorts, denied the luxury of full mental breakdown, were stuck on unforgiving videotape.

Philip Saville, a TV director with an apprenticeship stretching back to the dawn of ITV, was a keen experimenter who adored the lurid sheen of video. His 1964 *Hamlet at Elsinore* set the Dane on his home turf in moonlit chiaroscuro, and he was the first of the drama department to start fiddling with the new 'pick-a-back' electronic news gathering kit in 1974's *The Actual Woman*. For *Blackstuff*, he was given the BBC's latest acquisition to play with – a fully-fitted multi-camera mobile location unit which could capture the performances with the pin-sharp, wide-angle, bleached-out accuracy of sports coverage. Using tape rather than film preserved the sense of immediacy viewers knew from sport and, increasingly, current affairs reports. Saville could stretch and distort his shots with Grand Guignol flourishes and the thing was still visually locked somewhere between a riot and a second division match. Life on the social was a dismal sport, happening now.

'What were you doing during the Toxteth riots?' 'Well, I was down the supermarket quite a lot.' The Boys aren't comic types, they're semi-pro comedians. Deftly avoiding the rarefied pity-from-on-high of the earnest poverty play, Bleasdale shows the man first, and gets the social comment from his mouth, not over his head. He never slips into sentimental editorialising, even when the symbolism is spelt out, as when Snowy the proud Marxist artisan plasterer is literally killed by mass-produced shoddiness. Bleasdale knows the dramatist gets nowhere by battering stoic ciphers about, so his Liverpool becomes a music hall approached via the sewers. These are boys you could get on with in the pub.

But not the Green Man, where they repair after giving old socialist George the final send-off – an inferno full of sacked bouncers and faded speciality acts reduced to inebriated self-parodies by lunchtime, with the occasional frenzied redundancy party turning the ambience from Breughel to Bosch. This maelstrom of menace, psychosis and bird impressions was broadcast as the rest of the country's media either tossed off platitudinous editorials on the 'Liverpool situation' – treating Liverpudlians literally as boys, like teachers muttering about a problem child – or washed their hands of the matter entirely. 'They should build a fence around it and charge admission,'[371] as the *Daily Mirror* notoriously put it. *Boys from the Blackstuff* was a more humane alternative to that sort of brutal instruction. If you took the right cues, you *could* make it up.

ST ELSEWHERE (1982–8)

NBC (MTM Enterprises)

The chance encounter of realism and whimsy on an operating table.

THE PRODUCTION COMPANY FOUNDED in 1969 by Mary Tyler Moore and Grant Tinker gave American comedy and drama new texture: intricate, realistic, innovative; but also, to some, overly playful and indulgent. No series of theirs embodied this double-edged quality better than hospital drama *St Elsewhere*. The show began as, to all intents and purposes, Hill Street Wards. The *Hill Street Blues* formula was first tried out in 1979 pilot *Operating Room*, following the intertwining travails of three doctors in an LA hospital. NBC and MTM mulled over where to take this odd but promising concept, with Fred Silverman, as ever, having the final word. 'Let's try it as a cop show first, and if it works we'll do it with doctors.'[372]

They didn't even wait to see if it worked. With *Hill Street Blues* still bouncing along the bottom of the ratings charts after its first season, NBC gave producer Bruce Paltrow the go-ahead to make the medical version, now relocated to St Eligius: a crumbling, cash-starved teaching hospital on the wrong side of the Boston tracks. The three senior medics were kitted out with stories that, in précis, looked like pure cliché: Dr Westphall (Ed Flanders) was a widower with a severely autistic son; Dr Auschlander (Norman Lloyd) a liver specialist with incurable liver cancer. Then there was

Dr Craig (William Daniels), the most brilliant heart surgeon of his generation who, naturally, found the hearts of healthy people, his family and colleagues especially, an unfathomable mystery. It sounded like sub-*Kildare* soap, but Paltrow's writers, especially story kingpins John Falsey, Joshua Brand and John Masius, were adept at spinning gold from corn.

The many hospital dramas television had minted so far all featured the same elements: heroic senior doctors, awe-struck nurses, surgical races against time and an all-round setting of finely-chiselled profiles against the encroachment of death. Any viewer who'd spent time in a hospital knew this was nothing like the reality. Heroism was absent. Treatments didn't so much race to a nail-biting conclusion as involve hours of aimless hanging about. And never mind the ailment you came in with: shonky equipment, staff shortages and lack of funding were equally prevalent threats to existence. Drama, of the brow-mopping, double-door-crashing, defibrillator-clearing strain, was in short supply. Real hospitals exuded a weird, shapeless melancholy atmosphere that nobody, perhaps quite sensibly, had tried to condense into an hour of television before.

The pilot swarmed with exhausted medics, graphic descriptions of acute dysentery, low-level racism, doctors passing off patients on others, snatched romantic interludes in the morgue and general non-stop intra-staff bickering. Doctors were lazy, lustful, jealous, prejudiced and – the biggest taboo – variously incompetent. The assorted students presented as jokily frivolous (Dr Fiscus, played by stand-up Howie Mandel); bumblingly privileged (Dr Ehrlich, Ed Begley Jr.) right down to the resident pill-popping rapist (Dr White, Terence Knox). Taking its lead from Paddy Chayefsky's cynical 1971 film *The Hospital, St Elsewhere* established a new benchmark for realism in medical drama – *M*A*S*H* notwithstanding – from the beginning.

Almost immediately, it set about breaking that realism up. While the subject matter became ever more daring – including the first appearance of an AIDS storyline in late 1983 – the playful house style of MTM Productions began to assert itself with ever more extreme results. The usual trickle of in-jokes became a flood. Characters would appear or be paged with names familiar from a host of other TV shows, past and present, or (often suffering from embarrassing ailments) the names of network executives. Lines which seemed like plain non-sequiturs to most would, to the TV adept, be revealed as arcane references to old sitcoms, films or, as the show built up its own mythology after a few seasons, old episodes of *St Elsewhere* itself. Mandel reckoned this play-along aspect created a new hybrid genre, the 'drama game-show'.[373]

Occasionally the references threatened to take over. In one episode an amnesiac becomes convinced he's Mary Tyler Moore, and casts his fellow patients as Rhoda, Phyllis *et al*. In another, the three senior doctors repair to a bar across town, which happens to be Cheers. There they chat with Norm, Cliff and Carla from the NBC sitcom, in dialogue that drips with that show's expected wisecracks, although shorn of audience laughter and shot in *St Elsewhere*'s relentlessly grim visual style; America's favourite bar for a moment looks like a stagnant purgatory full of losers. On other occasions the conceit swamped the story. An episode where Fiscus, hovering between life and death, hallucinates a whimsical *Divine Comedy* populated by deceased characters from the series, ended with its flighty protagonist vowing to stick more closely to the straight and narrow in future. Some viewers were left wishing the writers would make the same pledge. The small art of deconstruction and the greater art of character development came together perfectly in 'Time Heals', a virtuoso two-parter in which fiftieth anniversary celebrations for the hospital trigger a series of personal memories for various characters going back through the decades to the opening of the place in the thirties. Past traumas shed light on well-known characters as they're relived (Dr Westphall's wife's death, Dr Craig's disastrous first operation) and social points are deftly made (the hospital is revealed to have been falling apart almost as soon as it went up). The dexterous use of visual cues to trigger flashbacks and the neat circular structure satisfy without shouldering the story into the background. Like the hospital itself, *St Elsewhere* somehow survived six seasons of dire ratings, relying on award nominations and the good favour of executives for a stay of execution. After a standoff over budgets in 1987, the end finally loomed, which raised the problem of exactly what that would look like. Finishing a continuing series is never satisfactory. Either the whole thing goes over the top to outdo the combined effect of what's gone before, or things peter out in an overly sentimental dimming of the lights. After toying with ideas ranging from Westphall confessing to the Kennedy assassination and a full-on nuclear holocaust,[374] the producers decided that the show that lived by self-reference should die by self-reference.

After a (relatively) sober parting of the ways for the staff, a strange coda was tacked on, recasting Auschlander, Westphall and Westphall's autistic son Tommy as a blue-collar family worrying over Tommy's constant fixation with a toy snow globe. The final shot of the series revealed the globe to contain a tiny model of St Eligius, implying the entire six series had been the boy's crazily elaborate daydream. Even more so than the end of *The Prisoner*, which nobody truly hoped to see neatly tied up, it was a masterclass in burning artistic bridges, undercutting years of accumulated drama with one last table-upsetting caprice.

It was also the kind of ending that could only be conceived in the days when TV drama was still ephemeral – syndication aside, everything was bet on the first transmission of every episode, after which all concerned simply moved on to something new. As cable channels became a low(er) pressure proving ground for drama, and the box set recast it as a permanent work of art, producers would have a little more control over when and how their creations came to an end, and bewildering reversals like *St Elsewhere*'s would fall decisively out of fashion (although the last few minutes of *The Sopranos* came close to bringing them back). The end of a long-running series will always sound a note of compromise and self-indulgence, and sabotaging everything you've created at the final hurdle is just another form of conceit. It's also part of a long artistic tradition: as Max Beerbohm observed when Ibsen summarily killed off an artist in his final play, 'It is but another instance of his egoism that he has reserved his most vicious kick for himself.'[375]

THE TUBE (1982–7)

Channel Four
(Tyne Tees Television)

The music show that talked itself off the air.

PRODUCERS OF YOUTH PROGRAMMES were used to being mocked for their 'groovy teacher' attitudes. In one case, such criticism had a point. At Ryhope School near Sunderland, Mr Malcolm Gerrie, 'Fuzzy' to his pupils, was a drama teacher with ambitions for the annual school play above and beyond the usual plywood-backed run-through of *Oliver!* His mammoth 1974 production of *Tommy* garnered the attention of the *NME*. The following year he topped it with a gargantuan version of the David Essex rock parable *Stardust*. Russell Harty of ITV's *Aquarius* arts programme marvelled at his effortless stewardship of a hundred-strong cast, baths full of dry ice and a revolving stage holding three different sets.

Having exhausted the possibilities of academic show business, Gerrie handed in his elbow patches and decamped to Tyne Tees, working on the production teams of youth-oriented shows such as *Check It Out* ('issues and news for the under-twenties') and *Alright Now* ('Big Den Hegarty hosts a happy half-hour of rock, pop, punk and funk'). In 1981 he gave children's ITV its most successful pop format since *Supersonic*. *Razzamatazz* was billed as 'a *Ready Steady Go!* for the teenyboppers of the eighties,' though Gerrie's description was more accurate: 'a rock 'n' roll party in a Rupert Bear environment.'

On a set decorated with clouds and rainbows, presenters Alastair

Pirrie and Lyn Spencer (later joined by a young Lisa Stansfield) introduced Kate Bush and Kiki Dee, items on roller discos and electronic T-shirts, Popscotch (a hopscotch-based competition involving kids jumping on images of pop stars' faces) and the Human Jukebox Man, who claimed to sing any song if you stuffed ten pence in his mouth. With the inky warhorses of the music press fast losing circulation to the shiny, knowingly naive *Smash Hits*, Gerrie's bubbly confection chimed perfectly with the times.

Razzamatazz impressed enough for Channel Four's Jeremy Isaacs to approach Fuzzy about making something a little more fifth-form. The commission was broad, and Gerrie broadened it further still: what began as a brief for eight half-hour magazine programmes ended up as twenty compendiums of live music and features running 105 minutes each. 'You've got the freedom to fail,' Isaacs told Gerrie. 'Just make sure you make it lively and give it some balls.' Gerrie, with fond *Ready, Steady, Go!* memories still fresh in his mind after two decades, knew what he wanted.

Scaffolding was erected, presenters were cast: dapper ex-Squeeze keyboardist Jools Holland, who struck just the right mock-formal tone and exuded a singular kind of laid-back anxiety; and Paula Yates, whose pop credentials included a long-running *Record Mirror* column, but who was still best known for her relationship with Bob Geldof and best-selling book *Rock Stars in Their Underpants*. They were assisted, in time-honoured fashion, by a rotating line-up of five 'rookies' recruited from over 3,000 applications. First, and longest lasting, was museum assistant Muriel Gray, who'd answered Tyne Tees's classified ad in the *NME*.

The inaugural edition of *The Tube* set out its stall with films on the LA music scene and African dance, alternating with valiantly uncool comedy monologues from Mark MiWurdz (né Hurst) and the latest video from Duran Duran. Holland interviewed Pete Townshend, Gray interviewed Paul Weller, and Yates 'chatted up' Sting on a double bed. The second half was devoted to live perform-ances from The Jam and Heaven 17, whose keyboardist Martyn Ware neatly summed up proceedings: '[Tyne Tees] might lack a bit technically, but they more than make up for that with their enthusiasm.'

The normally sniffy music press were enthusiastic too. *The Tube*'s launch made the *NME* cover and inside, the verdict was one of mildly qualified praise. 'If the presentation can be given more pace and punch,' mused Adrian Thrills, '*The Tube* will be on the point of becoming the first pop show really worth watching in years.'[376] A note of dissent came, ineluctably, from Julie Burchill. 'The presenters are no Cathy McGowans, or even Aysheas,' she sniped, before exclusively revealing, 'I personally have turned down THREE OFFERS to present TV teen shows for the simple reason that at twenty-two I am simply TOO OLD to tell teenagers what's what. *The Tube* – the weekend stops here.'[377]

The show's temperament largely matched the post-punk scepticism of the record business. Holland, for instance, abandoned industry etiquette when he introduced Tears for Fears with: 'Here's a bunch of posers. If you want a cup of tea, now's the time to go and make it.' On the other hand, the lasting achievement of the show's first series was the kick-starting of Paul Young's solo career.

As *The Tube* grew in stature, so did the list of complaints. Paula Yates, linking the programme from the studio roof, blurted 'it's fucking freezing up here,' unaware she was on air. Holland surprised goth act Lords of the New Church by taking a camera unannounced into their dressing room, only to find singer Stiv Bators stark naked. Rik Mayall opened one edition by voiding a mouthful of vomit. Robbie Coltrane was doused with paraffin. Mel Smith complained the studio catering was 'worse than the fucking Beeb'. The phrase 'hamster turds' was uttered. Barely a week went by without the IBA having to deal with something on the show that caused outrage.

With its only other competition coming from Jonathan King's BBC2 vehicles *Entertainment USA* and *No Limits*, the latter sending 'its well-scrubbed teen hosts to sundry British towns accompanied for no fathomable reason by a soundtrack of bland stadium rock,'[378] *The Tube* was out on its own, but not everything was going well.

Andy Allan, Tyne Tees MD and the show's most influential champion, left for Central Television at the end of 1984. A wave of budget tightening followed, meaning cutbacks on trips to the States and the loss of annual late-night knees-up *A Midsummer Night's Tube*.

Then came 1986 spin-off *Come Dancing with Jools Holland*, a New Year's Eve hootenanny with a celebrity audience, featuring comedy from Mayall and Edmonson's Dangerous Brothers and the *Who Dares Wins* team, involving evocations of a woman pissing into a wok and sexual relations between newsreader Alastair Burnet and Prince Charles. Home Secretary Leon Brittan, in the audience with his wife, was apoplectic. Foreign Secretary Geoffrey Howe, watching at home, made a formal complaint to the IBA, resulting in instant sackings for producers Royston Mayoh and Peter McHugh under charges, later rescinded, of gross misconduct. It was made clear to Holland that he would have to watch his step from now on.

This he conspicuously failed to do on 16 January. Just before half past five, in between the Gold Runs of *Blockbusters*, Holland fronted the show's usual cheeky live trailer reminding the cooler viewers of ITV's sixth form quiz to switch channels immediately. After announcing The Mission, Michelle Shocked and Timbuk 3, he improvised a sign-off line. 'I said, "Be there . . ." then I thought I'm not going to say ". . . or be square" so I said "or be a completely ungroovy fucker!"' he later recounted. 'It just slipped out. I nearly said "Oh shit" directly afterwards which would really have clinched it.'[379] Tabloid consternation followed, bringing a six-week suspension for Holland and the second reprimand in a month from the IBA. One more and Tyne Tees's licence to broadcast would be 'seriously reconsidered'.

With its every move now subject to crippling restrictions, *The Tube* was mortally wounded. Everything was examined for potential offence. The band Stump were made to alter their lyrics on the show, to remove the words 'Tupperware' and 'gonads'. Gerrie handed in his resignation in February, but stayed to the end of what would be the final series, disgusted at 'a cold wave of purit-anism blowing through the industry.' *The Tube*'s very final link summed up the once joyous programme's late-period frostiness. Paula hailed closing act Duran Duran as 'possibly the greatest band' they'd ever had on, prompting a grimace from Gray. 'Don't get any closer, Muriel,' retorted Yates. 'This isn't hot lesbo action time.' She was quite right – that was on Sundays after the racing.

M*A*S*H: 'GOODBYE, FAREWELL AND AMEN' (1983)

CBS (20th Century Fox Television)

The sitcom takes its final bow seriously.

THE TELEVISION SERIES, BOTH comic and dramatic, told its story at two paces. The first was the obvious, episode-long tale, an hour or twenty-five minutes in length, which set out its stall with characters already familiar to the audience, developed the action and brought things to an amusing or satisfactory conclusion before the end credits. The second pace covered more ground. Smarter series didn't just reset everything at the start of the episode – characters and situations developed over the thirteen or twenty-odd episodes of the season. This wasn't a full-blown serial, where a missed or out of order episode could lead to utter confusion, but it did endow its characters (and credit the audience) with memories slightly longer than that of a goldfish. The 'story arc' had arrived.

In sitcoms, this was kept firmly in the background – nice to have that extra layer, but a casual viewer needed to be able to stumble across a random episode for the first time and not feel hopelessly confused. In the 1970s, when demographic targeting led to increasingly sophisticated sitcoms with more dramatic qualities and complex characters, the successful ones could afford to make more of their own history. A viewer who began watching *The Mary Tyler Moore Show* with 'The Last Show' might have got a chuckle out of the clumsy group hug, but the emotional impact would have eluded them. Shows can fall into a pit of their own indulgence: *Friends* dissolved into a chorus of mawkishly quivering goodbyes, while *St Elsewhere* double-crossed its entire existence. Generally the temptation to coast along on the store of sentimental goodwill accumulated over the years proves too good for the creatively exhausted makers to resist. One sitcom, which had been straining at the boundaries of its genre for over a decade, broke into pure psychological drama.

Robert Altman's 1970 film *MASH* was a loose – very loose – adaptation of *MASH: A Novel About Three Army Doctors*, a fictionalised memoir of a military surgeon's chaotic tenure in the US army's 4077th Mobile Army Surgical Hospital during the Korean War, reworked to comment on the then ongoing conflict in Vietnam. Altman's fluid camera and editing combined with Ring Lardner Jr's transcendentally caustic screenplay and some ultra-naturalistic acting to create a new type of Hollywood film comedy, grossing over $20 million. Distributor Twentieth Century Fox offered CBS the series rights, but network executives initially worried it might be 'too hip for television'.[380]

Military sitcoms were surprisingly common in the sixties, but they tended to omit one crucial aspect: death. *McHale's Navy*, *Gomer Pyle USMC* and especially PoW pantomime *Hogan's Heroes* didn't so much draw black humour from the horrors of war as turn the whole thing into one big, silly game between stuffy top brass and klutzes in the ranks. If there was to be any point to a *MASH* sitcom, this taboo would have to be skilfully broken.

Gene Reynolds, producer of the re-punctuated *M*A*S*H*, enlisted writer Larry Gelbart, a TV veteran who started out on Sid Caesar's gag-writing team, to find a workable way to adapt Altman's bitter creation. The pair spent several weeks gathering situation and character ideas with a real MASH (this time the 8055th). The result was decidedly warmer than the film, though no less honest about the terror of the situation: medics larked about to keep themselves sane in between mortar attacks and waves of incoming wounded. All agreed the new template worked, but CBS still didn't know where to put it, initially scheduling it at 8 p.m. on Sunday opposite NBC's *Wonderful World of Disney*.

Sitcom conventions almost derailed the show. Creators were aghast at network insistence on a laugh track, and fought hard for it to be removed. Eventually a tepid compromise was reached, with CBS supplying an attenuated 'chuckle track' instead of the regulation torrent of hooting, which was respectfully switched off entirely during the operating theatre scenes. (A version with no laughter at all was shown by the BBC.) *M*A*S*H* soon became a national, then an international, favourite.

Gelbart left after the fourth season. His valedictory episode took every liberty with prime time comic practice. 'The Interview', patterned after a grim documentary made by Ed Murrow, was a semi-improvised affair based on 'in character' interviews conducted by an intern during free moments on set while filming the 'proper' episodes.[381] The result, complete with Father Mulcahy's unforgettable story of surgeons warming their hands in the steam from open wounds (a line directly taken from life), went out with no laugh track and in black and white.

After Gelbart departed, Alan Alda, established as the show's biggest star in the role of Lieutenant Benjamin Franklin 'Hawkeye' Pierce, became the driving creative force, directing and writing an increasing number of episodes himself. (Cast members Harry Morgan, Jamie Farr and Mike Farrell also got behind the camera.) The final episode, at the end of eleven seasons, was predominantly his work, and it was like no sitcom finale before or since.

Clocking in at over two hours minus commercials, 'Goodbye, Farewell and Amen' matched the original film for length and scope. For the most part, it was an emotionally charged tying up of loose ends and character stories in the manner of every sitcom finale before it. The haughty Charles Winchester finally engaged with the people whose country he was fighting to liberate. Cross-dressing discharge chaser Klinger married a local and stayed in Korea. After lasting three times the span of its real life counterpart, the TV Korean War came to an end, and several latrines were destroyed. All sound stuff, if unremarkable by the show's usual high standards.

Hawkeye's final story set it apart. He spends the first half of the programme in a mental hospital, as a psychiatrist homes in on the events of an ambushed charabanc outing to Inchon and what a civilian, overreacting to Hawkeye's desperate demand for silence, may or may not have done to what may or may not have been a chicken. All the small comforts of comedy were struck out of the frame in seconds: no small feat for a show that had made its name by giving and rescinding the reassurance of the sitcom, like a play-fully malicious parent proffering and suddenly withdrawing a dummy to a frustrated baby. No other sitcom, and few enough dramas, spent every episode in the shadow of death. Viewers may have thought they'd developed immunity after eleven seasons, but seeing the indestructible Hawkeye, previously always a cross between Superman and Groucho Marx by dint of his defiantly flippant worldview, brought to his knees was one last, magnificent, slap in the face.

The most widely publicised sitcom episode thus far received acres of pre-transmission press coverage and speculation on its tightly guarded contents. M*A*S*H had always bucked the American trend by combining fearless innovation with sky high ratings, but the last episode took things to a new level, reaching well over a hundred million viewers on transmission – three quarters of that night's audience – squarely beating previous record holder *Roots*.[382] That the top end of American TV popularity had such serious fare in it – with, of course, plenty of fluff like the shooting of J.R. as well – should have given the lie to US TV's dumbass international reputation but prejudices, as well as habits, died hard.

SATURDAY NIGHT AFFAIRS (1984)
BBC One

In which television is made by sticking some stars in a room, and then doing nothing.

FROM THE MOMENT GEORGE Orwell conceived the two-way telescreen, the thought of electronic voyeurism was tempting and terrifying. In 1956 maverick columnist Maurice Richardson, musing on the sort of programmes Britain's mooted third TV channel might show, decided the usual diet of drama and quizzes was old hat, and suggested 'a combination of concealed microphone and electronic eye, so that people could be televised without their knowledge, could be fascinating; but it is scarcely practicable; memories of Big Brother are too painful.'[383]

When Michael Parkinson vacated his beige swivel-throne in 1982, pundits predicted the end of the chat show. Said pundits can't have been paying much attention. From under Parky's dinosaur shadow scurried countless chattering mammals. Harty, Wogan and Aspel fought to unite their soft furnishings with the most exclusive showbiz bottoms. Breakfast television set commuters up for the day with nutritious anecdotes by the ton. Richardson had a phrase for chat show viewers, too: 'embarrassment perverts'.

With the market full of identikit mug-'n'-plug outlets, the BBC cast about for a celeb vehicle that could be called 'distinctive'. Its answer was 'a completely different new-style entertainment,' a star-studded mock party thrown at its Pebble Mill studios in honour of a distinguished guest, with a hundred other faces from their life paying tribute – some famous, some not; some aware of the cameras, some not. *Saturday Night Affairs* aimed to 'sidestep the set piece chat show and get natural entertaining conversation and music – just like you might get at a famous star's party.' Vidal Sassoon was lined up as the first guest of honour, with plenty of waspish indiscretion promised. 'There are no rules and no rehearsals,' said producer John King. 'There were times when I blushed to hear what they were saying.'[384]

At this point the fatal flaw of the enterprise became clear. King, Sassoon and pals were free to hear the juicy gossip and catty banter, as were the operators of the concealed cameras and mics. The forty-five minutes of each affair that made it to the screen, however, were of legal necessity the low calorie version. Beyond a minor spat between former *Generation Game* hosts Bruce Forsyth and Larry Grayson ('Oh, you're kidding,' groaned Brucie as the pair met at the studio doors. 'We're not walking on together!') and some digs at Richard Harris's prowess in the bedroom, the only distinction between this new-style chat and the school of Parky was its longueur-festooned aimlessness. Annie Ross asks Vidal if he knows Toyah Willcox. Vidal says no, he doesn't. The convivial ice remains stubbornly intact.

Next week was the turn of Dave Lee Travis. The public fled in droves, ignoring some encouraging critical notices. ('There has never been anything more gloriously awful in the history of television' – the *Guardian*.) The top brass hastily decided the party was over, leaving six editions untransmitted. We never got to see Pamela Stephenson's bash, which seemed the most likely to live up to the series' saucy ambitions, despite the Corporation vetoing her request for a drugs budget. (It was replaced with an emergency late film, *The Honkers*.) Or the party thrown by Spike Milligan, who wanted to invite people he hated, offer them bread and water and ignore them all evening. Or an entire forty-five minute celebration of the life and work of Lennie Bennett. It was the viewer's loss.

In hindsight, it's easy to see what *Saturday Night Affairs* lacked. Not the firm guiding hand of a seasoned chat show host, or some tighter editing to remove those shoe-gazing conversational cul-de-sacs – modern reality television is all but held together by awkward pauses and shifty coughs. What the new breed of all-star showcases have that *Affairs* didn't is the small but essential democratic element of *schadenfreude*.

'Presumably the champagne and prawns-the-size-of-lobsters, with which they were stuffing their faces,' inquired one disgruntled viewer, 'were paid for by millionaire Mr Sassoon himself and not by our licence fee?'[385] If only the stars had to sing, or do something much more demeaning, for their supper. 'There is a case for exhibiting people like Bruce Forsyth,' averred John Naughton, 'but *Affairs* provides the wrong kind of zoo for the job, not least because it insists on feeding its inmates.'[386] It would have been so much easier to stomach DLT fooling about with a set of bagpipes if the viewer had the knowledge that he could exact vengeance at a stroke, for the price of a premium rate phone call. But that quantum leap would have to wait.

THREADS (1984)
BBC Two

The bleakest television programme ever made.

I want some of you to stumble, and some of you actually to keel over and give up . . . it's not a very pleasant scene. And please, don't forget to shiver.

Mick Jackson directs nuclear holocaust survivors, Cumbar Edge, Peak District, February 1984

THE SECOND HALF OF the twentieth century unfolded in the shadow of a potential disaster everyone over the age of seven knew about, but nobody could fully comprehend. Peter Watkins, recalcitrant producer of perfectly observed mock documentaries, delivered *The War Game* to the BBC in the wake of the Cuban Missile Crisis. Lucidly detailing the effects of nuclear attack on Britain, and the inevitably inadequate response the authorities could be expected to supply, it was refused transmission by the Director General Hugh Carleton Greene (with guidance from Harold Wilson's cabinet). It was, of course, suppressed in the name of children – in an unfortunate turn of phrase, Mary Whitehouse claimed it would 'blow their minds'.[387] For the next fifteen years, while ITV produced bomb programmes both avowedly anti-nuclear (John Pilger's *The Truth Game*) and unrepentantly hawkish (Max Hastings's *The War About Peace*), the BBC made *Nuclear Nightmares*, offering four plausible Armageddon scenarios rendered slightly more palatable by some turns from Peter Ustinov.

With Soviet aggression in Afghanistan sparking panic, the BBC acquired a new urgency. *QED: A Guide to Armageddon* detailed the effects of a one megaton warhead detonated a mile above St Paul's cathedral. Produced by James Burke's prime collaborator Mick Jackson, it used a variety of deadpan techniques – most effectively the deployment of ripe fruit and cuts of meat to demonstrate the effects of flying glass and intense heat on the populace – to give a sane, honest and horrific glimpse of the apocalypse that felt, at the time, like a racing certainty.

In 1984, Jackson took charge of a much grander apocalyptic affair – a two-hour drama showing the effects of an all-out superpower confrontation on the people of Sheffield. *Threads* was written by Barry Hines, unsentimental chronicler of the northern working classes best known for his study of disaffected youth and wistful escapism, *Kes*. It was a fortuitous pairing: Jackson dedicated to factual accuracy, Hines attuned to social bonds and human grief. They carefully avoided taking any overt political stance, Hines claiming 'it was my duty to be as even-handed as possible'. Besides, it wasn't as if the bare scientific facts needed any partisan garnish.

Their research took in a Home Office training course at Easingwold for the civil servants expected to try and maintain some semblance of civilisation, during which they encountered gallows humour among the delegates so dark it bordered on pathological denial. The futility of that exercise impressed on Hines the problem with dramatising the Big One: the enormousness and enormity of the statistics reduce individual lives to motes in a desert. In *Threads*, human scale is provided by the story of engaged couple Jimmy and Ruth (Reece Dinsdale and Karen Meagher), he an apprentice joiner and – in an echo of *Kes* – parakeet fancier, she a teacher heavily pregnant with their first child, who experience 'the suffering without the understanding'.[388]

The programme itself had to make some attempt at understanding. To this end Paul Vaughan, authoritative voice of *Horizon* documentaries, provided a minute-by-minute commentary, turning a melodrama into a public information film. Actual information films concerning survival measures – made by the Home Office but never transmitted – punctuate the days before the attack with their chillingly deadpan instructions on shelter and improvised burial.

There's black humour – or rather fearful irony – in abundance. The first warhead is notable for its effects on various characters' bladders. In a more subtle physical gag, a young man rendered speechless on sight of the first mushroom cloud instinctively brings hand up to mouth in a thumb-sucking gesture. Human nature asserts itself in ways more varied than the expected chorus of despair. Kids take to the flimsy homemade fallout shelters with giddy excitement. Sealed in their bunker under the town hall, councillors retain their political tribal instincts and buck-passing games, despite knowing full well there's little above ground to administrate. Spike Milligan's 1963 play *The Bed-Sitting Room* played the nuclear aftermath as surreal farce, and, despite being its polar opposite in tone, *Threads* sometimes looks weirdly similar in its depictions of normal life vainly continuing in the face of Armageddon: jolly test card muzak heralds the arrival of emergency TV broadcasts, and a fleeing family are advised: 'Make sure you turn the gas off. Don't want the whole street going up!'

Jackson evoked a city's destruction on a tiny budget. Model shots are whisked off the screen just before the viewer's eye starts to get suspicious, and memorably small details like melting milk bottles take the place of fiery panoramas. Tightly framed locations and reaction shots do the majority of the work special effects can't manage, and only a select few of those well-worn nuclear test images – the shockwave ripping through a barn, the row of trees mown down – are wheeled out. It's an impressionism born of economic necessity and Jackson's solid documentary training.

So far there's nothing here that wasn't already covered by the programme's American precursor, ABC's *The Day After*. What sets *Threads* apart from its peers is the second act, where we're taken through a decade of nuclear winter. Cameras track through an interminable wilderness of the dead and dying, mountains of rubble and charred bodies, both still and twitching. The style turns from kitchen sink science fiction into anthropological observation: the post-bomb generation communicate only in a few mangled phrases ('Gissit!' 'C'mooan!') and are routinely gunned down by the remnants of martial law for looting hunks of mouldy bread.

This New Stone Age contains odd, almost mocking relics of the twentieth century: a Casio computer game and Sainsbury's carrier bags have somehow survived the holocaust. With power generation making a ramshackle return, kids and pensioners gather in a derelict school to mouth inanely along to the last shred of twentieth century learning – a VHS of BBC literacy programme *Words and Pictures*. The jarring nature of these mundane remains help the viewer relate these fantastical scenes to the real world, in a way the sometimes hastily-sketched protagonists don't quite manage. In the closing scenes, Ruth's adolescent daughter, impregnated by sexual assault, gives painful birth alone in a derelict farmhouse to a hideously deformed homunculus. Championship darts from Redcar follows after the news.

Threads was broadcast on 23 September 1984 – although nobody knew it at the time, almost a year to the day that a catastrophic failure in the Soviet Union's early warning system mistook a NATO exercise for the start of the third world war, and came within a whisker of retaliation. The world remained blissfully ignorant of this incident, and the main charge against *Threads* came from those who felt such ignorance should be maintained. What good could come of rehearsing the end of civilisation, they asked, other than to alienate an already fearful public even further?

If anything, *Threads* had a unifying effect, both on those who girded their stomachs to watch it (it proved very popular with children, whose minds could take more blowing than Mrs Whitehouse anticipated), and those who took part. When Jackson and Hines held auditions for post-apocalyptic extras, they expected a few dozen volunteers for what would be a gruelling few days' work. Over a thousand turned up, and startled the filmmakers with their enthusiasm. 'They have acted marvellously,' said Hines. 'I've been both touched and depressed.'[389] Enlightened if not uplifted, viewers could only say the same thing.

EVER DECREASING CIRCLES (1984–9)
BBC One

The sitcom becomes, in the best sense of the word, pathetic.

THE RISE OF ALTERNATIVE comedy brought many liberating bonuses to the craft, along with a few limiting stereotypes. Chief among these was the division of light from darkness. On the one hand, went the code, you had the jokey fluff of the old school sitcom; the polite clichés of a retrograde middle-class fantasy world that seldom generated controversy except by accident. Against this was the New Wave: cleansed of taboos, alert to modern life, and unafraid to explore – in the vernacular of the time – 'adult themes'. There was no mistaking one camp for the other, nor any question of mixing the two styles: old was old, and new was new, and *Never the Twain* was crap.

There were problems with this doctrine from the start. For one, 'adult themes' more often than not meant 'adolescent obsessions', which slightly offset any claim to maturity. More troubling was the old school sitcom's resolute refusal to conform to its new twee image. A close examination saw 'adult themes' – in the adult sense of the phrase – cropping up everywhere. There was no better illustration than the work of John Esmonde and Bob Larbey.

Their biggest hit, *The Good Life*, became shorthand for the lovely old guard when Adrian Edmondson's Vyvyan verbally and physically shredded it on *The Young Ones*: 'They're nothing but a couple of reactionary stereotypes, confirming the myth that everyone in Britain is a loveable middle-class eccentric and I hate them!' Richard Briers's Tom Good did exhibit a can-do cheerfulness that would have had Lulu reaching for the Valium, and a programme that recorded an edition in the presence of the Queen couldn't have been less anti-establishment. But the series ended on a jarringly bleak note, as the Goods return to their home after an evening out to find it trashed by vandals. They bravely soldier on, but the sitcom justice of niceness duly rewarded gets a sound kicking.

Esmonde and Larbey's next collaboration with Briers began at this level of desolation, and went downhill rapidly. *The Other One* packed Michael Gambon off to Spain as meek, lonely travelling salesman Brian Bryant in desperate search of fun, but finding only Briers's Ralph Tanner – equally sad, but possessing ironclad delusions of adequacy. He captivates his new-found posse of one with tall tales of a full life, but as Gambon probes deeper, ever more outlandish whoppers are needed to keep true intimacy, and the awful truth, at bay. This was a brave tone for a sitcom to take: Alan Bennett meets Samuel Beckett in a derelict Berni Inn. It worked its chilly trick for two quietly magnificent series, but two drips yoked together in chronic isolation would never match the audience of *The Good Life*.

For their third Briers vehicle, Esmonde and Larbey created a character somewhere between these two poles. Martin Bryce is, like Tom Good, an eternally busy chap with a boyishly chirpy disposition. Like Ralph Tanner, he's status obsessed, running the Rotarian social whirlpool of Horsham with military precision and childishly resentful if his achievements are outshone. The two sides combine to make the finest man-child role in British TV comedy. Permanently drunk on community spirit, Bryce fields enough displacement activity to win fifty Duke of Edinburgh awards a day. What he lacks in charisma he makes up for in fête organising. As he admits in a rare moment of self-awareness, 'for somebody like me to be centre stage, I have to write the play myself.'

Martin's position as de facto president of The Close's

highly-drilled leisure time is upended by the arrival next door of the easy-going Paul Ryman, a Cambridge blue with an address book to rival David Frost. Without trying, Paul knocks Martin off his pedestal in every activity, from cricket to snooker to breath-holding. A sweater idly tossed over the shoulder in a world of cardigans buttoned to the top, Paul gains the admiration of all in The Close, in particular Martin's multifariously frustrated wife Ann, while Martin hammers himself into the ground trying to match his idle feats.

Most suburban sitcoms have suburban normality visited by some stock crisis, of which the boss suddenly coming to dinner is only most widely parodied. *Ever Decreasing Circles* had a far more inter-esting premise: suburban normality is already a crisis, only just kept from disintegrating by the protagonists' desperate industry. For this to work, characters were kept within the bounds of credibility. Ann was granted just enough patience to keep her continuing marriage to Martin plausible, without making her a saint. Similarly, Martin occasionally let slip the odd intimation of an inner life, though it comes in touchingly infantile language. ('I've got a smile starting inside, Ann, but I'm not sure if I can make it come out of my face.') Even Howard and Hilda Hughes, an existential Janet and John in matching knitwear who spoke their innermost thoughts as if they were running their fingers underneath the words, occa-sionally exhibited enough backbone to explain their continued existence outside a secure institution.

Over four series, the characters were filled in, but rather than knock off the rough edges, the writers explained how they got there, making comic types into living creatures while keeping up the eccentricity. Martin slowly began to wise up, but only on his terms. We learnt the tragic nature of his proposal to Ann ('Why bother to cope? Let me do it'), and Paul's ex-wife spilled the beans on his less than heroic status outside The Close. Even Howard Hughes could occasionally silence Paul with a look somewhere between a baby's innocent ogle and a war veteran's thousand-yard stare.

Parts of such grotesque subtlety needed, and got, skilled actors. Nottingham Playhouse veteran Penelope Wilton made Ann a tragic heroine at bay, stoically channelling the rage of Lady Macbeth into a long, hard stare at a Laura Ashley table mat. Peter Egan, hitherto best known as the eponymous East End thug in notorious gangster drama *Big Breadwinner Hog*, worked brilliantly against type as the planet's most affable man. Most satisfying of all, Briers relished every moment as Martin Bryce, never happier than when he was undermining the 'sugar-flavoured snot' image he'd attracted with *The Good Life*. 'I hate the vacuous, the cheap,' he said, 'and [Esmonde and Larbey] aren't like that.' *Ever Decreasing Circles* contained scenes of such exquisite agony that his youngest daughter couldn't bear to watch. 'I was rather pleased, secretly.'[390]

HEIMAT: EINE DEUTSCHE CHRONIK (1984)

WDR/SFB (Edgar Reitz Film)

The TV novel reaches epic proportions.

The Americans have stolen our history.
Edgar Reitz on *Holocaust*, *Liebe zum Kino*, 1983.

HOLOCAUST, NBC's LAVISH ANSWER to ABC's *Roots*, an eight-hour chronicle of one Jewish family's persecution in Nazi Germany, provoked every kind of response from worthy plaudits to concerned voices over Hollywood's trivialisation of Europe's darkest hour. In West Germany, its broadcast had solid effects: the sudden mass release of repressed memories it triggered was a decisive step toward the government lifting the statute of limitations for war crimes. But Edger Reitz, one time leading light of the New German Cinema movement, now licking his wounds over the grisly notices for his recent period drama *The Tailor of Ulm*, was unimpressed by Meryl Streep's martyrdom. He decided that, after decades of wilful suppression, it was time the German experience of the war was televised. Reitz began working on his contribution, *Heimat*, in March 1979.

Heimat began with *Tales from the Hunsrück Villages*, a compilation of real life stories, gathered by Reitz and co-author Peter

Steinbach over a solid year of research among the people of the Hunsrück Mountains, an oral history documentary reaching from the end of the Great War to the present day. Steeped in folk memory, they devoted another four years to writing, casting over a hundred parts from the local population and filming a fifteen-and-a-half hour chronicle of the fictional village of Schabbach and its citizens, from matriarch Maria Simon and her prodigal husband Paul to the scarred outcast Glasisch-Karl. Shown in art house cinemas as two mammoth epics, or one all-dayer with lunch included, *Heimat* was a daunting prospect for all but the most seasoned aesthete. Televised in eleven ninety-minute chunks, however, with catch-up prologues courtesy of Glasisch-Karl, it beguiled an entire continent.

The TV audience did have to make some allowances, however. Reitz set a demand not usually asked by a television programme of its audience. 'Don't make other plans while this film is showing,' he asked, 'stop the hectic pace of your daily life and enjoy the beauty.'[391] The pace of the early episodes was laggardly even by continental TV standards. Even with fifteen hours to cover sixty years, did we need quite so much detailed footage of blacksmiths at work? The direction would slowly pick up as the technology of the twentieth century – and the agency that made use of it, the Third Reich – invaded Schabbach and brought the world with it, ending a centuries old rural idyll for ever.

Whenever TV gives birth to something strange and new, snobbery and mistrust are never far away. With *Heimat* it came in two flavours. The first was a blanket refusal – still doggedly intoned after a good thirty-odd years of constant refutation – to admit that television could work on such an exalted level. Film critic Derek Malcolm thought *Heimat* 'originally made for television but very much a piece of cinema.'[392] How else to explain it? Then there were misgivings over the format. Domestic, family-oriented, a celebration of life for life's sake – it all sounded horribly like those two words that traditionally signified the trashiest genre in all television. Richard Combs, early on in the UK screening, worried about the 'danger of *Heimat* becoming one more mammoth soap opera, in which respect for the mundane, the texture of everyday living, is also susceptible to mundane, conventional and trivial thinking.'[393]

The quality of the programme soon knocked these prejudices aside, as critics discovered how soap addicts felt, knowing the life stories of characters so intimately they began cropping up in their daily thoughts. One of the most derided aspects of the soap – its ability, by sheer weight of material, to swamp the viewer's attention – had been put to a higher use. *Heimat* came closer than any film to the *modus operandi* of Marcel Proust's *À la recherche du temps perdu*, the unparalleled depiction of *fin de siècle* Parisian high society which built a literary cathedral from a million tiny observations, thoughts and gestures; a timeless social panorama made up of countless trivial moments.

Too trivial, some argued. Just as Proust's world remains largely untouched by history until the Great War is well under way, so Schabbach seemed to have a relatively cushy time of it during the Second War. Local dignitaries converted to National Socialism out of opportunistic ambition, often laced with buffoonery, and the village held a Führer's birthday party while the Holocaust took place somewhere else. 'What about the other side?' demanded US critic Timothy Garton Ash. 'What about Auschwitz? Where is the director's moral judgement?'[394] Reitz was unmoved. 'If we are to come to terms with the Third Reich,' he wrote, 'it has to be by the same means we use every day to take stock of the world we live in.'[395] *Heimat* refused to streamline its characters' lives into the simple narratives expected of a war film. They were individuals with diverse motives and, much as it might have wished otherwise, even the Third Reich was powerless to change that.

Heimat's success on German TV was immense. Repeat screenings had to be hastily arranged so haughty viewers who'd avoided the early episodes could catch up. Other European countries were similarly smitten, including France, usually resistant to Germanic cultural exports. It didn't reach the UK until spring 1986, where it took up Saturday night peak-time residence on BBC Two, heralded by 'a fanfare of ludicrous pre-publicity, in which continuity announcers went hoarse reading excerpts of rave reviews.'[396] Very unlike the understatement and humility of the programme itself.

Heimat wasn't the first of its kind: *Matador*, Lise Nørgaard and Erik Balling's study of a Danish town from the Great Depression to the aftermath of war, had already kept northern Europe rapt from 1978 to 1982. It wasn't the first German giant to leap the channel: Britons had already lapped up white knuckle submarine misadventure *Das Boot* and gruelling lowlife promenade *Berlin Alexanderplatz*. But *Heimat*'s ambitions and successes were of a different magnitude, and in its wake more European blockbusters arrived. *The Octopus*, Italian television's answer to *The Godfather*, was a high-end example. Lower down the ranks were German medical soap *Black Forest Clinic* and *Chateauvallon*, a French *feuilleton* whose two rich warring families bore more than a passing resemblance to certain rival dynasties in real life Toulouse, and which was marketed in English as '*Dallas-sur-Loire*'.

If that wasn't enough, rumours were abroad about the EEC imposing a minimum quota for European programmes on British channels, setting the tabloids on a gleeful panic spree. 'LATIN LOVELIES COULD ELBOW OUT DALLAS!' shivered the *Daily Express*, anticipating a Brussels-imposed hell of pretentious French discussions, naked Italian housewives, farting Finnish comics and worse. 'The language barrier alone makes it extremely difficult to enjoy some Austrian folk singer warbling about his herd of goats.'[397] The supposedly worldly British press could act like the most obtusely isolationist residents of Schabbach at times, but millions had their curiosity piqued and, in the case of *Heimat*, rewarded with one of the most complex, finely crafted and emotionally scrupulous programmes ever seen on television.

MOONLIGHTING (1985–9)
ABC (ABC Circle Films)
The quirk factor goes through the roof.

IN TELEVISION MORE THAN any other entertainment industry, and American television most of all, the mainstream runs swift and shallow. Shows turn over rapidly and fashions change with the seasons, but depth and sophistication rarely intrude. When they do, when a series turns up in prime time bearing its nonconformity high and proud, a couple of seasons is often all it takes for it to either fall in line or completely drop out. Network caution, endless audience profiling and general creative exhaustion all contribute in various amounts, but however it happens, assimilation is almost inevitable.

Almost. Sometimes favourable conditions arise, often by accident, that let a singular series flourish. In 1985, ABC was in the doldrums, idling at a constant third in the network pecking order while NBC flew ahead in both popular and critical acclaim. Only when a network thinks it has nothing to lose does it give its producers carte blanche, and ABC were desperate enough to announce an experimental 'hands off' policy. Entertainment head Lewis Ehrlicht set up ABC Circle Films to produce a series of pilots, hiring fresh talent including Glenn Gordon Caron, a writer with a slim CV including *Taxi* and *Remington Steele*, taken on because Ehrlicht thought his work 'weird'[398] – possibly the first time a television boss had invested that adjective with approval. After two ideas floundered, ABC revoked a little of Caron's creative freedom by insisting the third pilot be a 'boy-girl' detective story.

This was hardly uncharted territory, and at the time already something of a crowded market. As well as *Remington Steele*, the schedules had recently been home to marital murder mystery *Hart to Hart* and secret agent romance *Scarecrow and Mrs King*. Looking for a way to differentiate the new pilot, Caron instinctively accentuated the part of the premise that interested him – the romantic comedy angle. Making the show predominantly a comedy created problems – sixty-minute comedies were practically unknown in prime time – but ABC gave him the benefit of the doubt.

What Caron was doing – unconsciously, as it took Cybill Shepherd, the first actor cast, to point it out to him – was restoring the screwball comedy to the American screen. Occupying a short but plentiful niche in the late 1930s and early 1940s, screwball was a brilliant, giddy cessation of American cinema's normal rules of combat. The standard issue square-jawed hero and sighing ingénue were jettisoned in favour of witty, fractious and above all equal partnerships between men who were not quite as cool as their sauntering suggested and women less haughtily unworldly than their bluestocking diction made out. They fell in and out of love as they stumbled from peril to peril, often having trouble taking deadly danger seriously. For a few glorious years silver screen romance was liberating, funny and empowering for both parties, until Doris Day turned up and schmaltz returned with depressing haste.

Shepherd and Bruce Willis became a Hepburn and Tracy for the Armani age. Shepherd's fashion model, fallen on hard times, investigates a deadbeat detective agency she set up as a tax dodge, finding only Bruce Willis's indolent detective David Addison, a frazzled receptionist and a non-ringing phone. ('Any appointments?' 'John Gavin was made ambassador to Mexico again.') With the minimum of ceremony, the reluctant sophisticate and the gung-ho oaf tackle cases from the pitiful to the squalid, the crossfire of antagonistic crosstalk only letting up in moments of utmost jeopardy.

Within a few episodes, the order of importance of the show's constituent parts became clear. Way out at the top was the chemistry between Willis and Shepherd: the shouting, the screaming, the slamming of doors, the way his ill-judged quip would be met with her well-bred disgust, which gradually softened into a condescendingly amused admiration. The promise of romance is always central to this kind of entertainment, but the appeal of the two leads, and the relish and skill the writers lavished on putting words in their mouths – rapid fire words at that, often delivered simultaneously – went beyond anything Robert Wagner and Stefanie Powers had previously clocked up.

Growing out of the stars' charisma came the second pillar of success: conversing with the audience. Not since George Burns stepped through his kitchen wall had fictional characters demonstrated such self-awareness. The first moments of the second series featured a minute of the leads bickering to camera to fill time, as 'the network says the show's a minute too short'. This soon became a semi-regular feature, as did the ending of shows with the characters walking off the set and driving home. Then, somewhere a few fathoms beneath all of that, came the need for a tangible mystery plot – nice to have, but it was no big deal if one didn't happen to turn up that week. This was television about television – by comparison, *St Elsewhere* was a paragon of production line realism.

Still, who needed realism when everyone was having so much fun? By the second series the show had reached that critical velocity which enabled any obstacle flung at it by the network to be absorbed and transmuted into an asset. 'The Dream Sequence Always Rings Twice' was the first episode to wander playfully away from the original premise, featuring two long scenes pastiching MGM showbiz musicals and Warner Brothers gumshoe adventures in every detail, right down to real black and white film stock. This gave ABC the fear; they insisted on the addition of an upfront warning to reassure the simple viewer that their set wasn't going on the blink. The producers made the warning, and got Orson Welles, in his last TV appearance, to deliver it.

The third season was yet more extravagant. A parody of *The Taming of the Shrew*, performed in period costume on a huge medieval backlot and written in iambic pentameter, trod a fine line between flash precocity and grating conceit (and admitted as much). Stunts like this made *Moonlighting* a stupendously costly show, regularly ringing up over $1.5 million an episode. Lavish production values and an all-consuming attention to detail often led to close runs with the show's broadcast deadlines: several times repeats had to be called up to fill in the gaps (with sheepish references to the hiatus tacked onto the start of the next episode when it finally arrived). Scenes were being shot and dropped into the show on the day of transmission.[399]

With such a fragile grip on its resources and its internal logic, *Moonlighting* couldn't last forever. The 'will they, won't they?' tease came to an abrupt end with the close of season three as Maddie and David consummated their relationship. Season four began in confident mode, with the cast larking about in a parody of *The Honeymooners* and a guest appearance from Ray Charles, but things were disintegrating fast. Shepherd, pregnant and increasingly at odds with the producers, appeared less and less. Willis, preparing for the first *Die Hard* film, had one foot out the door himself. Scenes featuring Willis and Shepherd together, the lifeblood of the series, became increasingly rare. Eva Marie Saint guested as Maddie's mother. David was put on a chain gang. Shepherd appeared in Claymation. As the heart of the show went AWOL, these cute bits of business lost their charm.

The fifth season opened with a jaunty musical number. 'Another season, another try/ To make twenty-two shows before we die/ A chance for critics to stop and sneer/ "We know they'll only make sixteen this year".' Despite a concerted effort to ditch the experimental fripperies and return to the original screwball exchanges, they managed just thirteen. The last of these trundled to a close with the dismantling of the detective agency set, and a fictional producer telling the fictional pair just why their fictional lives had to come to a real end – people had tired of it. At the outer limits of American television's long tradition of exhaustive self-reference, *Moonlighting* proved a series really can be too clever for its own good.

POB'S PROGRAMME (1985–7)

Channel Four (Ragdoll)

The threadbare origins of a children's television empire.

IT'S OFTEN SAID THAT children's television took a wrong turn somewhere: it began as an array of magical, prelapsarian programmes hand-crafted in potting sheds by committed artisans with an instinctive ability to think and feel like a child; and ended up as committee-designed, lifelessly loud franchises that exist primarily as a Trojan horse for branded lunchboxes. The only argument is when precisely the balance tipped from the first type to the second – it usually turns out to be when the person making the judgement hit puberty. Looked at more objectively, things aren't quite that simple – indeed, one producer achieved global domination with an equal mixture of commercial nous and childlike otherworldliness.

Anne Wood was an English teacher at a secondary modern school in 1965 when she founded child literacy magazine *Books for Your Children*. The campaign to encourage children to read slowly grew until she moved first to Tyne Tees, then Yorkshire Television in the late 1970s. Her first programme as producer, 1979's *The Book Tower*, continued the literacy-building theme and introduced Wood's signature style: an unabashed oddness. Few others would have set a programme designed to encourage reluctant junior readers in a forbidding stately home stalked by Tom Baker, who would spy on children 'testing' new books through peepholes and secret panels. But adult expectations of what children might find off-putting are often wildly wrong, and the programme and attached library campaign were a great success.

Wood cemented her reputation as consultant children's editor to nascent breakfast channel TV-am. As the main breakfast programme plunged in the ratings, her *Shedvision* segment, hosted by puppeteer David Claridge's egomaniacal creation Roland Rat, was another offbeat hit. In turn she became an independent producer under the guise of Ragdoll Productions, with a company philosophy borrowed from Carl Jung: 'Without this playing with fantasy, no creative work has ever yet come to birth'.[400] Channel Four, looking to explore the undiscovered country of preschool entertainment, were the first to seek out her talent for high-rating oddities. Wood gave them *Pob's Programme*.

In the time-frozen landscape of snooker, old westerns and farming news that formed the typical British Sunday afternoon, Pob, a part-sock, part-monkey puppet with the public speaking skills of Joe Pasquale undergoing heavy root canal work, stood out somewhat. The concept, as ever with Wood, was both highly specific and difficult to grasp. Pob lived inside your TV set, choosing two o'clock on a Sunday to make his presence felt by semi-communicating to the very young through the screen. At the same time, friendly celebrities (Roy Castle, Hannah Gordon) were mysteriously inducted by following a trail of wool through a garden (which proved to be Pob himself unravelling) and reading a story specially commissioned from respected children's writers like Catherine Storr and Alan Garner.

Then there was the 'spitting'. To put his garbled message across, Pob would often breathe onto his side of the screen and write or draw diagrams in the resulting mist. Unfortunately the effect used for this illusion made the mist seem more like foaming snow white phlegm. Parental concerns about children responding in kind, at a time when TV sets were still a) mainly rented and b) regarded as only mildly less dangerous than Three Mile Island, were rife. Add to all this some elaborate contraptions made by Alan Dart, and a confusing assortment of melancholy Victorian etchings, and you had a show that looked thrown together on a series of conflicting whims. But logic, as Wood knew, carries little weight with the under-fives. Having put up her Surrey house as security to start Ragdoll, she took Pob seriously. Unable to afford a replacement, she stored the precious puppet carefully away between filming sessions in a deposit box.

So much children's TV is created by adults mired for too long in business mode, trying to deduce from first principles what children want, like bewildered babysitting Aristotles. The end product can often seem a strange interpretation of youthful desires, especially to children. Wood got the concept of *Pob* from real world observation: 'I really got the idea from watching children in Tesco's – you see them trapped in those supermarket trolleys, trying to communicate.'[401] The idea of an unintelligible children's protagonist, communicating on a level below language to those who were yet to master it, became a Wood trademark, despite the trouble it caused.

Wood was one of the first children's producers to embrace that elusive quality: cult status. At Yorkshire Television she noted the ability of *Ragdolly Anna* to turn the Leeds flat where the title character supposedly lived into a place of parent-child pilgrimage. Wood was less interested in the other, ironic, kind of cult status enjoyed by *The Magic Roundabout*, but her work had this too: a survey of the most popular programmes with sixteen to twenty-four-year-olds in August 1989 placed *Pob's Programme* at number seven, amid more obviously teen-friendly shows like *The Chart Show* and *4 on the Floor*.[402]

Ragdoll's star rose through the nineties. *Rosie and Jim*, the adventures of two knitted puppets aboard a narrow boat captained by *Postman Pat* creator John Cunliffe, was Ragdoll's first step into the emerging sell-through video market, and a successful one, shifting two million copies. Its second cousin, the multi-lingual *Tots TV*, won that most lucrative goal, an American franchise. In 1996,

Wood channelled the money from this into her biggest, and most outlandish, venture.

Employing a lavish, purpose-built permanent outdoor set, equally extravagant mechanically assisted costumes and a battery of Day-Glo effects, *Teletubbies* transformed the BBC's venerable *Play School* slot into a Fisher Price hangover seemingly designed specifically to enervate fastidious parents. But wary tuts over its retrograde baby talk turned first to thankful sighs over its hypnotic power to keep toddlers quietly stationary, and finally to full-blown cult membership. With *Teletubbies* and its successor, *In the Night Garden* – a *Finnegans Wake* to the Tubbies' *Ulysses* – Wood established a highly marketable pre-school style, a visual Esperanto spoken in over seventy-five countries, defiantly unintelligible to anyone over six.

THE MAX HEADROOM SHOW (1985–7)

Channel Four/HBO (Chrysalis Visual Programming)

Enter the pop video, exit the pop presenter.

VIDEOS, OR TO GIVE them their original handle, 'promo clips', have been made, usually on a shoestring, since the sixties, but by the eighties they'd become an industry in themselves. In 1980, Blondie released *Eat to the Beat*, the 'first full-length album video-cassette' with production costs of $100,000. 'Video tapes of rock acts may some day be a hot item,' the *NME* speculated, 'if enough directors with imagination move into the field.'[403] The current state of the art certainly seemed to offer dizzying possibilities: 'You can now walk into a record shop and buy an hour-long Boney M concert for £37.75.'[404]

Video would soon become synonymous with corporate marketing might, but in its earliest days a relatively modest outlay could get you a workable promo, and there was plenty of indie experimentation. The first video-only album, *Emotional Warfare* by The Gas, arrived in 1981 on a budget of £300. The following year Scottish band Strutz released *Start/Stop*, the first video single, available only by mail order. Punters sent a blank cassette which was returned with the video dubbed on, 'leaving the rest of the cassette free for further taping'. This was all technically, though not necessarily visually, exciting. 'Not a verse goes by without someone furiously twisting the zoom lens,' opined Phill McNeill of a typical early video, 'or shoving a black and white image across the colour one and then, even more irritatingly (cos it's a good effect) flashing it off again.'[405] These off-the-peg tricks would form the backbone of indie video making for the next decade.

Perhaps the most commercially successful early 'video artist' was Toni Basil. Her 1982 album *Word of Mouth* – white backgrounds, kaleidoscopic costumes, legs-to-the-sky choreography – came out on both LP and VHS/Beta via video label Radialchoice ('music you can see on records you can watch'), and appeared on TV as *The Toni Basil Special*. Though her success was rapid, Basil became an early victim of the video credibility gap. 'I don't consider what I do as showbiz,' she protested. 'It's not insipid Broadway stuff. It's rock 'n' roll!'

In what would become a familiar pattern for the music industry, the sell-through video market began to struggle once someone invented a way to disseminate the product for free. Ex-Monkee Mike Nesmith, who knew a thing or two about the video credibility gap, had just inherited a small fortune from his mother, the creator of Liquid Paper. With it he made esoteric 1981 video-album *Elephant Parts*, mixing music videos with freeform comedy bits perched somewhere between Ernie Kovacs and *Saturday Night Live*. (The Monkees had form in the rambling oddity stakes, both in the cinema with psychedelic consumer satire *Head*, and on TV with pantomime music business satire *33 1/3 Revolutions Per Monkee*, the latter authored by Jack Good.) Nesmith also made *Popclips* in 1980, the first music video show, for Warner Brothers' fledgling cable channel Nickelodeon. In between unenthralling promos for Poco and Huey Lewis, assorted comedians would improvise links while pretending to DJ with prop laserdiscs, on a set constructed from polystyrene electrical goods packaging. Rickety as they were, the links often held more interest than the videos.

Spotting the germ of great things in this video lean-to, Warners poached the concept and launched MTV in 1981, with more graphical pizazz but less presentational wit. Not that it mattered: within two years sixty per cent of North America's cable-ready homes were consuming over an hour a week. By then much of the old DIY chaos had been replaced by efficient content delivery, with just enough quirk to avoid youthful ridicule. Conversely the videos, especially those made in the UK, reached new heights of invention. The all-American channel inadvertently facilitated pop's second British invasion.

While the UK's artists stormed America, their fellow countrymen, slow to change viewing habits, resisted music television's charms. Virgin attempted to kick-start the revolution in 1983, hooking up with major video producers Palace Pictures to create Cable Music, a channel mixing videos with 'proper' interviews and magazine programmes. Instead of Mike Nesmith it had Ringo Starr. Still, reworked for pan-European satellite transmission and renamed Music Box, it was picked up by various ITV regions hungry for cheap content to fill the newly deregulated broadcasting hours after midnight. Timmy Mallett, Gaz Top, Gary Crowley, Nicky Campbell, Anthea Turner and John Leslie were among those whose careers were sustained or created by the station. Later still BSB, Sky Television's foredoomed opponent, advertised its music outlet The Power Station by painting its other channels as 'four ways of persuading your parents to pay for a TV channel they'll hate!' Few kids took the bait.

The credibility gap closed slightly when video makers graduated to programme production. Peter Wagg, whose promo CV included everyone from Blondie to Billy Connolly, had been toying with the idea of a non-human linkman for a pop video showcase since 1981, on the basis that 'it's hard to find a human being who won't irritate most of the people most of the time.'[406] Rocky Morton and Annabel Jankel, whose Cucumber Studios created memorable promos for Elvis Costello and Talking Heads, moulded the very man – a sharp-suited amalgam of every arch show business tic and smooth line of patter, saved from cold super-efficiency by the occasional glitchy 'stutter loop' and a nice line in esoterically egocentric chat courtesy of Paul Owen and David Hansen, fugitive writers from *Russ Abbott's Saturday Madhouse*.

Max Headroom, self-proclaimed *bon vivant, gaucho amigo,* goombah, mensch and fifth musketeer, was introduced to the public via that venerable television institution, the po-faced April fool. The earnestly-titled *Channel Four Investigates . . . A Leap Forward In Television?* pitched Wagg against various concerned pundits debating the ethical implications of entirely artificial talent. The gag was blown three days later with the screening of *Max Headroom: 20 Minutes Into the Future*, a slice of dystopian science fiction which was very much in the current style: all shadows and fog, urban no-go zones and pre-stressed *Face* magazine clobber. Amongst the forest of angular black hardware was a wryly cynical take on pressure cooker advertising, consumer docility and the barrel-scraping possibilities of multi-channel television. TV was an amoral pap factory, and its salvation a sarcastic CGI lounge lizard with the diction of Porky Pig.

Two days after that, Max himself (i.e. actor Matt Frewer in a prosthetic skull cap) hosted the real *Max Headroom Show* (i.e. the fictional show within the previous show). Combining the shopworn professionalism of Bob Hope with the snippy camp of Russell Harty, Max was a true transatlantic creation. With his supercilious introductions, microsecond mood swings and complete lack of interest in anything beyond shoes, golf and pine furniture, he exposed the lacquered shallowness of the mainstream, even as the accompanying videos, grab-bags of electronic effects, silent movie footage and papier-mâché Rene Magritte rip-offs were frantically trying to dress it up.

The result was either a neat symbiosis or a zero-sum game, depending on where your interests and investments lay, but it worked. When TV tried to match pop for glamour or danger, it just looked gawky and cheap. But by playing the fool in the rock business court, it could boost both itself and its guest stars with a wit and humility so often absent from the music itself. Sting was just one of many to realise that arguing with a visual effect over a pair of golf shoes went a long way to atone for the lyrics of 'Synchronicity II'.

A VERY PECULIAR PRACTICE (1986–8)
BBC Two

Allegory goes peak time.

TV DRAMA HAS ITS fashions. Every few years certain subjects, styles and themes colonise the schedules: psychiatric soul searching in the late sixties, tricksy self-awareness in the seventies, roving-camera street realism in the early eighties. The late eighties hosted another sub-genre, identified by Hugh Herbert as 'bastard forms that draw on Gothic romance or that flirt with surrealism.' They took a dramatic genre, twisted it out of whack and decorated it with moments of supreme weirdness. In Herbert's judgement, 'often they reach for a deeper significance and almost as often they fall flat on their fancy.'[407]

Representing harsh reality with fantastic means was a strategy born of the Cold War. The threat of global destruction felt simultaneously very real and absurdly abstract. A realistic treatment, *à la Threads*, could only be done so many times before repetition set in and depression descended. *Z-Cars* creator Troy Kennedy Martin set realism aside to adapt *The Old Men at the Zoo*, Angus Wilson's 1961 conflation of international apocalypse and zoological administration, updated to 1983. Two years later came Kennedy Martin's own study of nuclear power, corporate greed and government cover up in the revered *Edge of Darkness*. For many, it was a smart melding of conspiracy thriller and environmental polemic. For others – well, for Hugh Herbert – it was 'the biggest collection of thriller clichés and trendy Thoughts for the Day you could sweep off a committee room floor'.[408] But *Edge of Darkness*'s 'clichés' were a means to an end, and it heralded a clutch of programmes that bent dramatic conventions to examine the modern world in oblique, dreamlike and often outrageous style.

Many big names entered this social hall of mirrors. In 1986, Fay Weldon's female revenge fable *The Life and Loves of a She-Devil* was burnished by director Philip Saville into high Greek tragedy with shoulder pads. Howard Schuman's *Up Line* refracted recession Britain through the prism of a cultish pyramid selling scheme. (Motto: 'shitty jobs for shitty times'.) *The Romans in Britain* writer Howard Brenton crammed diatribes on class and imperialism into *Dead Head*, a conspiracy film noir shot in what Julian Barnes dubbed 'super-murkovision',[409] which achieved notoriety for a highly symbolic rope-and-wellies sex scene.

Lower down the ladder of prestige came the psychotic pop video dystopias. *Brond*, a 'hallucinatory political thriller', brought *Z-Cars*'s Stratford Johns out of retirement to push kids off Glaswegian bridges and submit to a cattle-prod-wielding dominatrix in his underpants. That old favourite, the fascist future Britain where bedraggled hordes huddle round braziers while armoured vans full of rubberised riot police thunder down the overpass, was unpacked for *Boogie Outlaws*, a stilted rock-band-versus-the-state fantasy directed by Keith Godman, graduate of the 'Pick Up a Penguin' biscuit ads. At barrel's bottom, ultraviolent musical *Body Contact* boasted members of the Human League on the soundtrack, Timothy Spall as a Kalashnikov-toting gangster and Jack Shepherd as a hang-gliding, rapping sado-masochist priest. As sub-genres go, it was rarely dull.

The thriller wasn't the only genre that could be satirically super-charged. Andrew Davies, a lecturer at Warwick University who augmented his salary by writing children's programmes and period adaptations, worked the trick on that perennially unpromising format, the campus farce. Lowlands University was Davies's redbrick microcosm, a moribund seat of learning barely governed by vice chancellor Ernest Hemingway (John Bird), whose main priority was working out which bits to sell to Japanese corporations. Into this pit of despair Davies dropped Dr Stephen Daker (Peter Davison), a pleasant, open-minded new recruit to the medical faculty.

Daker's fellow doctors occupied various positions on the spectrum of acrimony: vampish, surname eschewing arch feminist Dr Rose Marie; faculty head Jock McCannon, a cynical ex-radical composed of equal parts R. D. Laing and Famous Grouse; and Bob Buzzard, a spineless, opportunistic entrepreneur, the free market incarnate in outsize Saatchi specs. Davies called them his 'sacred monsters': people who 'carry on as though they rule the world,'[410] the academic hothouse having distorted their fractious personalities into psychic gargoyles. Even Daker's one ally, down-to-earth behavioural psychologist Lynn, could intimidate him with, if anything, an excess of relaxed normality. In the background hovered staff and students varying in amiability and sanity, and two entirely unexplained feral nuns.

Having built the academic equivalent of a model train set, Davies put on his stationmaster's cap and began inventing ways to derail it. STD outbreaks, impotent professors, intrusive security measures and student riots assailed Daker and company week after week. Davies drew on his alma mater for odd details. Warwick was a research outpost for the Sinclair C5 electric buggy, and provided several senior lecturers with freebies, in which they solemnly trundled from lecture to lecture. A low-speed C5 chase was, however, excised from an early draft: slightly too ridiculous.[411]

For the second series, the rot took hold. Lowlands was bought by American developers, with a keen interest in cybernetics and defence and no use whatsoever for the philosophy department. In the closing one-off *A Very Polish Practice*, Daker and Buzzard duked it out in Eastern Europe as capitalism awaited its chance to move into the vacuum which would soon be left by communism in retreat. Throughout, Davies diligently ensured the allegorical elements remained subservient to the human drama. Daker's story

– a congenitally nice but often ineffectual man gets shafted by a sold-out, grudge-full world – was universal. This was crucial to the show's success. You can make your model railway as exquisite as you like, but tie a real person to the tracks.

The flogging of Lowlands coincided with the flogging of Britain, and few aspects of British life were flogged harder than British television. The popular allegory, however well crafted, became an increasingly difficult proposal. Proven talents like Dennis Potter and Alan Bleasdale were still given a fair degree of freedom, but in general the unusual was kept in check. *The Cloning of Joanna May*, Fay Weldon's sequel of sorts to *She-Devil*, was a flamboyant throwback, and Michael Dobbs's *House of Cards* (adapted by Davies) stood alone in arch defiance, the offspring of a messy one-night stand between Bertolt Brecht and Jeffrey Archer. In the main, though, nineties drama went back to its generic basics, its fancy Dan meditations on the human condition subordinated to the basic need for bums on sofas. Ambition hadn't deserted popular drama, but it seldom showed itself again in quite such lurid colours.

THE COMIC STRIP PRESENTS . . . PRIVATE ENTERPRISE (1986)

Channel Four (Comic Strip/ Michael White Productions)

TV gives alternative comedy carte blanche.

NOT ALL NEW WAVES break the same. Pop's New Wave, at a generous estimate, managed five years from swell to backwash. Its theatrical counterpart began a little earlier and ended a little later. The comic New Wave, while last to gather, lasted longer than its predecessors combined, mainly due to the media savvy of its practitioners.

The Comic Strip began as an alternative cabaret night, a splinter group of comedians from hip Soho club The Comedy Store. It was established in 1980 on the seedy, plastic-palm premises of the Raymond Revue Bar by writer and actor Peter Richardson, as a venue for his latest project, a William Burroughs musical. The musical was soon forgotten in favour of modern cabaret. 'It was,' reflected compère Alexei Sayle, 'quite a calculated move for us to enhance our careers.'[412] It worked: listings magazines *Time Out* and *City Limits* hailed the club; soon broadsheet hacks and TV producers were spotted in the back row. The next move was inevitable.

The TV Comic Strip centred around three double acts.

Richardson and Nigel Planer, aka The Outer Limits, were a musical comedy duo specialising in elaborate concept shows. Rival act 20th Century Coyote (Rik Mayall and Adrian Edmondson) worked at the other end of the sophistication spectrum. Keen students of *commedia dell'arte*, they combined terrible poetry with existential acts of tit-for-tat sadism. Dawn French and Jennifer Saunders completed the sextet with a roster of naturalistic character sketches, tending towards sulky sixth form strops. Other comics, notably Sayle and Keith Allen, augmented the core squad.

Their champion was BBC light entertainment production manager Paul Jackson, who after a couple of cabaret specials commissioned *The Young Ones*, a student sitcom that could switch from Chekhov parodies to farting hamsters with only the mildest crunch of gears. Richardson was the only Strip member not to feature – he was in talks with Jeremy Isaacs of the nascent Channel Four over an entirely different proposal.

The Comic Strip had already been immortalised in an eponymous 1981 short film by Julian Temple, visual architect of Sex Pistols post mortem *The Great Rock 'n' Roll Swindle*. Like that film, it was a mess of off-the-cuff doodles built around footage of the club's various acts. Sayle impersonated a Bertolt Brecht impersonator, pop-up toasters were celebrated in song, and green and magenta gels were applied to the lights with liberal abandon. It was disowned by everyone and buried for years.

What Richardson had instigated was far more ambitious than that punkish squib, but less countercultural in its pose. Channel Four's youth commissioning editor Mike Bolland called *The Comic Strip Presents...* 'the Ealing comedy of the eighties.'[413] Richardson himself compared it to the then profoundly unfashionable *Carry On* films, adding, 'I don't like jokes to no purpose. I like comedy that's about attitudes.'[414] This certainly applied to the first film, 'Five Go Mad in Dorset', which adorned the station's opening night schedule in 1982. The Famous Five, Enid Blyton's jolly gang of prep school vigilantes, were recast as dim, gluttonous bigots, giving the common folk and Johnny Foreigner a good lashing in between lashings of ginger beer.

The following films varied tremendously in style, content and tone. A breakneck, surreal farce would be followed a week later by a naturalistic, subtle character study. In an industry that was just starting to buy into the culture of branding this was, one critic remarked, 'a brave attack on television market research.'[415]

The stylistic jumble could be separated into a few distinct types. 'Five Go Mad . . .' headed one: the pastiches. These picked apart the visual and verbal clichés of cinema and TV: 'A Fistful of Travellers' Cheques' did spaghetti westerns; 'Consuela' filleted Hitchcock; the glam-grit cop show was skewered by 'The Bullshitters'; the fly-on-the-wall documentary skilfully aped in 'Bad News Tour'.

Chat show parody 'An Evening with Eddie Monsoon', starring Edmondson as a repellent Afrikaner TV star, had to be canned due to its extreme, potentially libellous content. Reworked as 'Eddie Monsoon – A Life?', it took its place in another fruitful category, the anarchic free-for-all. These films, though still well crafted, were closer to the team's tumultuous cabaret roots. Edmondson and Mayall enrolled Peter Cook as honorary member for 'Mr Jolly Lives Next Door', an alcoholic stagger through the junkyard of minor celebrity. Alexei Sayle's 'Didn't You Kill My Brother?' was a 200-decibel morality play combining the Kray twins, Brecht, Vittorio De Sica and a dead badger. More so even than *Monty Python*, this was a clash of the high and low brows, with little in between: cerebral satire meets brain-stem burlesque.

Somewhere between the scatological eruption and the cool technical spoof came a handful of more character-driven films. Adrian Edmondson's 'Private Enterprise' is the ideal example: a social satire populated with morally challenged characters of variously puny social standing, it's a concentrated burst of Essence of Eighties – *Only Fools and Horses* reconditioned by Ken Loach.

Keith (Richardson) is a toilet paper deliveryman on parole for God knows what, shacking up with girlfriend Debbie (Saunders) and temporarily harbouring his even dodgier pal Brian (Edmondson), who has a nicely exasperating line in dole queue philosophy. ('I do believe it's my superior intelligence that's secured my position in that small but elite body of men and women commonly known as Maggie's Millions.') Keith happens on the demo tape of Toy Department, a New Romantic band led by Mayall's fractious, boiler-suited neo-fop Ali ('So just because I dress more imaginatively than you, then I'm too fashionable to know anything about music, am I?') He punts it to the supercilious head of A&R at Hard Corps Records (Planer), who decides to release it as a tax loss. Unfortunately the anonymous drone becomes a massive hit, and Keith and Brian are tasked with conjuring a national tour out of thin air. Deceit is piled upon deceit, and desperation mounts. Keith's parole officer (French) closes in. Urgent action is required.

It was a prescient story. A couple of weeks after it was broadcast, Sigue Sigue Sputnik, a cartoon punk 'fantasy band' assembled by Tony James, released their first single, a shapeless mess of riffs, samples and posturing yelps eerily similar to Toy Department's 'Boots', a horribly catchy number concocted by the Strip's musical ace Simon Brint. James and company peppered their debut LP with paid adverts. The idealism of the musical New Wave had become a shameless devotion to private enterprise. The comic New Wave had the last laugh.

Rather like its central character, 'Private Enterprise' was a ramshackle operator, despite a solid plot, decent parts and enjoyable cameos from Roger Sloman and Lionel Jeffries. Edmondson handled his first directing gig gamely, but there's an unevenness to it that falls outside even the generous scope of rough-and-ready naturalism. When the series returned two years later, it began with Richardson's 'Strike', which couldn't have been slicker. By dovetailing a character story (Sayle's idealistic working class screenwriter pens a history of the miner's strike which gets butchered by Hollywood) with razor sharp film parody (the all-action end result of the commission), 'Strike' dragged the series far enough into the mainstream to win the 1988 Golden Rose of Montreux – despite it being screened to delegates without foreign language subtitles.[416] The Strip's constituent players duly took their places in the comedy establishment, but it was an establishment they'd helped change radically – one that was now more technically capable, more socially aware, and considerably more flatulent.

NIGHT NETWORK (1987–9)

LWT (Night Network Productions)

British television finally gets to stay up late.

Sniffing glue's over and Barclaycards are in.
Stuart Cosgrove, 'The Rise and Fall of Cult TV', *Listener*,
18 February 1988

IN THE USA, NETWORK television has run from early morning to the small hours since the 1950s, with magazine programmes populating mornings, and *Tonight* and its descendants occupying the night. British television, far more regulated and reserved from the outset, approached the depths of the night in a much more tentative manner, rarely staying up past midnight unless international sport or world events made extra time essential.

One early British all-nighter was composed entirely of American material. Granada's *The All-American All-Nite Show* sprawled over various ITV regions from 2 a.m. to 7 a.m. on 5 November 1980, marking the occasion of the USA's momentous Reagan-Carter election battle with a feast of clips from the hairier outposts of US television. Humiliating game shows, possessed evangelists, mad stuntmen jumping over speeding cars and losing a foot in the process, and Oscar the Wonder Rodent were wryly introduced by

Ned Sherrin. 'Remember,' he concluded ominously, 'that everybody you've seen tonight had a vote.' Such cretinous behaviour was kept firmly off our cultured British schedules, which still ended at a reasonable hour, even if they no longer came to a close with a thoughtful poem read by a cardigan-clad actor. But for how much longer?

Independent TV was regularly pushing out the post-midnight boat by the mid-1980s. Channel Four made highbrow treks past the dead of night with the moderately successful *After Dark*, an open-ended panel discussion, and the less successful *UK Late*, the same programme with a shouting studio audience. *After Dark* was memorable for its unflinching guest policy, booking at various times a drunk Oliver Reed, Klaus Barbie's defence counsel and a self-confessed child molester (though they decided against inviting Gerry Adams). *UK Late* was memorable for the terrible mess it made during its tiny lifespan. 'It's important to be constantly embarrassed by what you do,' mused John Peel on one edition. 'I hope, when I look at this programme on video, to be embarrassed by this, too.'

Otherwise, late night TV was a drowsy procession of veteran films, pop videos and cheap imports, notably over-excited US chat show *Donahue* and *Prisoner Cell-Block H*, a scraping from the Australian soap barrel which came to occupy a perversely high position in British popular culture. On *This Morning with Richard Not Judy*, Peter Baynham invented the game of switching randomly between different episodes of *Cell-Block H* being shown on different ITV regions to create entirely new plots ('I got Vinegar Tits to have an argument with herself the other night.') When London Weekend Television launched the first bespoke night-time programming at 1 a.m. on 29 August 1987, it had the *Prisoner*, rather than the *After Dark*, audience in mind.

Night Network was the creation of producer Jill Sinclair, graduate of *The Old Grey Whistle Test*, with help from future *Snub TV* founder Brenda Kelly. (Youth TV was largely female-led – Sinclair joined *Network 7* bigwigs Jane Hewland and Janet Street-Porter, and Katie Lander, architect of Jonathan Ross's *The Last Resort*.) Described by

LWT's Head of Entertainment Marcus Plantin as a 'night-time pot-pourri of youth-oriented fare'[417] and a suspicious *New Musical Express* as '*Saturday Superstore* with knobs on,'[418] *Night Network* filled the small hours of Saturday, Sunday and Monday with stripped mini-programmes that aimed to captivate easily distracted, high-spending youth with minimal production costs.

Like the first explorers of an uncharted wasteland, *Night Network*'s initial settlements were simple, makeshift affairs lashed together from whatever came to hand. Logos and livery were MTV in style: spiky luminescent graphics assembled themselves in a flurry of stylish animation to the sound of soft rock power chords. Pop videos were jammed into every available nook, alongside vintage transatlantic trash like *Batman* and *The Partridge Family*. Presenters Mick Brown and Paul Thompson addressed the sleepless thousands with the studied insouciance of the hipster journalist. Every trick was pulled to convince the viewer they were part of a tiny, clued-up elite, not a shiftless diaspora of lonely insomniacs.

Nicholas Parsons launched the 'ironic dotage' phase of his career with *The All-New Alphabet Game*, showering questions and film clips on celebrity contestants like Katie Boyle and Alice Cooper in an atmosphere of knowing tackiness. Despite Parsons's attempts to inject some edginess into proceedings ('Come on, this isn't a family show!') the mood was pure sequinned kitsch, a retro Day-Glo atmosphere that would soon usurp the earnest technophilia of *Network 7* to become the default setting for youth TV.

Slightly more successful in the sauce department was *Pillow Talk*, in which Emma Freud and guest (initially the BBC's star MP-cum-daytime-star Robert Kilroy-Silk) took coyly to bed for an 'intimate' interview lifted wholesale from Paula Yates's segment of *The Tube*. Most of the other mini-programmes were interviews, too. In *Leee's Place*, singer Leee John interviewed other musicians in a mocked-up bar, while in *The Bunker Show* Rowland Rivron chatted drunkenly to random star guests in a mocked-up fallout shelter, complete with a year's supply of toilet rolls. Angie Clarke, sister of motormouth Margi, had a shopping slot. Craig Charles ran a music video gong show. In between, bite-size snippets of Californian glamour and saucy fun (like the nation's top ten condoms) pinned *Night Network* irrevocably to its late-eighties habitat.

Not quite everything went: magician-comedian Jerry Sadowitz was given a slot to air some material from his Total Abuse live show, but a combination of self-exposure (on screen) and routines about the private life of Jimmy Savile (off it) got him banned from the programme after one appearance. As the show matured, the Sunday night edition frequently resorted to mouldering old films, and occasionally the entire night's billing would consist of three deadly words like 'Belgian rock festival'.

Beyond conquering the small hours in the name of entertainment, *Night Network* was a pioneer in less noble areas. Its producers worked closely with, and had their programming decisions formed by, the sales and advertising departments. Commercial television always kept the bottom line in sight, but *Night Network* was the first British show to tie itself firmly to its advertisers. Carefully keeping on the right side of the Independent Broadcasting Authority's ruling that 'advertising has to be clear and separate from programmes,' *Night Network* was still, in the words of sales manager Richard Holliday, 'product television,' where 'advertising becomes more of a complete part of the viewing experience than would normally be the case.'[419] These were not the words of establishment-shaking guerilla programme makers, but at a surprisingly healthy £1,000 for a thirty-second advertising slot, *Night Network* couldn't help but milk its affluent demographic for all it was worth.

Night Network lasted barely two years, but its various regional clones and successors kept the fast-moving capsule format and the rock-bottom budgets of the pioneers. Levels of sophistication may have varied, but the *i-D* magazine cool of *01 for London*, the laddish goofiness of *MTV's Most Wanted* and the tabloid leer of *The James*

Whale Radio Show were cut from the same dress pattern. The wasteland may have been colonised, but only a certain type of programme could flourish there: simple, hardy and low on sobriety; a night bus riding the ether.

MAHABHARAT (1988–90)

Doordarshan (BR Films)

All-singing, all-dancing, all-retina-burning dramatisation of the Indian epic poem.

Full of ideal romance, mystery, thrills, suspense, chivalry, adventure, awe-inspiring exploits and spine-shilling miracles, this wonderful epic . . . provides valuable guidance to the common householder for leading a pious, plain and virtuous life.

T. R. Bahnot, Introduction to
Mahabharat, Part 1, 1990

WHEN GLOBETROTTING THEATRE DIRECTOR Peter Brook staged the *Mahabharata*, the epic poem of India's mythic origins on Channel Four in 1989, he shaved a third off his open air theatrical version to leave a six-hour pageant of mysticism, ritual and deeply respectful mime. The due deference Brook gave the host culture was in turn served up to him by his fellow countrymen. There was a respectful *South Bank Show* special, an interview on *Signals*, and Channel Four published study guides and a lavish 160-page book. It was big, it was multicultural and it was deeply devout.

At about the same time, Indian television was putting its own version together, and it couldn't have been more different. Instead of respectful ritual and tasteful candlelight, the Indian *Mahabharat* was bombastic, heartfelt and epic in scope. Replicating the highly chromatic visions of the country's abundant religious murals, it pushed the medium to the limit, testing the limits of broadcastable colour saturation and seeing just how many flying demons could be superimposed on screen at any one time. It was every bit as devout as Brook's work, and fifteen times bigger, but unlike the impresario's version, this one positively romped along.

Television in India came late and grew slowly. Doordarshan, the state service, began in 1959, serving a handful of homes in a very restricted locale. The 1970s saw the partial adoption of advertising and a steady rise in audience, but full national coverage and colour only arrived in the early 1980s, bringing with them a boom in set ownership that was mainly fuelled by gargantuan serials and soaps.

From 1984, open-ended family sagas with huge casts proliferated, beginning with *Hum Log* (rough translation: People Like Us), closely based on the emotionally explicit 'Telenovela' format popular in Latin America. Focussing on a middle class extended family with the usual quota of illicit liaisons, feuds and black sheep, it reached an estimated audience of fifty million at its peak.

In 1987 director Ramanand Sagar applied the family saga format to epic Hindu poem the *Ramayana*. The series that resulted, *Ramayan* and *Luv Kush*, comprised over sixty hours of sumptuous palatial receptions, epic running battles and science fiction monster costumes as the bejewelled green hero of the piece searched for his kidnapped wife to a fully orchestrated musical commentary. It became essential Sunday morning viewing, with public screenings organised to maximise the audience – estimated at up to 100 million by the state's (admittedly not very reliable) ratings service.[420] As with many a popular fantasy franchise since, the success was milked by dragging the story out for as long as possible, and huge, seventeen-minute commercial breaks were inserted in the middle of each episode.

While India was hooked on Ram's quest, Doordarshan was already arranging a version of the *Mahabharat* to follow it. This was the big one. Weighing in at over 83,000 couplets – several

Bibles' worth of verse – this tale of the two warring families said to have founded ancient India was well-known to the vast majority of the population in all parts of the country. Some even had the entire thing off by heart. B. P. Chopra, taking a style only marginally less opulent than his predecessor, had the job of turning it into ninety-three hour-long episodes.

It was a mammoth task. In the story, heroines take multiple husbands and have innumerable sons, one of whom spends whole episodes conducting lengthy speeches while impaled on a bed of arrows. Warriors rip open their adversaries' chests and drink their blood, while ascetics stand on one toe in snowy wildernesses for years on end. Duels are conducted with gigantic spherical golden hammers, rhythmically swung by the combatants ('Hurgh!' *Doink*. 'Hurgh!' *Doink*). A hundred elephants charge into battle under hails of flaming arrows. Fifty-foot visions of Krishna spout fire and water and swallow populations. Men impregnate fish and women give birth to cannonballs of flesh. It's the most gob-smacking story ever told.

Chopra did the source material proud, marshalling episode-long battle scenes and baroque apparitions with conviction. *Ramayan*'s previous records were shattered. Estimates pushed the audience share towards ninety-five per cent of Indians with access to a television set. The government had to reschedule their Sunday briefing session after a clash with the programme's transmission led to several cabinet ministers bunking off to watch it.[421]

The series made its way to other countries, picking up a sizeable, if less strictly devout, following in each one. The BBC's regular Sunday afternoon and midnight screenings in the early 1990s became a source of unaccountable addiction for many non-Hindu viewers, who searched vainly for adequate cultural comparisons. ('*The Singing Ringing Tree* crossed with *Clash of the Titans*', said the *Listener*.[422]) Shortly after the final episode aired, a travelling stage version, complete with most of the original TV cast and some of the original elephants, played Wembley Arena, a fittingly outsize send-off for a programme that, against all good sense, took every monumental Cinemascope epic ever made and squeezed them all onto a twenty-four inch screen – something of a miracle in itself.

DEF II (1988–94)
BBC Two

The last stand of 'youth' TV.

LIKE AN OLD SATURN V rocket stack, pop is powered by the combustible mixture of two fuels – youthful ferocity and establishment unease. By the late 1980s, the second ingredient was becoming increasingly scarce. The country's great and good included ever more veteran rock fans in ever more powerful positions. Shrieks of moral abhorrence gave way to tuts of amused familiarity: the Man was once a kid himself. Television in particular was all over youth like electric Biactol, and it had learned to look relaxed about it.

Pockets of the square old guard held out, but the battles they fought started looking rather silly. Late-night ITV debate *Central Weekend Live* played host to Virginian panto-metal band Gwar, whose graphic live shows were causing consternation among upright Midlanders. In a perfect distillation of the absurdity of all encounters between the citizenry and feral youth, band members Sleazy P. Martini and The Sexecutioner, resplendent in head-to-toe latex stage regalia, lolled on swivel chairs while a scarcely less visually florid sea of blowsy councillors and pork-fed aldermen heaped righteous outrage on these 'rubber teddy boys'. The punk wars were repeating themselves, this time as slapstick.

The indie wars were similarly reduced to cartoon violence at televised pre-pubie jamboree *The 1991 Smash Hits Poll Winners' Party* when, after host Philip Schofield mocked the amp-trashing antics of Carter the Unstoppable Sex Machine ('blimey, that was original!'), the band's Fruitbat wrestled him to the ground as the kids screamed on. The same year, Carter's manager, the notorious Jon 'Fat' Beast, recorded a Channel Four pilot called *Beast on the Box*, a 'music and chat show incorporating a huge vat of baked beans'. Meanwhile Vic Reeves and Bob Mortimer made *Popadoodledandy* (working title: *What a Lot of Pop We've Got! A Copper Kettle Full of Pop!*), quizzing bands in detail about their National Insurance contributions. Generational conflict gave way to general daftness.

Elsewhere on the fourth channel, Janet Street-Porter's new Sunday morning magazine gave the new cultural relativism a more serious tone. Critics said many things about *Network 7*, but nobody could argue that it didn't put in the work. Items funereal and frivolous came and went at dizzying speed. Graphics popped up all over the place. Cameras swooped and cut about seemingly at random, in an austere, Jean-Luc Godard visual style as opposed to Mike Mansfield's exuberant Ken Russell look.

Its presenters, led by Murray Boland and Magenta Devine (née Kim Taylor, former PA to the Boomtown Rats), had two moods: knowingly grave for serious items, and knowingly detached for cultural matters. The viewer was kept regularly informed of the temperature in the studio, for reasons never revealed. It was, Street-Porter explained, 'what I like to call aspirational television. That kind of show shouldn't be too easy to understand: it ought to be television you can boast to your friends that you fully understood, even if you didn't.' She wanted *Network 7* to be the '*Tinker, Tailor, Soldier, Spy* of factual television.'[423] It was a sitting duck for critical disdain, but it did have the odd champion. 'Those who complain about "distractions" are really saying that *Network 7* isn't *Panorama*,' wrote Andy Medhurst. 'Very true, but then the Pet Shop Boys aren't Ray McVay and his Band of the Day, and I know whom I'd rather dance to.'[424]

Street-Porter's grand design transferred to BBC Two in May 1988. *Def II* sprawled over Monday and Wednesday evenings, a branded collection of programmes which overruled its parent channel's livery with scratch video barcode idents and some magnificently awkward rapped continuity announcements, sounding no more authentically ghetto than Central Television's Saturday night linkman did introducing milk-float comedy *Bottle Boys* in similar style back in 1984. ('They're likely lads, you can bet this lot'll/ Prove to you they've got the bottle!')

Other hip touches fared slightly better. Quirky links were obtained by allowing celebrities of the Stephen Fry variety to ramble on about *Captain Pugwash* and other bygone cultural ephemera, some of which (*The Invaders, Battlestar Galactica*) received repeat showings. 'We are watching a culture cannibalising itself and disappearing up its own backside,' noted an apprehensive Martin Walker. 'Which may not be the best place for it.'[425]

With *Def II*, however, nostalgia was part of the structure, like the corpses of victims built into an ancient despot's defensive walls. Throughout the 1980s the 'thinking man's' pop music of choice had become more and more influenced by the ideas, often half-digested, of post-structuralist philosophers, in the same way a slim volume of Camus peeped out from their predecessors' trenchcoat pockets. For these acts, inauthenticity and spectacle became plus points. Old pop music was resurrected and playfully spliced into the new. *Def II* did the same with TV history, sporting chunks of the ironically disinterred past in the form of out-of-context archive clips. (Cut from studio to Fyffe Robertson on an old *Tonight* report, standing next to a huge fish, saying 'I'm standing here with this huge fish!' Cut back to studio.)

Gradually the style, and indeed personnel, of *Network 7* resurfaced in the magazine *Reportage* and hip travel series *Rough Guide*, but music programming was *Def II*'s main strength. Three programmes came to define the strand. *Dance Energy*, a clubland *Top of the Pops*, was the most traditional, and least typical. *Rapido* was the big draw, a rock magazine boasting fifties kitsch stylings and the rapid-fire presentation of Antoine De Caunes, linking segments with suave Gallic ostentation, in the manner of a *Max Headroom* routine as retold by an espresso-fuelled Jacques Derrida.

Rapido sought out rising stars like the Stone Roses, but would happily accommodate big names like Paul McCartney if they deigned to appear. They often did, because, as Street-Porter explained, 'a lot of pop stars are snobs and like the idea of being done for a French show.'

The indie sector was catered for with *Snub TV*, product of artists Peter Fowler and Brenda Kelly. At the bottom of the food chain, *Snub* was initially funded by US cable channel Night Flight (where it became an unlikely favourite with veteran acid rockers the Grateful Dead), to the miserly tune of $1500 per show. Taking the DIY approach of the scene's print fanzines, Kelly and Fowler didn't bother with hosts or a studio, instead asking bands whereabouts they'd be at, say, four in the afternoon, and turning up with a camcorder. Specially shot music videos were made by independent artists, working for nothing more than national exposure. Here was a glimpse of the twenty-first century's financially exhausted music industry. In another sign of changing times, a headmaster rang the programme – not to complain of degeneracy, but to ask after a Mekons track he wanted to use in the end-of-term show.[426] Deal with a request like that and stay fashionable.

TWIN PEAKS (1990–1)
ABC (Lynch/Frost Productions)

The cult blockbuster takes America.

IN THE MEDIA PECKING order, television bows to film. Actors, writers and directors, from Dench to Chayefsky to Spielberg, learned their craft on the small screen before defecting to cinema's bigger budgets and greater acclaim. Movement in the reverse direction usually meant thin times for the talent. Ingmar Bergman switched between cinema and TV, but that was Swedish TV. *MASH* the movie satire became *M*A*S*H* the sitcom, and the Coen brothers' *Fargo* begat a *Twin Peaks*-style comedy-drama, but those were happy exceptions. The rule was clear: cinema was the grown-up cousin, the fully realised art form, where the cream of TV talent could only hope to finish up.

It took David Lynch, a born flouter of industry rules, to break this convention, and even he was motivated by necessity. To follow up his art house hit *Blue Velvet*, he and former *Hill Street Blues* writer Mark Frost wrote the film *One Saliva Bubble*, a wacky backwoods identity swap comedy set to star Steve Martin. Funding proved hard to scrape together, so the pair began tossing TV ideas around instead. Their first, *The Lemurians*, concerned two detectives on the trail of extra-terrestrial descendants of a lost continental civilisation (or something like that) and was knocked back by NBC. Undaunted, they took another, a *Blue Velvet*-like murder mystery called *Northwest Passage*, to ABC, then well into its five-year plan of innovation hunting that kicked off with *Moonlighting*.

A change of title, and the most unhinged prime time drama in network history was in production.

From the first moments of its long, freaky story of the death of prom queen Laura Palmer and the subsequent collapse of a peaceful lumber town as FBI agents interrogate the community, *Twin Peaks* was set against the American television grain. It wasn't the sporadic, random and – for American television – graphic moments of violence. It wasn't the systematic undermining of the wholesome myth of rural Midwestern life, formerly a backbone of comforting small screen entertainment from *Green Acres* to *The Waltons*. It wasn't the disturbing yoking together of soapy emotional outbursts with weird urban myths. More than anything, it was the pacing: soporific one-take scenes where characters took their time to haul themselves from one spot to another; ambiguous, ominous pauses in conversation, usually topped with a non-sequitur, the oddity of which was remarked by nobody. The camera made long, slow zooms into nothing in particular. The tightly cut, tightly framed, prescriptive visual grammar of network TV, with all its 'I's dotted and vagueness shunned, was swapped for a languid, leisurely style that took its time getting to wherever it was going. This was New Wave cinema plonked unceremoniously into the post-MTV mainstream, making the mainstream queasy.

Characters crashed out of their stereotypical roles. Seasoned police officers broke down in tears. High school girls possessed worldly knowledge well beyond what their rural upbringing would suggest, while FBI agents obsessed intensely over mundane food items. A seedy casino vied with the private lives of the town's residents for the title of most disturbing underlit scene. Odd relatives suddenly invaded the family house with half a dozen French baguettes. Norwegians deserted en masse. Best of all were FBI Agent Dale Cooper's divinatory dreams, a straight throwback to Lynch's hardcore frightfest *Eraserhead*, with reverse-speaking dwarves and psychotic spirits taking their bows on a herringbone parquet floor. Prime time drama was coming down with a severe case of post-traumatic stress.

The show was launched with huge publicity, and immediately snagged its target Yuppie market. The pilot was the highest rated TV movie of the 1989-90 season. The series proper would reach thirty-five million and held its own against venerable NBC sitcom *Cheers*. 'Something's right in America,'[427] beamed *Newsweek* approvingly. *Time* agreed, 'The medium has rarely seen anything as strange – or as superb.'[428] *The Washington Post* heralded 'the show that re-invents the [soap opera] genre and gives it class,'[429] and it became the focus of a *Village Voice* special report on 'Rad TV'.

When it landed in the UK in October, reception was more critical. Tabloids duly puffed the show with reference to its transatlantic hipness quotient. *Today* hailed 'the wacky soap you have to quote to prove you are not a philistine,'[430] and broadsheets reported, only slightly askance, on upscale America's penchant for *Twin Peaks* viewing parties fuelled by cherry pie, doughnuts and 'damn fine coffee'. As it got underway, though, it became clear that, transplanted to a country with a long history of weird peak time television, *Twin Peaks* struggled to stand out. Sheridan Morley in *The Times* compared the first episode to watching jelly set, and after watching the second issued an apology to jelly manufacturers. Andrew Goodwin in the *Listener* spotted a hollow centre. 'Rooted in a genre that will gain mass attention, while nodding and winking hysterically at the upscale audience who thought *Moonlighting* was terribly experimental, *Twin Peaks* is trying to have its formulaic cake and eat itself.'[431] James Saynor called Lynch out on a grand televisual con trick. 'He's now watching, smirking, from a safe distance, in no danger of being personally beaten up by his own art,'[432] he wrote. 'The right-hand side of the show's brain has had a stroke.'[433] Chris Dunkley in the *Financial Times* confidently predicted the show would top out at two and a half million UK viewers. In fact, combining the Tuesday showing and Saturday repeat, it comfortably broached eight million. The cult had translated. Criticism was moot.

As the show's two series unwound at different speeds on both sides of the Atlantic, the audience, many still expecting some kind of progress on the detection front, grew restless. The identity of Laura Palmer's killer came halfway through the second season, for what it was worth by then, but the show ambled on at the same sedated pace. With the nominal denouement out of the way, fans began paying attention to the man behind the red velvet curtain. Not since *The Prisoner* had so much money and prime time real estate been given over to a cosmic shaggy dog tale, the solemn guarding of a clearly empty casket. Even Frost and Lynch couldn't escape the ancient riddle: just how do you end these things? ABC didn't trust them to find an answer, and held a third series back.

Rushing to the show's defence, Lynch appeared on the Letterman show with a personal appeal for viewers to write into the ABC president pleading a stay of execution. 'If it has to end,' he said with typical eerie calm, 'that's all right. But if it doesn't have to end, that's even better.'[434] Such campaigns had worked in the past, most notably in the early years of *Cagney and Lacey*, but two series were all ABC were prepared to risk. A cinematic spin-off, *Twin Peaks: Fire Walk With Me*, took things to new depths of obscurity and squalor, but it didn't do it opposite Carol Burnett every Saturday night, which wasn't quite the same. Then, in a twist as implausible as anything in the show itself, Frost and Lynch announced that a new series, set 25 years on from the original, would be broadcast on the CBS cable channel Showtime in 2016.

Twin Peaks had an immediate, if localised, effect on US TV drama for the rest of the 1990s. 'Weirdness' cropped up everywhere. The *X-Files* and Oliver Stone's mess of virtual reality pottage *Wild Palms* brought disorientation back to TV science fiction. *Northern Exposure*, an Alaskan ensemble quirk from the creators of *St Elsewhere*, arrived just a few months after *Twin Peaks* but didn't suffer too greatly from superficial similarities. *Picket Fences* was a clear copy, larding its Wisconsin folksiness with decapitations and spontaneous combustion, even employing *Twin Peaks*'s 'dwarf' actor, Michael J. Anderson. It was the work of crack *LA Law* writer David E. Kelley, who would take this vanilla form of weirdness to popular heights with *Ally McBeal*, proving there was nothing so strange that the networks couldn't digest it and make it their own. But at least Frost and Lynch had given them a debilitating attack of wind on the way.

ABROAD IN BRITAIN (1990)

BBC Two

The arts documentary becomes art itself.

'It takes a clever dick to make an arse smart.'
Jonathan Meades, 1973

NOT MANY PROGRAMMES ABOUT church architecture begin with the line, 'God has been doted on since man, in his bewildered ignorance and reverential wonder, first conceived the notion that there must be some omniscient grease monkey who fitted all the parts together.' Not many histories of the Great British pub end with St George on horseback downing a can of lager in one gaseous gulp. Very few documentaries see fit to push their presenters off tall buildings onto the roofs of Ford Escorts. But then, as they chant from the terraces of the Royal Academy, there's only one Jonathan Meades.

The arts documentary comes in two distinct varieties. The most common is no-frills vanilla, bringing nothing to the screen that might distract from the subject, except maybe a tastefully chosen soundtrack. 'We're TV journalists,' Melvyn Bragg reminded everyone on the launch of archetypal pie-and-peas culture strand *The South Bank Show* in 1978, 'not arty-farty film-makers.' He was referring to the alternative, poetic flavour, which took boundless liberties with image and sound, as incubated during the 1960s on shows like Huw Weldon's *Monitor* – 'the only British experimental film school, ever,' according to its most notable graduate, Ken Russell.

The 'arty-farty' approach survived the eighties through the more playful entries in Alan Yentob's presenter-free arts slot *Arena*. In the early 1990s it assumed the shape of Nicholas Barker's *Signs of the Times*, a bone-dry cavalcade of domestic interiors of dubious taste, with their inhabitants musing stiffly on their choice of soft furnishings. More arch than a Victorian viaduct, it ostensibly withheld editorial judgement on its subjects while the camera trussed them up in their own awkwardness like an unwitting Gilbert and George, especially in the notorious shots where they stared blankly into space for seemingly minutes on end. Barker's work was, wrote one critic, 'packaged in the knowing, post-modernist manner . . . it hides behind a Sarah Dunant-style oleaginous irony.'[435]

Other approaches were available. Jonathan Meades, *Times* restaurant critic and RADA contemporary of Robert Lindsay and Stephanie Beacham, came to television in 1987, presenting Channel Four's *The Victorian House*, sporting huge prescription shades and ploughing unsteadily through a conventional account of nineteenth century domestic architecture. The delivery faltered as the words were not his. He fared better as one of the pundits on *Building Sights*, BBC Two's series of ten-minute visual essays the following year. The year after that he was given six half-hours to explore the country's architectural backwaters in a series provisionally titled *A Different Britain*.

Covering such recondite subjects as houses that abhor right-angles and the bodged folk dwellings of the Severn Valley, *Abroad in Britain* gave the manicured arts documentary a new kind of droll depth. It celebrated the underdogs of building and stood against the march of gutless, corporate postmodern detachment, in finely crafted programmes stylistically set against the blithely cocked eyebrow of the new ironic regime. Form followed argument. Meades's paean to the ragged Bohemian splendour of Hastings could easily apply to his own body of work: 'It's over-ripe, blowzy.

It has a bruised amiability that only the fallen can ever achieve. It really reeks of itself.'

Meades's words were provocative but serious, focused, sober. It was the landscape to which they referred, and in which they were delivered, that was out to lunch. Army platoons charged into frame from nowhere, pigs leapt from abandoned ovens and motorised golf caddies ran amok while Meades, in his unchanging FBI get-up, quietly struggled to make sense of it all – the previously common-place seen through a freshly de-scaled eye. Some critics just saw a good, straight documentary needlessly faffed about. Why, they asked, does he have to interrupt interviews with a house's inhab-itants by strolling about behind them, 'like Hitchcock making his ritual appearance in his own films . . . is this an out-take or a put-on?'[436]

With directors David Turnbull and Russell England, Meades perfected his brand of starched anarchy over three *Abroad . . .* series. Traditional, heroically perpendicular architectural photography – 'a vast institutional lie'[437] according to Meades – was junked in favour of wide angles, queasy tilts and compositions more likely to favour a nearby patch of waste ground notorious for dogging than the cottage or abattoir under discussion. By the third, *Even Further Abroad*, the look was of Peter Greenaway directing a public inform-ation film about the dangers of playing near postmodernist grain silos. Sound was exploited and perverted as much as image. Why accompany a cathedral interior with organ music when you can get a floating choirboy to sing 'Bat Out of Hell'? And who better to soundtrack the laudanum-soaked Victorian era than the Velvet Underground?

A new century, a new visual collaborator (Francis Hanly) and new technology led to even more exquisite shots and elaborate compositions in programmes ever more jokey, more wild, more compressed, with richer photography, dirtier gags, and lashings of Christopher Biggins. While other documentaries were rapidly cutting down on information, and obsessively worrying the viewer wouldn't understand the little that was left, Meades embellished his content, layer upon layer. He'd begin in a minuscule niche and end reaching out to the world. A programme set on the Hebridean isle of Lewis and Harris was carefully built from meticulously chosen individual shots to move from a prehistoric view of crags and standing stones, slowly evolving through pastoral scenes of sheep and primitive churches, to the eventual appearance of modern humanity, bathetically throwing up in the streets on a Saturday night.

With mainstream documentaries striving for ever more cloying inclusivity, Meades, the boy least likely to 'go on a journey' or be filmed studying archive footage on an iPad with mock intent, becomes ever more precious. In a schedule full of determinedly inoffensive steel-and-glass heritage interaction spaces, his programmes remain welcome intrusions of baroque, brutalist nonconformity. If it didn't go against his principles, he should be listed.

THE REAL WORLD
(1992–)
MTV (Bunim/Murray Productions)
Reality television takes off.

'THE AVANT-GARDE OF TELEVISION, way out along the boom, always tell you that the purest use of the medium should be unconscious. They would like to plant hidden eyes and ears all over the place and orchestrate by cross-cutting huge symphonies of social reality. It could be, but for reasons of humanity it obviously cannot be done.'[438] Despite that 'obviously' putting the very idea beyond the pale, Maurice Richardson, writing in 1960, was one of the first to set down the temptation for television documentary to do away with intermediaries and present the world to itself unmoderated, straight, complete – to serve up, in a word that steadily lost its meaning the more ubiquitous it became, reality.

The journey from ordinary fly-on-the-wall to full-blown reality began with a case of bad timing. Associated-Rediffusion's documentary crew built a reputation in the early 1960s for making smart, up-to-the-minute investigations into Britain's burgeoning youth culture with such films as *Living for Kicks* and *Beat City*. By the time they got themselves down the King's Road in 1966, however, they found it was swinging off its hinges, the groovy vibe long departed for pastures new. All they had left to point their cameras at was the well-manicured vacuity left behind, which they duly recorded and presented to the nation in shambling *cinema verité* study *Go, Go, Go, Said the Bird*.

The title, which sounds like a vacuously hip catchphrase until you realise it's a line from T. S. Eliot, pointed to a controlling intelligence behind the camera, which in turn pointed the camera at pure dumb chaos. You could tell by the dialogue that this was modern youth in all its splendour. 'I don't know what I feel at the moment, y'know, but one day I want to feel very calm, y'know, and next day I want to wear something ridiculous, y'know.' The beautiful people spoke their own private language: meandering nuggets of nothing. A fashion designer tried unsuccessfully to obtain a number from directory enquiries. 'They ought to be in concentration camps,' she huffed, hanging up in despair. The film-makers politely pointed out that she could just as easily look up the number herself in the phone book. 'If you've got to labour at anything it becomes too much,' she protested, 'and your thinking just dwindles away.' The temptation to sneer was there on a platter, but British viewers still felt uncomfortable doing this. 'I didn't like hearing myself making reactionary noises,' wrote George Melly, 'but I made them.'[439]

The next advance came in the USA in 1973, when PBS broadcast a twelve-part close study of the affluent Loud family from Eugene, Oregon. Produced by Craig Gilbert and filmed by Alan and Susan Raymond, *An American Family* presented the staid reactions of parents Bill and Pat Loud to the tumultuous activities of their five children, most famously Lance, who sensationally came out to his parents on screen. (Homosexuality was still officially treated as a mental illness in the States when the programme was filmed.) Antagonistic to his parents and camp beyond cliché, Lance emerged as the star of the show, a tempest of compulsive honesty in a mire of middle class repression. He also had the sharpest line on the show itself when he described it as 'the fulfilment of the middle class dream that you can be famous for being just who you are.'[440] Paul Watson's anglicised version made for the BBC the following year, *The Family*, took the lower-middle-class Wilkinses of Reading as its quarry and was several degrees more humble in every department, swapping pony riding and garage band jamming for brown Vymura wall coverings and earnest discussions about supplementary benefits over plates of crispy pancakes.

Though both these programmes became national obsessions, they were firmly rooted in the old documentary tradition – shot on film, carefully edited and broadcast as a crafted piece of reportage. In 1992 music channel MTV presented a 'social experiment' that kept the work of the programme makers well out of sight, to give the illusion of life brought fresh to the screen. Bearing more than a glancing similarity to *Nummer 28*, which appeared on Dutch station KRO the previous year, *The Real World*'s ethos was clumsily summed up in its introductory spiel: 'This is the true story of seven strangers picked to live in a loft and have their lives taped to find out what happens when people stop being polite and start getting real.'

'Real' in this case meant photogenic, flippant and nakedly aspirational. Assorted aspiring singers, dancers, models and actors piled into a spacious loft conversion in New York's SoHo to preen, argue, sulk and swap diet tips. The seven subjects wandered about in random states of undress, communicating more at than with each other in sentences that started out full of bravado before losing both energy and direction to finish in that familiar half-defeated, half-defiant 'y'know?' Low lighting and echoing sound gave proceedings a wash of streetwise drear, punched up by MTV's trademark rapid fire video editing. It simultaneously looked both glitzy and drab, and the stars were as pretty as they were dumb. A room full of kids mocked for being all surface by a station dedicated to the perfection of that surface, masquerading under the title *The Real World*, was a sitting duck for critics, but an instant addiction for viewers. One commentator could see why: 'post-adolescent lassitude is somehow acceptable when it has good muscle definition and straight teeth.'[441]

Almost as soon as its success registered, the spin-offs and copies appeared. A British version, *The Living Soap*, arrived in 1993 as part of BBC2's *Def II* youth annex, and was once again a lowlier affair, being set in a shared student house in Manchester. (And one with poor security at that, enabling locals to actively harass the show's more controversial contestants – the sort of reality feedback loop no programme wants to get stuck in, but plenty would.)

The MTV original rolled on throughout the 1990s, the carnival pitching up in a different US city each season. By 2000, as one commentator noted, the show had utterly changed 'from anthropological study to a mecca for the attention-starved and ego-maniacal.'[442] This was also the year *Big Brother* arrived in Britain, taking *The Real World's* format and welding game show elements onto the front. It arrived with similar boasts of sociological intent, and just as surely discreetly dropped them as the seasons rolled by.

Dwarfed by the programming dynasty it had spawned, *The Real World* shrank to the status of also-ran, but it was now an institution in the micro-history of MTV, and somehow kept going. In 2014 the ailing format was given a shameless tweak: *The Real World: Ex-Plosion* confronted the unsuspecting stars with the news that their ex-partners had come along for the ride. The promise of on-air mortification drove ratings up once more but, like every reality show, *The Real World* can only last for so many seasons before it milks its premise dry. Still, with nearly a quarter of a century on the clock, *The Real World* can claim to have outlived many of the more popular shows that came in its wake, including MTV's own family portrait, *The Osbornes*. Similarly, E4's recent 'structured reality' Sloane-basher *Made In Chelsea* carries the ancestral markings of *Go, Go, Go, Said the Bird*. These twentieth century ancestors may have been less symphonies of social reality than three-minute pop songs of social awkwardness, but they had a tune that producers the world over can't stop whistling.

COME ON DOWN
AND OUT (1993)

Channel Four
(Kudos Productions)

Television's most righteously cool channel starts confusing ends with means.

Hello there, all you lesbians, gays and black people!
Message that briefly greeted callers to Channel Four's
after hours Ansaphone, 1982

A COMMERCIAL STATION WITH a public service remit, the young Channel Four was radical in every department, but especially the factual. Series like *The Friday Alternative*, *20/20 Vision* and *Bandung File* wore their agit-prop hearts on their sleeves. Founding controller Jeremy Isaacs was famously asked by an irate Norman Tebbit why the minority channel the government had created for him was full of stuff about gays and Northern Ireland, rather than the sort of minority interests Tebbit had in mind: golf and yachting. Chris Dunkley of the *Financial Times* posited the stereotypical Channel Four documentary, a hopelessly obscure minority subject 'made exclusively by women of a certain sort (you know the sort)'.[443] This sort of criticism would only encourage them.

The channel's first problem was to snare a nation whose viewing habits had been largely unchanged for nearly two decades. Early efforts like earnest debate *Voices* dipped below 200,000 viewers, then the lowest measurable amount, thus earning the ignominious 'zero rating'. *Channel Four News*, Britain's first in-depth early evening bulletin, had similar audience issues in its first year. 'It would be cheaper to phone the news bulletins to people,' reckoned presenter Peter Sissons.[444] Under the editorship of ITN's Stewart Purvis it grew into Britain's most respected serious news programme, but anxieties remained. On laying out his heavyweight plan, Purvis was buttonholed by the channel's deputy chairman Richard Attenborough, who pleaded, 'darling, you will remember we are all in show business, won't you?'[445] As the channel grew larger on the landscape, and the British government less tolerant of televised dissent, big scoops got the chop. Ken Loach's union broadside *Questions of Leadership* and *The People's Account*, a look at the 1985 Broadwater Farm Estate riots from the residents' point of view, were just two high profile shows written off in the name of that mysterious entity, 'balance'.

In the latter half of the 1980s, Channel Four entered a new phase. *The Comic Strip Presents . . .* and *Saturday Live* put alternative comedy front and centre. Jonathan Ross threw out the last lingering formalities of the chat show. Entertainment elbowed its way to the front and came to define the channel with a new rakish swagger: less didactic, more off the wall, and far more comfortable in its own skin. Its factual output continued undaunted in the same ethical vein, but after Isaacs yielded to Michael Grade in November 1987, even that last bastion of the old guard would, slowly, be turned.

The 1990 Broadcasting Act made the previously subsidised channel a wholly self-funding body. Grade still vocally defended the old ethos, especially in the face of new threats to editorial independence, like the advent of fully sponsored programmes. 'There are two things which are absolute anathema to each other, and they are sponsorship and controversy.'[446] But then a subtle shift occurred. Politics were complex, dangerous and limited in impact to the informed and interested. Sex, meanwhile, though still a complicated and inflammatory topic, had universal appeal.

In 1991, the target was for thoughtful filth. *Dick*, a twelve-minute American film with a cast of a thousand penises, was put away on orders from the newly formed Independent Television Commission, but *WR: Mysteries of the Organism*, a psycho-sexual meditation with only a handful of penises, was shown, but with some hastily super-imposed goldfish swimming handily into view over the inappro-priate elements. By choosing material which kept to the channel's progressive, educational ideals, while still flushing out those who fancied a good gawp, Grade and friends had it, so to speak, both ways. Two years later *Love Weekend* repeated the trick, but with a noticeable shift towards untrammelled smut. *The Naked Chat Show*, a randy quiz and a 'snogging contest' hosted by Richard Jobson jettisoned the high-minded fig leaf of previous seasons.

In the spring of 1993, the Rubicon was crossed. *Come On Down and Out* was a purposefully crass game show in which three home-less contestants competed to win their dream prize: a home. Andrew O'Connor, ably assisted by Annabel Giles, put the hopeful down-and-outs through three gruelling rounds. First, a conventional quiz on the subject, naturally, of homelessness. What was the most common cause of death amongst the homeless? Suicide, guessed one contestant correctly. So, a bit of consciousness was raised. Immediately, however, O'Connor quipped, 'And that's why we removed all sharp objects from your dressing rooms tonight!' Humiliation was heaped on the hapless threesome in further rounds in which they had to 'build a bash' from assorted street detritus, and were subjected to demeaning hidden camera pranks while out and about. Scouse Jimmy made it to the final round, in which a dream house lay in one of three boxes. He picked the wrong one, and won a set of patio furniture. O'Connor oleaginously soothed his crestfallen nerves over the credits.

Then came a special continuity announcement: 'The programme you have just seen was not a real game show. All the contestants were actors.' And so the nation saw what they did there. The show was part of a wider season on homelessness, *Gimme Shelter*, which featured many more sober efforts like a retracing of Orwell's down-and-out odyssey and a repeat of *Cathy Come Home*. Even so, outrage broke out days before transmission. The soothing reveal was only added at the last minute as an emergency measure to offset the attacks, but it failed to placate many critics. The ethics of this sort of stunt were debated at length. The channel was accused of becoming too populist, indulging in controversy for ratings' sake, and abandoning its public service remit.

Such tactics were also being adopted by advertising agencies, unveiling 'shock campaigns' with relentless regularity, each one trying to go that bit further to offset the diminishing returns. In the process, shock value became an end in itself. A blood-soaked anti-fur campaign ad and a blood-soaked Benetton ad may differ in intent – one has real anger behind it, the other merely an eye on maximum publicity – but their effect is more or less the same, and it's the effect that generates the headlines. Upset becomes an end in itself.

Serious stuff was still being produced, but as the century turned, the channel's symbiotic relationship with tabloid consternation became one of co-dependence. Commissions like *When She Died*, an opera about the death of Princess Diana, were seemingly made with an eye for maximum free press advertising. ITV, of all institutions, criticised Four's populism. Even their own independent producers knew it. 'They're very safe,' admitted one, anonymously. 'They say they're radical, but it's all tits and willies, nothing very difficult.'[447]

Offence is a fossil fuel, requiring ever more desperate and destructive measures to extract it. When sex alone lost its power, dysfunction and outlandish peccadilloes were exhibited to attract the prurient. Extreme accidents of birth were paraded with a combination of sideshow rubbernecking and contrived compassion. Where once it was one tool among many, the ironic tone was now a mark of impregnable sophistication, a nod and a wink to help the producer disappear when awkward questions arose about motives. Assumptions were made rather than challenged. It all became a game, and a dodgy one at that, when real people were involved.

Finally, one of the station's central tenets was turned completely on its head. In 2014, *Benefits Street* catalogued the antics of a notoriously poor Birmingham neighbourhood. It was a rather old-fashioned beast, with only stylistic tics to distinguish it from the puzzled forays into the working class jungle made in television's formative years. Its publicity campaign, though, playing on the government's welfare crackdown, was a masterpiece. Viewers flocked, and kept on flocking when ministers name-checked the series in economic debates.

The old Channel Four would have been aghast at being co-opted to defend the status quo. Its mid-period incarnation might have tried to subvert the debate. Late-period Four just sat back and watched the numbers rise. In 2015 Love Productions began shooting a spin-off, *Immigration Street*, in Southampton's Derby Road. Locals, mindful of the company's previous work, organised petitions, protests and even staged disruptive direct action during location shoots. Channel Four's journey from streetwise scourge of the establishment to besieged enemy of the people was complete.

The director of Shelter, the homeless charity which collaborated with Channel Four on *Come On Down and Out*, said the game show aimed to highlight 'the hypocrisy of a society that sits in judgement, deciding who is worthy of help and who is not'. Defences of *Benefits Street* tended to skip any suggestion of intent, sticking to mollifying claims of 'getting a debate going', while naturally calling up the channel's long history of unimpeachably worthy programmes as a humanitarian shield. This wasn't tabloid telly. How could it be? It was on Channel Four, the thrusting young radical broadcaster that made minorities cool and compassion groovy. Once upon a time.

FRASIER (1993–2004)
NBC (Grub Street/Paramount)

Highbrow America in all its glorious stupidity.

THE HISTORY OF THE American sitcom since at least the late sixties is largely the history of smart kids from Harvard, Berkeley and Yale acting dumb for a paycheck. In the early days, when television was a suspicious little sideline for adventurous vaudevillians, gags were the product of tenement smarts, of blue-collar minds that had to be one beat faster than their fellows to stay on top.

Paul Henning was an exception to this rule. Born in a small Missouri town, he graduated from *The Burns & Allen Show* to create some of the most successful sitcoms of the sixties – *The Beverly Hillbillies*, *Petticoat Junction* and *Green Acres* – all based around the clash of urban and backwoods American lifestyles. When advertisers took to measuring audiences by demographics instead of raw numbers, Henning's creations were first against the wall. The college-educated, eighteen-to-thirty-four-year-old 'blue jean' set became television's prize quarry, and they demanded sophistication and social relevance. That the same generation would later wax nostalgic over soufflés such as *Gilligan's Island* and *The Brady Bunch* was a point slightly too sophisticated for the advertisers to measure.

For the best part of a decade, sitcom was dominated by two houses. MTM provided the upwardly mobile wit, while Norman Lear (with more than a little help from British writers like Ray Galton, Alan Simpson and Johnny Speight) put articulate, angry working class voices on screen. In 1978 a breakaway quartet of

377

MTM writers formed their own company to make a fusion of the two styles in *Taxi*. Though its nominal main characters were MTM types – a struggling actor and an art gallery receptionist – they languished in an authentically filthy yellow cab depot and were augmented, and soon upstaged, by their earthier cab-driving colleagues: a hyper-aggressive Italian, an otherworldly European immigrant, a dim boxer and a messianic space cadet. White and blue collars alike turned an indistinguishable oily black. It was a vibrant cross-section of American failure.

In turn, three star *Taxi* writers – James Burrows, Glen and Les Charles – refined this dead end melting pot formula with *Cheers*, the internecine affairs of staff and assorted hangers-on in a Boston bar. A broad social spectrum cohered through the magic of boredom and beer, with one sore thumb in the shape of frustrated intellectual waitress Diane Chambers (Shelley Long), a la-di-da graduate with pretensions that are mercilessly mocked by the rest of the gang. Taking charge of a home movie made for naive barman Woody to send to his concerned folks back in Indiana, she lards it with portentous symbolism, atom bomb footage and a Wagner soundtrack, titling it 'Manchild in Beantown Redux'. Her crass precocity leaves the bar agog, and we later learn Woody's dad wasn't keen on the film: 'He said it was too derivative of Godard.'

In the third season, Diane gained a partner in bookishness in the form of insecure psychiatrist Dr Frasier Crane (Kelsey Grammer), introduced as a foil to the show's central stop-start romance between Diane and bar owner Sam Malone, a smart but romantically feeble second banana based on Ralph Bellamy's roles in screwball comedies like *The Awful Truth*.[448] Long disliked the new character, but he proved popular enough to become a regular, acquiring an icy, bloodless wife and son over the next eight years. *Cheers* begat two spin-off shows: *The Tortellis*, focussing on acerbic waitress Carla's ex-husband, lasted just one season; *Frasier*, the second choice, had legs.

Cheers and *Taxi* avoided domestic situations, preferring to hint at characters' home lives rather than show them wherever possible.

Frasier was domestic to the point of imprisonment. His Seattle bachelor pad-cum-epicurean comfort zone is invaded first by his invalid ex-cop dad Martin, dragging a homely battered recliner in amongst the 'eclectic' array of Eames chairs and Chanel sofas, then by textbook kooky home help Daphne Moon, 'originally from Manchester, England' (though to British ears she was closer to Rochdale, Mars). Niles, Frasier's even more priggish brother, alternately ameliorated and added to the familial claustrophobia. Martin's role was to remind 'the boys' of their less than high flown origins, of the fact that brash wisdom will outclass well-spoken whimsy every time, and to throw their attenuated masculinity into sharp relief. Daphne and brazen radio producer Roz were there to point up their pampered lack of purpose and to throw their attenuated masculinity into sharp relief. Frasier's job as local radio shrink is consistently unrewarding and often downright humiliating; brother Niles, trapped in a marriage even more anaemic than Frasier's used to be, unspools a ceaseless litany of first world problems. Like Diane, he sees every flat farce as a Greek tragedy, constantly pleading that he surely deserves better than this, the answer always 'no'.

The pretensions of the brothers are a writer's gift. Their shared humour is an allusive, highbrow patois that, like most avowedly intellectual attempts at comedy, seem mainly restricted to bad puns about composers and European novelists. They chuckle indulgently at their immense erudition (Niles, at age six, drew not his parents but scenes from *Aida*) while everyone else looks on with an expression of, at best, muted pity. The sitcom itself had 'classy' touches – Grammer's ersatz blues theme tune, the gnomic captions between scenes, the roll-call of uncredited stars playing Frasier's phone-in patients from Cyd Charisse to Mary Tyler Moore – but snobbery and grandiose aspiration were always comic targets, not comic means.

At its best, the show was meticulously plotted. A satisfying comic plot requires greater precision, less wastage, than a decent drama. 'A concert pianist is allowed a wrong note here and there,' wrote Kingsley Amis. 'A juggler is not allowed to drop a plate.'[449] The show took pride in its ability to lay out a wide range of stories, taking old chestnuts like mistaken identity or an unsolved murder and adding a fresh comic spin. Frasier was sent running in frantic circles by a recurring homoerotic dream ('were there any cigars, bananas or short, blunt swords?') or an amateur revival of old fashioned live radio drama sinking under the weight of its company's incompetence and infighting. The obligatory minimalist episode, which all great sitcoms must foist on themselves on a point of technical honour, took the shape of a fractious, real time head-to-head chat in the Café Nervosa. The fourth season, capping half a century of television sitcom progress, represented the peak of the genre's wit and ingenuity – a long tradition taken to vertiginous heights.

Very rarely did *Frasier* experiment with sitcom's traditional self-reference, but one small indulgence stood out. Diane Chambers turned up like a bad penny, subjecting Frasier to a rehearsal of her theatrical atrocity *Rhapsody and Requiem*, a self-aggrandising *roman-à-clef* set in a suspiciously familiar-looking bar that made *Long Day's Journey Into Night* look like *Hellzapoppin'*. It was a scene that played clever games with the show's history, took a cheeky swipe at Long's original dislike of the Frasier character, and brought a long-standing emotional cliffhanger to a well-judged conclusion all at once. This was the smart sitcom in its element – throwing a perilously narrow bridge across the gap between its protagonists' formal intelligence and their emotional ignorance: then, when they're halfway across, giving them an encouraging sideways nudge. Gets 'em every time.

OUR FRIENDS IN THE NORTH (1996)
BBC Two

Drama thinks big.

By THE 1970S TALES of northern deprivation, whether romanticised by Catherine Cookson or polemicised by Jim Allen, claimed
so much British screen time they constituted a genre in themselves,
and thus awash with cliché. Clive James lamented the regularity
with which the hero's father would become trapped underneath a
collapsed pithead, and Nancy Banks-Smith noted that 'Yorkshire
seems infested with iron-fisted father figures much given to
shouting "Tha's nobbut nowt" and thus wounding the susceptibil-
ities of their sensitive southern sons.'[450] *Monty Python* made the
modern, media-savvy northern writer a rough-hewn D. H. Lawrence
hero, lamenting a life of backbreaking creative toil. ('There's nowt
wrong wi' gala luncheons, lad! I've had more gala luncheons than
you've had hot dinners!')

It had come to the point where the mere sight of a colliery on
the horizon or a clog-sparking child capering in front of some
back-to-backs provoked pre-emptive sniggers. Meanwhile the
breakdown of the British social contract dragged the north further
into debt. For jaded viewers still hooting at t'mill and its manifold
troubles a new language was needed; one compiled from the bottom
up.

Peter Flannery, a playwright from Jarrow-on-Tyne and grandson
of one of the Jarrow marchers of 1936, was a politically engaged

writer who wryly described his work as 'mainly about housing'.[451] His magnum opus *Our Friends in the North* had, even by the standards of most ambitious plays, a troubled genesis. It began as a stage play, slated to run at Stratford-on-Avon in December 1981 but was postponed for six months, finally surfacing to christen the Royal Shakespeare Company's new Pit theatre at the Barbican in the summer of 1982. It was ambitious stuff: a three-and-a-half hour epic in the style of recent broad Brechtian history plays like David Hare and Howard Brenton's *Brassneck* and David Edgar's *Destiny*; plays which started from current events and extrapolated backwards into Britain's ignoble imperial past.

Flannery's play took its four protagonists from Harold Wilson's 1964 election victory to Thatcher's in 1979, watching their youthful ideals slowly perish under the weight of establishment corruption, centring on the Newcastle of city councillor T. Dan Smith but reaching out as far as Rhodesia. It was a play firmly in the didactic mould, ending with a female character shooting smack, brandishing a machine gun and beseeching the audience to 'seize the power!' Flannery offered a hard-headed interpretation of post-war history, but not everyone was convinced. 'You don't prove a case simply by piling up incidents in a mountainous heap,' countered Michael Billington. 'What weakens the play's dramatic impact is the assumption of some mystical link between these specific, individual acts of corruption.'[452]

Our Friends was rewritten into a series for the BBC in 1984, and turned down. A second version returned to the controller's office in 1991, where Flannery's work was once again in good company. Controversial dramas based on real people and events were all over the news at that time: the BBC's Falklands War drama *Tumbledown* and Alan Bleasdale's Derek Hatton-inspired *GBH* grabbed as many headlines as they did awards. The Beeb's lawyers blocked production, uncomfortable over its reference to real events (the Poulson housing scandal, and the possible identification of several lightly fictionalised senior police officers). One lawyer suggested Flannery distance the play from reality by setting it in a fictional country called 'Albion'. Flannery hit back by sarcastically suggesting in turn that, to show it really was a work of fiction, all the policemen should be black.[453] This wasn't a good working relationship. 'It is making dealing with public life and real events in dramatic form impossible,' said Flannery. 'If my experience is typical, [we] should be concerned about the future of drama writers at the BBC.'[454]

Finally a nine-part series of Flannery's 'political *Heimat*' was green-lit in 1993, and the £8 million production was announced as part of a £174 million drama package attacked by the *Daily Mail* as a festival of 'under-age sex, lesbianism, violence and swearing.'[455] In an increasingly conservative dramatic landscape of bonnets, breeches and Darling Buds, *Our Friends* felt like something of a throwback to a less cowed televisual age. On the other hand, with a revamped Labour Party poised to take over the clapped out Tory government, it was as of the moment as ever. (Ironically, one prescient plot strand about the rise of spin doctors within the Labour ranks was removed from the drama during those protracted negotiations. The characters based on John Poulson and Reginald Maudling remained, as their originals had since passed on.)

The wait was more than worth it. Flannery had expertly integrated the countrywide, decade-spanning hauteur of the stage original with the material and emotional minutiae of individual life. (He admitted it was the protracted gestation that allowed him to convincingly age his characters, having aged along with them.) The four leads were, aside from being slightly too old to pass for students in the first episode, uniformly strong: Christopher Eccleston's political activist Nicky; Mark Strong's rocker-turned entrepreneur Tosker; Gina McKee's Mary, who vacillates between the two of them; and Daniel Craig's Geordie, going from Soho porn merchant to broken vagrant. All of them were caught in Flannery's web of corruption, now running up to the present day, but as strongly delineated as ever.

The look and feel of the programme may have been modernised, but the message came straight from the adversarial 1970s. A week after it came to an elegiac close, BBC Two began showing *This Life*, a thoroughly modern drama of liberal aspiration and déclassé identity politics. The odd politically committed exception like Jimmy McGovern aside, this would be the model for British drama from now on; *Our Friends* was a last hurrah. Even the conservative *Daily Telegraph* lamented the fact: 'We are not likely to look upon its like again.'

THIS MORNING WITH RICHARD NOT JUDY (1998–9)

BBC Two

Existential satire and blasphemy finally reach Sunday afternoons.

Don't you realise you're participating in a sophisticated satire on your own low expectations?
Stewart Lee to audience, *Lee & Herring Live*, Ashcroft Theatre, Croydon, November 1996

WHEN ALTERNATIVE COMEDY'S SECOND wave showed its colours on TV in the early 1990s, its distinctions were easy to spot. Politically they were just as far to the left as their predecessors, but the second wavers made politics less central to their act, partly because a left-wing stance had been ingrained over the past decade as the default consensus of the young comedy crowd (which meant conservatism would inevitably die through natural wastage within a couple of decades). Instead there was a more wide-ranging – all right, rambling – preoccupation with other social matters: religion, sexual acceptance or lack of it, and forensic poring over the detritus of recent pop culture.

It was more decadent, and more childish, in a way. *The Mary Whitehouse Experience* might start a sketch about Saddam Hussein, but within thirty seconds it became a philosophical enquiry into the significance of *Captain Pugwash*, forsaking the demolition of the realpolitik of late capitalism for some whimsical riffing on Peter Purves's World Cup electricity board adverts or the ontological implications of Baccara's 'Yes Sir, I Can Boogie'. A lot of it would later constitute the backbone of the new comedy establishment, full of well-scrubbed middle class male stand-ups with powerful agents declaiming inoffensive, banal observations to packed arenas. Some, though, married a head-banging obsession with mindless trivia to sharp social insight.

Stewart Lee and Richard Herring formed as a double act in the traditional way, bonding at an Oxford University student revue. Their roles were settled early on. Herring was the gleeful man-child whose world-view swung wildly from the touchingly credulous to the shabbily perverted; Lee the supercilious eternal sixth-former operating with absolute certainty that his opinions, tastes and achievements were superior to those of everyone else. Together they stumbled through pop culture, Herring getting the wrong end of every stick, Lee calmly disabusing and disparaging him. After years of work on the live circuit, they got into radio through milestone current affairs satire *On the Hour* before graduating to their own radio shows and, by 1995, television with the sketch show *Fist of Fun*.

Growing out of an improvised chat show the pair hosted at the Edinburgh Fringe, *This Morning with Richard Not Judy*, or *TMWRNJ* (pronounced 'Terwumwunjuh!'), was a forty-five minute sketch show nominally modelled on ITV's afternoon magazine *This Morning*, performed live at Sunday lunchtime. Even allowing for the annexation, in the wake of *Network 7* and *Def II*, of that previously fallow slot for various youth-oriented shows, this was risky in its conception to the point of mania. Lee and Herring threw everything into it, packing the long running time with a wealth of material, organising complex live routines and recorded items full of recondite references and elaborate premises in total contravention of what was normally considered easily digestible by the average viewer at that particular time.

Items were built on in-jokes and caprice, then fleshed out with the help of the BBC props department and a skilled repertory company including Paul Putner and Kevin Eldon. A pun on the title of a song by The Fall brought forth 'The Curious Orange', an outsize fruit with the mind of a small child. 'Sunday Heroes' was their attempt to represent religion, as was right and proper for the timeslot, in reconstructions of the gospels which ended up revealing Jesus as an obscurantist riddler, keeping his dimmer disciples in their place with wilfully ambiguous parables. Although these brief sketches contained a more thorough dissection of Christian teaching than had been aired in that time slot for decades, the devout were slow to show their appreciation.

Their skewering of the unsophisticated dogma of early alternative comedy was something entirely new. Herring, accused of some convoluted, shameful private act, pleads to the gallery: 'Who's the real sick man in our so-called society?' He argues – with textbook debating society rhetorical emphasis – it's not him, but 'the *busi-*ness*man*. In his *suit* and *tie*.' Later, the alternative establishment was forensically undermined in the sketch 'Angus Deayton's Authorised History of Alternative Comedy with Angus Deayton', parodying a recent clipshow on the subject with a series of thinly-disguised impersonations of New Wave acts intercut with their sadly wistful present day reminiscences of those 'amazing times' while nursing a commemorative SDP mug.

This was no reactionary attack. Equal scorn was poured on the trend, still fairly new but rapidly catching on, of post-political, self-reflexive controversy building. 'The Ironic Review' was a spoof fly-on-the-wall documentary of office life in a hip metropolitan magazine, not terribly loosely based on *The Modern Review*, a painfully arch culture compendium run by Julie Burchill and Cosmo Landesman in the first half of the 1990s. The staff's *raison d'être* was to manufacture opinions which were the opposite of what they assumed their peer group deemed acceptable, delivered with a childishly whinnying 'aaa-*aaah*!' At the time this niche target brought a muted response from the studio audience, but two decades on, with practically the whole of the opinion columnist's trade reduced to mindless contrariness in the desperate search for online ad revenue, it looks remarkably prescient.

This goes double for the throwaway gag that opened the show on the morning of the 1998 London Marathon, with Lee and Herring dressed as (the as yet undefiled) Jimmy Savile, cheerily looking forward to the race. 'I hope nobody dies!' 'If they do, bagsy I take them to the mortuary!' The programme's profile, low to begin with and rapidly diminishing, enabled this joke (again, to almost total silence in the studio) to be casually flung out without major controversy. 'Because we knew no-one [at the BBC] was interested in it,' Lee explained, 'we were able to do whatever we wanted.'[456]

As the second series progressed, a heady combination of the duo's obsessive industriousness and BBC management's almost total abandonment of the show meant that each of the already complicated running characters and sketches developed their own storylines, mutated out of shape, cross-bred and generally collapsed into a broiling, end-of-term chaos. This was what marked their act out in an increasingly mainstream, career-minded alternative comedy world where maximum acceptability and the thrifty re-use of material were standard practice. Lee and Herring's idea of a crowd-pleasing gesture could be summed up by the end of one especially abstruse *TMWRNJ* escapade, when Herring apologised to first-time viewers for any bewilderment caused, 'but hopefully you still enjoyed the colours and shapes'.

THE SOPRANOS
(1999–2007)

HBO (Chase Films/
Brad Grey Television)

US drama finally reaches critical mass.

Take a look at the television coverage of the quality press on both sides of the Atlantic in the early years of the twenty-first century, and you'll notice a minor miracle. For the first few years of the hopeful third millennium, television was following a slow spiral into an inescapable chasm of facetious self-assembly reality formats and drearily third-rate fiction. A few years on, however, and a new Golden Age had suddenly dawned, brought forth on a raft of original drama of unprecedented seriousness and ambition. *The Sopranos, Breaking Bad, The West Wing, The Wire* . . . series after series broke envelopes, pushed moulds and tipped points wherever you looked. The tube's sucking void was suddenly a horn of plenty. What happened?

There was, of course, no spontaneous generation of genius, more another step on the evolutionary trail that began with Paddy Chayefsky. Quality and complexity are nothing new. Innovation is continuous, but occasionally enough quality specimens clump together for the coarse filter of media journalism, and a Golden Age is solemnly declared.

Drama in the 1990s was a jumble after the self-aware MTM era. Upmarket soaps like *thirtysomething* brought drama back into the domestic fold. Meanwhile, cops and docs continued to dominate evenings with *NYPD Blue, Homicide: Life on the Street, Chicago Hope* and *ER*. Good shows, but together they didn't make something the glibber end of media journalism could rip an easy headline from. Into this network soup rode fast-rising cable channel HBO with a show that combined the crime and the domestic with the story of a middle-aged New Jersey mob boss under pressure from both his empire and his errant family – all inspired by *Goodfellas*, Martin Scorsese's filmed life of gangster-turned-witness Henry Hall.

The Sopranos worked the highly desirable trick of stuffing the scope of a novel into a popular weekly series. In most series a few main characters have full histories, with everyone else a cipher working in aid of the plot. In *The Sopranos* everyone, from Tony's therapist to the strippers in his 'office', was a rounded, living creation. The weekly doses kept it in the popular imagination, and when a series was over the boxed DVD version could stand there, like *War and Peace*, on the correspondent's coffee table.

With the 'literary' end of television drama – most conspicuously those beloved single plays of increasingly distant memory – drying up, innovation has to come from genre, of which the crime or police thriller is by far the most prevalent. Forty-odd years ago an ambitious writer would most likely not be drawn to genre television, though he would likely have learned his craft in it. A genre show was most often an assemblage of previously successful parts, sometimes animated by a guiding creative intelligence which clicked them into place in ways no-one had thought of before, but more often than not lashed together just well enough to weather a season or two. The network economy could operate in no other way.

The cable economy, on the other hand, could foster a show with comparatively little executive tampering, and few if any name actors demanded up front, where the creator/writer was king. (It's worth noting that only a macro-economy as big as the USA's can comfortably contain a micro-economy of this type big enough to make an impact, so critics from far smaller nations are being obtuse when they demand why their compatriots haven't come up with something similar.)

The Wire is far more than a police procedural, as *Battlestar Galactica* is more than space opera. With shows like this, genre is an emphasis, a lens through which the world is refracted rather than a set of rules for a game through which life can be endlessly avoided. Great things had always come from generic roots. Dickens wrote serialised stories for popular entertainment, and happened to over-fulfil his brief several times over. Tolstoy began *War and Peace* with no greater ambition than to write a Russian version of the English 'domestic chronicle' in the style of Anthony Trollope, but expanded to encompass Russian history and moral philosophy, the generic boundaries swelling to encompass 'the ever-changing, ever-great, unfathomable, and infinite life around him.'[457]

The auteured TV dramas of the 1990s and 2000s were similarly alive to the richness of the everyday as it's experienced, rather than the routine of the adventure as it's so often fictionalised. David Chase, creator of *The Sopranos*, aligned what he'd learned of crafting a TV script from his apprenticeship on quirky series like *The Rockford Files* and *Northern Exposure* with influences from beyond the Burbank backlot. For one episode involving Tony Soprano's hallucination of a beautiful Italian dental student, Chase pointed the director to the matter-of-fact surrealism of Luis Buñuel as a cue for the handling of the fantastic plot.[458] A committee-steered network series would have run a mile from that kind of influence in the unlikely event it even occurred to them.

Creativity needs freedom to work, and freedom has always been in short supply. In 1737, British spoken drama was segregated by parliamentary decree. Robert Walpole instigated the theatrical crackdown to curtail the many satirical broadsides against his government, introducing mandatory censoring of all plays. In the early twentieth century, modernist artists enforced the idea of 'literary' work as above and beyond the run of the fictional mill, focusing critical eyes on a small group of writers and leaving the mainstream to stew in its self-policing, market driven genres.

Walpole's Regulation Act was finally completely rescinded in 1968, about the same time that critics began to admit that the best practitioners of genre fiction could rival the highbrows. Television, as subject to the control of snobs and politicians as any medium, entered its most extraordinary period at about this time. From the mid-1960s to the early 1980s, British and American screens teemed with intelligent, lively, outlandish and fabulous comedy, drama and documentary. The excitable predictions of the twenties and thirties began to look like they had a point with their prognostications of a world forever changed by the UHF transmitter.

Unfortunately there was a third source of repression, which wasn't going away. In fact, it began to reassert itself to an ever greater degree. Economic necessity took hold in the 1980s and never let go. Privately owned broadcasters planted themselves across the TV landscape while state subsidised television was steadily pruned back. A profusion of new channels struggled to cover themselves with a dearth of old programmes. Market research and governmental compliance meant the making of new programmes became progressively less of a madcap art and more of a dismal science. Common denominators began burrowing their way to the Earth's core. After the briefest of spells in the ascendant, TV was hounded once more.

The melting pot of the new medium, with shows of different types and tones clashing every evening, gave birth to countless new dramatic shapes and gradually wore down the barrier between high and low. The single play – the aloof, often difficult work that stands alone – is a thing of the past. Any future innovation will come from the series, and the genre series at that. The concentrated art and wit of *The Sopranos* and many of the broadsheet-wetting prodigies that followed it show this is not necessarily the disaster twentieth century critics used to fear.

Perhaps the HBO microclimate is so celebrated because it feels like a last stand, the old forests of memory lovingly revived as a perfectly trimmed bonsai plot. At the same time, banishing these shows to subscription services and online niches away from the mainstream runs the risk of another kind of segregation. Among the genuine fans of the cable dramas, a new group of highfalutin dunces gets to feel superior to the reality-swilling masses just for being in the know. The single play flew too far from its roots and found itself starved of funds when the financial reckoning came. Today's Emmy-laden showrunners must ensure their rarefied end of the new, disconnected television system doesn't become a similar intellectual ghetto.

PEOPLE LIKE US
(1999–2001)
BBC Two

The mockumentary at its peak.

THE FIRST TELEVISION MOCK-DOC was the 1968 *Smothers Brothers Comedy Hour* extended sketch 'Pat Paulsen: the Making of a President'. Filmed on grainy, hand-held 16mm film, this perfectly deadpan skit laid out the electoral hopes of the show's semi-detached deadbeat, with everyone from Woody Allen to Bobby Kennedy in on the gag. Instantly the golden rule was established: your words and actions can be as demented as you like, as long as the presentation remains po-faced and precise.

In 1972, satirists John Bird and John Wells created several comedy specials for Yorkshire Television, each consisting of a behind-the-scenes pastiche of an area of factual programming; as Wells put it, a 'tiptoe through the grim hinterland of television'.[459] *Return to Leeds* depicted the fractious making of a 'writer revisits roots' documentary, with Bird as the left-wing subject and Wells as the metropolitan producer; while *Deadline Leeds* evoked a disintegrating current affairs programme, with the two Johns playing every character in front of and behind the cameras. The depiction of what gets shown and said on these programmes, and the thinking that makes them that way, was diabolically accurate, but real life behind-the-scenes problems meant the shows were transmitted piecemeal, with up to a year between episodes, dooming them to obscurity.

Through the next two decades, the mock-doc broadened its reach and sharpened its approach. Neil Innes and Eric Idle's fictional sixties pop group the Rutles began as a handful of Beatles pastiches with period visual accompaniment on *Rutland Weekend Television*, before having their ludicrous backstory filled in, again with a sprinkling of genuine stars, for 1978 NBC special *All You Need Is Cash*. The music business was mockumentary manna – the typical rock star's drug-flattened delivery, the insane decadence of the business and the increasing pretension of the music were a perfect combination. The *Comic Strip* depicted life at the bottom of the glorious heap with 1983's *Bad News Tour*, following a suburban metal band of honking fecklessness around Britain in a leopard-skin-trimmed van. The following year, Rob Reiner's cinema release *This Is Spinal Tap* covered the same territory, creating a sleeper cult hit.

Politics and news, the beachhead of media pomp, took their lumps from the genre. In the US, HBO's miniseries *Tanner '88* allowed Robert Altman to refine the roaming, overlapping style he'd popularised with *MASH*, trapping satirist Garry Trudeau's hopeful Democratic candidate in a web of pregnant pauses and fumbled rhetorical stabs. In Britain current affairs were demolished by the dynasty of radio and TV programmes marshalled by Armando Iannucci and Christopher Morris. *The Day Today*, their first TV manifestation, dressed as a news bulletin but impersonated everything. What looked like blunderbuss fire from a distance proved on close inspection to be a blitz of trained snipers. Picture, sound, style and speech of eras from the fifties to the present, and countries from the USA to France, were forensically restaged. A three second clip of a forgotten drama brought the sense of an entire series, even generation, with it – believable and familiar, but somehow fundamentally ajar. Countless delicately wrought moments piled up on each other to give the cumulative effect of television itself cracking up.

Brass Eye, Morris's demolition of the self-righteous *World in Action* crusading tradition, went even further, showing sanity a clean pair of heels from the interminable opening titles onward. Director Michael Cumming, who'd served an apprenticeship on sober science programmes like *Tomorrow's World*, was instrumental in keeping the wild script in contact with reality by furnishing the madhouse with authentic visual bric-a-brac. Cumming didn't direct the *Brass Eye Special*, the show's slight return in 2001, and the look of it suffered from the lack of visual unity: faked archive footage looked mannered, graphics too obviously wacky, and clips from supposedly different programmes not quite distinct enough. In this game the details matter.

The format reached its limit in writer John Morton's debut broadcast work *People Like Us*. It began on Radio Four in 1995 as a pastiche of the BBC's long tradition of earnest explorations of everyday life, which had grown into a recognisable formula. An everyday situation – a market stall, an accountancy firm – was visited by a reporter with a lugubrious, earthy, borderline sarcastic manner (Ray Gosling, Bernard Falk, and especially John Pitman) resulting in a half-elegiac, half-melancholy portrait of honest, humdrum Britain. Knowingly mundane titles like *The Beaminster and District Gardens and Allotments Society Goes to Chelsea* abounded. This had already been parodied in a running sketch on *Victoria Wood: As Seen on TV*. Authentic documentary reporter Paul Heiney and authentic documentary cameraman Philip Bonham-Carter were placed amongst characters created by Wood and her company of actors, creating a believably textured world that slowly but surely turned fully absurd.

In *People Like Us* Chris Langham was dogged interlocutor Roy Mallard, a distillation of the Gosling-Pitman manner with the bathos multiplied tenfold and the self-awareness stripped out, following honest working types through a typical day. ('Thursday.') His lugubrious voice plods through endless dollops of vapid scene-setting prose. ('Whilst those around him are bound for jobs in offices, shops or other offices, Rob's day may well take him to places he doesn't even know about yet, although equally it might not, in which case he doesn't know about that either.')

Mallard's inane questions, his subjects' only marginally less inane responses, and the tendency of both parties to become easily distracted from the task in hand, give the meandering format a deceptively quick-fire gag rate. Unusually for a sitcom, the director's main job was to make it look like it contained fewer jokes than it actually did.

Translated to television, the documentary conceit opened up further opportunities for self-sabotage. The visual constantly exposed defects in the verbal. Gaps in the film were arbitrarily plugged with Mallard's half-awake platitudes. ('Acting is a profession of extremes on the one hand, and on the other hand, too; an all-or-nothing world in which triumph and rejection, comedy and tragedy, go hand in glove like two halves of the same puppet.') The supposedly invisible filmmaking process becomes so gummed up in its own ineptitude it threatens to push its subject off the screen. The lives of dull fools are proudly explained by even duller fools, who still tell us plenty about life nevertheless, by sheer galumphing accident. It's a feeling every TV viewer knows well, so to have it intentionally replicated works as a welcome release: there's someone with brains in the zoo after all.

What followed *People Like Us*, though, was very odd indeed. The basic technical trappings of the fake documentary need a degree of observation and skill to pull off, but they're not that difficult to do. Unbolt the camera from the tripod, chop the dialogue into awkward, overlapping chunks and you're superficially halfway there already. The *Hill Street Blues* style of shaky realism becoming a one-stop application of grit for your drama output might seem logical, but its equally pernicious takeover of comedy a few years later (and soon everything up to and including ads) was more surprising.

Producers spotted that, just as the *Hill Street* technique could 'sell' a drama that might be lacking in other areas, it also added credibility to an undernourished comedy, soap or workplace injury advocacy commercial. Used cynically, it's an easy-to-apply prophylactic protecting the script's gaping holes from close inspection.

Suspend the camera from a woozy gimbal and the viewer's disbelief will follow. Until, that is, it becomes the default visual style and starts to count for nothing. 'In an age of naturalism,' wrote Eric Bentley, 'a writer's courage sometimes fails him and he tries to pass off a tame duck as a beast of the jungle.'[460] With their rag-bag of naturalistic tricks toted shamelessly up front, some programmes of the early twentieth century couldn't half quack.

John Morton addressed the courage deficit in *W1A*, his 2014 dissection of the BBC's bloated management culture. Given the run of the Corporation's spanking New Broadcasting House, Morton made it an anthill run by grasshoppers: uneasy, status-obsessed folk guarding their jobs with a jealousy that matched their inability to define what those jobs actually were, passing responsibility back and forth in a fugue of freshly-minted buzzwords that carried as little meaning as possible. Some critics dismissed it as a cosy dig in the ribs. As Morris and Iannucci discovered, satire's targets possess a sublime ability to mentally exempt themselves from attack. But at its best, the mockumentary lobs a message to the viewer over the social barrier – a valuable service when the official channels, as in *W1A*, aren't willing to offer anything more than an obtuse, 'No, yes. Right. Brilliant.'

BATTLESTAR GALACTICA (2004–9)
Sci Fi (NBC Universal)

Big, dumb science fiction smartens itself up.

No ENTERTAINMENT GENRE IS more patronised, in both senses of the word, than science fiction. Done right, it promises instant access to an audience large, loyal and lucrative enough to make crime writers retreat into their locked rooms and pull the trigger. And yet, even with a hit on their hands, TV people seem oddly ill at ease pushing space-age kicks. It's not . . . 'proper' drama, really, is it?

In literature, where it's been responsible for some of the most important and experimental works of the last century, science fiction enjoys a grudging tolerance. In the cinema it can choose between cultish esteem and mountains of cash, but almost never gets both. On television its reputation has long been lower still: an endless parade of beetle-browed men in one-piece polyester romper suits bellowing co-ordinates into silver hairdryers to a backing chorus of microwave oven alarms. It veers between the infantile and the psychedelically incomprehensible, often from minute to minute. Or at least that's the received opinion, and as a result it's generally the first thing to get the chop when a station tightens its purse strings.

Science fiction seems to come in three types. At the top there are the smoky fascist dystopias, which gain a few brownie points for fumbling at would-be 'adult' themes to the sound of rubber on brushed concrete. (This is the genre most 'proper' writers are likely to have a crack at – it seems easy enough.) Then come the one-shot plays with the dimension-warping twist in the tail, which are lauded for their wit, economy and cleverness, and then never referred to again. At the very bottom come the space operas, floating foil palaces full of jut-jawed men and well-proportioned women whose constant frowns are only there to prevent every meaningless speech dissolving into a fit of RADA giggles. All three are strapped for cash and drained of emotion. Brian Aldiss spoke of the bifurcation of fiction into literature (kosher) and genres like science fiction (suspect) some time after the war. Many practitioners of the TV variety have looked at the reputation of their trade and wondered if they didn't take the wrong turning.

It's a rough deal all round for the off-worlders. Come the twenty-first century, however, and American television caught the space bug again, even if the raw material it chose looked far from promising. Soon after the release of *Star Wars* (which was in turn shamelessly lifted from old movie serials – premise from *Flash Gordon*, helmets from *Fighting Devil Dogs*) producer Glen A. Larson had adapted a long-cherished pet project into a thirteen-part, million-dollar-per-episode George Lucas clone for ABC.

With its blonde hero, cute robots and evil, faceless Cylons, the original *Battlestar Galactica* was Lucas listlessly retrod: a slavish visual copy of its cinematic counterpart spiced with a gratuitous dash of Mormon theology and Lorne Greene in a purple cape. Mick Farren called it 'the product of Hollywood huck, jive and money shuffle.'[461] It was to *Star Wars* what another Glen A. Larson production, *Alias Smith and Jones*, was to Butch and Sundance – a luncheon voucher to a hundred dollar bill.

The show was the most perverse possible choice for a twenty-first century remake, but David Eick, producer of *Hercules: The Legendary Journeys*, and Roland D. Moore, writer for various reactivated branches of the *Star Trek* franchise, set upon it with the aim of fashioning a fully shaded drama that would take them out of 'the science fiction ghetto'.[462]

A two-part pilot cleared the decks of kitsch. Moore's remake was 'a character story about people who happen to be inside a science fiction universe.'[463] The cultural references to other TV shows, by now a network tradition, were still there – the station is introduced with a *M*A*S*H*-style camera sweep around the ensemble cast, much-cloned blonde female Cylon Number Six is named after McGoohan's Prisoner, and the *Hill Street Blues* cry 'let's be careful out there' makes several appearances. This time, though, the playfulness was kept in check – the story itself was too good to upstage.

Sci Fi, the show's host channel, had a chequered reputation among genre devotees. When *Galactica* came their way, they were bogged down with several unsuccessful adaptations of hard science fiction; an adaptation of Philip José Farmer's lauded *To Your Scattered Bodies Go*, set on an endless, alien-manufactured river valley where every human who ever lived is reincarnated, got no further than pilot stage, while a series based on Roger Zelazny's elephantine parallel world *Amber* series never escaped development. Grandiose ideas became inelegantly stuck in their tiny niche of appeal. Something altogether less esoteric was needed.

Galactica's budget had hardly swelled in the last quarter century to $1.5 million per episode: relative chickenfeed. Making the Cylons humanoid was first a money-saving choice, but took the show in a new, more fruitful direction; pouring off the spacey trappings expanded the possibilities. Flat broke and ghetto-bound, *Battlestar Galactica* stole a march on the mainstream of its cinematic sisters, where if something the size of Manhattan hasn't crashed into something the size of Belgium in the first reel, the film walks. For all the capable CGI battle scenes (framed in synthetic 'wobblyscope' for extra impact) the most memorable interludes consisted of two faces, talking.

Ever since Stanley Kubrick ended his space odyssey in an oak-panelled dining room, visual science fiction has delighted in spinning viewers' heads with the sudden appearance of retro props amongst the brushed chrome and pink perspex. *Battlestar Galactica*'s conceit – that these are humans from our distant past, who will eventually colonise Earth – was the one bit of Mormon detritus from the original that could be put to good use. With everything set in the past, the decision to go for rusting rivets, clockwork clocks, chunky buttons, sturdy ring-bound flight manuals and phones with flexes makes story sense and gives battle scenes a welcome physicality that virtual displays lack.

The commander can barely talk to his son, the Vice President is a duplicitous delusional paranoid and the President has cancer. Everyone from the top down is hugely vulnerable, becoming more wearied and brutalised as the series unfolds. They swap allegiances, question the point of it all, sometimes just give up. Religious conversions, class war, domestic violence and post-traumatic stress abound. It's no arid fantasy but a rich, living mess, rooted in the mundanities of life – characters endure vehicular breakdowns, act awkward with estranged relatives and eat mashed potatoes.

They also have sex. The two-episode pilot opened with a diplomatic human–Cylon snog. Sex in space opera was nothing new, but instead of Clark Gable clinches and girl-in-every-port fantasy, here it led to unwise relationships, betrayal and childbirth in every messy, complicated permutation. The often unacknowledged sexual tension that made RSC stalwarts collapse with mirth during futuristic speeches was thrust – or rather delicately placed – into the thick of the script. Wives and husbands populated the fleet, and the unisex crew were an army of sweaty-vested lovers from the start.

To get the general audience watching, smart science fiction needs a good reason for the effort and distraction of its whole invented world, when the real one seems to do well enough for others. *Battlestar Galactica* had a fine one: America's post-9/11 complex of fear, jingoist rancour and guilt was still too raw and inchoate to be addressed directly. Trussing it up in a prophylactic metaphor and bunging it to the other end of time and space allowed the writing team to treat recent events close-up. Though nominally set hundreds of millennia in the past, it was firmly attached to the times.

But War on Robo-Terror was only the most journalistically saleable angle of a complex scheme. The Cylons, who come in twelve flavours from hot blonde to sarcastic atheist priest, are mystically inclined, ultra-repressed and occasionally childishly vulnerable when the gaps in their emotional make-up come to light. According to Moore, 'They have aspects of Al Qaeda, and they have aspects of the Catholic Church [the Cylons worship one God, humans a selection box from Greco-Roman antiquity], and they have aspects of America.'[464] The allegory was turned on its head halfway through, as humans fought back against Cylon occupation with suicide attacks. The series grew deeper, not just more convoluted, as it grew longer.

Over four series *Battlestar Galactica* managed, more or less, to stay on top of its huge, ever-growing, pulsating agglomeration of mystical baggage to bring television science fiction back into favour. Many times in the past, whether through incomprehension or incompetence, producers have sorely underestimated the difficulty of the genre. The *Galactica* team not only got that right, they managed to marry science fiction's intellectual peaks with its trashy bottom line, in one Möbius strip of a serial. It's good science fiction; it's good drama. That's all.

FORBRYDELSEN (2007–12)

DR1 (Danmarks Radio)

European drama finally takes on the world.

IF THIS HAS BEEN a very Anglophone story, that's a symptom of the way television has enabled the culture with the most financial clout behind it to bulldoze the television of others into pidgin clones of its native formats, plus a few charmingly rustic local aberrations: emotionally incontinent Latin American soaps, impenetrably austere Albanian cartoons and childishly sadistic Japanese game shows. (It was chauvinistically assumed that these heightened qualities said more about the population of the programme's parent country than the genre it belonged to.)

When the original eight-nation Eurovision network started up in 1954, technical obstacles were soon dwarfed by language issues: 'a deadly self-criticism of what ought to be a mainly visual art.'[465] But it wasn't a mainly visual art; that pipe dream had died with silent cinema. Television was nearly all talk. The language barrier in television became high and immovable, but occasionally a show of sufficient cunning could still cross over.

For a long time, British productions used Europe primarily as a backdrop for middle class dramas with a holiday vibe. For the BBC, Michael J. Bird toured the islands of the eastern Mediterranean for exotically decorated thrillers such as *The Lotus Eaters* and *Who Pays the Ferryman?* Bird's Mediterranean, according to Jonathan Meades, was a place 'where the natives spout purplish aphorisms and specialise in looking meaningfully at strangers through eyes narrowed against the spitting fat of sheftalia.'[466]

In 1985, Bird relocated to Norway for the rural Gothic of *Maelstrom*, a psychological shocker stuffed with art-house longueurs, impenetrable plot twists and a surfeit of information about the salt fish industry, which became something of a public running joke. 'I would not want this to get around,' confessed Nancy Banks-Smith, 'but I have been following *Maelstrom* surreptitiously behind locked doors claiming defensively, when challenged, to be watching blue movies.'[467] Noting the package holiday landscape photography, Julian Barnes added, 'You half expect Cliff Michelmore or Frank Bough to turn up and explain about ferry bookings.'[468] But the gag was already reality: ferry firms were advertising exotic excursions to 'Norway: Land of the Maelstrom'.

Scandinavian countries built TV networks at various speeds in the early 1950s, with the single state broadcaster dominating. Sveriges Radio, Stockholm's answer to the BBC, exported Ingmar Bergman's six-part divorce study *Scenes from a Marriage* as far as the USA in 1973, albeit with Liv Ullmann dubbed by Annie Ross. National stereotypes informed the attendant press speculation that the 'gloomy' series might be responsible for the hefty recent increase in the Swedish divorce rate. On a lighter note, it was cited as a major influence by *Dallas* creator David Jacobs in the development of *Knots Landing*. But the general picture was of a TV landscape as bland as they came. Anthony Burgess, visiting Stockholm in 1981, noted that peak time was devoted to 'a highly instructive though sedative film on shoemaking in a remote Swedish village'.[469]

In 2009 Norway's national broadcaster NRK2 subverted this dreary reputation with a marathon broadcast of an uninterrupted live train journey in *Bergensbanen: Minutt for Minutt*, followed by *Hurtigruten: Minutt for Minutt* – live coverage of a five-day coastal cruise. 'Slow TV' was born, and quickly added to with live salmon fishing, close-up knitting and National Firewood Night. There was nothing new here: in TV's infancy, the BBC's intermission films of potters' wheels and kittens playing with wool were often eulogised as superior to their actual programmes. In the US, pioneering shows like *Garroway at Large* would rig up a camera on the studio roof and offer leisurely shots of the Chicago skyline, while in the mid-1970s a New York cable channel offered a constantly burning Yule Log service over Christmas, cited as 'evidence that daily life in America has surpassed surrealism and broken through into science fiction.'[470] Norway's programmes, though, amounted to a cult, with everybody in on the joke yet deadly serious about its telling. 'TV has mostly been produced the same way everywhere with just changes in subjects and themes,' claimed Rune Møklebust, the producer behind the movement. 'This is a different way of telling a story. It is more strange. The more wrong it gets, the more right it is.'[471]

The UK and US, with little to go on, were still getting Scandinavians wrong. Stereotype dictated that, though they themselves are incorrigibly morbid, their society was superhumanly idyllic, ordered and egalitarian. A new wave of crime writing, which explored the personal cliché and questioned the truth of the national one, took root in the 1990s with Henning Mankell's *Wallander* books. The brusque Swedish detective with an excessive love for opera and alcohol took a single murder and from it extrapolated a mare's nest of Mafia, drug cartels, far-right groups and corrupt politicians. Its TV adaptation in 2005 proved a surprise hit outside Sweden. British viewers especially couldn't get enough of 'Inspector Norse', and the quality channels started looking for more Nordic crime to import.

Denmark's public broadcaster, Danmarks Radio, was the first to go live in Scandinavia, but its creative peaks failed to travel. *Matador*, a huge saga of two influential families set during the Depression and WWII, remained a well-kept domestic secret, despite pre-empting *Heimat*. There was little else on Danish TV to challenge it, until Søren Sveistrup put a new crime series together for DR1. Like *Wallander*, it featured an emotionally reticent, case-hardened detective, and murder inquiries that touched on social problems. Instead of a new case every week, one incident was the trigger for twenty episodes of internecine connections and chilling discoveries.

Forbrydelsen ('The Killing') took the international language of crime literature and added Danish touches, from the murky half-light that pervaded every space to the co-operative nature of its production. Sveistrup, producer Piv Bernth and director Birger Larsen collaborated as the sort of free-associating team that used to be behind nearly every British TV production before manager-ial protocol swamped the process. In particular, Sveistrup worked closely with lead actress Sofie Gråbøl in the construction of DI Sarah Lund's personality. The pathologically taciturn inspector, fumbling male relationships from her estranged adult son to the assorted male colleagues she's teamed with, was a new and fascin-ating creation after a long line of similarly pensive male cops. A mystery as impenetrable as the motives of the mayor, it helped *Forbrydelsen* gain international status. For light relief, the Faroe sweater she constantly wore became a handily saleable signifier.

Sveistrup started from the personal. He was suspicious of what he claimed Mankell's books did, attacking social problems full on, preferring a subtler initiating incident whose repercussions affect all levels of society. 'It starts with an emotion,' he maintained, 'otherwise I don't see the point.'[472] That he could go from a single murder right up to the prime minister was down to the compact and bijoux nature of his homeland. *Forbrydelsen* could get its murder investigations to touch the depths of Danish society and still remain credible because Danish society, at around five and a half million strong, was so tight knit. Small countries work differently. As Bjork said of Iceland, 'if you go to the geothermal baths the prime minister is naked in the shower.'[473] Which sounds quaint, but with no-one deemed untouchable, a strangely sparse claustrophobia takes hold, a quiet village menace ideal for conspiracy's slow release.

British TV used to be able to capture the stillness and the mystery of its native countryside, but decades of period drama suffused fields and hedgerows with the soapy odour of the National Trust. The wilds were domesticated – even the most forbidding landscapes had to be shot imaginatively to remove the strong suspicion that there was a sizeable gift shop just out of view. Nordic scenery was wilder and free of 'Haywainification'. The people, too, were just exotic enough: though steeped in Americana, Danish culture was a lot less Americanised than the UK, retaining its own peculiar identity – both somewhere very vivid and nowhere in particular.

The Nordic incursion into the great Anglo-American TV narrative gathered steam with *Borgen, The Bridge, Mammon, Unit One* and more. Naturally they weren't allowed to do it all themselves; America demanded remakes. AMC's version of *The Killing* relocated the original's tranquil unease to the Pacific north-west and was compared by many to *Twin Peaks*, though without the 'metaphysical whimsy'[474] with which that show sabotaged itself. Though translations still had to be made, the Nordic renaissance was a harbinger of the new, more interconnected TV market. Where once subtitles signalled the presence of an obscure avant-garde film, they now adorn a much more accessible collection of international drama, from Sicilian procedural *Montalbano* to Parisian legal thriller *Engrenages*. The language barrier hasn't shifted, but world television becomes more accessible by the day, and the more we get, the more we'll watch it for edification and entertainment, not just to chuckle at funny customs or plan a fortnight's self-catering jaunt to Malmö.

APPLE ACTION NEWS
(2009–)

Apple Daily/YouTube (Next Media Ltd.)

The slightly silly dawn of virtual journalism.

IN THE 1990S, TOPICAL comedy underwent a change in emphasis. Instead of mocking public figures and social convention, many satirists turned their attention to society's reporters and pundits. In America, satirical paper *The Onion* used American journalism's bone dry verbal conventions to pull apart the self-generating forms and irrelevant content of much of its output.

In 1994 in the UK *The Day Today*, built from radio origins by a nexus of comedians centred around Chris Morris and Armando Iannucci, took the increasingly bombastic and tech-heavy direction British television news had been taking for the previous decade and projected it into idiotic space. One skit, a report on the NASA Space Shuttle's exhilaratingly pointless upcoming mission to leap over a line of twelve other shuttles in orbit, was illustrated with a 3D animation that looked exactly like a genuine news bulletin graphic, nudged just slightly into the realm of digital camp. Fifteen years later, that one-shot gag would be echoed in the birth of a new and rather suspect information industry.

Taiwanese animation studio Next Media began by creating 3D animated diagrams of serious news stories that needed detailed visual information: plane crashes, tanker spills and military manoeuvres. They did this in a style not too far removed from mainstream television news's in-house graphics departments, with perhaps a little more directorial licence on camera angles and the odd sound effect. With a huge bank of visual assets, slightly stiff but reasonably polished capsule reports could be turned out on their production line in a few hours. Hundreds of companies worldwide offered similar services, but Next Media quickly became one of the biggest in the field.

In 2009, they began branching out into stories on a more human scale. In a fast-growing and increasingly borderless video news market, it was becoming clear that the spoils were going not to the hack with the sharpest analysis or the inside line, but the organization with the most footage. For many stories, particularly those involving reports of personal indiscretion by celebrities, a fuzzy CCTV image was as good as it got, leading to a glaring gap between the breathless tabloid descriptions of Star X's crazed drug-fuelled antics and the solitary blue-grey blur viewers were assured was them caught mid-freak-out. Something was needed to bridge that gap, and CGI was the answer.

With a few additions to their basic set-up, Next Media began making human stories. Because of the lightning production schedule, results were far from polished. What was fine simplific-ation with vehicles and buildings looked humorous, even grotesque, on people. Faces were realistically proportioned and textured, but lighting, expressions and motion were only half there, creating an overlit world of glassy-eyed, karate-chopping stock figures bearing only the most basic similarity to whomever they were meant to be impersonating. It looked clunkily unreal to the point of demonic possession, but it put the story across in a memorable way.

Next Media's work initially appeared on two outlets – sister company Apple Daily's news website, and their own NMA.tv domain, though most of their international traffic naturally came via YouTube, helpfully showcased on traditional press and television reports. The first report to gain worldwide attention focussed on Tiger Woods's mysterious midnight altercation with his wife and subsequent low-speed car crash, recreated in glorious glassy-eyed, joint-popping 3D. Bits of dramatic emotional shorthand borrowed from Japanese *animé* – torrents of tears to indicate an upset protagonist, head erupting in flames for anger – added to the oddity.

Questions of taste that would trouble most mainstream TV outlets were brushed aside. To illustrate the Jimmy Savile scandal, what could be more appropriate than having a jogging, shell-suited avatar transform into the Child Catcher from *Chitty Chitty Bang Bang*, while children run away in all directions? Quite a lot as it happens, but as the lower end of print journalism had known for decades, the crass and the obvious get people's attention.

This new media was received with some very Old World attitudes. American and European pundits leapt on the viral success as a comprehensive dumbing down of core journalistic values by those inscrutable, childlike orientals. 'If this is the future of tabloid journalism,' thundered CNN's Howard Kurtz, 'then I want no part of it.'[475] Next Media intended it to be nothing of the sort, of course – the 'zanies', as they called them, were treated as the hi-tech equivalent of newspaper op-ed cartoons, with all the visual metaphor and irrelevance that came with it, rather than a news source in itself. It was a massively successful international calling card that initially helped to plug, and eventually overtook, their diagrammatic meat-and-potatoes work. By early 2014 their videos were averaging forty million views each.

The problem was that the wackiness was indeed starting to get confused with the serious reporting. TV news, especially in the English speaking world, was shedding the responsible restraint it had kept up for decades. In America, proprietary news outlets like Fox gave blocks of airtime to opinionated and animated pundits from the sweaty end of the far right, who manically outlined elaborate liberal conspiracies unchallenged for hours at a time. Britain had the opposite problem, a retreat into a kind of detached patrician superciliousness, looking askance at events through narrowed eyes as if the latest government initiative was a smudged drawing of a three-armed Santa from an unloved nephew. One took itself ultra-seriously, the other found it hard to respond to anything except as a bad joke. The two vastly different sicknesses produced the same symptom: prancing trivia.

This strangely wilful decline was encapsulated when, in 2013, editorship of BBC Two's flagship heavyweight news programme *Newsnight* went to Ian Katz, former *Guardian* deputy editor and complete television ingénue. Citing the very real lack of public engagement with contemporary politics, Katz loaded the analytical pantechnicon with gimmicks and stunts – anything to leaven that tedious political discussion, summed up by Katz's injudicious Tweet on Labour shadow minister Rachel Reeves's 'boring snoring' performance on the show.[476] The editorial tone fell somewhere between the world's oldest cynic and a ten-year-old child who'd won a competition.

The wall between serious news and mucking about, which had just about held up since Angela Rippon stepped out with Eric and Ern, collapsed. The 'and finally' item turned into a nugget of forced, end of term jollity – Kirsty Wark danced like a zombie on Halloween and a clearly reluctant Emily Maitlis covered children's channel CBeebies' collaboration with the makers of *Sesame Street* by interviewing the Cookie Monster. Serious reporting remained the programme's *raison d'être*, but the daft stunts got people's attention. As with *Apple Action News*, the objective was to generate a viral internet success by any means necessary. In a world faster, more connected and fractious by the day, reliable and quick news services were more important than ever. Perhaps it was in an honest reflection of the times that they spent so long goofing off.

LOUIE (2010–)
FX (Pig Newton Inc)

Comedy reaches new heights of philosophical rigour and infantile seediness.

'COMEDY IS THE NEW rock 'n' roll.' It's a sentence so corny and demonstrably wide of the truth (a large part of rock 'n' roll's impact relies on the wilful denial of absurdity) that it's amazing it hung around for a few months, let alone decades. It first surfaced in the USA in the late 1980s to help journalists crudely bracket an assortment of smoking, swearing truth tellers – most notably Sam Kinison and Bill Hicks – who provided welcome relief from the mass of jobbing actors in open-necked shirts cynically sliding behind the mic with the sole intent of securing a sitcom deal. The new breed eschewed network TV for raw cable channels and sweaty-walled basement clubs, firing out painfully honest material in assorted shades of adversarial rage. Skirting mainstream TV removed the cred-busting taint of show business from the acts, aligning them with Lenny Bruce rather than Bob Hope.

But TV comedians were often outsiders, fighting the medium and mocking its wares, ever since Ernie Kovacs and Spike Milligan pulled television apart when it had barely got itself together. Just as vaudeville troupes like the Marx Brothers filled theatre owners with as much trepidation as they did audiences with joy, the list of comedians who've properly embraced TV and of those who reduce channel executives to low, apprehensive mutterings are almost identical. Provide alternative comics with an hour of peak time and they'll blow it up. Give a whimsical folk duo their own comedy show and they become enemies of the state. Give a forty-something divorcee his own series and he'll show you the world. After a fashion.

Louis C. K. (real name Louis Székely) started out as a stand-up comic on the Boston circuit, but always had designs on television. 'It made me mad that the shows were so bad,' he recalled of his youth in front of the networks. 'People have a right to relax and watch theatre about themselves that makes them reflect and feel and have a good time doing it.'[477] He made a few art house films with his wife, but disliked the aloofness of the independent film scene, preferring the 'low self-esteem' of television.[478] His first sitcom for HBO, *Lucky Louie*, was a conscious attempt to slap a modern comic sensibility on *The Honeymooners'* old three-camera, dirty-walled kitchenette set-up. It passed through the 2006 summer schedules without touching the sides. The follow-up dropped conceptual gimmickry for street-level introspection.

Louie did things the modern way, taking a single camera out into New York for a mix of extended sketches 'from life' interspersed with stand-up bits based on their contents. Gradually themes took over whole shows, and Louie's fictionalised domestic life (divorced, two precocious daughters, struggling on the club circuit, shares an apartment block with a cast of oddballs) grew into a kind of half-sitcom with a running meta-commentary and, miraculously, no commercial break.

'The show we're doing has no precedent in American television history,' he claimed with mock grandeur, carefully adding, 'I can't speak for British TV.'[479] Something like it had been done in the UK before: Kelly Monteith, a Canadian comic working at the BBC, created a sitcom cutting between his slick act and the messy personal life that informed it a quarter of a century earlier. And just to dispel any hint of sophistication, Paul Squire, old school Mancunian comic who stormed the 1980 Royal Variety Performance, used the sitcom-about-making-comedy shtick for his TV début the following year. In formal terms, this postmodern nag had been ridden before.

The content, though, was another matter. 'Middle-aged man versus the modern world' had never been done with this level of raw honesty before. No plots where the hero takes up jogging and gets a hernia here. Instead, a curious Louis goes in search of an anal sex toy, only to put his back out in the shop pointing to the one he's after. Rock 'n' roll edge and middle-aged domestic farce collide, cruelly cancelling each other out. His regulation will-they-won't-they female buddy, played by Pamela Adlon, appraises him in terms varying from 'You're so afraid of life that you're boring' to 'You can't even rape well'. On the street, he's assailed by the randomness of the modern city. He goes apartment hunting and finds one with a toilet in the kitchen. He spots government agents swapping homeless people around on street corners. Another homeless ranter gets decapitated by a truck as he's on his way to a date: the ultimate visitation from blind fate. Incidents take on a fantastic turn, adding to the feeling of a dreamworld – a largely mundane and shitty dreamworld at that.

The show evolved from season to season. For the third, stories broke out of their twenty-three-minute confines and spread over several episodes. One three-part story brought the new and old ways of making television into a fantastic pileup. Louis gets, seemingly from nowhere, a chance to audition as a replacement for a supposedly retiring David Letterman. This biggest of big breaks turns into a nightmare as he finds himself in the starched throwback hands of Jack Dall, a veteran producer of Pre-Cambrian heritage. C. K. cast about the nation's entertainment grandees for the role: Jerry Lewis, Woody Allen and Martin Scorsese politely turned him down. Eventually David Lynch said yes.[480]

Remote and stilted, yet confident in an otherworldly way, Lynch proved the perfect choice to embody C. K.'s vision of the TV pioneers, being impossibly out of date to the point of total alienation, yet possessing a weirdly unflappable confidence and experience sorely lacking in the current generation. Louis is in awe of Dall, a buttoned up stiff working to cast iron show business laws only he can access; the wisdom of the ancients. The new rock 'n' roll rubs up against a wartime big band and finds its musical chops sorely lacking. It's the relationship modern TV has with its past – alternately raiding it for ideas and patronising it with smug nostalgia – in a nutshell of professional awkwardness.

Modern Jack Dalls are legion, but their collective usefulness is a matter of debate. Twenty-first century TV is subject to a ping-pong development process far more intensive and protracted than before, with each circle of development hell progressively more removed from the light of the studio floor. Mirages arise from endless boardroom table talk and budgets shrivel by the hour. Merely getting a programme on air is a triumph for the production team against an executive army that can seem endless, like Ray Harryhausen's regenerating skeleton brigades.

Louie was made in an uncommonly efficient way. Louis C. K. wrote, produced and directed the vast majority of the series, even editing early episodes himself on a Macbook Pro, before drafting Woody Allen veteran Susan E. Morse for the third season.[481] With a decision making chain that short, crises could be dealt with and on-the-hoof changes made in an instant. While the economic and distributive knots of television – channel, network, studio or online platform – can change with the seasons, the unit of production, the size of the crew who actually get the show made, is only as big as it needs to be. The numbers should stack up in descending order: an audience of millions for the labour of a dozen, working to the vision of one. Smaller, swifter and knowing all the angles, the makers will always get the last laugh.

Comedy, as much as any branch of the entertainment industry, has become a global leviathan. World tours and arena venues are the signs of stand-up success, and scale can't help but affect content. The restriction of British theatre to larger, approved venues like Drury Lane in the nineteenth century meant that Victorian acting, to fill the cavernous space, tended toward the loud, the unsubtle: literally playing to the gallery. Arena comedy has a similar effect: subtlety gets lost, and the size of the crowd means stand-ups metaphorically play to the gallery, going for laughs of easy recognition and steering well away from ambiguity, obscurity and offence. Treble-checked and hyper slick, arena shows are slow, lumbering beasts, at the mercy of the small club comic's instantaneous powers of reinvention. The close-up conjurer can work twenty tiny miracles while David Copperfield's still pouting through the overture to his set piece.

If Louis C. K.'s basement clubs were the opposite of arena shows, his FX show ran counter to the prevailing trends of TV comedy in many ways. *Louie* uses 'dark' comedy (the adolescent glee in gorging on childhood taboos) as decoration, but its bricks and mortar are the randomness of life, the terror of chance (what Anthony Burgess called 'the black borders of comedy').[482] There are no easy villains, no cardboard enemy for the crowd to round on, just one poor sap and his dumb luck.

Modern media make wild claims to girdle the Earth and serve huge populations. TV has been the most successful in doing this, but it did so by working on a small, human scale. Screens may now measure sixty inches or more, but they're also six inches or less. Like all great comedy, *Louie* shows the directionless mess of modern life can be redeemed through tiny pleasures. And if television isn't the biggest collection of tiny pleasures and telling details created by man, what is?

HOUSE OF CARDS (2013–)

Netflix (Media Rights Capital/Panic Pictures)

Television outgrows the television set.

To PREDICT THE FUTURE direction of television with any degree of confidence takes either extreme gumption or exquisite gormlessness. The traditional set-up of a handful of national terrestrial broadcasters per country, one of them funded by the state, has, after several decades under siege from the robber barons of cable and satellite, become critically enfeebled. The Internet has shown it can encompass television just as television could encompass cinema, and do a hundred other things besides. Doomy punters envision the death of TV just as they saw cinema's imminent demise when television first arrived, but they're no more likely to be right this time round. It is, however, changing shape drastically. The television of 2020 will differ massively from that of 2010.

Reality television is not so much a genre as a coalition of prurient documentaries and immense, season-spanning game shows engineered by producers who mould the gamely gullible as Isambard Kingdom Brunel manipulated cast iron. This is television as science, every element precisely calibrated to chime with the press and social media, expanding the reach of the franchise. As fewer and fewer people watch TV as it happens, these gilded tent-poles support the old broadcast channels for entire evenings, even weekends. But reality shows yield steadily diminishing returns, despite the dexterity of producers adept at shuffling and recombining the chunky building blocks of the trade (snap the community spirit factor off that old choir-in-a-council-estate singing show, clip it to the underside of this recreation of a wartime primary school syllabus, get an endearingly bumbling former home secretary to present, job done).

For anyone attempting to divine the future of broadcasting fifteen years into the twenty-first century, the interface between broadcast television and social media provides a damp set of tea leaves indeed. 'Live tweeting' takes television right back to the Victorian stage, when heckling and hissing were the audience's right, and the poor players targets for well-aimed veteran groceries. Producers scamper to social media portals, optioning the sensation of last Tuesday afternoon for a hastily bodged two-season package, but once they get down to business it all looks rather familiar. Musical YouTube sensations collapse under the pressure of that difficult second single; comic flavours of the month generate material that would shame a Basildon stag night from 1973. After a decade of this tentative symbiosis, social media has turned the 'and finally . . .' news item into an autonomous collective, but programmes proper are another matter.

This stand-off between frantic technological innovation and retrograde content is perfectly embodied by *House of Cards*, Beau Willimon's adaptation for Netflix of Andrew Davies's adaptation for the BBC of a political thriller written by Michael Dobbs, former chief of staff to Margaret Thatcher. Davies's version was of its time and place – Francis Urquhart, the Machiavellian chief whip, indulged in bloodless postmodern confessions to camera. Ian Richardson gave Urquhart a supercilious detachment to match the chilling words, becoming the charismatic presenter of a 'how to' guide for the power-crazed sociopath.

Frank Underwood, Urquhart's American avatar, was a Democrat with the ambition, guile and dark mental hinterland of Lyndon Johnson, but the dangerous aloofness remained. The main alterations involved the transposition from Westminster to Washington, and an expansion: the BBC's compact yet commercially inadequate four-hour series was expanded to a standard thirteen.

Netflix, having gamely commissioned two series without even a pilot, respectfully left the production well alone. (Still essentially a distribution company, they lacked the staff and the kind of corporate structure where meddling executives thrive.) David Fincher was tempted out of the cinema to direct by the simple advantage television has always had – more time than a feature film, and potentially more depth. Kevin Spacey was lured from the stage to play Underwood for similar reasons. With television's dramatic renaissance now widely acknowledged, neither saw it as a step down. *House of Cards* made history in 2013 when it became the first television show to win Emmys without a single episode being broadcast in the traditional sense. 'TV will not be TV in five years' time,' predicted Willimon in 2012. 'Everyone will be streaming.'[483] By early 2015 the prophecy looked solid as Netflix, broaching fifty million subscribers worldwide, was joined by other non-broadcast studios including an offshoot of cyber-vending behemoth Amazon, which commissioned pilots on spec, released them online and made series from the winners.

A future where television drama is released like multi-part films sounds grand: with programmes not only resembling but being distributed the same way as films, TV drama's unwarranted inferiority complex could easily vanish for good. Documentary, too, has outgrown the box. Adam Curtis, auteur of a series of left-field factual programmes that used found footage to demolish received wisdom, debuted his 2015 opus *Bitter Lake* on the BBC's iPlayer online service, bypassing broadcast entirely. 'I wanted to create something you wouldn't put on television,' he explained. 'It's a deal I have with the BBC: you can experiment, but don't cost any money.' Curtis could see where the talent was heading: 'in five years' time, everyone's going to watch everything on iPlayer, so let's get in there before the bureaucrats do.'[484]

Tales of digitally-distributed creative liberation abound, but with the fertile ecosystem of broadcast television gone – the wild cross-pollination that comes from all types of programming sharing the same transmission and production space, to which many of the shows in this book owe their existence – it could be at the expense of the biggest change of character ever undergone by a mass medium.

It will all depend on the speed and extent to which the original, mixed broadcasting model disappears. The current state of play suggests a future of straight-to-box-set prestige shows plus specialist channels for news, sport and the like funded by rental and subscription fees – economically lean, but shorn of its potential for creative chaos. State broadcasters will almost certainly continue to be cut down both financially and existentially, through targeted campaigns by rival commercial interests and the indifference of a public increasingly forgetful of the vital role they continue to play. Those rival commercial interests themselves will see their advertising revenue fall as the novelty of big top reality television wears off.

Television has fallen back on its past output in a big way, but perhaps not the right way. Instead of selecting well-remembered programmes to simply update and relaunch, it might be more profitable to try to rediscover the ideas, techniques and tricks it carelessly discarded on the way from there to here. Most of all it needs to recover the adventurous experiment of the pioneering decades, when the definition of television was still only half-written. Producers should stop timidly holding each other's hands and strike out across new terrain. They need to widen their search for talent of all kinds, especially writers, instead of waiting for other media to serve up ready-made stars. It might even be beneficial for TV to completely lose its head again once in a while, even if it results in the odd baroque flop. When everything's focus-grouped nothing surprises, and television's great power is its ability to shock and delight you in your own front room.

The global cottage industry of the late twentieth century is never coming back, but there's no reason why its tradition of intelligent risk-taking can't be salvaged and refashioned into exciting new shapes. Television's past isn't just good for a smug chuckle over atavistic attitudes and shapeless trousers, it's an education in making some of the most potent popular art ever created, and never was an industry in more desperate need of some last-minute revision.

Even yesterday's garbage can teach us something. In 1955 Associated-Rediffusion transmitted *You've Never Seen This!*, a 'series of canned filmlets' shot by a jobbing Gerry Anderson, in which sideshow organiser Pete Collins paraded human oddities in front of the camera – including dwarfs, giants and a 'human gasometer' – for the gawping amusement of the capital's early TV adopters. Bernard Levin was not impressed. 'It is not at all simply putting freaks in front of a camera and hoping the audience will stand up and cheer,' he claimed, and offered a piece of TV wisdom as true today as it was sixty years ago: 'No machine, as I believe the First Law of Thermodynamics tells us, will enable us to get more out of it than we put in.'[485]

ENDNOTES

1 'Coming "Frightfulness": America to see Cocktails by Wireless', *Manchester Guardian*, 28 February 1924.

2 'New Threat to Liberty', *Manchester Guardian*, 6 February 1926.

3 'Wireless and the Future', *Manchester Guardian*, 6 January 1924.

4 *Ibid.*

5 'A Liberal's Views on Sponsored TV', *Manchester Guardian*, 10 August 1953.

6 *Report of the Broadcasting Committee of Lord Hankey*, HMSO, 1945.

7 Mike Lloyd, quoted in *TV Times*, 1970.

8 'John Osborne Talks to Kenneth Tynan', *Guardian*, 30 June 1968.

9 Hamish MacRae, 'When it Comes to TV Viewing, Staring at Words or Figures Takes a Back Seat', *Guardian*, 25 August 1982.

10 Peter Fiddick, 'Human Brain', *Guardian*, 1 June 1982.

11 Philip Hope-Wallace, *Listener*, 5 June 1952.

12 Grace Wyndham Goldie, *Listener*, 18 August 1938.

13 Grace Wyndham Goldie, *Listener*, 2 March 1939.

14 Reginald Pound, *Listener*, 5 November 1953.

15 *Daily Express*, 21 May 1954.

16 'TV Cook Attacks Sparrow-Sized Breakfasts', *Daily Express*, 11 October 1949.

17 *Daily Mirror*, 26 April 1957.

18 Philip Harben, 'All For the Love of Good Food', *TV Times*, 1964.

19 *Manchester Guardian*, 16 May 1934.

20 Harry Castleman and Walter J. Podrazik, *Watching TV: Six Decades of American Television*, Syracuse University Press, 2003.

21 Keith Scott, *The Moose That Roared*, Thomas Dunne, 2000.

22 *Ibid.*

23 Donna Rico, *Kovacsland*, Harcourt Brace Jovanovich, 1990.

24 NBC script, quoted in Donna Rico, *Kovacsland*, Harcourt Brace Jovanovich, 1990.

25 Shaun Considine, *Mad as Hell*, Random House, 1994.

26 Paddy Chayefsky, *Television Plays*, Simon and Schuster, 1956.

27 Shaun Considine, *Mad as Hell*, Random House, 1994.

28 Paddy Chayefsky, *Television Plays*, Simon and Schuster, 1956.

29 Shaun Considine, *Mad as Hell*, Random House, 1994.

30 Oliver Postgate, *Seeing Things*, Sidgwick & Jackson, 2000.

31 John Crosby, *New York Herald Tribune*, 26 September 1955.

32 David Everitt, *King of the Half Hour*, Syracuse University Press, 2001.

33 *Ibid.*

34 *Ibid.*

35 C. A. Lejeune, *Observer*, 27 November 1949.

36 Peter Black, *Daily Mail*, 25 February 1956.

37 Peter Black, *Daily Mail*, 10 May 1956.

38 Bernard Levin, 'The Goons Give a New Dimension to Television', *Observer*, 12 May 1956.

39 Peter Black, *Daily Mail*, 17 May 1956.

40 Bernard Levin, 'The Goons Give a New Dimension to Television', *Observer*, 12 May 1956.

41 Philip Purser, *Daily Mail*, 31 May 1956.

42 Bernard Levin, 'Elephants Low Down – and The Only Treatment for Them', *Observer*, 19 May 1956.

43 *Person to Person*, BBC1, 2 August 1979.

44 'Broadcasters' Fees', *Hansard*, 11 February 1942, Vol. 377, cc1508-9.

45 'BBC Panel Game for American TV', *Manchester Guardian*, 10 July 1954.

46 James Laver, *Radio Times*, 17 October 1952.

47 David Attenborough, *Life On Air*, BBC Books, 2002.

48 'BBC Plan for Television', *The Times*, 30 August 1955.

49 *Manchester Guardian*, 30 May 1956.

50 *Manchester Guardian*, 16 May 1956.

51 *Ibid.*

52 'Youth Not Afraid to Ask', *Manchester Guardian*, 27 June 1956.

53 Clive James, 'Bernard Levin: Book Two', *London Review of Books*, 1979.

54 Bernard Levin, 'Opportunity Knocks – But No-one is at Home,' *Manchester Guardian*, 21 July 1956.

55 'Man With a Lemon in His Ear', *Manchester Guardian*, 16 January 1957.

56 Peter Fiddick, 'The Shows that Died of Embarrassment', *Guardian*, 20 March 1978.

57 *TV Times*, 6 November 1976.

58 Monica Sims, *The Singing Ringing Tree: a Cold War Fairytale*, BBC Radio 4, 28 December 2002.

59 *Evening Standard*, 23 January 1992.

60 *Radio Times*, 15 February 1957.

61 *Radio Times*, 22 February 1957.

62 Alley Cat, *New Musical Express*, 12 December 1958.

63 *Daily Mirror*, 23 May 1959.

64 Garth Bardsley, *Stop the World*, Oberon Books, 2003.

65 'Gurney May Be Dead . . .', *Daily Mail*, 28 November 1960.

66 'A "Diggable" Life for Anthony Newley', *TV Times*, 3 April 1960.

67 'The Strange World of Gurney Slade', *ATV Star Book*, 1961.

68 J. Piper, letter, *TV Times*, 27 November 1960.

69 Cecil Wilson, 'When a Teen Idol Hits his First Snag', *Daily Mail*, 29 November 1960.

70 Michael Wale, 'David Bowie: Rock and Theatre', *Financial Times*, 24 January 1973.

71 W. J. Weatherby, 'Anthony Newley', *Guardian*, 12 June 1961.

72 Michael Billington, *Harold Pinter*, Faber and Faber, 1996.

73 Letter, *TV Times*, 10 April 1960.

74 Letters, *TV Times*, 14 April 1960.

75 Philip Purser, 'The Landscape of TV Drama', *Contrast*, Autumn 1961.

76 *TV Times*, 24 April 1960.

77 Irene Shubik, *Play for Today*, Davis-Poynter, 1971.

78 'Tangled Quartet of TV Play', *Guardian*, 2 November 1960.

79 Roger Wilmut, *Tony Hancock – 'Artiste'*, Eyre Methuen, 1978.

80 *Radio Times* interview, 18 May 1961.

81 *Ibid.*

82 Roger Wilmut, *Tony Hancock – 'Artiste'*, Eyre Methuen, 1978.

83 *Omnibus: From East Cheam to Earl's Court*, BBC1, tx. 26 April 1985.

84 Anthony Cookman, Jr., *Listener*, 8 September 1960.

85 *Radio Times* 28 December 1967.

86 Martin Amis, *Experience: a Memoir*, Vintage, 2001.

87 Kingsley Amis, 'The World of Jazz: Rhythm and Blues', *Observer*, 21 October 1956.

88 Kingsley Amis, Letter to Philip Larkin, 19 April 1969.

89 *Daily Mail*, 14 September 1962.

90 Peter Black, *Daily Mail*, 15 November 1962.

91 M. Stowers, letter, *TV Times*, 2 December 1962.

92 Simon Reynolds, *Rip It Up and Start Again: Postpunk 1978-1984*, Faber & Faber, 2005, p524.

93 T. S. Eliot's personal note on *Beyond the Fringe* programme, Alan Bennett's Diary, *London Review of Books*, 3 January 2013.

94 *TV Times*, 25 October 1962.

95 'Satire in the Age of Television', *The Times*, 15 December 1962.

96 Peter Green, *Listener*, 29 November 1962.

97 'Satire in the Age of Television', *The Times*, 15 December 1962.

98 Anthony Burgess, *Listener*, 3 October 1963.

99 Peter Green, *Listener*, 13 December 1962.

100 Peter Green, *Listener*, 17 January 1963.

101 Peter Green, *Listener*, 10 January 1963.

102 *Private Eye*, 29 November 1963.

103 Interview, *New Release*, BBC Two, 22 November 1966.

104 David Mercer, *Radio Times*, 23 November 1972.

105 David Mercer, 'Birth of a Playwriting Man', *Theatre Quarterly*, Vol. 3, No. 9, 1973.

106 Don Taylor, *Days of Vision*, Methuen, 1990.

107 Derek Hill, *Listener*, 25 October 1962.

108 Michael Overton, *Plays and Players*, December 1962.

109 Don Taylor, *Radio Times*, 18 October 1962.

110 Michael Billington, *Harold Pinter*, Faber & Faber, 1996.

111 Kenneth Tynan, 'Sir Ralph Does it all by Numbers', *Evening Standard*, 13 June 1952.

112 John Russell Taylor, *Listener*, 7 December 1972.

113 Clive James, 'Lobbing-match Over a Cat's Cradle', *Observer*, 3 December 1972.

114 Mervyn Johns, *Listener*, 11 December 1980.

115 Laurence Leamer, *King of the Night*, William Morrow, 1989.

116 Kenneth Tynan, *Show People*, Weidenfeld & Nicolson, 1979.

117 Gordon, Corner and Richardson, *Public Issue Television: World in Action 1963-98*, Manchester University Press, 2007.

118 *Ibid.*

119 *TV Times*, 6 February 1965.

120 Peter Hillmore, *Guardian*, 15 August 1978.

121 Robert Waterhouse, 'Obituary: T. Dan Smith', *Guardian*, 28 July 1993.

122 Peter Fiddick, 'When the Action Replay isn't the Real Thing', *Guardian*, 17 November 1977.

123 Gordon, Corner and Richardson, *Public Issue*

Television: World in Action 1963-98, Manchester University Press, 2007.

124 *Ibid.*

125 Anthony Davis, *TV Times*, 9 June 1979.

126 Peter Fiddick, *Guardian*, 2 June 1981.

127 Andrew Culf, *Guardian*, 4 October 1995.

128 *A Fresh Start for ITV Current Affairs*, Granada, 1999.

129 Catherine Stott, 'I Kid You Not', *Guardian* 10 September 1971.

130 *Ibid.*

131 Maureen O'Connor, 'Humpty Dumpty's Big Break', *Guardian*, 27 April 1970.

132 *Ibid.*

133 Harold Jackson, 'Jackanory & Co.', *Guardian* 21 December 1966.

134 Angela Neustatter, *Guardian*, 23 December 1976.

135 George Melly, 'In McLuhan's Seat,' *Observer*, 3 September 1967.

136 *Children and the Mass Media* seminar, Hellebaek, Denmark, May 1973.

137 *Crossroads Revisited*, Central Independent Television, 1985.

138 Nancy Banks-Smith, *Guardian*, 30 March 1971.

139 Peter Fiddick, 'Signposts Point One Way for Crossroads', *Guardian*, 11 September 1981.

140 Alan Rusbridger, 'Meg Fans Crossroads' Embers', *Guardian*, 5 November 1981.

141 Tom Stoppard, 'Festival of Soap Opera', *Observer*, 29 September 1974.

142 Catherine Stott, 'Doggone', *Guardian*, 2 August 1972.

143 'A Dog for All Seasons', *Observer*, 23 April 1967.

144 Mary Samuel, letter, *Guardian*, 14 November 1966.

145 *Daily Mirror*, 7 December 1972.

146 'Puppets to the Tune of £250,000', *Financial Times*, 3 March 1969.

147 '2m More Watch Television', *Financial Times*, 21 July 1961.

148 'Paret Fight Not on TV', *Guardian*, 29 March 1962.

149 G. Reichardt, letter, *Financial Times*, 24 July 1968.

150 Dave Lanning, *TV Times*, 2 January 1965.

151 *Ibid.*

152 Mick McManus, *TV Times*, 3 May 1974.

153 Kenneth Tynan, 'West End Apathy', *Observer*, 31 October 1954.

154 Michael Billington, 'The Industry of John Hopkins', *The Times*, 23 March 1968.

155 George Melly, 'The First Masterpiece', *Observer*, 30 October 1966.

156 *Ibid.*

157 Edward Mace, 'Taking Telly

Seriously', *Observer*,
30 October 1966.

158 J. C. Trewin, *Listener*,
3 November 1966.

159 *Ibid.*

160 *Ibid.*

161 Clive James, *Listener*, 9 March
1972.

162 Nancy Banks-Smith,
Guardian, 1 March 1972.

163 Linda Christmas, 'The
Mourning After', *Guardian*,
4 March 1972.

164 David Bianculli, *Dangerously
Funny*, Simon & Schuster,
2009.

165 Harlan Ellison, *Los Angeles
Free Press*, 21 February 1969.

166 David Steinberg, interview,
*The Smothers Brothers Comedy
Hour: The Best of Season 3*,
Time-Life DVD, 2008.

167 M. A. Jones, *Memorandum,
RE: Elvis Presley*, Federal
Bureau of Investigation
Dockets, 4 January 1971.

168 Lee Langley, 'Dangerous but
Decent', *Guardian*, 8 June
1965.

169 T. C. Worsley, 'The Leaden
Touch', *Financial Times*,
25 October 1967.

170 Anthony Burgess, *Listener*,
2 November 1967.

171 Lew Grade interview, *Six Into
One – the Prisoner File*,
Channel Four/Illuminations/
Yo-Yo Films, 1984.

172 Anthony Burgess, *Listener*,
2 November 1967.

173 Patrick McGoohan interview,
*Six Into One – the Prisoner
File*, 1984.

174 P. J. Nee, letter, *TV Times*,
17 February 1968.

175 Andrew Billen, 'Come in
Number 6', *Observer*, 15
December 1991.

176 Johnny Speight, *For Richer,
For Poorer*, Penguin, 1991.

177 Tom Stoppard, 'Fact, Fiction
and the Big Race', *Observer*,
11 August 1968.

178 Robert Pitman, *Daily Express*,
6 August 1968.

179 Robin Thornber, 'Blacks and
the Prostitute', *Guardian*,
12 November 1969.

180 Dennis Barker, 'Changing
Views Overtake Speight's TV
Play', *Guardian*, 18 June
1973.

181 Johnny Speight, *For Richer,
For Poorer*, Penguin, 1991.

182 Joan Ganz Cooney and Dr
Edward L. Palmer, remarks
before the Regular Education
Subcommittee of the House
Committee on Education and
Labor, 2 October 1969.

183 Melanie Perrin Berson, 'Ali
Baba! What Have You
Done?', *Childhood Education*,
March 1970.

184 Linda Christmas, 'Sesame
Street Cul de Sac', *Guardian*,
24 November 1971.

185 'For Adult Children?',
Guardian, 11 August 1967.

186 Alan Garner, *The Edge of the*

Ceiling, Granada Television, 1980.

187 Robert Nye, 'A Question of Form', *Guardian*, 19 October 1973.

188 'For Adult Children?', *Guardian*, 11 August 1967.

189 Jenny Rees, 'Tea-Time Terrors', *Daily Mail*, 1 July 1978.

190 Peter Black, *Daily Mail*, 10 September 1969.

191 Mary Malone, 'A Glorious Bag of Disasters', *Daily Express*, 11 September 1969.

192 Richard North, *Listener*, 30 September 1976.

193 *Ibid.*

194 *Ibid.*

195 John Naughton, *Listener*, 21 July 1977.

196 *Ibid.*

197 'Teatime Treats,' *Listener*, 25 February 1982.

198 Robert S. Alley and Irby B. Brown, *Love Is All Around: the Making of the Mary Tyler Moore Show*, Dell, 1989.

199 Sally Bedell, *Up the Tube*, Viking 1981.

200 Robert Kubey, *Creating Television*, Routledge, 2009.

201 Ian Hamilton, *Listener*, 26 November 1970.

202 Nancy Banks-Smith, 'Miss TV Times', *Guardian*, 24 May 1973.

203 Reginald Pound, *Listener*, 25 October 1956.

204 Hilary Corke, 'Critic on the Hearth', *Listener*, 19 November 1954.

205 *Ibid.*

206 Christopher Walker, 'Miss World Was Not Amused', *Observer*, 22 November 1970.

207 *It's Your Time*, BBC Radio 4, January 1971.

208 Veronica Horwell, James Garner obituary, *Guardian*, 20 July 2014.

209 Fyodor Dostoyevsky, *Crime and Punishment*, Russkiy Vestnik, 1866.

210 Peter Brook, *The Empty Space*, McGibbon & Kee, 1968.

211 Henry Raynor, *The Times*, 12 February 1971.

212 John Gross, *Observer*, 14 February 1971.

213 T. C. Worsley, 'Familiar Faces', *Financial Times*, 17 February 1971.

214 Peter Black, *Daily Mail*, 12 February 1971.

215 Nancy Banks-Smith, *Guardian*, 12 February 1971.

216 Steven Awalt, *Steven Spielberg and Duel: the Making of a Film Career*, Rowman & Littlefield, 2014.

217 *Ibid.*

218 *Ibid.*

219 Shaun Usher, 'Enter Tom Jones, the Actor', *Daily Mail*, 13 May 1972.

220 Philip Hope-Wallace, 'Oh Dad at the Piccadilly', *Guardian*, 7 October 1965.

221 Jörg Türschmann, *TV Global: Erfolgreiche Fernseh-Formate*, Transcript Verlag, 2011.

222 'Man Alive', *Guardian*, 20 January 1972.

223 Brian Groombridge, *Television and the People*, Penguin, 1972.

224 John Ezard, *Guardian*, 9 June 1971.

225 Susan Pleat, *Pipkins Vol 2 (1973-1981)*, Network DVD, 2005.

226 Hartley Hare in Conversation, *Pipkins Vol 2 (1973-1981)*, Network DVD, 2005.

227 *Omnibus: Whatever Happened to Clement and La Frenais?*, BBC, 1997.

228 Mark Lewisohn, *The Radio Times Guide to TV Comedy*, BBC Publications, 1998.

229 Stacy Marking, 'No Laughing Matter', *Guardian* 15 March 1975.

230 *Ibid.*

231 *Daily Express*, 8 September 1976.

232 Brian Clemens interview, Network/Jeff Smart, 2005.

233 Eric Bentley, *The Life of the Drama*, Methuen, 1966.

234 'A Day with Dr Conan Doyle', *Strand Magazine* No. 20, August 1892.

235 Alix Coleman, 'The Kids Turn On to Saturday Pop', *TV Times*, 1975.

236 'BBC Chiefs Hit Back in the Children's TV War', *Daily Mail*, 4 September 1980.

237 'TV Notes', *Manchester Guardian*, 29 August 1956.

238 *TV Times*, 10 May 1975.

239 Magnus Pyke, *The Six Lives of Pyke*, JM Dent.

240 *Ibid.*

241 Michael Parkin, 'TV Shot Falls Even Shorter', *Guardian*, 18 August 1978.

242 Bart Mills, 'Box Pop', *Listener*, 12 February 1976.

243 *TV Times*, 1976.

244 Bart Mills, 'Box Pop', *Listener*, 12 February 1976.

245 Stephen Dixon, *Guardian*, 8 July 1975.

246 *TV Times*, 22–28 March, 1975.

247 *Daily Mirror*, 24 January 1983.

248 Julian Barnes, *Observer*, 27 February 1983.

249 Julian Barnes, *Observer*, 13 March 1983.

250 'Cassius Clay Walks off Sportsview', *Guardian*, 30 May 1963.

251 Bernard J. Mullin, Stephen Hardy, William Sutton, *Sport Marketing 4th Edition*, Human Kinetics, 2013.

252 Jonathan Lemire, 'Original Cable Guy', *Columbia College Today*, January 2005.

253 Paul Kane, *Australian Poetry: Romanticism and Negativity*, Cambridge University Press, 1996.

254 'ABC Plans a Vivid Colour', *Australian Women's Weekly*, 2 April 1975.

255 Roger Wilmut, *Kindly Leave the Stage!*, Methuen, 1985.

256 James Murray, 'Your Host, Gormless Gunston!', *Daily Express*, 18 November 1976.

257 Dennis Potter, *Radio Times*, 3 April 1976.

258 Dennis Potter, *Daily Herald*, 22 May 1964.

259 Dennis Potter, *Daily Herald*, 13 February 1964.

260 Dennis Potter, *Daily Herald*, 19 February 1964.

261 Dennis Potter, *Daily Herald*, 14 February 1964.

262 Dennis Potter, *Daily Herald*, 1 May 1964.

263 Dennis Potter, *Daily Herald*, 28 February 1964.

264 Dennis Potter, *Daily Herald*, 14 May 1964.

265 Dennis Potter, *Daily Herald*, 7 May 1964.

266 Dennis Potter, *Daily Herald*, 21 February 1964.

267 Dennis Potter, *Daily Herald*, 9 March 1964.

268 Dennis Potter, *Daily Herald*, 3 March 1964.

269 Letters, *Radio Times*, 1 May 1976.

270 Richard North, 'A Tricky Business', *Listener*, 8 February 1979.

271 Alan Coren, *The Times*, 30 November 1976.

272 *Daily Express*, 2 December 1976.

273 Nancy Banks-Smith, *Guardian*, 8 December 1976.

274 Reginald Whiteley, 'Charles Laughton Practises Stutter', *Daily Mirror*, 23 February 1937.

275 'Claudius to Reign . . . at Last', *Daily Mail*, 13 September 1976.

276 'J. M. Osborn, Public Opinion', *Daily Mirror*, 13 December 1976.

277 *I, Claudius: A Televison Epic*, BBC, 2002.

278 Peter Fiddick, *Guardian*, 19 October 1976.

279 Robert Giddings and Keith Selby, *The Classic Serial on Television and Radio*, Palgrave, 2001.

280 Clive James, 'Last of the Romans', *Observer*, 12 December 1976.

281 *Ibid.*

282 Harriet van Horne, 'The TV Week', *New York Post*, 5 November 1977.

283 Arthur Unger, *Christian Science Monitor*, 4 November 1977.

284 David Nobbs, *I Didn't Get Where I Am Today*, Heinemann, 2003.

285 *Ibid.*

286 Robert Tyrrell, *The Work of the Television Journalist*, Focal Press, 1972.

287 Jeremy Bulger, 'Battle of the Bulletins', *Listener*, 1 April 1976.

288 Public Eye, *Observer*, 24 April 1977.

289 Lesley Ebbetts, 'Be Your Age, Angela!', *Daily Mirror*, 7 April 1976.

290 Peter Fiddick, 'Not Just a Pretty Picture', *Guardian*, 8 March 1976.

291 Nicholas Harman, 'Read All About It', *Listener*, 18 March 1976.

292 Peter Fiddick, 'Not Just a Pretty Picture', *Guardian*, 8 March 1976.

293 Jeremy Bulger, 'Battle of the Bulletins', *Listener*, 1 April 1976.

294 *Ibid.*

295 Nicholas Harman, 'Read All About It', *Listener*, 18 March 1976.

296 Sue Francis, 'The Man Who Made a Goldmine Out of Trash', *Observer*, 15 April 1979.

297 Martin Amis, 'Trials of Strength', *Observer*, 28 December 1980.

298 Howard Schuman, 'Video-Mad: An American Writer in British Television,' Frank Pike (ed.), *Ah! Mischief: The Writer and Television*, Faber & Faber, 1982.

299 *Daily Mail*, 21 October 1982.

300 *Observer*, 3 July 1983.

301 David Housham, *Listener*, 29 January 1987.

302 'The Name of the Game is Audience Ratings', *Guardian*, 3 September 1984.

303 James Thurber, 'Onward and Upward with the Arts: Soapland', *New Yorker*, 29 May 1948.

304 Ellen C. Seiter (ed.), *Remote Control: Television, Audiences and Cultural Power*, Routledge, 1989.

305 Robert Kubey, *Creating Television*, Routledge, 2009.

306 *Susan Harris, Television Writer, Producer*, Paley Center for Media.

307 Robert Kubey, *Creating Television*, Routledge, 2009.

308 Martin Cropper, *The Times*, 2 August 1986.

309 Susan Harris, *Toronto Globe and Mail*, 8 January 1983.

310 Tony Schwartz, 'ABC had Adviser Known as a Psychic', *New York Times*, 13 March 1981.

311 *The Phenomenon of Roots*, The Wolper Organisation, 1978.

312 Richard Schickel, 'Viewpoint', *Time*, 24 January 1977.

313 Anthony Burgess, 'Firetalk', *Homage to QWERTYUIOP*, Century Hutchinson, 1986.

314 Mark Ottaway, 'Tangled Roots', *Sunday Times*, 10 April 1977.

315 'Getting Down to the Roots', *Guardian*, 11 April 1977.

316 Malcolm R. West, 'Black Historians Reflect on Criticisms of Roots', *Jet*, 28 April 1977.

317 *Daily Express*, 6 May 1952.

318 *TV Times*, 16 January 1965.

319 Oliver Pritchett, 'Mixed Reception for Sex Film', *Guardian* 17 April 1971.

320 Jonathan Coe, *B. S. Johnson: Like a Fiery Elephant*, Picador, 2004.

321 Peter Buckman, *Listener*, 9 May 1974.

322 Henry Fenwick, *Sunday Telegraph*, 24 September 1978.

323 Susan Willis, *The BBC Shakespeare Plays: Making the Televised Canon*, University of North Carolina Press, 1991.

324 *Ibid.*

325 Peter Fiddick, 'Burke's Steerage', *Guardian*, 30 December 1975.

326 *Ibid.*

327 Peter Lennon, *Listener*, 11 April 1985.

328 Clive James, 'The Burke and Burr Laugh-In', *Observer*, 4 January 1976.

329 *Ibid.*

330 Julian Barnes, 'Lost in a Noddy Universe', *Observer*, 24 March 1985.

331 Brian Winston, *Listener*, 7 December 1978.

332 Bella Bathurst, *The Wreckers*, HarperCollins UK, 2006.

333 JICTAR ratings, w/e 23 February 1979.

334 'Blank Shot Hits a Bullseye', *Daily Mirror*, 17 March 1979.

335 John Naughton, *Listener*, 8 September 1983.

336 JICTAR ratings, w/e 21 October 1979.

337 John Naughton, 'Barks and Whistles', *Observer*, 26 October 1980.

338 Television Notes, *Guardian*, 28 January 1958.

339 David Attenborough, *Life On Air*, BBC Books, 2002.

340 Manuel Alvarado and John Stewart, *Made for Television: Euston Films Limited*, BFI Publishing, 1985.

341 Leon Griffiths, *Minder Format*, 1978.

342 *Ibid.*

343 Cedric Cullingford, *Popular Television and Schoolchildren*, Oxford Polytechnic, 1982.

344 'Catch This If You Can', *Daily Mirror*, 9 March 1977.

345 Julian Barnes, 'View from Inside the Box', *Observer*, 25 May 1986.

346 Stanley Reynolds, *Guardian*, 27 September 1981.

347 David Hare, *Ah! Mischief, the Writer and Television*, ed. Frank Pike, Faber and Faber, 1982.

348 Herbert Kretzmer, *Daily Express*, 26 June 1964.

349 Michael Billington, *Guardian*, 10 November 1977.

350 Michael Coveney, 'Triumph of Death', *Financial Times*, 11 March 1981.

351 'Sting on a Wing', *Daily Mirror*, 28 December 1981.

352 Kenneth Hughes, 'Don't Worry . . . Just Enjoy It',

Daily Mirror, 29 December 1981.

353 *Ibid.*

354 Bill Pannifer, *Listener*, 20 May 1987.

355 James Murray, *Daily Express*, 2 January 1982.

356 Nancy Banks-Smith, 'Hitch in Time', *Guardian*, 30 December 1981.

357 Todd Gitlin, *Inside Prime Time*, Pantheon, 1983.

358 *Ibid.*

359 *Ibid.*

360 Feuer, Kerr, Vahimagi, *MTM: 'Quality Television'*, BFI Publishing, 1984.

361 Phill McNeill, *NME*, 9 January 1982.

362 John Craven, *Radio Times*, 14 November 1981.

363 Ian Penman, *NME*, 16 January 1982.

364 Norma Farley, Letter, *Guardian*, 2 October 1980.

365 Clive James, 'Marginally Better', *Observer*, 7 October 1979.

366 Jonathan Meades, *Peter Knows What Dick Likes*, Paladin, 1989.

367 Peter Fiddick, *Guardian*, 3 June 1974.

368 John Carey, *Listener*, 22 February 1973.

369 Peter Fiddick, *Guardian*, 6 August 1982.

370 Sean Day-Lewis, *Talk of Drama*, University of Luton Press, 1998.

371 *Daily Mirror*, 11 October 1982.

372 Joseph Turow, *Playing Doctor: Television, Storytelling and Medical Power*, Oxford University Press, 1989.

373 Scott Haller, 'Goodnight *St Elsewhere*', *People*, 23 May 1988.

374 Robert J. Thompson, *From Hill Street Blues to ER*, Continuum, 1996.

375 Max Beerbohm, *Saturday Review*, May 1906.

376 Adrian Thrills, 'Going Up the Tube', *NME*, 13 November 82.

377 Julie Burchill, *NME*, 13 November 1982.

378 Andy Medhurst, 'Def Sentences', *Listener*, 29 September 1988.

379 Jools Holland to Sean O'Hagan, 'Tube Disaster', *NME*, 7 March 1987.

380 Sally Bedell, *Up the Tube*, Viking Press, 1981.

381 Larry Gelbart, interviewed by Dan Harrison, *Archive of American Television*, 26 May 1998.

382 'Finale of *M*A*S*H* Draws Record Number of Viewers', *New York Times*, 3 March 1983.

383 Maurice Richardson, 'Third Programme?', *Observer*, 11 March 1956.

384 Sarah Bond, 'A Fair Celebration', *Daily Express*, 26 March 1984.

385 Deborah Ryan, letter, *Radio Times*, 16 June 1984.

386 John Naughton, *Listener*, 7 June 1984.

387 Mary Whitehouse, 'Shield for Raw Minds', letter, *Guardian*, 26 September 1980.

388 Mick Jackson, 'Tearing Threads', *Listener*, 20 September 1984.

389 Jim Crace, 'Acting Armageddon', *Radio Times*, 22 September 1984.

390 Tim Heald, 'The Luck of the Insecure Actor', *Radio Times*, 20 October 1984.

391 *Heimat* press kit materials, WDR Publishing, 1 August 1984.

392 Derek Malcolm, 'Soap and Glory', *Guardian*, 6 September 1984.

393 Richard Combs, *Listener*, 17 April 1986.

394 Timothy Garton Ash, 'The Life of Death', *New York Review of Books*, 19 December 1985.

395 Edgar Reitz, *Medium*, May 1979.

396 John Naughton, 'The Big Brains', *Listener*, 24 April 1986.

397 James Murray, *Daily Express*, 15 March 1986.

398 Joy Horowitz, 'The Madcap Behind *Moonlighting*', *New York Times*, 30 March 1986.

399 *The Story of Moonlighting*, Lions Gate, 2005.

400 Carl Gustav Jung, *Psychologische Typen*, Rascher Verlag, 1921.

401 Hillary MacAskill, 'Pob Launch', *Guardian*, 4 November 1985.

402 '16-24 Year Old's Top 10 by Index', *Listener*, 13 April 1989.

403 Richard Grabel, *NME*, 5 March 1980.

404 *Ibid.*

405 Phil McNeill, *NME*, 16 January 1982.

406 'Computer Wogan for Channel Four', *Guardian*, 23 March 1985.

407 Hugh Herbert, 'The Perils of Pye in the Sky Television', *Guardian*, 22 March 1986.

408 Hugh Herbert, 'Portion of Low Fibre Serial', *Guardian*, 5 November 1985.

409 Julian Barnes, 'Leaving the Latex Cabinet', *Observer*, 19 January 1986.

410 Nick Smurthwaite, 'Out of Practice', *Guardian*, 10 August 1989.

411 Christopher Kenworthy, 'What's Up, Doc?', *Radio Times*, 17 May 1986.

412 Roger Wilmut, *Didn't You Kill My Mother-In-Law?*, Methuen, 1989.

413 Jeremy Isaacs, *Storm Over 4*, Weidenfeld & Nicolson, 1989.

414 Mary Harron, 'A Strip Off the Old Block', *Guardian*, 3 January 1983.

415 *Ibid.*

416 Edward Durham Taylor,

'Blight Strikes the Rose', *Guardian*, 23 May 1988.

417 *Listener*, 20 August 1987.

418 John McCready, *NME*, 22 August 1987.

419 *Listener*, 20 August 1987.

420 John Stratton Hawley (ed.), *The Life of Hinduism*, University of California Press, 2006.

421 Ananda Mitra, *Television and Popular Culture in India*, SAGE Publications, 1993.

422 James Saynor, *Listener*, 14 December 1989.

423 Janet Street-Porter, 'Def Sentences', *Listener* 29 September 1988.

424 Andy Medhurst, *ibid.*

425 Martin Walker, *Guardian*, 4 December 1982.

426 'More Pop and Less Champagne', *Guardian*, 23 March 1989.

427 *Newsweek*, 8 April 1990.

428 Video, *Time*, 7 April 1990.

429 Tom Shales, *Washington Post*, 12 April 1990.

430 *Today*, 20 October 1990.

431 Andrew Goodwin, *Listener*, 10 May 1990.

432 James Saynor, *Listener*, 1 November 1990.

433 *Ibid.*

434 *Late Show with David Letterman*, 27 February 1991.

435 James Saynor, 'The Condemned Sell', *Listener*, 12 April 1990.

436 Hugh Herbert, *Guardian*, 20 October 1990.

437 Jonathan Meades, *Museum Without Walls*, Unbound, 2012, p. 11.

438 Maurice Richardson, 'A Triumph of Principle', *Observer*, 13 November 1960.

439 George Melly, 'Television's First Masterpiece', *Observer*, 30 October 1966.

440 Lance Loud on *The Dick Cavett Show*, ABC, 1973.

441 Nathaniel West and Steven Daly, 'Overt, Overdone and Over Here', *Observer*, 6 June 1993.

442 Jonathan Bernstein, *Guardian*, 24 June 2000.

443 Chris Dunkley, *Financial Times*, 20 January 1983.

444 Diary, *Observer*, 9 January 1983.

445 Jeremy Isaacs, *Look Me in the Eye*, Little, Brown, 2006.

446 Emily Bell, 'Not a Word from Our Sponsors', *Observer*, 21 April 1991.

447 Andy Beckett, 'Growing Pains', *Guardian*, 23 March 2000.

448 Brian Raftery, 'The Best TV Show That's Ever Been', *GQ*, 27 September 2012.

449 Kingsley Amis, introduction, *The New Oxford Book of Light Verse*, Oxford University Press, 1987.

450 Nancy Banks-Smith, 'Railway', *Guardian*, 15 May 1980.

451 Kate Kellaway, 'Behind the

Wire, in the Money',
Guardian, 8 October 1989.

452 Michael Billington, *Guardian*,
11 June 1982.

453 'Friends Come in from the
BBC Cold', *Observer*,
24 December 1995.

454 Richard Brooks, *Observer*,
14 July 1991.

455 *Daily Mail*, 12 May 1995.

456 *Richard Herring's Leicester
Square Theatre Podcast*,
Episode 8, 20 June 2012.

457 Leo Tolstoy, *War and Peace*,
Vol. 4, Russkiy Vestnik, 1869.

458 Martha P. Nochimson, 'Did
Tony Die at the End of The
Sopranos?', *Vox.com*,
27 August 2014.

459 John Wells, 'Don't Get Your
Johns in a Tangle', *TV Times*,
3 August 1972.

460 Eric Bentley, *The Life of the
Drama*, Methuen, 1966.

461 Mick Farren, 'Set the Controls
for Total Media Overkill',
NME, 28 April 1979.

462 Gavin Edwards, 'Intergalactic
Terror', *Rolling Stone*,
27 January 2006.

463 Walden Sadiri, 'Roland D.
Moore Re-Imagines science
fiction', *Manila Reporter*, 26
June 2005.

464 *Ibid.*

465 'Our London
Correspondence', *Manchester
Guardian*, 23 April 1954.

466 Jonathan Meades, *Observer*,
6 November 1977.

467 Nancy Banks-Smith,
'Maelstrom', *Guardian*,
13 March 1985.

468 Julian Barnes, 'Misery in a
Ravaged Land', *Observer*,
2 October 1985.

469 Anthony Burgess, *One Man's
Chorus*, Carroll & Graf, 1998.

470 J. Hoberman, 'Medium Cool
Yule', *Village Voice*,
29 December 1976.

471 Mark Lewis, 'Norway's "Slow
TV" Movement: So Wrong,
it's Right', *Time*, 8 July 2013.

472 Gerard Gilbert, 'An End to
The Killing', *Independent*,
28 July 2014.

473 Lucy Siegle, Observer Ethical
Awards, *Observer*, 15 June
2014.

474 David Bianculli, '*The Killing:
Twin Peaks* meets *24* on
AMC', *NPR*, 31 March 2011.

475 Elise Hu, 'For Taiwanese
News Animators, Funny
Videos Are Serious Work',
NPR, 27 January 2014.

476 Ian Katz, Tweet (deleted),
9 September 2013.

477 Joe Hagan, 'Can HBO
Save the Sitcom?', *New York
Observer*, 18 April 2005.

478 Emily Nussbaum, 'One-Man
Show', *New York Magazine*,
15 May 2011.

479 Joe Hagan, 'Can HBO Save
the Sitcom?', *New York
Observer*, 18 April 2005.

480 Dave Itzkoff, 'Louis C. K. and
the Ballad of Jack Dall', *New*

York Times, 5 April 2013.

481 Ned Hepburn, 'Louis C. K. Fires Self from Own Show', Death & Taxes Magazine, 27 February 2012.

482 Anthony Burgess, Urgent Copy, Jonathan Cape, 1968.

483 Scott Roxborough, 'Why Netflix's House of Cards is the Future of TV', Hollywood Reporter, 7 October 2012.

484 Paul MacInnes, Guardian, 25 January 2015.

485 Bernard Levin, 'House That ITV Is Building', Manchester Guardian, 19 November 1955.

The New Idea of a University

THE NEW IDEA
OF A UNIVERSITY

Duke Maskell

&

Ian Robinson

Lost was the Nation's Sense, nor could be found,
While the long solemn Unison went round.

Published in 2001 by Haven Books
An imprint of Dexter Haven Ltd
Burbage House
83–85 Curtain Road
London
EC2A 3BS

ISBN 1-903660-00-9

A full CIP record for this book is available from the British Library

Typeset in Caslon
Printed and bound by MPG Books Ltd, Bodmin

Contents

Preface

Anecdotes and Judgement

THIRTY YEARS AGO, snootiness about American secondary and higher education was widespread in Britain. The USA was frequently used in British academic circles as a cautionary example. Mass-market culture and television-addiction were thought to have reduced the number of potential American students at the same time as their universities were being swamped by too many students. There, we thought, was the blackboard jungle: the schools had no safeguards like the nationwide standards enforced by our excellent HMIs and visible in our O- and A-level. In the richest nation on earth, students were not properly supported by the state and many had to spend time that should have been given to reading working their way through college. The USA had far too many degree-granting bodies, with the results that there were no common standards and an American first degree often meant nothing: real university work was not started until the postgraduate level, where it could be delayed even longer by things called 'taught masters degrees'. Even research work was probably vitiated by over-specialization and subordination to the department programme of some high-powered professor; but a PhD was necessary because without one work in a university was not obtainable. American academics were often without any security in their posts and were constantly pressured to publish. Our own thorns being different, these were all things we thought we had to be on guard against.

How has it happened then that we have firmly established in Britain exactly the situation we used to attribute (rightly or wrongly) to the USA? Liberal education in England may survive in the twenty-first century, not very conspicuously, at two universities. In Wales (which we know) liberal education has no prospects, and we are not optimistic about its chances in Scotland or Ireland. We think this matters.

* * *

Much of this book is what the social scientists sometimes call 'anecdotal': if we can suggest why this is a proper mode of argument part of our work is already done. History is always anecdotal. Statistics, maps, charts come in, but a genuine history is the story of the public experiences of some representative individuals. We think our anecdotes are representative. We write straight out of first-hand experience of a very few institutions and of one subject, the one that used just to be called English. Literature itself consists of anecdotes raised to the level of art. Novelists do not write about life in general, or when they do their readers lose interest, but we are certainly not going to admit that literature is not thinking; our leading example of thought about education is a novel. Literary criticism normally works by comment on well-chosen quotation which by its nature is selective. A critical book rightly practises criticism.

It is also because we are offering criticism that we sometimes write in the first person singular, sometimes in the first person plural. The book is ours, a joint effort for which we are jointly responsible, but different parts arise from different individual experiences, about which we can only speak individually.

I nevertheless had some embarrassment at making detailed public criticisms of colleagues with whom I have worked for many years in reasonable harmony and sometimes friendship, for judgements they made in the reasonable expect-ation of confidentiality. When, however, they agreed to award high classes for theorizings of a kind I demonstrate below to be intellectually disreputable, the primary university obligation to the pursuit of true judgement had to override ordinary professional reticence. I am grateful, nevertheless, for my participation in university work, and I could not have survived so long had it not been possible for most of my time.

I stuck it out, doing what I could (I say with a clear conscience), but in the end I took 'voluntary redundancy' as the alternative to 'constructive dismissal', a device that would have enabled me to argue to an 'industrial tribunal' that I had been appointed as a lecturer in English Language and Literature, but was now required to acquiesce in the awarding of degrees in nonsense.

Our next step, as people still believing in liberal education, had to be to write this book.

Our hope must be that there are enough survivors of the educated class who have kept their heads down, or joined us in redundancy, to recognize the truth of what we say. We even hope that they can be persuaded to raise their heads, and make a difference. Barefaced power is important, but the educated do have great advantages in forming opinion.

I.R.
October 2000

GENERAL NOTE

Newsletter and *Newyddion* refer to the in-house journal of the University of Wales, Swansea, formerly the University College of Swansea.

Acknowledgements

A version of Chapter 3 appeared in *The Journal of the Philosophy of Education*, July 1999; the article used in Chapter 7 appeared in *The Independent*, 25 October 1990; part of Chapter 9 appeared in *The Spectator*, 6 August 2000. The quotation on the title page is from Pope's *The Dunciad*, Book IV.

I

THE ECONOMIC CASE FOR HIGHER EDUCATION

1 Education as Investment

In general economic success tomorrow will depend on investing in our schools today.

Gordon Brown[1]

Society benefits from higher education to the extent that a graduate pays higher taxes, as well as earning a greater amount post-tax. ... Thirdly, graduates may enhance the productivity of other people in ways not captured in their own incomes (one aspect of so-called externalities).

Dearing Report[2]

LIBERAL EDUCATION is not only not mentioned in either *The Charter for Higher Education*, 1993[3] or the Dearing Report of 1997; both documents are saved from being explicitly enemies of liberal education only by their 'completeness of unconsciousness'[4] that there has ever been any such thing in the world.

Universities are supposed by the *Charter* to 'deliver' a 'service', namely higher education, to 'customers', in two divisions, firstly students, and secondly business, which 'buys' both education and the results of commissioned research. The 'delivery' to students is by way of 'teaching' or 'effective management of... learning', in 'courses', all of which have 'aims and structures' clearly described in advance, and any of which includes 'transferable skills like problem-solving and effective communication'. The standards of these providers of teaching are guaranteed by 'quality assurance systems' which will be 'regularly audited' and will enable applicants to discover 'how well different universities and colleges are performing'.

Each of the phrases within quotation marks, and all of them cumulatively, betray a conception of higher education which is not only not that of the university, but is actively hostile to the university. They will be considered in the necessary detail below.

Education can be thought of in the modernized manner of the *Charter* because of a great discovery, made (like so much of our present civilization) during the 1960s, which has been transforming the whole 'education service' ever since: education is an investment. Education is the same as training; education is useful; education will make us rich.

Historically it has been the other way round: a nation gets rich then uses some of the wealth to endow more universities not as engines of economic growth but as centres of piety, learning and thought. The 'red-brick', 'provincial' universities were founded, as outposts of the spirit of Oxford and Cambridge, *after* the brass had been made out of the muck, and not to make more brass, but because, for instance, 'The rise of modern Universities has accredited an ambassador of poetry to every important capital of industrialism in the country.'[5]

To give just one reminder of the dawn of the new idea in the 1960s, from a source that is a kind of anti-classic:

> First, a simple statement about [education]. There is too little of it. ... Let us be crude. I am not imagining the extreme slowness of our growth in national production. The figures are these: for 1938 let us take the national product as 100 for each case. In the United States it has since gone up to 225; in West Germany to 228; in the OEEC countries on average to 164, and here to under 150 ... [five more lines of figures about GDP]. There is something wrong with us. A good deal of what is wrong, though of course not all, should be put down to our educational deficiencies.[6]

So we needed more education to get our GDP increasing as fast as Germany's. A quarter of a century further on, Snow's policies had still not been fully applied and

> last year, despite the success of a great many British companies, the [average] American produced 20% more.
>
> Now one of the many reasons for that is, a lot of Americans are better trained and educated for their jobs.[7]

Nearly a decade later there was, it seemed, still a long way to go. The incoming Education Minister of the 1997 Labour Government greeted the Dearing Report with, 'Our university system is in crisis. Our competitors in North America and the Far East have more young people going into higher education.' This despite the fact that 'Thirty years ago, one in 20 young [British] people entered higher education. Today the figure is one in three.'[8] One in three is not enough for the economy in the competitive world of the third millennium. Forty years after the great discovery nobody would get a hearing in the Commons on education except by affirming it. If we are still not as rich as we could wish, the reason must still be under-investment and the remedy is, naturally, under the free market as it used to be under socialism, still more education, apparently without limit.

The three establishment parties unanimously turn the great discovery into policy. In the government reshuffle that followed his beating-off of a leadership challenge in 1995, Mr Major reaffirmed his belief in it by amalgamating two ministries and appointing a Minister of *Education and Employment*, an implied cause-and-effect that his Labour successors were happy to keep. Labour outbid Mr Major at its subsequent October conference by announcing its desire for a University *for* Industry, which on assuming power it made haste to found.

So when in 1997 Mr Blair declared his three priorities to be Education, Education, Education, he uttered the wisdom of the age, and was rewarded with the biggest Labour majority in history. 'Invest in Education', as I was exhorted by a Liberal-Democrat poster hoisted in the marginal seat of Hereford the day before the 1997 general election, at which they gained the seat.

The consensus about education only leaves the parties to disagree about which can invest most. The Liberal Democrats, still at a safe distance from office, promised in the same general election campaign to put a penny on income tax to fund more education, and were rewarded by a doubling of their Commons representation; but the parties which have had the chance to Invest in Education have a very good track record that will be hard to beat. According to the latest available figures,[9] education in the UK costs about £38bn a year. This comes nearer to health (£46bn) than to defence, which at £24bn it comfortably exceeds. Education accounts for about 12 per cent of all government spending. Higher education costs about £6bn a year.

The investment is even greater when you take into account contributions by students and parents. In those dark days of minority élites 40 years ago we didn't have to pay a penny for our university fees or living expenses. Students from families rich enough to fail means tests now pay more than £1000 a year to fees and all their living expenses during their university years, and will graduate owing, as a matter of course, £10,000–12,000 or more.

All this could not have been achieved without the wholehearted co-operation of the university bureaucracies, which enthusiastically joined the post-1960s consensus. The 'mission statement' of one university in 1996 expressed the general mood when it declared as one of its principal aims, 'to facilitate regional economic growth and national wealth creation'. Philosophic academics as humane as the authors of *The Universities We Need* are in full accord: 'One of the functions of higher education is to meet the needs of the economy (a point, we should say here and now, that we do not dissent from) ....'[10] The universities' reward has been exponential expansion and the concomitant proliferation of careers and empires.

What a good job, then, that the investment, being so huge, is copper-bottomed and guaranteed by all the parties. They are so confident that none of them even needs to write into its prospectus the kind of warning which all other issuers of prospectuses are forced by law to use: the value of your investments can go down as well as up.

By education—be it in Beauty Science, Philosophy, European Food Studies, Pig Enterprise Management, Sanskrit or Early Childhood Studies with Sports Science—shall ye grow rich. But we are all prone to fears, and some of us to nightmares. What if education were not an investment? What if Mr Blair's election-winning cry of Education, Education, Education really means Money-down-the-drain, Money-down-the-drain, Money-down-the-drain? The facts and figures we need to allay any such fear must surely be abundant and easy to find.

Let us ask about education the questions that are asked about all other investments: what risk is there? and what return on capital? What dividends may education be expected to pay and to quite whom? It is a testimony to the strength of our belief in education as investment that such simple questions are hardly ever asked. They do nevertheless appear, though not in a way that attracts any attention, in the Dearing Report.

The Report doesn't doubt, of course, that higher education is a very good thing but, in its main part, doesn't make it clear quite who it's a good thing for. The individual student, it says, can make it a good thing for himself: we must 'encourage the student to see him/herself as an investor in receipt of a service, and to seek, as an investor, value for money and a good return from the investment.' [11] But whether or not the tax-payer can do the same is something it (with good reason—as we shall see) can't make up its mind about. Although it does call the £6bn of taxes that goes into higher education every year an 'investment', with a 'backlog' which needs to be 'addressed', it also calls it 'costs', 'expenditure' and 'funding', and looks forward to the government's 'delivering' a reduction in it.

Fortunately, the main report has attached to it two sub-reports by professional economists which do make it clear what returns graduates and tax-payers are each likely to get, no. 7 by Colin Sausman and James Steel of the Department of Education and Employment, on the 'Contribution of graduates to the economy: rates of return', and no. 8 by Professor Norman Gemmell of the Department of Economics, University of Nottingham, on 'Externalities to higher education: a review of the new growth literature'. These have the authority of the best economic judgement (in the government's judgement) the government could buy. Whatever economic case these two reports make out for the expansion is officially the economic case for the expansion. And the economic case for expansion is the official case for expansion. What other case, official or unofficial, could there be?

These two reports ought to be well-known—by everyone who pays taxes and especially by those who haven't got degrees. And no-one ought to be put off by the fact that they are technical reports written by economists, for, far from it being the case that only economists can understand them, economists are the last people (the authors included) likely to understand them.

So *is* higher education a good investment? Well, for many graduates, for many years, it has been, and its value as investment is easily understood. The student's investment is what he pays in fees and what he loses in (net) earnings during the period of study; his return is the higher net wages he can expect to earn over a working lifetime as a graduate and then the higher pension.[12] This is what the economists call the 'private rate of return'. If the graduate's costs are low enough, for instance because of generous subsidy by the state from taxes, and if the higher earnings are high enough, for instance in part because some jobs are reserved for graduates, it makes sound financial sense to get a degree. According to Sausman and Steel, the average yield has probably been about 12.5 per cent a year (Table 2.2).

The graduate's investment has some peculiarities. In one way it is rather like the purchase of an annuity. The capital invested in education is not retrievable and vanishes on the retirement or death of the graduate.[13] In another way educational investment is very unlike an annuity, and indeed almost any other kind of investment, in that it only begins to pay dividends when you also in person work hard enough to earn them. It is not so with dividends on shares. The workers work and the shareholders are paid dividends. What allowance should be made for this peculiarity in thinking about the return on educational investment nobody seems to have asked. There are other questions, too, about whether the education causes the graduate's increased income or whether the relation is more problematic. And then Sausman's and Steel's calculations are based on figures ten or more years old. In the intervening years the proportion of the population doing degrees has increased very considerably and grants have been replaced by fees and loans, so the likelihood is that the economic value of a degree is less than it was. Still, let us accept the best current official figures. Given government subsidies, the return is not bad for those who get it. The question is, what about everyone else?

The financial benefit their education confers on those with degrees supplies in itself no clue as to whether or not a large higher education system sustained by subsidies makes good economic sense either for non-graduates or for the economy as a whole. Do non-graduates benefit economically from subsidizing the education of graduates? If they don't, where is the justice of the subsidy and where is the political case for continuing to expand higher education through the tax system? If they don't, can there even be any economic case for the expansion? Professor Gemmell says,

> If the gains from HE (in the form of higher wages) are all reaped by graduates themselves there is no immediate economic case for subsidising the HE system. State-funded education would merely be taxing some individuals (with resulting efficiency losses) in order to enhance the private gains to others. Indeed the

subsidy will encourage some individuals at the margin to undertake a socially wasteful investment [1.3].

So, the semi-official (and wholly unpublicized) view seems to be that if it were only the graduates themselves who benefited from their subsidized education it would be both unjust and bad for the economy. Well, is it?

On the assumptions (which we will have more to say about later) that graduates are more productive than non-graduates, that it is their education that makes them so and that their greater productivity is measured by their higher pay, Sausman and Steel are able to calculate the 'standard social rate of return' —the economic benefit society as a whole gets from graduates, which is analogous to the 'private rate' which the graduates themselves get. The method of calculation is the same as that for the 'private rate' but the measures are somewhat different, and the results are more problematic because some of the costs and benefits cannot be measured directly but have to be inferred from proxies. The costs are the full cost of tuition and the GDP lost to the economy as measured by the students' foregone earnings. The benefit is the supposed higher productivity of graduates as measured by the greater cost of employing them, i.e. higher gross wages plus employers' higher national insurance and pension contributions. The 'standard social rate of return' accounts for the first two ways in which, Dearing says (see the start to the chapter), graduates benefit society as a whole, by earning more after tax and by paying more tax.

But economists also suppose that graduates are not only more productive themselves but make the non-graduates around them, both in their own and other firms, more productive too: in the phraseology of economics, there are beneficial 'externalities' or 'spillovers' to higher education, what a non-economist might think of as 'crumbs' (as in 'from a rich man's table'). Professor Gemmell again:

> If higher education does render educated individuals more productive, the case for subsidising them rests on there being beneficial spillovers (externalities) to others. There may be spillovers both within and between firms so that gains to the economy as a whole exceed those accruing to the educated individuals [1.4].

This is Dearing's third way. These three ways in which graduates, as a class, are supposed to benefit the economy need looking at more closely. Numbered headings might be helpful.

I. WAYS ONE AND TWO—EARNING MORE AFTER TAX AND PAYING HIGHER TAXES—THE 'STANDARD SOCIAL RATE OF RETURN'

From the raw results of Sausman's and Steel's calculations, it might sound to a non-economist as if everyone without a degree does quite well from their compulsory tax-investment in the education of people with them, for they share a return on the investment, apparently, of about 8 per cent (Table 2.1), which, though less than the 12.5 per cent the graduates themselves get, still sounds pretty good. But what non-economists are unlikely to guess is that this suppositious benefit to non-graduates is deduced almost entirely from the higher pay of the graduates. Whether the higher wages and taxes do measure higher productivity is a question we shall raise below but, whether or not, it is surely startling to realize, if we are looking for the economic benefits to non-graduates, that it would make no difference at all to the so-called standard social rate of return calculation if, as Professor Gemmell suggests is possible, 'the gains from HE [were] all reaped by the graduates themselves' (1.3). Even if the non-graduates got not a sniff of any benefits going, by way of taxation or otherwise, they would still be reckoned, according to the—what shall we call them?—counter-intuitive accounting procedures used by economists, to enjoy 'a standard social rate of return' on their subsidy of other people's education of 8 per cent. It's as if someone else could enjoy benefits on your behalf.

It would equally make no difference to the social rate of return, of course, if the Chancellor (like the Sultan in the story below) took all the graduates' higher earnings in tax. It would still make no difference if he handed it over to the non-graduates straight away.

The economist father of a friend of my son's explained the point to me. 'The *distribution* of the benefits,' he said, 'has nothing to do with Economics. The "distribution problem" belongs in Ethics.' He illustrated the point. 'Suppose,' he said, 'there was a very poor country which, because oil was discovered there, became, in a very short time, immensely rich; but all the riches were taken by the Sultan for himself; and not only that, but the Sultan, being a cruel and tyrannical man, used his new riches to increase his own power and to rob and oppress his subjects, making everyone but himself even poorer and more wretched than they had been before. Now, is that country, as a whole, richer or poorer than before? In the eyes of us economists, the country *as a whole*, all its increased poverty and wretchedness notwithstanding, is immensely richer and has come to enjoy a marvellously high "social rate of return" on its oil investment. After all, we mustn't forget that the Sultan himself belongs to the country (even if it does seem rather as if it's the country that belongs to him). All we economists are interested is total GDP. Everything after that is "the distribution problem". Nothing to do with us, old chap. You want someone in Ethics, down the road.'

Even if the greater productivity of graduates were proven, the 'standard social return' would not, then, in itself justify any subsidies to higher education. It does not—as it seems to—answer the question whether it is just or not for non-graduates to subsidize the education of graduates; and it does not—as it seems to—answer the question whether or not those subsidies benefit the economy as a whole. The economic question is whether public subsidy is more efficient than a free market in which all the investment comes from the graduate. Nobody discusses this. The economic case for subsidy must then depend upon:

II. THE THIRD WAY—CRUMBS
A. The theory

First of all, are there any economic theories that posit the existence of crumbs? Well, unfortunately, Professor Gemmell says, 'Traditional human capital theory has ... little to say about externalities', 'neo-classical growth theory [provides] no scope for externalities', 'traditional growth theory [gives] no role for education to play in the creation of "human capital"' (2.1). There have been, however, some 'recent advances in growth theory'. These new theories have (italics added) '*proposed* ... mechanisms whereby education affects productivity levels' but they

> typically incorporate ... *crucial assumptions [the] empirical basis [of which] is essentially unknown.* ... Firms are *assumed* not to be able fully to appropriate the gains from the production of knowledge so that spillovers occur.[14]

There are three types of new theory: '"sources of growth" equation models', an 'augmented "Solow" or neo-classical model' and 'endogenous growth models'. Unfortunately, only the third allows for crumbs (2.7, 2.13–14). Moreover, although it does make an 'assumption' that would 'allow' them to be 'inferred' (2.14),

> identifying the existence and extent of education externalities ... is ... fraught with difficulties ... and, until the methodologies and data used in empirical studies are developed further, all results should be treated with caution [3.3].

And that's the sum total of the theoretical justification for subsidizing a large higher education system.

B. The evidence
1. Direct or experimental

There is none.

> To identify HE externalities we ... need to observe the productivity of 'uneducated' workers with and without the presence of their HE-educated colleagues. Unfortunately such controlled experiments are almost never possible [1.7].

10

2. Indirect

In the absence of direct experimental evidence, we have to rely on inferences made from large-scale statistical comparisons between economies with more and less developed higher education systems. These might be comparisons between the economies of different countries ('cross-country') or between earlier and later stages in the development of the economy of a single country ('time-series'). Both studies belong to 'macro' economics, in contrast to the study of the wages of graduates dealt with earlier, which belongs to 'micro' economics.

(a) Findings

There is some tentative evidence that [there] may [be] indicati[ons of] possible externalities.

OECD countries which expanded their higher education more rapidly ... experienced faster growth. The direction of causation however is unclear.

The only specific group of graduates which have been examined for productivity growth effects are 'scientists and engineers'.

There is some evidence that education affects physical capital investment ... which ... raises income growth rates, though the specific role of higher education is less clear.

There is increasing evidence that research and development activities may be important for productivity growth and ... spillover. ... The additional link from higher education to research and development (R&D) is yet to be confirmed but some evidence is beginning to suggest that HE may be important.

The most direct evidence on HE externalities comes from comparisons of macro and micro rate of return estimates. There are currently very few of the former, but present evidence suggests, at most, very modest upward revision of standard social rates of return to account for externalities.[15]

(b) Warnings
(i) General (italics original)

data *quality* that is very different ... and ... proxy variables (of varying degrees of accuracy) [are used] because conceptually more appropriate variables are not available [3.6].

A particular problem concerns human capital measurement. To capture the production externalities of higher education it is clearly necessary to have an accurate measure of the extent to which HE augments the quality of labour input. However, measuring the output of education in general, and HE in particular, is notoriously difficult. As a result input measures tend to be used. ... It is very difficult to know how close these proxies are to their conceptual equivalents [3.7].

11

The cross-section regression methodology is a useful means of identifying *correlations* between variables of interest (e.g. HE and income growth). ... It is less good at identifying *causation* from one variable to another, and most regression studies make prior assumptions regarding causality with, at best, limited testing of these assumptions [3.8].

(ii) About 'cross-country' comparisons

One 'strange' finding of 'the most comprehensive evidence from cross-section regressions' is that 'female education (both secondary and tertiary) appears to be inversely related to growth' (3.11); another study throws up the 'puzzle' that although 'the number of scientists and engineers per capita is found to be significant ... similarly strong effects for years of university educational attainment' are not (3.12); and then another couple of studies 'report cross-section regression results in which educational attainment variables appear to be *negatively* related to growth' (3.15). Professor Gemmell sums up this section:

> Cross-section regression studies of growth have numerous methodological drawbacks and much more testing on better quality educational data, particularly for higher education, is required before firm conclusions can be drawn on the direct effect of education on economic growth [3.19].

He does immediately go on to say, 'In my view, the weight of evidence is increasingly that education is positively associated with income growth, and higher education seems to to be the most important variable' (3.19). But, as he has already himself pointed out, this does nothing to explain income growth; there is no claim to have established a 'direction of causality'. All it tells us is that when people have a lot of money they also very often have a lot of education (the same goes for wine). It's not a weight of evidence; it's a weight of doubt.

(iii) About 'time-series' comparisons

This kind of study is 'potentially more reliable ... not least because it avoids the questionable assumptions implicit in much cross-country work'. Unfortunately, 'in practice, limited numbers of observations often restricts [*sic*] the use of time-series methods (or their sophistication) and to date there are few studies of this sort' (3.20).

C. Conclusion

> The evidence ... for educational externalities (and especially for those associated with higher education) is still very limited in scope and extent. Any conclusions ... must be regarded as tentative, not least because the quality of both the available data and testing methodologies are [*sic*] ... flawed [4.4].

So there you are. *Everything* is tentative and uncertain—data, methods, conclusions. It's all guesswork. And what do you call an investment based on guesswork? A gamble? Well, you might, except that in this case the government goes on betting, year after year, with our money, without having any idea whether we're winning or losing. And calls it an investment. What independent financial advisor would recommend that the Chancellor put his own money where he puts our taxes? An independent financial advisor? A bookie would have scruples.

If no 'externalities' can be reliably identified, then, in Professor Gemmell's words, 'there is no immediate economic case for subsidising the HE system. State-funded education [is] merely taxing some individuals (with resulting efficiency losses) in order to enhance the private gains to others … a socially wasteful investment'—that is, no investment at all. The entire state-subsidized expansion of higher education, maintained by so many governments over so many years, with no semblance of justification offered for it that isn't economic, has been, it seems, a tremendous error, economically. And if the subsidies were withdrawn, the grotesquely bloated system they have created would shrink back to something that made economic (and educational) sense. The so-called customers would be found simply not to exist and the so-called need for this so-called education would vanish with them. In its present shape and size the whole thing is simply a creation of wastefulness. And that's according to what is in effect the government's own economic advisor, advising a government which, like all its recent predecessors, can't imagine any case for higher education that isn't economic. An investment? It's not even a bet. It's more like throwing money over your shoulder and wishing.

*   *   *

But it isn't just the fact that it has been subsidized through the taxes that makes the fifteen-or-more-fold expansion of the higher education system an error. It would still be an error, we believe, however it were funded. The case for it depends on two assumptions (made as a matter of routine by Sausman and Steel but questioned by Gemmell) which any ordinarily prudent investor would want to query: that people with degrees are more productive than those without and that it is their education that makes them so. Research is supposed to be one of the things that make universities an investment; research into the productivity conferred by the degrees they award is hardly ever undertaken and has never yet produced significant results.

How would you measure how much more productive a graduate was than a non-graduate? As Professor Gemmell says (and as one of us wrote before either had read Professor Gemmell), you'd have to observe the two performing similar tasks and see whether the graduates were more efficient. But, as we saw Professor Gemmell saying, 'Measuring the output of education in general, and HE in particular, is notoriously difficult' (3.7) and 'controlled experiments are almost never possible' (1.7). So the way economists do it is simply by taking the greater income of graduates as a measure of greater productivity: they measure, that is, how much more someone contributes to the economy by measuring how much more he takes from it (his net wages plus whatever else he costs his employer, taxes and national insurance and pension contributions) and treat the one as a proxy for the other. Now this, however scientific a practice, does make for some odd effects of language:

> the economic benefits from graduates ... their higher earnings [Report 7.1]

> the contribution graduates make to the economy ... the high salaries ... they receive [1.1]

These are the wonderland phrases Dearing is echoing when he says, 'Society benefits from higher education to the extent that a graduate [earns] a greater amount post-tax.' If this is how graduates benefit society, it must be more blessed to give than to receive in ways Jesus never dreamt of. Who in his right mind would agree to subsidize someone else's education for the somebody-else to get more pay than himself? What ordinary employer thinks a wage increase in itself evidence of an increase in productivity? It's logic through the looking-glass.

Pay may make, as Sausman and Steel call it, 'a straightforward measure' of productivity, but only in the sense that it is straightforward to make; it's hardly straightforward to think. Do we get what we pay for? Well, perhaps we do, but hardly as surely as we pay for what we get. All an employer can know is whether he is paying the going rate or not; the connection between that rate and the relative productivity of employees of different levels of education is as opaque to him as to any economist, and for the same reason: the experiments that would make it demonstrable can't be performed. The graduate wants more money for his higher qualification and to make up for his lost earnings; the employer is willing to give it him; and they settle, on average, for a certain sum. And that, in the absence of direct comparative evidence, is all that is known; and to know anything more is made all the harder by the fact that a great many jobs that graduates do are not open to non-graduates, so there is no direct competition. Nobody knows what part mere custom plays in setting such differentials.

But even if graduates could be shown to be more productive, it still wouldn't follow that it was their education that made them so. As Professor Gemmell says,

> There is a very credible economics literature which suggests that education (including higher education) may be no more than a screening device which allows employers to identify the more able potential employees from the rest. Thus graduates' wages are higher because they are inherently more productive, for example because they work harder or have more innate ability, but not because they are better educated. If this is the case then the current system of HE may simply be providing employers with a privately cheap, but socially expensive (i.e. wasteful), screening system. If firms know that the most productive individuals will choose

to go to (state subsidised) university, then they will select graduates in preference to non-graduates even if education has no effect on their productivity. Likewise, 18 year olds go to university to signal to employers that they are productive. There may still be a case for governments subsidising this 'screening system' if alternative screening devices are less efficient and if there are adverse social consequences from the mismatches which might result, such as unemployment or high labour turnover. However it is quite possible, if employers and/or employees had to fully fund a screening system privately, that they would be able to devise something more efficient than the current HE system [1.2].

Sausman and Steel acknowledge that it may be difficult to be sure how far it is a graduate's education rather than something else about him that makes him more productive (if he is) but they make their uncertainty a pretext for more calculations which any competent auditor would suspect. They rephrase Professor Gemmell's question, 'How can we know whether it is education that does the trick or not?' as 'How much of the trick does education do?' or, in their own terms, what is the correct value for the *alpha* factor? [16]

So what *is* the *alpha* factor?

Sausman and Steel first of all suppose that the higher productivity of a graduate can be portioned up like the higher wages which are supposed to measure it and each portion attributed to a separate, distinguishable cause: so much to family background, so much to innate ability, so much to education etc. These causes are named 'factors'; 'research' assigns each a numerical value; and education is singled out from them all to be distinguished as *alpha*. Sausman and Steel then talk about 'the *alpha* factor' in the tones of scientists investigating something as ordinarily and verifiably real as the stone Dr Johnson kicked in attempted refutation of Berkeley: 'Given the empirical uncertainties over the value of alpha, we present results for alpha values of 0.6 and 0.8', i.e. we are going to attribute between 60 per cent and 80 per cent of the higher productivity of graduates, which we have inferred from their higher wages, to their education—renamed 'level of human capital' (Annexe A, 11). But this is just verbal magic, mumbo-jumbo, superstition in a modern form. Why do they make this attribution? Where do they get their 0.6 and 0.8 from? These figures are 'suggested by the available research evidence' (Annexe A, 11)—which is no doubt as much to be relied on for any practical purpose as the other 'evidence' presented in these two reports. But wouldn't someone intending to risk his money on a new company with their 60–80 per cent in mind ('We must have graduates because of their much greater productivity') want to know how 'evidence' so scanty and imprecise could support figures so exact, and so large?

So who is right, those who like Sausman and Steel think that the education that graduates receive makes them more productive—'creates human capital'—or those others who think it is merely a 'screening device'? To give the crucial words of Professor Gemmell a little more fully:

> So, is it possible to discriminate between 'human capital' and 'screening' arguments in any systematic way ... ? Ideally one would hope to observe workers with different levels of education (but otherwise identical) undertaking similar tasks and see whether the more educated performed these tasks more efficiently. ... Unfortunately such controlled experiments are almost never possible [1.7].

And that is Professor Gemmell's last word on the subject. How can we know whether education makes people more productive or not? We can't. We just don't know in any such way as economists understand knowledge. But we invest billions every year on the assumption that we can and do know, all the same. On that assumption we have already increased the numbers in higher education from 1 in 33 to more than 1 in 3. On that assumption Gordon Brown proposed increasing them to 1 in 2 (*Today* programme, 16 June 2000).

If this is investment, put your money under the mattress.

*   *   *

For the layman—the taxpayer in the enforced role of venture capitalist—to be able to judge for himself whether the Dearing audit is favourable or not, he needs to grasp certain oddities, as they may seem, about the science of economics, and especially about the character of the precise-looking numerical methods it uses. Like other sciences, economics employs a vocabulary and methods which, to understand, you have to be expert in; unlike those of the physical sciences they ride on the back of assumptions that anyone might legitimately have an opinion about but which, as it happens, economists themselves, once they have made them, typically have no interest in whatsoever. When an economist assumes that the higher pay of graduates is proportionate to their higher productivity, he doesn't necessarily *think*, in the ordinary sense, that this is so. Making the assumption is just a technical matter for him, necessary to get him to the point at which he can begin to do what he really wants to do, his calculations. Not being able to measure relative productivity directly, he wouldn't be able to measure it at all if he didn't make some such assumption; therefore he makes it; and there's an end of his interest in the matter. Other economists do likewise; and there, if he needs it, is his justification. As Sausman and Steel say of their rate-of-return calculations, they are 'a long-standing economic technique'.

So it is quite possible for methods which are (at least to a layman's eye) expert and mathematically very sophisticated to depend on assumptions and reasonings which are not only unspecialized but imprecise or even crude. The mathematics can be (it is difficult for an outsider not to conclude) a disguise for guesswork or bluff.[17]

Parts of Gemmell's report a layman might think were mathematics ('Now, this looks something *like* an audit'):

Sources-of-growth equations are typically based on an aggregate Cobb-Douglas production function such as equation (E1) above which, when differentiated gives a relationship between the growth of output and the growth of factor inputs. For example, adapting (E1) to include human capital, H, gives:

Y=AKalbHg   a + b + g = 1   (E3)

(E3) can be written as:

y = a + ak + bl + gh   (E3.1)

where, again, lower case letters represent growth rates for their upper case equivalents and a is the growth of total factor productivity (TFP) [2.11].

But the certainty of the part (we presume it is that) is not shared by the whole. Above, below, all around the mathematical certainties are all sorts of uncertainties. The mathematical part—however cogent in itself—is really just uncertainty mathematized.

And on the other side of this seeming precision is real crudeness. The two words that dominate the conception of education in these two sub-reports (as in the main report itself) are, predictably, 'skills' and 'knowledge'. For Sausman and Steel the end result of education is 'appropriate labour skills', of two kinds (the 'specific skills gained from studying for particular degrees' and the 'superior analytical and communication skills' gained from any and all degrees) and many levels. Degree level skills are, of course, of a 'higher level' than A-level level skills, and, of course, correspondingly more valuable.

If 'skills' sums up your idea of education, as it does for Sausman and Steel, you are hardly free to think that higher qualifications mightn't mean 'more productive'. But you won't be any better off if your vocabulary includes, as Gemmell's does, 'knowledge', not if you think of knowledge as a sort of *stuff* that comes in quantities and may be spoken of in phrases like 'knowledge production' and 'the knowledge accumulation process'. If that's your idea of knowledge, then again, how can you think anything but such things as 'an education sector produces human capital for use in the production sector' (like coal mined for steel manufacture) and 'education creates human capital, which directly affects knowledge accumulation and therefore productivity growth' (which is like nothing recognizable at all)?

And if that's the mental world you live in you'd be better off *not* trying to say what education might mean if not jobs and wages. Otherwise you're likely to find yourself, like Sausman and Steel, defying the philistines by asserting that making money is not the only benefit to be had from education: there are 'consumer benefits' too, which may well include not just better health, 'and hence [lower] public health care costs', but also, even though they are very 'very difficult to quantify', the 'objectives that Robbins identified—promoting the general powers of the mind and the advancement of learning'.

Not to mention the spread of cant and accumulation of humbug.

Even if it were established that we do sensibly to invest in scientists and engineers, there are still to be considered the vast majority of graduates, graduates in the arts and in all those new dubiously vocational subjects like Leisure and Tourism. Isn't it *prima facie* likely that, if the philosophy or history or literary graduate has done some genuine work in his subject and acquired a taste for a kind of thought that is disinterested and contemplative, he will be less suited to the instrumental mental activity required in business? The folk-image of the absent-minded professor may after all, like other folk-images, have a core of truth. (We have met some professors like that.) And will it be any better if the graduate has done no genuine work? Isn't the likelihood that someone who has spent three years being trained to make a fake academic study of something practical and down-to-earth will be by so much made less fit for honest and productive work of any kind? It is often supposed that 'third world' economies are held back by large bureaucracies composed of graduates doing little productive work. How do we know that our increasing 'cohorts' of graduates, with their high salary expectations, are different? Education externalities—Gemmell might reflect—can come in the form of costs as well as benefits.

Take the case of economists themselves (perhaps social scientists generally) who have picked up from beneath the tables of the physical scientists any amount of crumbs and, as a result, are better fed than the physical scientists themselves (Report 7, 2.29). How sure can we be that what are, from their private point of view, undeniably crumbs, aren't, from the social, something more like grit? It may be that economists cost their employers an awful lot of money, but surely we can still ask, in our layman's commonsensical sort of a way, whether they are worth it? On the evidence of these two reports, economists themselves over-rate the importance of the mere calculating faculty. Perhaps their employers do too. On this one vexed question of whether or not there is an economic case for an immense, immensely-subsidized Higher Education System—and remembering that there is upwards of £6bn a year of public money risked—isn't it obvious that the way that economists combine rigour of calculation with looseness of thought is absolutely fatal to their pretensions to being socially useful? Perhaps, in calculating the relative worth of different classes of worker, we should make some allowance for the prejudices of a culture that, although faithless in other ways, has a naïve, if not downright superstitious faith in *technik* and numerical method. What value shall we assign to superstition as a factor—the *beta* factor?—to account for the high salaries economists get?

We propose an experiment, though not a numerically rigorous one. Compare the present remarks about the relative productivity of graduates and non-graduates with those of Drs Sausman and Steel and of Professor Gemmell. Which, the highly paid economists, or the two unwaged ex-lecturers in English literature, are actually more productive on what we believe we have demonstrated to be the vexed question of the value of education as an investment?

Financial history is spangled with curious manias and illusions which otherwise hard-headed people have mistaken for investments (black tulips, the South Seas). The 'investment' in graduates may turn out to be one of them.

Investment remains, until the bubble bursts, the magic word that freezes any possibility of protest. It's an investment that makes internet stocks look like gilt-edged securities; it's an investment on which neither of these literary redundants would dream of throwing away their severance payments. The difference from those advertisements (now banned?) for sure-fire can't-fail gambling systems is that the government itself runs this one and it is compulsory for all taxpayers to participate. This is an 'investment' the evasion of which is a crime.

But bubbles do burst—sometimes because they're pricked.

II

THE OLD IDEA
OF A UNIVERSITY

2　Newman

Thought kindling itself at the fire of living Thought

Thomas Carlyle

ABOUT THE MODERN CONSENSUS-VIEW of the good which is the *telos* of education, making money individually and nationally, we shall say little directly. The just and wise societies are not always the richest. The life of classical Athens would seem to us Spartan, and it took the eye of prophecy to see Old-Testament Israel as a land flowing with milk and honey. Even the best-educated modern Western nation, France, has had its periods of comparative poverty. Conversely the richest societies are not always the best educated. (Look across the Atlantic.) The assent to a world in which the only value is indefinite economic 'growth' is just too degraded for serious discussion. D. H. Lawrence imagined the consequent educational arrangements as what would now be called a 'worst case scenario': 'Teach the three Rs, and then proceed with a certain amount of technical instruction, in preparation for the coming job.' This would replace the ideals like 'to strive to produce … the perfect citizen' and 'disinterested nobility of heart to enable each one to vote properly at a general election' which in Lawrence's time had already become dead ideals.[1] Now that you can't publish anything whatever without a motto or cry, the DfEE[2] puts on the cover of the pamphlet *Financial Support for Students in 1999/2000* the motto 'It pays to aim higher.' That vision is just too low to be criticized.

What is more, this is not a harmless mistake which has benefited the universities by allowing easier access and consequent expansion. We shall show that in practice the changed notion of what universities are expected to do has damaged them, perhaps beyond repair. Before that, we would like to offer some beliefs about what liberal education really is, and what it really is not.

To join the modern consensus we have first to deny a number of traditional distinctions. To begin with we have to believe that education is the same as training; without this belief the doctrine that universities create wealth would be too implausible. Education is not the same as training nor as being instructed. Until recently these were truths generally known.

Philosophy came into being when Socrates went around Athens as one conscious of knowing little, looking for someone who knew more. The men Socrates talked to, those who had a *techne*, that is had been trained in a useful skill, turned out not to know more than he did because they knew *only* their skills. The distinction between liberal education and useful knowledge persisted strongly when the universities developed in the twelfth and thirteenth Christian centuries. The arts faculties' trivium and quadrivium, the three philosophies, the summit in theology, are all pure thought, of no earthly use. Theology of the kind discussed in the medieval universities was quite unnecessary, for instance, to the parish priests. Training was the province of the guilds. Between Chaucer's Clerk (modern English Philosopher) and his guildsmen there is a great gulf.

If education is not after all the same as training for wealth-creation, what is it? and is education a good? for the individual, for the community? and if so in what sort of ways? There has been classical thinking about education, some of it in English. The proper academic instinct is to begin by looking at what has been said, and the obvious place to start is *The Idea of a University*.

We shall have some adverse comments to make on the great J. H. Newman, so it will be good to recognize in the first place that he did some of the essential thinking, for our language and culture, about university education. Newman, moreover, asks precisely our politicians' question, if they were intelligent enough to ask it: 'What is there to show for the expense of a University; what is the real worth in the market of the article called "a Liberal Education"?':[3]

> Now this is what some great men are very slow to allow; they insist that Education should be confined to some particular and narrow end, and should issue in some definite work, which can be weighed and measured. They argue as if every thing, as well as every person, had its price; and that where there has been a great outlay, they have a right to expect a return in kind. This they call making Education and Instruction 'useful', and 'Utility' becomes their watchword. With a fundamental principle of this nature, they very naturally go on to ask, what there is to show for the expense of a University; what is the real worth in the market, of the article called 'a Liberal Education', on the supposition that it does not teach us definitely how to advance our manufactures, or to improve our lands, or to better our civil economy; or again, if it does not at once make this man a lawyer, that an engineer, and that a surgeon; or at least if it does not lead to discoveries in chemistry, astronomy, geology, magnetism, and science of every kind.[4]

The Idea of a University is Newman's attempt to say what the real worth—even in the market—of 'a Liberal Education' is. The attempt was, in practical terms, for a hundred years and more, triumphantly successful. Newman's idea of the university as providing a liberal education, even to those training for the professions—lawyers, engineers, surgeons and scientists of every kind—and thus making them even better lawyers, engineers, surgeons and scientists of every kind—became *the* idea of the university; and even today, though it may be lost sight of, it hasn't been replaced. The university has been remade not in defiance of Newman but in indifference to him. But he says things that, if anybody paid any attention to them, could not fail to kill instantly our new orthodoxy about the universities making us rich.

He describes the difference made by education:

> The Enlargement consists, not merely in the passive reception into the mind of a number of ideas hitherto unknown to it, but in the mind's energetic and simultaneous action upon and towards and among those new ideas, which are rushing in upon it. It is the action of a formative power, reducing to order and meaning the matter of our acquirements; it is a making the objects of our knowledge subjectively our own, or, to use a familiar word, it is a digestion of what we receive, into the substance of our previous state of thought; and without this no enlargement is said to follow. There is no enlargement, unless there be a comparison of ideas one with another, as they come before the mind, and a systematizing of them. We feel our minds to be growing and expanding *then*, when we not only learn, but refer what we learn to what we know already. [5]

Education is of the whole person, not the acquisition of skills:

> Such knowledge is not a mere extrinsic or accidental advantage, which is ours today and another's tomorrow, which may be got up from a book, and easily forgotten again, which we can command or communicate at our pleasure, which we can borrow for the occasion, carry about in our hand, and take into the market; it is an acquired illumination, it is a habit, a personal possession, and an inward endowment. And this is the reason, why it is more correct, as well as more usual, to speak of a University as a place of education, than of instruction, though, when knowledge is concerned, instruction would at first sight have seemed the more appropriate word. We are instructed, for instance, in manual exercises, in the fine and useful arts, in trades, and in ways of business; for these are methods, which have little or no effect upon the mind itself, are contained in rules committed to memory, tradition, use, and bear upon an end external to themselves. But Education is a higher word; it implies an action upon our mental nature, and the formation of a character; it is something individual and permanent, and is commonly spoken of in connexion with religion and virtue. When then we speak of the communication of Knowledge as being Education, we thereby really imply that that Knowledge is a state or condition of mind; and since cultivation of mind is surely worth seeking for its own sake, we are thus brought once more to the conclusion, which the word 'Liberal' and the word 'Philosophy' have already suggested, that there is a Knowledge, which is desirable, though nothing come of it, as being of itself a treasure, and a sufficient remuneration of years of labour .... [6]

Even though Newman does something here which is shockingly contrary to the habits of all recent, respectable thinkers on the subject, that is, to distinguish between education and instruction as if they were opposites, it is still hard to imagine that anyone who understands this passage will dispute it. Here, moreover, Newman was uttering the generally accepted understanding of his time. With Coleridge's view, 'Our gentry must concern themselves in the *education* as well as the *instruction* of their natural clients and dependents ... .'[7] Matthew Arnold would not have disagreed. We are not so far gone that what Newman says isn't recognizable as self-evidently true. People are instructed in such things as manual exercises, the fine and useful arts, trades and ways of business, methods for which there are rules; yes. The knowledge involved has little or no effect upon the mind itself and is not valued for its own sake; yes. It is an instrument or power bearing upon an end external to itself and aiming at a result beyond itself; yes.

Newman—rightly—doesn't attempt similarly to say that knowledge of some subjects will guarantee education. Anything, he argues, may be studied as a means to an end—not excluding virtue and religion themselves.[8] Instead Newman emphasizes the character of education as an end in itself: it 'dispenses with the necessity of ... looking abroad for any end to rest upon external to itself', it is 'excellent in itself', 'a good ... an end', 'desirable, though nothing come of it, as being of itself a treasure, and a sufficient remuneration of years of labour'.

The idea of education as an end in itself is bound up with another: that what educates us forms us: 'not a mere extrinsic or accidental advantage ... it is an acquired illumination, it is a habit, a personal possession, and an inward endowment;' it has an 'effect upon the mind itself ... it implies an action upon our mental nature, and the formation of a character; it is something individual and permanent, and is commonly spoken of in connection with religion and virtue.' And here again Newman was speaking for his age. In Mrs Oliphant's novel *The Curate in Charge*, the Newman position comes out as ordinary educated good sense. Mr Mildmay is on the point of declaring his love (as far as anyone ever does that in Mrs Oliphant) but is in no danger of losing his idea of education:

> 'Yes, I should like to be able to pass an examination and get a—what is it called?—*diplôme*, the French say. With that one's chances are so much better,' said Cicely, with a sigh, 'but I have so little time.'
>
> How the young man's heart swelled in the darkness!
>
> 'Self-culture,' he said, with a half laugh, 'must be disinterested, I fear, to be worthy of the name. It must have no motive but the advancement of your mind for your own sake. It is the culture of you for you, not what you may do with it. It is a state, not a profession.'[9]

Newman is absolutely right, isn't he, in connecting what we value as ends with what we essentially are? Our 'ends' are no mere extrinsic or accidental 'objectives' or 'goals', which we choose—the 'we' that does the choosing being thought of as separate from and set over against what it chooses, like someone choosing from a menu. The idea 'a person' and the idea 'ends' go together. A person values things not just for their usefulness, as instruments and means only, but as goods and ends in themselves. Take away 'ends' and the person collapses, becomes a mere sum of mechanical and random 'behaviours', not a person, but matter in motion.

He is also right, isn't he, to talk here as if it is persons not just minds that are educated? Throughout this passage his whole way of talking excludes the possibility that what he means by 'educated' is 'having a trained mind'—as if education developed our mental capacities much as lifting weights our bodily. He doesn't use the words 'intellect' or 'mind' or their cognates without significant qualification.

He describes both education and what he contrasts it with, instruction, as involving (as how could it not?) activity of mind. Plainly no-one can carry out instructions, or even listen to them, without using his mind—for 'manual exercises' as much as 'fine and useful art, trades and ways of business'. Remembering and applying 'rules' and 'methods' obviously involves the mind. With what do we remember if not our minds? Yet Newman treats all these kinds of mental activity as somehow failing fully to engage 'the mind itself'. When engaged in them, the mind falls short of being fully itself. And that's because (isn't this just what distinguishes between education, the 'higher' thing, and anything lower?) these are activities of the mind which have 'little or no effect upon the mind itself', have no 'action upon our mental nature', do nothing towards 'the formation of a character'; they are mental activities, what elsewhere he calls 'exercises of mind', which 'bear upon an end external to themselves'.

In such activities the mind is used, but *only* used—as an instrument, for ends: of comfort, convenience or necessity, supplied to it from elsewhere, ends that aren't its own. What could be more sharply antithetical to that other 'use' of mind in which it is employed better to discern what its own true ends are, what it is and might be? A kind of use in which the mind discovers its own nature and makes and remakes itself continually anew—Arnold's 'free play of mind'?[10] The mind in this latter sense is what else but the person? An educated mind in this sense is not a trained mind but an educated human being.

And that sense is reinforced when Newman describes the value of a liberal education to society: 'If then a practical end must be assigned to a University course, I say it is that of training good members of society. Its art is the art of social life, and its end is fitness for the world.'[11] We shall come back next chapter to the great question here raised, how education may be for the general good, and to this answer of Newman's. Obviously, educated minds in that sense—of anything like good members of society—are nothing like well-trained or healthy bodies.

It is quite possible to attempt to educate people on the assumption that they are their minds. James Mill tried with his own son, though in fact J. S. Mill's education was, to the extent that they can be separated, even more through the influence of his father than his father's programme. Which, the influence or the programme, was more disastrous may be debated. What a ghastly and horrible childhood he had—not an education but, as Dickens shows in his parody of it in *Hard Times*, a kind of crippling, in particular of the emotions, a trauma from which Mill's *Autobiography* shows him to have made only a very incomplete recovery. An 'experiment' is what J. S. Mill himself calls it, but without noticing what he has said, suggesting rather that the 'experiment' wasn't a success but might have been.

But, although such passages make *The Idea* the obvious place to go for an account and a justification of the university as a university and not a training school for dentists,[12] they don't make it the best or, perhaps, even a good place to go, for it isn't a coherent piece of work. There's a lot that's slack in it, and it suffers badly from equivocation. The trouble is that Newman wants to defend liberal education not just to his own satisfaction and on his own terms but also to the satisfaction and on the terms of his opponents, who want education to be above all else practically useful. He wants to convince them without convincing them they are wrong, to win them over to his side without making it necessary for them to give up their own. He finds it too easy to meet the practical-minded on their own ground, and he does not resist sufficiently the tendency of a wonderfully fluent mind to let eloquence substitute for thought. At this decisive moment, of sticking to the essential difference between education and the learning of useful skills, he should have told himself some such thing as Wittgenstein said to Rhees, 'Go the bloody hard way.'[13] But he didn't.

And we are now paying the price. He convinced Victorian England that education as an end in itself was the best means to the end of Utility, and thus paved the way for the defeat of his own party and the success of his opponents', whose descendants, a hundred and more years later, have noticed that they can have their end without his means.

The fault lies not in the bare fact of his claiming that a liberal education is useful as well as good but in his doing so by a sophistry. He is right not to be content to treat 'the good' and 'the useful' as mere alternatives or opposites, not to want to suggest that a liberal education, in being a good and an end in itself, is useless. Disinterestedness is the greatest of the intellectual virtues, but being disinterested doesn't mean 'serving none of my interests'; I have forms of interest which can only be served by my being disinterested. Newman couldn't have made a convincing *Apologia pro Vita Sua*, a project in which in an obvious way he had an interest, without being disinterested. Disinterestedness was in his interest.

It was the purity of his interest in the truth that enabled him to squash Kingsley as flat as he did (or rather: his disinterestedness did the squashing for him).

But Newman fudges this issue. He wants to put Oxford as well as Rome behind the seminarians, to make them more than bog priests, and perhaps also to make Victorian England educate its governing classes, in a university devoted to the pursuit of the good. And how better to do the latter—given the state of mind of the Victorian England which developed the steam age out of the eighteenth-century enlightenment and then gave birth to ours—than by persuading it that pursuing the good is the best way to catch the useful? Newman tries to justify, to a professional and practically-minded people, an education without any obvious professional or practical purpose, on the grounds that it's the best education, from a professional and practical point of view. The 'best aid to professional and scientific study' is not professional and scientific study itself but 'general culture of mind'. The best preparation for 'the successful prosecution of those merely personal objects'[14] means refusing the first place to them, postponing them, seeming to disparage them.

What is the very best means of gaining your professional ends? Having an education which is an end in itself. It doesn't sound honest, and it isn't. Newman was the last person (*pace* Kingsley) who would ever willingly have lied, but he has succeeded here in pulling the wool over his own eyes.

For a lot of *The Idea* Newman seems to be distinguishing between two kinds of education, 'Useful' and 'Liberal', only in order to deny that one of them is an education at all:

> In the one case it is called Useful Knowledge, in the other Liberal. The same person may cultivate it in both ways as once; but this again is a matter foreign to my subject; here I do but say that there are two ways of using Knowledge, and in matter of fact those who use it in one way are not likely to use it in the other, or at least in a very limited measure. You see, then, Gentlemen, here are two methods of Education; the one aspires to be philosophical, the other to be mechanical; the one rises towards ideas, the other is exhausted upon what is particular and external. Let me not be thought to deny the necessity, or to decry the benefit, of such attention to what is particular and practical, the useful or mechanical arts; life could not go on without them; we owe our daily welfare to them; their exercise is the duty of the many, and we owe to the many a debt of gratitude for fulfilling it. I only say that Knowledge, in proportion as it tends more and more to be particular, ceases to be Knowledge ....[15]

And—the implication seems unavoidable—Education, in proportion as it becomes particular, ceases to be Education.

But isn't there something of a fudge there? There are two uses of knowledge but one consists of not putting it to use and the other deprives it of its character as knowledge? You can use the hammer to knock a nail in or you can use it to ... heft about? But what a funny 'use' that is. Surely 'using knowledge' is a phrase that can properly be used of only one of Newman's two 'ways of using' it? The person who uses knowledge as an instrument for some further, external end of necessity or benefit uses it, but the person who 'uses' knowledge as a good and an end in itself doesn't use it at all—any more than he uses any other aspect of his own 'mental nature' or 'character', any more than he uses his 'religion' or his 'virtue'.

And the fudge isn't just a lapse, of the moment. It's part of a sophistry that undermines Newman's whole argument.

> Gentlemen, I will show you how a liberal education is truly and fully a useful, though it be not a professional education. 'Good' indeed means one thing, and 'useful' means another; but I lay it down as a principle, which will save us a great deal of anxiety, that, though the useful is not always good, the good is always useful. Good is not only good, but reproductive of good; this is one of its attributes; nothing is excellent, beautiful, perfect, desirable for its own sake, but it overflows, and spreads the likeness of itself all round itself. Good is prolific; it is not only good to the eye, but to the taste; it not only attracts us, but it communicates itself; it excites first our admiration and love, then our desire and our gratitude, and that, in proportion to its intenseness and fullness in particular instances. A great good will impart great good. If then the intellect is so excellent a portion of us, and its cultivation so excellent, it is not only beautiful, perfect, admirable, and noble in itself, but in a true and high sense it must be useful to the possessor and to all around him; not useful in any low, mechanical, mercantile sense, but as diffusing good, or as a blessing, or a gift, or power, or a treasure, first to the owner, then through him to the world. I say then, if a liberal education be good, it must necessarily be useful too.[16]

Well … *okay* … but rather obviously *not* the kind of usefulness 'some great men' are slow to allow the 'liberal' education Newman advocates. It was hardly diffusings of treasure of *that* sort they hoped a 'useful' education to provide. They were more interested in treasure on earth, of the ordinary bankable variety. Had Newman left it there, he couldn't have been convicted of sophistry but his audience might well have gone away feeling cheated.

But he doesn't leave it there. Claiming usefulness in the 'higher' sense for his idea of the university is only a preliminary to claiming it in the low and mercantile sense too.

He draws a specious analogy between a liberal education and a healthy body: as the latter doesn't of itself give you any particular bodily skill but is a prerequisite for all skills, so a liberal education, while it doesn't of itself make you a lawyer or businessman does enable you to become one more easily and more successfully, and so is useful in the lowest sense you could wish:

> Again, as health ought to precede labour of the body, and as a man in health can do what an unhealthy man cannot do, and as of this health the properties are vigour, energy, agility, graceful carriage and action, manual dexterity, and

endurance of fatigue, so in like manner general culture of mind is the best aid to professional and scientific study, and educated men can do what illiterate cannot; and the man who has learned to think and to reason and to compare and to discriminate and to analyse, who has refined his taste, and formed his judgement, and sharpened his mental vision, will not indeed at once be a lawyer, or a pleader, or an orator, or a statesman, or a physician, or a good landlord, or a man of business, or a soldier, or an engineer, or a chemist, or a geologist, or an antiquarian, but he will be placed in that state of intellect in which he can take up any one of the sciences or callings I have referred to or any other, with an ease, a grace, a versatility, and a success, to which another is a stranger. In this sense then, and as yet I have said but a very few words on a large subject, mental culture is emphatically *useful*.[17]

... That philosophical or liberal education, as I have called it, which is the proper function of a University, if it refuses the foremost place to professional interests, does but postpone them to the formation of the citizen, and, while it subserves the larger interests of philanthropy, prepares also for the successful prosecution of those merely personal objects which at first sight it seems to disparage.[18]

Newman evidently felt the need of the latter passage, which he added after the first edition, as the conclusion of his argument on the point. There, stated with all his lucidity, is Newman's fraudulent promise, which the university went on making to practical men (and taxpayers) for almost 150 years: that if it is left free to pursue the good, it will provide them also with the useful, that cultivating disinterestedness is the way to many self-interested ends, that an education which treats knowledge as its own remuneration will be very remunerative.

And how does Newman square the circle? How does he show that the higher mental culture associated with religion and virtue is emphatically useful in a low and mercantile sense? By a sophistry. Now by meaning one thing by 'mental culture', 'culture of the intellect', 'intellectual culture', 'cultivation of mind' and so on, now by meaning another. 'Mind' and its synonyms are, of course, very slippery words. They can be used to mean something very little short of 'the person'—not excluding all sorts of sensations and apprehensions that are just as much bodily as mental—and they can be used to mean 'conscious mind' only or 'intellect', the intellect as 'excellent' perhaps but, nevertheless, as an excellent 'portion' of the person only.

The 'parallel' between mind and body obviously holds for only the second of these senses. But what Newman does is slip and slide between the two, using the former sense when calling a liberal education a good and an end in itself, using the latter when calling it useful. He slides from 'the mind itself ... mental nature ... character' through 'mind' to 'intellect ... faculties ... exercises of mind ... intellectual powers' and comes to rest finally, fatally, in the idea of the mind as something which can be not just trained but trained scientifically:

We know, not by a direct and simple vision, not at a glance, but, as it were, by piecemeal and accumulation, by a mental process, by going round an object, by the

31

comparison, the combination, the mutual correction, the continual adaptation, of many partial notions, by the joint application and concentration upon it of many faculties and exercises of mind. Such a union and concert of the intellectual powers, such an enlargement and development, such a comprehensiveness, is necessarily a matter of training. And again, such a training is a matter of rule; it is not mere application, however exemplary, which introduces the mind to truth, nor the reading many books, nor the getting up many subjects, nor the witnessing many experiments, nor the attending many lectures. All this is short of enough; a man may have done it all, yet be lingering in the vestibule of knowledge ... he may have no power at all of advancing one step forward of himself, in consequence of what he has already acquired, no power of discriminating between truth and falsehood, of sifting out the grains of truth from the mass, of arranging things according to their real value, and, if I may use the phrase, of building up ideas. Such a power is the result of a scientific formation of mind ... .[19]

Although he only means by that last phrase something like, 'doing things systematically or methodically' or perhaps even just, as he says a couple of lines later, according to 'discipline and habit', he means something by 'mind' here very different from what he meant by 'the mind itself'.[20] It's true that he says that the proper object of the intellect is truth, and that cultivating the intellect is fitting it to apprehend and contemplate truth, but what he means by 'truth' here is certainly nothing like any truth that might belong with a way and a life; it is more like the modern philosopher's 'truth value' or 'correspondence', more like mere accuracy. As Newman speaks of it here, truth is an 'object'; truth, whatever and however it is, is so independently of our seeing it; we come to discern it by the conscientious employment of 'many faculties and exercises of mind'; learning to employ our minds in this way is 'necessarily' a matter of training; such training is a matter of 'rule', the result of a 'scientific' formation of mind.

Newman is now talking as if what gets educated is not us but mental skills and competencies which we can be trained to develop like muscles. We learn to contemplate truth by exercising the muscles of our mental eye in the same way a 'Bates practitioner' corrects short-sightedness by training the muscles of the bodily eye. This isn't even the analogy he started out with: mental culture as the equivalent of all-round bodily health. The activities of the mind described here are pretty much of the same sort as those which he elsewhere thinks of as not amounting to 'the mind itself'. This takes Newman to the top of a slippery slope at the bottom of which we meet, next century, something we shall mention in due course, 'personal transferable skills'.

The slide is present incipiently even in that phrase 'cultivation of mind'[21] which comes shortly after 'the mind itself'. The idea of the mind as something to be 'cultivated'—by a self or a will which is distinct from it—stands in marked contrast to the idea of the mind as something which is acted upon and formed by its own activity. Whether it's mind or potatoes we cultivate, we know in advance what end we seek, and all we have to do is find the means of obtaining it. We might be pleased by success but we aren't formed by either success or failure. The 'we' that did the cultivating remains as it was.

The other case couldn't be more different. For the mind's activity to have an effect upon the mind itself, act upon its own nature, form its character, that activity can't be a mere adapting of means to ends which are already known; it is the ends of its own activity themselves which the mind is learning to see more clearly. We are learning what to think *for*. We are learning not how to get what we want but what *to* want. It isn't powers that are being developed but the good that is being pursued. 'Truth' now is not accuracy but an aspect of the good; it isn't so much an 'object'—to walk around, scrutinizing—as a virtue, and capable of being lost, and found, but not necessarily in the same place.

Whatever else 'truth' is, it is certainly something that matters. And what could be more common than for thinking and feeling man to discover that what once mattered to him does so no longer—has become not so much false as dead? Hazlitt, for instance, discovering under Coleridge's influence that his own thoughts (in *An Essay on the Principles of Human Action*) had become to him not just untrue but *unthinkable*:

> I sat down to the task shortly afterwards for the twentieth time, got new pens and paper, determined to make clear work of it, wrote a few meagre sentences in the skeleton-style of a mathematical demonstration, stopped half-way down the second page; and after trying in vain to pump up any words, images, notions, apprehensions, facts, or observations, from that gulph of abstraction in which I had plunged myself for four or five years preceding, gave up the attempt as labour in vain, and shed tears of helpless despondency on the blank, unfinished paper. [22]

Now, *that's* what it is for thought to have an effect upon the mind itself. *There's* an instance of education: the differences between the Hazlitt-that-was who wrote the *Essay*, the Hazlitt-in-the-making who could write nothing and *Hazlitt*—who wrote the paragraph just quoted. Hazlitt, educated into the Scottish enlightenment by his father, had to be educated out of it by his new friends: not by their arguments or their opinions but *by them*. With the result that such truth as he was capable of, he discovered, had migrated or changed its form. It was no longer to be found in abstractions and analysis, it had passed into mere anecdote and description; truth not an object to be conscientiously observed but a virtue found in the 'observer' himself. Hazlitt describes there a moment in which truth had ceased to exist for him at all. One sort of truth had gone dead for him and another not yet come to life, that is, he had ceased to be one person but had not yet become another.

This is a way of talking about the matter that makes 'education' and 'society' practically the same thing, as it is for Shakespeare's Orlando, whose complaint at the beginning of *As You Like It* is just that by depriving him of education his eldest brother has deprived him of a gentleman's place in the world. He has been made to feed with hinds. Dickens's equivalent was the blacking factory and Chapter 11 of *David Copperfield*. It's the truth contained in Newman's remarks about the university's art being 'the art of social life' divested of Newman's fallacy of its 'training the mind'. As Hazlitt found, education for good and for ill belongs to the influence that people have on one another. It isn't courses that educate, it's persons, and not always the persons running the courses. If the education is genuine this influence is not of the form 'You must do it this way because I in authority say so' but because the lecturer's authority, that of the whole man or the whole woman, is shown in a mode of judgement the student can recognize as genuine, even when the recognition takes the form of dissent. And '… Successful collaborations often arise fortuitously and spontaneously. They share with friendship a resistance to planning.'[23]

It would be a mistake to think that this view of education, if true at all, is true only of 'the arts'. The force of personal example is what educates (if anything does) in the sciences too. Science, when it has the character of education, is a sociable and co-operative venture in which men and women have a direct personal influence on one another every bit as much as they do in the arts. You can see this in a book like James Watson's *Double Helix*—not because Watson gives it as his opinion that it is so; but because he just can't help showing it to be so. That Watson is plainly, outside science, a foolish man, whose opinions, whether of science or anything else, are of absolutely no interest whatsoever, makes his testimony to the sociability of the scientist's world all the more telling: he shows it like this not because (like Michael Polanyi) he has thought about it but because it can't be shown otherwise.

The 'course'—when it isn't simply a charade—is only a contrivance for providing opportunities for personal influence. In itself the course is inert. On the 'arts' side at least, the 'course' is most what it ought to be when it is least in evidence, when the classroom loses its character as a classroom and when the relations of teacher and taught are subsumed in those of partners in a particularly vivid and engaging conversation. As a friend, made during university days, said with aphoristic complacency—an older man (at thirty-six he seemed very old at the time)—'Seminars aspire to reproduce the talk in the pub the night before.' And as he said to a similar effect on another occasion—only with more emphatic self-congratulation as well as in extenuation of freedoms taken—'But *we* don't stop being students when we step out of the lecture theatre.' He might as easily have said (and perhaps did), 'Nor start when we step into it.'

(It follows that no genuine university can practise 'franchising', by which a university, instead of running a course itself, will let the staff of a college of further education [or whatever] run 'the same' course. 'The college delivers the whole or part of courses, units or programmes that are developed and validated

34

by the HE institution.'[24] This is the effort to apply the sometimes lucrative though risky formula whereby a commercial operation is carried out not by the firm that originated it but by licensees, quality guaranteed by the originator. 'Although the course is delivered outside, our quality procedures still apply.'[25] So the core activity of the new university is courses, whose quality depends on no-one in particular. By definition the franchised course is freed from the influence of those who devised it, and removed from the unpredictable discussions, questions and snags one actually meets in university work. The next step is franchising to computer.)

If 'truth' has a character anything remotely like the development Hazlitt discovered in himself, there can be no question of training the intellect by method and rule, scientifically, to get hold of such truth. All such mental exercises performed on the walkabout round the object are distractions, falsifications, impediments. What lays hold of truth is not exercise but a character allowing itself to be modified by thinking.

Newman was right, we believe, to say that it is a fallacy of Locke and his disciples that 'no education is useful which does not teach us some temporal calling, or some mechanical art, or some physical secret,'[26] but what he calls his own 'solution' is just another fallacy. If education is a good it is neither because it trains dentists nor because it trains intellects which help dentists become dentists more easily, gracefully, versatily and successfully than they otherwise would.

* * *

So who *will* show us what education is, how it may be both a good in itself and, without being training, in some sense useful too? Hazlitt will, when he puts his education to use in 'On My First Acquaintance with Poets'. Wordsworth will in his great poem about the growth of the poet's mind. Coleridge will. Newman himself actually tells us more about education in his *Apologia pro Vita Sua* than in *The Idea of a University*, though not by argument. Carlyle will. Matthew Arnold will. F. R. Leavis will. (What a scandal that *Education and the University* is out of print.) But more even than our distinguished tradition of thinkers on the subject—who from Carlyle to Collingwood and Leavis have understood the necessary connection between the intellectual disciplines and the pursuit of the good, in the formation of character and of an educated class—the great English novelists will. Education isn't just a particular subject a novelist may choose to deal with or not, like the poor law or madhouses, but something that must be part of any serious attempt to represent life. Dickens shows what education is. Lawrence does, especially in *The Rainbow*. But no-one does so more clearly or more convincingly than Jane Austen in *Pride and Prejudice*.

3 Jane Austen,
Leading Authority
on Liberal Education

The thing *I*'m afraid of is ... am I Mary Bennet too?

Brian Crick

A SCENE that often used to be found in the English departments of universities: seven people are sitting around a table, one man and six women, five young, one 'mature'. The man has a text, a letter, which he is familiar with but which none of the women has seen before. The man invites the women to say what they think of it but without—except in hints that take as much reading as the text itself—saying what he himself thinks. The man takes it for granted that what's called for is a judgement and that judging the letter is judging its writer.

Three of the six women aren't capable of thinking disinterestedly about anything because they judge things only by their bearing on themselves. Two of these don't think anything about the letter because all they can think about is men. The third takes to the writer because he seems to think as she does.

Of the other three women, one is a paradigm of academic disinterestedness, but only if that means 'personally, not involved at all'. She is keen to have a say but without, apparently, having anything to say. She has learned from the Biblical injunction, 'Judge not, that ye be not judged,' only as far as not to want to risk a real judgement, one that would lay her open to being judged in her turn. She won't hold the writer to account for his words and won't let herself be held to account for her own. She is perfectly objective and non-judgemental; in some eyes, a model student.

Both remaining women spot something in the letter—the same thing— which if they only follow it up will lead them to a definite judgement: that the writer apologizes for something he isn't responsible for and couldn't be supposed to regret. But where one woman lapses into 'candour' and gives non-sense the credit of sense—'Though it is difficult to guess in what way he can mean to make us the atonement he thinks our due, the wish is certainly to his credit'—the other, alerted by something in the style, follows up the clue she has given herself and, adding it to others, comes by steps, and in doubt, to a firm conclusion:

> Elizabeth was chiefly struck with his extraordinary deference for Lady Catherine, and his kind intention of christening, marrying, and burying his parishioners whenever it were required.
>
> 'He must be an oddity, I think,' said she. 'I cannot make him out.—There is something very pompous in his stile.—And what can he mean by apologising for being next in the entail?—We cannot suppose he would help it, if he could.—Can he be a sensible man, sir?'

And her conclusion is, of course, the man's own, the one he has been looking for and hoping to elicit all along. He is satisfied. He replies, 'No, my dear; I think not. I have great hopes of finding him quite the reverse.'

What could be more like a seminar in an English department (in a way that, on the whole, is to the credit of both seminars and breakfasts) than this family breakfast in Chapter 13 of *Pride and Prejudice*? This is exactly what we used to do under the name of 'practical criticism' until we abandoned it in favour of 'theory'. Such fathers and daughters—or teachers and students—are necessary to one another. It's easy to see why Elizabeth is Mr Bennet's favourite daughter, and why she would make anyone's favourite student. Jane Austen gives us a glimpse of what education is and of how it takes place—not by instruction, but by invitation, accepted or refused or just not noticed in the talk over the table— or in the pub—that seminars aspire to reproduce.

What a peculiar thing that the English should be in so hopeless a state of muddle and confusion about education when their favourite book—most read, best loved—is one of the best and most illuminating things on the subject in their own or any other language. It must mean that they read, and love, *Pride and Prejudice*, without understanding it. There is a piece of educating to be done, to teach them that what they read as a good and an end in itself is also immensely useful and capable of rescuing them from their state of confusion.

For no book has more to say to us about education than *Pride and Prejudice*; and it says it in the way we all most like things to be said, scenically and in art-speech, not discursively by consecutive reasoning and argument but by instances and patterns, showing us what education is and is not (but may be mistaken for) in pictures whose truth our own common sense and everyday experience can confirm.

Now *Pride and Prejudice* isn't about education in the way that *Hard Times* or *Educating Rita* is. *Pride and Prejudice* has plenty of breakfast and dinner scenes but no classrooms. But *Educating Rita* has so little to teach us about education, and *Pride and Prejudice* so much, that (if the respective authors had been anything like equals) one thing the contrast would suggest is that the best place to see education at work is not establishments specially set aside and dedicated to it but in the accidents of daily life. *Educating Rita* is supposed to be about … well … educating her, but though we repeatedly see her with her tutor in his room carrying folders which are supposed to contain essays, we don't really see the work that goes on there. We don't learn what work he sets her, how he wants her to go about doing it, what she writes, what criticism he makes of it or how she responds to his criticism. The change in the way she thinks and judges—from 'before' to 'after'—and the means by which it is brought about, are entirely hidden from view. We have to take them on trust. Whereas Jane Austen shows us changes in Elizabeth and Darcy which, however surprisingly, must be seen as education.

It isn't in question whether or not Jane Austen values education as ordinarily understood. For instance, when Elizabeth hears her uncle Mr Gardiner talking to Darcy, she

> could not but be pleased, could not but triumph. It was consoling, that he should know she had some relations for whom there was no need to blush. She listened most attentively to all that passed between them, and gloried in every expression, every sentence of her uncle, which marked his intelligence, his taste, or his good manners.[1]

And the book is full of a kind of disgust with those of its characters who are so variously uneducated: Kitty and Lydia—'silly and ignorant'; Mrs Bennet—'mean understanding, little information'; Mr Collins—'not a sensible man'; Lady Catherine de Bourgh, whose lack of 'breeding' makes Darcy feel ashamed of her, his aunt, just as Elizabeth feels proud of her uncle.

But what is in question, everywhere you look in the book, is what education *is*. Of course, *we* have no difficulty with this question. We know exactly what education is: unproblematic *instruction*; lifelong learning—of facts and skills. And yet those of Jane Austen's characters who share our view are all monsters. 'It shall ever be my earnest endeavour to demean myself with grateful respect towards her Ladyship,' says Mr Collins, obviously a monster of sycophancy with whom we have nothing in common. But Mr Collins is absolutely at one with us in his view of education: 'There can be nothing so advantageous to [young ladies] as instruction.'[2]

And Lady Catherine de Bourgh—'her Ladyship' herself—is another monster, therefore not a bit like us (not even those of us who are Ladies): 'I take no leave of you, Miss Bennet: I send no compliments to your mother. You deserve no such attention. I am most seriously displeased.'[3] But Lady Catherine is *just* like us in her view of education: 'I always say that nothing is to be done in education without steady and regular instruction, and nobody but a governess can give it.'[4]

Mary Bennet we all recognize to be a monster. But she is wonderfully instructed, as though for a circus, a kind of reverse Caliban, a person without a mind made to act as if she had one: not at all like us. And yet Elizabeth Bennet, everybody's favourite character, and intelligent and educable, contradicts us and Mary at once: 'We all love to instruct, though we can teach only what is not worth knowing.'[5]

What are we to make of the fact that it is the monsters who talk like us— saying things that we cannot, at the moment of reading, find to be anything but what Carlyle called jargon, falsity, hearsay and chimera? And that the one who is a pattern of loveable and intelligent womanhood says the exact opposite, with the full authority of her author?

Jane Austen consistently, systematically, presents the instructed mentality as the opposite of the educated, and the reception of instruction as one way of not being educated at all. And not just in *Pride and Prejudice*. Another set of Jane Austen's monsters is the Bertrams, in *Mansfield Park*. When cousin Fanny comes to live with them they express the same sort of shock at her ignorance as Tony Blair's at news of the nation's position in the international skills league table (see p. 74):

> 'I cannot remember the time when I did not know a great deal that she has not the least notion of yet. How long ago it is, aunt, since we used to repeat the chronological order of the kings of England, with the dates of their accession, and most of the principal events of their reigns!'
>
> 'Yes,' added the other: 'and of the Roman emperors as low as Severus; besides a great deal of the Heathen Mythology, and all the Metals, Semi-Metals, Planets and distinguished philosophers.'[6]

Fanny 'does not know the difference between water-colours and crayons' and 'does not want to learn either music or drawing.' But the Bertrams, like Lady Catherine, and Tony Blair, know what remedial measure to take. Fanny is to have what all modern British schoolchildren have, 'a regular instructress' and 'proper masters', professionals. And by this means—the magic wand of professional instruction—she is to be turned into the sort of young lady who can, as Bingley, in *Pride and Prejudice*, mockingly says, 'paint tables, cover skreens, net purses,' someone like the Bertram girls themselves, who 'exercise their memories, practise their duets, and grow tall and womanly,'[7] someone like George Eliot's Rosamond Vincy in *Middlemarch*, who 'was admitted to be the flower of Mrs Lemon's school, the chief school in the county, where the teaching included all that was demanded of the accomplished female—even to extras, such as the getting in and out of a carriage.'[8]

What those nineteenth-century girls were expected to know is, naturally, very different from what our own twenty-first-century girls are. Whereas Lady Catherine de Bourgh and Sir Thomas Bertram want girls to be taught ladylike accomplishments, playing the piano, singing and drawing, Tony—and William—want them, like boys, to be taught the unisex and economically valuable skills of numeracy, literacy and information technology. And these two could scarcely be further apart, could they: the practically, the commercially useful versus the ornamental?

But in a world in which, for a girl, there are no jobs to be had, only husbands —and men want what George Eliot not very forgivingly calls 'a paradise with sweet laughs for bird-notes, and blue eyes for a heaven'... where everything is given to you and nothing claimed'[10]—what is more commercially useful than ornamental femininity? A girl wasn't expected to earn her living by her accomplishments directly. She didn't play for a paying audience or sell screens to tourists. But she was expected to earn her living by them indirectly—and perhaps the livings of other members of her family too, as Miss Maria Ward does in *Mansfield Park*. There was a point of view—the Bertram or de Bourgh point of view—from which her accomplishments gave her added value as a wife. The common alternative was the awful fate (as the Brontës show it to be) of becoming a governess: and what, after all, was a governess but a woman who had a job instead of a husband? And what governess wouldn't rather have had the husband even if he wasn't quite a Mr Rochester or a M. Paul Emmanuel? In Charlotte Lucas's case any husband is better, even Mr Collins. Marriage can even be seen as the reward of training and skill of the kind Charlotte Lucas recommends to Elizabeth Bennet for her sister Jane, the skill of 'fixing' a man by 'shew[ing] *more* affection than she feels'.[11] Playing the piano proves just such a useful skill for Rosamond Vincy. It's one of the things that fixes Lydgate.

Nowadays we don't want our daughters to be accomplished, we want them educated. We want them to read and to think, to know. But this view too has a spokesman in *Pride and Prejudice*—and a less monstrous one than Lady Catherine de Bourgh. When Caroline Bingley says that, to deserve to be called accomplished, a woman 'must have a thorough knowledge of music, singing, drawing, dancing, and the modern languages ... and besides all this, she must possess a certain something in her air and manner of walking, the tone of her voice, her address and expressions,' Darcy adds, 'All this she must possess, and to all this she must yet add something more substantial, in the improvement of her mind by extensive reading.' (Elizabeth Bennet replies, 'I am no longer surprised at your knowing *only* six accomplished women. I rather wonder now at your knowing *any*.')[12]

And the novel has, too, an example of a woman who reads very extensively just in order to improve her mind. She 'worked hard for knowledge and accomplishments'[13] and, even without professional help, is the best-instructed person in the Bennet household. She would make—according to a very common idea of what a student should be—a model, one who would certainly go on to do research (perhaps in Gender Studies or The Invention of the Idea of 'Englishness',

1790–1820), with which 'project' she would enter the broad, well-trodden path of an academic career: Mary Bennet—'who piqued herself upon the solidity of her reflections', such as

> 'Pride is a very common failing I believe. By all that I have ever read, I am convinced that it is very common indeed, that human nature is particularly prone to it, and that there are very few of us who do not cherish a feeling of self-complacency on the score of some quality or other, real or imaginary. Vanity and pride are different things, though the words are often used synonimously. A person may be proud without being vain. Pride relates more to our opinion of ourselves, vanity to what we would have others think of us.'[14]

Like the ideal examination candidate she has learned not only the lesson but the style. Allowing for the distance of time and phraseology, her style—when she can find nothing from a text-book to quote—is just like that of the modern career academic: cagey to the point of self-extinction. Mary has as a gift what in real life is only obtained at the cost of many pains and great sacrifice; she has expelled all trace of herself—of any living, breathing woman—from her own words. Who that has ever worked in an English department could fail to recognize her comment on Mr Collins's letter? 'In point of composition his letter does not seem defective. The idea of the olive branch is perhaps not wholly new, yet I think it is well expressed.'[15] Here's prophecy for you. What modernization does it need beyond a few conditionals, in place of indicatives? —a 'would seem' or two? In spirit what modernization does it need at all? Her first sentence gets the question on to the safe ground of the technical, made safer still by a caveat. Her second parodies academic 'balance'.

When Mary speaks, no-one replies; there is no-one there to reply to. Is her sister Elizabeth to walk three muddy miles from Longbourn to Netherfield— and back—to see Jane who is unwell? Mary's advice is: first do a cost-benefit analysis: '"I admire the activity of your benevolence," observed Mary, "but every impulse of feeling should be guided by reason; and, in my opinion, exertion should always be in proportion to what is required."'[16] But no-one can hear: 'We will go as far as Meryton with you,' say Catherine and Lydia as if Mary weren't there (as she isn't). Mary doesn't talk, she makes observations.

When the Bennets learn that Lydia has ruined not just her own but the reputation of the whole family by running off with Wickham, it's true that the one thing they can give one another in the dreadful circumstances is consolation. But the very last thing any normal person could find consoling is Mary's way of stating the fact:

> 'This is a most unfortunate affair; and will probably be much talked of. But we must stem the tide of malice, and pour into the wounded bosoms of each other, the balm of sisterly consolation.'[17]

When she unsurprisingly gets no reply, she adds:

41

'Unhappy as the event must be for Lydia, we may draw from it this useful lesson; that loss of virtue in a female is irretrievable—that one false step involves her in endless ruin—that her reputation is no less brittle than it is beautiful,—and that she cannot be too much guarded in her behaviour towards the undeserving of the other sex.' [18]

The necessary judgement comes—silently—from Elizabeth, who 'lifted up her eyes in amazement, but was too much oppressed to make any reply.'

Mary Bennet is the deconstructionists' ideal. Her speech hasn't just been invaded by others', it is over-run, authorless. The things she says can't be replied to, only ignored—or deconstructed. Her father sometimes forestalls them by deconstructing them in advance:

'What say you, Mary? for you are a young lady of deep reflection I know, and read books, and make extracts.'
Mary wished to say something very sensible, but knew not how.
'While Mary is adjusting her ideas,' he continued, 'let us return to Mr Bingley.' [19]

And who in the novel most resembles Mary Bennet, the ideal student? Wickedly, Jane Austen makes it Mr Collins, who isn't educated at all. The sense Jane Austen gives to 'uneducated' is worth some attention:

Mr Collins was not a sensible man, and the deficiency of nature had been but little assisted by education or society; the greatest part of his life having been spent under the guidance of an illiterate and miserly father; and though he belonged to one of the universities, he had merely kept the necessary terms, without forming at it any useful acquaintance. [20]

She talks as if formal 'education' and 'society' serve the same purpose. What confirmed the deficiencies of nature in Mr Collins was not any want of schooling, either as a child or young man, but, firstly, the influence upon his own character of his father's (his father's illiteracy being thought of not as a want of skills but a quality of character on a par with miserliness) and then his own independent failure to take advantage of university—his failure there lying not in his not studying hard enough but in his not forming 'any useful acquaintance', people, that is, who might have been useful to him by acquainting him with an educated standard to think, talk and behave by.

The uneducated in this sense and the studious have a natural affinity for one another, it seems. None of the other Bennet girls can bear him but Mary would have him: 'She rated his abilities much higher than any of the others; there was a solidity in his reflections which often struck her ....' [21] Though she thinks he needs encouraging to read and improve himself by her example, he doesn't in fact need her example at all. His own talk about and to Lady Catherine is every bit as premeditated as her own. Just like her, he doesn't talk but makes speeches and gives lectures.

Although the deficiencies of his nature haven't been much assisted by education, his mental habits conform so perfectly to those recommended in a not at all uncommon kind of teaching that, when he proposes to Elizabeth Bennet, he does so in the form of a well-structured essay, much on the model recommended by cribs to A-level candidates. He is going to propose, to ask a young woman to marry him, be his wife etc etc. And 'he set about it in a very orderly manner, with all the observances which he supposed a regular part of the business.'[22] He does use to Elizabeth the words 'marrying', 'marriage', 'wife', 'happiness', 'feelings', 'affection', 'love'—and not in ways that any computer programme or teacher of EFL could rule to be ungrammatical—but he does so without ever managing to say or, apparently, even realizing that he is called on to say, that he loves and wants her. He doesn't lie, like Pierre Bezuhov in *War and Peace* proposing to his first wife: he can't get that close to speaking the truth. He has, of course, reasons—quite good ones—for marrying, reasons— quite good ones—for coming to Longbourn for the purpose of arranging a marriage and reasons—quite good ones—for selecting Elizabeth from the girls he finds there. He does not neglect to 'state'[23] them, general and particular, sub-divided and numbered, and—with an emphasis here and a repetition there—as clearly as if he were obeying an A-level rubric: 'Candidates are reminded that the assessment criteria include the ability to organize and present information, ideas, descriptions and arguments clearly and logically, with correct use of grammar ... .' Unfortunately, all this is to a proposal of marriage what, in Bingley's words, conversation is to dancing: 'Much more rational ... but ... not ... near so much like a ball.'[24] The first, last, best reason Elizabeth could have for refusing him is his proposal itself.

> 'My reasons for marrying are, first, that I think it a right thing for every clergyman in easy circumstances (like myself) to set the example of matrimony in his parish. Secondly, that I am convinced it will add very greatly to my happiness; and thirdly —which perhaps I ought to have mentioned earlier, that it is the particular advice and recommendation of the very noble lady whom I have the honour of calling patroness.'[25]

He then appropriately expands—unpacks—this last point, before moving on (but not without glancing back):

> 'Thus much for my general intention in favour of matrimony; it remains to be told why my views were directed to Longbourn instead of my own neighbourhood, where I assure you there are many amiable young women. But the fact is, that being, as I am, to inherit this estate after the death of your honoured father, (who, however, may live many years longer), I could not satisfy myself without resolving to chuse a wife from among his daughters, that the loss to them might be as little as possible, when the melancholy event takes place—which, however, as I have already said, may not be for several years. This has been my motive, my fair cousin,

and I flatter myself it will not sink me in your esteem. And now nothing remains for me but to assure you in the most animated language of the violence of my affection.'[26]

And having said so—and therefore having done so too—all that does remain is to add the footnotes:

'To fortune I am perfectly indifferent, and shall make no demand of that nature on your father, since I am well aware it could not be complied with; and that one thousand pounds in the 4 per cents which will not be yours until after your mother's decease, is all that you may ever be entitled to. On that head, therefore, I shall be uniformly silent; and you may assure yourself that no ungenerous reproach shall ever pass my lips when we are married.'[27]

Pursuing this line of thought (and it is that, thought, as well as the most marvellously entertaining art) of the studious as a form of the miseducated, Jane Austen (Terry Eagleton thinks he's an iconoclast?) yet more wickedly gives Darcy a style that has recognizable affinities with Mary's and Mr Collins's. Darcy is, of course, a genuinely educated man with a kind of seriousness derived from being so which, when the novel opens, Elizabeth Bennet stands more in need of than she knows. Bingley has 'of his judgement the highest opinion'; and he is right: 'In understanding Darcy was the superior. Bingley was by no means deficient, but Darcy was clever.'[28] But, until he comes under Elizabeth's influence, he makes being educated seem like a personal disadvantage (like Richardson's Mr Walden in *Sir Charles Grandison*). It has allied itself with social pride to make his conversation rather wooden, pompous, theoretic. We shouldn't mistake it for Mary Bennet's or Mr Collins's. It is all the same a bit would-be Johnsonian—Johnsonian without also being conversational, too bookish, and too proud of it. It is a style of talking which bears out what Bingley says about his writing: 'he does *not* write with ease. He studies too much for words of four syllables:'[29]

'Your list of the common extent of accomplishments has too much truth. The word is applied to many a woman who deserves it no otherwise than by netting a purse, or covering a skreen. But I am very far from agreeing with you in your estimation of ladies in general. I cannot boast of knowing more than half a dozen, in the whole range of my acquaintance, that are really accomplished.'[30]

'Undoubtedly there is meanness in all the arts which ladies sometimes condescend to employ for captivation. Whatever bears affinity to cunning is despicable.'[31]

'The country can in general supply but few subjects for such a study [of intricate characters]. In a country neighbourhood you move in a very confined and unvarying society.'[32]

(No wonder Mrs Bennet is provoked to reply, 'I assure you there is quite as much of *that* going on in the country as in town.' One can sympathize.)

'Nothing is more deceitful than the appearance of humility. It is often only care-lessness of opinion, and sometimes an indirect boast.'[33]

'Will it not be advisable, before we proceed on this subject, to arrange with rather more precision the degree of importance which is to appertain to this request, as well as the degree of intimacy subsisting between the parties?'[34]

And so on; too much like T. S. Eliot remembering he is serious; and when he is trying to be light, heavy. In this character Mr Darcy makes his own first proposal to Elizabeth.

In the most important respect of all, nothing could be more different from Mr Collins's. Darcy does propose, not just carry out the regular observances: '... how ardently I admire and love you.'[35] But all the same there are curious, modified, reminders of Mr Collins in him, a not unlike emphasis on the history of his own reasons, motives, considerations, for and against—as if what were wanted here were explanations. He 'spoke well' and is 'eloquent' when, again, perhaps something other than excellence of performance is what is wanted.[36] And what the character of his eloquence is we can gather from the indirect speech Jane Austen summarizes his conclusion with:

He concluded with representing to her the strength of that attachment which, in spite of all his endeavours, he had found impossible to conquer; and with expressing his hope that it would now be rewarded by her acceptance of his hand.[37]

We again recognize these well-formed eighteenth-century periods as (without its being implied that there is some other particular style that is called for) not quite the thing called for. He is too much master of his words, and his words are too much those of a species—the educated eighteenth-century gentleman. They are too familiar a part of 'the regular business'. At any rate, that, more or less, is how Elizabeth sees them—and in this there is another passing resemblance to Mr Collins, to the difference between saying things and meaning them: 'He *spoke* of apprehension and anxiety, but his countenance expressed real security.'[38] So here, again, is a proposal which supplies the grounds on which it is to be rejected; and, again, we see Elizabeth as a true judge and critic.

The changes that take place in Elizabeth and Darcy as a result of this proposal and its refusal—the changes they bring about in one another—show us how (in modification of Elizabeth's dictum) we can teach what is worth knowing, even if we can't do it by instructing. As Mr Bennet, without aiming to, just in the ordinary course of domestic life, educates his daughter Elizabeth, so Elizabeth re-educates the formally educated Darcy, and is educated by him in turn.

What Darcy might have to learn from Elizabeth that he did not learn at university is beautifully suggested in the conversation between them that con-cludes Chapter 12. The conversation is something like an eighteenth-century version of the wit combats of Beatrice and Benedick—except that, it being the turn of the eighteenth not sixteenth century and the participants being a kind of lady and gentleman that Beatrice and Benedick are not, the conversation *is* a conversation as well as a game. There's more stating, and no puns. It's 'polite'. But this combat differs in another, more particular way too. All the playfulness (until the very end) is on one side. It's not so much a combat of wit as a combat between wit and what evidently takes itself for wisdom. Elizabeth is playful, ironic, jokey—without being frivolous. Darcy is literal-minded and discursive —as if anything else were beneath him. The subject of the conversation, unfortunately for him, is whether he's a fit subject for laughter or not (the poor man having to suffer not just Elizabeth Bennet's jokes but Jane Austen's too). It's Caroline Bingley who has let him in for it by saying—but not as a joke—that he's no subject for laughter. Elizabeth takes it up; and, as the ball is batted back and forth, quickly, neatly, tellingly from one side, ponderously from the other, it seems as if she has not just all the humour but all the intelligence too:

'Mr Darcy is not to be laughed at!' cried Elizabeth. 'That is an uncommon advantage, and uncommon I hope it will continue, for it would be a great loss to *me* to have many such acquaintance. I dearly love a laugh.'

'Miss Bingley,' said he, 'has given me credit for more than can be. The wisest and the best of men, nay, the wisest and best of their actions, may be rendered ridiculous by a person whose first object in life is a joke.'

'Certainly,' replied Elizabeth—'there are such people, but I hope I am not one of *them*. I hope I never ridicule what is wise or good. Follies and nonsense, whims and inconsistencies *do* divert me, I own, and I laugh at them whenever I can.—But these, I suppose, are precisely what you are without.'

'Perhaps that is not possible for any one. But it has been the study of my life to avoid those weaknesses which often expose a strong understanding to ridicule.'

'Such as vanity and pride.'

'Yes, vanity is a weakness indeed. But pride—where there is a real superiority of mind, pride will always be under good regulation.'

Elizabeth turned away to hide a smile.

'Your examination of Mr Darcy is over, I presume,' said Miss Bingley;—'and pray what is the result?'

'I am perfectly convinced by it that Mr Darcy has no defect. He owns it himself without disguise.'

'No'—said Darcy. 'I have made no such pretension. I have faults enough, but they are not, I hope, of understanding. My temper I dare not vouch for.—It is, I believe, too little yielding—certainly too little for the convenience of the world. I cannot forget the follies and vices of others so soon as I ought, nor their offences against myself. My feelings are not puffed about with every attempt to move them. My temper would perhaps be called resentful.—My good opinion once lost is lost for ever.'

'*That* is a failing indeed!'—cried Elizabeth. 'Implacable resentment *is* a shade in a character. But you have chosen your fault well.—I really cannot *laugh* at it. You are safe from me.'

'There is, I believe, in every disposition a tendency to some particular evil, a natural defect, which not even the best education can overcome.'

'And *your* defect is a propensity to hate every body.'

'And yours,' he replied with a smile, 'is wilfully to misunderstand them.'[39]

And there he at last relaxes under the warmth of her teasing, and replies, with a smile, in kind; and we glimpse a side of him that is both more educable and more likeable than we had perhaps seen before. Until then it has seemed to be precisely his understanding, not his temper, which is deficient; until then superiority of mind has looked to be the last quality he could justifiably claim. But with that last remark and the smile that accompanies it, we can see that he is capable of learning, not from instruction but from—again—the invitation implicit in example, the invitation he shows himself ready to accept. (This is process and progress, not instant conversion. Their education is still incomplete at the end of the novel when Elizabeth holds back from mocking the now-accepted lover: 'She remembered that he had yet to learn to be laught at, and it was rather too early to begin.'[40]) Not quite by the way we also notice that this passage tells us much more about vanity and pride than the academic authority Mary, quoted above.

Short as it is, this conversation makes it clear why Elizabeth is so irresistibly attractive to Darcy. It's not just that she has qualities that might attract any man; it's also that he is peculiarly in need of them. As he says later, he 'admires her for the liveliness of her mind';[41] he can't help himself; her sort of liveliness is the very thing he lacks; he's incomplete without it.

And if learning from her example, in whatever measure he can, isn't being educated ... nothing is. (It's a lesson the modern academy is as far from learning as Mary Bennet is: that intelligence and seriousness belong as much with playfulness as with propositions possessing truth-value.)

The book is the story of Elizabeth's education out of prejudice as well as Darcy's out of pride, and prejudice of a more interesting kind than her initial dislike of Darcy. These glimpses of what it is to be educated are opened out in the story of her changing relations with him and Wickham. It proves to be one thing for a clever young woman to see what Mr Collins is made of, another thing altogether to see through Wickham—not because, as Jane Austen shows it, he is intrinsically any harder to fathom, but because he is so for a marriageable young woman, however clever. Elizabeth Bennet isn't, like her sisters Kitty and Lydia, just any (in the Johnsonian phrase) 'unidea-ed' girl but she is, like Kitty and Lydia, a girl, as much at the mercy of good looks and a charming manner as any other. And that she is, is part of the marvellous truthfulness of Jane Austen's art.

The two crucial tests for Elizabeth (and the reader) are what Wickham says about Darcy in the conversation in Chapter 16 in which he blames Darcy for the bad relations between them, and what Darcy says about Wickham in the letter in Chapter 35 in which he defends himself and puts the blame on Wickham.

When Elizabeth, with her sisters, meets Wickham in the street, in Chapter 15, Jane Austen conveys with a beautifully light touch the character both of Wickham's appeal and Elizabeth's response to it, which, for all her superiority to her sisters, is no less automatic and undifferentiated than theirs:

> This was exactly as it should be; for the young man wanted only regimentals to make him completely charming. His appearance was greatly in his favour; he had all the best part of beauty, a fine countenance, a good figure, and very pleasing address. The introduction was followed up on his side with a happy readiness of conversation—a readiness at the same time perfectly correct and unassuming.[42]

There, irony doesn't, quite, precipitate from description but it does in the next chapter; and it leaves the reader with no-one to blame but himself if, by the chapter's end, he hasn't seen how thorough a charlatan Wickham is and how thoroughly Elizabeth is taken in.

Not that Elizabeth is satisfied just to admire him. She both admires him and finds her admiration to be justified: She 'felt, she had neither been seeing him before, nor thinking *that* of him since, with the smallest degree of unreasonable admiration.'[43] What makes her admiration reasonable? His superiority of 'person, countenance, air' and (beautifully) 'walk': 'He was the happy man towards whom almost every female eye was turned, and Elizabeth was the happy woman by whom he finally seated himself.'[44] And it is her happiness, in the conversation that follows, to be shown every last twist and turn of his— as Mr Bennet later calls it—impudence and hypocrisy, without being able to recognize it. It is true that he is very adroit at sounding her out and seeing how far he can go in blackening Darcy's character without risking his own; but his adroitness, his calculation and caution, are, after all, themselves there to be seen—if Elizabeth had her eyes as well open as when she is looking at Mr Collins. As entirely convincing as it is that she should be taken in, the means by which she is taken in are, by any account, pretty crude. What else—being means—could they be? Wickham may be adroit but that doesn't make him any less transparent.

He begins not with Darcy at all but the distance Netherfield is from Meryton. He brings Darcy in only 'in an hesitating manner'[45] and as no more than what might be taken for an indifferent conversation piece, asking how long he had been staying there. Then, on Elizabeth's frankly owning her interest in Darcy, he ventures as far as his estate, and—without venturing off it—invites her to invite him to approach the man himself: it is an estate about which he can give 'certain information' because of the 'particular manner' in which 'I have been connected with his family ... from my infancy'.[46] To make quite sure of his ground: is Elizabeth much acquainted with the man? As much as she ever wants to be? Perfect. The way is clear.

But that doesn't stop it being devious. Elizabeth may frankly avow her dislike of Darcy, Wickham is too good a man to do any such thing. He has no right to give his opinion, he is not qualified to form one—for, after all, he has known Darcy too long and too well … to be a fair judge or impartial. If Darcy is generally disliked, he can't pretend to be sorry, but only from a love of justice: he wouldn't want any man to be thought better of than he deserved. It's true that Darcy has used him very badly—scandalously badly—but he regrets that not for his own but for Darcy's sake … and Darcy's father's. He could forgive Darcy for what he has done to him. The disgrace and disappointment he has brought to his own father—'one of the best men that ever breathed … the truest friend I ever had … a thousand tender recollections … excessively attached to me'—he never can forgive.[47]

And so it goes—wonderfully—on, even to Wickham's claiming to have (like Mr Collins speaking of the 'violence' of his affections) a 'warm, unguarded temper'.[48] Wickham is not a bit less impossible a prospect as a husband than Mr Collins, and his impossibility is not (for someone with eyes to see) a bit less visible. The clever man who calculates the impression he makes can no more disguise what he is and what he is doing than the man who is too stupid to know he is making any particular impression at all. Language is such, the conditions of life are such, that the one as helplessly reveals what he is as the other ('Each mortal thing does one thing and the same;/Deals out that being indoors each one dwells'[49])—but not to Elizabeth. She and Wickham talk 'with mutual satisfaction'. His account of Darcy seems a 'very rational' one, and she goes away 'with her head full of him'.[50] Later, of course, under the influence of Darcy's repudiation of what Wickham tells her, she sees 'the impropriety of such communications to a stranger' and 'the indelicacy of putting himself forward as he had', and she sees also that she ought to have seen it at the time: she 'wondered it had escaped her.'[51]

She might well wonder. For, in a way, she does at the time recognize the impropriety and indelicacy, sufficiently so at least to feel scruples on her own account. At the start of the conversation she knows that, much as she would like to, she 'could not hope' to hear about Darcy from Wickham, and 'dared not even mention that gentleman';[52] and part way through, as keen as she is to hear more, 'the delicacy of it prevented farther inquiry.'[53] So 'all' she has to do is to apply to Wickham a standard which she applies to herself: if it would be indelicate of her to ask, what is it for him to volunteer? Similarly, she is perfectly capable of reading Caroline Bingley's 'high flown expressions' with 'all the insensibility of distrust'[54]—so why not Wickham's? In a way, she does already know what Wickham is and, from that, what Darcy cannot be. She just (as if it were so easy) needs to recognize it.

The first and last thing to be insisted on is that whatever else is effectual in education, it isn't 'facts'. Facts are necessary but they won't do the job for Elizabeth. She has to agonize before she even decides what the facts are, but only because of what the facts might mean to her. The fact that Wickham, having said he would never avoid Darcy, does avoid him at the Netherfield ball, is no help to Elizabeth—she blames Darcy. The fact that Wickham drops her to go after Miss King because the latter has come into £10,000 is no help either—she excuses him on the grounds of his need. She discounts Bingley's testimony because it must rest on Darcy's. She discounts Bingley's sister's because it is tainted by snobbery (even though, if she thought, she'd recognize that it must be disinterested). Charlotte Lucas's advice not to risk offending a rich man for the sake of a poor one condemns itself. And Mrs Gardiner's caution is scarcely distinguishable from Charlotte Lucas's: if only Wickham were rich, Elizabeth could scarcely do better; as it is …. Jane is no use, of course: she speaks up for Darcy … and Wickham. And in this case Mr Bennet is no help either: like everyone else, at this stage, he is 'partial' to Wickham.[55]

Darcy is not just the one who happens to open Elizabeth's eyes. He seems to be the only one capable of opening them. But that isn't *only* because he has information other people don't have. It isn't the information that opens her eyes. It's true that Darcy does give her 'another side of the story', which makes it 'impossible not to feel that there was gross duplicity on one side or the other,'[56] but the question remains for her … which?

> She … weighed every circumstance with what she meant to be impartiality—deliberated on the probability of each statement—but with little success. On both sides it was only assertion.[57]

The most that the new information can do is show her that the affair was 'capable of' a turn she hadn't expected.[58] The question still remains: but which man is honest, which the liar? It's not facts she needs, to vouch for character, but a judgement of character to vouch for 'facts'.

Now, Darcy's letter has a definite character. To begin with it's long—not so far short of 3000 words, longer than some of Jane Austen's own chapters, longer than a broadsheet review or a mid-length learned article—and it's well-organized. It has things in common with Mr Collins's proposal. It has a beginning, middle and end; and its middle divides into sections and sub-sections, which we should have no difficulty in numbering. It's the letter of a man accustomed not merely to write at length but at the same time to develop a train of thought, to analyse, to use evidence, to blend argument and narrative. It's the letter of an educated man, a university man who has done more than keep the necessary terms.

But whereas the degree of organization Mr Collins gives his proposal is part of what stops it being a proposal, the organization of Darcy's letter is part of what makes it a self-vindication, and, in its own, odd way, a real love letter too—made so just by avoiding any hint of love. Its organization is part of what justifies his saying, 'I demand your attention ... I demand it of your justice.'[59] He has to earn the right to make such a demand, and he does: the length, thoroughness, connectedness of part with part—and distinctness of part from part—of his letter, all help him to. These things are not just signs of the strenuous sincerity of his effort to make himself clear to her, they are a form that that sincerity takes. He is seeking earnestly to come to a disinterested judgement of himself which she can concur in. So he has to distinguish— between topic and topic, the more from the less grave, where he has been in the right from where he has been in error, error that is innocent from error that isn't quite so innocent, the effects of his actions from their motives, cases where his judgement is certain from cases where—though definite—it may be corrigible. What else can the letter be but long and highly organized? Who but an educated man could write it? 'I believed it on impartial conviction, as truly as I wished it in reason.'[60] Who but an educated man could say such a thing? Here is education not as a training in mental gymnastics or form of social advantage but as character, something individual and permanent, desirable, though nothing come of it, as being of itself a treasure, and a sufficient remuneration of years of labour. To Darcy, of course, it proves something else Newman calls it, not only a good but productive of good, useful, emphatically useful, the means of his winning his wife, 'dearest, loveliest Elizabeth!' (not only 'worthy of being pleased' but by his letter made more worthy to please[61]). Darcy vindicates himself to his future wife and in doing so does something to vindicate a liberal education too.

He would never have written such a letter, of course—one so free of complacency—except under the influence of Elizabeth herself. Without some such shock to his opinion of himself as the terms of her refusal give him, any account he gives of himself would be likely to be very different. We have his own word for it:

> a selfish being all my life ... taught what was *right*, but ... not taught to correct my good principles, but left to follow them in pride and conceit ... spoilt ... allowed, encouraged, almost taught ... to be selfish and overbearing, to care for none beyond my own family circle, to think meanly of all the rest of the world ... Such I was, from eight to eight and twenty; and such I might still have been but for you, dearest, loveliest Elizabeth! What do I not owe you! You taught me a lesson, hard indeed at first, but most advantageous. By you, I was properly humbled. I came to you without a doubt of my reception. You shewed me how insufficient were all my pretensions to please a woman worthy of being pleased.[62]

And we can see for ourselves the change in him in the difference between the way he describes his objections to her family when he proposes and the way he describes them when he writes. It's not, though, that he softens them in the letter. Actually, they are more severe there, but disentangled from any taint of social pride.

But just as the effect on him of Elizabeth's rejection depended on what he should make of it, so the effect of his letter on her—no matter how good it is—is out of his hands. That depends on her and what she makes of it. His letter may vouch for his honesty as plainly as Wickham's conversation does for his dishonesty, but there's nothing to guarantee that Elizabeth will see the one any more than the other. His letter is only an invitation, after all, which she can always refuse. And at first, on the subject of her family, to refuse to see him or Wickham in any light but the one she is accustomed to seems the thing she is likeliest to do: she's amazed that he thinks he can make any apology, steadfast in the belief that he can have no explanation, strongly prejudiced against everything he might say, instantly resolved that he's untruthful, too angry to wish to do him justice, convinced his letter is all pride and insolence. And even though she reads the part about Wickham 'with somewhat clearer attention', she nevertheless 'wished to discredit it entirely', repeatedly calling it 'false' and putting it away 'protesting that she would not regard it, that she would never look at it again.'[63]

But that, in her honesty, she acknowledges, 'would not do'. She gets out the letter again and 'commanded herself so far as to examine the meaning of every sentence ... she read, and re-read with the closest attention'—not to learn anything new but to learn whether or not she must look at what she already knows in a new light. She goes back over Wickham's behaviour and conversation—just as she does over Darcy's letter—and finds that the parts that compose it, all familiar, each no different from what it was before, take up a new pattern contradictory of the old. She now sees what had previously escaped her: that all her good opinion of Wickham derived from his 'social powers' alone, his 'countenance, voice, and manner ... charm of air and address' but no 'instance of goodness ... trait of integrity or benevolence', no more 'substantial good than the general approbation'. And then, going back over that first conversation, from which 'many of his expressions were still fresh in her memory', she sees everything she ought to have seen at the time.[64] But to do so she has had not just to be shown it but to look for herself: the truth of Darcy's letter can't be communicated to her without herself laying hold of it. And when she does, it is not just Wickham that she comes to judge differently, or even Darcy along with him. Everything changes for her. She sees her family in a new, harsher light, and herself too:

> She grew absolutely ashamed of herself.—Of neither Darcy nor Wickham could she think, without feeling that she had been blind, partial, prejudiced, absurd.
> 'How despicably have I acted!' she cried.—'I, who have prided myself on my discernment!—I, who have valued myself on my abilities! who have often disdained the generous candour of my sister, and gratified my vanity, in useless or blameable distrust.—How humiliating is this discovery!—Yet, how just a humiliation!—Had

I been in love, I could not have been more wretchedly blind. But vanity, not love, has been my folly.—Pleased with the preference of one, and offended by the neglect of the other, on the very beginning of our acquaintance, I have courted prepossession and ignorance, and driven reason away, where either were concerned. Till this moment, I never knew myself.' [65]

The echo of the Delphic oracle is unusually grave for Jane Austen, but fully justified. Know thyself—and realize that it's difficult. Darcy's letter, having, in one section, effected that change in her, also makes it possible for her to read its other section, on her family, quite differently. Her first reading ('all pride and insolence' [66]), she comes to see, is a misreading. But, it must be said, misreading or not, it is a real reading, even in its lapses, and in itself illustrates what it is about her that attracts Darcy and makes her new understanding possible. She has a kind of hunger for meaning (which is the basis of all knowledge, all understanding, all real education—Jane Austen has put a lot of herself into her):

how eagerly she went through [its contents], and what a contrariety of emotion they excited. Her feelings as she read were scarcely to be defined. ... She read, with an eagerness which hardly left her power of comprehension, and from impatience of knowing what the next sentence might bring, was incapable of attending to the sense of the one before her eyes. [67]

And although her second reading is 'widely different', because her judgement of the writer has become so ('How could she deny that credit to his assertions, in one instance, which she had been obliged to give in the other?' [68]), it has in common with her first a fallible but passionate sincerity in her

giving way to every variety of thought; re-considering events, determining probabilities, and reconciling herself as well as she could, to a change so sudden and so important ....

Mr Darcy's letter, she was in a fair way of soon knowing by heart. She studied every sentence: and her feelings towards its writer were at times widely different ....[69]

This is what 'studying' is—when it is what it ought to be—the antithesis of Mary's studiousness. This is what it is to be disinterested: to follow a sense passionately even if it is the one one wants most to deny. This is education, the opposite of instruction. Darcy's letter does educate Elizabeth but it couldn't do so without her co-operation, any more than her refusal of him could have taught him the lesson it did without his. Each is changed by the truths the other teaches, but they wouldn't be without actively reaching for and laying hold of those truths themselves. Each educates and is educated but neither has anything delivered to them. They have acquired no new skills, not even new life skills or ones of the personal transferable kind. (The person in the novel who possesses those is the odious and shallow Wickham.) They have become better critics, better judges of the value of things, better people. Liberal education has to be more or less like this.

Jane Austen doesn't just tell us that Elizabeth firstly misjudges Wickham and Darcy, and then comes to judge them rightly, she shows her making her judgements, shows the judgements in the making, for us to judge. Jane Austen puts her readers and her characters on an equal footing, tests and (let's hope) educates the judgements of the one as she does those of the other. We may very well misjudge Wickham along with Elizabeth, and without her excuse. The judgements we are called on to make in reading *Pride and Prejudice* are the same sort of judgements (often the very same judgements) that the characters of the book are making, for good or ill, in their lives, and the same sort that we make in our own.

It is in the exercise of judgement, and the modification of one judgement by another, that education is seen: not of judgement in any particular professional or specialized sphere but of it in—as Carlyle calls it in *Sartor Resartus*—'the "Science of Things in General"', practised everywhere, and on matters great and small. *What party shall we vote for? Shall we get married? Whom shall we appoint? Shall I buy this newspaper? Can I be bothered with this?* It makes not for the lifelong learning we are told we must all undertake on pain of not getting a big pension, but for a lifelong growth in discrimination which is the same as development of character. Jane Austen not only puts it at the very centre of our lives, entering into and intertwined with every other aspect, even the power of love, but shows it to be a good and a value in itself.

She gives us a picture of life which a great many people, if they were consistent, would dislike and disapprove of, as irredeemably élitist. 'The unreasoned life,' said Socrates, 'is not worth living.' Jane Austen goes further: a life without judgement, her books strongly imply, would not be a human life at all. But she goes further, in the direction of the offensive, still: the more alive in judgement, she implies, simply, the more alive. The better the judge, the better the critic, the better the man or woman—the better, the more alive as a man or woman. The characters in the novel who are most alive, Darcy and Elizabeth, are those who judge best and whose judgements are most open to being educated. Jane Austen writes as if we are the sense we make and as if that sense were not only judgeable but most plainly judgeable in the way we talk and write.

It could almost be said that this is her great theme. Let us learn what we can from Elizabeth and Darcy but not overlook Emma's education under the influence of Mr Knightley, Captain Wentworth's and Miss Anne Elliot's mutual education, and not least Henry Tilney's as well as Catherine Morland's. Nor can her other ineducable monsters be safely ignored: Sir Walter Elliot, Miss Elliot and Mr William Elliot; General Tilney. We have already mentioned the Bertram girls.

*   *   *

So what an odd relation Jane Austen has to modern England: our most popular classic novelist (and, currently, perhaps, dramatist too) but in defiance of the incorrectness in our world of the 'judgemental' that is the centre of hers. Unless we can be brought to recognize that our current idea of education not only collides with hers (with that of our great writers generally and with our own common sense), there is no hope for 'education' in this country and nothing to be done about it. It is doomed to be a monstrosity and a millstone around the national neck. Unless directed by an intelligent, by an educated conception of education, all 'reform' will prove to be a process without purpose and without end, a delusion. The long sequence of reforms and improvements made from the 1960s onwards can already be seen to have about as much consistency to it as the movements of the ball on a pinball machine. The ball, of course, for all its vagaries of movement on the way, is steadily drawn to the low point on the table—but the analogy holds there too, for education may not have become better over the last 30 years or so, or even more democratic; it has undoubtedly become—along with newspapers, radio, television and public utterance of any and every kind—steadily lower. That is the significance of the Dearing Report and and the Dome, Tony Blair's Cool Britannia and the People's This, That and the Other: the plebification not just of the ruling but of the educated class. Or, as we might say: for all that Britain may contain a great many educated individuals, it now questionable whether it has an educated class.

It is a great misfortune that English literature counts for so little in English public life. Literature is, of course, in one way and another, a prominent and flourishing business. There is the Arts Council and the arts pages, the Lottery money, the Booker and the Whitbread, and the publishing and teaching industries; there is even a Minister for the Arts, with a PhD, in English literature; but none of these gives English literature any authority in English public life, not even in university departments of it.

And yet English literature, with its testimony to other possibilities, is still, triumphantly, there; and it can be—it is—still read, not just studiously but with pleasure; and while that is so, there is hope, even for our education system. For the pleasure stories and poems give us is bound up with the degree and varieties of assent they draw from us. Our pleasure depends on our assent, or, we might say, is one form it takes.

No-one, I suppose, can read *Pride and Prejudice* without taking pleasure in its happy ending. Except perhaps for some of Shakespeare's comedies (and perhaps not even those) no book has a greater power to make us share the happiness of its characters. 'Had Elizabeth been able to encounter his eye, she might have seen how well the expression of heart-felt delight, diffused over his face, became him; but, though she could not look, she could listen....' [70] But the happiness we feel in their happiness isn't self-indulgent or merely vicarious. It is a response to what is there in the novel. It's a kind of assent to what we have been shown, and to the judgements that belong to it. We shouldn't feel the pleasure we do if we couldn't recognize Darcy's case, for instance, as being what it is meant to be, that of a man in love, whose happiness depends on success in love. It's not only that this is how the author means us to take him—and we can see that it is—but that we actually do take him so, can't help but say, 'yes, this is what love is like.' Without that assent, the entire anxious comedy of, firstly, his tongue-tied awkwardness, then of his happiness, would fall flat.

So when we observe that the British educated classes love *Pride and Prejudice*, we are also observing that they acknowledge, even if they don't know it, the picture of education it gives them to be a true one—even though that picture is utterly irreconcilable with the way they themselves habitually talk about the matter.

Our modern educationists and politicians read Jane Austen's novel as if one thing were true, and then talk as if something not merely different but precisely opposite were. How are we to resolve that contradiction? In a way—we *want* to believe—that is to the credit of their real, underlying good sense: they know better than they think they do; they read more sincerely than they speak; they only think they think that training and education are the same and that the usefulness of education lies in the profitability of the skills it inculcates; really —though for the most part they don't know it—they think something quite different; what they really think is not gauged by what they say in their official capacities as Vice-Chancellor of This and Minister of State for That—which is very often just role-play and affectation—but by what they do as private men and women, when they are free to do as they please; and then what they do is read *Pride and Prejudice*, with pleasure and with assent.

And that is why there can be some practical point to the present book. We are not trying to change what people think, just persuade them to recognize what they know. 'Look at *Pride and Prejudice*,' we say. 'There, that's what you actually believe, isn't it? What can you find there to disagree with? Don't believe us. Believe her. Believe yourselves.'—not the selves that pretend to think the international skills league table anything but a chimera, but the selves whose pleasure in *Pride and Prejudice* is a form of assent to its author's wisdom, and a sign that they can still recognize genuine speech when they hear it.

So it isn't too much to hope, is it, that a minister of education or a prime minister (especially one who tells us he has a 'passion' for education [71]) might read a book like *Pride and Prejudice*, and learn something from it—even about education?

That's what we want to think. For the alternative is that our educated classes read our classic literature without it meaning anything to them at all. ('Hearing they hear not, neither do they understand.') And if it doesn't mean anything to them, what does?

III

THE NEW UNIVERSITY FOR LIFE

4   The Vision and the Mission

But I say unto you, That every idle word that men shall speak, they shall give account thereof in the day of judgement.

For by thy words thou shalt be justified, and by thy words thou shalt be condemned.[1]

MR COLLINS AS THE LEADING MODERN AUTHORITY

UNIVERSITY DONS are traditionally accused by practical men of logic-chopping and of finickiness about language. Milton as controversialist did spend too many pages attacking his opponents' grammar. But there is no way of objecting to disputes about language without also objecting to the university itself in its role of critic and former of judgement.

Jane Austen's judgements of persons are regularly expressed as judgements of their language. This does not mean that the standards she judges by are schoolma'amish or snobbish. She doesn't value correctness—social or linguistic —for its own sake. Her standards aren't narrowly intellectual or 'literary' either—ones that would necessarily find against the unintellectual or unread or those who might stumble over their words. Although no-one could be more fluent than she herself is, no-one else could think she values fluency for its own sake. Who could be less at a loss for words than her monsters, Mr Collins, Mrs Bennet, Mr Wickham, Lady Catherine de Bourgh—even, when she can fit an 'extract' to an occasion, Mary Bennet? And although she is as witty a writer as there is in the language no-one could think Jane Austen values wit for its own sake either. Mr Bennet is a clever man. He has a mind as lively as his daughter Elizabeth's and is much better read. Jane Austen makes him as witty as she is herself—in fact, his lines are even better than her own—but no-one could come away from *Pride and Prejudice* thinking wit an end in itself or that he doesn't misuse his great gifts. Mr Bennet's wit—for all the truth and justice to be found in it—has too much in common with the way he shuts himself up in his library and fails to provide for his family after his death. Being witty at his wife's and daughters' expense may be necessary for his mental health, but at the same time the wit is plainly one of the forms his irresponsibility takes.

There is no saying in advance how we ought or ought not to speak, no prescribing the best style. There are judgements to be made but no rules to follow, no skills to be exercised. Not even 'speaking well' *will* always be speaking well. Sometimes clumsiness, or silence, might be better. When Darcy first proposes to Elizabeth he 'speaks well', and is 'eloquent', but only because, it seems, he doesn't feel what he should. He doesn't yet know how much his happiness depends on success in love; and when he learns, the knowledge makes him speechless. And then his tongue-tied awkwardness says more of his love and the power love has over him than his eloquence ever did. As he says to Elizabeth when she later tells him he might have talked more, 'A man who had felt less, might.' But the instant he knows he is loved in return, love, that tied his tongue, unties it, and releases him into an articulacy that is nothing like eloquence. He doesn't speak well now, he just talks freely. He and Elizabeth 'walked on, without knowing in what direction. There was too much to be thought and felt, and said.'

Clichés similarly might be a bad sign—or not. As Jane Austen reports it, Darcy's style in his first proposal is very much a stock one. He is to be found saying the sort of thing that men like himself generally do say when called on to say such things, and he does it well—that is, ill. And yet that same style, in all its stereotypicality, is, as Jane Austen also reports it, the one in which Elizabeth accepts his second proposal; and there it is, it seems, just the thing called for, the sign that Elizabeth feels every bit what she might:

> Elizabeth, feeling all the more than common awkwardness and anxiety of his situation, now forced herself to speak; and immediately, though not very fluently, gave him to understand, that her sentiments had undergone so material a change, since the period to which he alluded, as to make her receive with gratitude and pleasure, his present assurances.[2]

The difference is that what prompts Elizabeth to have recourse to the ready-made is more or less the opposite of what prompted Darcy. Whereas his stock phrases came to him easily just because of what he didn't feel, hers, as the signs of what she does feel, are the nearest way out of a crisis. We might expect that Darcy, having failed to find the right words for his first proposal, might need to find new ones for his second. But no. It wasn't different words he needed, just different feelings. His feelings having changed—he having changed—those original, wrong words have become the right ones. They are redeemed and their intended meaning reclaimed. So he doesn't need to propose afresh, only to say that he stands by what he said before: 'My affections and wishes are unchanged.'

The standards, then, by which Jane Austen judges her characters (and readers) might be those of any or all classes and sorts of person. They are to be found wherever English is found, and—translation not being an impossibility—even where it is not. They are truly the standards, that is, of the best part of the language, present—potentially so—everywhere in English life. Jane Austen writes as if language were important, all-important, but only for the life to be found in it, only for the sake of the life it makes possible (and not).

Words and the styles they combine in have no fixed values but acquire them from the life they express. They enable us to give meaning to our lives; but only to the extent that we bring their meanings to life. We have to live the meanings possible to words for words to have those meanings; if we don't, their meaningfulness is simply an illusion. The 'power of speech' *is* a power but a power to make nonsense as well as sense. Language fills the world with meanings it wouldn't otherwise have but, by the same token, it has the power to make it meaningless too. Language creates the world, our world; and can uncreate it too.

This is why Mary Bennet and Mr Collins have such fascination for Jane Austen, as people who are not really human because their language is a sort of anti-language. Never mind Samuel Beckett; here is meaninglessness, here is silence, in the midst of loquacity. Mr Collins is one of Jane Austen's—of English literature's—greatest creations. Only a very great writer could have done him. Of course, considered as a person, he could hardly have less to him and still be recognizable as one. But the significance his author discovers in him is a different matter. He may be shallow; his author's contemplation of him is anything but. He is one of her versions of Pope's dunces. A similar playfulness and inventiveness has gone into the making of him and there's a similar fascinated horror with the result. Mr Collins is no 'great Anarch', Emperor of Chaos or Goddess of Dulness; he is a country parson, proud of his wife, his garden and—most of all—his patron's permission regularly to abase himself at her dinner table. But his is the authentic 'uncreating word'. When he speaks, as when the Goddess of Dulness yawns at the end of Pope's mock-epic *The Dunciad*, Light dies, the Arts go out, Truth flees, Morality expires—''Till drown'd was Sense, and Shame, and Right, and Wrong'—not because he is a liar or immoralist but because, in his commonplace way and in his limited sphere, he makes all distinctions, all thought, all judgement, impossible.

To the creating eye of Jane Austen, as the dunces are to Pope, Mr Collins is a sort of ultimate horror, portending a world from which the possibility of meaning has been expelled, or never entered—a horror contemplated as a joke. What makes him a monster is that he is so obviously a man, and a quite harmless one, but without anything to justify his being so. He has the faculty of language (he's not Dr Frankenstein's monster) but without, apparently, anything in him—or anything but the most rudimentary egotism—to express, nothing to give meaning to the familiar words he uses. We think of the purpose of language as being to make sense; and he uses it to make nonsense, of a deep, radical but perfectly respectable kind. He is no Mrs Malaprop or Flora Finching. He speaks and writes perfectly ordinary, fluent, correct and idiomatic English (at least it isn't French). He doesn't make mistakes in grammar or spelling and he plainly uses words in the sense of their dictionary definitions. (He would probably do very well in his GCSE exam.) In every way (but one) he falls within the socially acceptable: a perfectly acceptable parson, dinner guest, master, son-in-law, husband. It's just that he has this one oddity, of using language in such a way as to destroy its capacity for making sense. Words, to him, are just counters or tokens, to be moved around and exchanged: useful but not for meaning anything.

It has been said of both Macaulay and Richard Nixon that they have styles in which it is impossible to tell the truth. But that's not much compared with Mr Collins, whose language makes no sense of any kind. He is as incapable of lying as of telling the truth. He is beyond good and evil—even if not quite as Nietzsche meant. As he is himself only going through the motions when he proposes to Elizabeth, he naturally takes her to be going through similar motions when she refuses him. She doesn't *mean* anything by it ('it' being several paragraphs of very plain speaking), it's all 'merely words of course ... the usual practice of elegant females'.[3] He is like a creature from another planet, giving a quite expert imitation of human behaviour but without having any under-standing of it. He is ineducable.

*   *   *

If we say that the language in which universities now habitually conduct their affairs, and the language of public debate about education, denies the existence of the university—whatever in particular is being said about the university—we are making use of this fact that there is no separating judgement from language. It is not nit-picking to object to titles like *Management Aspects of Implementing Flexible Learning*: they are from a language which is itself the destruction of thought.

The chosen phrase comes from a document from the University of Salford.

> Consensus to a concept or vision of the desired shape and purpose of the organi-zation not only makes the organization more effective in carrying out its mission, but also makes it more capable of dealing with future change in a positive and pro-active manner.

When Charlemagne offered the Saxons the alternative of baptism or the sword he did not add the insult of demanding 'consensus to a concept'. The smallest objection to this is that 'consensus to' is not an English idiom. This style is not only inadequate, but a kind of virus rendering blank the minds that try to use it.

We had a vacant post for a linguist with special emphasis on dialectology. The Department's practice was to ask candidates to make a short 'presentation'. One distributed a sheet of quotations (obligatory on the modern lecturer though of course the students naturally start reading the quotations instead of listening to the lecture) including this:

> … The language question in Wales is sufficiently highly charged that some might infer that even to pay analytic attention to English in Wales, or 'Welsh English' … represents an ideological position, perhaps even a form of capitulation, or collusion with forces threatening the Welsh language.[4]

The elementary points about English grammar ('highly charged' takes 'for' not 'that'; 'capitulation' needs a 'to', etc) are, again, just another facet of the necessary judgement that this (politically motivated) 'thinking about' language gets expressed in a kind of dissolution of language. This was offered not as a cautionary example but as modern thinking, and was successfully taken as such: the candidate was appointed and has, I believe, been thinking in the same style ever since.

Are we not, after all, rather monstrous? Our monstrosity is not quite Lady Catherine's, or Mary Bennet's. But had Mary lived now she too would have been discussing consensus to a concept.

Pope concludes *The Dunciad* with a vision of the end of the world. The world is destroyed—by the Goddess of Dulness, in a parody of the creation of the world at the beginning of Genesis—as it was made, by the word:

> Lo thy dread empire, Chaos, is restor'd;
> Light dies before thy uncreating word.

Though Chaos restored by Dulness will be, like the original, void, it will not be without form. In Pope's vision of the end of things, the physical world goes on as if nothing had happened. In ours, mankind will continue not only to be fruitful and multiply, but to speak and write in well-formed sentences, make bullet-points and spider-graphs, to pass GCSEs and meet government literacy targets (or else be subjected to procedures put in place to ensure they do next time), to be the customers who will receive, from cradle to grave, lifelong learning, duly monitored and quality assured. There is just this difference. Henceforth they will all sound like David Blunkett. The world ends, for Pope, not with a bang nor even a whimper, but stupefied with a yawn. It isn't comets or nuclear war or aliens that destroy it, or the Devil in any very sulphurous form. It's clichés, rubbish-talk, what Jane Austen calls 'nothing-meaning terms'. The world ends with the destruction *by* the word *of* the word. If you can't imagine this, try and read the Dearing Report.

SIR RON DEARING, SON OF COLLINS

Jane Austen always knew when to stop. After the end of her story, Charlotte *née* Lucas found that she had made an incorrigible mistake, that no establishment could compensate for Mr Collins's society. She showed herself less practical than she had imagined; she pined away and died. Mr Collins reverted to his original intention of marrying a Bennet and Mary, still available, after mature deliberation had no doubt about accepting him. More surprising, they had issue. Among their distant descendants, still keeping the breed true, is Sir Ron (as he was at the apogee of his fame) Dearing, the most influential modern example of Collins-like monstrosity.

We haven't, we confess, read all 1700 pages of Sir Ron's committee's report into higher education.[5] We made do, largely, with the 20-page summary. Strictly speaking, we can't claim to have *read* even that. But that's not our fault, for, strictly speaking, *reading* isn't something that can be done with it. The report can be down-loaded, scanned, studied, used, say, by a Government wanting to justify something-or-other, or, in its printed form, for landfill; but the one thing no-one can do with it is read it, except, like Mr Collins's letters, as symptoms. If you are exposed to the Dearing style you run—as we also see with Mr Collins's letters—a truly horrible risk: you either diagnose the disease and inoculate yourself against it by something like reading Jane Austen, or you catch it.

Sir Ron and his committee—with all its many members of a broad expertise divided into working groups—had what they call a 'vision' of Higher Education in the Third Millennium. It is a vision of a 'learning society' in which the entire population is 'learning for life'. It is a vision of high standards, rigour, search for truth, love of knowledge and understanding for their own sakes, disciplined thinking, critical analysis, culture, civilization (and cognitive skills such as an understanding of methodologies)—all things life-enriching and desirable in their own right, or whatever. Unfortunately, though Sir Ron and his Committee knew that Higher Education possessed these things, it didn't occur to them that their own Inquiry needed to. They knew they needed to travel—to France, Germany, Holland, Australia, New Zealand—but had no idea they needed to think. Or, if they had, one of the things they must have thought was that aeroplanes, trains and taxis were more use to them than the words 'university', 'thought' and 'literature' or its cognates, 'literate', 'literary' and 'literacy' (in place of the last, the more impressively technical-sounding 'communication'), for though they made extensive use of the former they found no use for the latter at all. They went into education, and came out with a report that isn't an effect of it and could only be a cause by being seen as an example of its opposite.

You might be surprised that a 1700-page report on higher education (we word-searched the full version) could find no real use for the word 'university'; you shouldn't be. A National Committee of Inquiry is a government quango and naturally looks upon the objects it inquires into—especially when they are paid for from taxes—as things subject to the powers of government. The word 'university' does occur, but usually as an adjective and never as the object of thought. But the kind of power over things that derives from paying for them is subject to rather obvious limits, even when, as in the case of a government that has got rid of constitutional checks and balances, to that power is added the power to make law. A government can do all sorts of things; what it can't do is say what those things mean. It can decide who is to get 'family allowance' but not what we are to understand by the word 'family'. It has the power to confer the legal status of 'university' upon whatever set of activities it pleases but not the power to prevent us from understanding the result as a joke. Its powers in this respect are no greater than those of the prostitute's client, who may choose what she does but not what it means to her. There, her freedom remains absolute ('the undefil'd, tho' ravish'd night and morn', as Blake puts it).

The word 'university' has a history which makes some things almost impossible to say, for example that the university should be for all, or for job-training, or to make us rich. The beauty of terms like 'higher education' and 'higher education sector', for someone with a remit, like Sir Ron, is that, denoting things that governments invent, they can be used however governments please, without fear of contradiction. The higher education sector—of the education system—doesn't exist except as a government conceives it or apart from the legislative and financial instruments that maintain it. It isn't a branch of education (which has no sectors and isn't a system), it is a branch of government. It is part not of education but of education-as-organization, 'education' as so much of *matériel* and of men and women, doing whatever they happen to be paid to do, be that what it may. Over the meaning of such things a government naturally does have power. Of an expression like 'higher education sector' Sir Ron might truly say, like Humpty Dumpty, 'When *I* use a word, it means just what I choose it to mean—neither more nor less.'

Two things ought to be noticed, though: firstly, that if Sir Ron says things about 'higher education' that can't be contradicted it's only because they are beyond the true and the false altogether. They are non-sense, for the freedom to give words what meaning we please is much like the freedom to walk, or even skate, without friction—self-contradictory. Secondly, as soon as Sir Ron starts to imagine that what he says about education-as-organization applies to education itself he ceases to talk the sort of pure non-sense which is immune from contradiction and starts talking the ordinary sort.

Doing without the word 'university', it is only natural that Sir Ron should do without 'thought' too. He does use it in his summary, once, and then in a way that is very revealing, as of something that comes in measurable, in investable, amounts, like time or 'resources': 'implementation [of the recommendation for the innovative use of the new Communications and Information Technologies to improve the quality of Higher Education] requires investment, in terms of time, thought and resources.' This is why, presumably, he speaks of the work of university teachers as if it had no definite character to it but was made up of various 'combinations' of different 'roles' or 'functions' which are 'likely to change ... at different stages of their careers'. The retort to which must be that a member of a university has just one 'role', and that is to think. He justifies himself by thought, or not at all. Thinking is to members of a university what playing is to a football team or worship to a congregation. To exchange that 'function' for some other or combination of others is to cease to *be* a member of the university, whether officially accredited by an Institute for Learning and Teaching in Higher Education (see below) or not.

'Thought' having no place in Sir Ron's vocabulary, it is again only natural that 'literature' and 'literate' should have none either. It won't have occurred to him that there could be any sense in which he was wanting in literacy himself. But what a terrible revenge the language takes on him! He has no place in his report for literature, and what he gets in its place is cant. His exemplary instances aren't Jane Austen and J. H. Newman but ... the anonymous authors of journalist cant, advertiser cant, politician cant, educator cant. What a sucker for the stuff Sir Ron is. His mind has for it the adhesiveness of fly-paper. A cliché has only to brush against it, and that's it: stuck. The Dearing Report will prove in centuries to come a sort of archaeological record of the clichés current amongst the English great and good in the summer of 1997. I have picked a whole basket of dead flies off the fly-paper (just of one species); lorry-loads remain.

The habit of metaphor is sometimes thought to be the mark of a poet. With Sir Ron, it's just a habit. Ever since Kenneth Baker (now there *was* a poet!) discovered that standards are the sort of thing that can be 'levered up' (by the National Curriculum—remember?), the literal-minded have (in Coleridge's phrase) talked of mind, and thought of bricks and mortar. So it's Sir Ron's way to use a certain range of terms in any sense but the literal (the art not so much of coining new expressions as clipping old):

> quality of life [*except as something immeasurable*]; quality assurance [*of anything that can't be audited*]; mission [*but not of anything spiritual*]; vision [*ditto*]; management [*of anything but a busine*ss]; franchise [*ditto*]; partners [*likewise*]; customers [*except of shops*]; clients [*except of solicitors and suchlike*]; delivery [*of anything but milk, coal or the post*]; provision [*but not of provisions*]; investment [*but not in the stock market*]; leading edge [*except of aeroplane wings*]; professional [*except to mean 'paid'*]; freestanding [*of anything but buildings*]; to produce [*anything but physical goods*]; drive [*anything but vehicles*]; seek continuously to improve performance of [*anything but an engine*]; generate [*anything but electricity*]; communications [*especially where no transmitters or receivers involved*]; target [*of anything but arrows*]; strategy [*except in warfare*]; mechanism [*of things immaterial*]; global market place [*for things spiritual*]; outcomes [*especially invisible*]; monitoring [*except in a schoolroom*]; etc etc.

He puts together little bits like these to make ... bigger bits. It's the verbal equivalent of meccano, lots of standardized bits put together in a few standardized ways. As with meccano, you best see what it's for *dis*assembled. A list of the report's clichés does more than convey an idea of its style, it makes the report itself superfluous. All the report's got that such a list hasn't (except a lot more of the same) is the grammatical links that join, or separate, the bits listed.

Mostly—but not always—the bits are put together grammatically, but then in sentences that might have been meant to prove the futility of grammar. The ungrammatical sentences are at least grammatically interesting, as illustrating the subtleties of usage. For Sir Ron and his Committee of Experts are not perfectly at ease amongst the subtleties of usage. Because they aren't using words to think with but are just fitting clichés together, they sometimes miss the native idiom, as in 'we received tremendous support and commitment to our task from …' or 'we support the diversity between …' or 'it is a strength in responding to …' or 'to take an imaginative leap in devising …' or (a bit of stage-French?) 'UK qualifications have standing.'

Sir Ron's cliché-aggregations are sentences in the sense that they aren't anything else. But if, as the linguists tell us, sentences make sense, they are only sentences in the way that Mr Collins's are. Mr Collins imitates sense and thereby parodies it. Sir Ron does the same. Typically Sir Ron's sentences combine a sort of windy assertiveness with banality, or something less:

> It should, therefore, be a national policy objective to be world class both in learning at all levels and in a range of research of different kinds. In higher education, this aspiration should be realised through a new compact involving institutions and their staff, students, government, employers and society in general.

> Higher Education must create a society committed to learning throughout life. That commitment will be required from individuals, the state, employers and providers of education and training.

> But over the next two decades, higher education will face challenges as well as opportunities. The effectiveness of its response will determine its future.

> The higher education sector will comprise a community of free-standing institutions dedicated to the creation of a learning society and the pursuit of excellence in their diverse missions. It will include institutions of world renown and it must be a conscious objective of national policy that the UK should continue to have such institutions.

> Higher education … will contribute not only through … and by … but also by … and … and promoting the values that characterise higher education … Equally …

This is the way with words that Mr Collins and Mary Bennet have. Look what he does to the word 'compact'. What sort of compact is made between parties that not only aren't in any distinct logical relation to one another but even include one another, making up a list you could stretch out or shorten like a piece of elastic? How could you imagine these parties being separately represented? Often the weird emptiness of Sir Ron's well-constructed sentences is best brought out by trying to imagine what it is they *deny*: that it ought to be a national policy objective to be less than 'world class'? or to be 'world class' in learning but not research? or in learning at some levels not others? or in a range of research all of one kind?

Sir Ron's 'will' and 'must' are an endless tease (though no more so than his 'should'). You can't tell whether he's giving Leninist-bureaucratic orders, making predictions, making judgements or speaking in tautologies. In one passage which begins 'The future will require ...' he seems to be doing the four at once. Leaving aside the ludicrousness of the ambition to make our universities renowned (rather than just good), why *must* it be a conscious objective of national policy that they be anything at all? Is it somehow not enough just *to be* good, and to strive to be so, like Pele or Mozart or Mother Teresa? What's gained by making it, consciously, an objective—and of national policy—to be so? (See some remarks below about 'goals'.) I don't suppose Sir Ron's committee made it their conscious objective to write a report that's world class, but would it have made any difference if they had? I don't suppose, either, that they had the conscious objective of being world class at having conscious objectives but world class at *that* is the one thing they undoubtedly are world class at.

Where are Sir Ron's imitation sentences going? Not—as you might think—nowhere. These cliché-agglutinations may not be the work of intelligence but they aren't the work of mere chance either, any more than those of the ancestral Collins. They have as good a reason for existing as Sir Ron himself. They are the solution to an insoluble problem: how to affirm the truth of the new master idea—that the purpose of education is to make us rich—without causing offence by denying the truth of the old—that it is to make us wise. Sir Ron is an evangelist for the new idea, and he must have seen, like other evangelists before him, that a new belief most readily supplants an old not by opposing but by merging with it. And how else could he bring wisdom to merge with riches except through the happy, distinction-annihilating power of the cliché? How else could oil and water be made to mix, chalk taste like cheese or Labour to lie down with the Tories? How else could the new idea of the university as a mass institution selling instruction in saleable skills be made compatible with the old idea of it as an élite institution giving a free and liberal education? Sir Ron does unite these opposites, but only by removing sense from both. For as we have shown there is no more genuine sense in the belief in education as investment than (from Sir Ron) in belief in the life-enhancingness of education.

In his prose all edges meet in the middle. It is the discursive equivalent of a spider-chart (see below) in that every single, distinct, plottable point on it gives directly on to every other. You don't have to *get* from A to B (or even *alpha* to *omega*) in this universe, you're already there. And it is the intelligence-defeating power of the cliché that puts you there. It is a power that makes all things possible. It makes Sir Ron to mental knots what Alexander was to string. The White Queen could believe six impossible things before breakfast. Alice should have met Sir Ron.

In Sir Ron's world there are no problems, only solutions. Lions lying down with lambs? No problem. Oil and water? No problem. Did Newman write a whole book on whether education is an end in itself or a means to an end? False problem. In Sir Ron's world (fortunate world!) it is both, simultaneously. It is life-enriching and desirable in its own right, of course, *and* a good investment (*excellent* personal investment, return averaging between 11 per cent and 14 per cent, *and* fundamental to the economic health of the nation, enabling it to compete at the cutting edge of innovation). Education and training are one and the same thing under different names. They (or it) both (or either) indifferently equip people for work *and* foster culture for its own sake. Both (or either) *both* increase knowledge and understanding for their own sakes *and* foster their application for the benefit of the economy. Things which are good in themselves are also, thank goodness, Sir Ron finds, *immensely* useful. They are even saleable. Higher education has, of course, always had the role of guarding and transmitting culture and maintaining the values which make for civilized society, but now, with the development of information technology, it faces the challenge and opportunity of selling its products, competitively, all over the world. It can now both promote, as it always has, the values which characterize itself *and also* turn them into programmes that can be marketed in the global marketplace. Good leads to goods, improving the quality of life in quantifiable and quite unmysterious ways.

Nor is there any need to fear that past, present or future expansion of the universities is incompatible with the maintenance of standards. We don't set targets but we do envisage a rise in the national average of young people participating in full-time higher education to 45 per cent, or more; we deplore the continued under-representation of socio-economic groups III to V, people with disabilities and specific ethnic minority groups; and in future we must enable *all* students, even those who have struggled to reach the threshold of higher education, to ... [better be careful here] ... to achieve beyond their expectations. But there is no need to fear that any of this will lead to lower standards because we can at the same time *make a commitment to high ones*, and thus not only have many more students, including the strugglers, but pursue quality, sustain a culture which demands disciplined thinking, and safeguard the rigour of our academic awards all at the same time.

It is just as well, of course, that the pursuit of civilization and high standards on the one hand and the pursuit of sales and expansion on the other go so conveniently together, because the need for greater investment in education-and-training to meet the international challenge and the demand, the informed demand, from all those people ready and willing to move on to higher education would drive a resumed expansion of student numbers *anyway*—that is, even if the civilization and the high standards had to (as they say in the building trade) go the journey.

The overall increase in participation in higher education (an achievement in which higher education can take justifiable pride) is to be welcomed—because it is democratic. Culture and civilization are things to approve of, and so is democracy. Never mind that some senses of 'democratic' diverge from some senses of 'cultured' and 'civilized', there's no need to choose. Get the right throb in your voice and no-one will notice. Imagine you're George Washington and you won't even notice yourself:

> higher education … part of the conscience of society [but not any old society, *democratic* society] …

> part of its task to accept a duty of care for the well-being of civilisation [but not any rotten old civilisation, *democratic* civilisation] …

> a major role in shaping society [but a society that is democratic, civilised and inclusive] …

> rights of the individual … responsibilities of the individual …

> respect for the individual and respect by the individual … respect for evidence; respect for individuals and their views [respect for everything except genuine thinking] …

> the search for truth [in a style that turns it into the blind leading the blind] …

For Sir Ron all is possible—not just to believe, but to do. You just put in place, firstly, your national policy objective—to combine participation for all with high standards from top to bottom—and then your mechanisms for achieving it—a participation strategy, a progress monitoring mechanism and an achievement review provision, *plus* a Quality Assessment Agency with expert teams, benchmark information, a framework of qualifications and threshold standards. And Bob's-your-uncle. You've not only widened participation without lowering standards but reduced your need for an apparatus of quality assessment and audit too. You've got it all. You *can* drink simultaneously from the mouth and the source of the Nile. All you need is a long enough straw.

And Sir Ron has all sorts of straws, which he strongly recommends we suck. One (a very short one, some university members might think) is the establishment of a professional Institute for Learning and Teaching in Higher Education, whose purpose would be to establish university teaching as a profession in its own right. It would do this through its accreditation function. University teaching in the UK will never be a profession in its own right, or be world class, until it's the norm for all permanent staff with teaching responsibilities to be trained on accredited programmes. So, over the medium term, it should become the normal requirement that all new full-time academic staff with teaching responsibilities achieve at least associate membership of the Institute, for the successful completion of probation.[6]

And there we have the centrepiece of Sir Ron's vision: there at the very tiptop of the higher education tree sits Sir Ron, at the head of a Committee of his clones; immediately below, the Institute, staffed, similarly, by his clones; and below that, the universities (as it were), staffed, from top to bottom—from the medium term onwards—by virtue of the powers invested in the clones of the Institute, by no-one who is not a clone, by *accréditation*. To be a bit of Blu-tack or a bad sector on a floppy disk, yes, but to be Mary Bennet or Mr Collins, to be a clone of Ron Dearing's ... I'd rather be Dolly the Sheep.

And what will the students of the third millennium have to show for all this many-sided educational excellence? Among other things, a 'Progress File', for life. Sir Ron gives the File a paragraph to itself; and the paragraph is worth quoting in full. It is a sign of what those mysteries 'the learning society' and 'learning for life' mean:

> Young people entering higher education will increasingly come with a Progress File which records their achievements up to that point and which is intended for use throughout life. We favour the development of a national format for a transcript of achievement in higher education which students could add to their Progress Files.

And it won't end there: 'We envisage individuals building up a portfolio of achievements at a range of levels over a working lifetime,' and having them too, no doubt, conscientiously entered into their Files, as permanent measures of Progress made, and not. In this brave new world, we are to have our school reports always with us, like the *biografi* the Albanians carried under Hoxha.[7]

Sir Ron has a vision of us learning all our lives, but not just in the course of living, as we all do, like Elizabeth Bennet and Darcy, or don't, like Lydia and Wickham. His vision is not of life as a classroom, and as including criticism with breakfast, but of the classroom as life, with cant for breakfast, dinner and tea, administered by a Mr Collins or a Mary Bennet who has at least associate membership of the ILTHE, *avec accréditation*. The only alternative he can imagine is that 'individuals manage their own development and learning', which is, of course, just what Mary Bennet does, an accredited teacher with herself for her own pupil. Here is the form Big Brother is to take on our little island in the third millennium. Here's what Fate has in store for *us*. Not Hitler or Stalin or Mao (and certainly not Cromwell) but Mary Bennet, Mr Collins, Sir Ron, a Dunce and a Headmaster rolled into one and forever checking our Progress Files. A vision of a life without literature, without criticism, without thought, but *with* education—as a life sentence.

5   The New University as Training in Skills

THAT PROFESSIONAL INTERESTS are best served indirectly, Newman made the keystone of his argument for the university; and, for a hundred years, that made the keystone of many such arguments—though not the Newbolt Report's, and not Leavis's, to which ours is much indebted. Newman's dodge worked for a century, until Mrs Thatcher came along and called the bluff about the graceful versatile dentists. But where *is* the use? she asked. Where are all these graduate wealth-creators that liberal education promised to supply us with? What have we *really* to show for the expense? Useful is what you say a university is? Then let it *be* so—and *directly*.

It's simple and it's candid. And in the long run it can't be anything but healthy. Mrs Thatcher forced the university to face the questions Newman enabled it to avoid. His dodge permitted the university to flourish dishonestly, without enquiring too closely into its own nature, and to take public money on false pretences. Her challenge, if it doesn't just crush the university out of existence altogether, will force it to justify itself on more intelligent and more honest grounds.

Immediately, however, the results have been otherwise.

When it was proposed to 'break down the barrier between academic and vocational training', as *The Independent* headlined it—a 'barrier' also noticed by *The Times* and *The Daily Telegraph* [1]—there was, not for the first time in this free country, no public debate. No murmurs were heard from the universities. The journalists sang in unison.[2] The opposition parties had no need to consider. They were able to complain that the Conservatives had stolen their ideas: that is, there was all-party consensus, usually a dangerous sign in the Commons.

The nub of the White Paper's proposals was therefore to eliminate 'the distinction between polytechnics and universities' (*Telegraph*), and introduce a new 'vocational' school qualification of equal esteem with academic qualifications, handing over control of this latter sixth-form area to regional bodies dominated by businessmen. The White Paper was quoted as saying:

The title of polytechnic has never been widely understood. The British academic world realises that the polytechnics are higher education institutions achieving the same academic standards and giving the same quality of education as most universities. Many able school-leavers and their parents still tend, however, to regard the title as a reason for making them a second choice.

It was this foretaste of spin-doctoring, the emphasis on the doing away with the old academic snobbery, that allowed participants in the non-debate to avoid the awkward question whether the universities are really as useful as the polytechnics. The universities' reply to the challenge consists, in the first place, of the claim that they just are: if there is no distinction between education and training, education *is* training. The *unum necessarium*, all agree, is the supply of graduates essential to the expansion of the national economy—any graduates in anything, for the supply is offered as in itself the universities' mode of being useful.

Any suggestion that the distinction between training and education was, is, and imaginably still could be, *real*, is literally unsayable in the 'heavy' dailies, the weeklies or the Commons. Any propensity to say this ineffable is defused in advance: it would be mere *snobbery*, the snobbery of the academic looking down on the vocationally qualified mechanic. (The reverse snobbery of the practical man who looks down on the academic, like the old carpenter in *The Miller's Tale*, no longer bothers anybody.)

The then Prime Minister, John Major, led the way in breaking down the barriers and removing the distinction. 'It is a distinction well worth removing,' he said. He knew, having suffered as an outsider from the snobbery of the educated. *The Independent*, complaining that the proposed reforms were 'timid'[3] twice used the word 'snobbery' in its editorial. *The Daily Telegraph* stood out in qualifying its own support with the proviso that different things should not be confused; it didn't, however, get as far as saying what the different things are.

The proposal to allow the polytechnics to rename themselves universities naturally followed from the breaking down of the barriers and, in the absence of opposition, was enacted with remarkable speed and smoothness. The former polys devised romantic names like Northumbria (later to be judged the number one university in England[4]) or took over ones well-known already like Oxford (with an addition in small type). There was no parallel proposal to allow the universities to rename themselves polytechnics, which they have in fact been making feeble efforts to become.

The next stage after the renaming of the polys, the speed and smoothness of which was even more remarkable, was an explosion in the number of 'universities' such that the former polys themselves began to be thought of as 'old' universities. In 2000 there are more than five times as many 'universities' in the UK as there were in 1980.

With the simultaneous announcement[5] of the establishment of a University for Industry and a Life Long Learning system whereby tax reliefs would be given to workers embarking on courses (to be 'delivered' to terminals in public libraries and workplaces), any special place in the scheme of things for an institution devoted to liberal education seems finally to have vanished.

So at the turn of the millennium, on the verge of the competitive world of the twenty-first century, we had vast amounts of university education—though, of course, still not enough—all officially of equal esteem and all useful.

*   *   *

There may still be lurking doubts about whether Philosophy is as useful as Dentistry. The universities have hit on the perfect way of putting them to rest and of persuading Chancellors of the Exchequer to keep their cash-flow increasing, like the growth of the national economy, indefinitely. This, unfortunately, is by way of another dodge, and one, moreover, plainly descended from Newman's.

If the challenge is made to show the return on the investment in universities, the academics will give a simple and complete answer. What have we to show for all this money spent? Answer: 'skills'.

If you are a public figure and want to be taken seriously on the subject of education, you call it skills. You won't be taken seriously if you don't. It's a word that in itself obliterates the snobbish old distinction between education and training; and it makes education straightforward and definite, at one and the same time something you can 'do something about' and something worth the doing because it will increase GDP. Skills (always plural, usually adjectival) is a word that puts you in control—like Tony Blair, in control, on the *Today* programme[6] promising to do something about our shocking position in the World League Skills Table (we were forty-second). It also shows that you know that there is more to education than facts. Dickens's Gradgrind may have proceeded on the assumption that two and two make four and nothing left over, but we now know that there is something practically even more important, training in skills.

Whether training itself will do all or even most of what is expected of it is a question we need do no more than glance at, this being a work about universities not economics. 'Is training a waste of money?' is a question we would not presume to ask, though it was the title of a serious article in *The Financial Times* which even used one of our phrases,[7] and which discussed, for instance, the in-house 'universities' started by American companies, like Motorola University and 'the famous Hamburger University where Macdonald's graduates 3000 store managers a year'. 'Does training affect the bottom line? Or is it a … PR exercise in pouring money down the drain?' It was argued that in some cases the answer may be the latter. Another article in the same financial heavyweight raised the question of the use of 'gap years'.

> 'Taking a year off between school and university can not only be made to pay,' says Simon Targett, 'it can also help your chances of landing a good job.'[8]

This is because

> The one thing that blue chip companies complain about, year in and year out, is the paucity of job skills among today's graduates. ...
>
> Such skills can be acquired in other ways ... .

If the useful training offered by universities is actually better acquired by staying away, why go? Let us grant, however, that if, as yet another article put it, 'the courses fit a very specific business need, and ... "this morning's learning can be applied to this afternoon's job"',[9] the money spent on training may be well invested. These are precisely not the skills offered by the universities, which can keep their promise of being useful only by a drastic reinvention of the notion of 'skill'.

For the new universities' offer depends on a double slide about 'skill' much like Newman's single one about 'mind', though less defensible because dependent on a much more obvious misuse of a word.

'Skill' is not one of Wittgenstein's family-resemblance words. A skill is a teachable way of doing a particular thing. Riding a bicycle is a skill; making a spongecake calls on several skills. Some of the traditional trades like signwriting or wheelwrighting demand skills of a high order. On the other hand, skill, as Frank Palmer says, in an essay that should be classical, cannot be stretched to 'a sense of wonder' or 'to adjust to different social contexts' or 'to accept responsibility', all of which have been offered by educationists as examples of skills to be taught in schools.[10] Nor can PSE (Personal and Social Education) be thought of with any sense as a set of skills. *The Universities We Need* quotes an SCAA document—'The value of PSE was seen by some in developing interpersonal skills, including managing feelings, understanding others and learning to take responsibility for one's actions'[11]—and asks, 'What are "interpersonal skills"? Aren't interpersonal relationships more a matter of what kind of *person* you are rather than what skills you deploy? ... As for "managing feelings", there is something worrying about a person of whom you could say that he was skilled at managing his feelings.' The SCAA document includes 'the skills that enable people to make wise decisions and develop acceptable values ... .' 'But how could morality be reduced to skills?'[12]

Are the skills that education claims to use itself any more like genuine skill? The answer to the question 'What are study skills?' given by one authority begins,

> A skill is a 'practised ability'. No doubt you will already have, or be learning, many skills—you may be able to play tennis or football well, having learned the basic skills and then practised so you get better and better at the game.[13]

Some objections could be made: not all practised abilities are skills (talking, for instance) and more goes into games than skill. But so far we would not dissent much. The question is whether education 'skills' are analogous.

There are skills which will enable you to become a good student. These skills can be learned and then practised in the same way as you learned to swim, ski or play tennis. ... This Guideline will look at developing good STUDY HABITS, improving your MEMORY, LISTENING & NOTE-TAKING, REVIEWING your work, improving your READING and ESSAY WRITING, and finally REVISION and EXAM TECHNIQUES.[14]

Are there such skills? The University of Birmingham School of Continuing Studies advertised 'two self-contained but linked half-day sessions' on 'Note-taking and Listening Skills' and 'Improving Your Essay-writing Skills'.[15] The offer was necessarily vacuous because there is no general good advice to be given about listening but 'do—if what is being said is worth listening to,' and about taking notes but 'don't if you can help it.' (People vary and some do help themselves by taking notes, though generally note-taking is a distraction from the critical attention required in a lecture audience.) In both these titles skill is redundant. Nothing is lost and, it seems to us, much gained if the word is deleted. But it couldn't possibly be, in the new university. Without skills the vacuity of the offers being made about note-taking, listening, thinking etc would be undisguisable.

The skill to end all skills was brought home by my son from a Careers lesson, supplied by the Hereford & Worcester Careers Service in 1998. 'What are key personal skills?' was a question answered, of course, in a series of multi-coloured bullet-points. For the most part they fulfilled my prediction that the genuine skills on offer are the three Rs, for they began with

- use numbers correctly
- read, write and communicate effectively

The correct use of numbers can take place in many contexts, and if you can read one document you ought to be able to read many. But after this came things that are not skills at all, like '• work as part of a team' and '• show enthusiasm and interest.' The latter may really be a skill (that is, *fake* an interest) but if so is undesirable. The one that took my fancy, though, was in the middle:

- learn new skills

Now there's a skill for you. Learn the skill of learning skills and what else do you need? In fact it makes redundant even the more advanced skills also listed: '• problem solve [*sic*] ... • action plan [*sic*] ... • speak different languages.' Why worry if you have the skill of learning new skills? Wait until you need to action plan or to problem solve, or to use new languages, then use your universal skill of acquiring skills as required. (The putting into practice of the '• speak different languages' skill was first recorded on the Day of Pentecost, but was then rightly regarded as miraculous.) There is not, and in the nature of genuine skill could not be, such a skill.

The following year, even glossier and with even more colours, the equivalent brochure listed 'employability skills' that included 'interest in the job' and 'experience of the job' which would also have to be miraculous (though not a skill) to someone trying to get their first job.

In this age of the marriage of the entrepreneur with education, a number of businesses have naturally been marketing the sale of educational skills. The samples I have seen have much in common with Victorian marketing of patent medicines, Fenning's Fever Curer and the like, though that, being made of sulphuric acid, actually did something: if you survived the Fever Curer you were likely to have survived the fever also. The concern quoted above that offers listening as one of the key skills says in the same document what it means by listening as a skill:

> You need to be an ACTIVE LISTENER. Only 10% of what you hear or read is KEY INFORMATION. If you can learn to pick out KEY WORDS AND IDEAS from lessons, lectures, videos or books and record them in a way which is easy to review, you will greatly improve your memory skills. Your teacher may say things like:
> the main reasons/points are …
> it is important to remember …
>
> > LISTEN actively by looking for new
> > IDEAS which are shown by words which are
> > SIGNALS.
> > TAKE PART in lessons by asking questions to
> > EXPLORE the subject in greater depth and take
> > NOTES of key ideas and words [16]

How would you identify the KEY WORDS AND IDEAS? The teacher would tell you. (Key words are in any case a trap. One GCSE Biology board, I am told, gives the impression that key words are self-sufficient by docking marks if they are not used. But you do need the lock: the understanding of why the words are 'key'.) Why the teaching profession is thought to be so grossly incompetent as to waste 90 per cent of the available time we are not told.

This mind-boggling layout does seem to me actually demented. If a student wrote it in an exam, the board would call for a medical report. Which 90 per cent of *it*, by the way, is discardable noise, and what skill could tell me?

The other side of the sheet explains the same thing by an even madder 'spider plan'. This is incoherent in the sense that there is no way of knowing how or in what order the parts are supposed to be connected. 'Listening' is the spider at the middle, but whether it rushes out to bite and digest 'Ideas', 'Explore' or 'Take Part', must depend on whim. It seems to follow that if you 'Take Part' or 'Take Notes' you are probably not having 'Ideas'; which is probably true, but not helpful. Why is this imaginable as a skill (what work is being done and how?) or as having anything to do with learning except, possibly, as an inoculation against it?

Today's radio [17] reports a government 'initiative' for thinking to be taught in schools as a skill. This would certainly be a short-cut; unluckily it can't work.

The work of the university just *is* thinking, in the different modes represented by the subjects. Thinking in philosophy is just a long phrase for philosophy; to think in philosophy is just to do it, and there is no short cut to doing it by way of acquiring elsewhere the skill of thinking then applying it to philosophy. The mastery of any subject, the getting inside it, is the same as mastering its particular modes of thought. Learning at any level higher than the three Rs cannot be either a skill or a set of skills.

All the same, all this learning-skill stuff might be thought at worst harmless nonsense (though if education is devoted to making sense how can it tolerate nonsense?). But go on to the skills not needed for learning itself, and the shams may be vicious. Hereford College of Technology advertises an '8 week evening course' in 'Basic Counselling Skills'. 'So what exactly will I learn?' asked one section. Answer: 'active listening, exploring thoughts and feelings, use of language, empathy and the use of questions'. Somebody might actually need help from someone certificated in this course. Those who think empathy is a skill are unlikely to be able to share anyone's feelings. There must be human damage as a result of these shams.

But then again, the skills might be genuine and useful. On 21 October 1998 it was announced that in Sheffield, in the millennial year, would be established the University for Industry. According to Radio 4's *Today* programme, its aim was to 'promote basic literacy and numeracy skills'. 'Sounds like a good idea,' said James Naughtie, interviewing the country's first Professor of Life Long Learning. Quite possibly, though one wonders how many illiterate adults will be able to find their way to Life Long Learning. A good idea—but a *university*? If universities are there to teach you the three Rs, what are primary schools for?

*   *   *

But is not this just a peripheral muddle that leaves unscathed the basic offer of the universities to provide a trained workforce? The doubt that philosophers might not be quite as useful as dentists is answered by a different refinement of the concept of 'skill'. What the graduates have received is not skills only, but 'personal transferable skills'. How will the universities produce graduates guaranteed to increase GDP? By teaching you one useful skill in particular (like golf-course construction or tar-macadaming) but—and here is the beauty of it—a skill which will come in equally handy when you do something else. This is not quite the purely magical skill of learning skills mentioned above, though closely related, but is even more convenient. Any university degree whatever will give you 'the general (and therefore transferable) intellectual skills which lie at the heart of higher education'.[18] I first noticed the idea in one of the multi-signatured documents (a number of the signatories being philosophers) with which academics try to influence politicians:

All university Arts courses have vocational relevance in that, far more than present-day Science courses, they develop, and are recognised by employers to develop, certain skills valued over the whole range of industry, commerce, education and other services, and administration—skills such as the ability to cope with long cumbersome documents, the ability to express themselves clearly in a variety of contexts, and the ability to think on their feet.[19]

This idea appears in the *Charter* in the already quoted phrase 'students are taught transferable skills like problem-solving'; it would be impossible to justify the subsidies to Arts faculties by the *Charter*'s lights on any other assumption; and, as Blake, Smith and Standish report,

It is taken for granted [by the Green Paper on Lifelong Learning, 1998] that there is a significant corpus of skills or bodies of knowledge whose attainment facilitates performance in a range of significantly disparate activities, so that learning them makes the employee more readily switch to a different job ....[20]

This, too, is why (as my fourteen-year-old son reported from a Careers lesson) all university degrees are of equal status. Whatever skill you learn will be useful in itself (if, for instance, you want to manage a Pig Enterprise, take the course in Pig Enterprise Management), but because it is compounded out of elemental skills that are the same anywhere will also enable you, when you have one of the mid-career changes we are told to expect, to switch smoothly to Floristry or the teaching of History.

This is yet another thing that doesn't sound honest and isn't.

In the nature both of genuine academic thinking and of genuine skills, the offered programme does not and cannot work. 'Transferable skills' is a contradiction in terms. Skills are not transferable. I do the washing up most days and I vacuum-clean the house most weeks. I enjoy computer chess. I have just finished writing a book with an appendix on medieval grammatical categories which, I do hope, reads lucidly, but over which I sweated blood. I have (please God) become surprisingly clear-minded about medieval grammar, but alas there has been no consequent improvement in my chess, and I wash up in just the same way that I did before I proved that the Modistae did not discover the well-formed sentence. Why should this surprise anybody? Any skills involved are so called just because they can't be transferred. Learn how to mend your car engine and you will also learn how to work out the difference between stress and beat in English sixteenth-century metrics. As one trying to do both I assure you that neither gives any assistance at all with the other.

Some work with machines or with computers resembles other work with machines or computers, but that is not because skills are transferable but because some skills extend over more than one task.

Let us hope it is true that an educated person will have some general sense of tackling new problems different from an uneducated person's, though 'problem' is so vague as to be problematic. But as Carlyle said,

> Abbot Samson had no experience in governing; had served no apprenticeship to the trade of governing,—alas, only the hardest apprenticeship to that of obeying. ...But it is astonishing, continues Jocelin, how soon he learned the ways of business; and, in all sorts of affairs, became expert beyond others.[21]

This is not because lecturing in the schools, or the monastic life of poverty, chastity, obedience and prayer, formed a set of transferable skills, but because of the man Samson was after that discipline. This is one of the many places where education is in fact sharply distinct from training in skills.

Where actually, in the real world that the electronic faces are always telling us we must enter, are these transferable skills? A meeting of Birmingham tutors in continuing education was questioning the necessity always to be nagging mature students (who quite often do spare-time degree work for pure academic motives like wanting to master an academic subject) to accumulate 'credits'. The woman in charge said that testing all the time is necessary to make sure the students are acquiring the personal transferable skills to take back with them to the world of business. 'Yes, the Government says that,' I objected, 'but none of us believe it, do we?' After the obligatory apology for saying anything in favour of the then government, the reply was that she did believe in personal transferable skills. Asked for just one example, she gave her chairing of the meeting then in progress. Chair one meeting, I suppose, chair the lot. But if even chairing meetings is thought of as a skill, not an art, or not common sense, it is no wonder that so many meetings are badly run.

Another clue to what 'personal transferable skills' might be intended to refer to, beyond my guess 'reading, writing, and PC operation', was given when one of our HEFCW (Higher Education Funding Council for Wales) inspectors (see Chapter 6) pounced on a marginal comment made by one of my colleagues that cross-heads and bullet points are not appropriate to English essays. In the real world there are cross-heads and bullet points. *The Times* now obligingly saves us the trouble of reading its editorials ('long cumbersome documents'?) by giving the gist in one line at the top. This is communications skills, and if you can do it in Classics or Philosophy you can no doubt also do it in *Times* editorials. It was also intimated that our assessments were far too much based on the written word. We should be paying more attention to the skills of oral presentations (and no doubt to the eye-contacts and smiles which are so important a part of interview skills; one may smile and smile and be a villain).

Our Classics Department, similarly visited, prepared a leaflet to explain what personal transferable skills are. Some of these 'skills' are not even desirable, like 'make quick, appropriate decisions'; see 'the ability to think on their feet' above. An academic discipline is not the mental equivalent of speed-reading; in genuine academic thinking (as in ordinary life) it may not be possible to solve a problem against the clock. The Classics Department included things like 'show resourcefulness' and the even more immediately relevant 'withstand and deal with pressures', which would be useful if the phrases were not too vague to say anything, but also 'explain clearly' and 'give appropriate examples'. This is a version of the *Charter*'s 'problem solving' and is necessary to the whole programme. Learn how to solve problems in one context and carry over the skill to another. The reason why, as already reported, this does not work, is that what constitutes a solution of a problem in one subject will not in another. 'Explanation', as Aristotle recognized, will vary with context. Even if there were anything here properly called skill it would not be transferable. The sense of what examples are appropriate must belong within a particular discussion.

Transferable skills remain the foundation on which the new university is built, and are about to be inserted into the old. The North Commission is to impose them on Oxford, 'including computer literacy and leadership', along with '"non-examination-based" forms of assessment',[22] in order to 'meet the demands of employers'. Does it really require any penetration to see that computer skills and leadership do not belong in the same category, or even that one of these can be taught and the other can't? Whether Oxford retains its own leadership after the imposition of transferable skills remains to be seen.

If there are no such things as personal transferable skills, the consensus reason for supporting the Arts subjects collapses. We hope it need not follow that the university must be entirely abolished, but to the extent that it is supposed to be a direct preparation for wealth-acquisition that does follow. This belief in an *organon* of transferable skills may, however, go some way to explaining the sort of farce I heard of when a man with a degree in Management Consultancy turned up to run a newly-privatized power station and had no idea what to do.

Another part of the current political rhetoric about the competitive world of the next millennium flatly contradicts the part about transferable skills, for it is often recognized that skills are not transferable, that training in one process will not do anything to prepare you for other processes; we must therefore be ready and willing to retrain. (Readiness is a disposition not a skill.) Macdonald's, the worldwide fast-food chain, employs chefs who (I am told, though I have not confirmed the information) are always retrained and duly certificated by Macdonald's University as fit to cook in any Macdonald's on the face of the earth. (The training programme takes two days.) The assumption is not that they have skills which can be transferred, but that the two days will give them brand new skills.

During the general election campaign of 1997, the lecturers' union, the AUT, obtained from all the establishment parties statements of higher education policy. Unsurprisingly, they were virtually indistinguishable. Labour and the Conservatives agreed that (i) as Gillian Shephard put it, 'many will switch career more than once in their lifetime,' which demands 'flexibility' (David Blunkett's version: the demand for 'innovative and creative workforces'). On the other hand, (ii) Mrs Shephard promised to 'ensure that they are equipped with the skills ... needed by the labour market of the 21st century' (Labour: 'highly skilled ... workforces'). The skills are precisely what will have to be relearned if we are to have flexibility; they will serve only in the first job, after which new skills will have to be learnt. The complete self-contradictory propositions therefore ran: Conservative—'the skills and flexibility needed by the labour market' (if skills needed, flexibility not needed); Labour—'highly skilled, innovative and creative workforces' (if creative and innovative, no need to be highly skilled).

Even if personal transferable skills are a con-trick, the skills the universities teach must be genuine? Some (we have a list in Chapter 9) do look useful, though most would have been beneath the dignity of a polytechnic. If you want to sell scent and have the leisure not to learn the trade while working at it, perhaps Perfumery Business will give you some good advice. Then if you wish to branch out into mail order, Packaging will come into its own. But World Studies? Will they give you the skill to deal with the World?

The ex-universities sometimes lose *both* their own true role of providing opportunities for thought, *and* the polytechnics' true role of training in the higher reaches of useful knowledge, *and* the adult-education sorts of low-grade usefulness; for they lay on courses which, without making any pretence to thought, are not, either, at any level, useful.

Penguin sent me a catalogue called *Essential Reading for Women*.[23] This was aimed at the growing Women's Studies market. 'Women's' is surely a dative, meaning studies for women; if so it confesses in its title that it has students but neither subject nor object. University College, London was offering in the year 2000 'taster' courses for prospective students on 'Women in Mathematics', 'Women in Earth and Planetary Sciences' and 'Women in Engineering (2 days residential)'. Would any knowledge of maths be required to follow the first or of engineering for the last? Is the interest supposed to be psychological? historical? What is the aim of the 'women's studies' in terms either of thought or of usefulness?

'Women's Studies' has grossly reintroduced sex discrimination into universities by way of the repulsive and untrue principle that some academic activity is restricted to members of one sex:

> Their anthology ... has no male contributors, and all its essays deal either with theoretical questions or with the work of women writers. This woman-centred approach has now become the dominant trend within Anglo-American feminist criticism.[24]

'Woman-centred' cannot but remind us of 'child-centred' (though it has not yet become the dominant trend that children's books are written by children), and with that gives the even more repulsive hint that women are the more imbecile sex. The other sex can sometimes, however, be admitted on a kind of honorary-imbecile basis.[25]

It is hardly to be pretended, is it, that Tourism is a subject calling for the disinterested pursuit of truth for its own sake? It does not follow, however, from the non-academic nature of the activity that anything useful is going on. Can Tourism even be made to sound as if it is of any use to the local boarding-house keepers (who in fact mock it)?

If only a few students are sitting an exam it is labour-saving to amalgamate several groups into one exam hall, which can become a sort of microcosm of the new university. In one such, the handful of English students who had opted to read some Chaucer (unread by the rest) were alongside a few students writing on French Modernist Poetry, and more than a dozen on Language and Reality, no doubt discussing Plato, Rorty and so on; but the bulk, 80 or 90, drawn from the Faculties of Engineering, Science and Arts, and pursuing courses in 'Business Studies, Management Science, European Business Studies, European Management Science, American Management Studies, Modern Languages with Business Studies [and/or the still catch-all subject], Geography', were sitting a three-hour paper called Tourism Studies.[26]

A misdistribution of papers to confront the Language and Reality philo-sophers with this one might have led to interesting academic results. The answers that could have been made, in a sort of way, to some of the questions, could only have been Arts-faculty kinds: opinion based on impressions or experience, or refined common sense. This was evidently not what the setters had in mind; the questions were all invitations to be pseudo-scientific:

1 Explain briefly what is meant by each of the following:
   (a) Tourism destination segmentation
   (b) Sustainable tourism development
   (c) Carrying capacity (in relation to tourism development)
   (Each part of the question carries one third of the marks.)

2 Enumerate and discuss the dimensions of the tourism industry and their interrelationships with each other.

The dimensions: as if of a warplane. They must really be arbitrarily decided by the experts in Tourism. Tourism is to be defined as what is discussed in the Department of Tourism. Arbitrary definition naturally leads to pseudo-scientific treatment of very vague matters. 'With positive host–guest interaction and, therefore, socio-cultural impacts, can tourism become a worthy effort towards fostering world peace? Cite examples to support your answer.' The one-word answer to that is 'No'; otherwise it is the kind of 'question' that would actually be better treated in a primary school, where the debates may be at their own level quite sensible and unmarred by academic cant and pomposity.

This examination couldn't in any way provoke to thought. Really to do academic work in this examination would be to reject the questions. If I were recruiting for a tourist agency I would consider a completed course in Tourism a positive drawback. It would certificate something worse than a simple waste of time, namely that the graduate had successfully 'taken on board' a lot of pretentious waffle, with the likely upshot of enhanced self-importance and salary expectations.

Tourism may be thought to be a sitting duck (though it's worth insisting that the mansion-house of the goodly family of the Sciences should not breed sitting ducks), but what about Business Management? Is not that directly useful?

'Management', though it pretends to be a subject teachable at university level, is actually one of the great bluffs of the age, along with its first cousin skills. The two together, management-skills, is a double-whammy that few of the recipient 'customers' can resist. But where is the definable content or method that makes Management a subject? And how can it avoid the gross fallaciousness of supposing that the organization of human beings is a collection of general skills that can be taught on courses?

Management magazines being amongst the ephemera discarded on railway trains, I have sampled a few, and am still surprised that they bear out so consistently my prediction that they *must* be childish. Pick up examples on any inter-city. If we must have one quoted:

> As part of the National Health Service drive to implement Opportunity 2000—the Business in the Community initiative to get more women into management posts— senior NHS women have been given the chance to learn vital management skills.
>
> The women, a mixture of clinicians and managers, spent three days exploring The Industrial Society's unique five way management model. This looks at managing not only those who report to us, but also managing ourselves, our colleagues, those above us and the strategic picture.[27]

Perhaps this should be recommended to the Church of England, which seems to be having some difficulty managing 'ourselves' (some of its members), and even more in managing 'those above us' (God). The uniqueness claimed for The Industrial Society's 'model', I regret to report, does not consist in its absolute meaningless. That is something it shares with the rest.

Meanwhile, in the 'real world' of commerce, which does effectively confirm or contradict the judgements of investors by way of share prices, 'BTR was built by one man—Sir Owen Green—on a single premise: that management was a generic skill, and that good managers could manage anything. In the end, this proved false ....'[28] See 'The idea that a good manager can manage any business has been largely discredited.'[29] If so, what is taught at management schools?[30]

And what about a Centre for European Business Studies? Well, business studies of any sort—and what is added to them by 'European': is European Business somehow academically different from American Business? When I asked in the College *Newsletter* nobody told me. (The members of the Centre maintain a large output of what they call 'double-blind-refereed papers',[31] which one takes to be publications adjudicated by experts blind in both eyes.) 'Fatuous non-university subjects' was a phrase in a letter the *Newsletter* did print from a much-respected professor of Geology, whose subject has been got rid of in the college, about Tourism and Business Studies.[32] Nobody tried to refute him.

Again, we may be thought to be picking off the unhealthy stragglers on the periphery of the useful herd. But everything we have said of Football Management or the poor little European Business School at Swansea applies *a fortiori* to the Oxford Business School, the development of which made a long-running story in *The Financial Times*. 'Oxford University wants a leading MBA course but academics oppose the £40m project.' At last, I thought, a genuine debate. They will surely not let Oxford down to the level of Harvard. At Oxford they still know that there is no intellectual substance in business schools? This, however, was not to be the subject of the debate. The building proposed is to be 'on a greenfield site in the heart of the city'. It was an environment issue, not an academic one. That sharp journal was not on the *qui vive* for signs of academic nervousness from the business school. They were there, however. The same issue carried a letter from the Chairman of the Council of the School of Management Studies, University of Oxford, in which he declared his hope

> that as Oxford, and even Cambridge, wholeheartedly develop their business schools, more of our brightest students will perceive a career in business as a respectable intellectual challenge, and thereby increase the quality of our national management resource.

(Though if, as he also hoped, the students come from across the world, we shall also be increasing the quality of the management resource of our competitors.) There is room for improvement, then, and not all the brightest students manage to notice the respectable intellectual challenge?

The following week, the dons voted no. 'Some dons fear that academic freedom would be restricted by the foundation.'[33] This, however, was because the benefactor whose millions were to endow the school had prudently allotted to himself 'controlling influence on the foundation', not because nothing calling itself a Business School can possibly have any academic standards—a remark no doubt too ungentlemanly for Oxford. The following year the dons relented and the prestigious development is to go ahead by which the great university dangerously recognizes as belonging to it a set of activities which are neither inductions to thought nor to useful skills.

If Oxford goes, can Cambridge be far behind? 'The course is particularly attractive to overseas students', at £17,500 a year.[34] Is the idea then that our national economy gets the £17,500 and is then further advantaged by the sending back to Asia, the USA etc of competitors crippled by the management course?

In our less ambitious way at Swansea we offered 'Evening Programmes for Management Development'[35] about things like 'Project structures and features', 'Planning of projects: estimating costs and duration' and 'Computers in project management'—which might all be common sense or, more likely, common sense adulterated by jargon—for which the fee for ten consecutive Thursday evenings was a more modest £220.

The one sure thing about the relation to wealth creation of both expensive Cambridge and downmarket Swansea is that sums of money make their way from individuals and/or their employers to the universities and their employees. If any useful skill is involved it is in the extraction of £17,500 and £220 respectively.

For though many university departments can have nothing to do with either thought or usefulness they do have a function, and an economic one at that: to increase the size of universities by getting more money from government, students and students' parents. This is the one and only genuine bit of economic growth inspired by the new university. Sometimes this is said with surprising frankness. 'On the question of research, this College has been in the forefront of expansion with the express purpose of providing additional funds with which we could bring in active new staff.'[36] The universities do contribute to the local economies by employing labour, but in much the same way (though without the justification of meeting human needs) as old folks' homes and prisons.

The very worst thing in the post-university—and that is saying something—is the appropriation to and by universities of the styles of 'marketing'. They 'market' their own courses; they lay on courses in Marketing. Put the university prospectuses in the same folder as the holiday brochures and see if you can tell the difference.

The corruption of language naturally comes to a head in the departments that create themselves out of it.

> The College is pleased to announce the establishment of the British Rail Chair of Marketing in the Department of Management Science and Statistics. Welcoming the announcement the Principal said 'Both the College and British Rail view this appointment as the next vital step in the development of Business and Management research and teaching activities at Swansea.'
>
> The new professor will provide a full undergraduate option in marketing for business students....[37]

Marketing is persuading people to buy goods and services. Sometimes, coincidentally, this may be done by pointing out some truths about the goods and services, but the persuasion is the defining factor. A genuine university could not conceivably find room for such a chair, supposedly the final mark of recognized academic status: it would have to be called British Rail Professor of Lying.

It may seem unduly heavy to invoke Socrates again, but let us bear in mind that the institutions we are considering were quite recently supposed to take to their limits and beyond the serious thought of which the human race is capable. Socrates was put to death for making the worse appear the better reason, and for corrupting youth. History has vindicated the judgement of his friends that Socrates was not guilty, and that on the contrary he had been following reason as far as he could and wherever it led. But had he pleaded guilty, he would not have thought the punishment unduly severe.

A bad style will make the worse appear the better reason, and if this happens in 'the education service' the result cannot but be the corruption of youth. The marketer, interested in persuasion not truth, exactly fits the bad name that Socrates tried to give rhetoricians and sophists. The effort to persuade regardless of truth is by definition an enemy of that pursuit of truth which has always been the inspiration of the university. It again does not follow that the aim has been achieved. Not everybody who wants to be a professional liar succeeds—not even when the skill is dignified by the name of 'spin doctoring'.

*   *   *

So ... we have achieved Newman's ideal, and allowed Pig Enterprise Management and Wine Studies to sprout as new shoots of the one tree of knowledge. Contemplated by the human mind they form part of the one large system. There are no natural or real limits between part and part; Lighting Design is ever running into Knitwear Studies, and both into Sanskrit.

In the bad old days, the Newbolt Report quotes a witness as saying, 'education was purely utilitarian; its object was limited to giving children the instrument for earning a living.'[38] The compulsive 'modern' in new educational policy only falls short of indicating a return to the bad old days because then what was taught was genuinely useful. The 'modern' points to something worse, because the modern utilitarianism only makes a promise that cannot be kept.

A degree in a non-subject will not qualify anybody to do anything, not even to become a successful con-man. The more likely result is demoralization. It is almost equally untrue that a degree even in a genuine subject will do as much to prepare anyone for running a company or a factory as experience of the relevant concern.

What happened was not that the polys became universities but that both polytechnics and universities went on using a name the significance of which had evaporated even in the act of immense proliferation. Are there 261 universities in this country, or two, or none?

6   How to Run a New University in Seven Easy Lessons

Idleness is a disease which must be combated; but I would not advise a rigid adherence to a particular plan of study. I myself have never persisted in any plan for two days together.

Dr Johnson[1]

HAVING ATTAINED THE FIRST, overriding objective, and got funding, management's challenge is to run the new university so as to get it well up the league tables while satisfying the highest international standards, and the customers.

The word 'customer' appears three times in the short Introduction to the *Charter* signed by the then Secretary of State, and recurs throughout. Not long since, at the doctor's you were a patient, on the train a passenger, at the solicitor's a client, and at a university an undergraduate or student. Now everybody is a customer, everywhere, even on the trains. This may seem common sense. If the relations are basically the same in all these cases why not use the same word? (Has the usage extended yet to penitents in the confessional or prisoners?) But *are* they basically the same?

To customers are supposed to be delivered goods or services, in this case education. Education is obviously not goods, but must it follow that it is a service? So the Minister thought: 'Universities and colleges are more and more aware of the need to deliver high-quality services, responding to the needs and demands of customers.'

Service itself, which may cover quite an area, has a core idea that something is done for somebody in return for a fee: a case argued, an illness treated, hair cut, a meal served, possibly, even, a skilled trade taught to an apprentice. University education does not do anything for anybody. We know in advance what we expect from a service. No student knows except in the most embryonic way what is going to happen to him as a result of education.

What happens in the real thing is that students join in a community of scholars, by practising a style of thinking which they demonstrate in examinations. How is that a service? Where a service is being offered, the university has ceased to function, because nobody is being inducted into thought, and the real university is replaced by the sham. In the sham, the customers are to be satisfied: as follows.

(i) TEACH

> Instruction, that mysterious communing of Wisdom with Ignorance, is no longer an indefinable tentative process ... but a secure, universal, straightforward business, to be conducted in the gross, by proper mechanism, with such intellect as comes to hand.[2]

The service universities promise to provide to the customers can only be the delivery of knowledge and skills, which can only be done by teaching, as Lady Catherine's 'regular instruction' is now called. A way of downgrading a university is to turn it into a 'teaching only' institution, that is, with no research going on: so 'teaching' must be the irreducible basic university activity, to which 'research' adds a touch of upmarket class.

'Teaching', unluckily, though the word is universally used without qualms, is not what happens in the real university. 'I see the word "teaching" in inverted commas,' wrote Leavis; 'I don't like it, because of the suggestion it carries of telling—authoritative telling.'[3] This perhaps derives from Quiller-Couch's pointed quotation of the terms on which he had been appointed professor, 'But I ask you to note the phrase "to promote, so far as may be in his power, the study"—not, you will observe, "to teach"....'.[4] Rush Rhees 'wrestled with philosophical problems before the class as if for the first time.'[5] That is university work, but 'teaching'?

There are times when 'authoritative telling' does properly come in. Characteristically it is introductory work. I am permanently grateful to my colleague and friend David Parry for teaching me some Old Norse and for enormously improving my Old English. That certainly involved a great deal of 'teaching', the well-judged authoritative imparting of information and correction of mistakes. The sign of the success was that towards the end of the Old Norse course I began to be able to form an opinion and join in a discussion. But as soon as I was capable of making any kind of judgement of the difference between the *Vǫlsunga* and *Laxdæla* sagas, teaching in the primary sense was at an end, the introductory phase was over and—I want to say—the real university work was starting. I am not now the equal of David Parry on Old Norse and never shall be, but I can talk to him about it with some common basis in knowledge, and it is this talk, if anything, that is going to get me further in the subject—as well, possibly, as him. There is no positive good, and an open invitation to confusion, if we stretch the word 'teaching' to cover this kind of discussion.

Tutorials (now abolished) were a central part of my work over the years. A small group, a tutor and perhaps only one student or perhaps as many as four, meets often enough to get to know one another and discuss, often on the basis of a student essay, some question connected with English literature (and in my experience the smaller the scope for one tutorial the better). I have had some of my best and some of my worst university experiences in tutorials. I used to forbid notebooks in tutorial because the usual meaning of the appearance of the notebook is to turn the conversation of the tutorial into a teaching hour. In goes the transferred information or, worse, the transferred opinions.

I know what it means to teach French, also to teach pupils, but what does it mean to teach *Macbeth* or *The Rainbow* (suchlike phrases being commonly heard in the new university), if not to give students a, or even the, correct way of taking a book? And what is that but, one way or another, the replacement of thought by indoctrination? or of something yet lower down the intellectual scale, the mere repetition of a tutor's notes?

The quality of teaching in my department was assessed by a team led by a management consultant (an ex-chemist) sent down from HEFCW. We were all told as soon as we heard of this visitation that we could give up all hope of any academic work for the next six months, preparing for it, and some of my hardest-working colleagues duly spent their long vacation manufacturing minutes, mission statements and the like for the perusal of the Assessors. The latter told us what to expect. 'The assessment is concerned with the reception and conveyance of material by and to the students.'[6] The customers will have material conveyed to them and will convey it back to us by way of assessed essays or examination scripts. This two-way shifting of information is to be expected if we are teachers and they taught. Simultaneously a number of us were concerned about the previous summer's Shakespeare scripts, which had been doing exactly that and were in consequence at once eccentric and deadly dull. One of the worst things that happens when marking exam scripts is to have one's not-very-inspired thoughts conveyed back to one in script after script. Did I really say that? Oh! I probably *did*! There is all the difference in the world between that and the still exhilarating experience of reading a script which shows that a student has really listened and made something of what one was driving at. The usual sign is either some taking further of a lecturer's line of thought or some disagreement. The ordinary word for this activity is discussion, and it cannot subsumed in 'teaching'.

During my final session in the University of Wales I was asked seriously, by two students on separate occasions, whether they were allowed to use the first person singular in essays. Their tutors in the first year had recommended the third-person (Mary-Bennet-style) appeal to those popular authorities 'many critics', whom they were to repeat uninspected. The essays that year were the worst I have ever seen, being full of indiscriminate quotation of second-rate criticism as authoritative, and showing no sign of thinking (thought is individual). The university that tries to reduce thought to teaching actually stifles thought.

In universities, undergraduates read for degrees, with what help they can get from the senior members. (Some of the best students virtually ignore the senior members without being visibly the worse for it.) The mark of progress is for the students to be able to continue the intellectual activity that constitutes their subject beyond anything they are taught. Different ways of offering help are appropriate in different subjects. Sometimes this goes well, sometimes badly, and it is never possible to predict good years or bad years in advance, until the university is degraded to a mechanism for conveying information and has ceased to be a university.

What I wanted to say about 'teaching' came to me one somnolent afternoon when I was training to be an 'appraiser' (what *that* is is something we can be spared); as phrases about 'performance' and 'system' and 'management' floated around, and as I shut off and looked through the window at the warm May mist over Swansea Bay, a sort of catch came into my mind:

> Thought
> can't be taught.

(Elizabeth Bennet would not have put it like that, but I hope she would agree.) If so, 'teaching' cannot be the central, defining activity of the university. Or, as Newman put it, 'Gentlemen ... you have come, not merely to be taught, but to learn.'[7]

(ii) IN COURSES

If our customers are, like the Bertram girls, to be professionally instructed, how is it to be done? What can be taught? The answer, obviously, is *courses*. Anything called a course can be planned as to content and method, and then delivered by way of teaching. At the end of the ideal course you will ideally know and be tested on just what the course has taught you, no more and no less. So it is a full answer, in the twenty-first century, to any objection that a graduate is lacking in knowledge of some part of his subject (Shakespeare, let's say, in the case of an English graduate) for the graduate to say, 'It wasn't on the course.' Courses also have the great advantage of being inspectable (see section v). The quality of a course can be assured whether or not the course has anything to do with education.

This contradicts an older fashion, when we used to be told that learning should be 'heuristic', but then, you can't have everything. I was subjected to some pressure (not, to be fair to my former colleagues, much) because I always refused to publish a contents list of my Chaucer option. We used to spend the first few weeks sampling the poet's very various kinds of poetry. Then I asked the students to go on sampling while we discussed the dream poems. At the end of the first term I then asked them what they would like to discuss next. Occasionally we had to resort to votes. This seemed to me a good way, and one in the spirit of university study, of conducting the class; but it couldn't be called a 'course'.

The whole conception of a statable course belongs to the useful, instrumental knowledge which we deny to be the province of the university. Machine maintenance is rightly taught in courses. The knowledge aimed at can be described in advance, and the aim is simply to attain it. University knowledge is not structurable in the kind of way demanded. Leavis's seminars had no structure whatever: they were determined by the relative urgency of what he was trying to think about.[8]

I was glad to see at the Cambridge Music Faculty open day that even in a subject where a fairly well-defined body of material is to be covered, titles of series of lectures were such as 'European Counterpoint 1580–1750', which does give scope for different emphases and treatments.

The new university, however, can operate only in courses of a different and more modern kind.

(iii) WITH AIMS, OBJECTIVES AND GOALS

According to the *Charter*, 'Your university or college should explain the aims and structure of your course.'[9] This in fact applies at all levels of education, from the demands made by national testing of seven-year-olds up through GCSE and A-level to honours degrees. If information is to be conveyed to and from the students, *what* information must be precisely specified. (The New A-level schemes have dropped the old name 'syllabus' and are called 'specifications'.) So the statable aim is to convey such-and-such information.

Examining boards therefore go into detail about what their aims are, at GCSE or degree level. University prospectuses now state the aims and objectives and goals both of the whole institution and of particular courses. The style for formulating such aims shows, unfortunately, that whatever the paraphrasable content, the real aim is to make nonsense. There used to be an organization called PICKUP 'on campus'. Ours exhorted us to 'Make sure your college's strategic and tactical aims include improved performance goals, more flexible procedures and more creative thinking....'[10] To the small extent that this means anything at all it just means 'do better', but nobody with any advice on how to do better could possibly put it like this.

To make us take 'Goals' with proper seriousness a refinement of vocabulary was needed. Aims, for instance, have to be distinguished from objectives. One official document told me on the authority of HEFCW that aims are 'what the institution wishes to become or achieve in measurable terms' while objectives are 'the means and methods by which these aims are realised'.[11] In English an objective cannot mean a method. It is always a bad sign when bureaucrats resort to the redefinition of common words. In common speech aims and objectives are not far off synonymous.

If a subject is well studied a department has no further aim, and any general statements about what 'well studied' means are vapid without the actuality of the study itself.

In extreme cases the effort to state an academic aim becomes a self-contradiction. If the aims could be clearly stated, the course would already have finished. 'What do you say in your new book?' I once heard one academic ask another after a meeting of the Arts Faculty. 'You will have to read it,' was the inevitable reply.

Practical questions are of course important. Is most of the work done in tutorials or lectures? What is the library like? But it is logically impossible for the student to understand the 'structure of the course' in advance of reading; the structure is internally related to the subject. On the other hand it is quite possible for a student to make his own coherence within a subject. Oddly enough this can hardly be said in the age of infinite student choice.

The 'mission statement' that accompanied Dr R. S. Thomas's letter set out the aims (not the objectives) of University College, Swansea. They included, as well as the already quoted 'to facilitate regional economic growth and national wealth creation' a final one (of only three) even more splendid: 'to contribute towards meeting the needs of society as a whole.'[12] Imagine this even in the next manifesto of New Labour: 'to meet the needs of society as a whole.' Like what? Breakfast, dinner, lunch and tea/Are all the human frame requires? or do we also need the National Lottery? Turn it into a party game: give an answer to the question what it could possibly mean to meet the needs of society as a whole.

Must there not be something wrong with an institution devoted to thought which announces as its aim something that anyone without the benefits of higher education can see at a glance is quite vacuous? But any statement of 'goals' will necessarily be either vacuous or tautologous or just plain wrong.

It is better to avoid phrases like 'the goal of a university', as a road liable to subsidence. The aim, the objective and the goal of the university is just to be a university; the aims of the departments are to pursue their respective subjects as best they can. Improvement should always be striven for, but just as part of the ordinary well-being of the university, not as a goal. A goal can be scored, but there is no point at which the university can pass a resolution to the effect that its goal has been attained, and that the effort to improve is no longer necessary. On the other hand there is a real possibility of a university's losing its nature, even as part of its aiming at goals, if the goal is facilitating regional economic growth and the like.

Many human institutions are like this. The goals defined are either plati-tudinous or false. A nation has no goal as a nation except to go on realizing its character. If a nation confuses this with reforms or improvements or party politics and says the nation must be democratic (or whatever) the goal is false; if the goal is something like making the national life better and more whole-some the use of 'goal' just leads to tautology. It is even possible for an unlucky academic politician to be both platitudinous and false at the same time, as when it is said that the goal of the university is to aid the national economy. (The word-processor keeps trying to make me write 'gaol'.)

To these conceptual objections to 'goals' I have to add a theological one. 'First define your goal, then set about achieving it,' an engineer exhorted us; he naturally joined 'goals' and 'customers':

> 'Quality' is defined as 'fitness for purpose', the customers indicating the purpose, the educators providing the fitness. Put more precisely, this amounts to 'the specifying of worthwhile educational goals and enabling students to achieve them'.[13]

'Worthwhile' is a slide: there is no more need for these customers *qua* customers to keep to the worthwhile than the customers of Woolworths, nor is there any indication of how they are to recognize what is worthwhile. But let us stick to 'goals'. The once-hackneyed tag from Burns about the best-laid schemes of mice and men is relevant. Even in the Soviet Union the aims of five-year plans were not always attained. And, 'The good that I would, I do not, but the evil which I would not, that I do.' Giving the universities' intentions the benefit of all the doubts, we know what road good intentions proverbially pave. 'To this project ... it can only be objected, that, like many projects, it is, if not generally impracticable, yet evidently hopeless, as it supposes more zeal, concord and perseverance, than a view of mankind gives reason for expecting.'[14] The talk about goals and objectives has too little sense of the necessary chanciness of education. One can do one's best to prepare a lecture and still give a bad one. Sometimes, even, it seems afterwards that what made the lecture bad was the effort at preparation or the need to keep to aims and objectives. Conversely, to be at one's best at one's least premeditated is a very common experience, and not just in universities.[15]

What staff might look to be doing in universities is some thinking ourselves, if we can manage it, and some discussion and conversation (that is, thinking in groups) with our students. That's all, but it will be impossible if we also have to set ourselves the goals of achieving well-defined course objectives and of customer satisfaction. But what a difference it would make to the world if the universities were allowed to pursue the goal of going on being universities!

(iv) IN MODULES

If, however, universities are there to teach the magical personal transferable skills by way of imparting information through courses with well-defined aims, it probably follows, as declared by a Swansea document, that 'The quality of teaching provision may be enhanced if modular degree programmes are introduced.'[16] A 'module' does indeed sound like a manageable, goal-directed, teachable object.

> DEFINITION OF MODULARITY
> ... reduced to its basic form, it may be described as:
>> division of a degree scheme into individual components, each with its own learning goal;
>> assessment of student performance in each component during or as soon as possible after the completion of teaching associated with it;
>> frequent feedback to students on their academic performance.[17]

Degrees in the future will consist of a certain number, usually 36 (yes, 36), of modules, added up.

I have never met an academic who believed that modularization will improve the university academically, that is, in its nature, and no academic advantages were mentioned in the list of pros and cons given by the Swansea *Report of the Teaching Committee on Modularisation and Semesterisation*.[18] In fact that ten-page document nowhere mentioned principles at all. My own Dean of the Swansea Arts Faculty (who steamrollered modularization through the Faculty in gross defiance of the Faculty's majority opinion and was rewarded with a Vice-Principalship) remarked that 'there are no convincing academic arguments in favour of [modularization],' and that 'On a purely academic basis ... I have not seen any argument which leads me to believe that modularity has any intrinsic academic superiority.' Though he is an Egyptologist not a logician, it is still remarkable that he thought that this follows: 'Therefore, for me, the issue has to be decided on the basis of practical considerations.' The possibility that modularization might academically be a change for the worse did not enter his head, though he heard that opinion repeatedly argued, and though in one of the discussions the practicalities resolved themselves, for him, into damage limitation.

Comments were invited on the question, sent top-down, as to what progress we could make with modularization. (We were never asked what we thought of it in principle.) My own comment in a letter to the same Dean was:

> Amongst the possible objections to modularity [mentioned in a circulated document] is:
>
> [Modularity] may lead to a lack of coherence in a student's scheme of study.

This is seriously understated. It follows a definition of modularity as 'division of a degree scheme into individual components, each with its own learning goal'.

If a degree scheme can be so divided, no questions of coherence can arise. If a degree scheme cannot be so divided without loss of coherence, lack of coherence is not something that modularity may (or may not) 'lead to', but is part of the definition of modularity. Modularity *per se* is, in these circumstances, incoherence.

Item 5 on the same agenda, also from the Academic Board, a report on the 'New Procedures for the Approval of Degree Schemes', told us that 'In putting into effect any arrangements for the approval of schemes of study to be introduced in October 1992 or thereafter' the first principle that has to be 'addressed' is 'The need to preserve and enhance academic standards'.

If this is meant seriously it automatically rules out modularity in the subjects I know anything about, the degree schemes of which do aim at coherence, because modularity by definition renders them incoherent.

(Dear non-academic Reader: guess which if any of the quoted phrases about academic standards and modularity were meant to be taken seriously.) This communication having received no attention, we expand it a little.

I am told that one of the explanations of the old fact that some doctors 'do men to dyen through their drinkes · ere destinee it wolde' is that medical degrees are traditionally constructed on modular lines: one set of memorizings (information conveyed to and from the medic) for first MB, another for second MB and never the twain shall meet. Learn the brain and then forget it and learn the lungs and giblets and forget *them*. My only experience of this kind of thing was learning Linotype typesetting, which indeed was a course divided into parts (keyboard, casting, distribution etc); but all the time it was necessary to keep in mind what the parts were doing in the whole machine. Nobody would have thought of doing one bit without the rest, and if they had they certainly wouldn't have learnt Linotype operation and maintenance. Nor would the Linotype course have been turned into a degree scheme by the introduction of a bit of Greek tragedy or midwifery.

By the quoted definition of modularity, university studies must be divisible into discrete units, each with its own definable goal, teachable in 12-week courses some of which may be taken at different institutions, and which in principle can be mixed. This is a simple contradiction of the idea of a university subject. The mastering of a genuine subject does include some pondering and frequenting. The belief, for example, that one bit of a literature can be studied at degree level satisfactorily in 12 weeks, without a context of other such studies, is a nonsense. Nor is the nonsense confined to the Arts Faculty. In the top-of-the-league-table University of Northumbria the word 'unitization' is employed for the same thing, defined by a member of the Chemistry Department as 'the destruction of academic subjects'.

Even if modular degrees are awarded in genuine subjects rather than in indisciplined mixtures, the modular principle is vicious. It is obvious, for instance, that there is no sense in learning one bit of the grammar of a language in the hope that it will be self-sufficient. But hardly anything academically worth doing, *possibly* excluding mathematics and the mastery of musical techniques, can be reduced to discrete parts and then built up step by step, and even in these examples the steps have to be taken in order. In philosophy, you don't progress from the simpler problems to the more difficult. As soon as you ask questions in a certain way you are doing philosophy, however primitively. Progress consists of asking them more intelligently or more insistently or from a base in a more thorough knowledge of philosophizing. And although different areas of the subject can conveniently be examined separately (aesthetics, moral philosophy, epistemology, logic), I don't believe that the parts can be done properly in isolation, without the kind of analogies, comparisons, glimpses from one bit to another that make the subject a whole. 'For him, philosophy was one subject, not a collection of specialisms.'[19]

Modularity, anyway, is supported not as a way of studying the academic subjects, but by the offer of infinite mixture. I read an American student's cv after noticing that her contributions to class discussion were at once strange and uninteresting. She was majoring in Health Care Studies but had also done a bit of mathematics somewhere and also, unless my memory is playing tricks, the ancient civilization of the Aegean islands. Now she was completing the all-roundness of her degree by studying women in medieval English literature. I only saw the last bit, but having read the print-out it didn't surprise me that she wasn't making much of the medieval women.

It may be that some bits of one subject can be used in another, including the study of a fragment of a literature; but in that case it still needs a different whole to belong to. Notoriously, in my subject, Chaucer and Langland used to be used (before they were judged too difficult) as sources for social history. Fair enough, as long as we know what is going on and as long as the sources are read with reasonable sensitivity. But studied in themselves (this is quite possible, despite the defeatist schools of critics who deny it), works of literature take time to sink in, they have to be compared with others, and with many other matters, in the formation of educated judgement. This is one reason why some 'taught MAs' are shallower than undergraduate work: they deal, hastily, with one bit of something. Educated judgement is simply not analysable into discrete fragments.

Take the case of Classics. This consists of the study of Latin and Greek, in particular the literatures, but with a good deal of history, some philosophy, and since the great generation of Jane Harrison, much anthropology. The point of the study is to put these things together, to see, for instance, that the study of the Latin language acquires a new sense if it is part of the study of Classics.

But still, everything does have to start somewhere. Perhaps a bit of philosophy or a bit of Latin is better than none? *Soit*, especially at school, where beginnings are made—or, in the case of the University of Wales, Swansea, Part One, with its excellent Greek, Latin, Welsh, Italian for beginners, and an introduction to philosophy that presupposes no previous acquaintance with the subject.

Universities, however, are for taking things further. Graduation is a certificate that a student may now go all lengths of research if he wishes, not that he has made three dozen starts.

Modules are generally designed to last 12 weeks with, in unsemesterized universities, a vacation coming during the 12; the teaching will normally occupy two hours a week or less. Modules belong with 'teaching' because each of the starts will have to be in a course that has been intensively taught. What can be done in 24 hours spread over 12 weeks? Crash courses, introductions for students totally ignorant—computer programming, grammar of Old English or whatever. What can be reliably expected in subjects taught in modules that do not lend themselves to crash-introductions is short bursts of jargon. It is easy enough to pick up an academic jargon in 12 weeks without taking in with it any hint of the possibly serious thought of which the jargon is a deformity.

The great attraction of modularity is said to be the freedom of choice it gives students (and consequently the pressure on course tutors to be popular). Even if modular courses are in some sense chosen, regimentation in the following of courses is a *sine qua non* of modularization, for it is only the following of a course, as against demonstration of thinking about a subject, that can constitute completion of a module. The awarding of a print-out of details of courses completed, with grades, instead of the old-fashioned overall class of degree, is already held in check in this country only by employers' distrust of it. A departmental power-broker to the committee that is his special creation, on the effect of modularization on the presently permitted transfers from one subject to another during the first month of the university year: 'That degree of freedom's gonna disappear.' [20]

The *Charter* exhorts students to attend lectures, which is more than I ever did. (My advice to students to ask themselves whether the lectures were as much use as the same time spent reading or talking once or twice got me into hot water.) But an ordinary lecture series is often by different people with various points of view, and will look to an examination which can be approached in various ways. Students will be able to pursue different interests and emphases on, say, Victorian Poetry, while showing knowledge of and intelligent interest in the subject. What happens when Victorian Poetry is treated as an option (an embryo module) with one Tutor offering one 'correct' point of view we shall see below.

Modularity may nonetheless look like a healthy step away from specialism. Subject boundaries are not rigid. Before we know where we are we find ourselves doing a bit of philosophy or history or even theology when we thought it was literary criticism. If the tree of knowledge is one, the more of it we climb the better. Plato and Aristotle must remain the ideals, and imagine either of them as a one-subject specialist! And what about Oxford Greats or Mods, combinations of subjects, or the Cambridge Tripos system, which is an open invitation to undergraduates to change subjects midway? Are they not proto-modules? The differences are that a tripos consists of two big bites at possibly different cherries, and that its aim is at putting the two together, for which the system presupposes sufficient general culture in the undergraduate. In the provinces, before general degrees were renamed joint honours, the joint honours degree was thought harder than single honours, and only the ablest students were permitted to sit for one.

Newman thought that the tree of knowledge is one, and the subjects are the branches. Modularity gives us a bunch of twigs but no tree.

Each Module, said the 'Minutes', 'attracts [*sic*] a *credit* which is related to its weight within the scheme' and 'can be a free-standing piece of work, or may have *pre-requisites* or *co-requisites* according to the particular scheme.' This is the attempt to disarm the objections I have been making. A judicious set of regulations will ensure that the modules will not be free-standing if their free-standingness would damage the coherence of the degree-scheme. Directors of studies will be appointed to guide the customers along paths which will often enough coincide with the old degree subjects. Damage-limitation will take some such forms, undertaken in the new names of counselling, guidelines and suchlike exercises of power without responsibility.

If my (commonly held) fears are alarmist, if the subjects are to be allowed to retain some coherence, would it not be better to say so and drop the modu-larity jargon? If the choices are not after all going to be free, why had we to go through the trauma?

But I just don't believe that modularity can be transformed into something coherent. It is beyond even the ingenuity of academic politicians to turn round so cleanly a system whose first principle is that the units are 'freestanding'. The first reason for modularization we were offered was: 'Students will have greater freedom to construct their own degree courses out of a wide range of elements.' As one academic put it,

> In the end though, the question is whether you are prepared to trust students (most of them, most of the time) to make sensible decisions in a relatively free intellectual environment. Most of the time they do, I'm glad to say—and since they're legally adults, it's only right that they should have the chance.[21]

By definition, though, undergraduate students are not mature enough to make their own syllabuses or to examine themselves. If they were they would not need a university. Sensible decisions presuppose an experience which by definition the students have not yet had. I also notice that *we* know what is sensible. Nothing can be done, however, if the decisions are not sensible. 'The integrating principle in other words is their interest rather than any presupposition on our part on what should be covered.' [22] This does to my certain knowledge cover the student of English literature uninterested in English poetry or Shakespeare or both. But why is this university equivalent of child-centred learning thought to have an integrating principle at all?

Modularity is obviously intended to make university subjects student-centred not subject-centred. The extreme example is the graduate in 'Independent Studies', i.e. a degree put together by the student, who designs projects and coursework to suit his interests, in order to emerge with a degree which makes no formal claim to coherence. Of course these are degrees without finals examinations.

> John Wakeford, director of the school of independent studies set up at the University of Lancaster in the early 1970s, argues that a reason for establishing it was to 'isolate people with wild ideas in one school and let them get on with it.' [His words not mine.]
> Modularisation of courses will bring many mainstream courses more in line with the Lancaster model as students compile unique degrees. [23]

The same article reports that 70 per cent of students completing these degrees at Lancaster get a first or an upper second. How such a degree can be meaningfully classified is a nice question which can only possibly be answered if we allow that to graduate is not to have mastered a coherent discipline. A practical question more in tune with the post-university is to inquire whether these degrees impress prospective employers, and if so why.

Choices of modules within subjects are usually made in ignorance. If a student has enough glimmerings and hints to be able to make an intelligent choice of subject, that is as much as can be hoped. As a medievalist I know what it is for the university to suffer from bogus freedom of choice: how many students, asked to choose one or two from 57 options, are going to plump for English Literature 1150–1250, the interest of which they are most unlikely to discover within the first month's work? (And it *is* very interesting. I know. So do the students who for various reasons have found themselves doing it.)

The subject has been transformed in the interests of 'freedom'. If we are free we shall decide for ourselves what to read, unhindered by élitism. It is not always realized even in universities how limited this freedom must be, just by the nature of publication and the size of libraries. Genuine freedom would be indistinguishable from chaos. In practice, students' choice is severely restricted by what academics are willing to 'teach'. Hence the Heinz-numbered modular options in the department I left. Fifty-seven is a large number of varieties but not compared with the number of possible topics.

Modularization in English in fact dictates a much more restricted 'canon' than the Cambridge English Tripos ever did (though with no guarantees against wild eccentricity) but forces the student to ignore much of it. So much you must read, but need read no more. And within each course there is no freedom whatever. The students are free to pick from Shakespeare, Crime Fiction etc, but in any of them they will be told exactly what to read and subjected to 'authoritative telling' about it.

In this way 'freedom of choice' reproduces just the circumstances which were first judged objectionable—except that the old dictation was largely imaginary (the Cambridge English Tripos has no set texts), the new very actual. The last unsurprising thing is that all the new freedom-imposers agree with each other. There are Marxist options but not fascist options, feminist courses but not anti-feminist courses, deconstruction but not reconstruction. As I write, the fashion is for New Historicism, the doctrine that old writings are never self-evidently interesting, but to be used as a mode of self-congratulation by us on our escape from previous incorrectnesses, as described by authority (see Chapter 8 for some examples). Such is the new freedom to study anything— provided it is studied in a politically correct manner and on the list. Students rapidly learn the various patters (or as a Canadian friend says, 'put in the sprin-kles') but God knows what if anything they think in their hearts.

The overwhelming *practical* argument for modularization is to get into line with the majority of European universities. If we continue unmodularized we shall be out on a limb. The vaunted academic independence of our universities routinely takes this form of the dread of being out of step. Recruits, as potential customers are also known, would think of finals-oriented degrees as old-fashioned; it is unthinkable that any recruit worth having would want to go anywhere old-fashioned. Yet simultaneously it is common knowledge that Oxford and Cambridge, which just won't have modularity, still have their pick. What happens to being in line with Europe if, as seems probable, the brave new 'Europe' breaks up even before it has been formed, we are not told. It is perhaps also worth asking, though nobody of academic standing seems to be doing so in public, how this squares with the repeated assurances that the 'European Union' is not aiming at a homogenized and uniform European culture, and why our great step towards European Union has to be by way of abandoning our tradition of half a millennium.

Modularity, we are told, has been successfully used in Germany and the USA for many years. Not all that long ago we would have turned up our noses. German academic life has always been much respected in England but it has not previously been thought good to turn the respect into imitation.

What cannot be denied is that modularity in principle dissipates exami-nations. Courses are examined piecemeal as they run or as soon as they are completed, sometimes after only 12 weeks in the first year of the university. There is no fortnight in a student's life during which he is required to show mastery of a subject. By the outgoing finals system, whole subjects were examined.

Students please note: the belief that one degree is as good as another in 'the real world' is fanciful. That is something we really have learned from the USA. Employers please note: a degree from a modularized British university will certify (reliably or not) that on 36 occasions the graduate has been able to exhibit, during or after 12-week courses, disconnected bits of what is judged by course tutors to be skill. It will certify nothing else.

(v) TOTAL QUALITY CONTROLLED

Naturally, the performance of the new university must be properly monitored. The *Charter* promises that the universities will be subjected to proper quality control, including in their examinations. Oh, by whom? Any inspector of an educational establishment is in a position of superiority to it. The inspector possesses the standards by which to judge the performance. Schools used to be in dread of surprise visits by HMIs because of the Inspectors' powers, but their authority was also generally respected. Universities, however, recognize no superiors in the intellectual world. They could only be inspected if there were a higher level of thinking by which to judge them. The system of external examining is quite different. Until it breaks down into tolerance (you pretend my jargon is acceptable and I pretend yours is: see Chapter 8) it maintains a common standard by the presence of scholars of one intellectual community at the deliberations of another. The external examiners, however authoritative, are peers, giving advice to a board which may nevertheless in the end reject it, not superiors giving instruction about intellectual standards. In an extreme case an external examiner may veto, but so may an internal. If examiners' meetings fail to maintain standards there is no remedy within the system, as we exemplify below (see Chapter 8).

So when the universities began to be inspected, in the 1990s, the word 'inspection' was not used inside the universities, though it appeared freely enough in the press. 'All universities are now subject to inspection by the funding councils of their research and teaching programmes.'[24] Phrases like 'quality audit' were brought in, and departments were instructed to produce a 'self-assessment document' in advance of the inspectors' visit, so that the fiction could be maintained that the assessors would judge only what the departments themselves claimed to be doing.

The HEFCW-appointed Assessors were coming, we were reassured, to adjudicate our 'teaching methods', not what is 'taught', and to place us in one of three categories, unsatisfactory, satisfactory or excellent.[25] We have already seen what they understand by 'teaching'.[26]

The dust was consequently removed from the computers (acquired for about £15,000 each, a year's salary for a junior member of staff, and which are never otherwise used) by which we can get at literary databases; feeble but attractively printed poems were hung, beautifully framed, in all the corridors, and the washbasin in the gents', cracked for many years, was renewed. (During one of the later financial crises that are normally a sign of the season of mists and mellow fruitfulness in universities, the thing not to be cut was preparations for Quality Assessment. Money was still available for window-dressing.[27])

My department duly produced its 'self-assessment document'. On the document itself I forbear comment, and on the visit, which included episodes like the sitting in on a few of my classes by a grim-faced lady phonetician, so strictly in the spirit of inspecting only method that she professed herself entirely ignorant of the subject of the seminar. As I mentioned, when the great moment arrived—would we be declared excellent or only satisfactory?—we were disappointed: because we did not lay claim to be 'teaching' the 'personal transferable skills' discussed above.

Universities are not only being inspected but, despite the self-assessment fiction, judged by standards not proper to them. A self-respecting university would treat the whole thing with open contempt, but the universities take the gradings seriously, presumably because applicants for admission do too. They are thought to be part of the Quality Assurance promised by the *Charter*.

There arrived on my desk a document beginning with a preliminary sheet called, with an oddity I hope is generally perceptible, 'Mission Statement, Aims and Objectives', that went on to what ought to be an even odder title 'Total Quality Management', called afterwards in the document and here TQM.[28]

This TQM text, from 'Prof W. D. Morris, Vice Principal, and Chairman of the Teaching Committee', is not fully literate and has phrases that would be sub-edited in, say, *The Daily Telegraph* or *The Guardian*. 'Because the overall governance procedures of the College are currently under active review, the concept of fine tuning existing procedures has been felt to be the most appropriate manner to proceed.' A concept cannot be a manner to proceed and I am not sure that it can be a feeling either. 'Thus a well designed quality assurance system should obviate against the need for time-consuming "fire fighting" activities.' 'Obviate' takes a direct object. This may seem academic and pettifogging. Or, alternatively, it may not. When Air Marshal Sir Hugh Dowding received documents containing illiteracies he initialled them and returned them to the sender without further comment or action, and we won the Battle of Britain. This is, anyway, the tip of another Dearing-age iceberg of non-language.

The aim is 'the detailed development of a total quality management methodology covering all aspects of teaching, research, central administration and student welfare'. The assumption has to be that any 'quality' in a university is capable of being 'managed' in a way that makes talk of methodology appropriate, beside which the feeding of the five thousand must seem an everyday event, though regrettably lacking in the proper management procedures and not following correct guidelines. According to Prof. Morris,

The importance of developing a corporate quality awareness must start at the highest management level in any organisation and then cascade down to all departments and employees. In the context of the UCS, this means that academic departments, administrative departments and all departments responsible for student support services and welfare *must accept and embrace a quality ethos* which is 'top down' driven.

I should no doubt have recognized 'cascade' as a term brought in from Management Science,[29] but as a mere English academic I took it at face value as a fatuous poeticality. In 1997 I participated in the last examiners' meeting of my department to discuss joint honours degrees. The following year, degrees were to be awarded by a computer into which marks had been typed. I do not know whether it is coincidence that this degree-awarding machine is called Cascade. What a shower!

The most strictly proper intellectual response to Prof. Morris is something short and offensive. 'Argument' implies that a case has been offered to criticism, which here it has not. We have already met the phenomenon. You can't argue with Mr Collins. But I will try, even with that amazing 'cascade'.

'Management' is a recent word in universities, of course brought in from industry. The College civil service, the registry staff, were traditionally quite separate from the academics. It was a surprise in 1987 to receive through the College internal mail a document about courses from the Registrar headed by a summary ending *'You must …'*. In the previous quarter of a century I had never as a member of academic staff been told by the Registrar what I 'must' do about academic matters. Naturally this will come easier to registries if they can call themselves 'management'. At my son's school the more important teachers are called 'the senior management team'. The Management of the University of Wales offered me voluntary redundancy, on condition that it was 'in the management interest'. (I made sure it was.) Real schools and universities do not have managements; they have things like deputy headteachers, Faculties, Senates, Councils, Governing Bodies, Registrars, Vice-Chancellors.

Well, it's all management isn't it, whatever name you use, just as we're all customers? As a matter of fact, no. 'Management' applies to things like estates, households, and in the present ethos, above all, limited liability companies. If all bodies are managed by managements why does not the body imposing these changes use the term of itself? But the Secretary of State for Education and Employment is not going to be renamed a Manager, nor are the officers in the Civil Service with whom he works. Her Majesty the Queen is not going to be renamed General Manager of the Realm, nor even is 'Manager' going to be brought in for the President of the European Commission.

TQM links with the 'customer' talk like this:

Quality is about meeting 'customer needs'.… Without top level management commitment, drive and direction quality issues in an organisation will soon 'wither on the vine'. Taking a line of least resistance by non-management involvement will leave those who operate the day to day activities of an organisation with little direction, low morale and uncompetitive. Quality has and must be managed, one cannot leave it to chance and those who think otherwise are sadly misguided.[30]

What is the sense of the clause beginning 'Taking a line …'? 'Quality has and must be' should be 'Quality has been and must be'. Again, the ordinary sub-literacy is remarkable as a sign of something deeper, the supposition that in a university morale will be low and we shall be 'uncompetitive' if we just get on with our work.

But if quality is 'about meeting customer needs' it is not the quality we talk about in everyday life. Something is being attempted with 'quality' rather like what has been done to 'skill', and with the same purpose. As W. A. Hart says,

> In short, 'quality' in 'quality assurance' is a technical notion, only tenuously linked to 'quality' as the term is used in ordinary speech. It is quality in the sense of 'fit for a purpose' (and crucially also within a certain price range) rather than quality in the sense of 'good of its kind'.[31]

We are told by Prof. Morris that 'quality assurance' is quite different from 'quality control' and demands the establishment of *'quality objectives* appropriate to our role in the higher education sector' so that we must *'establish procedures* within the College whereby these objectives may be realized'. All these phrases, anyway—and I do not pretend to be able to follow the distinction between 'quality assurance' and 'quality control'[32]—depend on an understanding of 'quality'. I was employed by 'UCS' to lecture in (not 'teach') English Language and Literature. My understanding of 'quality' is that I have to engage in the thoughts that constitute my subject to the best of my ability, with such students as will join in, and if I (or my peers) find that I cannot do it reasonably well I should resign. 'Quality' here is just the day-to-day thinking, the university subject itself. How can the Principal, whose subject I believe was acoustics, or the Council, or the Senate, tell me, top-down, what counts as quality in English Language and Literature, and hold me to it? (Any Principal might be able to, coincidentally, but in fact mine would not have made that claim.) The belief is that thinking in the university can be 'top down' driven or main-tained by properly established 'managerial structures' and the 'development of employee attitudes which, when followed, results in the quality objectives being fulfilled'. It is on my authority as an experienced university lecturer that I assure the reader: these quoted words are simply and straightforwardly meaningless, and they could not have been used by anyone with any under-standing of a university. Nobody who was actually acquainted with the relevant kind of quality—nobody, that is, who wasn't, by the relevant standard, unintelligent and uneducated (a Mr Collins)—could possibly use them except in contempt and parody.

They cannot even be neutral. Their actual meaning is as an attack upon thought. Thought can't be taught; it can't be managed either, and the attempt to manage thought could only damage it.

Insofar as quality ever can be assured, the university has always had procedures for assuring it: they are not managerial and bureaucratic; they are the procedures of educated conversation, debate, argument, procedures which, in the present instance, lead to the judgement that all this management-speak is self-interested claptrap. In general the present aim is to replace judgement with system. The formal exclusion of judgement culminates in the replacement of examiners' meetings by computer programmes.

That there is one uniform system controlled from the level of top management which can ensure a cascade of quality down throughout the university is not merely a harmless fallacy. It is a sign of a blankness about thinking that must lead at best to irritation with thinking. If 'quality' could be top-down driven in universities the first requirement would be that the top consisted not of managers or bureaucrats but of the best thinkers. They could not express themselves in language remotely like Prof. Morris's.

The analogy with manufacturing industry was inevitable.

> For a number of years manufacturing companies have been adopting management techniques to assure the total quality of their products. Management methodologies devised to assure total quality for manufactured artifacts and products have also been adapted for application to the service industries ....

The attempt to see them as like industries is either stupidly or intelligently malevolent to universities (the former, I think; but I also think that in universities stupidity is the unforgiveable sin). Even if we accept for the sake of argument the huge assumption that TQM has improved quality or consistency in manufactured goods, there is no reason to suppose that it can have any bearing on quality in universities.

The one and only assurance of quality in universities is in the examinations that count towards degrees. If people of little judgement trained only in cliché are allowed to graduate with good degrees there is no quality. If they get to the top and from those cloud-capp'd towers cause these cascades of TQM (Gardeyloo!), the university is in process of committing suicide.

(vi) GIVE FIRSTS

Now that we have the whole course, with properly defined aims and objectives, taught modularly, with copper-bottomed quality guarantees, what is to prevent the performance of universities going up and up? And so we show our success by awarding more and better degrees than ever before.

At a preliminary examiners' meeting it looked as though no student was going to get a first; and though there was also only one third, and the long list had a small majority of upper seconds, we had a speech from a middle-aged senior figure telling us that it was a very bad and depressing list and will do us harm. One way or another we are going to be paid by results. If we don't publish lists containing firsts and more upper seconds, the department will be downgraded and the students disadvantaged. Other departments give more firsts and have more students going on to postgraduate work. We must not let 'antiquated' ideas of standards get in the way of producing the star-spangled class list required by government, the prosperity of the department, and the future of our graduates. That this belies the repeated talk of maintaining standards is too obvious to be worth saying, and perhaps it is not as scandalous as it sounds, merely recognizing a fact and asking us to play on the new and easier pitch. As long as nobody supposes our 2–1 means the same as before, there is no deception. 'In recent years,' as the Chairman of the Higher Education Quality Council was reported as saying, 'the upper second class degree has replaced the lower second grade as the standard honours degree.'[33] But this does overlook the way we have to think in classifications as we mark. Any experienced examiner has a good sense of what a solid 2–2 feels like, and to call it a 2–1 involves a more than mathematical exercise.

Another obvious decline has been in what we expect by way of knowledge. If a present student has read anything outside the texts prescribed for courses we treat it as gratuitous good luck. This has not always been so. It used to be known that education presupposed a level of common knowledge, including factual knowledge, but mainly (in our case) a wide enough acquaintance to make gestures towards an idea of a whole literature not just absurd. Leavis sometimes used a perfect imperative: 'Have read' so-and-so. It used to be assumed, not altogether fancifully, that we had. For instance our Shakespeare paper at Swansea was always on Shakespeare, not a list of set texts. In the years I set it, it always began with a compulsory critical-commentary question on unidentified passages. Any such paper would now be unthinkably difficult.

*   *   *

At present we have moral chaos, regimentation of 'teaching', and laxity in examining.

Moral chaos? And even if so, does it matter? Of course, the idea that the university is a semi-religious institution demanding moral commitment from its members, an institution whose 'output' if any is the clerisy, has been hibernating for a long time. It was not accidental, though, that universities originated as bodies of *clerkes* intellectually free but associated with the Church. The sceptical Chaucer gives in his Clerk a beautiful example of a student whose dedication involves a life of strict moral discipline. With recent changes in the law the senior members are no longer *in loco parentis* and no ordinary morals are enforced either on them or on the undergraduates. Counsellors have largely replaced chaplains.[34] The most blatant moral degeneracy, though, is that there is no longer any pretence that the 'customers' are being prepared for anything more onerous than earning a lot of money. There is no other connection of the modern university with virtue or the pursuit of the good. Aristotle would not have recognized it. Academic seriousness cannot long survive in these circumstances.

'Laxity of examining' may seem unjust. Examiners generally take the work seriously, even to the point of illogical agonizing over borderline cases. (Illogical because in a genuine borderline case justice is done whichever side of the border-line the student comes. That it *was* a borderline can then be stated on references. The real question is whether examiners agree about where the borders are, which, as we shall see in Chapter 8, they no longer do.) But it is not seriously disputable that students can now graduate in many Arts subjects without being able to write decent English prose and without any general culture. The know-ledge required of them is that of their courses, a requirement that modularization makes the only requirement, and which is only by lucky chance knowledge as ordinarily understood, knowledge that has some home in common speech.

This topic, however, is important enough to need a separate chapter.

(vii) PUT ON THE CROWN JEWELS: RESEARCH, OR, GREAT HEAPS OF NOTHING

Having got our new university up and running, with the modularly taught getting firsts and upper seconds, it only remains to make sure we get our fair share of the crowning glory. Teaching, we saw, is the basic university activity, but to be a 'teaching only' institution is to be downmarket.

It must be reasonable to address questions about 'production' to the new universities, confident as they are of having at last got across to government the message that their products are making an essential contribution to the national economy. If you claim that we are all producing, there follows the little question *what* are we producing? What do English Literature departments produce? English Literature? As a matter of fact, they are busily engaged in denying there is any such thing.[35]

The first answer that is always given is 'graduates'—without embarrassment, although, in these early days of cloning, human beings can still produce more human beings only by way of procreation. Cloning nevertheless seems the ideal here: an ever-increasing supply of those skilled in the skill of acquiring skills etc etc. Commonplace example of the link between this possibly RUR[36] process and the wished-for prosperity: 'The College was committed to producing graduates who would make a major contribution to the future prosperity of the country....'[37] Graduates are produced by teaching.

If you ask, however, what it is that our graduates themselves might be able to produce, you get back quickly to the word 'research', research which everybody including the government expects the government to fund. Controversies rage about which universities should get what research funding, but not about whether any should get any. The permanent members of the university have to give a lead and themselves spend any time they are not 'teaching' on 'research', in accordance with the simple equation: the university = teaching + research.

There have to be questions, mysteriously overlooked by the TQM regime, about the quality of the 'research' (a word that has spread to the schools, so that on UCCA/UCAS forms I constantly saw that Julie's essays are 'well-researched'). But giving all benefits of doubts, and again admitting that in the science departments this notion that they produce research has at least some plausibility, we still have to ask what sense can it make for me in English Literature? or in Philosophy? or in Classics?

A few good books, a decreasing number (see below) of new editions, some new information, do still come out of these departments. But these products of research are hidden in a mass of published matter of a most peculiar kind.

It might be expected that 'research' would have obeyed the demands of the age, though how the productions of philosophers or historians could do so is not easy to imagine:

> In future, research will be increasingly assessed on the contribution that it will make to the national economy, and Research Council grants will go to those whose research is seen to be benefiting the economy in either the short or the long term.[38]

To be fair to the arts departments they have not tried very hard to apply this, but have understood their productivity in a very simple way. For, in this hard-nosed age, this no-nonsense age, the answer you get to the question about what we produce is another question, sometimes threatening: 'How many pages have you published last year?'; or, if you want promotion: 'Have you got a firm contract with a publisher and if so how many pages long will the book be?'

One odd consequence: the other year I was able to ensure that a publication of mine was short and competitively priced. Legible and with reasonably sized type it got into around 60 pages, paperback. With a few pushed buttons on the computer the same work would very easily and without unduly large type have made 120 pages hardback (such is printing), to be published at about eight times [*sic*] the paperback price. Through the folly of seeking readers I was only half as productive as I might have been.

After the foregoing paragraphs were written the 'models' grew more sophist-icated. There is a sort of league-table in which editions are, incredibly, worth less than critical essays; with other refinements. 'Sheer quantity,' however, 'whatever the technical restrictions of the Research Assessment Exercise, carries much more weight than it ought.'[39] The refinements do not include any exercise of judgement about what work if any is of value. University depart-ments have what is called a 'Research Rating' that depends still, for the most part, on how many pages they get out per annum. Members of staff who refrain from issuing pages drag down the department average, and departments are then in danger not only of getting considerably less money but of being assessed as 'teaching only' departments not capable of 'research'. Whether either the 'teaching' (above) or the 'research' has anything to do with thinking is the question never, never asked. In such circumstances appointment committees will tend to ask not, 'Who thinks best?' but, 'Who'll do the most for our Research Rating? Who'll bring us the most money?'

In this little island alone there are, I am told, over a thousand members of staff just in the English departments of the 'old' universities. In practice, the 'canon' of the literature consists of works by about 30 authors. Few of us (though the few do include Sir Frank Kermode) are vainglorious enough to expect to join the select number of the widely read; few indeed expect an audience outside the university. But even that is extravagant. Actually we are not read inside the university either. If the thousand conceived any hopes of being read only by the other 999, just think of the congestion. In practice, the system tacitly recognizes that our publications are not going to be read by anybody at all. Publication is to be taken as numbers of pages receivable into the library. Publications without readers does seem an extraordinary class, but it is the answer to the question what we produce.

Two new professors were to be appointed in my department: a week before the interviews the list of shortlisted names (about which the department was not consulted) was made available to us. These were, of course, academics with energetic publication records, and ones we had heard of. We sat round a table to consult about them. So and so is very impressive on paper, but such and such has done even more. Nobody had read more than a fragment here and there, and most of us hadn't read any of it. This, surprisingly, surprised nobody, nor did it prevent anyone from commenting. We really don't expect anyone to read our publications, and have no intention of reading our colleagues'.

In one case, we were told off the record, a candidate had simply declared himself to have published over two hundred articles, without bothering to list them. He seemed to have got the rationale of the system.

One thing I know for sure is that many books published by people in arts departments are literally never seen by mortal eye. You think, once more, that I am exaggerating? What evidence is there, to begin with, that they are ever read by their authors? The editor or publisher may (or may not) send the typescript to a 'referee', who may or may not read it. Or there may not be a typescript, for many publishers now prefer the book to be submitted either in the form of a camera-ready copy or floppy disk, which can be fed into a typesetting machine without anybody glancing at what it contains. Even typescript can be electronically scanned and turned into text without human intervention. Proof-reading is largely a thing of the past, 'for reasons of economy'. So, one way or another, the book gets made and sent to reviewers, and … they read it? Don't make me laugh: I have been reviewed. When I have reviewed a book myself and read it all the way through I have more than once known for sure from the state of the printing that I am the first person to have done so. Some books are full of the kind of typographical error that could not have survived a cursory reading.

More machines produce the publisher's catalogue and other machines or human beings imitating machines scan the catalogues, make the appropriate orders, catalogue the work when it arrives at the library—and then consign it to the library stacks and the oblivion from which it has at no stage ever emerged. It may well get on reading lists, be occasionally borrowed and so keep its place in the library,[40] still without ever being read. Nobody has ever read it and nobody ever will. At length, the inevitable happens to 'that vast mass of literature which is kept with a view to being looked at some day', it

> finally drifts unread to the bourne of all waste paper, and is ground into pulp again, and rolls over the endless web again, and comes back into the world printed with more intellectual food … .[41]

which in turn will never nourish anybody.

If on publication these books went, instead of into the stacks, straight into recycling bins, the national economy would be infinitesimally improved (production of waste-paper, savings on library administration) but there would be no other consequence whatever.

I can't give an exact figure—my research is not complete—but more than 90 per cent of university 'research' does not, strictly speaking, exist. The late Roland Barthes tried to establish a distinction between literary 'works' and 'texts'. The former are thought to be physical objects having existence on shelves, books, CD-roms, microfilms or the like; the latter exist in their active interplay with the reader. The distinction is untenable, for the object on the shelf is *only* an object, not a 'work', until read.

> In Books, not Authors, curious is my Lord;
> To all their dated Backs he turns you round,
> These Aldus printed, those Du Suëil has bound.
> Lo some are Vellom, and the rest as good
> For all his Lordship knows, but they are Wood.[42]

On the other hand, bring it into existence by reading it and the 'work' is already a 'text'. (It *is* possible to read works in a drilled way, which presumably Barthes was trying to get at.) Books exist in reading, and nowhere else. An unread book is *only* an object on a shelf, to be for instance occasionally dusted, and literally does not exist as a book.

The great effort of the Arts Faculties is being directed to the production, strictly and precisely, of NOTHING. We are straining every nerve to produce more nothing. The individuals who produce the most nothing are given chairs, and the departments that produce the greatest heaps of nothing get the best research ratings, and so, more money with which to produce more nothing. But: infinity times nothing is ... ?

The first possible answer to this riddle is 'Deconstruction'. If the demand is to look academically impressive not to make sense, output will be increased if we reduce Mr Collins to system. All works of Deconstruction are written to formula (beginning with references to Saussure, the indeterminacy of the sign etc etc.) whether by computer or living creatures. I shall quote from some Swansea examination scripts the first steps of initiation into the process.

The second possible answer seems to be 'poetry'—understood in a sense peculiar to the new university and its colonies in the literary press. One agenda item at a department meeting: whether to get some sort of honorary fellowship in the department for a Poet who works in the Department of Health Care Studies. The Department of Health Care Studies cannot list his poems under their annual publications, but we can, and they are many. We saw a publications list over a page long and the departmental mouth watered at the prospect of what this would do for our Research Rating.

In preparation for this *démarche*, the Poet had addressed a meeting of our department seminar. The address had taken the form of a new Poem, read by the Poet at the length of about 20 minutes, after which he answered questions. The answers showed him to be a well-read and intelligent man, and I could well imagine he would make a useful member of an English department. The Poem itself, I remarked at the subsequent department meeting, put me in mind of that moment of *Waiting for Godot* when Lucky (is it?) is commanded to 'think', and does so for several pages. It was as if somebody had said 'Poetize!' and out it all came. There were Images, occasionally Rhymes, recognizable Lines, mentions of Bones and Sex. Even a drift was discernible: it was about the Poet's thoughts as he looked across Swansea Bay at the smoke of Port Talbot, a theme that permitted considerable latitude. The lines, the images, the Bones went on, with occasional mentions of Swansea Bay and Port Talbot, and all much faster than a BBC newscaster would have read, and in a more monotonous voice. That it would last about 20 minutes had been announced in advance, otherwise I don't know how the end would have come. As it was we all sat it out, Poet and audience; but nothing had happened at all. I recall a Thurber story in which a pigeon is sitting on a wall, being a pigeon. Nobody in that audience could have had any perception beyond the fact that here was a Poet BEING A POET. When I said this at the department meeting nobody argued or put in a good word for the poetry. I think one of the eighteen people present had read some, but cannot vouch for that as reading was not mentioned. This Poetry was non-existent as surely as our published critical essays.

Thy No thing of an Intended Poem, O Poet...behold it has not yet become a Thing.... The Thing, in philosophical uncommercial language, is still a No-thing, mostly semblance and deception of the sight;—benign Oblivion incessantly gnawing at it, impatient till Chaos, to which it belongs, do reabsorb it! [43]

Carlyle's mistake was to suppose that this would matter to the Poet. Not in the least. What matters, as with any other non-existent 'publication', is the number and frequency of pages.

*   *   *

The situation does ask to be made fun of, but it means that there is a probably incurable corruption in our universities. It is an absurdity to suppose that numbers of published pages have any direct correlation with the real work of any university. During Wittgenstein's tenure of his Cambridge chair, when with a number of pupils he did the most important philosophical work since Plato, he published one review. I refrain from the complementary examples of compulsive publication of nothing. A university which doesn't know itself as the enemy of absurdity is already ceasing to be a university; all the universities that go along with this nonsense are subscribing to absurdity.

I hope that the politicians will latch on to this primary fact, that in the terms they understand the arts departments produce, literally, *nothing*. There is, according to market logic, an obvious enough conclusion, which we shall draw.

When Arts academics do have anything to publish, it really is addressed to the world: we still have to assume the possibility of common sense as embodied in the common reader. It may be that some Arts dons have a role in the world by way of addressing the common reader. We even hope this for the present work.

If the academic and bureaucratic mind could be cleared of that cant about our contribution etc, we might even get as far as regaining some understanding of what the arts faculties ought really to be doing in national life, which is very far from nothing.

IV

LEVERING UP STANDARDS, OR, TOP-DOWN DRIVEL

Introduction to Part IV

THE POWER GOVERNMENTS HAVE over educational 'provision' is of course great; and the richer the country and the higher the taxes, the greater the power. But the power governments have over education ... isn't power at all. The best educated government can't achieve more than the general level of culture permits. The worst can't escape the limitations of its own character. What could Mr Collins do as Prime Minister or Education Secretary? (No more than Mr Blair or Mr Blunkett.) Governments might as well claim the power to make people more religious or more virtuous as better educated. (For an example, drawn from first-hand experience, of what such power amounts to in practice, see pp. 177–82.)

In 1993 (an eternity ago in 'politics'; otherwise yesterday), John Patten, as education minister, said he 'fought' for A-levels as an unashamed élitist. But you can't brag you're an élitist in clichés—can you?[1] Maybe you can in football, if you're Ron Atkinson. But in Education? If you're the Secretary of State for it? To call A-levels (they were ... they still are ...) 'the hallmark of educational quality and excellence', 'a high-quality currency' (for entry to work and the burgeoning college and university sectors), 'a jewel in the crown' (of secondary education), 'a benchmark for excellence' (not just in this country but throughout the world)—is that how an élitist talks?

Mr Patten 'fought' for A-level but not as if it were an exam—a hieroglyph that means only as much, or as little, as we can make it mean; he fought for it as if it were a historic monument—in need of a preservation order. Touch of dry rot in the Jewel Tower? Send in Rentokil. A-levels threatened? Do the same. Be in charge. Be Ministerial. Announce that you are making three important announcements. Number one: that you will augment A-level ('augment', now, that is a fine word) with a new Starred Grade which will give a real incentive to our highest flyers, as well as greatly assisting the university talent spotters; number two: that you will encourage the greater use of AS qualifications, which in the other direction can do a great deal to broaden the options (and which in

117

fact paved the way for the subsequent government's phasing out of A-level); and number three: that you will announce the Government's Response to the Inspectors' Report (and make the levelling parties livid).

But is that how an exam standard is maintained? Bureaucratically?

Where does 'an exam standard' come from? How many or how few are the judgements—how wide or how narrow is the community—it depends on? Could exam standards be kept up by the political establishment, for instance, if the whole political establishment talked in clichés? Or worse—if it did, and the wider educated public didn't notice? Or does that (élitist?) sort of thing not belong to the defence of élitism? What counts is the will of the Secretary of State for Education, enforced through the proper procedures by Her Majesty's Inspectors of Schools? So an education minister and his *officiers* can just decide that standards be maintained? All he has to do is speak the word, and see that HMIs do the same, and it shall be so? Let there be an élite and an élite there is? Time and tide wait for no man but him?

The standard of an examination—any examination, but especially one such as A-level which, even in the sciences, has always demanded a high degree of literacy—is upheld—if it is upheld—by a wide daily life. It is the outcome of influences widely diffused and largely obscure. It is maintained or lost as the result of a multitude of people thinking a multitude of different things on a multitude of subjects in a multitude of circumstances—thoughts which act and re-act upon one another in ways that are invisible to the people thinking them. All exam marking—even in the most technical subjects with the most explicit marking schemes—depends on distinctions between what is more and less important, more and less true, better and worse sense, better and worse expression, which are themselves untechnical and inexplicit. If our hold on these general and unspecialized distinctions weakens, exam standards fall, not merely without deference to the say-so of boy secretaries of state for education but without even being recognized. 'Standards' depend, helplessly, on culture. And boy secretaries—whether of state or of stamp clubs—command that as much as they do the weather.

The impossibility of Mr Patten's doing what he announced himself as doing is proved by the style in which he announced it. We may suppose that he would have avoided clichés if he could, because, we may speculate, as an ex-don he has some inkling of what they are: not a shorthand used for convenience's sake—where we might, if we wished, have chosen something different—but a deadly automatism. We don't choose clichés, they choose us. We don't use them, they use us. They are not words that are merely unoriginal or conventional but words that, without our knowing it, have lost their meaning. Words in combinations that reveal us as—without knowing it—having lost our meaning. Words that have lost their status as words, for men who have lost their status as men. And when they get a hold on us we become updated versions of

Mr Collins or Mary Bennet. It is possible to become to clichés what Midas was to gold. It happened to John Patten when he was Education Secretary. He was able to turn to cliché words as unsuspected of it as 'Thirty years ago' or 'when I was in the sixth form'. He could turn to cliché 'already', 'some' and 'and' (as in, 'Already, some 1000 schools and colleges …').

When a politician like Mr Patten says that quite a lot of people doing General National Vocational Qualification exams means 'a richness of vocational and academic choice', the voice is the voice of Mary Bennet, and like Mr Collins he is telling neither truth nor lies. These aren't words that can be believed or disbelieved, by Mr Patten or anyone else. He isn't saying something, about something, true or false. He's croaking.

And he's got company. When a Secretary of State—in a quality newspaper—makes as many as three important announcements—including naming a new top priority—all in one go, he is not likely to be the sole author of what he says. His drivel will be other men's too. It will have been sieved and picked over, scrutinized and passed (even supplied) by the finest critical intelligences on the government's pay-roll—high flyers whose talents, like Mr Patten's own, were spotted by other high flyers with talents like Mr Patten's own. Now that 'New' Labour has displaced 'Old', it is the drivel of the entire political establishment. Mr Blair's Education, Education, Education doesn't mean, 'We will show an understanding different from the Tories.' It means even more of the same, and it sounds awfully like Mr Patten—and Mr Collins.

When a Secretary of State for Education mistakes boastful inanity for good sense forcefully expressed; when there is no-one around him in his department, the Government, the civil service, his party, his family or his friends, to supply him with the judgement he lacks himself; and when the editor of a newspaper read by two million or so of the best-educated people in the country (social classes AA and AB, all) prints the inanity, confident that his paper's readers won't know it from sense either; when inanity is current and orthodox, throughout the educated classes … how simple a matter can it be to maintain the standards of public examinations? What can Legislation and Administration do? How can anyone—any of the anyones of whom Mr Patten is an example—know whether standards are being maintained or not? Or why it matters? Mr Patten fought for A-level as an unashamed élitist. His Labour successors have decided to dilute and diversify A-level as even more unashamed anti-élitists. But where is the difference? If Mr Patten's an élitist, is Baroness Blackstone a leveller?

Policies for keeping standards up in school count for nothing unless the standards have been kept up widely outside school, in the educated class from which government members, civil servants, teachers and examiners are drawn. The sort of standard in question isn't, after all, like those guaranteed by the British Standards Institute or that metal bar kept in ideal conditions in Paris that defines how long a metre is. You can't go and look at it; it isn't an independently existing criterion; it *has* no existence aside from the acts of judgement that constitute it. It is real none the less. An exam board *can* be a good place to find it and, as we see from *Pride and Prejudice*, so can breakfast.

But it isn't something you can impose, through any variety of British, or European, Weights and Measures Act. The attempt to raise standards—'lever them up'—by a species of force is self-defeating. It can only mean that we go on for the next 20 years or so as we have for the past 20 years or so, going round in circles and multiplying cures that aggravate the disease: solving the problem of teachers doing what they like by giving them an insanely detailed National Curriculum to follow; solving the problem of them no longer having enough time for reading, writing and 'rithmetic by giving priority to National Literacy and Numeracy Hours (something teachers themselves, of course, had never ever thought of doing and never ever done). Having saved all the time infants waste in play by making school exclusively workful, we go on to solve the problem of Jack's being such a dull boy by adopting the very latest 'European' method—'learning through play'. We have just solved the problem of A-levels that are narrow and élitist by making them broad and anti-élitist. What scope this gives us for solving the problem of university entrants who are unprepared for university work!

The real problem is not a kind for which there can be an administrative solution. 'What is to be done?' asked Carlyle:

> It seems to be taken for granted ... that there is some 'thing' or handful of 'things', which could be done; some Act of Parliament, 'remedial measure' or the like, which could be passed, whereby the social malady were fairly fronted, conquered, put an end to; so that, with your remedial measure in your pocket, you could then go on triumphant, and be troubled no farther.

Instead, what was to be done—first, before anything else could be—was the doer change himself:

> ... a radical universal alteration of your regimen and way of life ... a most agonising divorce between you and your chimeras, luxuries and falsities ...
>
> ... when jargon might abate, and here and there some genuine speech begin ...
>
> If thou ask again, therefore, ... What is to be done? allow me to reply: By thee, for the present, almost nothing. Thou there, the thing for thee to do is, if possible, to cease to be a hollow sounding-shell of hearsays, egoisms, purblind dilettantisms ... .[2]

Jargon, falsity, chimeras, hearsays ... they're the problem. It isn't Research Assessment Exercises or Quality Assurance Agencies or money or national curricula or concentration on literacy and numeracy skills in whole class teaching that education in this country needs. For thou there, David Blunkett, and thy Shadow, on the front bench opposite, more money to spend, for the present, will produce nothing but more money spent. More whole class teaching will produce nothing but more classes taught as wholes. The more the national curriculum, the less the reading, writing, 'rithmetic; the more the 'rithmetic, the less the music and art; the higher up the results go, the lower down the standards come; the nearer we are to England the further off from France.

We need to divorce ourselves (and some will find it agonizing) from the crippling and delusive idea that education is a service industry like dry-cleaning, identical with the material arrangements through which we seek to provide it. You might as well identify the Church that is the bride of Christ with the Church that runs a pension scheme. You might as well try to lever up the standards of love or virtue as of education. The standards successive governments strive to raise or maintain are either widely diffused throughout the educated class or else are missing even from the agencies supposed to do the raising and maintaining.

The two following chapters illustrate (with certainly not too *little* detail) how examination boards themselves are likely just to reproduce the standards of the world around them, the world from which examiners as well as candidates are recruited. What is true of one A-level and one degree level examining board has general significance for standards in the whole modern university. We are not making a wild leap from an anecdote to a world. These two examining boards are a very small part of the world, but a part of a whole; and the whole is one of those whose character can be seen in all its parts. It is little more than a bare possibility that two public examinations such as these should show such signs of collapse and the collapse not have occurred elsewhere: in these two English examinations but not others, in English but not Philosophy or History. That the rot spreads is evidence of the wholeness of the body.

7 A-level, the Jewel in the Crown

INTRODUCTORY

THE LONG but not now very thorny road to the new university probably starts officially at age seven, with the first national tests, but the first real low hurdle is GCSE. If the subject is English and if you can get an English degree unacquainted with English literature it should not be surprising that English literature is not required for GCSE English. I nevertheless was surprised. At a public school where in the first four years they have read no Shakespeare, my son followed a syllabus including a verse Anthology for which my formula is Blake + Crap. Blake is admitted, to the extent of six lyrics, as a revolutionary. Wordsworth is represented, but only by 'Daffodils' and a poem, 'Nuns Fret Not', characteristic of his elderly dull phase. Otherwise there is hardly anything capable of being read with attention. Dyer, not the *Fleece* but the sixteenth-century dullard. A very minor poem by Herbert. A section by Seamus Heaney in which his trailing after Wordsworth would be painfully apparent to anyone who knew Wordsworth. That is before you get down to the real dregs. Alice Walker (see below) is represented: the true, the unblushful E. J. Thribb, accompanied by two photographs presumably of Ms Walker, looking studiously at her pen. All poems written before 1900 are prominently labelled 'Pre-1900', just like the cigarette packets warning us of health risk. My son says: imagine applying this to music or art (he studied Van Eyck with real interest). The principle is no less absurd applied to literature. There are lots of 'poems from other cultures' (which on this showing aren't cultures at all), though not from Pre-1900 poets like Homer, and pages of stuff by the quite nice would-be poet Gillian Clarke. This is for boys and girls who for the most part are unacquainted with English poetry and have no terms of comparison. My grandmother, who went to school in the bad old days before GCSE, had to learn a lot of English poetry by heart.

Then there is GCSE fiction: one short story by Hardy and another by John (*Triffids*) Wyndham. The Hardy is deadly dull and incredible, one of the ones he couldn't be bothered with. When this is said the teacher replies, 'But look at what it says about women's rights.' Written in about 1896, this Hardy represents Pre-1900 (in the new millennium will it be Pre-2000?) to boys and girls who for the most part have never read any Dickens or Jane Austen. Then they read one scene of *The Tempest*—the one where Trinculo and Stephano discover Caliban. Why this one? Because it tells you about the class system and colonialism (New Historicism). Nowadays we treat monsters as equals?

This GCSE, from the Northern Examinations and Assessment Board, is just Aged Ignorance clipping the youthful wings. Well, perhaps GCSE has to be adapted to the capacities of the mass of children, and of teachers. But was not A-level, the final stepping-stone into the university, still so reliable ('specialist', élitist) that it had to be done away with? Is not that the reason? Politicians seem to think so.

EXAMINING THE EXAMINERS

I marked an A-level English paper in 1993,[1] and if Mr Patten had only studied that one paper, the marking scheme for it, the answers to it and the marking of those answers, he might have begun to get some idea of the difficulty of doing in fact what he thought he had done by announcement. The paper was a thoroughly bad one, bad in the most fundamental way, originating in the selection of texts and passage for comprehension.

Firstly, the distribution of answers in the 193 scripts I marked: of the eight set texts, the two classics of English literature amongst them (which were also the only texts on the paper not written in the last 30 years) received no answers at all; of the six contemporary texts, one, the most ancient (some very ordinary journalism written as long ago as, and about, the sixties) also received no answers; of the remaining five set texts, two received two or three answers each. Of the three texts preferred by almost all candidates, one (the book of the film) was answered on by every candidate.

Given the texts chosen by the examiners, this was predictable. Were *Tristram Shandy* and Pope's *Essay on Criticism* chosen deliberately as being unlikely to be read? Who is going to do Sterne when they can do Susan Hill and Alice Walker (both as much alive as they ever were, both women and one black)? If a genuine invitation was to be issued to the English literature of the eighteenth century, why not *The Dunciad*? Would the Board have been afraid of being identified? If this syllabus and examination educated anyone, it was by accident.

The Assistant Examiner who tried to raise the matter at the Co-ordination meeting was bad-temperedly and pompously silenced as having raised a question for which, 'This was not the appropriate forum.' (What other forum was there?) 'Had she written to the Board?' She had not (as the Board well knew). Collapse of female party. And warnings all round.

Two books of particular worthlessness typified the selection: Philip Howard's collection *The State of the Language* and Alice Walker's novel *The Color Purple*.

Philip Howard's own language is in such a state that he's the last person to have anything intelligent to say about anyone else's. His style (as anyone may verify from his journalism—he is the long-serving literary editor of *The Times*) is a mish-mash of mutually contending clichés. The only consistent thing about it is that it consistently betrays him. The opinions which his book are fabricated from add up to two. One is that language is always changing. The other is that style must be 'appropriate' (clichés, appropriately, he thinks may be useful, when appropriate). Both opinions he has borrowed from academic linguisticians (as journalists daily borrow and are forced to borrow from all and sundry). The second question on him in the exam paper asked the candidates what they had learned from his book. The only thing anyone could learn (owned to by one candidate) is the lesson taught by this syllabus and examination paper as a whole: don't be critical.

Answers on *The Color Purple* showed the same lesson learned. Alice Walker's book is just soap opera, but that is not how it was seen.

This selection of texts couldn't have been made by anyone with any capacity to judge books. It couldn't have been made by anyone with any taste or judgement of language at all, and it dared the candidates (and their teachers) to question the taste that had made it. None (in the 193 papers I saw) dared. All treated these books in the way they were plainly meant to, with the same undifferentiated respect they would treat any set text, any 'classic'. If the text *is* a classic no harm is done. Most eighteen-year-olds won't go far wrong taking the merits of Shakespeare and Jane Austen for granted. But Alice Walker? I read two good answers out of 193, both by candidates who had a way of speaking for her which didn't tempt you to think they were speaking for themselves. They weren't critical but they did the next best thing: they kept their distance.

And then, in the passage for 'comprehension', hostility (or just blankness) to literature gave way to hostility (or blankness) to sense itself. To get a good mark on this, the one compulsory question, the candidates had either not to understand the passage or pretend they didn't. That—of an examination that's the jewel in the crown and a benchmark for excellence—may seem far-fetched but it's the simple truth. Let me say it again, deliberately: the examination board responsible—through its question-paper, its marking scheme and its 'team leaders' who oversee the work of the assistant examiners—required that its candidates should not understand the passage it had set them for comprehension. It did not require that knowingly; it was just that none of its senior members understood the passage himself.

It was not, of course, that they had failed to understand any of the individual words or grammatical constructions, that someone had made 'slips' of a kind that could be (easily) corrected. It was much worse than that. It was that they had all failed to see what was in front of them, failed to judge it aright—both in detail and overall. They took as cogent and reasonable—and required their assistant examiners and the candidates to take as cogent and reasonable—what was in one part foolish and conceited and in another indifferent to foolishness and conceit. They had been unintelligent. And—because examination boards are excellent examples of institutions in which Quality is Top-down Driven—they saw to it that intelligence wasn't what their juniors looked for in the candidates. The initiation into a community of thinkers took the form of rewarding candidates who could prove they shared the examiners' unintelligence. Such is the crown and benchmark.

I'll look in detail at just two sets of questions and answers, on the comprehension passage and on *The Color Purple*.

The Comprehension Passage

The passage set was the theatre column from *The Independent* for 25 October, 1990. In it a group of jet-setting English theatrical celebrities are quoted, with journalistic approval, as agreeing with one another that the English (excepting their jet-setting theatrical celebrities and their journalistic hangers-on) don't understand Shakespeare as well as foreigners do—because they have the disadvantages of speaking his language and knowing his plays. Put yourself in the place of an A-level candidate faced with this:

> Amid the storm of praise that greeted Peter Brook's production of *The Mahabharata* when it came to Glasgow two years ago, there was the odd murmur of dissent. When, said some critics, were we going to see another Shakespeare from the director whose *Midsummer Night's Dream* was a landmark in British theatre? Well, Shakespeare it is that he brings to Glasgow next week, but not quite the Bard as nature intended: his long-awaited production of *The Tempest* is in French.
>
> This is not a mischievous move: the production has just opened at Les Bouffes du Nord, the theatre in Paris that Brook has made his home for twenty years. Following Yukio Ninagawa's exquisite Japanese productions, the arrival of Brook's *Tempest* in Britain prompts speculation as to what can be lost, and what can be gained, in foreign-language Shakespeare—and whether the best productions can be even more exciting than the familiar English plays. How well do texts survive the crossing?
>
> 'The plays are so dense and so rich, that even when you lose the music of Shakespeare's poetry, it's like cutting the head off a worm—a complete worm is still left,' says Brook. 'It can also be fascinating. I saw *Hamlet* once played in Azerbaijani. "To be" is "alom", and "not to be" is the same word pronounced slightly differently— "alum". To show these two total opposites you say the same word with a faintly different intonation. That's very moving, and brings a completely new meaning to it.'
>
> *La Tempête* was translated by Jean-Claude Carrière, who has done most of Brook's translations. Even a hop across the channel however, brings a different attitude to language. 'You can't have two languages more incompatible than French

and English,' according to Brook. 'In English a word is marvellous because it can have many meanings and in French a word is only marvellous if it is clear, transparent, and has only one meaning. Sometimes you have to sacrifice one phrase and then capture the feeling of it in the following phrase.'

'I shifted the alliteration for "Full fathom five", using "p" as the alliterative letter,' says Carrière. 'But occasionally you've got to be bold enough to translate directly. For "we are such stuff as dreams are made of" [sic] most translations use "matière" for "stuff". I used the exact translation—"étoffe"—and hidden rhymes appeared.'

Carrière has always wanted to translate *The Tempest*—he admits to having practised secretly on passages for years. 'It is the one in which Shakespeare is most free with the form—it jumps from one to another, sometimes in the middle of a line. This is very attractive for a translator ... It is fascinating to try to make your own language flexible enough to follow the secret rhythms of a writer. Of course there is something you can never quite reach.'

There may, however, be things that a translator can reveal in a Shakespeare text. 'I read and re-read the play until I can feel the words which are the most frequent,' says Carrière. 'There are always two levels; there are words which reflect the obvious themes, and words which let you know what was interesting Shakespeare at the time. In *The Tempest* the first words are "island, sea, prisoner". But the secret word, which keeps coming back, is "freedom".'

Carrière translates into modern French, and Brook points out that this can often assist the actors with comedy. Michael Bogdanov, who has directed several Shakespeares at the Hamburg Schauspielhaus, agrees: 'Because the plays are frequently re-translated for each production, they come much closer to the language of today'. Working abroad has other advantages for an English director. 'There is a much greater freedom about directing it in another language,' Bogdanov feels. 'The restrictions and taboos aren't there.'

Richard Eyre, artistic director of the National Theatre, feels finding a fresh approach can be difficult: 'Every time we do a Shakespeare play in Britain we have sitting on our shoulders this huge weight of myth.' The National recently brought over a Romanian *Hamlet* and is about to host *The Kingdom of Desire*, a Taiwanese version of *Macbeth*. 'For us,' Eyre says, '*Hamlet* is a play full of quotes—quotes of incidents as well as of language.

'When the Romanian company approached it, they didn't have that baggage. Also if it's a play about tyranny and assassination, we're not terribly in touch with that. But they've had a master-class in Eastern Europe. So they don't have to create imaginary universes ... Shakespeare has served as a great ally of dissent in Eastern Europe. In Japan he is phenomenally popular, partly because there is something about the way that he treats elemental stories that they find very attractive.'

The Romanian *Hamlet* was played with such urgency that the play seemed newly written. Audiences for Kurosawa's film *Ran*—taken from *King Lear*—or Ninagawa's stage versions of *Macbeth* and *The Tempest* often saw the plays in a new, vivid light. In a sense the language barriers may assist the audience to focus on the play differently. It could be said that the very familiarity of Shakespeare's poetry sometimes dulls our response.

'Productions from abroad can be an eye-opener,' says Bogdanov, adding that directors have far more time to work on a play in almost every country outside Britain. 'So much of the good work on Shakespeare is going on in other countries. In Britain we tend to skate along on the surface and think it is the poetry of the language that is most important. People try and seduce with the language rather than the ideas.'

Bringing a different culture to the plays, as did Ninagawa, can unlock new meanings. Peter Brook is using actors from different theatrical traditions for Shakespeare's most elusive, magical play—Sotigui Kouyaté, who plays Prospero, and Bakary Sangaré (Ariel) are both from Mali. 'It seemed to me that actors whose culture means they have no problem with believing in the reality of the invisible world bring something different from actors produced by urban culture,' he explains.

'I do think that if one tries to interpret *The Tempest* in terms of master–slave relationship and so forth, one can easily miss the real qualities of the play... Reading a Shakespeare play one is touched by all manner of ambiguities, and in staging it one can easily be tempted into trying to resolve those ambiguities for the audience. But a play can't be about freedom, it can't be about power. It has to be about what's in between the fifty definitions that you can give of "pardon", the 300 things that you can say are "freedom".' Seeing Shakespeare through other eyes may help open up such possibilities, and send us back to the original refreshed. Peter Brook hopes so: 'Theatre lives on freshness. Anything that helps you discover freshness is of great value.'

Nothing much is lost in translation, after all: just the music of the poetry, the poetry of the language, the language. Without the language, you've still got the ideas. (Where, though?) You've still got the plays. It's like cutting off the head of a worm (or a theatrical jet-setter) and finding you've still got the worm complete. In fact, a worm that's more than complete. For Shakespeare's English keeps the English skating on the surface of his plays. Without it, the Romanians, Taiwanese, Azerbaijanis and Malians are free to dive in deep.

And if the foreigners don't know what to expect of a production, because they've never seen one before, so much the better. All that baggage, that huge weight of myth is removed: 'The restrictions—the taboos aren't there.' And who aren't they there for? For the foreign audience? Well, actually, no. For the jet-setting English celebrity: 'There is a much greater freedom about directing in another language.' So that's what's at the bottom of these paradoxes. The jet-setter wants to be free. The understanding of a native audience—and the expectations that understanding gives rise to—constrain him. And, very understandably, he doesn't want to be constrained. He wants to do as he likes. So the idea of the 'new and exciting' does as it likes with him; and freshness becomes another (stale) cliché.

These and other deep thoughts the journalist, Sarah Hemming, then stitches together as if they were authoritative, and as the most painless way of getting her copy. (And because the piece didn't take up enough room, someone—Sarah herself? a copy-editor?—stuck part of Hamlet's 'to be, or not to be' speech at the bottom of the page, in English, in French, in Welsh, in Basque and in Esperanto. Pity about the Azerbaijani.)

And then the board presents this stuff to its candidates, not for criticism but for 'comprehension', i.e. requiring them to treat it as if it were all the most plain and obvious good sense. As if it could be comprehended without ridicule. As if anyone with any interest in Shakespeare or in English or in ideas could feel anything for it but savage contempt.

Aren't such arty-farty thought-stutterings the very worst sort of thing to put before an average lot of eighteen-year-olds? Bullying them on the one hand, despised by them on the other, just the thing to leave them not knowing what to think or feel or dare to say.

The questions (especially in conjunction with the marking scheme) were of a kind to conceal the differences between the better and the worse candidates. It would take a very unusual eighteen-year-old to express contempt for a passage set for comprehension in an exam but, given the right questions, one might reasonably expect the better candidates to wonder whether there was not something suspect about the relation between 'language' and 'ideas', 'poetry' and 'the play' proposed by Monsignors Brook, Bogdanov and Eyre. An intelligent, well-taught eighteen-year-old who liked Shakespeare ought to be capable of discussing whether Shakespeare's 'ideas' exist apart from his language, whether his poetry is just a distracting 'music', whether it is an entirely unqualified advantage to come to a play (or symphony or football match) without expectations— because without knowledge—and whether (though no-one wants plays any more than bread to be stale) 'freshness' is quite the all-valuable quality Brook and his colleagues think it. A clever eighteen-year-old might even want to ask how someone who was seeing Shakespeare performed for the first time could know whether the performance was fresh or not.

The questions asked were of a kind to make any real comprehension of the passage a maddening distraction, for example:

> (a) Explain in your own words the different attitudes of the French and English to language as expressed by Brook and Carrière in paragraphs 4 and 5.
>
> (b) In your own words explain why Shakespeare is popular in (i) Romania and (ii) Japan. Use the material in paragraphs 9 to 11.

The unintelligence of the questions was then reinforced by a marking scheme which told the examiners that what the candidates mainly had to do was locate 'the correct point'. What the examiners then had to do was tick it:

> (a) Four points are to be made, each carrying two marks. Give a tick when you are giving one mark and two ticks when you are giving both marks. Place the ticks in the body of the script at the point where you decide to award the marks. At the end of the answer add the ticks and place the total in the right hand margin.

The four points to be credited are:
(i)   Brook: multiple meanings for a word are ideal in English
(ii) single meanings are the goal in French
(iii) Carrière: in translation you have to achieve the same effect by different means
(iv) sometimes a literal translation brings stylistic richness.

For each point award ONE mark for the point being found and attempted and ONE extra mark for successful expression showing understanding by using own words.

(b) There are five possible points here … etc.
(i)   Romania: tyranny and assassination
(ii) don't have to create imaginary universes
(iii) Shakespeare an ally of dissent
(iv) Japan: way that he treats elemental stories
(v)   unfamiliarity with the poetry enlivens the response
For each of four points … etc.

The questions prevented the candidates judging the passage as a whole and the marking scheme prevented the examiners judging a candidate's answer as a whole. A tick for circling the point, a tick for paraphrasing it; and for writing intelligently or for glimpsing stumbling blocks where jet-setting celebrities, journalist and examining board saw only a clear, fourteen-lane highway—*nothing*. Even if the passage had been cogent and the questions made up by someone who had understood it, this kind of task—circling points (half-way to ticking boxes)—isn't a proper one for A-level English candidates; any more than ticking the points circled is a proper task for their examiners.

Ticks were used particularly stupidly in question (d), where one had to be given for the 'purpose' of the article's headlines, captions and photograph and another for their 'impact', when 'purpose' and 'impact' are one and the same thing seen from different angles. 'The purpose of all headlines is to make an impact', as you might say, or—as one candidate did say—'the purpose and impact is to attract the reader's attention'. It might do for O-level. It might do for EFL. But for A-level English Language and Literature? The jewel in the crown and benchmark of excellence? For university entrance?

A third of schoolchildren (I hear) now go on to do A-level. A lot of them—nearly a hundred thousand a year—do English. And a lot of *them* don't see or read or like Shakespeare. Robbie Williams might be part of their world, Shakespeare isn't. And it showed—in candidates who had noticed that the passage set them … well … it might be all right for *them* but it wouldn't be everyone's cup of tea. Not when it 'dropped play-names like *Hamlet*', 'appeared to assume that everybody is aware of Shakespeare is [*sic*] a prominent play writer,' 'expected its readers to have come into contact with Shakespeare's work and indeed particular plays such as *The Tempest* and also *Hamlet*' and expected even that 'the reader would understand "using 'p' as the alliterative" when a reader may not know.' It might be 'very cultural' and 'show quite a high understanding of English' but—it had to be said—it was really for 'those with interests in the "finer" sections of society, middle-aged and elderly members of society whose knowledge of literature is somewhat advanced.' The truth was that 'more than the books, appealing to most are films, plays etc. as they are not quite as heavy going and easier to understand.'

Every A-level English paper must now be sat by lots of candidates like that, who, when they hear *Hamlet* mentioned, reach for their Walkmans. This question invited them to come out, unembarrassed and unashamed. And out they came. They saw what the jet-setting celebrities thought about Shakespeare, and that what they thought, though it was here and there offensively allusive or used long words, wasn't all that different from what *they* thought. And they saw that the journalist on *The Independent* approved it and that the Board didn't mind it. So they repeated it, but more plainly. They said things that showed they understood Peter Brook better than he understood himself:

Shakespeare's English could almost be a foreign language.

You have to contend with Shakespeare's poetry.

The poetry of the plays, which is sometimes confusing in English, and so blinds the reader to the true meaning of the play, is often lost when translated and so the audience can then picture the real story without hindrance.

Shakespeare is performed so often that people concentrate on the language e.g. blank verse and rhyming cutlets [*sic*] instead of the actual acting.

In Japanese, Shakespeare's poetry is lost and therefore you have to look at the story and what Shakespeare is actually saying and this is good.

The Japanese are seeing a new product without a stereotypical sequence of old incidents and speeches.

The Romanians don't have a history of producing Shakespeare hanging over their heads.

They were lucky in that they didn't have to wade through all Shakespeare's quotes as us English do.

Shakespeare is popular in Romania as they do not have the handicap of the English language.

These candidates really did understand the passage and deserved more ticks than were available to give them.

But they weren't the only ones who understood it better than the examiners. There were others who, if the questions had helped instead of hindering them, might have been able to say what was wrong with it.

Question (a) asked the candidates to 'explain the different attitudes to language of the French and English as expressed by Brook and Carrière'. Now, that could mean 'find and paraphrase their (four) main points'—which is what the examiners took it to mean. But—because it doesn't dictate what counts as 'explaining'—it permits something more (more interesting). You can see that this is so if you compare it with (b).

Whereas in (b)—'explain why Shakespeare is popular in Romania and Japan'—'explain' means 'find the cause of' and does invite answers that invite marks in the form of ticks (and crosses), in (a) 'explain' means something more like 'give a reasoned account of'. It leaves—it ought to leave—the candidate freer to answer according to his own sense of what counts as 'explaining'. Part of the point of this question (for an examiner who is himself alive to the way the word shifts its meaning) is to test what the candidates can make of 'explain'. There can't be any question of the examiners merely awarding ticks for each of 'four correct points' and ignoring everything else. Yet that was just what the marking scheme required them to do—even though not a few students showed that, put to the test, they might prove capable not just of paraphrase but of thought.

'A reasoned account' of what Brook and Carrière say about the differences between the French and the English attitude to language—an account that really did explain something—ought to go a good deal further than paraphrase, however sensible. What they say isn't obviously friendly to Brook's larger argument that Shakespeare gains from being translated. On the face of it, the differences described suggest that translations into French must be travesties. And quite a few candidates, without any help from either the question or the passage, did, in the very short space they had available (about 40 separate 'points' to be located and paraphrased in 60 minutes), tug and pick at the knot Brook had tied. They showed a capacity for thinking which the assistant examiners were forbidden to credit.

I didn't record every instance where a candidate said something deserving a tick I couldn't give but I know that I not infrequently felt indignant, sometimes sufficiently to say so in the margin of the script (putting messages in bottles and throwing them in the sea—now forbidden for fear they get back to the candidates: see p. 145). And I did record the following instances where I thought the candidate was doing something more interesting and more valuable than merely finding and paraphrasing, was making a start on criticism:

> Brook thinks that the French and English languages are incompatible because the essence of the language is so different. It is difficult then to translate one language, in which words have many meanings, into a language where the words need to be clear in meaning. He feels that both languages have very little in common.
>
> You can't have two languages more incompatible than French and English. By this he means that both languages are difficult to translate into the other.
>
> This highlights a fundamental difference in attitude to language between the English and the French, to the extent that Brook calls them the most incompatible languages. The differences are not negative though ...

This last candidate has seen what neither Brook himself, nor the journalist, nor the Board has seen, that Brook's larger argument needs rescuing. Is that worth one tick or two? or, following the marking scheme, none?

It isn't that an examiner couldn't in these cases find some plausible excuse for putting a tick or two in the margin but that he couldn't properly take into account the fact that something better was being supplied than was wanted, that he was being required to overlook exactly those qualities he should have been looking out for. It was like being told to prospect for fool's gold.

The following says exactly the opposite of what Brook says (and couldn't be given a tick by the most lenient or inconsistent examiner) but it is saying something which is not only sensible in itself but needs to be said: that for the audience of a Shakespeare play it can be an advantage to be English:

> In England we have a heritage of great Shakespeare plays and from childhood are 'brought up on' certain quotes from his plays. Shakespeare is part of a literary heritage that we are all proud of, and in some ways possessive of—in the way in which we use quotes from the plays as part of our everyday language. Other countries do not have the same background.

Now isn't this, at worst, the necessary counter-truth to Brook's own? Shouldn't Brook have thought of it for himself? Shouldn't the journalist? As they didn't, shouldn't the examiners have welcomed and rewarded it, instead of sending it away tickless?

A lot of candidates, I thought, understood the paragraphs which question (b) is based on (9 to 11) better than the examiners did. The question asks why Shakespeare is popular in Japan and Romania, but these paragraphs are only about Shakespeare's popularity where the speaker forgets what he is talking about. As pretty well all the candidates spotted (how could they miss it?), the subject of these paragraphs is the same as that of the piece as a whole: how much more foreigners make of Shakespeare than the English (unless they are jet-setting celebrities). 'Popularity' is, at most, a side issue. Many candidates seemed to me hindered by the obtuseness of the question. If they understood the passage, their answers were pulled one way; if they wanted a tick, they were pulled another.

The Color Purple

This is the book which all the candidates answered on. It is a really rubbishy, boring book—soap opera plus ishoos, the race ishoo and the sex (or rather the gender) ishoo—sentimental trash. Check this opinion if you have a few days spare: the book is very easily available. Nothing like it could ever pass as literature anywhere there was an educated class, intact as a class and confident of its taste. Only in a culture like our own, where the dominant standard is plebeian and uneducated, could such a book ever be used to prepare candidates for university entrance. Only in a culture where the contemporary standard prevailed in defiance, or ignorance, of any standard that had ever gone before could *The Color Purple* be 'studied', alongside—what shall we say?—*King Lear*, *Pride and Prejudice*, Homer? (except that of course on this A-level list the latter were unavailable).

The book is rubbish of a peculiarly American sort—something low with pretensions to the 'higher' and more 'spiritual'. The high brought horribly low by familiarity. Fake, democratic modesty, real conceit. Who needs read further than the dedication?

> To the Spirit:
> Without whose assistance
> Neither this book
> Nor I
> Would have been
> Written.

But if that sets your teeth on edge, the way Alice Walker signs off will make you wish you'd had them out:

> I thank everybody in this book for coming.
> A.W., author and medium

One of the two questions on the book could have been taken advantage of by a candidate who was inclined, and dared, to dislike it: what does it have to say about love? The other question required the candidates to think that Alice Walker has something called 'writing techniques'. (The novel is, like *Pamela*, epistolary, and presumably the different styles of the various correspondents, beginning with Celie to God, were intended.) As you couldn't possibly attribute any such thing to her, except in derision (see—as the candidates had to—the last chapter), the candidates had either to ignore that side of the question (there were several others) or to bluff their way round it. It was bluff that was wanted. (I hope that one of the things I was judged too lenient for was not penalizing its absence.)

But it was what the book prompted these young people to say about love and about life generally that interested me. All had pretty much the same thing to say—which was pretty much the same thing the book itself has to say. All the candidates, the worst and the best, seemed to understand the book equally—indistinguishably—well. As, being what it is, how could they not? The book was evidently congenial to them, they receptive to it. ('His nonsense suits their nonsense, sir.') But it was more than that. Understanding the book presented no difficulty to them because they already knew what it had to teach. It summed up what they themselves knew. They didn't read it or judge it or think about it. They merely reproduced it: that is, they innocently, candidly, expressed—produced—themselves. They and it are precipitates of the same moral chemistry, the same assumptions, the same grammar.

In reading these exam papers I felt I was being shown something much stranger and more exotic than any merely Elizabethan or medieval—or aboriginal—World Picture. I was being shown the World Picture of the present all around me, the World Picture of the young, of my own and my neighbours' children. Not the picture of the world held by the Inter City Firm on the Meadowell council estate but that held by the respectable and well-behaved, middle class, educated young of the suburban Tyne Valley. 'Great kids,' sometimes say their teachers. Great kids, all.

And I was to mark this stuff, to distinguish the better in it from the worse, in numbers out of 80. When it was all—all (all answers but two)—equally, because absolutely, worthless. To mark it, when what one felt for it (off a council estate oneself) was pure, aristocratic disdain, *desdeyn*—for what the candidates were writing; for the book they were writing about; for the Chief Examiner who not only set the book but claimed (as I was told) that the more he read it the more he saw in it; for the Team Leaders and Assistant Examiners who carried out his instructions like lackeys and footmen (Quality—Top-down Driven); for the teachers (more lackeys) who chose to 'teach' the book, as just more stuff to teach; for the parents of the candidates and the candidates themselves who would rejoice or sorrow over the marks as if they meant something, as if they were the mark of something real; and disdain, of course, for the university admissions tutors and the employers (not to mention journalists and politicians) who would treat the results as the record of real events.

The candidates' language made me feel like the residue of some extinguished nobility. Not the errors of 'SPAG' (spelling, punctuation and grammar) and idiom, common enough and bad enough though they often were. Nor the Americanized, soap opera vulgarisms like *mouthed off at, love has to be a two-way thing, can't handle relationships* (because no mum and an inattentive dad), *relationships can work* (with the components of love and mutual respect), *on a high, calling the shots*. Nor even a vocabulary full of media-words—if not homegrown then naturalized—like *lifestyle, image* and *relationship, concepts* and *factors, positive, negative, caring, supportive* and *bonding, totally, basically* and *actually* (as in *to actually do any and everyfing*). Nor the fact that no-one, not one candidate, ever tried to rise above, or sink below, plain matter-of-fact statement, that no-one liked or disliked or joked or was ironical. Nor even that everyone was more or less the same as everyone else.

All this was bad enough. I shouldn't want to pretend it didn't matter. But in the examination answers of eighteen-year-olds, mere ignorance and tastelessness, or the absence of individual character, wouldn't, on its own, seem prophetic. But something did, something which seemed to me to underlie, or surround and bind together, all these lesser failings and give them their special virulence (as AIDS can make a cold fatal). This something was a new common sense—the common sense that underlies abortion and divorce and euthanasia and privatizing prisons; pop, fashion and deodorant adverts; Alice Walker, Elizabeth Taylor, Tony Blair, Princess Diana, the 'European Union' and BS 5750; the common sense that underlies and supports the whole modern form of life—here, made candidly and unselfconsciously plain, as only youth can.

I say 'new'. In a way it's respectably old and familiar. It's certainly been a few hundred years in the making. In this country Newman called it 'liberalism' and F. R. Leavis called it 'technologico-Benthamism', in Canada George Grant called it 'technology and liberalism'. But such phrases suggest something having the character of an idea, something examinable. What these exam papers contained was something far beyond that: the idea become the underlying, unexaminable ground of any and all ideas whatsoever—unexaminable, to the holder, because comprising the language in which he conducts any conceivable examination of anything, including of the language in which he examines things. How to get far enough outside this language in order to see it? Impossible, except by learning another language. Shakespeare's would do. What could be more commonsensical than such assumptions as these: that what is real is material-mechanical, and can be manipulated and measured; that all values are relative; that there is no judgement ... that doesn't infringe some-one's freedom; that if there is any final good it is that freedom, and equality in freedom; that there are no ends ... that aren't means to other ends (not even that end of all ends, happiness). This isn't new in itself, of course, but the frank brutality with which these respectable eighteen-year-olds say it, without apparently being aware that they are saying anything at all—that's new.

What are these truths which they hold to be self-evident, and which Alice Walker helps them state? They're the good ol' American truths—life, liberty and the pursuit of happiness, rights to—after 200 years of development and a new land-fall in the Old World. They're our own chickens, come home to roost—as crows, with sentiment. I quote the candidates themselves:

The important thing is to manage to sort out your life.

People can only benefit from love in the long run.

Love can help you exist happily/gain confidence/survive/get through life/carry on.

You need love to give a sense of self-worth.

We must learn to love and appreciate ourselves.

Love is about being completely content with yourself.

We must learn to accept each other for what we are and give ourselves the freedom to enjoy it.

Sexual love can transcend the borders of gender/is transferable and need not be mechanically fixed to one gender/need not be confined within its stereotypical contexts and sometimes the more unusual it is the more wounds it can heal.

Love of women for women is acceptable but love for men and women is also fine. Love is the important thing in any way you can find to suit yourself and your partner.

It doesn't matter what form it arrives in/whether of man or woman, your husband or lover/be it love for a person, love for an animal, or love for an object.

A religion that does not judge ...

God no longer the white man but a thing that is everywhere/a something, a beholder of beauty instead of the white ideas of an old white man with a white beard and white hair/not a he but an it, pleased with creation. 'If people don't admire the color purple it pisses God off.'

God simply loved people to be happy and appreciate the things around them and the feelings they experienced. 'God loves everything you love' and 'God loves all them feelings. That's some of the best stuff God made' and 'me and God make love just fine.'

Love is the right of all of us.

And then there's the way these truths work themselves out in Celie's life, before and after Shug (Shug—Avery—is her Saviour and her, and her husband's, and others', lover). B[efore] S[hug], Celie

is inadequate as a woman in her own right/isolated from her own feelings;

makes no effort to discover/get in touch with her inner feelings;

has a poor self-image/no self-prestige/a lot of negativity;

has no concept of the pleasure of sex and it being a tool which can be manipulated to express love;

protects Nettie from Pa as she has no feeling of self-worth;

is timid and lacking in self-esteem and has no fighting spirit, but she does have redeeming characteristics: she knows how to survive and her sexual urges are awoken by Shug Avery. However she is no paragon;

is far too sympathetic to others and careless of herself, too considerate, but she learns, through Shug Avery, to become more aggressive and self-seeking.

Under Shug's influence, Celie becomes a paradigmatic, modern woman. Her development is multifaceted, and the facets all fit—'everything comes together for her': Her

search for herself begins;

life becomes her own/her feelings are allowed to be heard;

husband's love for Shug highlights his weakness and this is important to Celie because it shows what a woman can do to a man and how she can treat him if she tries.

She

begins to try to be her own person/becomes a person in her own right/comes to terms with who she is/recognises herself as an individual;

becomes strong enough to be her own woman/comfortable with herself/at ease with herself;

explores herself and becomes proud of what she discovers. This experience gives Celie a worth that she must also love herself;

gains the advantage of self-acceptance;

appreciates herself/can accept without being put down for feeling good about herself/makes herself feel better/is transformed to a life of self-esteem/feelings of self-love waken within her/obtains self-esteem, independence and self-love;

becomes strong/assertive/aggressive/proud/a confident assertive woman who knows what and whom she wants;

can finally live the life she wants/enjoy the lifestyle she wants;

gets control of her own life;

grows from being unhappy and unloved to someone who has gained what she wants;

becomes happy once she discovered this happiness and realized she had a right to happiness/happy to be the person she is/finally happy to be herself, and not some-one's wife;

learns much in her expressions of love and anger/the love she felt let her mouth off to him, and eventually stick a fork in his hand/this is the first real anger she feels;

comes to terms with what life is all about;

realizes that life is to be enjoyed not endured;

becomes capable of living for herself, instead of through others;

develops from being self-sacrificing to someone who 'struts a bit';

so that whereas she starts off blaming herself for all the bad things that happen, in the end she blames others;

resents God because he doesn't help her in suffering/save her from bad experiences/take any notice of her. 'What God do for me?' she says;

loses her faith in God [when things go wrong], regains it [when things go right];

grows to love herself and therefore to love sex/achieves sexual liberation;

learns to relate to other women;

realizes her own and Shug's needs/realizes the concept of enjoying sex/has some flesh to direct her feelings at/utilizes her body to gain pleasure;

Sex activity enables her to gain self-confidence/the two women are naturally lovers because both are women, both have the same experiences and the same feelings;

Shug is caring and supportive/Celie and Shug are an example of the way women must support each other/the idea of sisterhood helps Celie in the area of bonding/ if women work together, they can achieve anything, can be in control/by quilting together they succeeded in creating female continuity in a world that represses female expression/Celie and her sister, Nettie, don't just love one another, like sisters. They have 'sister' love, which is an indication of the unity of women and oppression of men.

The unity of women is tried by a man (that is, by the urge for one, that is, by the wish to know that one can still get one, if one wants) but not overcome. The mature wisdom acquired in the trial brings it through:

It's important to Shug to know that she can still get a young man.

The time comes for Shug to have a fling with Grady.

Even when Shug leaves Celie for Grady, she still loves Celie, who learns that just because someone leaves you for someone else, it doesn't mean the end of love.

It does not mean that Shug loves her less but that she needs her freedom. Celie, broken hearted at first, comes to terms with that. 'Just cause I love her don't take away any of her rights.'

Love is about sharing but love is also about letting the person you love go. Celie has to learn this and she does. 'I try to teach my heart not to want what it can't have.' [*There's spiritual for you.*]

And through the unity of women—the unity of all, as women (who have taken the place of the proletariat), in the genderless society:

Celie and Albert are united by their love for Shug.

At the end when Celie's sister returns, the family is united, and Africa and America are united.

All the characters are re-united in a feminized space. Alice Walker makes all males females, all differences equal.

And what's so strange about all that then? It's no mere jargon or set of notions adopted to pass an exam with. These are the new commonplaces of—as Lawrence called it—'a newspaper-reading democracy': Christianity Benthamized, Marxized and sentimentalized. It's a new common sense (which turns the old on its head). Look at the number of different ways it offers of saying the same thing, the way the new combines with the old in it, the vulgar with the pretentious. It's not just flexible and various but organic—able to turn anything and everything it touches into a form of itself (like the vegetable from outer space in one of the Quatermass films). Here is a language capable of making sense of the world. It's a language and a common sense that draws the world together. (No wonder the French fear English.) It doesn't draw together just the Black American feminist–novelist and the (mainly) white English students writing about her. The teachers who examine the latter know a branch of the same language. Examiners need (we nod in agreement with the Chief Examiner who says so) 'sophisticated reading skills' in order to 'interact' with candidates who may not be very 'sophisticated communicators'. (Well, you wouldn't expect them to be—doing A-level English—would you?)

This new common sense joins together what used to be thought opposites. San José and Slaggyford, Christ and Jeremy Bentham, love and anger, soap opera and literature. It joins together Elizabeth Taylor—telling the audience at a pop concert for Aids sufferers to 'stay alive'—and a British Prime Minister—telling the nation he wants it to be 'at ease with itself'. All differences, as the candidate said, made equal—annulled, melted down in 'pop'. 'Love to the loveless shown that they might lovely be'... become ... 'all you need is love'.

*   *   *

What subject has been examined here as A-level 'English'? Not the one I did 38 years ago. Not the genuine subject of English at all. Something as little that as alchemy is chemistry. Wherever 'English' is a genuine subject of study—at whatever level—the standard that is appealed to, however remotely, however tacitly, is that of the literature as the best of the language. But the active standard here—throughout the paper, from the selecting of texts to the policing of marking—is that of journalism. Not the standard of the best thought and said, wherever English is spoken, over centuries, but the standard of the moment, in Wapping.

What this exam does is to make hostility to the genuine subject of English respectable and to certify proficiency in that hostility. But if so, the literature itself can still be a kind of antidote—while it can still be read. And if it could not still be read it would not need to be kept off the syllabus.

That's why this particular board, which exists to establish and preserve standards, can't allow any genuine literature into its exam. The real thing would judge the exam and the board that devised it. If only one Shakespeare play were on the same list as Alice Walker's novel, and read, the absurdity of solemnly discussing *The Color Purple* or 'comprehending' Miss Trot's 'piece' on Monsignor Block would be undisguisable. Let the students see what Jane Austen, in *Pride and Prejudice*, makes of Mr Collins, and then ask them what they have learned from Mr Howard.

INSPECTING THE INSPECTORS

How Not To Do It may have been the whole science of government in the days of the Circumlocution Office and rotten boroughs but it is hardly enough today. The science of democratic government is a bit more refined than that. It includes the art of How To Do What Can't Be Done. Nowadays when something's wrong we put initiatives in place to put it right. We want action. So action is what we get.

Somebody's dog's bit somebody's child, and you want a law against it? You've got it. Somebody's husband's dodged off and not paid up? You want him made to pay? You've got it.

You want a better education for your children? You've got it.

What hasn't been done to give you it? Parental choice, League Tables, Local Management of Schools, the National Curriculum, Quality Assurance, Baker Days, bigger sixth forms, more nurseries, more universities, bigger universities, more inspections, reform of inspections, reform of teacher training, reform of examinations, reform of the National Curriculum ... more and still more reform of the National Curriculum? What has been left undone that could possibly be done?

And yet the more done, the more there seems to do.

How could that be?

Could it be that, for some things, something more—or different—is required than sheer blind activity?

Inspection—it's sometimes called monitoring—is a very important cog in the system of pulleys and levers by which educational standards are to be—as Mr Baker used to say, 'levered up'. If teachers and examiners are likely to fall below the mark—and how could they not be—what could be more sensible than to send in the inspectors to bring them back up to it and to keep them there? That's doing something, isn't it? Who can deny it?

In Circumlocution Office times, when asked, 'What is to be done?', Carlyle did once famously reply, 'By thee, for the present, almost nothing.' But that was then, and could scarcely apply now, to a body of men and women who (unlike Matthew Arnold) are all professionals—trained, interviewed and appointed, with job descriptions. A body, moreover, which has been reorganized, semi-privatized upon the most up-to-date and businesslike lines, and has a name that's an acronym, Ofsted, a logo and a colour scheme. You couldn't fairly say to them, could you, 'Thou there, the thing for thee to do is, if possible, to cease to be a hollow sounding-shell of hearsays, egoisms, purblind dilettantisms; and become, were it on the infinitely small scale, a faithful and discerning soul'? Such an old, exploded style of speech as Carlyle's couldn't apply, could it?

The same year as I marked A-level, all boards were inspected by Ofsted. The amount of work it had to do was immense: inspecting the work of seven boards examining three quarters of a million candidates writing two million scripts in eleven subjects, all over the country. Ofsted covered—that is had headings and sub-headings for—everything: every aspect of syllabuses, from principles to presentation; every aspect of exam papers, from design to marking schemes; every aspect of marking and grade awarding, from the selection and training of examiners to borderline re-marking. It covered the schools as customers too, satisfied or otherwise. No wonder it took from January to August. What an immensity of measurable activity must have been entailed: hours of listening, watching, conferring; pages of typing; miles of travelling; miles upon miles of central heating pipework and telephone and electrical cable kept employed. What organization. What a contribution to the economy—or a cost.

We can get some idea from the report it produced.[2] Did it do the job? Does it tell us whether the quality and standards of A-levels are high or not? Actually, no. Not that it has failed to. It didn't try. It judges and sets out to judge—in the ordinary sense of that common English word—nothing at all.

The 'quality and standards' Ofsted concerns itself with have nothing to do with quality and standards as ordinarily understood. Whatever the Inspectors do do with their pudding, the one thing they don't do is eat it.

An examination candidate needs not just to possess information but to make sense of it—according to the canons of his subject, according to what, within the subject and at his level, matters more and less. A student in the act of studying develops a new scale of values. Things which don't matter outside the subject and to laymen (to himself before his own initiation), within it become important. This new scale of values won't just sit alongside his old but will be incorporated into it, modifying it, modifying—if ever so slightly—him, permanently, for good or ill. As he enters more deeply into the subject, the subject enters more deeply into him.

And what is true of the candidate is true of his examiner. What qualifies the one to judge the other is not just that he knows more but that he knows better what is and isn't worth knowing in the subject. What he has more of is not only information but, as it were, the morality of the subject.

And what is true of candidates and examiners must be true of inspectors. The inspectors can no more judge the work of the examiners from a position outside the subjects being examined than, from such a position, can the examiners judge the work of the candidates, or the candidates know how to answer the examiners' questions. The work of inspection is done—if it is done—from within the subjects and within what they have in common. To inspect the 'quality and standards' of the examining boards, inspectors have to think primarily, essentially, like men and women who care—can one say?—for the honour of their subjects and of the larger order the individual subjects compose.

But not at Ofsted. Ofsted attempts the impossible—impossible not because merely very difficult but because self-contradictory: to judge the examining of the arts and sciences from a standpoint outside all art and science.

Ofsted's standpoint is, as the report itself says, 'quality assurance', 'quality control procedures', 'auditing'. The kind of 'quality' and 'standards' that is in question is that of industry, a kind that can be ascertained by rule and method, by (as an Ofsted inspector said to me in a letter) 'methodology', a kind that can be controlled (like portions), that is familiar to trading standards officers and is expressed, ideally, in quantities. We are in the world not of mere fallible judgement but of measurement and certain results. ('Never mind the quality, feel the width.') It's a world in which, if you've got 'quality', you can get a British Standards Certificate, BS 5750, to prove it.

An audit may gain in 'objectivity' over mere judgement, but only by losing sight of everything that isn't auditable, which may be—for all your audit can tell you—the most important things of all. Despite the report's sub-title, 'Quality and Standards', and its ostensible purpose, it has next to nothing to say about quality. In what it does have to say, it is like a (perfunctory) school report, handing out mere grades of approval:

Syllabuses—Appropriate

Questions—Appropriate

Demands—Appropriate

Standards—Appropriate

Quality of Papers—Sound to High

Marking—Satisfactory to Good

Overall—Immensely professional

But the report gives the reader no glimmer of an opportunity to test these verdicts, no hint of its evidence or reasoning, no hint of what makes standards appropriate or of what they might be appropriate to. It gives no hint, that is, what its own standards are. You've got to take them on trust—or not. It has no interest, really, in its own judgements. It makes them to get them out of the way and to get on with other, auditable, things. On what is ordinarily understood by the terms 'quality' and 'standards' it is practically inarticulate, as—if it's an audit—what else can it be?

The core of the report would be, you'd think, the sub-section 'Quality and Standards' within the main section 'The 1993 Examination Papers', and perhaps it is, but it consists of only one short and one longish paragraph. The short one says that quality was satisfactory to high but gives no hint what made it so. The longish one begins with a windbag's statement of the obvious, couched in an abstract jargon meant to make it seem like a discovery: 'The key criteria for effectiveness in question-papers are the appropriateness and consistency of their level of demand.'

Then it repeats what it says in the paragraph before: 'Questions were almost always judged to be pitched at an appropriate level.'

Then, without hinting what made them so, it gets on with one of the things it can talk about, the 'tighter co-ordination' required to make all demands perfectly uniform.

What the report is about is not quality and standards but 'practices and procedures', the 'examination process' as a process, a kind of industrial production line manufacturing grades. If you consider examining at a sufficiently high level of abstraction, it *will* seem to be a variety of manufacturing, and to be subject to the same quality control procedures and analyses as 'any other' manufacturing process. (Looked at from outer space, the Los Angeles smog is reportedly beautiful.)

The report notices three things and three things only about the process: how explicit all the various bits of documentation are ('Syllabuses offer a satisfactory specification of the examination requirements'); how well one section of the production line, or one input, fits in with another ('need to devise more sophisticated mechanisms for relating dissimilar components'); and how consistent practices and procedures are within and between the Boards ('variations need resolving').

The desirability of these three things—perfect explicitness of statement, harmonization of parts, uniformity of practice—the report rehearses in slightly varied phraseology over and over and over again. Look at all the ways it finds to say, in its thousand words on syllabuses, that it really does like things to be spelled out (it certainly couldn't be accused of saying one thing and doing another):

> clear indications ... satisfactory specification ... clearer statements ... specify requirements ... specific indication ... fuller account ... make clear ... say little ... guidance adequate ... less clarity ... clearly and fully ... helpful guidance ... little guidance ... how far specify ... no indication ... some guidance ... closely specifying ... clearly presented ... more clearly presented ... additional guidance ... lack clarity

But that quality assurance finds the production line to be running smoothly says nothing about the standard of the examining, the 'goods produced'. The senior examiners who selected the texts, set the paper and supervised the marking of the paper I marked didn't know good books from bad or sense from nonsense. Their examination blurred the difference between good and bad candidates. But that's nothing, to quality assurance. What matters is this:

> Some schemes were exemplary. They reflected the assessment objectives set in the syllabus very well indeed. The marks awarded corresponded with the demands of questions. Where questions required discursive answers, the marking schemes

often included criteria relating characteristics of expected answers to mark bands and, occasionally, to grades. Outstanding examples of marking schemes were those provided for English in two of the Boards [p. 20, para. 30].

Terrific: marking schemes reflect assessment objectives, marks correspond with demands, answers are related to grades by criteria—it all fits together—but *so what* if the 'objectives', the 'demands', the 'criteria' are all wrong, because the examiners are philistines? Where's the merit in their being consistently so?

Quality assurance has nothing to say about quality. Standards can't be audited. That Ofsted thinks that it has done so shows itself a collapse of standards, not among those who do badly at school, but amongst those who do so well that they go on to inspect those who examine and teach those who do best of all. The real crisis in British education is not at the bottom, amongst an underclass, but at the top, amongst those in charge. As we saw, Ofsted isn't alone in thinking that the quality of academic institutions—of thought—can be audited.

Carlyle was right: before these people can do anything they must become different people. And Nietzsche, a bit later, was right too: we need educators who are themselves educated.

There is one thing that puzzles me though: the thought that there is—there *must* be—a discrepancy between Ofsted, the organization whose logo appears on the covers of the report, and the inspectors who work for it. The latter can't be—they absolutely cannot be—as individual men and women, what they seem to be from this report, brainless philistines. They must surely be, many of them, civilized men and women. If you write to them or speak to them on the telephone, that's what they are likely to seem: nice, reasonable, thinking people. And then you look at this report they produce, and the poverty of the interests they bring to it. The contrast is bizarre. *There's* a mismatch between components for them to audit: that between themselves as living men and women and as servants of Ofsted.

What could any Minister do in the circumstances? Via the system of levers and pulleys that constitutes his mere brute power, nothing at all. As an influence perhaps a good deal, but then only with the co-operation and assent of the educated generally. The trouble is, in this country today, that many supposedly educated people aren't, and that they occupy positions for which education is necessary. The 'educated' need educating first. And what could the Minister do about that? even if he were Matthew Arnold himself?

THE NEW, MODERN A-LEVEL

English A-levels used to be very various, like university degrees. We have instanced a bad one. There were other bad ones. Examiner to Team Leader: 'You don't really believe these answers are worth the marks you are telling me to put on them, do you?' Team Leader: 'These people pay me.'

Some A-levels were very much better, quite recently; A-level did not go wobbly at a uniform pace. The Northern Ireland Board's A-levels were worth as much as some mainland degrees at a time when others, like the one we have instanced, were practically worthless. There was and is shopping around by schools to find the boards most likely to award most As and improve ALIS ratings.[3] On the other hand there are still schools that look for the genuine article, and at least for some years and in some subjects they could find it with the Oxford and Cambridge Board, in which I was an examiner in English for three years.

The Oxford and Cambridge syllabus was a good introduction to English literature (some Chaucer, at least two Shakespeare plays, poetry including Milton and Wordsworth, a classical nineteenth-century novel ...) and included a compulsory practical criticism paper.[4] At my first standardization meeting the Chief Examiner refused to give hard and fast grade outlines and emphasized that we were exercising judgement. (He was later forced to resign because our standards were said to be slack.) We formed groups of half a dozen to mark sample papers, discussing them with each other and then with the three team leaders, who once or twice modified their opinions. The spirit was of discussion, not correction. For this board I *often* marked work much better than I was accustomed to see in finals papers at Swansea, by students who were capable of writing convincingly about genuine works of literature. So there was about a decade, roughly the 1990s, when the general collapse of the universities became unmistakeable but, at least here and there, A-levels flourished.

Other cracks appeared, however, even before the millennial reorganization. Boards had to change their methods of examining quite radically in response to the demands for increasing openness and transparency. By *diktat* since 1999 students have had the right to see their marked scripts. And why not? Human judgement is a process not an event; and why should not the examined see the process and form a judgement about its justice? There is much to be said for this view. Generally speaking, though, unless there is confidence in the examiners, no procedure will save the examinations. And as human beings it is much less likely that examiners will express their true opinions on scripts if the examined are likely to see them. Some examiners were not even sure that they would be immune from legal challenge, for example libel actions. The road to other endless litigation (sexual and racial discrimination would certainly be alleged) was open.

So: from 1999 onwards candidates are permitted to see their marked scripts, but with the little drawback that henceforward there will be no comments on them. One Board's general instruction to examiners in June 1999 began, 'NO SCRIPT MAY BE ANNOTATED IN ANY WAY, with tick, cross, comment, explanation or opinion, either in pencil or in ink.' Spelling mistakes must not be corrected. Unofficially, examiners were advised to make notes for their own guidance on yellow stick-on-removable slips, or to keep notes on private sheets, but not to allow anyone else to see either. I can well imagine the resultant organizational nightmare.

By another rule every page has to have some evidence of having been read by an examiner. To get round this apparent contradiction examiners were instructed to initial every page they had read, but not in such a way that the initials could make a comment. (That any examiner should put his or her initials on an unread page is of course unthinkable.)

But though marginal and interlinear comments are strictly forbidden, customers must be satisfied and the openness of the process respected: so examiners *must* write a comment at the end of every A-level answer, even if they don't want to. This too is subject to a drawback. The comment is not permitted to be their own. They are not allowed to use their own words. A phrase has to be chosen from the 'Mark Band descriptors' (why descriptors not descriptions?) put out by boards to define what different marks mean. These are necessarily vacuous. The sense of grades is inherent in relation to the subject and the questions asked. No mark descriptor can mean more than 'Jolly good!' 'Bloody awful!' or the like. They can be actively misleading if they try to define abstractly qualities that must be present in a given grade; which is impossible in English, where there is no general form of intelligent criticism. As *The Universities We Need* puts it,

> Where checklists such as grade descriptors are drawn up, they draw from this well of experience of judgement in practice, and in their application they rely on an appropriateness of interpretation that that experience makes possible. Explicit formulation, however, can mislead us into thinking that they themselves are the authoritative source and final safeguard of standards.[5]

So the new rule that only band-descriptor phrases can be used means that no genuine individual comment will ever get back to the examinee. It also means that the comments will be virtually useless to second examiners, merely an expansion of the mark given.

Why do examiners like to write in the margins anyway? Sometimes just to let off steam. 'Rubbish!' or, less frequently, 'Yes!' But also as a record of the steps towards making a judgement—even at the elementary level of the correction of grammar and spellings, which is second nature to all teachers and cumulatively helps to form judgement. Glancing back at one's notes may concentrate the mind about a mark.

More important, examining is collaborative. I annoyed an external examiner by ignoring his instruction not to annotate scripts. His idea was that remarks by a first examiner would prejudice the 'moderator' and the external examiner, who would be second- or third-reading scripts. It would be fairer to the examined for every examiner to come to the script completely fresh and uninfluenced. I thought he had misunderstood the collaborative nature of judgement. It would be strictly on a par to say that trial by jury would be fairer if the jurymen were not allowed to hear anyone else's opinion before expressing their own. Discussion is permitted before the issue of a class list (though that too is on the way to being replaced either by computers or the disuse of classes), so why restrict it to formal meetings? It can be very helpful to see why a colleague has come to a particular judgement, particularly if the second examiner can modify the train of thought and hence the judgement. I always used to read my colleagues' remarks to see whether I could disagree—and was surprisingly often cheered up to find that I couldn't; it is encouraging that there can be standards in subjects where no opinion can be proved right or wrong.

Our new openness means that examiners are not allowed to record their judgements moment by moment, answer by answer, or on a script as a whole. And if reasonable frankness is impossible to examiners, they are certainly inhibited.

*   *   *

From now onwards good A-levels will not just be here and there; they will be impossible. I don't know whether the new system has been dubbed 'modern' or 'The People's A-level', but it is certainly what others call dumbed down, though it is still possible to imagine further steps along the same road, and it may get worse.

The old two-year A-level in three subjects examined in three-hour exams at the end of the second year is replaced by 'new modular specifications'. ('Specification' is a technical term insisted on in official literature to replace 'syllabus': guess why, and where it came from.) Students will normally take four subjects in the first year, acquire an AS (Advanced Subsidiary) level in one and continue the rest in the second year for the award of full A-level. So each full A-level 'specifies' six units arranged in two groups of three. The first three are 'free standing', completed in the first year, and can lead to the award of an AS grade. Full A-level is attained by adding the other three in the second year.

In theory it will still be possible for a whole course to be examined at the end of the second year. In practice all the schools we have heard of are embracing modularity. It is open to all the objections we made vis-à-vis degree schemes, but more so. A-level is a big step up from the fifth form. The student, though still often too much taught, has to progress in individual thinking and organize work accordingly. Progress really is often made. Then at the end of two years the mind is concentrated as the work of the whole course is drawn together for the exams. Revision can be formidable, but is worthwhile: literal revision, seeing again, and probably differently. At the end of the course the student should be much better at the subject than at the end of the first year; the whole is a fore-taste of what should happen during the reading for a degree. In the new scheme

147

the possibility of progress is recognized; the modules comprising the AS-level year are to be marked at a lower standard than those for the second.

The basic objection to modularity is that it reduces a whole to disconnected parts. To answer this objection, all new A-level specifications, unlike modular degrees, have to have a 'synoptic element'. 'This unit demands a synthesis of the knowledge and skills acquired during the course as a whole ... ,' says one board.[6] They sensibly make this unit practical criticism. But in the old A-level the whole examination demonstrated what is now a special requirement. The 'synoptic assessment' becomes itself another bit. Whether in general one of six bits can be made to unite the others remains to be seen, but I doubt it.

Simultaneously, the percentage of coursework marks will be increased to '30% in most subjects'.

'Key skills' becomes a compulsory component in all A-levels in all subjects. I can offer no direct report because the A-level candidates I know cut all the key skills lessons without being caught. According to the document cited, the skills looked for, bearing out my guess reported above, will be 'application of numbers', 'communication' and 'information technology'. Number has no natural application in the central Arts subjects. 'Communication' is necessary in all subjects, but is not a skill. The fallacy is the one we discussed above, the supposition that if you can communicate in Maths you can also communicate in Latin or to the postman.

The demands made on students are to be much reduced. The OCR English tells us that 'The Advanced Subsidiary GCSE specification covers, within a programme of wider reading, a minimum of four texts ... .'[7] The four texts to be read include one Shakespeare play 'and at least one other pre-1900 text', which may be Mary Shelley's *Frankenstein*. The full A-level gives the opportunity, though not the requirement, to read another Shakespeare play. Though other selections from the specification can be made, a typical requirement for A-level reading over the two years would be *A* [sic] *Winter's Tale*, *Frankenstein*, Ivor Gurney's Selected Poems, Coleridge's Selected Poems, Ian McEwan, *The Child in Time* and L. P. Hartley, *The Go-Between*. By the board's own previous standards this is very lightweight.

The 'OCA Subject Criteria for English Literature (1999)' require that candidates meet assessment objectives including

> A04 articulate independent opinions and judgements, informed by different inter-
> pretations of literary texts by other readers.

This in itself looks harmless; it would be satisfied by good class discussion, and the 'independent opinions and judgements' are certainly necessary. The 'other readers' requires, not superfluously, that any discussion should be based on knowledge. This applies to the discussion of published criticism as well as discussion in class. There is, though, one flaw. Unless 'interpretation' is understood as in musical performance, where the existence of the interpreted work is assumed, and 'interpretation' can be discussed like critical opinion, it is necessary to say that we read, not interpret. Interpretation is bounded by the work interpreted. 'The Lady of Shalott', for instance, is not (see Chapter 8) about Victorian industrialism. Into that possible crack, with unerring aim, is in fact being introduced the blunt instrument of compulsory 'theory'. For instance the English Association (of all people) ran a day conference on 11 March 2000 in which the assembled teachers were assured that for the future all examining boards will insist on knowledge and practice of deconstruction, defined as 'not a dismantling of the structure of a text, *but a demonstration that it has already dismantled itself.* Its apparently solid ground is no rock but thin air.' (Naturally this is just at the moment when deconstruction is fading away in the theoretical centres.)

If you happen to believe that a poem is indestructible, you are ruled out on theoretical grounds. Thin air is insisted upon. Why this is called 'theory' will be a question raised by anyone familiar with genuine theory in the arts, musical theory for instance, and it is discussed elsewhere.[8] The present point is that if the theorists have their way, and concentrate the seventeen-year-old minds on the indeterminacy of the sign, the trace, the always and only self-referentiality of language and so on, instead of encouraging them to read attentively some books worth reading, even the most serious of the young people will get bored, quite quickly. Their attention is unlikely to be revived by the other 'theoretical' demands, 'Literature and Gender'[9] and 'Literature and Psychoanalysis'.[10] The problems of English will rapidly solve themselves in the fading away of the subject.

In the new AS-level History at least one board does not require any essay writing. Imagine History tested by multiple-choice questions, bullet points or spider charts! Well, by the time you read this it will not be imaginary. It remains true that the arts subjects have no effective alternative, for the organization of thinking, to English prose. The intelligent sigh can certainly demonstrate judgement but is not examinable. Ticks from multiple-choices can no more display thought than answers on *University Challenge*. They can't even display any meaningful kind of knowledge.

The school whose report I have been using, an independent school, showed no signs of independence and was intent only on assuring parents that it was fully prepared to co-operate. There was a page about the advantages of the new system, things like 'expands horizons' (vague enough to be safe) and 'postpones decision' (a good thing?).

The latter was in support of the great claim that the new A-level will be less specialized. Why three subjects counts as undue specialization at age sixteen I don't know. In fact the student will now ordinarily pursue four (easier) subjects in the first year sixth instead of only sometimes pursuing four subjects throughout.

The pressure will be on them to mix subjects and include 'useful' ones like Business Studies.

Taken together, these changes can only mean that the sixth form will be even less of a preparation for university than at present.

So why this major change to what was so recently on all sides 'the jewel in the crown'? The A-levels of the last 40 years have been, the Minister told us, 'wrong', too narrow, too specialist, too élitist, and 'designed for a world which no longer exists'—the world, it may be, in which education had some place.[11] The old A-levels were, moreover, British. 'Blackstone ... is an enthusiast for broad-ranging European qualifications ....'[12] Some schools, accordingly, have brought in the continental-style Baccalaureate. Have we really got to such a pass that we can no longer organize our own examinations? After all, we have been having public exams for quite a while, and only in the last decade or so has there been a real collapse. Some examiners still survive. Ampleforth has already taken the more promising route of setting its own A-level in English.

Meanwhile, any surviving university has a problem about judging the qualifications of applicants. All universities are equal but somehow there are so many applications to Oxford and Cambridge that they are effectively lottery tickets. Some colleges are unwise enough to rely on interviews; these are inherently unreliable, even setting aside the scare stories of Oxford dons who put their predilections (usually feminism or Marxism) before the search for promising intelligence. Many colleges give themselves quotas of state-educated applicants, ethnic minorities and so on, so it can help to have been to a good state school. But with the collapse of A-level, colleges have no reliable unbiased evidence on which to decide who are the strongest candidates. Some schools' references are optimistic; other schools underestimate their candidates, and yet others hardly know them. Until A-level is restored nationally, genuine universities are going to have to bring back their own entrance exams. Why ever did Oxford and Cambridge discard theirs?

8 An Examining Board in the New University

If there is no common sense: what is there?

Brian Lee[1]

I GOT A SHOCK marking a set of exam scripts; I thought them bad in a quite remarkable way. The subject was supposed to be Victorian Poetry. Here are a few passages from essays most of which ended up with 2–1 marks, and which I marked at third or lower. The quotations are *verbatim* and I observe in passing that the students' standards of ordinary literacy have certainly improved recently.

> Christina Rossetti uses an even more subtle approach in her poems, often cleverly hiding the subject of women in her poems to subvert male patriarchy cleverly from inside this culture. Her poem, By the Sea, hides women literally and symbolically; literally, because the Stanzas two and three begin respectively with the words 'Sheer' and 'Shells' both of which contain the word 'she'. Symbolically, the poem emphasizes women in many ways, and it is soon clear that it is women, not the sea, which is the subject of Rossetti's poem. Of the sea, she says 'It frets against the boundary shore' suggesting woman's attempted resistance of male dominance.

> The position of women in the patriarchal society of Victorian England was one of absolute dependence. Women were marginalised into the home, had no vote, no political or earning power. This repression and domination was so absolute that it was largely accepted by women. However, some tried to rebel, and Christina Rossetti's method was through poetry.

> Rossetti writes about the oppression of women using poetry, which was marginalised and linked to the feminine.

> The subjects [Mariana and the Lady of Shalott] are further isolated by the fact that they are women, who were repressed by Victorian patriarchy ....

> In Mariana, Tennyson also seems to point to the uprisings which were occurring in Victorian society at the time his poems were written, for example Chartism. Outside Mariana's 'grange', he tells us 'Hard by a poplar shook alway'; and we can

151

see that 'poplar' can be read as a subtle pointing to the word 'popular', and the people fighting for their 'popular' cause constantly 'shook' in their anger and attempts to change the society in which they lived.

Both the Lady and the reapers are set outside the commercial capital city of Camelot, and … indeed both maybe the victims of the industrial society—forced into labour by the exploitation of the Capitalist Society and thereby representing an alienated form of labour. [You can't win: 'marginalized' at home or exploited in industrial Camelot.]

Lancelot is very much a part of the industrial society, with 'coal black curls' and 'armour'.

Technology is shown as an intrusive force in the lady's life, in the form of Lancelot; she brings the curse upon herself by looking down on his shining armour and 'coal-black hair'; Lancelot appears as a machine.

The 'Lady' moves from her 'web' and 'loom' (perhaps suggesting the weavers moving to factories in towns—urbanisation) to 'gray', industrialised Camelot.

Orthodox religious faith during the Victorian era was thrown into chaos and confusion owing to scientific discoveries and higher criticism.

O 'Jesus quicken me,' a call for annihilation it seems because to quicken nature is to whither and die. … [She] turned into a Royal cup in an incredible inversion of traditional images in which she becomes the saviour of Christ.

The poem [Clough, 'That there are Powers'] therefore seems unsure as to the true nature of God; yet it uses as the basis of its text, the narratives of the monotheistic Christian God. This implies that faith is actually stronger than doubt, for in doubting God Clough uses the language of God himself in the form of the biblical narratives.

Whilst Arnold and Clough maybe considered to be agnostic poets, deconstructing the poems seems to reveal the potential for a greater faith to emerge from the trials of darkness of 'the darkling plane'. Whilst such readings may distort the poet's original intention, there is evidence that faith may be restated, perhaps not in its original form, but as a stronger faith, purged of previous doubts.

Clough's poem, too, inevitably speaks with the language of faith; the narratives of Christ walking on the water, his calming of the sea of Galilee and a half-reference to Noah's Ark, the 'evanescent spectrum', are powerful examples of the strength of faith and what it can perform.

Arthur Hugh Clough was also affected by industrialisation and subsequent doubt, but was eventually able to proclaim, 'That there are powers above us I admit.'

Peter took his eyes from Jesus and began to sink. Thus, it is implicit within the poem that one's faith will always let one down. … Doubt poems do assert faith but faith poems also assert doubt.

At the meeting for vetting questions, months before, I had asked to see any exam paper I would be marking, but it had not then been decided who was to mark what, and I did not see the Victorian Poetry paper. Given the chance, I would have objected to it as a whole and in its parts, and would have declined to mark the answers unless the questions were drastically altered, because (a) they were not about Victorian poetry and (b) most were grossly biased in that they invited answers only from one point of view, presumably (see Chapter 6) that of 'the course'. The tutor, it transpired, did think that the questions could only be answered by students who had followed the course, not students of Victorian poetry.

Not a single question addressed the matters which indisputably do belong to the study of literature—style, feeling, movement, what poetry makes of the thought and spirit of an age; and not one question allowed for the possibility that any one poem might be more interesting than any other. The questions on individual poets were without exception directed away from poetry, generally towards the class war, the industrial revolution, the subordinate position of Victorian women. 'How far and in what ways is Browning's poetry concerned with both sexual and class politics?' An ingenious student might turn that into a question about poetry, but it is much more natural to take it as a question about sexual and class politics. 'How can the voices and concerns of Chartist poetry be located in middle-class Victorian verse?' is plainly about certain opinions that may be represented in 'middle class' verse (whatever that is), not about verse.

As to bias: 'What specific strategies do Victorian women poets employ to challenge and subvert the man-made world of patriarchy?' This simply assumes that Victorian women poets did employ specific strategies etc, also that the Victorian world is properly called man-made and properly described as patri-archal. Those positions can be argued: the objection is that the question assumes them to be beyond challenge, and that no other opinion, such as that Christina Rossetti made no effort to subvert anything, is permissible. This paper, not approved by me, was quite improperly approved by an external examiner.[2]

Howbeit, I was faced simultaneously with the question-paper and the answers. So: why did I put low marks on them?

About the poems mentioned, most of the scripts—no doubt following the approved line of the seminars—made the same comments, often in the same words, and using the same quotations. My first objection was that there was hardly any independence or individuality of thought (see above about 'con-veyance of material' to and from students).

The scripts showed, secondly, very small acquaintance with Victorian poetry. Most Tennyson answers mentioned only 'The Lady of Shalott' and 'Mariana'; in the Christina Rossetti answers (Dante Gabriel was unmentioned) there was one lonely reference to *Goblin Market*; the answers were almost exclusively on the same three minor lyrics.

Thirdly, in obedience to the questions, the scripts were not about Victorian poetry at all. They were, if anything, a kind of history—the kind sometimes called the New Historicism—trying to use poetry to comment on Victorian power relations, though it was not history that a historian could have recognized. All these comments were risible, for instance the ones quoted about the absolute oppression of Victorian women. Tell that to the Queen, or to Mrs Oliphant, or to my grandma.

Finally, the link by which this pseudo-history was joined to Victorian poetry was consistently made by 'interpretations' that are nonsense: of a very odd kind, but certainly nonsense. Faced with the question how a text that seems to have nothing to do with Christianity is really about Christ and the Church, the medieval exegetes came up with their fourfold method of interpretation. This was made necessary by the demand that the text bear a Christian meaning. The course tutor now demands that these poems should say the correct things about the role of women, the industrial revolution and so on. The snag is that in literary criticism one is entitled to ask whether they really do. For the reader without the benefit of the course, there is no reference to industry in 'The Lady of Shalott' and Camelot bears no resemblance to Sheffield. In these scripts the problem of finding the industrial/feminist significance was again and again solved by impossible allegorical interpretations of the Lady as the oppressed weaver making her way to the grey industrialized centre of Camelot, with Lancelot as technology. Offered as a reading of the poem this is simply impossible, and as there is no external information that Tennyson is coding messages about the industrial revolution the allegorical reading is mindless, though fanciful in a way that ordinary stupidity could not be. Similarly hopeless attempts were repeatedly made to read the poplar which shook outside Mariana's window as the populace, shaking with democratic rage. It isn't, it's an ordinary poplar, never still.

These answers were based on simple misreadings, but of a fantastic kind. They are made possible by the Eagletonian contradiction[3] whereby (1) signifiers are related only to each other, i.e. words have no determinate meanings but (2) everything is really about modes of production and exchange.

Another supporting interpretative method was to pick words out from other words, more or less like the children's game of the word-square. If Christina Rossetti uses the words 'shell' and 'sheer' they are to be taken as codes for 'she' because both include 'she'. A poem about the sea chafing against the shore is therefore *really* about the Victorian female chafing against male domination. If 'It is women, not the sea, which is the subject of Rossetti's poem' what would Ms Rossetti have done had she wanted to write a poem about the sea chafing against the shore? It is just a linguistic impossibility for 'shell' to express 'she'. One might as well notice that 'shell' includes 'Hell' or that 'she' and 'her' both always include 'he'; any use, therefore, of the feminine pronouns would also always suggest the masculine. *Quod est absurdum*. The method has academic precedents, but as Johnson remarked, no precedent justifies absurdity. One critic quotes another's remark that 'the central names [of *Wuthering Heights*] are clearly (but not obviously) anagrammic.'[4] 'CATHERINE and HARETON contain HEART and EARTH' and (what can hardly be disputed) 'HEATHCLIFF... compounds HEATH and CLIFF'; so that, the critic concludes,

> the text's cryptic incorporations and inclusions compulsively enclose or contain one identity within another in an unsettling play of textual phantoms, with the result that the novel unfolds nothing less than a poetics of haunting.[5]

Wow! And all this from the names, anagrams 'in the rather loose sense', before anybody gets haunted at all, and with so much left unsaid! 'HARETON' and 'CATHERINE' both also contain 'HEAR', 'THAN', 'RAT', 'RATE', 'NEAR' and 'RATHE', so perhaps both characters are to be rated early rats ('HARETON' has the long medieval form 'RATON'). Hareton includes 'NOTE' as well as 'TONE', but Catherine's alternative is 'NOCE', hinting with 'THINE' and 'NEAR' at their long-delayed nuptials. 'THAR' (Middle English 'need') it be stated that this is a game with no rules, i.e., a bit crazy? I would have given Dr Vine a gamma, too.

That every statement includes its contradiction is untenable as a general proposition about language because if it were true it would include its own contradiction. In these scripts it was offered not as something speculative but, of all things, as unchallengeable common sense. Poems of faith are said always to *assert* doubt, and *vice versa*. NB it was not being said that the poetry of doubt has to use the language of faith, which might have led to something interesting, but that when Clough writes that our Lord is in the tomb mouldering low he *asserts* the resurrection, and when Hopkins celebrates the grandeur of God he is expressing doubt. Nonsense.

My discovery was that in the new university nonsense is no disadvantage.

When the Course Tutor saw my marks he said that there had been 'a disagreement at a high theoretical level'. His own marks often came out two classes higher than mine, and he supported them with remarks such as that there were ideas floating about. We agreed that there was no point in trying to reach agreement, and that the scripts should be referred to the external examiner —who did not want to be involved and thought that if the internal examiners had been locked up together for long enough they might have agreed marks, presumably by the exhaustion method so efficacious in the negotiation of international treaties.

I didn't agree about the high theoretical level. What I had objected to was irrationality. If there were ideas floating about it mattered to me that they were nonsensical ideas, as well as that they were all the same and belonged, it seemed, to no individual. There is nothing theoretical about the opinion that nonsense gets low marks. I know the retaliatory moves about 'sense' being ideologically conditioned, male-dominated and the like, but I am not impressed. Nonsense remains nonsense, and if nonsense does not get low marks, all marks are meaningless.

The external examiner generally ruled against my marks. He remarked, quite rightly, on the fragility of the whole system; he said that there was here an 'ideological problem'—there *was*, namely that my colleague was in the grip of an ideology—and that we had been looking for very different things. Yes indeed: I had been looking for literary criticism of Victorian poetry. Different people approach in different ways. Yes; but my first objection was to the mono-maniacal sameness of these scripts. There were arguments both ways, said the external; the scripts I had objected to had indeed been reductive, but they showed sufficient evidence of thought and knowledge. In some cases he had gone down the middle, but on the whole had gone for the more generous mark. 'Generosity' is a word often heard in these discussions; it is of an economical kind that costs the giver nothing except, perhaps, integrity.

There are only two alternatives. Either, 'interpretation' is unlimited—and we have no category of mistake or nonsense, and are unable to make a meaningful class list—or, the convening of an examining board presupposes a general consent to standards of sense. But if there is then no general agreement about what is sense and what nonsense, it is again true that no class list can be made. One or both of these is our present state, and in either case a class list using the disputed marks is unreliable.

Another script was not disputed between myself and the course tutor, but was marked down by the external examiner from the top of class 2–2 to the top of class 3. About this script I think there was general agreement: it was humane, showing a feeling for poetry, nicely written, but not rigorously argued and with a rather poor sense of relevance to questions. The rights and wrongs of this one could indeed have been argued two ways. Some might be inclined to emphasize and give credit for sensitivity and others to penalize irrelevance, though my own view was that anyone trying to write about Victorian poetry had to ignore these questions. What I will never accept is that if scripts full of outright nonsense are respectable, this one was a third. I could not avoid the inference that this candidate was being penalized for not including the required amount of nonsense, though the external examiner did explicitly deny this.

Well, perhaps it was an eccentrically bad run of scripts. Here are a few more examples, from less advanced students (again quoted *verbatim*: their grammar is not so good) examined in the same season. The topic this time is James Joyce's *Dubliners*. They were nonsensical in much the same way. The same phrases were again used time after time, phrases unconnected with reading or, often enough, with any sense at all. The mindless fancifulness was of the same *ethos* as the stuff about Victorian poetry. Here the theme is not industry or downtrodden women or faith-and-doubt but intellectual paralysis:

The colours yellow and brown are continually used—yellow being the Symbolic colour of paralysis. [The Liberal Democrats paralytic?]

The man [in 'An Encounter'] also questions them about which books they have read and this can be interpreted as intellectual paralysis. The picture of 'Romeo and Juliet' above the piano in 'The Dead' and 'The Two Murdered Princes in the Tower' are other examples. [Read and be paralysed? So don't risk it?]

There is plenty to eat and drink at the party but the 'Goose' is rather symbolic being brown and cooked (preventing flight).... [*We* eat *our* geese on the wing?]

The snow completes this scene for us being a symbol of paralysis.

The whole of Dublin is covered in snow, which as frozen water signifies paralysis. [Again. But do not despair: release is at hand.]

Snow, the final paralysing image, falls 'generally all over Ireland'.... Snow, however, must melt, giving water—life-enhancing and purifying. [For those unfamiliar with Dublin slush. We must open ourselves up to this water of life but:]

Gabriel also shows paralysis by wearing Galoshes, keeping water (a source of life out) from him.

To be fair, religion was sometimes also mentioned, though, as it seems to me, with an even wilder play of fancy:

The boy could see no fault with the priest, when he heard that he had died, that night he had a dream of Father Flynn smiling showing his big teeth and a connection with Persia.

After his death the sisters offer a parody of communion whilst they look into an empty fireplace.

He has a red handkerchief which he uses to clean his clothes. This is a parody of Christ's sacrificial blood shed for the sins of mankind. It is symbolically not sufficient in this story as the priest has his hand on it.

Can these students be said in any sense to have read and understood either *Dubliners* or their own scripts? These caused no flurry, though: I was marking only one third of the paper, only a pass was required, and heavy scoring elsewhere ensured that all these students passed.

In our arts faculties there is a lot of *dis*education going on. The students come in, sometimes after A-level at a good school, interested, intelligent, ready to learn; they go out as bored but salary-expectant manufacturers of nonsense. Our graduates are *often* worse equipped to read and think about literature than our freshmen. A fairly steady decline is often observable. A-level is worth more than BA, BA is worth much more than MA,[6] MA is worth more than PhD.

Many lecturers are far from unaware of the state of affairs. One of the great developments at Cambridge in the 1920s was the secure establishment, at the heart of 'English', of 'practical criticism'. This is just the demand that a student, faced with a short English text (or preferably two, for comparison) in prose or verse, without any information about date, author or what is not contained in the text itself, should be able to say something reasonably intelligent about it. This is an essential test of the English student because it epitomizes the common judgement the whole degree is supposed to foster. If you can't make *some* initial response to a couple of short poems you have never seen before—making all allowances for the differences made by knowledge, and, more importantly, the better judgement that comes of allowing something to sink in—how are you any sort of judge of language? We were agonizing about the place of practical criticism in the new university, and I will cite at this point a paper issued by one of my younger colleagues.

I mentioned a fundamental impoverishment, both cultural and linguistic, which runs right back through the students' education and which leaves them at a loss when faced with poetry whose vocabulary, syntax and allusive range are all problematic. It seems curious that a university student having read English for a year can write of the Hardy piece 'this poem is boring and has lots of difficult words,' but it seemed only an open avowal of what the majority of candidates evidently thought but had tried to disguise. Not more than two or three demonstrated any responsiveness to poetic language. Most were anxious to write about anything but; either firing off a scatter of technical terms (onomatopoeia, alliteration, personification) in the hope of a few hits, or speculating wildly about the poem's occasion, in the 'how many children had Lady Macbeth' tradition but without any historical, literary or general knowledge to back it.

Many students appeared unused to and totally unprepared for the sort of test practical criticism sets. The increased role of coursework and the shifting of exam question approaches at A-level clearly contribute to this. I think we at least need to consider the point that such exams may be counterproductive and futile given the world our present students actually inhabit. Should we be examining them on things they can't do, or searching for those they can?

If we continue with some such exercise we need to address it in a different way; the lectures and seminars in Part One seem poorly attended in part because the students do not feel pressed to devote much attention to the subject; it allows itself to be regarded as an optional extra rather than as the centre of the year's study. This would involve a reappraisal of Part One tutorials, of course. There may well be a strong case for including some form of practical criticism, close reading or whatever we want to call it, in finals; either through a separate paper or through some variant of gobbet-type questions on many, if not perhaps all, of the current papers, if only to impress on students' minds the value we place on it—if we do.

In my naivety I may have only belatedly realised that one can no longer assume university English students will possess at least a basic command of what the close reading of literature involves. As a department we need, I think, to make a positive decision as to whether close reading is to be the centre and prerequisite of the study of English, and if so, to design and promote our teaching and examining accordingly. If not, I think we need equally to clarify what we *are* doing and what we are expecting our students to do in order to merit a degree.

The Department's response was to do away with Practical Criticism altogether, to replace it by a course on Literary Theory. There is no point, the feeling was, in trying to deal with close reading or judgement, which cannot any longer be attempted. We should concentrate on things that we (and they) *can* manage, like theory based on 'readings' of Mary Shelley's *Frankenstein*. The question what it is that we expect our English students to be able to do at the end of their courses remains unsolved, though I do not believe it is a difficult one.

The answer can only be generally the one we derived from Newman and Jane Austen: to feel one's way into something real which may go towards setting a standard of reality, and to begin to remake and judge the literature—and everything else. This, however, does assume that, as Leavis thought, English literature is 'there' as more than an academic invention, and it does mean that the subject has to be centred in attentiveness to real works of literature. If the students can't read attentively and if we can't help them, the academics are right to suppose that there is no subject of English Language and Literature: but then there isn't anything else in their departments either, except, of course, salaries.

There is no need for things to be so bad, even given the current state of the world. Simultaneously with the Victorian Poetry I was reading a set of first-year scripts about Middle English which impressed me by their knowledge (I picked up a few things) and sensitivity. They were not all saying or noticing the same thing. Also simultaneously I marked a few scripts by Spaniards to whom I had been teaching elementary Old English. The Spanish have to be told forcefully that they are allowed to utter their own opinions. More than one took to this like a duckling emerging from the nest, and after a few uncertain steps launched out on the waters of genuine literary criticism—*not* by any means always agreeing with me.

The External Examiner put the incident of the disagreement about Victorian Poetry thus in his official report (which I was not shown; I had to 'obtain' a copy, as the newspapers say of leaks):

> I was asked to adjudicate in the case of one paper where first and second markers were often three classes apart. This was in fact an ideological battle: basically the first marker disagreed violently with the thrust of the course, as reflected in several of the scripts.

So the course, not Victorian Poetry, was to be examined, and a university must 'teach' by 'courses' in which the student has to adopt the 'teacher's' 'ideology'? This is not only untrue, it is hostile to the pursuit of truth that constitutes the university. It does explain, however, why the external examiner had no qualms about judging my marks—which, I remind you, were penalizing nonsense, not any particular political opinions—unduly harsh, and thereby, on his own account, affirming one ideological position. He added that 'the whole exam system would break down if the externals' marks were regularly challenged in this way.' It already had, because there was no longer any common judgement. The unusual thing was the challenge. When common judgement goes, one sign will inevitably be that the loss is shared by the external examiners who are supposed to guarantee it.

When the external examiner ruled against me I should have demanded that no degree list be issued before an investigation by the Dean of the Arts Faculty or whatever competent body. To my shame I did not do so—because it immediately occurred to me that I would have to put my argument to the reading public, in the hope that there is still some common judgement in the world, if not in our arts faculties. So I refused to sign the class list, but did nothing more drastic to inhibit the proceedings. It is too late to prevent the graduation of these students, though I have no confidence at all in the worth of their degrees. I make my appeal instead—to common sense.

V

CONCLUSION

9   The Tree of Knowledge or
       a Shopping Mall?

This purifying of wit, this enritching of memory, enabling of iudgment, and enlarging of conceyt, which commonly we call learning ...

Sir Philip Sidney [1]

The man we are proud to send forth from our Schools will be remarkable less for something he can take out of his wallet and exhibit for knowledge, than for *being* something, and that 'something' a man of unmistakable intellectual breeding, whose trained judgment we can trust to choose the better and reject the worse.

Sir Arthur Quiller-Couch [2]

The end of learning is to repair the ruins of our first parents by regaining to know God aright.

Milton [3]

KNOWLEDGE IS ONE, argued Newman, beautifully:

> All that exists, as contemplated by the human mind, forms one large system or complex fact, and this of course resolves itself into an indefinite number of particular facts, which, as being portions of a whole, have countless relations of every kind, one towards another. Knowledge is the apprehension of these facts, whether in themselves, or in their mutual positions and bearings. And, as all taken together form one integral object, so there are no natural or real limits between part and part; one is ever running into another; all, as viewed by the mind, are combined together, and form a correlative character one with another ... . [4]

This, we think, needs an addition about the kind of value knowledge has; but when Newman sketches the alternative he is flawless. If the university is not the garden of the tree of knowledge, what is it? Newman's nightmare 'university' in which specialisms have no common ground is more alarming than it could have been in his own day, for we need only look around us to see his prophecy horribly fulfilled. The university becomes a sort of bazaar, or pantechnicon, in which wares of all kinds are heaped together for sale in stalls independent of each other ... to save the purchasers the trouble of running about from shop to shop; or an hotel or lodging house, where all professions and classes are at liberty to congregate, varying, however, according to the season, each of them strange to each, and about its own work or pleasure; whereas, if we would rightly deem of it, a University is the home, it is the mansion-house, of the goodly family of the Sciences, sisters all, and sisterly in their mutual dispositions.[5]

The difficulty for us in recognizing Jane Austen's authority on education is not that we have any doubts. We have no lurking fear that Elizabeth and Darcy's mutual education might turn out to be another rabbit-out-of-the-hat like Newman's. No, the difficulty is the move from *Pride and Prejudice* to the academy.

After all, even at best, how much of what goes on there remotely resembles the mutually correcting judgement and developing understanding of Mr Darcy and Elizabeth Bennet? And it's not just that few universities' members will resemble them in personal qualities, that most, inevitably, will resemble more closely Elizabeth's sisters or Mr Wickham; it is not just that Darcy and Elizabeth show us an ideal that not many people will be able to live up to. It is, even more, that, for perhaps the great majority of university members, the relations between Elizabeth and Darcy will only with difficulty be recognized as an ideal of university life at all.

What bearing, it might be objected, could it have on any possibility open to the student of Dentistry or Astro-physics or Marketing-with-Early-Childhood-Studies? These are subjects which test their students' technical grasp, not their personal qualities, and, in doing so, are typical of university studies. For, in the modern university the general forms of intelligence have been buried under a lumber of specialization. They are still there, but for the most part invisible, their presence a matter of inference.

Of course, distinctions between subjects aren't the invention of the modern university, and, from their antiquity and the barrenness of experiments in 'inter-disciplinarity', we might reasonably suppose them to be necessary; but the form they now take, outside the sciences, *is* an invention of the university and is regarded there—when it isn't simply taken for granted—as a proof of progress.

The modern university is a place bewitched by science, or by a sort of folk idea of science—by its practices and language, of course, but also by its organization or structure. The extreme specialization that now characterizes the organization of knowledge in the university, the proliferation of subjects and of fields within subjects and the accompanying insistence that only someone expert in a given field can speak authoritatively on its subject matter, and then only in terms of trade, does seem to resemble, or to imitate, that of science, the non-sciences modelling themselves on the sciences in the (sad) hope of reproducing their success.

One of the things science owes its success to—its practical, working success—is undoubtedly its own version of the division of labour. As science has developed, over four centuries, so its 'fields' have been constantly dividing and sub-dividing, proliferating into ever smaller sub-divisions of sub-divisions, each with the capacity to develop into a full-grown 'parent' field itself. So, notoriously, scientists in one field, even within the same 'subject', will have no more authoritative understanding of the work being done in fields distant from their own than will laymen. A working scientist need know no more of the work going on in fields other than his own than he needs in order to do his own. And yet, marvellously, this process of division and multiplication has gone ahead not only with great accuracy of distinction between the parts but without the whole falling into unintelligibility and becoming a mere chaos of bits that have no bearing on one another. It has managed to remain—despite whatever local and temporary inconsistencies may have from time to time arisen—a self-consistent whole. And it has done so because, unlikely as it might seem, common standards of what counts as good scientific work have contrived to apply right across a whole body of activities and practices of which no one person can possibly know more than a tiny fraction. Its growth has been like that of some wonderfully successful organism, continually extending itself, adapting to and colonizing new parts of its environment—a version of Newman's tree of knowledge, continuously budding and branching.

But the—it might seem, amazing—feat of creating, across centuries, a self-consistent whole from infinitely and unpredictably proliferating parts has only been accomplished because the scientific community polices itself strictly and unforgivingly. No one scientist may be able to survey all fields of science but each can survey more than just his own; all fields either overlap with other fields or are overlooked by them. There is no police force to oversee the whole and enforce common standards, but no police force is needed; for neighbours oversee neighbours and do the enforcing themselves. The continuous budding of part from part has had to be accompanied by something else, an equally continuous rejecting of parts which don't develop 'true' to the organism as a whole. To be as successful as it has been, science has had to be as intolerant of foreign bodies as it has been welcoming of new growth. If it hadn't, it would have become corrupt; ceased to be a whole; ceased to be intelligible; ceased to develop; it would have merely proliferated at random, and turned from a tree into a bunch of haphazardly fallen tent poles and blocks of dressed wood.

Which is precisely what has happened, as Newman foresaw, to the university as a whole which science is part of. The universities at large have been every bit as welcoming of new growth (that is, money) as science has, but have shown no accompanying intolerance of foreign bodies whatsoever. At any one moment the list of university 'disciplines' may be finite but it increases every year upon a principle that admits of no limit. It includes not just all the traditional Arts and Sciences—and not quite so traditional Social Sciences—and all their sub- and sub-sub-disciplines evolving into disciplines of their own—but all those vocational, quasi-vocational and pseudo-vocational courses which *all* universities, not excepting Oxford and Cambridge, now run, courses like the following:

> Arts Management; Asset Management; Beauty Science; Beauty Therapy and Sciences; Broadcasting Studies; Business Decision Analysis; Business (or Catering) Management and Sports and Exercise Sciences; Business Mathematics; Business Studies; Coaching Science; Consumer Studies; Cosmetic Sciences; Costume and Make-up; Counselling; Early Childhood Studies with Sports Science (or Marketing or Tourism with Early Childhood Studies); Embroidery; Enterprise, Entrepreneurship, Innovation; European Food Studies; Facilities Management; Fashion and Fashion Design, the Promotion of; Fine Arts Valuation; Floristry; Footwear Design; Garden Design; Global Futures; Golf Course Management; Golf Green Keeping; Golf Studies; Health and Fitness; Health Promotion; Hospitality Management; International Tourism Management; Investment; Knitware Studies; Leather Technology; Leisure Management; Lighting Design; Model Making; Packaging; Perfumery Business; Personnel; Pig Enterprise Management; Popular Music Studies; Real Estate Valuation; Sports and Exercise Sciences and Leisure Management; Sport, Recreation and Tourism; Travel and Tourism; Turf Science; Wine Studies; Women's Studies; World Studies…

Businesses are so various and—as technologies and fashions come and go—so ephemeral that there is, literally, no limit to the number or the character of the courses that at different times might (supposedly) serve them. And each of these separated courses goes its own way without reference to any other or the standards of any other. Are the examination papers in Tourism and Leisure Management simply *rubbish* by the standards of those set in Moral Philosophy (see pp. 83–4)? Firstly, it doesn't matter if they are. The Moral Philosophers have no say in Tourism and Leisure Management. Secondly, by definition they can't be. Only those expert in Tourism and Leisure Management can say what its standards are. Or: once you're in you're in, and that's an end of it. And to get in? The funding has to be in place, that's all. The modern university can't recognize foreign bodies because it has no idea what its own tissue is. What might be part of it? Quite simply, anything. What is it then? Big.

It has imitated science in one respect—in welcoming new specialisms and all the new money and jobs and opportunities for empire-building they bring, but not in another—in vetting them for fitness to belong, for that would mean turning away new money and jobs and opportunities for empire-building. Science is good but butter is better.

We do not say that, until about 1963, the university in this country was just what it should be or that in 2000 none of it is what it should be. If the university system had been anything but very imperfect in 1963, how did it come to be the fraud it is now? For the changes it has undergone in the last 30 years weren't forced on it. We might say that it co-operated in bringing them about—except that even 'collaborate' would be too weak a word. As Hamlet said of Rosencrantz and Guildenstern, 'Why, man, they did make love to this employment.' And, the university system is now—quite apart from anything else—so big and so various that it would be strange if there weren't some good in it somewhere. There are continuities between what it was then and is now, both for good and ill. It would be astonishing if there weren't.

What we do say is: that, as big and as various as it is, the modern university system may be judged as a whole, may be summed up; that the summing up can only be that it is a fraud; that, in order to say so, we don't need to graduate in any more subjects than our own, English Literature.

This last contention will, we know, seem to many people self-evidently absurd. 'How,' they will say, 'can you possibly judge the whole university—composed of very many, very different specialisms—on evidence drawn from one alone? Pyramids stood on their tips fall over.'

This *has* force, but only the rhetorical or debating-point kind. Its force fades as soon as you ask how many (let alone which) subjects it would be necessary to judge before you had judged the university as a whole. One piece of advice we had was that four would be the minimum (mention was made of science as if it were one subject, maths, theology and law). But could the force of this objection, if real, be dissipated so cheaply? *'What?* Only *four*—from hundreds? You need at least *six/twelve/twenty-four* ....' However many subjects were dealt with short of all, it might still, from this point of view, be objected that by so much had less than the whole been dealt with. And yet to offer to sum up more than a very few, close disciplines (each with its own proliferation of sub-disciplines) is, for any one man (or even two), self-evidently impossible. They wouldn't be the separate disciplines they claim to be, otherwise. And, on the other hand, the judgements of many men of many subjects cannot be amalgamated to form a single judgement, though the government does in a manner try.

So what does that mean? That the university—as a whole—*can't* be judged? We can't say whether it's any good or not? As if we couldn't know that a cat was dead without examining every last cell. This is Zeno's paradox. If the universe is divisible into parts that don't add up to a whole, the hare can't catch the tortoise, the arrow never moves and no-one knows whether cats or universities are dead or not. And yet, as we all know, arrows do fly, hares pass tortoises and men judge the health of cats not infallibly but pretty reliably all the same. Perhaps universities too.

This follows from Newman's tree of knowledge. The university (like the universe) is a whole not a sum of parts, and it is the kind of whole which—while it continues to *be* the university and not another thing masquerading under that name—may be judged (like a cake or a piece of music or a man or woman) from its parts. If it can't, then *ex hypothesi* it isn't a university at all. It's something for which we need that useful word which George Grant and Mohammed Mujeeb Rahman and others in America and Canada have coined: a 'multiversity' (our local variation must, presumably, be 'polyversity'—which has the additional benefit that it sounds as if it might have something to do with 'perversity'). It's Newman's bazaar of independent stall-holders.

It is only when we assume that the university is, properly, just such a collection of separated and diverging specialisms—i.e. that it isn't a whole—that the objection to our judging the whole from a part will be thought to have any force. The objection depends on the objector's unadmitted assumption that a bazaar of independent stall-holders is not what the university has merely happened to have become, in error and as a corruption, but just what it was always meant to be, 'in ideal perfection'. The real objection isn't to the narrowness of our range of evidence but to our (and Newman's) idea of the university. It is an unexamined expression of disbelief in the idea of liberal education itself.

Our universities are dominated by such a disbelief. University departments don't like being 'assessed'—inevitably it is more or less unpleasant—but they don't dislike the way 'assessment' recognizes their characters as independent stall-holders. The government doesn't pretend to have departments 'judged', according to how well or badly they educate their students; it has them assessed, by objective criteria, according to how well or badly they have met their own objectives. On the one hand, the University of Oxford still aims to educate its students in French and still judges the study of French literature necessary to that end; on the other, the University of Northumbria at Newcastle aims to teach its students what it once summed up as 'French for Export' and to acquaint them with the culture not of France but of Peugeot–Renault– Citroën; and above both, but not designed to register any such difference as that, is the government apparatus of assessment—whose verdict is that Modern Languages at Northumbria is worth 23 out of 24 but at Oxford only 21.

The government doesn't quail before the problem of summing up a university divided into infinite parts. It just employs enough people to cover the lot. It employs a team of people—a team of teams—to rate all courses, for both teaching and research, in all universities, numerically, on a scale (for research) of 1 to 5, according to standards appropriate to the subjects taught on them. Then—weighting for size and so forth—it takes the average for each university. And it could, of course, do what it hasn't yet got round to doing: weighting for size and so forth, take the average of all 261 or so of those averages, and thus obtain a rating for the entire British University System (of something between 1 and 5).

But that rating wouldn't be a judgement, certainly not of British universities as a whole—and not just because a score isn't a judgement, but also because, here, sameness of score doesn't mean sameness of judgement. The scores averaged together are arrived at entirely independently of one another, according to standards that are not just widely different but, in many cases, mutually hostile: as in the case of Physics and—let's say—Beauty Science; or of Philosophy and International Leisure and Tourism Management; or Art and Arts Management; or, on the one hand, let us say, Counselling and Business Studies and, on the other, Mathematics and every other branch of thought that is either carried on honestly or not at all. The scores which are averaged together as if they had a single absolutely homogeneous meaning—just like cardinal numbers—have (as the interested parties pretend not to know) wildly different meanings. Averaging these meanings as scores is perfectly rational and utterly senseless. (And there, not quite incidentally, we do get a glimpse of how you might go about coming to a judgement of the modern university: by asking the question: 'Are such exercises taken seriously in it? And by those in government educated by it?')

The very process of university 'assessment' in fact concedes the case we are making: that what we now have in this country, as an ideal not an error, is not the university at all but a mere bazaar of specialisms, the polyversity. When the Professors of Theological and Cosmetic Science or Philosophy and Tourism sit on Senate side by side, the university *has* no definite character any more, except the character of not having one.

If the universities do still make sense as a whole (if they and their place in the national life, for good and ill, can still be judged, and not just 'assessed'), then the parts will partake of the character of the whole and the whole of the parts. The character of the whole will be discernible, with greater or lesser difficulty, in the individual subjects that make it up. That Theology and Ethics are part of the whole will be discernible, for instance, in at least what does *not* go on in Anatomy and other branches of investigation into the human body. Certain experiments performed in concentration camps can't be performed in the university... without the university taking on the character of a concentration camp. No more can the ethos and practices of advertising be introduced into it, as they have, without its taking on the character of an advertising agency, as it has.

But not even the bad imitation of good science or the good taste of best butter wholly explains the disintegration of the university into what Leavis called a 'mere collocation of specialist departments',[6] the 'bazaar, or pantechnicon,' that Newman foresaw, 'in which wares of all kinds are heaped together for sale in stalls independent of each other... to save the purchasers the trouble of running about from shop to shop.' For that, all idea had to be extinguished of what sort of whole the non-sciences might make, of what might hold them together as one body of knowledge, seen in different lights or from different perspectives, and of where that body's centre might lie; the idea of a university as a place of liberal education had to be replaced by the idea of it as an investment in training and skills. Only then could the modern multiversity flourish.

And only some renewed understanding of liberal education will give us anything better.

The mutual correction of judgement that takes place between Elizabeth Bennet and Darcy, or Elizabeth's groping for a judgement of Mr Collins in response to her father's invitation to judge his letter, is, to our minds, a perfect example of what education is, and unless it is realistically claimed that universities offer inductions into such judgement, they had better give up. We can see from those instances that judgement is personal ('or nothing') but not private or 'subjective'. Judgements are made within traditions of judgement, in particular settings like law courts or seminar rooms or at breakfast tables. And they are formed in a world where many values are assumed, like the worth of integrity, or the hope for happiness in marriage to be based on love. Not all such values appear on syllabuses. Together they make a world.

All education is induction into the life of a world even as it renews and changes that life; academic education is just a more deliberate induction into what Leavis sometimes called 'cultural continuity'. The continuity of academic thinking with common sense is essential—but broken under the stress of extreme specialization. Academic judgement, when it has not been corrupted by specialization (as it seems to us it has been in, for example, some of what we have shown of economics), is not different in kind from common judgement, but is developed by more extensive acquaintance with 'the best that has been thought and said' and with the attendant modes of discourse and argument as embodied in the people we meet at university.

The personal influence we see at the heart of education is similar whether it be T. F. Powys educating his adoptive daughter quite unconsciously,[7] or Wittgenstein or Leavis wrestling with their angels in the company of their pupils. The difference between a university and that breakfast table at Longbourn or Powys's influence on his daughter is just that the first has to make a more formal use of knowledge and that the judgement it aims at is more public. Universities maintain common judgement (if they do) by the use they make of the knowledge we can also have in common.

Newman's one tree of knowledge is common knowledge academically developed and taken in a particular light. The educated person has to be knowledgeable, of course, and the knowledge is of what T. S. Eliot in one of his more grandiose moments called 'the mind of Europe'. The cultured person knows as much as possible of 'the best that has been thought and said in the world', by all available routes—including the low ones—though the universities award degrees in separate subjects, and efforts to amalgamate the subjects have not succeeded. The knowledge has to be of a whole, though, as it is in science, by way of different glimpses. Our view of knowledge is distorted by the present predominance of rather marginal matters (as Tolstoy called them) like the physical sciences. 'The proper study of mankind is man': in the universities, by way of history, literature, philosophy, theology .... These do all belong to the one tree; they all demand much knowledge as well as thought; they are all interrelated, though—like the sciences—separately examinable; they all depend on human judgement as well as offering to develop human judgement.

And although it is true that universities aim to develop and refine common knowledge, it is also true that those 'developments' and 'refinements' can prove shams, and that one of the necessary proofs of them is their capacity to survive outside the special atmosphere of the university in the rough and tumble of common life. It's always a bad sign if the technical terms of arts subjects wilt when introduced to common speech.

If education drifts too far from life it defeats itself. You certainly won't understand Shakespeare or the Renaissance or the Reformation if you know in your own life nothing of love, family life, politics, religion, good and evil. Shakespeare may then show you some of these things more deeply or terribly, or may provoke you to protest that life is not such as he depicts. The student's experiences will not be the same as those Shakespeare enacts, but will go towards forming the language in which human relations can have sense, and towards forming judgements of that sense, for of course not all senses are desirable. (I remember students who have said they 'identified' with Macbeth. Heaven forfend!) Formal education in schools and universities tries to take further, and in academic ways, the education that every child engages in by growing up in the human world, but if there is a discontinuity between education inside and outside school there is something wrong—with the school.

The appeal to the tree of knowledge is necessary, but to be educational, university studies have to be more than extensive reading, more than 'knowledge for its own sake' or 'pursuing the argument wherever it leads', more even than 'the disinterested pursuit of truth' and the formation of judgement under the influence of the educated. The tree is of the knowledge of good and evil. University studies have to be undertaken in a certain spirit and from a certain point of view, the spirit and the point of view embodied in Darcy and Elizabeth Bennet. Education has to be a form of the pursuit of the good.

This is the principle missing from the modern university which, if brought back into it, would rid it of its clutter of corrupt specialization and turn back a pile of twigs into a living tree again.

*   *   *

Elizabeth and Darcy are both seeking the good, though that isn't one of their phrases. It is, in one necessary way of putting it, the morality in Elizabeth Bennet that involves her in concentrated reflection and the organization of her natural gifts. Mary might claim to be pursuing the good, but can't be allowed to be so in an educated way because of her mental disqualifications which are at the same time moral. The two youngest sisters and their mother are not pursuing the good at all, but would be more educable if they were. Education, the education they administer to one another, is necessary to the kind of good Elizabeth and Darcy achieve. Let us bear in mind, on the other hand, that Darcy's education is a by-product of his love. Without love education will not get far.

Education and morality do lean on one another but are still distinguishable. There are many good but uneducated people. On the other hand education is not always undertaken in the right spirit—though when this happens we would say it does not bloom as it ought.

What should human beings be, to attain their full humanity? Aristotle thought you should be what we have to translate as 'a philosopher' (or lover of wisdom) or what we have to translate as 'a politician', by which he meant someone taking a full part in the life of the community; the very best thing was to be both at once.[8] Education should make anyone fitter to take a thoughtful part in public life, even if only the public life of the polling station, by developing common knowledge and common judgement. The benefit of university education for the individual and the state is, as Coleridge said, the formation of the clerisy, the class that judges in public.

The educated person can take up one of the roles belonging to the clerisy better than the uneducated—being a judge in the ordinary law-court sense but also teaching, preaching, writing for the newspapers, and so on. Here the commitment to the good is an obvious necessity. The journalist devoted to corrupt ideals like economic growth as a sufficient end for a community will spread corruption, and more effectively if he is a powerful and educated thinker, though the conjunction here is hard to imagine. But for instance there are notorious examples of effective MPs who are not in any sense committed to the good. Education here consists of some disciplined knowledge that enables the educated person to use knowledge, and some mature judgement of human affairs; without a simultaneous commitment to the good these powers of the educated will be at best useless and at worse vicious, but they can nevertheless be seen as the ones belonging to education that a moral but uneducated person, or a highly skilled person, may not possess.

*   *   *

Does it work? Education is not inoculation. Many students will not be educated. If Jane Austen had issued a class list (in Carlyle's 'Science of Things in General') it would by modern standards have included too large a percentage of failures, and, even worse, no upper seconds; for Kitty and Lydia must have failed outright along with the untypically bad 'mature student' their mother, Mary would be a third, Jane a lower second and Elizabeth a first. A high real failure rate does not invalidate education in the university any more than it does in the Bennet family. Contemporary universities, when they do not hide this situation by the easy route of declaring the failures successes, agonize over many failures which are not theirs. Our complaints are not about seed that fails to bring forth a hundredfold, but systemic failure that makes university education impossible. Does it work? Try asking instead whether we can do without it.

And as for that question we began with, 'What bearing could the example of Mr Darcy and Elizabeth Bennet have on the study of such technical subjects as Dentistry and Astro-physics?', we have to say, frankly, that the more genuinely technical the subject the less possible bearing the example could have on it. But, we insist on adding, what that means is, the further that subject is from the centre of the university's life. The university could afford the loss of Dentistry or Astro-physics (though we'd be sorry to see the latter go); it couldn't afford the loss of History, Philosophy, Literature ... .[9]

But we don't admit that Jane Austen's example has no bearing on any of the subjects practised as if they were essentially technical. We have shown that it has a bearing on economics. Economics is a subject presently but not necessarily devoted to a corrupt ideal, that economic growth—never mind the form, never mind the consequences, never mind whose—is a good in itself. We *have* helped to illustrate how its unexamined devotion to that ideal helps to make the subject not only more immoral than it need be but less intelligent too. Is it really so outlandish to think that the subject would benefit from a more intelligent conception of wealth than that it presently has? or that when it offers to study the economics of education it would benefit from a more intelligent conception of education too?

And the bearing of Darcy and Elizabeth Bennet on Business Studies, and all its variants, could hardly be plainer: they should be treated by the university like the foreign bodies they are, flushed out of the system and all the money they bring into it with them.

* * *

Near the beginning of Chapter 5 of *Apologia pro Vita Sua*, Newman—a genuinely educated intellect if ever there was one—has some marvellous, still pertinent things to say about the self-destructiveness of the educated intellect which, rejecting all constraint, insists on its own freedom and self-sufficiency. He sees (we believe, truly) that what characterizes the modern, free-thinking intellect is that it won't accept a boundary and a foundation from outside itself and in the nature of the case cannot provide them from within. In consequence it has become randomly destructive.

Newman speaks—in fear and admiration—of 'the restless intellect', 'the wild living intellect of man', 'the immense energy of the aggressive, capricious, untrustworthy intellect', with its 'all-corroding, all dissolving scepticism', 'that universal solvent', 'the energy of human scepticism', 'that deep, plausible scepticism [which is] the development of human reason, as practically exercised by the natural man' and which leads us away into 'a bottomless liberalism of thought'. He calls freedom of thought both 'one of the greatest of our natural gifts' and something that needs 'rescuing from its own suicidal excesses'.

Newman says, tentatively, modestly, that he does not think he is wrong in saying that reason tends towards 'a simple unbelief in matters of religion'. More than a century later we can be a bit bolder. Reason as understood in the modern technologico-Benthamite world tends towards a simple unbelief in *everything* —everything but the things it can make visible to itself and whose existence it can verify, 'objectively', buy and sell.

When Newman made war on liberalism he did not go as far as predicting that unbelief in religion would also appear in politics and literature (that took Carlyle). Before the twentieth century it was hard to realize that literature, civilization, the nations themselves need for their existence something very like faith. But what else but a shared unbelief makes it so easy for our liberal estab-lishment to have Terry Eagleton in its midst? What else makes it so easy for him to be there? Well, the 'what else' is pseudo-science, 'literary theory' and the like, but its role is the legitimization of 'all-corroding, all-dissolving scepticism'.

It may still seem hard to credit that it is orthodox in university departments of English to deny the existence of 'English Literature' except as a deceit and a sham, a trick of the ruling class, serving the same purpose as the game laws but less honestly. It may seem even harder to credit that this orthodoxy is only a particular application of a more general but correspondingly less articulated one. But look around you.

Begin with the other university subjects. If there isn't a Faculty of Social Sciences, then Sociology, Psychology, Economics still belong to Arts, and dominate it. And what is their mainspring but to displace the distrusted unverifiable judgement of human things by a reliance on measurement and system? The proper study of mankind can only be allowed if done by the proper pseudo-scientific methodologies. What else do they do but teach people to distrust anything not measurable and verifiable? Latterly, when students asked me *how* to do literary criticism and I said, 'There are no methods,' they thought that was the same as admitting a fraud. What a terrible co-operation and mutual reinforcement there is between these institutionalized superstitions and the unpremeditated habits of modern correctness—all those variations on 'Be objective', 'Don't be judgemental', 'One opinion is as good as another' and the rest. Geography, which always became a ragbag the minute it diversified beyond maps, became a proper subject by quantifying itself. History, which for decades past has been frantic to get itself out of the subjective Arts Faculty, has turned itself into Sociology-of-the-Past and believes every bit of the past is as important as every other bit. (The right sort of unbelief allows you to believe anything.) Classics dissolves into Ancient History and Civilization, a particular fragment of Sociology-of-the-Past no longer boringly dependent on dead languages and their living poetry. Modern Languages are increasingly without literature, and have mechanized themselves to the point where you can graduate in French without any idea of what makes French worth knowing.

What wonder that the genuine subject English can no longer be tolerated in an academy dominated by science on the one hand and misplaced and/or pseudo-science on the other? Liberal education is an anomaly in the new university. The fault-lines between liberal education and everything around it are too pronounced. Hence the landslips which buried 'English' and threw the present writers out onto the street, luckily uninjured. We, not they, are the survivors. Where is the Arts Faculty now except amongst the redundant? (We are, however, open to offers.)

What are Chris Smith's qualifications to be Culture Secretary (and Sport at the same time)? Unlike Mr Major, he went to university and unlike Mr Collins he did more than keep terms. He made useful acquaintance, very useful. He worked; he has a doctorate; in English Literature; on the romantic poets; from Cambridge University. What more could we want? And asked by *The Spectator* whether Bob Dylan's 'poetry' is as [of course] *valid* as Keats's, Chris Smith, PhD (Cantab.) replied, 'Yes, I do believe that. The distinctions between the higher and popular arts are meaningless.' [10] Asked whether Dylan's music is as good ('valid') as Beethoven's: 'Beethoven and he are different. You can't put them in a pecking order. I wouldn't want to establish hierarchies.' We must not discriminate. That is not to say that the arts are unimportant in the only way that matters. 'The point about the popular music industry, for example, is its serious value to the economy.' *There* is the large return on a genuine investment. But how could the Arts Faculty survive for long in a nation with such a government?

Modern, 'educated', liberal-minded man can no more believe in literatures, or the nations from which they spring, than he can in God or the hierarchies of the heavenly host. Having dissolved the foundations of the religious world, secular 'reason' has made a very satisfactory start on dissolving the foundations of the secular too: if God can't be verified, can King, Noble or Gentleman? Or any of the virtues once associated with them? Can man or woman—except as a certain complexity of organs, energies and infinitely variable roles? Husbands and wives—except as partners? Manliness and womanliness? Englishness? The humanness of the unborn baby less than twenty-six weeks old? Are art and literature verifiable, 'objectively'? Good and evil? Crime and punishment? Murder—except as unlawful homicide? Quality, except in a form that may be audited, controlled and driven (top-down)? Standards, except in a form that may be levered up? Politics—as anything but climbing up or slipping down the greasy pole? Even as particular and localized a thing as the university—the idea of the university—can that be found? Can it be delivered, except as a congerie of courses? What is a university but whatever we call so? Take that complex of buildings, bodies and activities over there. Yesterday it was a polytechnic, today it is a university. It has been decreed. Who can say otherwise?

And where will it end, the march of progress into unbelief? This is a later phase than the one Carlyle found in the French Revolution, in which he saw 'the whole *demonic* nature of man ... hurled forth to rage blindly without rule or rein ....'[11] We are well beyond the blindly raging stage. Newman's answer, in 1864, was that it could be brought to an end by the Catholic Church and Infallibility. Conrad's answer, in *Nostromo*, 40 years later, follows the logic of Newman's argument without Newman's belief in the Catholic Church: where will it end? In suicide for the 'educated', and the tyranny of 'material interests' over everybody else; the place where religion and art was shall be occupied by Alice Walker. This is the way our world ends. Well, let it—and let's hope afterwards to regain the recognition of a few realities. What educated judgement remains can see these things, and can even 'carry us through' to something better.

> If indeed these also fail us, and ... cannot vindicate themselves into clearness here and there, but at length cease even to try it,—then indeed it is all ended: national death ... well-deserved annihilation, and dismissal from God's universe, that and nothing else lies ahead for our once heroic England too. ... [but] if this small Aristocratic nucleus can hold out and work, it is in the sure case to increase and increase.[12]

It is actually the case that some people can still read English poetry. While that remains true, the university is still possible.

An Anecdote of
Institutional Life

But infinitely beautiful the wondrous work arose…

William Blake[1]

THE STATE'S OBJECTIVELY EXISTING MACHINERY of standard-raising and measurement is just a figment but, when treated as a reality, perfectly capable of doing more harm than good. When the 'education system' really is thought of as a system—a complicated arrangement of levers, pulleys and wheels—the parts put in place at the top to ensure that the parts lower down work properly may very easily make them work worse. I believe I saw this happen, on a small scale, at first hand, when I was in the Humanities Department at Newcastle Polytechnic (before it became the University of Northumbria) in the 1970s.

*   *   *

Until the mid-1970s, our students did London external general degrees. They were taught by one set of people and examined by another, and they generally got lower seconds or thirds. The meaning of the arrangement was clear and (it seemed to me when I arrived in 1972) just: 'This institution is fit to teach at degree level but not examine at it.' When we switched to the (now defunct) Council for National Academic Awards degrees, we became (like all the other polytechnics) an anomaly, something that was neither fish nor fowl, fit both to teach and examine but only under the supervision of a centralized bureaucracy.

The purpose of the CNAA was to ensure that institutions that weren't universities (I mean in fact not just in name) could do what only universities can, award degrees. Its actual function proved to be, not surprisingly, different: to provide a professional leg-up for those who joined its committees. It gave them another line on their cvs and membership of an academic equivalent of the Lions or Masons. It didn't make the polytechnics universities (that came later, and more cheaply) but it did ensure the promotion into positions of power of those who were happier in committee meetings than classrooms or libraries. It was a wonderful instance of the plasticity of things bureaucratic. Set up to serve an official purpose that was a self-contradiction, the CNAA was instantly bent to private purposes that weren't.

When we switched to the CNAA we became our students' examiners as well as their teachers, but that made no immediate difference to ... well ... anything: not to the way we taught, not to the way we got on (or didn't get on) with the students and with one another, not to the marks the students got. We hadn't yet twigged, that is, that henceforth *our* 'performance' was to be measured by the students' and the security of our jobs to depend on it. The continuity between London and CNAA days was, in one aspect, a very good example of quality control, assured not by machinery but something much more reliable (much cheaper too), if not conscience, quite, then the next best thing, habit.

What this meant for our students, though, was that they continued to get lower seconds and thirds (and that we didn't see why they shouldn't). What it meant for us was that the first time we applied to have our CNAA licence renewed, it was refused. Lower seconds and thirds (even if they were, now, mainly honours degrees), along with our drop-out rate, were inconsistent with our new status as an institution different from but equal to a university, and also with the typical class lists of other polytechnic Arts departments. The Visiting Panel that made the decision found other things amiss too: damaging criticisms from students, book lists that weren't up to date ('Chesterton on Dickens? *Chesterton?* In *1978?*'), a language course that was amateurish ('There is a proper discipline for the study of language—it is called linguistics. Teach your students *that*') and, as an aggravation of the rest, dislikeable manners ('Those two treated us like fools'). The Chairman of the Visiting Panel summed us up: 'There's no room in Higher Education for amateurs.'

Our jobs being in danger, we pretty quickly professionalized ourselves—or were made to, by a new Head of Department brought in from outside to save us from ourselves. We swapped our old, easygoing habits (or consciences) for something more strenuous, and our re-application the following year was successful. The key to our keeping our jobs was that our class list was sufficiently improved to promise further improvements to come. And come they did, year on year: the general degree disappeared, the thirds followed, the lower seconds became fewer and fewer, the upper seconds became common and above them began to appear an increasingly respectable sprinkling of firsts. Within two or three years our bad, old amateur ways were things of the past; we had somebody in charge who *was* in charge, and instead of a course on Language that had something to do with Literature, we had one that hadn't.

Previously, we had, probably, most of us, taught as well as we could, but we had done so, as it were, casually and with no aim in mind beyond that of being as interesting and intelligent as we could, that is, without really, in one very influential sense of the word, teaching at all. We taught without having any very definite idea of what we wanted the students to learn. And our examining showed a similar aimlessness. We marked up what we liked, marked down what we didn't, purposelessly and without thought of consequences. It was the same with the booklists we drew up and, even, with our treatment of the students (it was certainly the same with our treatment of one another). Wherever you looked, we did—you might say—as we pleased.

But not after 1978. From then on we had an aim, one that was simple, clear and measurable: to get as many students through the degree every year with as high marks as possible. We became focused and properly professional, in four … no … five key areas: course design, teaching, marking, student welfare and (the fifth, or the first) staff discipline.

We began, when we drew up courses, to ask ourselves, for the first time, what our courses looked like from the students' point of view. Were they adjusted to the students' interests and abilities? Would they be accessible and manageable? Was it possible for the students we got (no different from the ones we had got before) to get upper seconds in them? The other key principle we adopted for course design was that no course was to be too strongly marked by the particular interests and opinions of the person designing and teaching it. It ought to be such that any fellow professional could take it over if need be. This principle was well summed up by one of us as, 'Courses aren't like books.'

Whereas previously exams had tended to be rather an afterthought, they now became the very first thing we thought of. 'Set the exam paper and teach to it,' 'Make sure they're prepared,' 'Make sure they know what's required of them'—such became our guides. What some people deride as 'spoon feeding' we learned to think of as responsible and conscientious teaching. You knew in advance what you wanted your students to learn—that is, what to say in the exams—and you made sure you taught them it. What's wrong with that? We were encouraged to adopt a more encouraging style of class teaching too.

And we started marking differently. No-one cynically gave marks he didn't believe could be defended in public, but we did all, more or less as a matter of policy, begin giving marks at the very top end of what we thought we could defend, which had the effect, of course—not that we especially intended it to—of bringing that top end down, lower and lower. I don't say that by marking high ourselves, right across the board, we were deliberately putting pressure on external examiners to mark high too but, probably, our marking did tend to have some such effect—especially as, of course, the externals, in their own institutions, were under exactly the same pressure to mark high as we were. Internals/externals: we were all in the same boat.

We had to get our drop-out rate down too, so, as a matter of deliberate policy, we became more caring. Our way of welcoming new students to the department became much better regulated, for instance. We didn't welcome them haphazardly any longer, according to someone's individual disposition and temperament, and with other members of staff free to come along or not. We now gave them—all of us—a welcome that was official and collective. And we made sure the Polytechnic Student Welfare Officer was present too. It was a pity that, personally as well as professionally, he was a bit of a dampener, but at least he was another means for us to demonstrate our concern.

We became more conscientious as personal tutors too, requiring our students to see us at regular intervals and recording their failures to turn up. Only two of us weren't routinely conscientious; both were male; one had the gift of making the role of personal tutor a way of getting students into bed; the other could never be bothered even to learn their names. Apart from the second of these two, we all started keeping a close check on attendance and progress generally. We kept on the look-out for warning signs and when we thought we spotted them kept one another informed. If a student didn't turn up for an exam one of us would drive to his home and bring him in. We started taking student opinion seriously too. Their official representatives sat on one of the committees, and we always made a point of asking them what they thought and listening politely to whatever they said.

The key to our success was the much higher level of staff discipline imposed by the new Head. Previously we had not been used to having many meetings and had been used to going to them or not just as we pleased. Now we had a lot of meetings and were expected to attend all of them. We had also been used to treating one another very unprofessionally, in meetings even more than out. There was a general air of licence about the place. Sometimes, it is true, it could be very stimulating but it had the disadvantage of making co-operation between some members of staff more or less impossible. Even though it was a joint English/History course we were running, it was impossible, for instance, to have some members of the English staff teach jointly with some members of the History staff. If they were put together, you could never be sure how they would get on. One of the English staff in particular was very easily irritated by people who didn't think quite as he himself did. Quite small things would set him off, and then he'd insult his colleagues, openly, to their faces, in front of students, and even in front of the external examiner. And the worst of it was, you'd never know in advance what might offend him. Sometimes you didn't know afterwards either.

But all that sort of thing was put an end to. The concept (and not just the concept) of 'the actionable' was introduced into the Department. What had been a perfectly respectable argument for avoiding work, that 'if one were made to do things one didn't want to do, one would do them badly,' lost its respectability. The departmental administrative machinery was elaborated, and everybody was expected to be responsible for some part of it. We started to get into the habit of treating one another less as individuals and more as functionaries—as Admissions Officer or First Year Co-ordinator or some such.

That way, at work, foes could be friends. Our new Head himself set the example. Meetings became much more procedurally correct, with less talking out of turn and fewer personal attacks. Although, in some ways, there was less fun in the department, what there was was more equally shared. Certainly, from one point of view, the work went ahead more smoothly. The most important administrative development was the creation of the Senior Management Team, which put a real distance between those who were on it and ran things, and those who weren't and didn't. Departmental policy was no longer made (and unmade) in public dogfights but peaceably by those in positions of responsibility. This made it easier, for instance, to ensure that on the English side only those sympathetic to deconstructionist theory taught it. To have let the students see members of staff violently disagreeing with one another would have been a very retrograde step—especially as one of the likely parties to any such dispute had the habit of making professional disagreements personal. It was much better to make sure that he got nowhere near the subject. (Managers ought to manage.)

Of course, the creation of the Team might itself have become a cause of discontent, but two measures were taken to prevent it: firstly, the Team members, one by one, for a time, took to holding departmental dinner parties, to which everyone was invited and at which the new spirit of working co-operation could be reinforced; secondly, everybody was made to feel that their professional achievements were all equally valued as contributions to the department's success. Too often in the past people had felt they weren't. One of the first things the Team did was to invite people to notify it of anything they had achieved— getting a PhD, say, or an article into a refereed journal, or writing up a CNAA submission—and then it would send them a memorandum of congratulations with copies to the rest of the department. The congratulations were read out at department meetings too.

I shouldn't want to pretend, of course, that everything was now perfect. It is true that business went more smoothly and without obvious clashes. But, of course, people continued to differ from one another as much as ever; they just kept their differences hidden. Discord and friction hadn't gone away, they'd gone underground; and that, perhaps, in some ways, gave them a settled virulence they hadn't had before.

Certainly, there was something odd about the position in the department of the new Head who had been responsible for the transformation in its fortunes. He *had* saved us from ourselves, and half his reward was that on all matters and occasions of official business, including departmental dinner parties, he had our unanimous, or near unanimous, support. But the other half of his reward was, at all other times, by some instinct of mutual preference, to be solitary. With one exception (a woman, of course, with a woman's loyalty), he was never to be seen taking coffee with the members of his own department, not even his closest allies (and, as in the song of the Miller of Dee, they never took coffee with him). And it wasn't that he was unsociable by nature or boring or dis-agreeable. He was rather a clever man, literate and cultivated and (off the subject of work) with a lively sense of humour. (I remember once being brought to a stop by his saying to me, 'Maskell, when Blake said, "Opposition is true friend-ship," he meant it as a paradox.') He was no Mr Collins. We *had* a Mr Collins in the department but with him people were ordinarily sociable.

His superiors (whose backsides he had saved too) were no more grateful. When the Faculty was reorganized he didn't even get onto the subs bench. He got a new title, a bigger salary and an office somewhere out of the way, but no job. The system of official relations and officially approved judgements, which for ten years he had been treating as something real, had suddenly given way to a personal one. He made you feel uncomfortable: get him out of the way. But I expect they gave him a good reference for the job he got as an Inspector.

He did have the last laugh though—where he could—not on his superiors, on the Department. Before he left he made sure that his successor was the one of us most widely disliked by the rest.

Quite likely, our CNAA re-application of 1978 deserved to be turned down, but no more so than our original application of 1975 or any of our successful re-applications from 1979 onwards. We may not have impressed the 1978 CNAA Visiting Panel but its members were no essentially fitter, it seemed to me, than we were, merely a more concentrated essence of the managerial. Supposing they were right, and we weren't very good, what was achieved by trying to *make* us better, by their means, means themselves only dubiously good? Our results got better and better, of course, but largely because, by one means and another, we made sure they did. The students graduating in 1987 weren't better educated than their predecessors of ten years earlier, just better qualified. Departmental business was conducted with fewer public dog-fights but with correspondingly more behind-the-scenes back-biting and flank-rubbing. The improvement in results mostly meant a decline in standards; the more correctly we behaved towards one another in public, the more sincerely we disliked one another in private. There were only two unequivocal improvements, and neither had anything to do with top-down drivel or the managerial machinery it set in motion: one was that the History staff surrendered the selection of students to the English staff, and the other was that we began favouring mature students (mostly married women) over school-leavers.

An Education
Policy Document

THERE ARE SEVERE LIMITS to what even an enlightened government could do for education. No educational reform can take place in disconnection from society. How could a nation with our opinion-formers have decent universities? —or *vice versa*? At worst, it may be that if the reforms we need were possible they would not be necessary. Educational reform presupposes a certain level of existing education, whereas we are close to having to start from scratch—which would only be possible after something more like conversion than reform. There are additional difficulties in the *soi-disant* democracies of the twenty-first century. Our task, within the limits of the possible, would have been easy in the time of King Henry VIII. Simply catch the attention of the intelligent tyrant at a suitable moment. Nowadays we not only need a strong minister of education, we need 'public opinion', and the catch obviously is that the state of public opinion is part of the disease. Howbeit: we make a start. Imagine that enough of the clerisy come to see the sense in what we say: what then should be done by way of policy? We must state one assumption, as part of the hypothetical case about the clerisy. The judges, teachers, commentators and critics, clergy … ought not to fear want, but ought not on the other hand to be very rich. Scholars are traditionally poor; which is not ideal, but it is positively a bad thing for them to become fat cats, or to expect to be courted by company boards looking for rising entrepreneurs. The educated ought to have a reasonable chance of a comfortable life in the clerisy, but not to expect a direct link between a degree and the creation of wealth.

What follows is based on our reply to an invitation to submit a policy document on education to a political party: it is free for all now; no copyright claimed for this part. The agents of the changes proposed are to be imagined to be not ourselves but a political party convinced by our book. (Of course, we are both just as open to offers of education secretaryships as to regius professorships.)

SIX PRINCIPLES

1 Education is valuable for its own sake both to the individual and to the state.
2 Because education is valuable to all, and because universal suffrage demands it, the education of the less academically able must receive as serious attention as the education of the academically more able.
3 But because there is no upper limit at which education loses its value, and because not everyone either wants or is able to pursue education as far as it can be pursued, the formation of an 'élite' must be a natural and desirable end of education.
4 Education and training are often close together in our early experience but diverge more and more the higher in education we go, and must not be confused.
5 Education is, like the armed forces and pensions, a legitimate public cost not an investment, but there can be sensible financial limits to that cost.
6 Training, on the other hand, is an investment, the cost of which should be shared by those who expect dividends from it.

The proposals that stem from these principles will at once improve the quality of both training and education, and save immense sums of public money.

*   *   *

Basic literacy and numeracy is already better in the schools than it was during the liberal hegemony, and we shall build on this improvement. All children will be introduced to at least the beginnings of knowledge of the best of our own form of life. English poetry will be read, and British history, and for all children there will be a sketch of European history from Greece and Rome to the present. No child will leave school ignorant of the Bible. All children will be expected to be musically literate and have some acquaintance with Western music.

A National Curriculum will be maintained, but made less dictatorial and less of a burden on teachers. The bias towards science and technology, introduced in the mistaken belief that it would help to make us rich, will be removed. As a result the smaller proportion of pupils wishing to pursue scientific subjects will be able to do so in smaller classes and with better resources. It will again be possible for a child to study to GCSE level two foreign languages and both History and Geography.

SIXTH FORMS

The attempt to create in the GNVQs a vocational 'equivalent' to A-level is badly misguided and deeply confused. The GNVQs have undermined the character and function of the old academic sixth form as preparation for university by making it too large and depriving it of its coherence; and they have done little to create a new technical sixth form in recompense. The whole apparatus of GNVQs must go. If business values the training the GNVQ subjects provide, there can be either training in the workplace or specialized technical schools.

The well-established two-year A-level in, usually, three subjects, examined at the end of the second year, will be reinstated.

Sixth forms will naturally be much reduced in size when it is realized that university entrance is not automatic and that university degrees will not necessarily lead to lucrative careers, but that preparation for university is for those of all classes and backgrounds capable of and interested in university work.

FURTHER AND CONTINUING EDUCATION

We strongly support the extramural activities of the universities, and the work of the WEA and local authorities, provided that they are genuinely educational. There is no call for the state to subsidize local classes in flower arrangement and Feng Shui, which now make up, by a very long way, most of what is 'taught' in what used to be called 'night schools'. The schools of continuing education have allowed numbers of adults who missed higher education to make contact with it. We support the principle of part-time degrees for extramural students, though we think universities should be abstemious about awarding honours after six years of part-time modular work.

One good recent development has been the recognition that not everybody is ready at age eighteen or nineteen to decide to embark on a university career. Some of the best university entrants have come in as mature students at any age from twenty-five to seventy and more, often after access courses or extramural work. This, though nobody will expect retired people to use their degrees in wealth creation, is to be strongly encouraged. For the comparatively small number of students involved there will be scholarships large enough to mitigate the hardships which three years without earned income entail for some potentially excellent but middle-aged students.

UNIVERSITIES

Educated judgement is necessary to the nation, absolutely; without it the nation loses its mind. The universities must be the seminaries of the class of opinion-formers that Coleridge called the clerisy.

During the last decade, the genuine university subjects have collapsed, often into nonsense. They have also on the one hand been adapted to the capacities of the weaker students and and on the other to the practices of some continental European and American universities which cannot be grafted on to ours.

Put together, the proliferation of useless non-subjects and the dilution of the genuine subjects mean that most of the academics at present employed in higher education, and the 'cohorts' of students they 'produce', are wasting their time. The dilution and/or nonsense in some institutions has got to the point of making genuine university work impossible to any minority still capable of pursuing it. The situation brings learning into contempt, wastes national resources, and has a demoralizing effect on the staff and students.

There will be an immediate and decisive transformation of this situation for the better with four principal measures.

1 University subjects that are neither use nor ornament will be phased out and degrees awarded in the traditional core of liberal arts subjects at every institution permitted to call itself a university.

   Genuine training courses will be transferred to other institutions. Foreign language departments that teach no literature will be classed as suppliers of training.

   A lot of universities will consequently be closed or revert to their former status, for which the name polytechnic will be reintroduced. The new polytechnics, unlike the old, will not run liberal arts courses parallelling those in the universities.

   This reform will reduce the numbers both of universities and of university students by more than three quarters, and will encourage a return to real university standards.

   We anticipate that with the re-establishment of academic standards, modular degrees will fade away.

2 Reformed universities will be adequately funded; British students' fees will normally be paid by the state and maintenance grants will be restored. Students need to concentrate their minds, and this cannot be done when they have to take paid work in the evenings, at weekends and in vacations when they should be reading. On the less inflated scale we project for the universities, the cost of this will be much more than covered by the savings we propose (as will redundancy payments). Overseas students already contribute substantially to university budgets, and we envisage that with the international reputation of our universities restored this will continue; but universities will be not be permitted to reduce their intake of UK students in order to accommodate overseas students.

   There will be encouragement of genuine endowment of universities and scholarships by tax reliefs, and a promise not to tamper with endowments.

An unparsimonious level of funding will be ensured for research projects that are at once genuine and necessarily expensive, like many scientific projects with no commercial application, and like scholarly editions which will not pay for themselves.

3 Once the universities have been rescued and funded on a more realistic scale, they shall be left strictly alone. If they really are autonomous trees of knowledge without superiors they cannot be inspected. The reformed universities will return to the system of external examining by peers, not 'appraisal' and 'academic audit' by pseudo-superiors.

4 Genuine vocational training will be subjected, within reason, to market discipline.

The last is such a new proposal that quite a lot of work will be required filling in the details. The general logic is, however, clear.

If the economy must have training as investment, the resultant wealth-creation will necessarily one way or another pay for the training. It is sometimes thought that a well-trained labour-force is rather like the 'infrastructure', that the state should provide training like roads or power-lines; though many states in fact pay for roads with tolls on their users, and National Grid plc is now denationalized. The question is whether the cost of training should be borne mainly by the direct beneficiaries, or mainly by the beneficiaries of increased wealth in general, the taxpayers. We believe that the former is both fairer and quite practicable, and that the investment should be subscribed for by the investors, that is, the trained and those who use the training commercially.

It is in the interests of the state that standards of training should be reliable, and the state must have as effective an inspectorate for technical institutions as it has for schools. It does not necessarily follow that the costs of such inspection should come out of the taxes.

The state's interest in technical education will be recognized in supporting it, but not *in toto*. There are various possibilities for the mechanics of financing the new system. As a beginning, three quarters of the cost of technical tertiary education will be transferred to the fees, leaving one quarter for the exchequer, though this may vary somewhat from course to course. The national interest may possibly require some specialist training beyond what the market will support. But in general, if a business cannot do without trained personnel, three quarters of the cost will come from the business or from the trained.

A system will be introduced, along with the appropriate inspectorate for making sure that firms don't cheat, whereby firms will pay levies to the institutions whose qualified personnel they need, to a total of one quarter of the costs of such courses.

The remaining half will come from the trained. This follows from the status of their training as genuine investment. The present loan system will be much extended, with proper safeguards against any resultant hardship due to changes that make the training irrelevant, and ceilings will be fixed so that the possibility of crippling debt will not arise. Very expensive courses can have a higher proportion of fees coming from the state.

The difference between necessary skills and pseudo-academic waffle will consequently be more sharply understood. If it is really necessary to have a qualification in Leisure Studies to run a leisure centre, and if the owners of the leisure centre have to share the cost, they may well influence the qualification-granting body to make their courses more realistic. It may dawn on those running the 'tourist industry' that they don't need to employ people with qualifications in tourism. It is even possible that the new MBA schools will collapse. But that will be for the markets to decide by way of finance directors. Students who face the prospect of paying for their qualification will similarly be readier to treat the training as a genuine investment and ask whether their time and money are being well spent. This can only be good for genuine wealth-creation.

Though in the present educational fog we call this proposal new, it is little more than an adaptation to the modern world of the old ideas of apprenticeship: youths were trained partly at their own expense (by way of low pay in the years of the apprenticeship) and partly at the expense of their masters who stood to gain skilled workers. The principle continues to be sound and usable.

There are some borderline cases. Teacher training must continue to be supported by the state, as must the colleges of nursing and midwifery, though an improvement in the whole atmosphere of education will in both cases lead to a greater emphasis on experience and a reduction of theorizing. The medical schools fall halfway between true academic study and useful training, and since also their courses are longer than those for other first degrees the state will continue to support them substantially, though some considerable contribution to cost can reasonably be expected from doctors and dentists. There is no reason, however, why the supply of solicitors, so many of whom end up in the House of Commons, should make any charge on the exchequer; though as an academic subject law must be subsidized.

POSTGRADUATE STUDIES

The Conservatives insisted on universities setting up 'taught MAs', partly under the mistaken belief that these would qualify students for postgraduate work proper. By definition, graduation being the certificate that the graduate is competent to continue the study unaided, postgraduate study cannot be taught; the taught postgraduate degrees are therefore contradictions in terms, and will be phased out.

All higher degrees will be awarded by dissertation not by examination. State funding will be available for the minority of genuine postgraduate students who show themselves capable of original research and may be expected to make a career in universities.

*   *   *

As a consequence of these reforms there will be a drastic overall reduction in the size of secondary and tertiary education, releasing for productive work many middle-aged people, as well as the young who are now often wasting three of the best years of their lives on nonsense. The net direct savings anticipated from our policies will make a considerable difference to the budget. Whether they will appear as tax-reduction or be used otherwise cannot be predicted at this stage. The Liberal Democrats want to increase income tax for more education. Income tax could be reduced by at least 1 per cent within the life of one parliament and education much improved at the same time.

Can it be done? Not without another renaissance, which seems unlikely. Politics is the art of the possible, said Butler—'but we create possibility,' retorted Leavis. We think there is enough of an educated nucleus to create possibility. It is not impossible, for instance, that the present little polemic may make a stir. Let a political party once adopt something like our policies, for our reasons, and people will start to listen—and then the mainstream parties will take fright and begin to listen too. And genuine education will once more be something thinkable.

Notes on the Text

CHAPTER 1

1 *Financial Times* report of Mr Brown's first Budget speech, 3 July 1997, p. 17.
2 National Committee of Inquiry into Higher Education, *Higher Education in the Learning Society*, Stationery Office, 1997, Annexe C, para. 19.
3 Called henceforth *Charter*.
4 F. R. Leavis, *Education & the University*, 2nd edn, 1948, p. 16.
5 *The Teaching of English in England* (*The Newbolt Report*), 1921, p. 259.
6 C. P. Snow, 'Education and Sacrifice', *The New Statesman*, 17 May 1963, p. 746.
7 Advertisement in *The Financial Times* by the National Council for Vocational Qualifications, 26 January 1988.
8 David Blunkett, 'The Tough Truths of Dearing', *The Times*, 24 July 1997, p. 20.
9 Sources, *Whitaker's Almanac*, the *Blue Book*, *Education Yearbook 2000*, the *Annual Abstract of Statistics 1999*.
10 Nigel Blake, Richard Smith and Paul Standish, *The Universities We Need*, 1998, p. 51.
11 Ch. 22, para. 19.
12 Oddly, despite the present fashion for retiring at about age fifty-five, the pension advantage is not mentioned in these reports.
13 It is not stated whether the figure for average return depreciates the investment over the working life, but bear in mind that the capital invested is never seen again.
14 'Growth Theory'.
15 'Empirical Evidence'.
16 Report 7, 1.8–1.12 and Table 2.1; also Annexe A, 'Measuring the Social Rate of Return', 3, 11 and tables 1–3.
17 See Paul Ormerod, *The Death of Economics*, 1994, for a great many very similar remarks about economics.

CHAPTER 2

1 'Education of the People', *Phoenix*, 1936, pp. 594–5.
2 Department *for* Education and Employment.
3 *Newman: Prose and Poetry*, sel. Geoffrey Tillotson, 1957, p. 498. Like many eminent Victorians, Newman was always tinkering with his work, and the book generally known as *The Idea of a University* exists in a number of states. We quote the first edition as reprinted in this attractive Reynard Library volume; Newman page references are to it unless otherwise stated.
4 p. 498.
5 p. 481; cf. an equally good passage in Newman's novel *Loss and Gain*, ed. Alan G. Hill, Oxford, 1986, p. 15.
6 p. 467.
7 S. T. Coleridge, second Lay Sermon, quoted Richard Holmes, *Coleridge: Darker Reflections*, 1998, p. 448.

8   p. 462.
9   *The Curate in Charge*, 1875, repr. Gloucester, 1985, p. 203.
10 'The Function of Criticism at the Present Time', *Essays in Criticism*, first series, 1865.
11 p. 521.
12 The glance is at Professor Sir Randolph Quirk, whose doctrine as a grammarian is that he should not tell people how they ought to speak, but describe, in a spirit of scientific neutrality, how they actually do speak. It is a principle with him that from the practical point of view his profession is utterly useless. But how, as Vice-Chancellor of his university, did he justify universities to the University Grants Committee? and the public at large? By the training it gives dentists. (Cf. 'The New Battle of Britain for Our Universities', *The Times*, 2 February 1982, cited *The Gadfly*, February, 1984, pp. 5–6.)
13 Cf. the last chapter of Rush Rhees, *Without Answers*, 1969.
14 See the fuller quotations on pp. 30–31.
15 p. 465.
16 p. 503.
17 p. 505.
18 *The Idea of a University*, ed. George N. Schuster, New York, 1959, p. 183.
19 p. 497.
20 Cf. above, p. 25, from *ed. cit.*, p. 467.
21 *Ibid.*
22 William Hazlitt, 'My First Acquaintance with Poets', *The Liberal*, April, 1823, repr. *Selected Essays of William Hazlitt*, ed. Geoffrey Keynes, 1930, p. 510.
23 *The Universities We Need*, p. 82.
24 Leah Sims and Maggie Woodrow, *Franchising for Wider Access: Executive Summary*, University of North London, 1993, A1.
25 *Ibid.*, D1.
26 pp. 505–6.

CHAPTER 3

1   Ch. 43 (modern numbering), p. 276. (Chapter and page references for Jane Austen and George Eliot novels are to current Penguin editions.)
2   Ch. 14, p. 113.
3   Ch. 56, p. 368.
4   Ch. 29, p. 199.
5   Ch. 55, p. 353.
6   Ch. 2, p. 54.
7   Ch. 2, p. 56.
8   Ch. 11, p. 123.
9   Ch. 11, p. 122.
10 Ch. 36, p. 385.
11 Ch. 6, p. 68.
12 Ch. 8, p. 85.
13 Ch. 6, p. 71.
14 Ch. 5, p. 67.
15 Ch. 13, p. 108.

16 Ch. 7, p. 78.
17 Ch. 47, p. 305.
18 *Ibid.*
19 Ch. 2, p. 55.
20 Ch. 15, p. 114.
21 Ch. 22, p. 165.
22 Ch. 19, p. 146.
23 Ch. 19, p. 147.
24 Ch. 11, p. 100.
25 Ch. 19, p. 147.
26 Ch. 19, p. 148.
27 *Ibid.*
28 Ch. 4, p. 64.
29 Ch. 10, p. 93.
30 Ch. 8, p. 84.
31 Ch. 8, p. 85.
32 Ch. 9, p. 88.
33 Ch. 10, p. 93.
34 Ch. 10, p. 95.
35 Ch. 34, p. 221.
36 *Ibid.*
37 *Ibid.*
38 *Ibid.*
39 Ch. 11, pp. 102–3.
40 Ch. 58, p. 380.
41 Ch. 60, p. 388.
42 Ch. 15, p. 116.
43 Ch. 16, p. 119.
44 Ch. 16, p. 120.
45 Ch. 16, p. 121.
46 *Ibid.*
47 Ch. 16, pp. 122–3.
48 *Ibid.*
49 G. M. Hopkins, 'As Kingfishers Catch Fire'.
50 Ch. 16, p. 127.
51 Ch. 36, p. 235.
52 Ch. 16, p. 120.
53 Ch. 16, p. 122.
54 Ch. 21, p. 157.
55 Ch. 26, p. 181.
56 Ch. 36, p. 234.
57 *Ibid.*
58 *Ibid.*
59 Ch. 35, p. 227.
60 Ch. 35, p. 228.
61 Ch. 58, p. 378.
62 *Ibid.*

63　Ch. 36, p. 233.
64　Ch. 36, pp. 234–5.
65　Ch. 36, p. 236–7.
66　Ch. 36, p. 233.
67　*Ibid.*
68　Ch. 36, p. 237.
69　Ch. 36, p. 237; Ch. 37, p. 241.
70　Ch. 58, p. 375.
71　27 August 1997.

CHAPTER 4

1　Matthew, xii. 36–7.
2　Ch. 58, p. 375.
3　Ch. 19, pp. 149 and 150.
4　Attrib. Algeo 1991 and Coupland and Thomas 1989: I have lost the reference sheet.
5　Available not only in paper form (see note 2 on Ch. 1) but on the internet, the full report at www.leeds.ac.uk/educol/ncihe/natrep.htm, the summary at www.leeds.ac.uk/educol/ncihe/sumrep.htm.
6　The immediate result is that far-sighted lecturers have invested in the relevant certificates obtainable from the USA at a going rate of about $200 plus two recommendations/reports from friends. (You write mine and I'll write yours.)
7　See Lloyd Jones, *Biografi: A Traveller's Tale*, 1994.

CHAPTER 5

1　Reports of the White Paper *Higher Education: a New Framework*, 21 May 1991.
2　A partial, honourable exception was *The Daily Telegraph*.
3　'Timid Tory Plan for Training', 21 May 1991. Perhaps 'training' was suggested only by the tempting alliteration.
4　'A former polytechnic in Newcastle, now the University of Northumbria, tops the Financial Times performance indicators table.... Predictably Oxbridge scores badly....' (*The Financial Times*, 4 December 1999).
5　25 February 1998.
6　27 November 1996.
7　27 August 1997, p. 8.
8　Subtitle-blurb for Simon Targett, 'Plug the gap—with cash and experience', *Financial Times* Weekend, 21 August 1999, p. XIII.
9　Mr Frank Nigriello, Communications Director of Unipart, quoted in Simon Targett, 'Graduates with a BAe', *The Financial Times*, 7 June 1997.
10　Cf. Frank Palmer, 'Skillsology *vs* Culture', *'My Native English'*, pp. 53–60. This essay is a good example of the criticism of language that one should expect from a university. Cf. also William Hart, 'Against Skills', *The Oxford Review of Education*, vol. 4, no. 2, 1978, repr. *Our Schools/Our Selves*, September 1992, pp. 117–37; p. 117. We recommend this excellent essay.
11　p. 57.

12 p. 58.
13 *The Complete Careers and Higher Education Guidance Scheme*, Independent Schools Careers Organisation, Camberley, 1998.
14 *Ibid.*
15 25 October and 22 November 1997.
16 *The Complete Careers and Higher Education Guidance Scheme*, as above.
17 20 January 2000.
18 William Birch, 'Cloistered Against the Real World', *THES*, 2 February 1990, p. 18.
19 A letter from the Deans or other Representatives of University Faculties of Arts and Social Studies to Sir Peter Swinnerton-Dyer, Chairman, University Grants Committee, 30 March 1984.
20 *The Universities We Need*, pp. 148–9.
21 *Past and Present*, Book II, Ch. IX.
22 *Financial Times* report of the report of the North Commission, 29 January 1998, p. 8.
23 January 1997–May 1998.
24 Toril Moi, *Sexual/Textual Politics: Feminist Literary Theory*, 1985, repr. 1990, p. 51.
25 That Penguin anthology had one book by a male author (James F. McMillan, *European Women: Social History 1780–1945*). *Mother Courage* was not by Brecht but 'Letters from Mothers in Poverty at the end of the Century'.
26 Prifysgol Cymru: University of Wales Degree Examinations 1994, R/S/157/1.
27 *Briefing Plus* (The Monthly Focus on Management and Training Matters), November 1993, p. 1, published by The Industrial Society, registered charity no. 290003.
28 Tony Jackson, 'One-man Shows', *The Financial Times*, 24 November 1998, p. 25. Jackson reports that 'ostensibly, its skill was to buy ill-run companies and make them more efficient. In reality, it relied heavily on one tactic: pushing up prices.'
29 City Comment, *The Daily Telegraph*, 12 February 2000.
30 *The Times* carried a picture of 'Some of the first class of graduates from the first Football Management course, run by Liverpool University', and an accompanying article in which I could not detect any irony (15 December 1998). 'The hard-nosed message offered by the course is that football is big business. Clubs cannot afford to carry on hiring former professional players to carry out difficult, specialised jobs.' As a matter of fact, the present fashion is for businesses to focus on their 'core activities' in the hope that executives will know what they are doing. Either there is an abstract management skill, in which case it needn't specifically be football, or to run a football club demands knowledge of the game, in which case the former professional player has an advantage over the bespectacled mortar-boarded lady sitting in the middle of the front row of *The Times*'s picture. It will be interesting to see whether any football clubs take on any of these managers, and if so whether their place in the league tables improves.
31 'Some 250 delegates attended the conference and a total of eighty double-blind-refereed papers were included in the Conference Proceedings. The European Business Management School was represented by Dr A. Diamantopoulos and Professor Bodo Schlegelmilch, who presented a paper entitled "Determinants of Charity Giving: An Inter-disciplinary Review of the Literature and Suggestions for Further Research".' (*Newyddion*, 19 March 1992, p. 2).

32 *Newyddion*, 26 May 1988.
33 *The Financial Times*, 12 November 1996, front page.
34 'Cambridge has bowed to market pressures to offer a one-year MBA course' and 'Where the US lags behind', *The Financial Times*, 25 November 1996, p. 15.
35 Management Development, Advanced Professional Training, University College of Swansea, 1991.
36 Letter from the Principal of University College, Swansea, to All Members of Academic and Academically-related Staff, 10 June 1992.
37 *Newsletter*, 5 November 1987.
38 p. 253.

CHAPTER 6

1   Johnson, Boswell, Saturday 9 July 1763.
2   Carlyle, 'Signs of the Times' (1829).
3   F. R. Leavis, *English Literature in Our Time and the University*, 1967, pp. 65–6; cf. *The Human World* editorial 'Authority and Concern in the University', no. 2, 1971.
4   Sir Arthur Quiller-Couch, Inaugural, *On the Art of Writing*, Cambridge University Press, 1916, repr. 1925, p. 7.
5   *Rush Rhees on Religion and Philosophy*, ed. D. Z. Phillips, Cambridge University Press, 1997, p. xviii.
6   Minutes of a Meeting of the [University College of Swansea English] Departmental Teaching Committee with Dr Geoffrey Penzer ... 5 July 1994. There ought to be a name for the particular feeling of hopelessness inspired by this phrasing.
7   J. H. Newman, 'Discipline of Mind', repr. *The Idea of a University*, New York, 1959, p. 440.
8   Cf. Ian Robinson, 'F. R. Leavis the Cambridge Don', *The Use of English*, 43/3, 1992, pp. 244–54.
9   *Charter*, p. 3; the assumptions are pre-modular.
10 *Newsletter*, December 1987.
11 A letter from (Dr) R. S. Thomas [*non poeta*], Director of Planning and Marketing, entitled 'Strategic Plan', 5 August 1996.
12 Executive Summary of the Strategic Plan presented [by the University of Wales Swansea] to the Higher Education Funding Council for Wales, June, 1996. Whoever said that grandiloquence went out with Milton?
13 John Sparkes in *The Hire*, 5 February 1993, p. 12.
14 Johnson, *Life of Swift*.
15 Cf. Mark xiii. 11.
16 *The Approach to Total Quality Management Being Adopted at the University College of Swansea*, paper H.5536, 1994, para. 19.
17 Minutes of the First Meeting of the Academic Board Working Group on Modularisation of the University of Wales, held on 20 December 1991 ... via the Videoteaching Network (hereafter shortened to *Minutes*).
18 N.d.; ref. H.4491/HLM/LP.
19 *Rush Rhees on Religion and Philosophy*, ed. D. Z. Phillips, Cambridge University Press, 1997, Introduction, p. xi.
20 3 October 1994.

21 Colin to Jim, 8 June 1992; passed on to me by Jim.

22 *Ibid.*

23 *The Hire*, 2 July 1993, p. 4.

24 *The Times*, 27 May 1994. *The Times* thinks that this produces an 'intelligent competitiveness' that 'reflects a new and invigorating mood in British universities'.

25 The methods-only semi-fiction presumably explains why Modern Languages at Northumbria got 23 out of 24 for teaching but at Oxford only 21. Northumbria (one of whose slogans used to be—and perhaps still is—'French for Export') must teach French for business better than Oxford teaches French for education.

26 See above, 'Teaching', p. 90.

27 October 1996—all departmental grant allocations reduced by 15 per cent, etc, five paragraphs of emergency cuts ....

28 See note 16 above to p. 95.

29 Cf. 'Management control is formalised at all levels and is regulated by cascading limits of authority.' (Tesco plc Annual Accounts 1997, 'Policies and Procedures', 'Corporate Governance', p. 2.) Sell.

30 A. M. D. Armitage, letter in *The Hire*, 5 February 1993.

31 W. A. Hart, 'The Qualitymongers', *Journal of Philosophy of Education*, vol. 31, no. 2, 1997, p. 299.

32 I should no doubt have consulted the experts. 'Quality is high on the management agenda in education today' and so a specialist magazine quickly materialized, *Quality Assurance in Education.* By subscribing, 'you can keep abreast of current questions such as 'what is the relationship between Total Quality Management and quality assurance?' But you are more likely to get an answer to 'what are the costs of non-conformance?' for, as we were warned, 'Those institutions which fail to demonstrate a commitment to, and a strategy for, the management and development of quality are likely to be penalized, in a number of ways.'

33 *The Financial Times*, 4 December 1996.

34 Counsellors have to help students with private problems including the ones thrust upon them by modern life, but without any authority and without any principles. This is responsibility without power. All the counsellor has to fall back on is the aim of getting the student graduated: the functioning of the system is the only available criterion. In one institution not long ago students who wished to withdraw were routinely referred to a psychiatrist. (And, weren't there reports in the papers a year or two ago of some American research which showed that counselling did more harm than good?)

35 Cf. Ian Robinson, *The English Prophets*, 2001, Ch. 8.

36 *R.U.R.*, a play by Karel Capek about robots who destroy their human masters.

37 Principal's Address to the Court of Governors, *Newyddion* 331, 3 December 1987.

38 Circular from the Principal of University College, Swansea, 7 December 1987.

39 *The Universities We Need*, p. 165.

40 Academic libraries habitually discard books that have not been borrowed for a few years. If this had been the practice in the Middle Ages, Old English poetry would not have survived.

41 M. E. Braddon, *The Fatal Three*, 1888, repr. Stroud, 1997, p. 301.

42 Pope, 'Epistle to Burlington', pp. 134–8.

43 *Past and Present*, Book III, Ch. XII.

INTRODUCTION TO PART IV

1 'Why I'm fighting the A-level Cause', *The Daily Telegraph*, 12 November 1993.
2 *Past and Present*, Book I, Ch. IV.

CHAPTER 7

1 The basis of this account is a report I wrote to the board as the last of my duties as an assistant examiner. Though I asked for a reply I got nothing that could be called one—except that I had been inconsistent and lenient, and wouldn't be required as an examiner again.
2 GCE Advanced Supplementary and Advanced Level Examinations: Quality and Standards 1993, HMSO, £3.50.
3 These predict A-level grades from GCSE: schools take the credit for any 'value added' and may expect to be punished for any value lost, though how the schools are supposed to prevent many young people going to the bad by the age-old paths such as drink, with consequent academic effects, who knows?
4 For my reasons for thinking this a very good thing see Ian Robinson, 'UCCA to What?', *The Use of English*, 34/3, 1983.
5 p. 41.
6 OCR [Oxford and Cambridge and RSA] 'recognising achievement'. *English Literature: Approved Specifications for Teaching from September 2000*, p. 29. Should not academic authorities resist the mania for 'tab-lines'? Another board is Edexcel ('Success through qualifications'). Does it inspire confidence in their examining standards?
7 p. iv.
8 Ian Robinson, *The English Prophets*, Edgeways Books, 2001.
9 'Gender', a term in grammar, is always misused by theorists to mean 'sexuality'; but not of the kind the young folk may be expected to be interested in. The invitation will be to contemplate and disapprove of the subjection of women to men in the ages of Chaucer (e.g. the Wyf of Bath) or Queen Elizabeth or Queen Victoria.
10 If this can be done at all it is obviously postgraduate stuff for graduates well read in both literature and psychoanalysis.
11 Baroness Blackstone, Higher Education Minister and former Master of Birkbeck College, reported in *The Financial Times*, 3 October 1998.
12 *Ibid.*

CHAPTER 8

1 *'My Native English'*, eds Roger Knight and Ian Robinson, 1988, p. 157.
2 This was not the external who objected to a question of mine, 'Can one assume a consensus on what "poetic" means?' But if not what is our subject?
3 Cf. 'False Prophets' in *The English Prophets*, 2001.
4 Steven Vine, 'Crypts of Identity', *English* [the quarterly of the English Association], Autumn, 1999, p. 171. He is quoting Stevie Davies.
5 p. 172.

6   The content of at least some of these postgraduate courses is either identical with or less demanding than that of undergraduate courses, and their subject matter very elastic. In my own department, quite on Eagletonian lines, a whole literature was invented for the sake of having an MA in it, and you can become a *Magister* in this literature in twelve months flat, that is to say, three times quicker than it is possible to become a bachelor in English Language and Literature. This is 'the non-English anglophone literature of twentieth-century Wales', as the Swansea self-assessment document hopefully put it—asking us to believe in something that uses the sounds (and also, as a matter of fact, all the other features) of a particular language without being in it.

CHAPTER 9

1   *Apologie for Poetrie*, ed. Churton Collins, Oxford, 1907, repr. 1955, p. 12.
2   'Inaugural', *On the Art of Writing*, Cambridge University Press, 1916, repr. 1925, p. 10.
3   *Of Education*, p. 2; Prose Works II, facsimile edn, Menston 1968.
4   p. 402.
5   p. 441.
6   F. R. Leavis, *English Literature in Our Time and the University*, 1969, p. 3.
7   Cf. Theodora Gay Scutt, *Cuckoo in the Powys Nest*, Brynmill Press, 2000.
8   *Nicomachean Ethics*.
9   The new university naturally doesn't see it like that. Newcastle, for instance, has, for some years, felt perfectly well able to afford the loss of Philosophy.
10   Emma-Lou Montgomery, 'Bob Dylan? He's just as good as Keats', *The Daily Telegraph*, 27 March 1998. Does Charles Moore edit any of this newspaper apart from the editorial page and the one facing it?
11   *The French Revolution*, Boston, Mass., 1884, vol. I, p. 16.
12   *Shooting Niagara: and After?*, ed. cit., pp. 316, 317.

AN ANECDOTE OF INSTITUTIONAL LIFE

1   From the building of the 'Mundane Shell' in *Vala, or the Four Zoas* ('Night the Second'), William Blake: *The Complete Poems*, ed. Alicia Ostriker, 1977, p. 312.